INBRED AND GENETICALLY DEFINED STRAINS OF LABORATORY ANIMALS

Part 2
Hamster, Guinea Pig, Rabbit, and Chicken

III

INBRED AND GENETICALLY DEFINED STRAINS OF LABORATORY ANIMALS

Part 2
Hamster, Guinea Pig, Rabbit, and Chicken

COMPILED AND EDITED BY

Philip L. Altman and Dorothy Dittmer Katz

Federation of American Societies for Experimental Biology

BETHESDA, MARYLAND

PRINTED IN THE UNITED STATES OF AMERICA

Library of Congress Catalog Card Number: 78-73555

International Standard Book Number: 0-913822-13-2

FOREWORD

In approaching the many complex problems of biology, the ability to restrict the biological variables affecting an experiment has led to major discoveries about fundamental mechanisms and to rapid developments in the biomedical sciences. Paramount among these experimental tools are the inbred and genetically defined animals. Their use has led to profound insights into the mechanisms of gene expression in mammals, tumor growth, tissue transplantation, host defense, responsiveness to drugs, and many other biological processes of basic scientific and medical importance.

The tremendous power that genetic insight gives to biological experiments has led to the rapidly increasing use of inbred and genetically defined laboratory animals. The difficulties in organizing the genetic information about the different strains and species, and in developing a perspective on the number and availability of such animals, have presented a formidable barrier to those who are not primarily geneticists. The objective in preparing *Part 1* and *Part 2* of this volume was to organize and present the information on inbred and genetically defined laboratory animals in such a way that the range and nature of the data would be immediately accessible to those who wish to use the information for experimental purposes. It is expected also that the volume will be a useful reference work for geneticists.

The spectrum of resources among inbred and genetically defined animals is quite broad and probably not adequately appreciated. The mouse is the prototype of such animals, and it has been the best studied and most extensively developed. The information on the rat is also fairly well developed, although it is not yet near the level attained by the mouse. It has some interesting differences from the mouse, and further studies on these differences may increase our understanding of the organization and expression of genetic information in mammals. The data for these species are summarized in *Part 1* of the volume. The hamster, guinea pig, rabbit, and chicken have been studied in varying, but lesser, detail, and the information about them is tabulated in *Part 2* of the volume.

The Editorial Board wishes to acknowledge partial support for the preparation of this book by the American Cancer Society under grant number RD-5 and by the National Cancer Institute under grant number 1 R01 CA 26665-01.

1 August 1979
Pittsburgh, Pennsylvania

Thomas J. Gill III, M.D., *Chairman*
Biological Handbooks Editorial Board

ADVISORY COMMITTEE ON INBRED AND GENETICALLY DEFINED STRAINS OF LABORATORY ANIMALS

FASEB PUBLICATIONS COMMITTEE

OFFICE OF BIOLOGICAL HANDBOOKS STAFF

CONTRIBUTORS AND REVIEWERS

ABPLANALP, HANS
University of California
Davis, California 95616
ADAMS, RICHARD A.
Bio-Research Institute, Inc.
Cambridge, Massachusetts 02141

BACON, LARRY D.
USDA, Regional Poultry Research
Laboratory
East Lansing, Michigan 48823
BAILEY, DONALD W.
Jackson Laboratory
Bar Harbor, Maine 04609
BEAUCHAMP, GARY K.
University of Pennsylvania
Philadelphia, Pennsylvania 19104
BENEDICT, ALBERT A.
University of Hawaii at Manoa
Honolulu, Hawaii 96822
BERMAN, LEONARD D.
Veterans Administration Hospital
Boston, Massachusetts 02130
BITTER-SUERMANN, D.
Johannes Gutenberg University
Mainz 65, Federal Republic of
Germany
BLOOM, STEPHEN E.
Cornell University
Ithaca, New York 14853
BRILES, W. E.
Northern Illinois University
DeKalb, Illinois 60115

CHAI, C. K.
Jackson Laboratory
Bar Harbor, Maine 04609
COE, JOHN E.
NIH, Rocky Mountain Laboratory
Hamilton, Montana 59840
COGGIN, J. H., JR.
University of South Alabama College
of Medicine
Mobile, Alabama 36688
COHEN, CARL
University of Illinois Medical Center
Chicago, Illinois 60612
CRARY, DORCAS D.
Jackson Laboratory
Bar Harbor, Maine 04609
CRITTENDEN, L. B.
USDA, Regional Poultry Research
Laboratory
East Lansing, Michigan 48823

DE WECK, ALAIN L.
Inselspital Bern
3010 Bern, Switzerland

DUNCAN, WILLIAM R.
University of Texas Southwestern
Medical School
Dallas, Texas 75235

EDIGER, RAYMOND D.
Animal Health Laboratory
Frederick, Maryland 21701
ETCHES, R. J.
University of Guelph
Guelph, Ontario, N1G 2W1, Canada

FAIRFULL, R. W.
Animal Research Institute
Ottawa, Ontario, K1A 0C6, Canada
FESTING, MICHAEL F. W.
MRC Laboratory Animals Centre
Carshalton, Surrey, SM5 4EF,
England
FOX, RICHARD R.
Jackson Laboratory
Bar Harbor, Maine 04609
FRENKEL, J. K.
University of Kansas Medical Center
Kansas City, Kansas 66103

GECZY, A. F.
Australian Red Cross Society
Sydney, New South Wales 2000,
Australia
GILMAN-SACHS, ALICE
University of Illinois Medical Center
Chicago, Illinois 60680
GILMOUR, DOUGLAS G.
New York University Medical Center
New York, New York 10016
GOWE, R. S.
Animal Research Institute
Ottawa, Ontario, K1A 0C6, Canada
GREEN, IRA
NIH, National Institute of Allergy and
Infectious Diseases
Bethesda, Maryland 20014

HANAFUSA, HIDESABURO
Rockefeller University
New York, New York 10021
HANLY, W. CAREY
University of Illinois Medical Center
Chicago, Illinois 60680
HART, DAVID A.
University of Texas Southwestern
Medical School
Dallas, Texas 75235
HAWES, R. O.
University of Maine
Orono, Maine 04469

HEFFRON, DONADEE
University of South Alabama College
of Medicine
Mobile, Alabama 36688
HOMBURGER, FREDDY
Bio-Research Institute, Inc.
Cambridge, Massachusetts 02141
HUBBELL, H. R.
University of Texas Health Science
Center
Houston, Texas 77030

KITE, JOSEPH H., JR.
State University of New York
Buffalo, New York 14214
KREMER, A. K.
Rijksuniversiteit te Utrecht
3508 TD Utrecht, The Netherlands

LANCKI, DAVID W.
University of Illinois Medical Center
Chicago, Illinois 60612
LEE, E.
NIH, Medicine Branch
Bethesda, Maryland 20014
LEHMAN, JOHN M.
University of Colorado Medical
Center
Denver, Colorado 80262
LISAK, ROBERT P.
University of Pennsylvania
Philadelphia, Pennsylvania 19104
LYMAN, CHARLES P.
Harvard Medical School
Boston, Massachusetts 02115

MARSH, RICHARD F.
University of Wisconsin
Madison, Wisconsin 53706
McBRIDE, RAYMOND A.
Baylor College of Medicine
Houston, Texas 77030
McCORMICK, JAMES G.
Bowman Gray School of Medicine
Winston-Salem, North Carolina
27103
MURPHY, MICHAEL R.
NIH, National Institute of Mental
Health
Bethesda, Maryland 20014

NIXON, C. WILLIAM
37 Ox Bow Lane
Randolph, Massachusetts 02368
NORDSKOG, A. W.
Iowa State University
Ames, Iowa 50011

O'CONNELL, ROBERT J.
Worcester Foundation for
 Experimental Biology
Shrewsbury, Massachusetts 01545
ORSINI, MARGARET W.
University of Wisconsin
Madison, Wisconsin 53706

PETERSON, DANIEL W.
University of California
Davis, California 95616
PETERSON, J.
Boston College
Chestnut Hill, Massachusetts 02167
PEVZNER, I. Y.
Iowa State University
Ames, Iowa 50011
POLAK, L.
F. Hoffmann-La Roche & Co., Ltd.
CH 4002 Basel, Switzerland
PURCHASE, H. GRAHAM
USDA, Science and Education
 Administration
Beltsville, Maryland 20705

RICARDO, MANUEL J., JR.
University of Tennessee Center for
 the Health Sciences
Memphis, Tennessee 38163
ROBINSON, PETER J.
Northwestern University
Chicago, Illinois 60611
ROBINSON, ROY
St. Stephens Road Nursery, Ealing
London, W13 8HB, England
ROSE, NOEL R.
Wayne State University School of
 Medicine
Detroit, Michigan 48201

SCHIERMAN, LOUIS W.
University of Georgia
Athens, Georgia 30605

SCHWARTZ, BENJAMIN D.
Washington University School of
 Medicine
St. Louis, Missouri 63110
SHAW, DAVID C.
Glaxo Research Limited
Harefield, Uxbridge, Middlesex,
 England
SHEVACH, ETHAN M.
NIH, National Institute of Allergy
 and Infectious Diseases
Bethesda, Maryland 20014
SHOFFNER, R. N.
University of Minnesota
St. Paul, Minnesota 55108
SLATER, GILBERT M.
Charles River Breeding Laboratories,
 Inc.
Wilmington, Massachusetts 01887
SMYTH, J. ROBERT, JR.
University of Massachusetts
Amherst, Massachusetts 01003
SOMES, RALPH G., JR.
University of Connecticut
Storrs, Connecticut 06268
SPENDLOVE, W. H.
North Oxfordshire Technical College
 and School of Art
Banbury, Oxford, England
STEIN-STREILEIN, JOAN
University of Texas Southwestern
 Medical School
Dallas, Texas 75235
STONE, HOWARD
1827 Lyndhurst Way
Haslett, Michigan 48840
STRANZINGER, GERALD
Eidgenössische Technische Hochschule
CH-8092 Zurich, Switzerland
STREILEIN, J. WAYNE
University of Texas Southwestern
 Medical School
Dallas, Texas 75235

TISSOT, ROBERT G.
University of Illinois Medical Center
Chicago, Illinois 60612
TOOLAN, HELENE WALLACE
Putnam Memorial Hospital Institute
 for Medical Research
Bennington, Vermont 05201
TRENTIN, JOHN J.
Baylor College of Medicine
Houston, Texas 77030
TURTON, JON A.
Middlesex Hospital Medical School
London, W1P 7LD, England

VAN DONGEN, C. G.
Bio-Research Consultants, Inc.
Cambridge, Massachusetts 02141
VAN HOOSIER, G. L., JR.
University of Washington
Seattle, Washington 98195
VETTERLING, JOHN M.
USDA, Agricultural Research
 Service Western Region
Ft. Collins, Colorado 80522

WHANG-PENG, J.
NIH, Medicine Branch
Bethesda, Maryland 20014
WILSON, BARRY W.
University of California
Davis, California 95616
WRIGHT, SEWALL
University of Wisconsin
Madison, Wisconsin 53706

YERGANIAN, GEORGE
Northeastern University
Boston, Massachusetts 02115
YOON, CHAI H.
Boston College
Chestnut Hill, Massachusetts 02167

ZBAR, BERTON
NCI, Biology Branch
Bethesda, Maryland 20014

CONTENTS

IV. GUINEA PIG

INTRODUCTION

INBRED AND GENETICALLY DEFINED STRAINS OF LABORATORY ANIMALS is volume III in the new series of Biological Handbooks. This volume is divided into two parts with *Part 1* covering Mouse and Rat, and *Part 2* covering Hamster, Guinea Pig, Rabbit, and Chicken.

Contents and Review
Part 2 of this volume contains a short chapter on the history, uses, classification, and definition of inbred animal strains; 25 tables on the hamster, 21 on the guinea pig, 12 on the rabbit, and 26 on the chicken. The contents of *Part 2* were authenticated by 86 outstanding experts in animal genetics. The review process to which the data were subjected was designed to eliminate, insofar as possible, material of questionable validity and errors of transcription.

Headnote
An explanatory headnote, serving as an introduction to the subject matter, may precede a table. More frequently, tables are prefaced by a short headnote containing such important information as units of measurement, abbreviations, definitions, and estimate of the range of variation. To interpret the data, it is essential to read the related headnote.

Exceptions
Occasionally, differences in values for the same specifications, certain inconsistencies in nomenclature, and some overlapping of coverage may occur among tables. These result, not from oversight or failure to choose between alternatives, but from a deliberate intent to respect the judgment and preferences of the individual contributors.

Conventions and Terminology
The main conventions used throughout this volume were adapted from the fourth edition of the *Council of Biology Editors Style Manual,* published in 1978 for the Council by the American Institute of Biological Sciences. Terminology was checked against *Webster's Third New International Dictionary,* published in 1961 by G. & C. Merriam Company.

Contributors and References
Appended to the tables are the names of the contributors, and a list of the literature citations arranged in alphabetical sequence. The reference abbreviations conform to those in the *Bibliographic Guide for Editors and Authors,* published by The American Chemical Society in 1974. References in some tables are to review articles rather than to the original papers from which the data were obtained. The objective was to conserve space while providing the user with the latest citation from which earlier references could be identified and retrieved.

Enzyme Nomenclature
Enzyme names and Enzyme Commission numbers were verified in *Enzyme Nomenclature,* the 1972 recommendations of the Commission on Biochemical Nomenclature, published by Elsevier Scientific Publishing Company for the International Union of Pure and Applied Chemistry and the International Union of Biochemistry.

Range of Variation
Values are generally presented as either the mean plus and minus the standard deviation, or the mean and the lower and upper limit of the range of individual values about the mean (either observed or statistical). Usually, it is of greater importance that the range be given rather than the mean. The several methods used to estimate the range—depending on the information available—are designated by the letters "a, b, c, or d" to identify the type of range in descending order of accuracy.

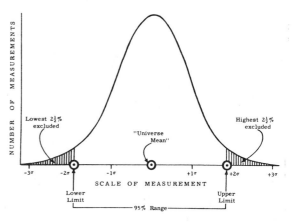

"a"—When the group of values is relatively large, a 95% range is derived by curve fitting. A recognized type of normal frequency curve is fitted to a group of measured values, and the extreme 2.5% of the area under the curve at each end is excluded (*see* illustration).

"b"—When the group of values is too small for curve fitting, as is usually the case, a 95% range is estimated by a simple statistical calculation. Assuming a normal symmetrical distribution, the standard deviation is multiplied by a factor of 2, then subtracted from and added to the mean to give the lower and upper range limits.

"c"—A less dependable, but commonly applied, procedure takes as range limits the lowest value and the highest value of the reported sample group of measurements. It underestimates the 95% range for small samples and overestimates for larger sample sizes, but where there is marked asymmetry in the position of the mean within the sample range, this method may be used in preference to the preceding one.

"d"—Another estimate of the lower and upper limits of the range of variation is based on the judgment of an individual experienced in measuring the quantity in question.

HOLDERS

ACC   J. Lloyd Spencer
Agriculture Canada
Ottawa, Ontario, Canada

AGS   Genetics Research Laboratories
C.S.I.R.O. North Ryde
P. O. Box 90
Epping, NSW 2121, Australia
(B. L. Sheldon)

AMU   L. S. Yakovleva
Academy of Medical Sciences
Moscow, U.S.S.R.

ARC   A. A. Grunder
Animal Research Institute
Ottawa, Ontario, Canada

ARI   R. S. Gowe
Animal Research Institute
Research Branch, Agriculture Canada
Ottawa, Ontario, Canada K1A 0C6

ATCC   American Type Culture Collection
12301 Parklawn Drive
Rockville, Maryland 20852

BII   Andrew S. Kelus
Basel Institute for Immunology
Basel, Switzerland

BIO [Guinea pig]   Institut für biologische Forschung
4114 Füllinsdorf
Switzerland

BIO [Hamster]   Bio-Research Institute, Inc.
9 Commercial Avenue
Cambridge, Massachusetts 02141

BSRA   J. P. Boyer
Station de Recherches avicoles, C.R.V.Z.
B.P. no. 1, 37380 Monnaie, France

BVG   V. V. Bulow
Bundesforschungsanstalt für
Viruskrankheiten der Tiere
Tübingen, Federal Republic of Germany

CAL   D. W. Peterson and F. H. Lantz
Department of Avian Sciences
University of California
Davis, California 95616

CAS   Karel Hála
Institute of Molecular Genetics
Czechoslovak Academy of Sciences
Prague, Czechoslovakia

CASM   I. Mlozanek
Czechoslovak Academy of Sciences
Prague, Czechoslovakia

CBC   W. Staples
Cobb Breeding Corp.
Concord, New Hampshire 03851

Cbi   Chester Beatty Research Institute
CBI   Institute of Cancer Research
Fulham Road
London, S.W. 3, England

CDN   G. F. de Boer
Virology Department
Centraal Diergeneeskundig Instituut,
Lelystad
39 Houtribweg
Lelystad, The Netherlands

CIT   J. H. Richards
Division of Chemistry and Chemical
Engineering
California Institute of Technology
Pasadena, California 91125

COH   City of Hope Medical Center
Duarte, California
(C. W. Todd)

CONG   Paul F. Goetinck
Animal Genetics Department
University of Connecticut
Storrs, Connecticut 06268

CONS   Ralph G. Somes, Jr.
Nutritional Sciences Department
University of Connecticut
Storrs, Connecticut 06268

COR   Stephen E. Bloom
Department of Poultry Science
Rice Hall
Cornell University
Ithaca, New York 14853

Cpb CPB	Centraal Proefdierenbedrijf TNO P.O. B.167 Woudenbergseweg 25 NL-Zeist, The Netherlands
CSIRO	Genetics Research Laboratories Division of Animal Production C.S.I.R.O. North Ryde P. O. Box 90 Epping, N. S. W. 2121, Australia
CUD	O. P. Settnes University of Copenhagen Copenhagen, Denmark
CZ	Milan Hasek Czechoslovak Academy of Sciences Institute of Experimental Biology and Genetics (Budejovicka 1083) Prague 4, Czechoslovakia
DEN	Dennen Animal Industries Leo G. Arsenault 405 Essex Avenue Gloucester, Massachusetts 01930
DKFZ	Institut für Virusforschung Deutsches Krebsforschungzentrum Im Neuenheimer Feld, 280 D-6900 Heidelberg 1, Federal Republic of Germany
DT	Department of Tuberculosis National Institute of Health Tokyo, Japan
DUKE	Duke University Medical Center Department of Microbiology Jones Building Room 414; P. O. Box 3020 Durham, North Carolina 27710 (R. E. Smith)
ENG	Engle Laboratory Animals, Inc. Everett Engle RR #1, Box 23 Farmersburg, Indiana 47850
FLA	A. Tanaka Laboratory of Molecular Virology Life Sciences, Inc. St. Petersburg, Florida 33710
FOX	Richard R. Fox The Jackson Laboratory Bar Harbor, Maine 04609

FSIPR	J. Folkerts, Jr. Instituut voor pluimveeonderzoek 'Het Spelderholt' (Spelderholt Institute for Poultry Research) Beekbergen, The Netherlands
GAR	Klaus Gärtner Zentrales Tierlabor Medizinische Hochschule Ernst-Wiechert-Allee 3000 Hannover Federal Republic of Germany
GEO	K. Washburn Poultry Science Department University of Georgia Athens, Georgia 30601
GUE	B. S. Reinhart Department of Agriculture and Poultry Science University of Guelph Guelph, Ontario, Canada N1G 2W1
He	W. E. Heston (retired) National Cancer Institute Bethesda, Maryland 20014
HNW	D. V. Zander Heisdorf and Nelson Redmond, Washington 98052
Hprs HPRS	Houghton Poultry Research Station Houghton, Huntingdon Cambs., PE17 2DA, England (L. N. Payne)
HSN	Institute for Medical Genetics University of Uppsala V. Agatan 24 S-75220 Uppsala, Sweden
IAF	H. G. Grant Institute of Food and Agricultural Science Gainesville, Florida 32604
ICRF	Imperial Cancer Research Fund Central Laboratories Burtonhole Lane, The Ridgeway Mill Hill, London, NW7 1AD, England
ICRL	Imperial Cancer Research Fund Laboratories P. O. Box 123 Lincoln's Inn Fields London, WC2A 3PX, England (R. A. Weiss)

IIB R. Kasabov
Institute of Immunology
Sofia, Bulgaria

INM J. Gonzales
Departmento de Virologia
Instituto Nacional de Investigaciones Pecuarias
Apdo. Postal 41-652
Mexico City 10, Mexico

IPP P.-A. Cazenave
Analytical Immunochemistry
Institute Pasteur
Paris (Cedex 15), France

IUA A. W. Nordskog
Department of Animal Science
Iowa State University
Ames, Iowa 50011

IUMS Department of Immunology
Indiana University Medical School
Indianapolis, Indiana 46202
(J. S. Ingraham)

J The Jackson Laboratory
JAX Bar Harbor, Maine 04609

JLV H. Bauer
Institut für Virologie
6300 Giessen
Frankfurter Strasse 107
Federal Republic of Germany

JNAH Department of Veterinary Science
National Institute of Health
10-35 Kamiosaki, 2-Chome
Shinagawa-Ku, Tokyo 141, Japan
(Masuro Nakagawa)

Lac Medical Research Council Laboratory
LAC Animals Centre
Woodmansterne Road
Carshalton, Surrey, SM5 4EF, England

Lak Charles River Lakeview
LAK P. O. Box 85
Newfield, New Jersey 08344

LPC Claude Petter
Laboratoire de Physiologie Comparée
Université Paris
VI, 9, quai Saint-Bernard
75-Paris 5ᵉ, France

LSH London School of Hygiene and Tropical
Medicine
Winches Farm Field Station
395 Hatfield Road
St. Albans, Herts. AL4 0XQ, England

LSI Life Sciences Research Laboratory
1509½ 49th St., S.
St. Petersburg, Florida 33707
(J. Beard)

LUN S. Lundberg
Department of Medical Microbiology
Rikshospitalet, Univ. of Copenhagen
22 Juliane Maries Vej
DK2100 Copenhagen Ø, Denmark

LVR I. V. Patrascu
Laboratorul de Virusuri Tumorale Aviare
Bucharest, Romania

MAR O. P. Thomas
Poultry Science
University of Maryland
College Park, Maryland 20742

MAS J. Robert Smyth, Jr.
Department of Veterinary and Animal Sciences
University of Massachusetts
Amherst, Massachusetts 01003

MCD R. B. Buckland
Department of Animal Science
P. O. Box 228
Macdonald College
Macdonald College, Quebec, Canada H0A 1C0

MCN R. A. McBride
New York Medical College
Valhalla, New York 10595

MIN University of Minnesota
Institute of Agriculture
Animal Science Department
St. Paul, Minnesota 55101
(R. N. Shoffner)

MLGF P. Merat
Laboratoire de Genetique Factorielle,
C.N.R.Z.
78350 Jouy-en-Josas, France

MSC E. C. Hahn
Memorial Sloan-Kettering Cancer Center
New York, New York 10021

MSD M. R. Hilleman
Merck, Sharp, & Dohme Research
Laboratories
West Point, Pennsylvania 19486

MUM W. A. Marquardt
Poultry Science
University of Maryland
College Park, Maryland 20742

N NIH	Division of Research Services Veterinary Resources Branch National Institutes of Health Bethesda, Maryland 20014	NYS	Bruce W. Calnek Department of Avian and Aquatic Diseases New York State Veterinary College Cornell University Ithaca, New York 14853
NCI-BB	National Cancer Institute Biology Branch Bethesda, Maryland 20014	NYU	New York University New York, New York (G. J. Thorbecke)
NCI-LIB	Laboratory of Immunobiology National Cancer Institute Bethesda, Maryland 20014	OHI	Karl E. Nestor Poultry Science Department Ohio Agricultural Research and Development Center Wooster, Ohio 44691
NCRPBL	North Central Regional Poultry Breeding Laboratory Agricultural Research Service, USDA Poultry Science Building, Purdue University West Lafayette, Indiana 47907	ORE	Fred H. Benoff Poultry Science Department Oregon State University Corvallis, Oregon 97331
NEB	J. A. Brumbaugh School of Life Sciences University of Nebraska Lincoln, Nebraska 68508	OSU	N. S. Fechheimer Department of Dairy Science Ohio State University 625 Stadium Drive Columbus, Ohio 43210
NIAID	Laboratory of Immunology National Institute of Allergy and Infectious Diseases National Institutes of Health Bethesda, Maryland 20014	OUJ	S. Kato Osaka University Osaka, Japan
NIHK	R. Krause National Institute of Allergy and Infectious Diseases National Institutes of Health Bethesda, Maryland 20014	OXF	Department of Biochemistry Oxford University South Parks Road Oxford, OX1 3OO, England
NIHR	National Institutes of Health Bethesda, Maryland 20014 (R. G. Mage)	PAK	Packham Hawkesbury Agricultural College Richmond, N.S.W. 2753, Australia
NIMR	National Institute for Medical Research Mill Hill London, NW7 1AA, England	PBE	A. E. Churchill Poultry Biologicals Ltd. Houghton, Cambs., England
NMS	D. L. Zartman Dairy Department New Mexico State University Las Cruces, New Mexico 88003	PEN	Edward Buss Poultry Science Department The Pennsylvania State University 203 Animal Industry Building University Park, Pennsylvania 16802
NSA	D. C. Crober Department of Animal Science Nova Scotia Agricultural College Truro, Nova Scotia, Canada B2N 5E3	PET	Peterson Hamstery Burlington, North Carolina 27215
NU	Northeastern University Laboratories of Environmental Biomedical Sciences 360 Huntington Avenue Boston, Massachusetts 02115	PH	Milan Hasek Institute of Molecular Genetics Czechoslovak Academy of Sciences (Budejovicka 1083) Prague 4, Czechoslovakia

PRC   Poultry Research Centre
Kings Buildings
West Mains Road
Edinburgh, Scotland

PSAM   M. J. Petitjean
Station experimentale d'Aviculture de
    Magneraud
B. P. 52, 17700 Surgères, France

R   The Rockefeller University
Tower Building, Room 1135A
York Avenue & 66th Street
New York, New York 10021
(Hidesaburo Hanafusa)

RIT   N. Z. Zygraich
Biologics Department, RIT
Geneval, Belgium

ROST   W. Rudolph
Sektion Tierproduktion
Universität Rostock
Wissenschaftsbereich Tierzucht
DDR-25 Rostock
Liebigstrasse, Fachnr.: 27-08
Democratic Republic of Germany

RPM   R. L. Witter
Regional Poultry Research Laboratory
East Lansing, Michigan 48823

RPRL   USDA-SEA-AR-NCR
Regional Poultry Research Laboratory
3606 E. Mt. Hope Road
East Lansing, Michigan 48823
(L. B. Crittenden)

RSAM   F. H. Ricard
Station experimentale d'Aviculture de
    Magneraud
B. P. 52, 17700 Surgères, France

SAS   R. D. Crawford
Department of Animal and Poultry Science
University of Saskatchewan
Saskatoon, Saskatchewan, Canada S7N 0W0

SCH   ARS/Sprague-Dawley
R. D. Fortney
P. O. Box 4220
2826 Latham Drive
Madison, Wisconsin 53711

SDA   Walter Morgan
South Dakota State University
Brookings, South Dakota 57006

SIM   Simonsen Laboratories, Inc.
Harry C. Simonsen
1180 Day Road
Gilroy, California 95020

SKI   H. Oettgen
Sloan-Kettering Institute for Cancer Research
1275 York Avenue
New York, New York 10021

SPAFAS   Spafas, Inc.
R.F.D. 3
Norwich, Connecticut 06360

SRPGL   Southern Regional Poultry Genetics
    Laboratory
Agricultural Research Service, USDA
University of Georgia
Athens, Georgia 30602

Ss   Willys K. Silvers
Department of Medical Genetics
University of Pennsylvania School of Medicine
Philadelphia, Pennsylvania 19104

SVC   F. Lesnik
University School of Veterinary Medicine
Košice, Czechoslovakia

TBH   Országos Allatégeszségügyi Intezet
Budapest, Hungary

TUE   Setsura Ebashi
Department of Pharmacology
University of Tokyo Faculty of Medicine
Bunkyo-Ku, Tokyo 113, Japan

UCD   Hans J. Abplanalp
Department of Avian Sciences
University of California
Davis, California 95616

UCDM   T. Mikami
University of California
Davis, California 95616

UCLA   Department of Surgery
University of California at Los Angeles
Los Angeles, California 90024

UCS   L. van der Heide
Storrs Agricultural Experiment Station
University of Connecticut
Storrs, Connecticut 06268

UGA   C. S. Eidson
Poultry Disease Research Center
University of Georgia
Athens, Georgia 30602

UGAS   Louis W. Schierman
Poultry Disease Research Center
Department of Avian Medicine
University of Georgia
953 College Station Road
Athens, Georgia 30605

UIGC   Carl Cohen
Center for Genetics
University of Illinois Medical Center
Chicago, Illinois 60680

UIMC   Sheldon Dray
Department of Microbiology and Immunology
University of Illinois Medical Center
Chicago, Illinois 60680

UMAS   M. Sevoian
Department of Veterinary and Animal
  Sciences
University of Massachusetts
Amherst, Massachusetts 01002

UMI   A. Zanella
Institute of Infectious Diseases
Veterinary Faculty
University of Milan Research Laboratory
Cip-Zoo, Breschia, Italy

UPJ   Upjohn Co.
Animal Rearing and Procurement Unit
Kalamazoo, Michigan 49001
(W. R. Graham)

UQA   A. Mustaffa-Babjee
University of Queensland
St. Lucia, (Brisbane), Queensland, Australia

USA   D. Harman
University of Sydney
Camden, Australia

USC   Department of Microbiology
University of Southern California
Los Angeles, California 90033
(P. K. Vogt)

UTA   Department of Microbiology
University of Texas at Austin
Austin, Texas
(W. J. Mandy)

UTR   Vakgroep Zoötechniek
Faculteit der Diergeneeskunde
Rijksuniversiteit Utrecht
Yalelaan 17, de Uithof
3508 TD Utrecht, The Netherlands
(J. Bouw)

VA   Virus Research Laboratory
Veterans Administration Hospital
Gainesville, Florida 32601
(C. Moscovici)

VRH   H. N. Thakur
Veterinary Research Institute
Budapest, Hungary

VUB   R. Hamers
Laboratory of Animal Physiology
Vrije Universiteit Brussel
Pleinlaan 2
1050 Brussels, Belgium

VUC   V. Jurajda
State Veterinary Institute
Brno, Czechoslovakia

WE   O. L. Weiser
Microbiology Division
U.S. Army Medical Research and Nutrition
  Laboratory
Fitzsimmons General Hospital
Denver, Colorado 80240

WEK   A. deWeck
Institute for Clinical Immunology
Inselspital Bern
Bern 3010, Switzerland

WFEB   Worcester Foundation for Experimental
  Biology
Shrewsbury, Massachusetts 01545
(H. L. Robinson)

WIS   W. H. McGibbon
Department of Poultry Science
University of Wisconsin
Madison, Wisconsin 53706

WRE   J. F. Blaxland
Wellcome Research Laboratories
Beckenham, England

WRL   J. Ivanyi
Department of Experimental Immunobiology
Wellcome Research Institute
Beckenham, England

WSM   Department of Microbiology
Wayne State University
Detroit, Michigan 48201

WSU   B. R. Cho
Washington State University
Pullman, Washington 99163

7HILL   Poultry Research Station
Seven Hills, N.S.W. 2147, Australia

INBRED AND GENETICALLY DEFINED STRAINS OF LABORATORY ANIMALS

Part 2
Hamster, Guinea Pig,
Rabbit, and Chicken

INBRED ANIMALS

HISTORY, USES, AND CLASSIFICATION

The investigator requiring animals for research can choose his subjects from a large number of species. These include a variety of domestic animals (ranging from cattle, swine, and chickens, to dogs and cats), non-human primates (such as monkeys, chimpanzees, baboons, and marmosets), and the small laboratory mammals. The latter are by far the most commonly used.

In addition to selecting the ideal organism for the experiment, the investigator must also choose the genetic state that makes the model a valid representation of the target population. In experiments using mice, rats, hamsters, guinea pigs, rabbits, dogs, or chickens, the research worker's options are random-bred, inbred, F_1 hybrids, and haphazardly bred animals. In this volume, the inbred or genetically characterized animal is presented as the research tool of choice.

Historical Development of Inbred Lines

The great variability of living organisms accounts in part for the fact that biology has lagged far behind physics and chemistry in precision. The ideal scientific method enables the investigator to distinguish the variables that play roles in a particular phenomenon, and to reduce to one the number of variables being tested. With the development of measurement standards and the preparation of reagent and analytical grade chemicals, repetition of experiments in various laboratories, under essentially defined conditions, became possible. Such experiments were the foundations on which physics and chemistry have been built.

The development of lines of inbred animals can be considered an equivalent achievement in the biological and biomedical sciences. The "reagent grade" animal, the result of carefully controlled inbreeding, now permits repetition of experiments requiring fine discrimination within an animal species.

The inbred line is a population of animals that has attained homozygosis at nearly every locus through the use of a mating system that reduces the number of genetically unlike ancestors. The most common practice is rigid brother by sister mating over many generations, although other systems may be used (see Definition of Inbred Strains, p. 422). Thus, all members of an inbred line have essentially the same genetic constitution.

The history of the inbred laboratory mammal is actually the history of the use of the mouse in cancer studies and the guinea pig in studies of multifactorial inheritance. The rediscovery of Mendel's work in 1900 led to the reexamination of cancer as an inherited disease. Studies of human families over successive generations disclosed that the occurrence of cancer was more frequent in some families than in others. Although common environmental conditions might well have been implicated, it apparently was intellectually more satisfying at the turn of the century to seek possible genetic factors as an explanation for such incidences. Unfortunately, there was little evidence that the mode of cancer inheritance conformed to any of the Mendelian patterns.

The observed inconsistencies stimulated the use of animal systems in which uniform or controlled conditions could be applied. The initial experiments involved spontaneous cancer in breeds of mice raised by fanciers. Attempts by Jensen, Ehrlich, Tyzzer, Loeb, and others to transplant these tumors to other mice produced some successes and many failures. The variance in results was explained when Little and Tyzzer found that several loci were involved in transplanting tumors between two mouse populations. Partly in response to this finding, Wright, who had a particular interest in the mathematics of genetics, developed the theoretical expression of the manner in which genes segregate during the inbreeding process.

In order to attain repeatable and controlled systems for studying factors affecting tumor transplantation and for providing insight into why cancer develops, Little began to inbreed mice to obtain the necessary genetic homogeneity. His inbreeding originated in a line that had been maintained for coat color studies since 1909. By the early 1920's, a number of other lines were developed by Little, Murray, Strong, Bagg, and Lynch.

Many of the early inbred strains of mice originated from a small number of stocks (see Genealogy of the More Commonly Used Inbred Mouse Strains, p. 16, Part 1 of this volume). This relatively restricted gene pool accounts for the similarities and differences in the classic inbred lines. The history of each inbred mouse line is included in the listing of Standardized Nomenclature of Inbred Strains of Mice published regularly in *Cancer Research*.

The original lines of inbred guinea pigs were started by Wright who published an important series of papers dealing with the effect of inbreeding and crossbreeding on general characteristics such as vigor and reproductive effectiveness (see Origin of the Domestic Guinea Pig and of Inbred Strains, p. 505). Most importantly, his work on the inbreeding of the guinea pig led to an understanding of some of the complexities of multiple factor inheritance. Wright's scientific studies also gave rise to the formalization of a method of analysis of breeding systems, called "path analysis," which has been most useful in estimating levels of in-

continued

breeding. The coefficient of inbreeding is the calculated probability that two allelic genes united in a zygote are both descended from the same gene found in an ancestor common to both parents (*see* Definition of Inbred Strains, p. 422).

Philosophy Underlying Use of Inbred Animals

An inbred line consists of a population of great genetic homogeneity, and experiments performed within such a population can test the treatment variability which in the usual, haphazardly bred animal might be confused with genetic variability. Thus, homogeneity of animal stock allows for more sophisticated experiments.

Although the inbred mouse was not originally developed for the purpose of improving experimental design, the use of specifically named and defined animals has served this purpose extremely well. New inbred lines permitted comparison of the characteristics of individual inbred strains within a species. Characterization of each of the several inbred lines also demonstrated that each line might have unique properties because of the random fixation of the genome. The fixed genome of one strain did not resemble that of another strain, and gene action during development and during the life-span, after endogenous or exogenous stimulation, resulted in differences in phenotypic expression.

The use of inbred animals permits (i) the testing of the influences of a specific treatment or manipulation on the response of the animal, with the potential for repetition of the experiments at another time or in another laboratory; and (ii) the exploitation of the unique properties of a particular strain obtained by inbreeding or by selection during the inbreeding process. The concept of uniqueness also includes the introduction of specific alleles into an inbred background to provide a line specifically created for particular studies.

The number of inbred lines and sublines available for experimental use is constantly increasing as new lines are created by inbreeding, by genetic manipulations to create a specifically characterized, genetically homogeneous animal, or by variations discovered within sublines derived from the original parental stock. The qualities of the inbred animal—namely, genetic homogeneity, defined responsiveness to certain stimuli, and the possession of unique behavioral, biochemical, or developmental attributes—allow the investigator to carry out experiments with a much-reduced number of variables. Great precision with small numbers of animals thus becomes possible. One attribute that is lost, of course, is genetic variability, and the investigator who fails to realize that inbred animals may be missing some of the characteristics essential to his research could be in difficulty. He may select a line popular for cancer research but one which is totally unresponsive to the biochemical or behavioral treatment under investigation.

Experiments Requiring Use of Genetically Defined Stocks

Although the well-known inbred lines of mice and the fewer lines of inbred rats, hamsters, guinea pigs, rabbits, and chickens have been available for a long time, it is only in the last 15-20 years that investigators without extensive genetic training have used inbred strains rather than face possible criticism for not having done so. In many instances, both the investigator and critic fail to recognize that the purpose of the experiment may not require the more expensive, inbred animal. Some investigations may even lose their meaningfulness if an inbred animal is used. For example, such an animal is obviously inappropriate for experiments designed to exploit the variability present in a population.

Research requiring laboratory animals falls into three major categories: (i) bioassay, (ii) studies of the attributes of the specific animal or species, and (iii) studies in which the animal serves as the model for another species.

For the bioassay, the ideal animal is one in which the genetic variance is reduced so that the effect of the test substance on the animal can be attributed to the dose, route, or exposure time. The number of animals used can be restricted to the number necessary to give statistically meaningful results, especially if a pilot experiment was performed to establish the variance for the test. The investigator should not assume, however, that the marked reduction in genotypic variance achieved by inbreeding will necessarily eliminate all phenotypic variance. Some experimental evidence suggests that homozygous individuals are less well buffered against minor environmental agents, and that inbred animals may be no more uniform in response than random-bred animals. Use of the F_1 hybrid from two inbred strains, however, retains the advantage of genetic uniformity while adding superior development and physiological homeostasis. The cost of the hybrid also is generally lower than that of pure strains.

When the animal species itself is the target of investigation—either for the development of concepts or for investigation of the animal's attributes—the selection of the strain, strain combination, or substrain should be based on the characteristics necessary to answer the scientific question under consideration. The well-defined inbred strain is probably the most suitable for this kind of study.

The object of the third type of investigation is to discover models for the exploration of human problems, particularly those in which the nature of the knowledge sought involves a treatment or manipulation that for ethical or legal reasons cannot be carried out in man. Since the genetic variability and resultant physiologic differences in man are the products of a haphazard breeding system based on geographic, cultural, socio-economic and other influences, and since an important consideration is that the study be based on population characteristics, the non-inbred is the most desirable animal for such research.

An exact animal model which retains the characteristic of human genetic variability cannot be achieved, but there are several types of heterozygous populations available from which to select the one most closely approximating the extent of variability for the specified line of investigation. The population most commonly used, but in many ways the least suitable, is the so-called random-bred animal, such as the Swiss mouse or the commercial rabbit, rat, or

continued

guinea pig. These populations have an unknown amount of genetic variability, and frequently have much more restricted variability than can be assumed from the term "random-bred."

A wild population or a mixed multi-strain population is useful when a truly heterogenous population is desired. These animals are suitable for the study of population dynamics, but they are not convenient for the separation of genetic from environmental factors.

An interesting population, not commonly available, is one made up of F_1 offspring from many distantly related, highly inbred strains in many combinations of crossbreeding. Although this population is quite different from the human population, it allows the investigator to retain genetic control, as well as to reproduce the identical, defined population. It has the further great advantage of mimicking the genetic diversity of man's genotype, including heterozygosis and its concomitant variability and epistatically acting genotypes.

Since a great many different kinds of experimental animals are now available, the experimental design must include consideration of the best choice of animal. The value of the research results ultimately may be dependent on the selection of the experimental animal. It is essential, therefore, that the investigator be deliberate in his choice of animal and be cognizant of the reputation of the supplier. Fortunately, many sources of laboratory animals use breeding systems that maintain either the homogeneity of the inbred animal or the heterogeneity of the random-bred animal.

Nomenclature

More than 300 strains of inbred lines of mammals are available today; over 250 of these are mouse strains. The nomenclature for all inbred strains reflects both the independent development of the strains and the rugged individualism of the investigators who attach a designation to their particular inbred creation.

Efforts, started in 1932, to achieve a standardized nomenclature for the inbred mouse, have resulted in some degree of uniformity and orderliness (*see* Nomenclature and Rules

Contributor: Carl Cohen

for Mouse Genetics, p. 9, Part 1 of this volume). Wide variety in names and symbols still persists, however, and it is essential that an investigator recognize and understand the symbols designating the specific strain or substrain with which he is working.

There is a standing committee for the nomenclature of the mouse, and regular publication of a standardized nomenclature. The most recent compendium appears in *Cancer Research* 36:4333, 1976, and includes the rules governing the committee's judgments. No other species except the rat has had the benefit of committee action and symbol designation.

A key rule set forth by the committee on mouse nomenclature pertains to the definition of an inbred strain: For a strain to be considered inbred, it must have had the equivalent of 20 generations of brother by sister mating. This rule is rigidly applied in the designation of the mouse, but, because of operational factors, may need to be modified for other species.

In some instances, the designation "inbred" indicates only reduced genetic variability within the strain. Such use of the term generally is in connection with (i) species having lines which represent fewer than 20 inbred generations, but in which skin grafts may be exchanged between all members of the designated line; and (ii) species with long intervals between generations, but to which the term "inbred" may be applied after only a few generations of brother by sister mating.

Other important rules which apply to mouse nomenclature include the designation for substrains and the factors which define a substrain, and the designation for animals having an unusual derivation or experimental background (congenic stocks, foster nursing, ova or ovary transplantation, complex crosses, or embryos preserved by freezing).

It is strongly recommended that the most recent publication of the list of inbred strains be consulted so that an investigator using an inbred mouse fully understands the development and the qualities of the animal used. Although the inbred mouse is referred to as a "reagent," each strain has a long and interesting history which merits attention.

Inbred strains of experimental animals have come into widespread use in research because of their increased genetic uniformity and constancy. These highly valued attributes for experimental strategy in the biomedical and agricultural sciences are gained through the genetic effects of inbreeding.

Inbreeding is the mating of individuals that have at least one ancestor in common. Any one gene from the common ancestor has a chance of being transmitted through both parents, so the resulting offspring will have two homologous alleles identical by descent. In this way the genetic homogeneity in inbred individuals will tend to increase, and progressively so if inbreeding is continuously applied generation after generation.

The *inbreeding coefficient*, F, is a useful theoretical measure of the progress of inbreeding. It is defined as the probability that both alleles at a locus are identical by descent. It therefore indicates the proportionate decrease of heterozygous loci in the inbred individual relative to those in a representative individual of the starting population.

F increases at different rates, depending on the amount of ancestry shared by the systematically mated individuals. Repeated backcrossing to an already existing, highly inbred strain is the most intensive inbreeding attainable in vertebrates. If there is no existing inbred strain, then brother by sister, or younger parent by offspring,

is the most intense type of inbreeding. Brother by sister mating is the regimen conveniently applied to laboratory mammals; regimens of more distant relationships have been found more practicable for experimental farm animals.

The changing values of F in three different mating regimens are presented in Table 1. In all three, F theoretically approaches but never reaches unity. In practice, however, inbreeding gains will tend to level off even before unity, due to the countering effect of new mutations. This reservoir of mutations, although very small, prevents the highly inbred strain from ever being genetically constant through time, and it permits separately maintained sublines of the strain to become genetically divergent because of the genetic fixation of mutant alleles at different loci. Long-separated sublines of inbred strains therefore should always be appropriately identified by the conventional symbols to avoid confusion in comparing research results that would otherwise be taken without question as applying to the strain in general.

F is a theoretical value calculated from a pedigree, and not only does it ignore mutational effects, it also ignores effects of selection favoring heterozygotes. For a species in which inbreeding is difficult, i.e., when many matings fail to produce viable offspring, one can assume that selection has favored heterozygotes. The calculated F in such cases is an over-estimate.

Table 1. **Inbreeding Coefficients Under Three Systems of Close Inbreeding**

Data were modified from reference 1.

Generation	F		
	Repeated Backcrosses to Highly Inbred Line[1]	**Full Brother x Sister, or Offspring x Younger Parent**	**Half Sib**[2]
0	0	0	0
1	0.500	0.250	0.125
2	0.750	0.375	0.219
3	0.875	0.500	0.305
4	0.938	0.594	0.381
5	0.969	0.672	0.449
6	0.984	0.734	0.509
7	0.992	0.785	0.563
8	0.996	0.826	0.611
9	0.998	0.859	0.654
10	0.999	0.886	0.691
11	1	0.908	0.725
12	1	0.926	0.755
13	1	0.940	0.782
14	1	0.951	0.806
15	1	0.961	0.827
16	1	0.968	0.846
17	1	0.974	0.863
18	1	0.979	0.878
19	1	0.983	0.891
20	1	0.986	0.903

[1] Generation 0 is equivalent to generation N_1 in Figure 1. [2] Females are half sisters to males.

continued

The ultimate objective of inbreeding is to attain uniformity and constancy of genotype. Theoretical probabilities of attaining three different aspects of this objective by brother by sister mating are presented in Table 2. One aspect is *homozygosity* [ref. 3]—the homozygous condition *an individual* attains at a locus that was heterozygous at the outset of inbreeding. Another is *genetic fixation*—the homozygous condition *both individuals* of a generation attain for the same allele at a locus that was heterozygous at the outset of inbreeding [ref. 2]. Such a genotypic mating combination perpetuates itself in succeeding generations; it is irreversible, barring mutation.

A third aspect is *genome purity*. This is a theoretical concept based on the assumption that parents of the first in-

bred generation are heterozygous at all loci in the genome. As inbreeding progresses, the *heterogenic tracts* (those chromosomal segments that have not yet become homogeneous through genetic fixation) will decrease in number and mean length [ref. 2]. The proportion of the genome involved in these tracts is estimated by the difference between unity and the value in the genetic-fixation column of Table 2. From this it is clear that relatively few genes would be included in these tracts in later generations. Nevertheless, there is a sufficient number of such tracts present so that it is not until generation 60 that one has a 99 percent chance of being completely rid of them—the condition of genome purity.

Table 2. Effects of Brother by Sister Inbreeding on the Genotype

Calculations are based on the methods of Fisher [ref. 2]. For **Probability of Homozygosity** and for **Probability of Genetic Fixation**, a locus is selected at which the two parents in generation 0 are both heterozygous with four alleles, i.e., a double cross (ab x cd). **Probability of Purity**: The probability that no heterogenic tract (chromosomal segment of heterogeneous origin) remains in the genome; it has been assumed that the genome length is 1500 centi-Morgans.

Generation	Probability of Homozygosity[1]	Probability of Genetic Fixation	Probability of Purity
0	0	0	0
5	0.594	0.409	0
10	0.859	0.785	0
15	0.951	0.925	0
20	0.983	0.974	0
25	0.994	0.991	0.009
30	0.998	0.997	0.140
35	0.999	0.999	0.500
40	1	1	0.728
45	1	1	0.883
50	1	1	0.953
55	1	1	0.982
60	1	1	0.993

[1] Homozygosity is equivalent to F, but, unlike F in Table 1, it is delayed one generation due to starting with a double instead of a single cross.

For those species easily inbred, such as the laboratory mouse, the conventional criterion for declaring a strain "inbred" is that it be continuously maintained by matings of brother by sister for 20 generations (when F = 0.986). Before then, it is an "incipient" inbred strain. For other species, such as poultry, which are difficult if not impossible to inbreed at the intensity of the brother by sister regimen, the term "inbred" is commonly used to describe any line which is more inbred than the population from which it arose.

Contributor: Donald W. Bailey

References

1. Falconer, D. S. 1960. Introduction to Quantitative Genetics. Oliver and Boyd, Edinburgh.

2. Fisher, R. A. 1949. Theory of Inbreeding. Oliver and Boyd, London.
3. Wright, S. 1921. Genetics 6:167-178.

III. HAMSTER

DESCRIPTION OF SYRIAN HAMSTER

The Syrian hamster (*Mesocricetus auratus*) is a small rodent that has been used increasingly in biomedical research since it was domesticated in 1931. Adult animals of this species weigh approximately 100-150 g, and can fit comfortably in the cupped palm of the human hand. The coat is short and soft, and its color, being characteristically agouti, has given rise to the animal's popular name, "golden hamster."

Hamsters possess only a rudimentary tail. On their flanks are two relatively conspicuous pigmented areas (more prominent in males) that are known as "sex spots." From a comparative anatomic standpoint, the most unusual feature of the hamster is the presence of two eversible cheek pouches. These relatively large, epithelially lined outpouchings from the buccal cavity are used by the animal to carry food and to bring materials to its burrow.

The native habitat of the Syrian hamster is the agricultural region surrounding Aleppo in northwestern Syria and extending into southern Turkey. In this relatively fertile area, the animal is a nocturnal forager and is usually regarded by the local farmers as a pest. The animals live in small breeding units, located in burrows 3-6 feet underground, and during the often harsh and prolonged winters may hibernate. Syrian hamsters new to experimental domestication are usually regarded as vicious, and frequently must be handled with forceps, or forceps and gloves. They quickly adjust, however, to human handling, and are widely used as pets in western Europe and the United States.

The table below shows the appropriate taxonomic location of the Syrian hamster (*M. auratus*).

Hierarchy	Scientific Name	Common Name
Class	Mammalia	Mammals
Order	Rodentia	Rodents
Family	Cricetidae	New World rats, mice, hamsters, muskrats, gerbils
Subfamily	Cricetinae	Hamsters
Genus & species	*Cansumys*	Gray long-tailed hamster
	Cricetulus alticola	
	C. barabensis	
	C. barabensis griseus (C. griseus)	Chinese hamster
	C. lama	
	C. longicaudatus	
	C. migratorius	Armenian hamster
	Cricetus	European hamster
	Mesocricetus auratus	Syrian or golden hamster
	M. brandti	Kurdistan hamster
	M. newtoni	Rumanian hamster
	Phodopus roborovskii	Desert hamster
	P. songorus	Djzungarian hamster

Until 1970, all experimental hamsters used in the United States and Europe were derived from three littermates caught in 1930 in the wild near Aleppo, Syria. The detailed account of their capture and ultimate dissemination to laboratories around the world has been fully documented by Dr. George Yerganian in reference 2. All inbred lines commercially available at this time in the United States and England were derived from these three littermates, and therefore represent the progeny of a very restricted gene pool.

In 1970, an expedition to Syria by Dr. Michael R. Murphy resulted in the capture of at least a dozen wild Syrian hamsters from scattered areas around the city of Aleppo. Genetically inbred lines are being developed from these animals, but no fully isogenic strains have yet emerged. None of these animals is commercially available at this time.

Experimental work for which the Syrian hamster seems to be particularly well-suited is highly diverse. A listing of such investigations is given on the following pages.

Contributor: J. Wayne Streilein

General References

1. Hoffman, R. A., et al., ed. 1968. The Golden Hamster. Iowa State Univ. Press, Ames.
2. Homburger, F., ed. 1972. Prog. Exp. Tumor Res. 16.
3. Streilein, J. W., et al., ed. 1978. Fed. Proc. Fed. Am. Soc. Exp. Biol. 37:2023-2108.

INVESTIGATIONS FOR WHICH THE HAMSTER IS WELL-SUITED

Data have been adapted and updated from information of G. P. Fulton, page 5 in *The Golden Hamster, Its Biology* *and Use in Medical Research*, 1968 (R. A. Hoffman, et al., ed. Iowa State University Press, Ames).

Investigation	Reference
Aging	86,126, 131,132, 146,184, 188,189
Bacteriological & viral studies	
Colorado tick fever	59,60
Influenza virus	103,182
Influenzavirus & *Paramyxovirus* infections of the central nervous system	104
Leprosy, human	14
Leprosy, rat	21,24
Newcastle disease	158-161
Non-viral intracellular infections	66
Oncogenic viruses[1]	19,58
Plague	128
Poliomyelitis	148,190
Rabies	113,162
Range of specificity to viral infections	201
Scrapie	124
Staphylococcus infection	114,214
St. Louis encephalitis	36,37
Tubercle bacilli	46,51,81
Tularemia	116
Virus pneumonia	57
Cardiovascular research	
Arteriosclerosis	18,76,184
Cardiomyopathy	22,23,74, 84,200
Experimental hypertension	193
Lipemia	48
Microcirculatory studies	45,67-70, 110,121
Dental caries	20,102, 107-109, 133,134
Experimental animal model use in study of diseases	
Alloxan diabetes	195,199
Cancer	136
Central nervous system cancer	139
Larynx (cigarette smoke-induced) cancer	27,53,89
Lingual cancer	72,123
Lung cancer	118,119, 127
Mammary cancer	13,50
Pancreatic cancer	17,153, 154,196
Tracheal cancer	82,178
Cancer chemotherapy	11
Chemical carcinogenesis	91,93,94, 96,97, 152

Investigation	Reference
Chronic bronchitis & emphysema	87
Experimental goiter	33,63-65
Experimental syphilis	207
Interaction of chemical carcinogens & parasites	38
Obesity	25
Polymyopathy	73,74,90
Prostatic hypertrophy	92,177, 205
Teratology	95
von Recklinghausen's disease	151
Experimental carcinogenesis in cheek pouch	75,91, 137,172, 174,180, 181,215
Experimental psychology studies	
Hoarding behavior	187,204
Maze learning	170
Hibernation	34,35,39, 106,122
Host for parasitological studies	
Entamoeba histolytica ⟨*Endamoeba hystolytica*⟩	49
Hymenolepis	115,157, 194
Kala-azar	16
Leishmania	15,71,77, 78
Schistosomiasis	47
Taenia	176
Trichinella	32,101
Nutritional studies	31,143
Experimental rickets	105
Vitamin A deficiency	88,173
Vitamin A in gallstone formation	80
Vitamin A in neoplasia of larynx	129
Vitamin B_6 deficiency	179
Vitamin B_{12} requirements	175
Vitamin C requirements	42
Vitamin E & muscle degeneration	98,125
Pharmacological studies	26,40,79, 85,169, 200,213
Pineal gland: illumination, melatonin, & reproductive function	197,198, 202,203, 208,209
Research in genetics & immunogenetics	
Colchicine	145
Delayed cutaneous inflammatory reaction	156
DNA & cytotaxonomy	138
Graft versus host ⟨GVH⟩	192

[1] There is a rich and abundant literature on all aspects of viral oncogenesis in hamsters that cannot be documented adequately here; those interested are encouraged to trace the many fine additional reviews.

continued

Investigation	Reference
Heterologous GVH	130
Major histocompatibility complex ⟨MHC⟩	54-56
Mutations	166-168, 210-212
Predicting histocompatibility	191
Sex chromosomes	111,112
Sex behavior & pheromones	52,144, 183
Tooth transplantation	43,140-142,163, 165
Transplantation of embryonal, neonatal, and/or adult tissues in cheek pouch	
Adrenal cortex	150
Cheek pouch morphology	155
Embryonic explants	83,185, 186,206
Heart	149

Investigation	Reference
Pancreas	99,100, 171
Skin	44,164
Transplantation of normal and/or malignant tissues in sites other than cheek pouch	
Cell cultures	6,8,10,61, 62
Heterotopic transplantation of cheek pouch	4,30,215
Human infectious mononucleosis cells	10,12
Human leukemic cells	8,9,135
Skin	1,2,7,28-30
Tumor growth in cheek pouch, both homografts & heterografts	3-5,28,41, 67,83, 117,120, 147
Cheek pouch test for malignancy of cultured cells	61,62

Contributors: Freddy Homburger and Richard A. Adams

References

1. Adams, R. A. 1956. Anat. Rec. 125:646.
2. Adams, R. A. 1958. Ibid. 5:24-26.
3. Adams, R. A. 1963. Cancer Res. 23:1834-1840.
4. Adams, R. A. 1963. Ibid. 23:1841-1846.
5. Adams, R. A. 1964. Science 146:944-945.
6. Adams, R. A. 1970. Cancer Res. 30:338-345.
7. Adams, R. A., et al. 1956. Transplant. Bull. 3:41-42.
8. Adams, R. A., et al. 1967. Cancer Res. 27:772-783.
9. Adams, R. A., et al. 1968. Ibid. 28:1121-1125.
10. Adams, R. A., et al. 1971. Cancer 27:651-657.
11. Adams, R. A., et al. 1972. Ibid. 29:524-533.
12. Adams, R. A., et al. 1973. Ibid. 31:1397-1407.
13. Adams, R. A., et al. 1979. Prog. Exp. Tumor Res. 24: 408-413.
14. Adler, S. 1938. Int. J. Lepr. 6:467-596.
15. Adler, S. 1947. Trans. R. Soc. Trop. Med. Hyg. 40: 701-712.
16. Adler, S., and O. Theodor. 1931. Proc. R. Soc. London B108:453-463.
17. Althoff, J., et al. 1975. Cancer Lett. 1:21-24.
18. Altschul, R. 1946. Arch. Pathol. 42:277-284.
19. Ambrose, K. R., and J. H. Coggin. 1975. J. Natl. Cancer Inst. 54:877-880.
20. Arnold, F. A., Jr. 1942. Public Health Rep. 57:1599-1604.
21. Ashbel, R. 1947. Trans. R. Soc. Trop. Med. Hyg. 40: 457-458.
22. Bajusz, E. 1969. Nature (London) 223:406-407.
23. Bajusz, E., et al. 1969. Ann. N. Y. Acad. Sci. 156: 105-129.
24. Balfour-Jones, S. E. B. 1939. Int. J. Lepr. 7:77-83.
25. Bernfeld, P. 1979. Prog. Exp. Tumor Res. 24:118-126.
26. Bernfeld, P., and F. Homburger. 1972. Toxicol. Appl. Pharmacol. 22:324.
27. Bernfeld, P., et al. 1974. J. Natl. Cancer Inst. 53:1141-1157.
28. Billingham, R. E., and W. K. Silvers, ed. 1961. Transplantation of Tissues and Cells. Wistar Institute, Philadelphia.
29. Billingham, R. E., et al. 1960. Proc. Natl. Acad. Sci. USA 46:1079-1090.
30. Billingham, R., et al. 1964. Proc. R. Soc. London B161:168.
31. Birt, D. F., and P. Pour. 1979. Prog. Exp. Tumor Res. 24:145-156.
32. Boyd, E. M., and E. J. Huston. 1954. J. Parasitol. 40: 686-690.
33. Braun, H. G. 1953. Berl. Muench. Tieraerztl. Wochenschr. 66:160.
34. Brock, M. A. 1960. Am. J. Physiol. 198:1181-1186.
35. Brock, M. A. 1960. Ibid. 199:195-197.
36. Broun, G. O., et al. 1941. Proc. Soc. Exp. Biol. Med. 46:601-603.
37. Broun, G. O., et al. 1941. Ibid. 48:310-313.
38. Bulay, O., et al. 1977. J. Natl. Cancer Inst. 59:1625-1629.
39. Chatfield, P. O., and C. P. Lyman. 1954. Electroencephalogr. Clin. Neurophysiol. 6:403-408.
40. Chen, K. K., et al. 1945. J. Pharmacol. Exp. Ther. 85: 348-355.
41. Chute, R. N., et al. 1952. Cancer Res. 12:912-914.
42. Clausen, D. E., and W. G. Clark. 1943. Nature (London) 152:300-301.
43. Coburn, R. 1960. J. Dent. Res. 39:707.

continued

44. Cohen, S. N. 1961. Proc. Soc. Exp. Biol. Med. 106: 677-680.
45. Copley, A. L. 1948. Fed. Proc. Fed. Am. Soc. Exp. Biol. 7:22-23.
46. Corper, H. J., and M. L. Cohn. 1944. Am. J. Clin. Pathol. 14:571-576.
47. Cram, E. B., and J. Bozicevich. 1944. Trop. Med. News 1:16-17.
48. Cullen, C. F., and R. L. Swank. 1954. Circulation 9: 335-345.
49. DeLamater, J. N., et al. 1954. Am. J. Trop. Med. Hyg. 3:1-8.
50. Della Porta, G. 1961. Cancer Res. 21:575-579.
51. Dennis, E. W., et al. 1949. Ann. N. Y. Acad. Sci. 52: 646-661.
52. Di Nicolo, A. 1953. Ph.D. Thesis. Bucknell Univ., Lewisburg, PA.
53. Dontenwill, W. 1973. J. Natl. Cancer Inst. 51:1781-1832.
54. Duncan, W. R., and J. W. Streilein. 1977. J. Immunol. 118:832-839.
55. Duncan, W. R., and J. W. Streilein. 1978. Transplantation 25:12-16.
56. Duncan, W. R., and J. W. Streilein. 1978. Ibid. 25:17-22.
57. Eaton, M. D., et al. 1945. J. Exp. Med. 82:329-342.
58. Eddy, B. E. 1972. Prog. Exp. Tumor Res. 16:454-496.
59. Florio, L., et al. 1950. J. Immunol. 64:257-263.
60. Florio, L., et al. 1950. Ibid. 64:265-272.
61. Foley, G. E., et al. 1962. Natl. Cancer Inst. Monogr. 7:173-204.
62. Foley, G. E., et al. 1962. In M. J. Brennan, ed. Biological Interactions in Normal and Neoplastic Growth. Little, Brown; Boston. pp. 75-87.
63. Follis, R. H., Jr. 1959. Proc. Soc. Exp. Biol. Med. 100:203-206.
64. Follis, R. H., Jr. 1959. Ibid. 102:425-429.
65. Follis, R. H., Jr. 1959. Trans. Assoc. Am. Physicians 72:265-274.
66. Frenkel, J. K. 1978. Fed. Proc. Fed. Am. Soc. Exp. Biol. 37:2063-2064.
67. Fulton, G. P., and B. R. Lutz. 1957. Boston Med. Q. 8:13-19.
68. Fulton, G. P., et al. 1946. Anat. Rec. 96:537.
69. Fulton, G. P., et al. 1946. Ibid. 96:554-555.
70. Fulton, G. P., et al. 1953. Blood 8:140-152.
71. Fulton, J. D. 1944. Ann. Trop. Med. Parasitol. 38: 147-158.
72. Fujita, K. 1973. J. Dent. Res. 52:327-330.
73. Gertz, E. W. 1972. Prog. Exp. Tumor Res. 16:242-260.
74. Gertz, E. W. 1973. Am. J. Pathol. 70:151-154.
75. Ghadially, F. N., and O. Illman. 1961. J. Pathol. Bacteriol. 81:45-48.
76. Goldman, J., and O. J. Pollak. 1949. Am. Heart J. 38: 474.
77. Goodwin, L. G. 1945. Nature (London) 156:476.
78. Goodwin, L. G. 1945. Trans. R. Soc. Trop. Med. Hyg. 39:133-145.
79. Goodwin, L. G., and F. B. Marshall. 1945. J. Pharmacol. Exp. Ther. 84:16-25.
80. Granados, H., et al. 1977. 13 Congr. Latinoam. Cienc. Fisiol. 20 Congr. Nacl. Cienc. Fisiol. Mex. Resume. Comun., p. 173.
81. Griffith, A. S. 1941. J. Hyg. 41:260-265.
82. Grubbs, C. J., et al. 1979. Prog. Exp. Tumor Res. 24:345-355.
83. Handler, A. H., and G. Yerganian. 1954. Proc. Am. Assoc. Cancer Res. 1:18.
84. Handler, A. H., et al. 1975. Proc. Soc. Exp. Biol. Med. 148:573-577.
85. Harris, P. N., et al. 1946. J. Pharmacol. Exp. Ther. 87:382-388.
86. Haverland, L. H., et al. 1972. Prog. Exp. Tumor Res. 16:120-141.
87. Hayes, J. A., et al. 1977. Lab. Anim. Sci. 27:762-770.
88. Hirschi, R. G. 1950. J. Oral Surg. 8:3-11.
89. Hoffmann, D., et al. 1979. Prog. Exp. Tumor Res. 24:370-390.
90. Homburger, F. 1972. Ibid. 16:69-86.
91. Homburger, F. 1972. Ibid. 16:152-175.
92. Homburger, F., and C. W. Nixon. 1970. Proc. Soc. Exp. Biol. Med. 134:284-286.
93. Homburger, F., and A. B. Russfield. 1970. Cancer Res. 30:305-308.
94. Homburger, F., et al. 1962. Med. Exp. 6:339-345.
95. Homburger, F., et al. 1965. Toxicol. Appl. Pharmacol. 7:686-693.
96. Homburger, F., et al. 1972. Cancer Res. 32:360-366.
97. Homburger, F., et al. 1978. Fed. Proc. Fed. Am. Soc. Exp. Biol. 37:2090-2092.
98. Houchin, O. B. 1942. Ibid. 1:117-118.
99. House, E. L., et al. 1958. Endocrinology 63:389-391.
100. House, E. L., et al. 1958. Anat. Rec. 130:316.
101. Humes, A. G., and R. P. Akers. 1952. Ibid. 114:103-113.
102. Hurst, V., et al. 1949. J. Dent. Res. 28:430-432.
103. Jennings, R., and C. W. Potter. 1978. Fed. Proc. Fed. Am. Soc. Exp. Biol. 37:2072-2073.
104. Johnson, K. P. 1978. Ibid. 37:2074-2075.
105. Jones, J. H. 1945. J. Nutr. 30:143-146.
106. Kayser, C. 1939. Ann. Physiol. Physiochim. Biol. 15:1087-1219.
107. Keyes, P. H. 1956. J. Dent. Res. 35:95-101.
108. Keyes, P. H., and P. P. Dale. 1944. Ibid. 23:208-209.
109. Keyes, P. H., and P. P. Dale. 1944. Ibid. 23:427-438.
110. Kivy, E. 1951. J. Morphol. 88:573-593.
111. Koller, P. C. 1938. J. Genet. 36:177-195.
112. Koller, P. C. 1946. Proc. R. Soc. London B133:313-316.

continued

113. Koprowski, H., and H. R. Cox. 1948. J. Immunol. 60:533-554.
114. Krasner, R. I., and G. Young. 1958. J. Bacteriol. 76:349-354.
115. Larsh, J. R., Jr. 1946. J. Parasitol. 32:477-479.
116. Larson, C. L. 1945. Public Health Rep. 60:839-841.
117. Lemon, H. M., et al. 1952. Science 115:461-465.
118. Little, J. B., and A. R. Kennedy. 1979. Prog. Exp. Tumor Res. 24:356-369.
119. Little, J. B., et al. 1973. Eur. J. Cancer 9:825-828.
120. Lutz, B. R., et al. 1950. Cancer Res. 10:231-232.
121. Lutz, B. R., et al. 1951. Anat. Rec. 109:412.
122. Lyman, C. P., and D. W. Fawcett. 1954. Cancer Res. 14:25-28.
123. Marefat, P., and G. Shklar. 1979. Prog. Exp. Tumor Res. 24:259-268.
124. Marsh, R. F., and R. P. Hanson. 1978. Fed. Proc. Fed. Am. Soc. Exp. Biol. 37:2076-2078.
125. Mason, K. E., and W. T. West. 1954. Anat. Rec. 118:327-328.
126. McCay, C. M. 1951. J. Gerontol. 6(Suppl.):123.
127. McDowell, E. M., et al. 1978. J. Natl. Cancer Inst. 61:577-586.
128. McMahon, M. C. 1944. Public Health Rep. 59:234-236.
129. Meade, P. D., et al. 1979. Prog. Exp. Tumor Res. 24:320-329.
130. Merk, L. P., et al. 1974. Proc. Am. Assoc. Cancer Res. 15:132.
131. Meyers, M. W. 1950. Anat. Rec. 106:282-283.
132. Meyers, M. W., and H. A. Charipper. 1956. Ibid. 124:1-25.
133. Mitchell, D. F., and M. J. Johnson. 1957. J. Dent. Res. 36:372-374.
134. Mitchell, D. F. and W. G. Shafer. 1949. Ibid. 28:424-429.
135. Miyoshi, I., et al. 1978. Proc. Am. Assoc. Cancer Res. 19:12(Abstr. 48).
136. Mohr, U. 1979. Prog. Exp. Tumor Res. 24:235-244.
137. Morris, A. L. 1961. J. Dent. Res. 40:3-15.
138. Moses, M. J., and G. Yerganian. 1952. Genetics 37:607-608.
139. Mukai, N. 1975. Year Book of Cancer. Year Book, Chicago. pp. 31-33.
140. Myers, H. I., and V. D. Flanagan. 1955. J. Dent. Res. 34:715.
141. Myers, H. I., and V. D. Flanagan. 1958. Anat. Rec. 130:432-433.
142. Myers, H. I., and V. D. Flanagan. 1958. Ibid. 130:497-513.
143. Newberne, P. 1979. Prog. Exp. Tumor Res. 24:127-138.
144. O'Connell, R. J. 1978. Fed. Proc. Fed. Am. Soc. Exp. Biol. 37:2099-2101.
145. Orsini, M. W., and B. Pansky. 1952. Science 115:88-89.
146. Ortiz, E. 1955. Anat. Rec. 122:517-537.
147. Patterson, W. B., et al. 1954. Cancer Res. 14:656-659.
148. Plotz, H., et al. 1942. Proc. Soc. Exp. Biol. Med. 51:124-126.
149. Poor, E. 1957. Transplant. Bull. 4:143-144.
150. Poor, E. 1958. Proc. Soc. Exp. Biol. Med. 97:535-539.
151. Pour, P. 1977. Abstr. Symp. Syrian Hamster Toxicol. Carcinogenesis Res., p. 39.
152. Pour, P. 1979. Prog. Exp. Tumor Res. 24:391-396.
153. Pour, P., and J. Althoff. 1977. Cancer Lett. 2:233-238.
154. Pour, P., et al. 1974. Am. J. Pathol. 76:349-358.
155. Priddy, R. B., and A. F. Brodie. 1948. J. Morphol. 83:149-180.
156. Ramseier, H., and R. E. Billingham. 1966. J. Exp. Med. 123:629.
157. Read, C. P. 1951. J. Parasitol. 37:324.
158. Reagan, R. L., et al. 1948. Am. J. Vet. Res. 9:220-224.
159. Reagan, R. L., et al. 1948. Cornell Vet. 38:418-420.
160. Reagan, R. L., et al. 1948. Proc. Soc. Exp. Biol. Med. 67:234-236.
161. Reagan, R. L., et al. 1948. Ibid. 68:293-294.
162. Reagan, R. L., et al. 1953. Ibid. 83:793-794.
163. Reece, C. N. 1959. Oral Surg. Oral Med. Oral Pathol. 12:736-743.
164. Resnick, B., et al. 1960. Arch. Dermatol. 81:394-399.
165. Robinson, P. J. 1978. Fed. Proc. Fed. Am. Soc. Exp. Biol. 37:2059-2060.
166. Robinson, R. 1962. Am. Nat. 96:183-185.
167. Robinson, R. 1962. Genetica (the Hague) 33:81-87.
168. Robinson, R. 1962. Heredity 17:477-486.
169. Rogers, W. I., et al. 1963. Cancer Chemother. Rep. 29:77-83.
170. Rowland, J. A., and R. H. Waters. 1955. Psychol. Rep. 1:437-440.
171. Sak, M. F., and I. A. Macchi. 1962. Am. Zool. 2:443-444.
172. Salley, J. J. 1953. J. Dent. Res. 32:679.
173. Salley, J. J., and W. F. Bryson. 1957. Ibid. 36:935-944.
174. Salley, J. J., and S. J. Kreshover. 1959. Oral Surg. Oral Med. Oral Pathol. 12:501-508.
175. Scheid, H. E., et al. 1950. Proc. Soc. Exp. Biol. Med. 75:236-239.
176. Schiller, E. L. 1949. J. Parasitol. 35:37-38.
177. Schmidt, T. J., and W. J. Visek. 1977. Proc. Soc. Exp. Biol. Med. 155:105-110.
178. Schreiber, H., et al. 1975. J. Natl. Cancer Inst. 54:187-197.
179. Schwartzman, G., and L. Strauss. 1949. Fed. Proc. Fed. Am. Soc. Exp. Biol. 8:369.
180. Shklar, G., and E. Eisenberg. 1979. Prog. Exp. Tumor Res. 24:269-282.

continued

181. Shubik, P. 1959. Acta Unio Int. Contra Cancrum 15:554-558.
182. Sigel, M. M., et al. 1949. Proc. Soc. Exp. Biol. Med. 72:507-510.
183. Singer, A. G., et al. 1976. Science 191:948-950.
184. Smith, J. W. H. 1951. J. Gerontol. 6(Suppl.):151.
185. Smith, T. E., Jr., and D. I. Patt. 1958. Anat. Rec. 130:374.
186. Smith, T. E., Jr., and D. I. Patt. 1958. Ibid. 131:160.
187. Smith, W. I., and S. Ross. 1950. J. Genet. Psychol. 77:211-215.
188. Soderwall, A. L., et al. 1956. J. Geront. 11:441.
189. Spagnoli, H. H., and H. A. Charipper. 1955. Anat. Rec. 121:117-139.
190. Stebbins, M. R., and S. G. Lensen. 1949. Proc. Soc. Exp. Biol. Med. 71:272-274.
191. Streilein, J. W., and R. E. Billingham. 1968. Transplantation 6:694.
192. Streilein, J. W., and R. E. Billingham. 1970. J. Exp. Med. 132:163.
193. Stroia, L. N., et al. 1954. Am. J. Physiol. 179:154-158.
194. Stunkard, H. W. 1945. J. Parasitol. 31:151.
195. Sudak, F. N., et al. 1956. Anat. Rec. 124:367.
196. Takahashi, M., et al. 1977. Lab. Anim. Sci. 27:336-342.
197. Tamarkin, L., et al. 1977. Science 198:953-955.
198. Tamarkin, L., et al. 1977. Endocrinology 101:631-634.
199. Tassoni, J. P., et al. 1955. Anat. Rec. 122:485.
200. Taylor, G. J., and R. T. Drew. 1975. Toxicol. Appl. Pharmacol. 32:177-183.
201. Toolan, H. W. 1978. Fed. Proc. Fed. Am. Soc. Exp. Biol. 37:2065-2068.
202. Turek, F. W. 1977. Proc. Soc. Exp. Biol. Med. 155:31-34.
203. Turek, F. W., et al. 1975. Science 190:280.
204. Waddell, D. 1951. J. Comp. Physiol. Psychol. 44:383-388.
205. Wang, G. M., and C. P. Schaffner. 1976. Invest. Urol. 14:66-71.
206. Waterman, A. J., and J. F. Wohnus. 1952. Anat. Rec. 113:599.
207. Wile, U. J., and S. A. M. Johnson. 1945. Am. J. Syph. Gonorrhea Vener. Dis. 29:418-422.
208. Wurtman, R. J., and M. A. Moskowitz. 1977. N. Engl. J. Med. 296:1329-1333.
209. Wurtman, R. J., and M. A. Moskowitz. 1977. Ibid. 296:1383-1386.
210. Yoon, C. H. 1972. J. Hered. 63:344-346.
211. Yoon, C. H. 1973. Ibid. 64:305-307.
212. Yoon, C. H. 1975. Invest. Ophthalmol. 14:321-325.
213. York, I. M., et al. 1963. J. Pharmacol. Exp. Ther. 141:36-49.
214. Young, G. 1954. J. Exp. Med. 99:299-306.
215. Ziegler, M. M., and C. F. Barker. 1978. Fed. Proc. Fed. Am. Soc. Exp. Biol. 37:2057-2058.

USEFULNESS OF THE HAMSTER IN THE STUDY OF HIBERNATION

Two genera of hamsters, *Mesocricetus* and *Cricetus*, have been used in the study of hibernation. The Syrian or golden hamster, *M. auratus*, has been used extensively in the United States and to a lesser extent in Europe. The Turkish hamster, *M. brandti*, was imported to the United States in 1965 and has been used in hibernation research in a few laboratories since that time. The European hamster, *C. cricetus*, has been used in Europe but rarely in the United States.

The Syrian hamster may enter deep hibernation at any season of the year if exposed to the cold ($5 \pm 2°C$) and given ample food and bedding. Cold exposure results in the desaturation of white adipose tissue, so that this animal is an adequate model for the study of factors controlling the saturation of fat [ref. 1]. Hibernation, however, is unpredictable in this species, and a large percentage of the animals never hibernate when exposed to the cold. There is evidence that some laboratory strains hibernate more readily than others. Failure to do so cannot be attributed to laboratory breeding over the past 45 years, since animals newly obtained from Syria hibernate no more readily than do laboratory animals [ref. 2].

The total season of hibernation for the Syrian hamster is shorter than for the golden mantled or thirteen-lined ground squirrels, and the periods of continuous hibernation are shorter. Syrian hamsters are also very sensitive to external stimuli when in hibernation, making them difficult to manipulate without causing arousal. Because of these characteristics, *M. auratus* is not the animal of choice for multiple measurements involving physical manipulations. It is suitable for single experiments in the hibernating state, particularly when it is desirable to use animals of known history and lineage.

The region native to the Turkish hamster surrounds that of the Syrian hamster and extends across Turkey into the Caucasus and northern Iraq and Iran. The Turkish species can be raised in the laboratory, but the offspring must be separated soon after weaning or fights to the death will ensue. It usually hibernates when exposed to cold in the autumn. The hibernating season and periods of continuous hibernation are longer than for the Syrian hamster, and are comparable to those of the golden mantled and thirteen-lined ground squirrels [ref. 2]. Although the Turkish hamster is larger than the Syrian hamster, its small size is a disadvantage if the animal must be fitted with bulky recording apparatus, particularly since it does not tolerate readily any type of extraneous equipment. Nevertheless, it is the animal of choice when known history and lineage, as well as the tendency to hibernate readily and for long periods, are required.

The European hamster, *C. cricetus*, is much larger than the Syrian or Turkish species, being about the size of a guinea pig. It apparently can be raised in captivity, but there is no detailed account of its laboratory care. Although its larger size may be advantageous for some experiments, the animal is said to be vicious and not inclined to tolerate encumbering apparatus. [ref. 3]

Contributor: Charles P. Lyman

References

1. Fawcett, D. W., and C. P. Lyman. 1954. J. Physiol. (London) 126:235-247.

2. Lyman, C. P., and R. C. O'Brien. 1977. Breviora 442.
3. Malan, A. 1969. Arch. Sci. Physiol. 23:47-87.

NORMAL HEMATOLOGIC VALUES IN SYRIAN HAMSTER

Specification	Value	Reference
Strain (CB × MHA)F$_1$		
Reticulocyte count, %	2.0 ± 0.4	6
Hematocrit, ml/100 ml blood	51.6 ± 0.7	6
Leukocyte count, 10^3/μl	6.5 ± 1.2	6
Neutrophils, %	21	6
Eosinophils, %	1	6
Basophils, %	0	6
Monocytes, %	12	6
Lymphocytes, %	66	6
Platelets, 10^3/μl	600 ± 60	6
Outbred Strains		
Blood volume, ml/100 g body wt	7.97 ± 0.64	3
Erythrocyte count, 10^6/μl	6.96 ± 0.7	4
	6.96 ± 1.51	1
Reticulocyte count, %	1.3 ± 0.05	2
Hemoglobin, g/100 ml blood	16.0 ± 0.7	1

Specification	Value	Reference
	16.1 ± 1.3	2
	16.2 ± 1.3	4
Hematocrit, ml/100 ml blood	49.0 ± 5	1
	49.1 ± 2.1	2
	50.7 ± 3.0	4
	51.9 ± 3.4	3
Erythrocyte sedimentation rate, mm/hr	1.2 ± 0.6	1
	1.6 ± 0.5	4
Leukocyte count, 10^3/μl	3.4 ± 7.6	4
Neutrophils, %	30	4
Eosinophils, %	1	4
Basophils, %	0	4
Monocytes, %	3	4
Lymphocytes, %	66	4
Platelets, 10^3/μl	297 ± 73	4
Unspecified Strains		
Leukocyte count, 10^3/μl	5.78 ± 1.29	5

Contributor: J. Wayne Streilein

Specific References

1. Eddy, H. A., and G. W. Casarett. 1972. Prog. Exp. Tumor Res. 16:98-119.
2. Friedell, G. H., and P. D. Bannon. 1972. Ibid. 16:87-97.
3. Kutscher, C. 1968. Comp. Biochem. Physiol. 25:929-936.
4. Schermer, S. 1967. Blood Morphology of Laboratory Animals. Ed. 3. F. A. Davis, Philadelphia. pp. 75-84.
5. Sherman, J. D., and D. I. Patt. 1956. Cancer Res. 16: 394-401.
6. Streilein, J. W., and J. Streilein. 1972. Transplantation 13:378-390.

General Reference

7. Hill, B. F., ed. 1973. Charles River Dig. 12(1).

NORMAL SERUM PROTEINS IN SYRIAN HAMSTER

A variety of proteins in the serum of Syrian hamsters has been quantified by agar-ring diffusion assay [ref. 4], using specific antisera. Serum levels of four known immunoglobulins (IgG$_1$, IgG$_2$, IgA, and IgM) in inbred hamster strains (LHC, LSH, CB, BIO PD4) [ref. 2] have generally fallen within the ranges detected in serum from normal adult outbred hamsters (see page 471). Average serum concentrations of IgM in females frequently were higher than those in males of various strains. The relative amounts of serum β$_1$C-globulin were also determined in the previously mentioned strains and found to be comparable; average serum levels of β$_1$C-globulin were higher in females than in males [ref. 2].

The relationship between sex and serum proteins was particularly obvious with Female Protein, an α-globulin found in sera from all normal inbred and outbred female Syrian hamsters (1-2 mg/ml) [ref. 1]. However, Female Protein was not detectable by simple gel diffusion in serum from normal adult male hamsters (inbred or outbred), although it was present during a neonatal period [ref. 1].

Additional serum proteins have been analyzed by other techniques; e.g., haptoglobin levels (40.3 ± 8 mg/100 ml) have been reported in normal hamster serum by Streilein, et al. [ref. 5], and electrophoresis patterns of sera obtained from normal hamsters at various ages have been published by House, et al. [ref. 3].

Contributor: John E. Coe

References

1. Coe, J. E. 1977. Proc. Natl. Acad. Sci. USA 74:730-733.
2. Coe, J. E. Unpublished. Rocky Mountain Laboratory, Hamilton, MT, 1977.
3. House, E. L., et al. 1961. Am. J. Physiol. 200:1018-1022.
4. Mancini, C., et al. 1965. Immunochemistry 2:235-254.
5. Streilein, J. W., and J. Streilein. 1972. Transplantation 13:378-390.

Inbred strains not included below are ALAC and CLAC, maintained at the Medical Research Council Laboratory Animals Centre, United Kingdom; and APG, maintained at the University of Tokyo.

Part I. Strains Maintained at Bio-Research Institute and Trenton Experimental Laboratory Company

Data in light brackets refer to the column heading in brackets. Figures in heavy brackets are reference numbers.

Strain	Coat Color [Coat Color Genes]	Origin	Number of Generations Inbred	Characteristics ⟨Gene Symbol⟩
BIO 1.26	Acromelanic white [c^d/c^d]	LaCasse, Schwentker	F59	....
BIO 1.5	Acromelanic white [c^d/c^d]	National Institutes of Health	F43	Susceptible to dental caries [8]
BIO 2.4	Agouti [+/+]	London School of Hygiene	F49	Benign prostatic hypertrophy [3]
BIO 4.22	Agouti [+/+]	Schwentker	F62	....
BIO 4.24	Agouti [+/+]	Schwentker	F55	Benign adenomas of the adrenal cortex [1]. ♀ obese; hepatic cirrhosis & amyloidosis [4].
BIO 7.88	Cream [e/e]	Toolan, Gulf	F52	....
BIO 10.37	Piebald [s/s]	Whitney	F23	....
BIO 11.10	Dominant spot [$Ds/+$]	Whitney	F32	....
BIO 12.14	Pale cream [$e/e\ T/T$]	Warren	F43	Hindleg paralysis ⟨pa⟩ in ♂ [7]
BIO 14.6	Acromelanic white [c^d/c^d]	Schwentker, LaCasse	F49	Myopathy ⟨my⟩ [5]
BIO 15.16	Tawny [T/T]	Warren	F38	Highly susceptible to tumor induction with 9,10-dimethyl-1,2-benzanthracene ⟨DMBA⟩ [2]
BIO 40.54	Agouti [+/+]	Schwentker, LaCasse, Toolan, Gulf	F26	Myopathy ⟨my⟩ [5]
BIO 41.56	Cream band [$Ba/Ba\ e/e\ p/p^{1/}$]	Larmore, Whitney	F36	Heterochromia iridis [6]
BIO 45.5	Cream [e/e]	Ingham, Toolan, Gulf	F36	High incidence of hepatic cirrhosis & amyloidosis [1]
BIO 53.58	Acromelanic white [c^d/c^d]	Subline of 14.6	F19	Myopathy ⟨my⟩ [5]
BIO 54.7	Amber [$p/p^{1/}\ f/f$]	Warren	F42	High incidence of hepatitic cirrhosis & amyloidosis [1]
BIO 72.29	White [$Wh/Wh\ \&\ Wh/+$]	Ingham, Larmore, Whitney	F30	Anophthalmic white
BIO 82.62	Acromelanic white [c^d/c^d]	Toolan, Gulf, Schwentker, LaCasse	F35	Myopathy ⟨my⟩ [5]
BIO 82.73	Lilac [$p/p^{1/}\ T/T$]	Warren	F41	....
BIO 84.9	Cream [e/e]	Manor Farms	F37	....
BIO 86.93	Albino [$c^d/c^d\ e/e\ p/p^{1/}$]	Toth	F32	Spontaneous seizures ⟨sz⟩ [9]
BIO 87.20	Rust [$b/b^{2/}$]	Ingham, Gulf, Toolan	F43	Benign prostatic hypertrophy [3]
BIO IPI	Rust [$b/b^{2/}$]	Ingham	F37	....
BIO PD4	Acromelanic white [c^d/c^d]	Pee Dee Farms	F70	....
BIO X.3	Acromelanic white [c^d/c^d]	LaCasse	F50	....
BIO X.68	Acromelanic white [c^d/c^d]	LaCasse, Schwentker	F47	Hepatic amyloidosis & cirrhosis [1]
BIO XX.B	Agouti [+/+]	Whitney	F47	....

1/ Pink-eyed dilution; formerly b ⟨brown⟩. 2/ Brown; formerly r ⟨rust⟩.

Contributors: Chai H. Yoon and J. Peterson

References

1. Homburger, F., ed. 1972. Proc. Exp. Tumor Res. 16.
2. Homburger, F., and S. S. Hsueh. 1970. Cancer Res. 30:1449-1452.
3. Homburger, F., and C. W. Nixon. 1970. Proc. Soc. Exp. Biol. Med. 134(1):284-286.
4. Homburger, F., and A. B. Russfield. 1970. Cancer Res. 30(2):305-308.
5. Homburger, F., et al. 1962. Arch. Intern. Med. 110: 660-662.
6. Magalhaes, H., et al. 1962. Am. Zool. 2:537.
7. Nixon, C. W., and M. E. Connelly. 1968. J. Hered. 59(5):276-278.
8. Volker, J. F. 1952. J. Dent. Res. 31:478.
9. Yoon, C. H., et al. 1976. J. Hered. 67:115-116.

continued

94. ORIGIN OF INBRED STRAINS: HAMSTER

Part II. Strains Maintained by Charles River Breeding Laboratory

Origin: For full name of originators, *see* list of HOLDERS at front of book. Data in brackets refer to the column heading in brackets.

Strain	Coat Color	Origin	Source [Date Obtained]	Number of Generations Inbred	Characteristics
CB/SsLak	Golden	CBI	Billingham & Silvers, Univ. of Pennsylvania [11-5-65]	F58	Small; hypersensitive; small litter size (1-9). Frequently cannibalizes baby hamsters.
LHC/Lak	Cream	LAK	Non-inbred LVG [6-8-58]	F53	Gentle
LSH/SsLak	Golden	LSH	Billingham & Silvers, Univ. of Pennsylvania [11-5-65]	F61	Gentle
MHA/SsLak	White	NIMR	Billingham & Silvers, Univ. of Pennsylvania [4-30-65]	F51	Susceptible to dental caries; prone to diarrhea. Chatters; ♂ frequently sterile.
PD4/Lak	White	....	George Sawchuck, Univ. of Pennsylvania [5-14-70]	Fx + F21 [1]	Large; placid disposition.

[1] Fx indicates that number of generations prior to acquisition is unknown; F21 gives the number since acquisition by Lakeview.

Contributor: Gilbert M. Slater

Reference: Billingham, R. E., et al. 1960. Proc. Natl. Acad. Sci. USA 46:1079-1090.

Part III. Strains Maintained at the Massachusetts Institute of Technology

All strains are partially inbred. **Parentage**: Each number represents one of the twelve animals captured from the wild in Syria, in 1971, by Dr. Michael R. Murphy. These numbers indicate those animals of the original 12 who contributed to the specified strain during the first few generations when the strain was in its formative stage. **Number of Generations Inbred** as of March 1977.

Strain	Parentage	Number of Generations Inbred	Characteristics
2.12	♂ 2; ♀ 12	F10	Light golden agouti
6.8	♂ 6; ♀ 8	F8	Animals somewhat smaller than normal
28.36	♂ 2, 6; ♀ 3, 4	F11	Low incidence of microphthalmia
28.94	♂ 2, 6; ♀ 3, 8	F4	Dark agouti coloration
30.70	♂ 2, 6; ♀ 3, 8	F13	Normal agouti
49.19	♂ 6, 10; ♀ 5, 8	F11	Normal agouti
79.43	♂ 6, 10; ♀ 4, 5	F11	Normal agouti
BF	♂ 2, 6, 7; ♀ 4, 9, 12	F8	New mutant "pinto" occurred and is carried in this line
CD	♂ 2, 6, 7; ♀ 4, 9, 12	F8	Light golden agouti

Contributor: C. William Nixon

General References: 1. Murphy, M. R. 1971. Am. Zool. 11:632.
2. Murphy, M. R. 1974. Lab. Anim. 3:45-47.

95. GENETICALLY DEFINED BUT NON-INBRED STRAINS: HAMSTER

Gene Name	Gene Symbol	Strain	Reference
Dark gray	dg	....	4
Dermal pigmentation	..	....	9
Frost	f	BIO 29.66	6,15
Furloss	fs	BIO 1.14	17
Hairless	hr	....	3
Hydrocephalus	hy	BIO 35.97	18
Jute	J	BIO 37.39	7
Lethal gray	Lg	BIO 65.67B[1]	4,5
Light undercolor	..	....	10

Gene Name	Gene Symbol	Strain	Reference
Longhair	l	BIO 1.83	14
Mottled white	Mo	....	2,12
Naked	N	....	1
Rex	rx	....	16
Ruby eye	ru	....	8
Satin	Sa	....	13
Spontaneous seizure	sz	BIO 11.34	19
Tortoise shell	To	....	11

[1] The original BIO 65.67 lost the lethal gray gene. The strain was started again and is designated here as BIO 65.67B.

Contributors: Chai H. Yoon and J. Peterson

References

1. Festing, M. F. W., and M. K. Wright. 1972. Nature (London) 236:81-82.
2. Magalhaes, H. 1954. Anat. Rec. 120:752.
3. Nixon, C. W. 1972. J. Hered. 63:215-217.
4. Nixon, C. W., and M. E. Connelly. 1967. Ibid. 58:295-296.
5. Nixon, C. W., et al. 1969. Ibid. 60:74.
6. Peterson, J. S. 1975. Ibid. 66:102-103.
7. Peterson, J. S., and C. H. Yoon. 1975. Ibid. 66:246-247.
8. Robinson, R. 1955. Nature (London) 176:353-354.
9. Robinson, R. 1959. Genetica (the Hague) 30:393-411.
10. Robinson, R. 1960. J. Hered. 51:111-115.
11. Robinson, R. 1966. Nature (London) 212:824-825.
12. Robinson, R. 1968. In R. A. Hoffman, et al., ed. The Golden Hamster. Iowa State Univ. Press, Ames. pp. 41-72.
13. Robinson, R. 1972. J. Hered. 63:52.
14. Schimke, D. J., et al. 1973. Ibid. 64:236-237.
15. Whitney, R. 1963. In W. Lane-Petter, ed. Animals for Research. Academic Press, New York. pp. 384, 388.
16. Whitney, R., and C. W. Nixon. 1973. J. Hered. 64:239.
17. Yoon, C. H., and J. Peterson. Unpublished. Boston College, Dep. Biology, Chestnut Hill, MA, 1978.
18. Yoon, C. H., and J. Slaney. 1972. J. Hered. 63:344-346.
19. Yoon, C. H., et al. 1976. Ibid. 67:115-116.

96. CHROMOSOMES AND KARYOLOGY: HAMSTER

Hamsters belong to the order Rodentia, family Cricetidae. **Chromosome:** Unless otherwise indicated, chromosomes are arranged in order of decreasing size, with each assigned a number. No standard numbering system is presently available for these species, and the designations given below should not be considered as such. **Position of Centromere:** A = acrocentric; MM = median metacentric; SMM = submedian metacentric; ST = subtelocentric; T = telocentric.

Species [Common Name]	No. of Chromosomes	Chromosome	Position of Centromere	Reference
Calomyscus bailwardi [Mouse-like hamster]	2n = 32	10[1]	MM & SMM	7
		2[1]	ST	
		18[1]	A	
		X[2]	ST	
		Y[3]	A	
Cricetulus barabensis [Daurian hamster]	2n = 20	1	SMM	8,12
		2	MM	
		3	MM	
		4	SMM	
		5	SMM	
		6	ST	

Species [Common Name]	No. of Chromosomes	Chromosome	Position of Centromere	Reference
		7	SMM	
		8	SMM	
		9	SMM	
		X[4]	ST	
		Y[2]	SMM	
C. barabensis griseus[5] [Chinese hamster]	2n = 22	1	SMM	1,2
		2	MM	
		4	SMM	
		5	MM	
		6	ST	
		7	ST	

[1] Number of autosomes. [2] Medium-sized. [3] Small. [4] Equals size of chromosome 3. [5] Synonym: *C. griseus*.

continued

Species [Common Name]	No. of Chromo-somes	Chromo-some	Position of Centromere	Ref-er-ence
		8	ST	
		9	SMM	
		10	SMM	
		11	MM	
		X[6]	SMM	
		Y[7]	SMM	
C. migrato-rius [Arme-nian ham-ster]	2n = 22	1	MM	5,14
		2	MM	
		3	MM	
		4	MM	
		5	MM	
		6	ST	
		7	ST	
		8	ST	
		9	ST	
		10	ST	
		X[8] Y[8]	ST	
Cricetus cri-cetus [Eu-ropean hamster]	2n = 22	1	SMM	4,13
		2	SMM	
		3	SMM	
		4	SMM	
		5	MM	
		6	SMM or ST	
		7	A	
		8	SMM	
		9	SMM	
		10	SMM	
		X[2]	SMM	

Species [Common Name]	No. of Chromo-somes	Chromo-some	Position of Centromere	Ref-er-ence
		Y[2]	MM	
Mesocricetus auratus [Syrian or golden ham-ster]	2n = 44	1	SMM	3,10, 11
		2	SMM	
		3	SMM	
		4	SMM	
		5	MM	
		6	ST	
		7	ST	
		8	SMM	
		9	SMM	
		10	MM	
		11	ST	
		12	SMM	
		13	SMM	
		14	MM	
		15	SMM	
		16	A or T	
		17	A	
		18	A	
		19	A	
		20	MM	
		21	A	
		X[9]	MM	
		Y[10]	SMM	
M. brandti [Azerbai-dzhan or Kurdistan hamster]	2n = 42	40[1]	MM & SMM	6,9
		X	SMM	
		Y	SMM or ST	

[1] Number of autosomes. [2] Medium-sized. [6] Equals size of chromosome 4. [7] Equals size of chromosome 5. [8] Sim-ilar in size; second and third longest chromosomes. [9] Long-est. [10] Equals size of chromosome 15, but Y's of different sizes & morphologies have been described.

Contributor: John M. Lehman

References
1. Hsu, T. C., and M. T. Zenzes. 1964. J. Natl. Cancer Inst. 32:857-869.
2. Hsu, T. C., and K. Benerschke, ed. 1967. An Atlas of Mammalian Chromosomes. Springer-Verlag, New York. v. 14(13).
3. Ibid. v. 14(14), 1967.
4. Ibid. v. 4(166), 1970.
5. Ibid. v. 6(269), 1971.
6. Ibid. v. 7(315), 1973.
7. Ibid. v. 8(364), 1974.
8. Ibid. v. 8(365), 1974.
9. Lehman, J. M., and I. Macpherson. 1967. J. Hered. 58:29-31.
10. Lehman, J. M., et al. 1963. J. Natl. Cancer Inst. 31: 639-650.
11. Popescu, N. C., and J. A. DiPaolo. 1932. Cytogenetics 11:500-507.
12. Rajabli, S. I., and E. P. Kriukova. 1973. Mamm. Chro-mosomes Newslett. 14:112.
13. Wolf, U., and D. Hepp. 1966. Chromosoma 18:438-448.
14. Yerganian, G., and S. Papoyan. 1964. Hereditas 52: 307-319.

97. DAILY OBSERVATIONS OF REPRODUCTION: HAMSTER

Plus/minus (±) values are standard errors, unless otherwise indicated.

Part I. General Development and Time of Sexual Maturity

The female golden hamster is larger and heavier than the male. The latter's small size is probably due to the effect of testosterone, as castration results in increased size and weight. The two sexes show sexual dimorphism in the

continued

Part I. General Development and Time of Sexual Maturity

weights of the pituitary (heavier in the female) and of the adrenals (heavier in the male). [ref. 16] There is also a sexual dimorphism in spleen weight among adults, with the female spleen the heavier [ref. 3]. The male lives longer than the female [ref. 2, 5]. Parous females have a shorter life-span than virgins (pseudopregnancies have no effect on life-span) [ref. 2]. *Abbreviations:* SD = standard deviation; SE = standard error.

Age [1]	Observation	Reference
Day 10 of gestation	Primordia of gonads appear, but sex not visibly distinguishable	10
Day 12 of gestation	Sex visibly distinguishable	10
Birth	Time of parturition is 15 d & 7-17 h after ovulation	11
	Body weight of young = 2.052 g	13
	Sex determined with difficulty by using size of urogenital papilla, & distance between urinary & anal openings; both larger in ♂	8
6-7 d	Sex easily distinguished by presence or absence of prominent milk lines, the developing mammary glands, visible as two noticeable dark lines on lateral-ventral aspect in ♀	12
10-15 d	Vagina becomes patent	6
25 d	Spermatogenesis commences	7
26 d	Antral follicles appear	4
27-29 d	First antral follicles appear	7
28.4 d	17 ♀ reared in 12 h light:12 h dark, checked for cycle from 20th day on, showed first post-estrous discharge at 26-33 d	1
30 d	Earliest spontaneous ovulation	4,7
33.58 d	Appearance of first post-estrous discharge, in 696 ♀ checked daily from 25 d after birth, occurred at 33.58 d ± 4.055 (SD), 0.15 (SE), with range of 27-51 d; mean weight at first ovulation, as judged by this discharge, was 66.78 g ± 11.36 (SD), 0.43 (SE), with a range of 41-99 g	12
36 d	Mature spermatozoa appear	7
	Fertilizing life of sperm is 13 h	9
40 d	♂ sexual maturity	7
42.5	Sexual maturity in group of 20♂, as judged by penile smear, occurred at 42.5 d ± 1.76 (SD)	17
14 mo	Usually cease littering, and if bred thereafter, ♀ abort at continually earlier stages of pregnancy [2]; ♂ continue to be functional breeders for a longer time	15
2 yr	Approximate life-span for ♂ & ♀	15

[1] Unless otherwise specified. [2] Wheat germ oil given to aged ♀ increases fertility, percent conceiving, and number giving birth [ref. 14].

Contributor: Margaret W. Orsini

References

1. Alleva, J. J., et al. 1968. Endocrinology 82:1227-1235.
2. Asdell, S. A., and S. R. Joshi. 1976. Biol. Reprod. 14: 478-480.
3. Blazkovec, A. A., and M. W. Orsini. 1976. Int. Arch. Allergy Appl. Immunol. 50:55-67.
4. Greenwald, G. S., and R. D. Peppler. 1968. Anat. Rec. 161:447-458.
5. Kirkman, H., and P. K. S. Yau. 1972. Am. J. Anat. 135:205-220.
6. Kupperman, H. S., et al. 1944. Anat. Rec. 88:441-442.
7. La Velle, F. W. 1951. Carnegie Inst. Washington Contrib. Embryol. 223:19-53.
8. Magalhaes, H. 1968. In R. A. Hoffman, et al., ed. The Golden Hamster. Iowa State Univ., Ames. pp. 15-24, 91-110.
9. Miyamoto, H., and M. C. Chang. 1972. J. Reprod. Fertil. 31:131-134.
10. Nakano, A. 1960. Okajimas Folia Anat. Jpn. 35:183-217.
11. Orsini, M. W. 1961. Proc. Anim. Care Panel 11(4):193-206.

continued

Part I. General Development and Time of Sexual Maturity

12. Orsini, M. W. Unpublished. Univ. Wisconsin, Bardeen Medical Laboratories, Madison, 1979.
13. Purdy, D. M., and H. H. Hillemann. 1950. Anat. Rec. 106:591-598.
14. Soderwall, A. L., and B. C. Smith. 1961. Fertil. Steril. 13:287-289.
15. Soderwall, A. L., et al. 1960. J. Gerontol. 15:246-248.
16. Swanson, H. H. 1967. J. Endocrinol. 39:555-564.
17. Vandenbergh, J. G. 1971. Biol. Reprod. 4:234-237.

Part II. Cycle

Since the post-estrous discharge is the most prominent feature of the cycle in the female hamster, the day of its appearance is herein designated as day 1, thus making it possible to parallel the first days of pregnancy and pseudopregnancy with the cycle. Many authors, however, designate the appearance of "heat" as day 1, which is the day prior to the post-estrous discharge. The data below are based on the premise that "heat" begins on the evening before the designated day 1 and extends into the early hours of the morning.

External vaginal phenomena are identical for the first three days for all three physiological states (cycle, pregnancy, pseudopregnancy) [ref. 17]. Estrus can be induced in the ovariectomized female by injection of 10 μg of estrogen, followed 24-48 h later by 0.05-0.5 mg of progesterone. After this regimen, estrus resembles that in the normal female. [ref. 4] Starvation for two cycles results in no ovulation, suppression of FSH production and release, and probable increase of LH production and release; the ovary is like the ovary in the lactating female, with much interstitial tissue [ref. 20]. The FSH release center is located in the mammillary bodies, and is inhibited by a center in the ventral tegmental nuclei [ref. 21]. *Abbreviations*: FSH = follicle-stimulating hormone; LH = luteinizing hormone.

Day	Structure, Organ, or Hormone Studied	Observation	Reference
1	Ovary	Fresh corpora lutea in morning	15
		Ovulation occurs 10-11 h (0100-0200) after peak of LH in plasma	16
		Under light from 0500-2100: ovulation occurs 9-10 h (0030-0110) after peak of LH in plasma	5
		Under light from 0600-1800: ovulation occurs within 2-h period (0100-0300) in animals up to 4 mo old, but at 6 mo of age it occurs within a 4-h period (2300-0300). Under light from 1200-2400: ovulation occurs 6 h earlier (1700-2100 on day 4). Transfer of animals from one regimen to the other results in shift in ovulation time within 2 mo; environmental light determines ovulation time.	1
	Corpora lutea	Average weight per corpus luteum = 0.28 ± 0.02 mg	15
		Average diameter per corpus luteum = 546 ± 12.5 μm	8
	Oviduct	Ova in cumulus	24
	Uterus	Contains highest number of mast cells, 42.7 ± 5.6 per 12 μm section of endometrium	10
	Vagina	Post-estrous discharge is opaque, white mucus, with columnar epithelial cells having oval nuclei	17
	FSH	High, but drops during day; peaks at 0800, ∿900 ng/ml serum, and declines thereafter to 300 ng	3
	LH	Low, <100 ng/ml serum	3
	Estradiol	Low, 13.8-22 pg/ml plasma	2
	Estrone	High in peripheral blood, 79.1 ± 13.9 pg/ml at 2200	2
		Daily cycle, higher at 2200	3
	Progesterone	Content per corpus luteum = 2.7 ± 0.15 ng; level in plasma = 14.3 ± 1.6 ng/ml	15
	Prolactin	Varies cyclically between 10 & 17 ng/ml serum	3
2	Ovary	Corpora lutea well established	15
	Corpora lutea	Average weight per corpus luteum = 0.33 ± 0.1 mg	15
		Average diameter per corpus luteum = 628 ± 12.1 μm	8

continued

Part II. Cycle

Day	Structure, Organ, or Hormone Studied	Observation	Reference
	Oviduct	Ova in zona pellucida	19
	Uterus	Mast cells = 21.8 ± 1.3 per 12 μm section of endometrium	10
	Vagina	Discharge waxy; leukocytes predominant, few columnar cells	17
	FSH	Lower than during day 1	3
	Estradiol	Rises gradually	15
	Estrone	Peak of 114.6 ± 30.8 pg/ml reached at 2200	2
	Progesterone	Peak values for cycle: content per corpus luteum = 8.2 ± 0.80 ng; plasma level = 19.9 ± 1.68 ng/ml	15
3	Ovary	Leukocytes found within corpora late on day 3; follicular atresia occurs between days 3 & 4, reducing number of large follicles in ovary by half	6
	Corpora lutea	Average weight per corpus luteum = 0.35 ± 0.04 mg	15
		Average diameter per corpus luteum = 627 ± 15.3 μm	8
	Oviduct	Ova in oviduct in morning; by ∿1500, ova pass into uterus and begin to break up within zonae	18
	Uterus	Peak labeling of uterine luminal epithelium with [³H]thymidine occurs in afternoon	12
		Mast cells = 22.5 ± 4.1 per 12 μm section of endometrium	10
	Vagina	Discharge negative; amorphous debris, few epithelial cells & decreasing number of leukocytes	17
	FSH	At basal level for cycle, $^1/_5$-$^1/_{12}$ of day 1 level	3
	LH	Essentially low & constant	2
	Estradiol	Reaches peak of 90 pg/ml at 1400	2
	Estrone	Rises to 71 pg/ml at 2200	2
	Progesterone	Content per corpus luteum = 1.8 ± 0.29 ng; plasma level = 6.6 ± 1.99 ng/ml	15
		Level drops by 0200 when luteolysis commences, rises again at 1200-1600, and then drops again	22
4	Ovary	Corpora small & pale	15
		Under light from 0500-1900: critical period occurs at 1300-1430; release of ovulatory gonadotropins 30-60 min later; LH increases 30 min after critical period; ovarian progesterone rises at 1600 in response to gonadotropic release, peaks at 2000, begins to drop at 2200 (interstitium of ovary & follicles is probably main source of progesterone); follicles increase in size, and ♀ goes into heat	7,9, 14, 16
		Under light from 0600-1800: heat occurs at 1800-2100; majority ovulate 8-9 h after initiation of estrus	11
		Under natural lighting: heat occurs at 1800-1900, & ovulation at 2400-0115, with peak at 0100. In some parous ♀, heat observed as late as 1000 on day 1	24
		Ovulation results when 1 μg LH & 10 μg FSH are administered concurrently, thus showing synergistic action of these two hormones	9
		Ovulation can be prevented by blocking with anti-estrogens before critical period; thus showing positive feedback of estrogen for release of ovulatory hormone	13
	Corpora lutea	Average weight per corpus luteum = 0.14 ± 0.02 mg	15
		Average diameter per corpus luteum = 454 ± 13 μm	8
	Oviduct	Empty	18
	Uterus	Zonae are not lost from ova, which are difficult to recover from uterus on this day; material from ovum is dispersed within zona pellucida	19
		Mast cells = 10.7 ± 1.3 per 12 μm section of endometrium	10
		Peak uptake of thymidine in connective tissue & muscle of uterus	12
	Vagina	Discharge is slight, stringy, translucent	17
	FSH, LH, & prolactin	Serum levels high, with peak at ∿1600	3
	FSH	Low, rises at 1400, drops after LH surge	3
	LH	Surge in plasma LH from 1430-1730, otherwise base level is 11 ng/ml; half-life of LH in plasma = 33 min; level of plasma LH on other days of cycle is low	23

continued

97. DAILY OBSERVATIONS OF REPRODUCTION: HAMSTER

Part II. Cycle

Day	Structure, Organ, or Hormone Studied	Observation	Reference
	Estradiol	Linear increase from 0900; peak of 186.6 pg/ml at 1500; drops to 24.2 pg/ml by 2200	2
	Estrone	Peak at 1400 of 99.4 pg/ml, and again at 2000 of 80.6 pg/ml	2
	Progesterone	Content per corpus luteum = 1.2 ± 0.04 ng; plasma level = 9.8 ± 1.92 ng/ml	15
		Surge in afternoon; peak of 50 ng/ml in early evening; non-luteal in source; comes from interstitium & large follicles	14, 16
	Prolactin	Rises in afternoon, as does LH	3

Contributor: Margaret W. Orsini

References

1. Alleva, J. J., et al. 1968. Endocrinology 82:1227-1235.
2. Baranczuk, R., and G. S. Greenwald. 1973. Ibid. 92:805-811.
3. Bast, J. D., and G. S. Greenwald. 1974. Ibid. 94:1295-1299.
4. Frank, A. H., and R. M. Fraps. 1945. Ibid. 37:357-361.
5. Goldman, B. D., and J. C. Porter. 1970. Ibid. 87:676-679.
6. Greenwald, G. S. 1961. J. Reprod. Fertil. 2:351-361.
7. Greenwald, G. S. 1967. Endocrinology 80:118-130.
8. Greenwald, G. S. 1968. J. Reprod. Fertil. 16:495-497.
9. Greenwald, G. S. 1971. Endocrinology 88:671-677.
10. Harvey, E. B. 1964. Anat. Rec. 148:507-516.
11. Harvey, E. B., et al. 1961. J. Exp. Zool. 146:231-236.
12. Kupperman, H. S., et al. 1944. Anat. Rec. 88:441-442.
13. Labhsetwar, A. P. 1972. Endocrinology 90:941-946.
14. Leavitt, W. W., and G. C. Blaha. 1970. Biol. Reprod. 3:353-361.
15. Lukaszewska, J. H., and G. S. Greenwald. 1970. Endocrinology 86:1-9.
16. Norman, R. L., and G. S. Greenwald. 1972. Anat. Rec. 173:95-108.
17. Orsini, M. W. 1961. Proc. Anim. Care Panel 11(4):193-206.
18. Orsini, M. W. 1964. 5th Int. Congr. Anim. Reprod. Artif. Insem. Trenton 7:309-313.
19. Orsini, M. W. 1965. Ciba Found. Symp. Preimplant. Stages Pregnancy, pp. 162-167.
20. Printz, R. H., and G. S. Greenwald. 1970. Endocrinology 86:290-295.
21. Printz, R. H., and G. S. Greenwald. 1971. Neuroendocrinology 7:171-182.
22. Ridley, K., and G. S. Greenwald. 1975. Proc. Soc. Exp. Biol. Med. 149:10-12.
23. Turgeon, J., and G. S. Greenwald. 1972. Endocrinology 90:657-662.
24. Ward, M. C. 1946. Anat. Rec. 94:139-162.

Part III. Pregnancy

Pregnant hamsters display a slow, gradual increase in weight during the first 9 days; from day 10 on, weight rises sharply until parturition, at the rate of ∿5 g/d [ref. 25]. Hamsters will mate during pregnancy [ref. 18], and will do so repeatedly if males and females are maintained together [ref. 30].

During the first 8 days of pregnancy, each ovary contains an average of 11 large follicles, 277-553 μm in diameter [ref. 6], and from day 10 of pregnancy to parturition, each ovary contains 22 follicles, 277-600 μm in diameter [ref. 9]. The number of ova discharged ranges from 7-17, with a mean of 10; fertilization rate is 85.7% [ref. 1]. In 1057 hamsters, the number of corpora and implantations were associated with maternal weight; corpora ranged from 10.3 ±

0.22 in females under 100 g to 14.3 ± 0.21 in those over 130 g; the fertility index for all was 92-94% [ref. 37]. Among 18 control females, ovulations numbered 12.9 ± 0.5, implantations, 12.2 ± 0.5, and live fetuses, 11.6 ± 0.5 [ref. 12]. After being bred at 28 days of age, the youngest female to litter had 5 young; a littermate bred at 39 days of age had 9 young [ref. 38]. In 107 deliveries, number of young per litter ranged from 2-15, with a mean of 6.93 ± 0.23 [ref. 3]. Gestation lasts 15 days and 7 hours in young animals, 15 days and 17-20 hours in older animals, and 16-17 days in senescent animals [ref. 25, 30].

Antral follicles are the source of estrogen in the pregnant hamster [ref. 9]. Unilateral ovariectomy during pregnancy decreases peripheral level of ovarian steroids; the lowered

continued

Part III. Pregnancy

steroid level reduces inhibition of gonadotropin, and subsequent rise in gonadotropin results in ovarian compensation [ref. 4]. Antiserum to LH given before day 4 prevents implantation, and if given anytime between days 5 and 11, pregnancy is terminated. A combination of progesterone and estradiol-17β could maintain implantation and pregnancy. Antisera to FSH-LH postpones parturition, but FSH antisera alone has no effect. Deprivation of LH affects luteal function in pregnancy. [ref. 36] Administration of LH antiserum at days 6-11 causes termination of pregnancy, indicating dependence on LH for first 11 days of pregnancy [ref. 35]. *Abbreviations:* FSH = follicle-stimulating hormone; LH = luteinizing hormone.

Day	Structure, Organ, or Hormone Studied	Observation	Reference
1	Ovary	New corpora lutea in ovary are luteinized during this day	17,29
	Corpora lutea	Average weight per corpus luteum = 0.29 ± 0.03 mg	21
		Average diameter per corpus luteum = 539 ± 22.4 μm	8
	Oviduct	Pronuclear stages of ova	39
	Vagina	Post-estrous discharge (plug), consisting of columnar epithelial cells & sperm, strings out on contact	25
	FSH	Level is five times as high as level in later stages of pregnancy	2
	LH	Level has dropped; varies little	2
	Progesterone	Content per corpus luteum = 3.5 ± 0.3 ng	21
	Prolactin	Low, 27.9 ± 1.6 ng/ml	2
2	Corpora lutea	Average weight per corpus luteum = 0.39 ± 0.03 mg	21
		Average diameter per corpus luteum = 667 ± 11.1 μm	8
	Oviduct	Two-cell stages of ova	39
	Vagina	Waxy discharge containing leukocytes	25
	FSH	Decreases to near 200 ng/ml, and remains fairly constant thereafter	2
	LH	Decreases from day 1	2
	Progesterone	Content per corpus luteum = 8.3 ± 1.0 ng; plasma level = 25.9 ± 4.2 ng/ml, significantly higher than in cycle	21
	Prolactin	Serum level = 46.0 ± 3.9 ng/ml; rises on days 2 & 3, stays elevated until day 6, drops gradually thereafter to day 1 level	2
3	Ovary	No reduction in number of large follicles, such as occurs during days 3-4 of cycle	5
	Corpora lutea	Average weight per corpus luteum = 0.35 ± 0.02 mg	21
		Average diameter per corpus luteum = 718 ± 12.1 μm	8,11
	Uterus	Ova enter uterus in afternoon of day 3	27
		Mast cells = 9.4 ± 3.5 per 12 μm section of uterus	14
	Vagina	No discharge	25
	Estrogen	Increases	15
	Progesterone	Content per corpus luteum = 9.5 ± 0.4 ng	21
		Plasma level significantly higher than comparable day of cycle; rises gradually thereafter	15
4	Ovary	First significant increase in ovarian weight	21
	Corpora lutea	Average weight per corpus luteum = 0.50 ± 0.02 mg; first significant increase in weight	21
		Average diameter per corpus luteum = 781 ± 10.4 μm	8
	Uterus	Zona pellucida lost, probably by lysis; blastocyst is free; implantation is initiated with adhesions and first attachment between epithelial cells of lumen; decidualization begins	24,26-28,31,41
		Mast cells per 12 μm section of uterus = 8.4 ± 3.3 at 3 d & 7 h postovulation (early day 4), and 4.7 ± 1.1 at 3 d & 21 h postovulation (late day 4)	14
	Vagina	Discharge clear, stringy, fluid	25
	Estrogen	Reaches plateau	15
	Progesterone	Content per corpus luteum = 12.5 ± 0.9 ng; level in plasma = 19.9 ± 4.4 ng/ml	21
		Plasma level is rising	15
		Implantation can take place on progesterone alone	13,33

continued

Part III. Pregnancy

Day	Structure, Organ, or Hormone Studied	Observation	Reference
5	Corpora lutea	Average weight per corpus luteum = 0.50 ± 0.03 mg	21
	Uterus	Blastocyst penetrates epithelium; giant cells are prominent; decidua involves antimesometrial & lateral aspects of lumen, and walls of lumen fuse above (mesometrial to) the implantation site	26,32, 39
		Mast cells per 12 μm section of uterus = 4.2 ± 0.5 at 96 h postovulation, 5.6 ± 1.2 at 4 d & 7 h, and 2.1 ± 0.07 late in day 5	14
	Vagina	May look sealed; discharge clear, stringy	25
	Estradiol	Secretion plateaus from day 4 to day 9	15
	Estrone	Rises	15
	Progesterone	Content per corpus luteum = 10.9 ± 0.2 ng; level in plasma = 19.6 ± 2.9 ng/ml	21
6	Corpora lutea	Average weight per corpus luteum = 0.53 ± 0.04 mg	21
	Uterus	Decidual cavity appears; peak of antimesometrial decidual development & ectoplacental cone stage of embryo	23
		Mast cells per 12 μm section of uterus = 3.0 ± 0.07 at 5 d & 7 h (early day 6)	14
	Vagina	Discharge clear, stringy, bubbly	25
	Progesterone	Content per corpus luteum = 12.7 ± 1.0 ng; plasma level rising	21
7	Corpora lutea	Average weight per corpus luteum = 0.65 ± 0.04 mg	21
	Uterus	Well-developed yolk sac placenta; giant cells found within peripheral vascular spaces of endometrium	23
		Mast cells per 12 μm section of uterus = 2.2 ± 0.3 (6 d & 7 h postovulation)	14
	Vagina	Discharge stringy, bubbly or flocculent, beaded	25
	FSH	Slightly higher	22
	LH	Antiserum causes regression of corpora & termination of pregnancy	22
	Progesterone	Content per corpus luteum = 14.6 ± 0.3 ng	21
8	Corpora lutea	Average weight per corpus luteum = 0.75 ± 0.03 mg	21
		Average diameter per corpus luteum = 843 ± 20 μm	11
	Uterus	Chorion begins to fuse with Träger, i.e., ectoplacental cone	23
	Vagina	Discharge clear, stringy, bubbly; flocculent, stringy, beaded	25
	FSH	Pituitary content drops during first half of pregnancy, reaches lowest level during day 8, and plateaus from days 8-14	11
	Progesterone	Content per corpus luteum = 14.1 ± 0.6 ng; level in plasma = 31.0 ± 2.8 ng/ml	21
9	Corpora lutea	Average weight per corpus luteum = 0.92 ± 0.0 mg	21
	Uterus	In latter part of day, allantois vascularizes chorio-allantoic plate and circulation begins; conceptual swellings increase markedly in size; antimesometrial decidua degenerating. Giant cells present in circumferential & mesometrial arteries and are penetrating sheathed arteries of placenta	23
	Vagina	Discharge clear, stringy, bubbly; flocculent, stringy, beaded	25
	LH	Plasma concentration drops and remains low for days 10, 11, 13-15	16
	Progesterone	Content per corpus luteum = 16.9 ± 0.8 ng; plasma level drops	21
10	Corpora lutea	Average weight per corpus luteum = 0.98 ± 0.03 mg; second growth phase of corpora begins	21
	Vagina	Discharge stringy, flocculent, beaded, waxy	25
	FSH	Slightly higher	15
	Estrogen	Acts at uterine level to maintain normal-sized conceptual swellings and to prevent constriction of uterus	9
		Secretion rises between days 10 & 12	15
	Progesterone	Content per corpus luteum = 19.6 ± 1.7 ng; plasma level = 18.1 ± 2.55 ng/ml (lowest level)	21
11	Corpora lutea	Average weight per corpus luteum = 1.07 ± 0.04 mg	21
	Vagina	Discharge waxy & stringy	25
	Progesterone	Content per corpus luteum = 17.1 ± 1.3 ng; plasma level = 19.5 ± 3.5 ng/ml (level begins to rise again)	21

continued

Part III. Pregnancy

Day	Structure, Organ, or Hormone Studied	Observation	Reference
12	Ovary	Pregnancy can be maintained by a single corpus luteum from day 12 on	40
	Corpora lutea	Average weight per corpus luteum = 1.0 ± 0.02 mg	21
		Average diameter per corpus luteum = 913 ± 23.9 μm	11
	Uterus	Establishment of definitive vascular pattern of placenta & vascular knot	24
	Vagina	Discharge waxy & stringy	25
	Pituitary gland	Hypophysectomy prior to day 12 causes involution of corpora, and after day 12 corpora are maintained histologically; hypophysectomy at any stage of pregnancy causes interruption of gestation; after hypophysectomy at day 12, only FSH is required to maintain pregnancy	7
	Progesterone	Content per corpus luteum = 14.8 ± 1.2 ng; plasma level = 36.4 ± 5.5 ng/ml	21
		Reaches second peak	19,21
	Prolactin	Elevation to 23,000 ft for 4 d or more before day 12 causes interruption in pregnancy, with regression of corpora lutea, but follicular development remains normal; no effect noted if elevated at 12 d of pregnancy, apparently because placenta provides prolactin after day 12	34
13	Corpora lutea	Average weight per corpus luteum = 1.2 ± 0.05 mg	21
	Vagina	Discharge waxy & stringy	25
	Progesterone	Content per corpus luteum = 19.4 ± 1.3 ng; plasma level = 26.3 ± 5.7 ng/ml (decline in level)	21
14	Corpora lutea	Average weight per corpus luteum = 1.4 ± 0.04 mg; diameter = 1044 ± 17.9 μm	11,21
	Vagina	Discharge waxy & stringy	25
	Progesterone	Content per corpus luteum = 18.3 ± 0.9 ng; plasma level = 42.2 ± 5.6 ng/ml (third & highest peak in pregnancy)	21
		Peak production	19
15	Corpora lutea	Average weight per corpus luteum = 1.5 ± 0.06 mg	21
	Vagina	Discharge waxy & stringy	25
	Progesterone	Content per corpus luteum = 16.6 ± 1.7 ng; plasma level = 23.5 ± 3.0 ng/ml	21
		Levels decline	19,21
16	Corpora lutea	Average weight per corpus luteum = 1.2 ± 0.06 mg; diameter = 1061 ± 18 μm	11,21
	LH	Rises sharply to level found on day 1 of pregnancy	16
	Luteotropic complex	Consists of 1 mg prolactin, 200 μg FSH, & small amount of LH; estrogen is also needed	10
	Progesterone	Content per corpus luteum = 8.2 ± 1.0 ng	21
		Drops in plasma & in corpora	19-21

Contributor: Margaret W. Orsini

References

1. Austin, C. R. 1956. J. R. Microsc. Soc. 75(3):141-154.
2. Bast, J. D., and G. S. Greenwald. 1974. J. Endocrinol. 63:527-532.
3. Bond, C. R. 1945. Physiol. Zool. 18:52-59.
4. Chatterjee, A., and G. S. Greenwald. 1971. Anat. Rec. 171:221-226.
5. Greenwald, G. S. 1961. J. Reprod. Fertil. 2:351-361.
6. Greenwald, G. S. 1964. Anat. Rec. 148:605-610.
7. Greenwald, G. S. 1967. Endocrinology 80:118-130.
8. Greenwald, G. S. 1968. J. Reprod. Fertil. 16:495-497.
9. Greenwald, G. S. 1972. Endocrinology 91:75-86.
10. Greenwald, G. S. 1973. Ibid. 92:235-242.
11. Greenwald, G. S., et al. 1967. Ibid. 80:851-856.
12. Hahn, E. W. 1972. Lab. Anim. Sci. 22:649-651.
13. Harper, M. J. K., et al. 1966. Acta Endocrinol. 52:465-470.
14. Harvey, E. B. 1964. Anat. Rec. 148:507-516.
15. Joshi, H. S., and A. P. Labhsetwar. 1972. J. Reprod. Fertil. 31:299-302.
16. Joshi, H. S., et al. 1974. Biol. Reprod. 10:39-46.
17. Kent, G. C. 1968. In R. A. Hoffman, et al., ed. The Golden Hamster. Iowa State Univ., Ames. pp. 119-138.
18. Krehbiel, R. H. 1952. Anat. Rec. 113:117-121.
19. Leavitt, W. W., and G. C. Blaha. 1970. Biol. Reprod. 3:353-361.
20. Lukaszewska, J. H., and G. S. Greenwald. 1969. J. Reprod. Fertil. 20:185-187.
21. Lukaszewska, J. H., and G. S. Greenwald. 1970. Endocrinology 86:1-9.
22. Mukku, V., and N. R. Moudgal. 1975. Ibid. 97:1455-1459.
23. Orsini, M. W. 1954. Am. J. Anat. 94:273-331.

continued

97. DAILY OBSERVATIONS OF REPRODUCTION: HAMSTER

Part III. Pregnancy

24. Orsini, M. W. 1957. J. Morphol. 100:565-600.
25. Orsini, M. W. 1961. Proc. Anim. Care Panel 11(4): 193-206.
26. Orsini, M. W. 1963. In A. C. Enders, ed. Delayed Implantation. Univ. Chicago, Chicago. pp. 155-169.
27. Orsini, M. W. 1964. 5th Int. Congr. Anim. Reprod. Artif. Insem. Trenton 7:309-313.
28. Orsini, M. W. 1965. Ciba Found. Symp. Preimplant. Stages Pregnancy, pp. 162-167.
29. Orsini, M. W. 1968. J. Endocrinol. 41(Proc.):vii-viii.
30. Orsini, M. W. Unpublished. Univ. Wisconsin, Bardeen Medical Laboratories, Madison, 1979.
31. Parkening, T. A. 1976. J. Anat. 121:161-184.
32. Parkening, T. A. 1976. Ibid. 122:211-230.
33. Prasad, M. R. N., et al. 1960. Proc. Soc. Exp. Biol. Med. 104:48-51.
34. Printz, R. H. 1972. Anat. Rec. 173:157-171.
35. Rao, J., et al. 1970. J. Reprod. Fertil. 23:353-355.
36. Rao, J., et al. 1972. Ibid. 29:239-249.
37. Robens, J. F. 1968. Lab. Anim. Care 18:651-653.
38. Selle, R. M. 1945. Science 102:485-486.
39. Ward, M. C. 1948. Am. J. Anat. 82:231-276.
40. Weitlauf, H. M., and G. S. Greenwald. 1967. J. Reprod. Fertil. 14:489-491.
41. Young, M. P., et al. 1968. J. Embryol. Exp. Morphol. 19:341-345.

Part IV. Pseudopregnancy

Day 1 is designated as the first day following mating with a vasectomized male. When females in heat are placed with vasectomized males for 10-30 minutes, pseudopregnancies rarely fail to occur. Attempts to induce pseudopregnancy by cervical stimulation were more time-consuming and less successful. [ref. 15] Pseudopregnancy elicited by cervical stimulation of a definite pattern—electrical stimulation 30 times over 300 seconds—resulted in 83% pseudopregnancy [ref. 2]. Pseudopregnancy could be elicited in 75% of cyclic females by injection of 4 mg prolactin and 200 μg FSH, in a twice-daily regimen initiated on day 1 or 2 of cycle, but could not be extended beyond 9 days [ref. 3]. Pseudopregnant hamster will not mate on evening of day 4 [ref. 9].

Duration of pseudopregnancy extends from the initiation of mating to the onset of "heat" marking its termination. Post-estrous discharge immediately following pseudopregnancy is sometimes obscured and appears more waxy; "heat" therefore is the best criterion. The rest of the cycle following pseudopregnancy is usually distinct, with no mucus on days 2 and 3. [ref. 9] Corpora in pseudopregnancy are larger than cyclic corpora; vaginal epithelium undergoes changes as in pregnancy, and the mammary gland shows partial development [ref. 1]. Duration of pseudopregnancy: 8 days in the young, 9 days in most, and 10 days in the old

(hamsters a year or so in age) [ref. 15]. In 19 cases, the range was 7-9 days [ref. 19]; in 22 cases, the mean was 9.64 days, with a range of 7-13 days [ref. 1]; in 51 hamsters, the mean was 9.08 ± 0.84 days, with a range of 8-10 days [ref. 6]. Traumatizing the uterus in varying amounts (2-15 loops) is ineffective in prolonging pseudopregnancy; the duration in 52 normal animals was 9.08 ± 0.84 days; with 2 loops, duration was 8.95 ± 0.48 days, and with 15 loops, duration was 9.44 ± 1.35 days. [ref. 6]

During pseudopregnancy, a gradual rise in body weight is noted over the first 6-7 days, with a drop in weight on the day of "heat" [ref. 9]. Sometimes pseudopregnancy terminates with a silent heat [ref. 14]. Some young hamsters may return to heat during the evening of day 8; in most animals return to heat is delayed until the evening of day 9 [ref. 16, 18].

The life of the decidual cell response can be extended, to date, only by evoking it in the sterile horn of a pregnant hamster. In such a situation, the endometrial portion resembles an absorption or abortive implantation site; sheathed arteries develop in the mesometrial endometrium, but no giant cells are found in this horn. [ref. 14] *Abbreviation:* DCR = decidual cell response.

Day	Structure or Organ Studied	Observation	Reference
1	Ovary	Contains freshly ovulated corpora lutea; luteinization begins	9
	Oviduct	Ova in cumulus; cumulus disperses at approximately 1200	9
	Vagina	Same as for Cycle (*see* Part II)	9
2	Ovary	Corpora lutea very vascular	9
	Oviduct	Ova lie within the zonae, and are single-celled	12
	Uterus	Passage of a thread into uterus, and through lumen, in evening of days 2-5 can elicit a decidual reaction, deciduomata, DCR	18
	Vagina	Same as for Cycle (*see* Part II)	9

continued

Part IV. Pseudopregnancy

Day	Structure or Organ Studied	Observation	Reference
3	Ovary	Differs from Cycle in that corpora are still growing; no evidence of any involution of the corpora	9
	Uterus	Ova pass from oviduct into uterus at approximately 2 d & 12-14 h; ova are still enclosed within zonae, but are individual units, and are not degenerating	12
		Traumatic stimuli (cutting uterus with scissors, or passage of thread into uterus) will elicit deciduomata	3,5
		Non-traumatic stimuli (air injection into uterus, or via oviduct into uterus) will not elicit deciduomata until following day	15
	Vagina	Same as for Cycle (see Part II)	9
4	Ovary	Corpora lutea continue large & functional	9
	Uterus	Ova lie within uterus, still essentially intact; in morning of day 4 zonae expand, become thin, and are lost, probably by lysing. Ova spread out within uterus, and if Pontamine Blue is given, tracts show localized areas of increased capillary permeability as sharp in coloration as those of pregnancy; luminal changes also mark site of freed ova. In areas sectioned, one ovum (nestled against the antimesometrial epithelium) was found; edema was present within uterus at this area. For this ability of the ovum in pseudopregnancy to elicit a reaction so similar to first adhesion stage of implantation, the term *pseudoimplantation* has been proposed.	11-13
		Non-traumatic stimuli applied 3 d & 9-22 h post-ovulation will elicit deciduomata resembling in size & pattern the normal conceptual swelling	10
		Sequence & pattern of decidualization of such deciduomata resembles those of the normal conceptus	17
	Vagina	Same as for Cycle (see Part II)	9
5	Ovary	Corpora, ovulated 4 d before, still functional; no fresh ovulations occur	9
	Uterus	In normal pseudopregnant hamster, site of ova can be observed in cleared uterus by luminal changes, but Pontamine Blue does not mark site; ova, which appear shrunken & distorted, still can be recovered from uterus during days 5-7	12,13
		Where DCR's have been provoked by non-traumatic stimuli, small swellings containing glycogen are present; sites of traumatically induced DCR's also contain glycogen, but size of swellings varies with technique used. In all cases, first decidua is at antimesometrial side of lumen, then at antimesometrial & lateral sides, and finally all about lumen; then antimesometrial decidua disappears.	12
		Traumatic stimuli still may elicit a DCR; old hamsters may respond to a non-traumatic stimulus on this day	15
	Vagina	No post-estrous discharge apparent; instead, clear translucent fluid still present	9
6	Corpora lutea	Average diameter per corpus luteum = $753 \pm 36.7 \mu m$	4
	Uterus	On days 6 & 7, extracts of the uterus contain luteolytic factor, whereas immature & pregnant uteri do not	8
	Vagina	Discharge is mucous, translucent fluid becoming flocculent	9
7	Corpora lutea	Average weight per corpus luteum = 0.52 ± 0.02 mg; progesterone content per corpus luteum = 11.5 ± 1.01 ng	7
	Uterus	Maximum DCR; decidual cavity appears within DCR of size comparable to normal conceptus; DCR may also undergo initial regression late on day 7 just as some areas of decidua degenerate at varying times within a definite time pattern in the normal course of pregnancy	17
	Vagina	Same as on day 6	9
8	Ovary	Corpora lutea show definite signs of regression	9
	Uterus	Gross changes indicative of necrosis appear in periphery of DCR	18
9	Uterus	Cell boundaries are less distinct; DCR begins to peel from endometrium	16
		If decidualization has been extensive, hamster may show dark blood at vaginal orifice, indicating necrotic condition	15
10	Vagina	Post-estrous discharge indicates initiation of another cycle	9

continued

Part IV.   Pseudopregnancy

Contributor: Margaret W. Orsini

References

1. Deanesly, R. 1938. Proc. Zool. Soc. London A108: 31-37.
2. Diamond, M., and R. Yanagimachi. 1968. J. Reprod. Fertil. 17:165-168.
3. Grady, K. L., and G. S. Greenwald. 1968. J. Endocrinol. 40:85-90.
4. Grady, K. L., and G. S. Greenwald. 1968. Endocrinology 83:1171-1180.
5. Kent, G. C. 1968. In R. A. Hoffman, et al. The Golden Hamster. Iowa State Univ., Ames. pp. 119-138.
6. Kent, G. C., and G. Atkins. 1959. Proc. Soc. Exp. Biol. Med. 101:106-107.
7. Lukaszewska, J. H., and G. S. Greenwald. 1969. J. Reprod. Fertil. 20:185-187.
8. Mazer, R. S., and P. A. Wright. 1968. Endocrinology 83:1065-1071.
9. Orsini, M. W. 1961. Proc. Anim. Care Panel 11(4): 193-206.
10. Orsini, M. W. 1963. J. Endocrinol. 28:119-121.
11. Orsini, M. W. 1963. In A. C. Enders, ed. Delayed Implantation. Univ. Chicago, Chicago. pp. 155-169.
12. Orsini, M. W. 1964. 5th Int. Congr. Anim. Reprod. Artif. Insem. Trenton 7:309-313.
13. Orsini, M. W. 1965. Ciba Found. Symp. Preimplant. Stages Pregnancy, pp. 162-167.
14. Orsini, M. W. 1968. J. Endocrinol. 41(Proc):vii-viii.
15. Orsini, M. W. Unpublished. Univ. Wisconsin, Bardeen Medical Laboratories, Madison, 1979.
16. Orsini, M. W., and N. B. Schwartz. 1970. J. Reprod. Fertil, 21:431-441.
17. Orsini, M. W., et al. 1970. Am. J. Obstet. Gynecol. 106:14-25.
18. Turnbull, J. G., and G. C. Kent. 1963. Anat. Rec. 145:97-99.
19. White, G. V. S. 1949. J. Tenn. Acad. Sci. 24:216-219.

Part V.   Lactation

Weight drops slowly but steadily throughout lactation, then a slight gain occurs prior to the first postpartum estrus; after the first few days, weight loss can be prevented by daily feeding of fresh greens. [ref. 8] Cycle will return in lactating females 4 days after young are removed; one young can maintain lactation [ref. 3]. Lactation can continue after ovariectomy on day 7 [ref. 3]. All investigators agree that during lactation, the hamster has no postpartum ovulation. Acyclic animals (those that suddenly cease cycling) show only waxy, bleb-like lactation; ovary has no large follicles or corpora lutea; and cycling usually starts again spontaneously several weeks later. [ref. 8] *Abbreviations:* FSH = follicle-stimulating hormone; LH = luteinizing hormone.

Day Postpartum	Structure, Organ, or Hormone Studied	Observation	Reference
1	Ovary	All vesicular follicles undergo atresia	3,6,7
	Corpora lutea	Average weight per corpus luteum = 0.68 ± 0.08 mg. Luteolysis destroys corpora.	3,6,7
		Average diameter per corpus luteum = 1019 ± 15.0 μm	4
	Progesterone	Plasma level = 1.4 ± 0.5 ng/ml; level dropping	6
	Prolactin	Level high	1
1-4	Vagina	Bloody discharge for first 3-4 d	8
	Estrogens	Low level	5
2	Corpora lutea	Average diameter per corpus luteum = 854 ± 7.6 μm	4
	FSH	Increases to peak of 850 ng/ml serum; diminishes thereafter [L/]	2,3
	Prolactin	Level drops	1
2-3	Ovary	Filled with interstitial tissue, no antral follicles; this histology may be due to continuing LH and low FSH production after day 2	3
3	LH	Rises to peak of 70 ng/ml serum, diminishes somewhat, and then remains constant [L/]	2,3
3-8	Prolactin	Rises to day 1 level and remains fairly constant at 35 ng/ml serum	1,2
4-5	Vagina	Discharge becomes white, non-mucous, or waxy, or there is no discharge	8
8-19	Progesterone	Non-detectable in plasma	6
26	Ovary	Vesicular follicles reappear	3
28-30	Ovary	Ovulation ensues	3

[L/] This "lactation picture" of FSH and LH levels can be maintained by 1 or 2 young [ref. 3].

continued

97. DAILY OBSERVATIONS OF REPRODUCTION: HAMSTER

Part V. Lactation

Contributor: Margaret W. Orsini

References

1. Bast, J. D., and G. S. Greenwald. 1974. Endocrinology 94:1295-1299.
2. Bast, J. D., and G. S. Greenwald. 1974. J. Endocrinol. 63:527-532.
3. Greenwald, G. S. 1965. Endocrinology 77:641-650.
4. Greenwald, G. S., et al. 1967. Ibid. 80:851-856.
5. Joshi, H. S., and A. P. Labhsetwar. 1972. J. Reprod. Fertil. 31:299-302.
6. Leavitt, W. W., and G. C. Blaha. 1970. Biol. Reprod. 3:353-361.
7. Lukaszewska, J. H., and G. S. Greenwald. 1970. Endocrinology 86:1-9.
8. Orsini, M. W. 1961. Proc. Anim. Care Panel 11(4): 193-206.

98. VALUES FOR REPRODUCTION AND DEVELOPMENT: HAMSTER

Part I. Reproductive Performance of BIO Inbreds

Matings: exposure of two females to two potentially fertile males for seven days. **Animals Lost:** difference between the number of animals **Born/Litter** and the number of animals **Weaned/Litter**, expressed as percent of animals **Born/Litter**.

Strain	Matings			Born/Litter		Weaned/Litter		Animals Lost %
	Total No.	Fertile No.	%	Mean	Mode	Mean	Mode	
BIO 14.6	853	317	37	5.6	..	3.7	..	34
BIO 15.16	3769	2277	60	7.0	7	6.1	7	13
BIO 72.29	288	160	56	5.5	..	4.8	..	12
BIO 87.20	175	75	43	7.1	..	5.0	..	29

Contributor: C. G. Van Dongen

Reference: Van Dongen, C. G. Unpublished. Bio-Research Consultants, Inc., Cambridge, MA, 1978.

Part II. Effect of Parity on Reproductive Performance of BIO 15.16 Inbreds

Percent Lost: Litters—calculated from **Total Litters; Animals**—difference between the number of animals **Born/Litter** and the number of animals **Weaned/Litter**, expressed as percent of **No. Born/Litter**.

Parity	Total Litters No.	No. Born/Litter		No. Weaned/Litter		Sex Ratio at Weaning % ♂	Percent Lost	
		Mean	Mode	Mean	Mode		Litters	Animals
0	325	5.9	6	5.1	6	48.7	0.7	14.2
1	245	7.0	9	6.5	7	48.6	1.7	7.6
2	203	6.5	7,9	6.0	9	47.6	13.8	8.9
3	142	5.4	7	4.7	5.7	49.1	18.7	13.1
4	63	4.1	3,5	2.4	5	52.3	22.0	41.0
5	19	4.0	3,7	2.3	5	48.7	15.8	42.1
6	0	...	...	...	...	...	...	...

Contributor: C. G. Van Dongen

Reference: Van Dongen, C. G. Unpublished. Bio-Research Consultants, Inc., Cambridge, MA, 1978.

98. VALUES FOR REPRODUCTION AND DEVELOPMENT: HAMSTER

Part III. Development and Sexual Maturation of BIO Inbreds

Plus/minus (±) values are standard deviations.

Strain	Gener- ations Inbred No.	28-Day Body Wt, g ♂	28-Day Body Wt, g ♀	Age at First Litter, d
BIO 1.5	38	35.0 ± 5.8	34.4 ± 5.2	86.0 ± 13.8
BIO 7.88	51	37.0 ± 11.1	38.8 ± 10.7	89.5 ± 36.0
BIO 14.6	47	45.5 ± 10.5	46.2 ± 9.4	103.7 ± 32.1
BIO 15.16	40	46.3 ± 7.7	47.0 ± 7.6	70.6 ± 8.5

Strain	Gener- ations Inbred No.	28-Day Body Wt, g ♂	28-Day Body Wt, g ♀	Age at First Litter, d
BIO 40.54	30	32.4 ± 7.1	33.9 ± 6.5	100.8 ± 32.8
BIO 72.29	29	52.9 ± 8.8	50.4 ± 8.8	88.4 ± 7.5
BIO 82.62	32	35.6 ± 5.6	37.6 ± 5.7	76.2 ± 19.1
BIO 87.20	40	44.3 ± 9.6	42.1 ± 9.1	89.0 ± 15.0

Contributor: C. G. Van Dongen

Reference: Van Dongen, C. G. Unpublished. Bio-Research Consultants, Inc., Cambridge, MA, 1978.

Part IV. Body and Organ Weights of BIO 15.16 Inbreds

Plus/minus (±) values are standard deviations.

Age wk	No. & Sex	Weight, g Body	Brain	Liver	Kidneys[1]	Adrenals[1]
20	12♂	111.9 ± 11.8	0.957 ± 0.052	5.5 ± 0.5	0.905 ± 0.180	0.031 ± 0.005
	12♀	121.6 ± 13.9	0.984 ± 0.039	6.1 ± 1.1	1.115 ± 0.115	0.017 ± 0.005
30	37♂	122.5 ± 8.2	0.959 ± 0.045	5.7 ± 0.5	0.937 ± 0.074	0.031 ± 0.006
	38♀	127.9 ± 11.4	0.983 ± 0.039	6.7 ± 0.9	1.254 ± 0.190	0.020 ± 0.005

[1] Both.

Contributor: C. G. Van Dongen

Reference: Van Dongen, C. G. Unpublished. Bio-Research Consultants, Inc., Cambridge, MA, 1978.

99. BODY AND ORGAN WEIGHTS: HAMSTER

Data are for males and females from the colonies of two inbred strains: ALAC/Lac and CLAC/Lac [ref. 1, 4]. ALAC/Lac is an acromelanic albino strain developed at the Medical Research Council Laboratory Animals Centre. It was obtained in 1966 from a commercial breeder, and is presently at F40. Origin of this strain is obscure, probably from a mutation arising in Russia. CLAC/Lac is a cream-colored strain developed by the Medical Research Council Laboratory Animals Centre from one litter supplied by Glaxo Laboratories Limited in 1965, and is presently at

F42. Origin of this strain is from a mutation arising in a non-inbred colony of golden (wild-type) Syrian hamsters maintained by Glaxo Laboratories.

All animals were given two-star "conventional" status [ref. 3], and were fed a PRD diet and mixed seed. The animal-room temperature was 20 ± 2°C, and the lighting cycle was 15 hours light:9 hours darkness. All animals were weaned at 21 days. Data are previously unpublished.

Part I. Growth

Adult animals were kept as monogamous pairs. After wean-ing (21 days), the sexes were separated. The members of

each colony were maintained separately in groups of 3 to 6 for the duration of the investigations, and were weighed

continued

Part I. Growth

at approximately fortnightly intervals for a period of 6 months. Thus, the data are based on sample weighings, and reflect ranges of variation in body weight for each colony. Values for animals 2-16 weeks of age were calculated from body weights at each particular time period, plus or minus

3 days. Weights for animals older than 18 weeks were computed from the observations available from 18 to 26 weeks. Values in parentheses are ranges, estimate "b" (*see* Introduction).

Age, wk	Male		Female	
	Body Weight, g	No. of Observations	Body Weight, g	No. of Observations
		ALAC/Lac		
0 (birth)	3.2(2.0-4.4)	20	3.0(1.8-4.2)	19
2	11.7(8.8-14.6)	36	12.0(7.6-16.4)	37
4	43.4(18.7-68.1)	16	42.9(18.4-67.4)	23
6	64.6(45.0-84.2)	23	64.2(53.0-75.4)	29
8	75.2(57.5-92.9)	17	75.3(57.7-92.9)	26
10	83.7(68.5-98.9)	18	85.7(67.0-104.4)	15
12	84.5(70.3-98.7)	26	88.6(68.5-108.7)	34
14	85.1(66.2-104.0)	24	90.2(65.9-114.5)	33
16	89.9(74.6-105.2)	25	102.3(82.4-122.2)	18
>18	91.9(62.9-120.9)	10	124.2(97.9-150.5)	28
		CLAC/Lac		
0 (birth)	3.1(1.7-4.5)	34	2.8(1.4-4.2)	28
2	13.1(8.5-17.7)	43	13.9(3.8-24.0)	47
4	36.6(12.5-60.7)	22	40.8(22.5-59.1)	26
6	72.3(55.5-89.1)	19	70.9(56.1-85.7)	28
8	85.5(64.2-106.8)	29	89.4(70.6-108.2)	27
10	98.4(84.6-112.2)	16	105.3(89.6-121.0)	19
12	106.6(80.0-133.2)	17	107.3(86.9-127.7)	6
14	105.9(85.6-126.2)	19	121.6(94.9-148.3)	17
16	114.6(89.7-139.5)	8	120.1(71.2-169.0)	9
>18	118.7(106.0-131.4)	9	135.6(81.4-189.8)	29

Contributors: David C. Shaw and Jon A. Turton

References: *See* Part II.

Part II. Weight of Body Structures

At a selected age, each hamster was killed with an overdose of CO_2, body weight determined, the animal dissected, and the various organs removed and weighed. For paired organs, only the left was removed (consult ref. 2 for anatomical descriptions). A total of 26 ALAC and 32 CLAC males,

and 28 ALAC and 32 CLAC females were dissected, and a curve of the second degree polynomial ($\hat{Y} = a + bx + cx^2$) was fitted to each set of organ weights for each sex of each strain. In this way, the estimated weight of each organ at a particular age (*see* below) was determined.

Specification	Male						Female					
						ALAC/Lac						
Age, d	25	40	55	70	85	100	25	40	55	70	85	100
Body weight, g	37.4	56.1	71.2	82.7	90.5	94.7	34.9	54.0	71.0	85.9	98.7	109.5
Weight of structure, mg												
Liver	1868.6	2522.0	3017.9	3356.3	3537.3	3560.8	1697.9	2322.4	2876.9	3361.4	3775.8	4120.3

continued

99. BODY AND ORGAN WEIGHTS: HAMSTER

Part II. Weight of Body Structures

Specification	Male						Female					
Lung	326.4	361.3	391.5	417.0	437.7	453.6	349.0	377.9	409.7	444.5	482.2	522.9
Heart	181.1	236.1	281.0	316.0	340.8	355.7	174.1	245.5	307.5	360.0	403.1	436.7
Spleen	103.4	94.6	87.7	82.6	79.4	78.1 [L/]	104.8	101.1	100.8 [L/]	103.9	110.4	120.3
Kidney	261.9	324.0	371.2	403.7	421.3	424.1	255.1	326.0	387.5	439.4	481.8	514.8
Testis	213.3	777.5	1209.5	1509.1	1676.5	1711.6	....	....	....	....	....	....
Testis fat	116.5	414.0	645.7	811.4	911.2	945.0	....	....	....	....	....	....
Ovary	....	....	....	....	....	....	11.5	13.7	15.4	16.7	17.5	17.7
Uterine horn	....	....	....	....	....	....	25.3	76.9	117.7	147.4	166.2	174.1
CLAC/Lac												
Age, d	25	40	55	70	85	100	25	40	55	70	85	100
Body weight, g	36.7	61.7	82.2	98.2	109.8	116.9	35.8	61.7	83.7	101.7	115.8	126.0
Weight of structure, mg												
Liver	2229.1	3446.4	4405.1	5105.2	5546.6	5729.4	2201.1	3169.8	3980.7	4633.8	5129.1	5466.5
Lung	293.5	345.8	389.6	425.1	452.1	470.8	309.0	390.8	458.2	511.2	549.8	574.0
Heart	160.3	227.3	283.5	329.0	363.6	387.5	161.6	234.7	298.1	351.9	395.9	430.2
Spleen	59.1	69.7	78.2	84.8	89.4	91.9	57.9	81.9	102.6	120.0	134.1	144.8
Kidney	256.2	323.6	377.8	418.8	446.6	457.8	246.4	326.9	394.4	448.7	490.0	518.2
Testis	232.9	789.6	1222.9	1532.6	1718.8	1781.6	....	....	....	....	....	....
Testis fat	121.5	591.2	974.6	1271.7	1482.5	1606.9	....	....	....	....	....	....
Ovary	....	....	....	....	....	....	7.5	12.2	16.2	19.4	21.9	23.7
Uterine horn	....	....	....	....	....	....	29.1	81.4	123.6	155.6	177.5	189.3

[L/] Indicates an apparent reduction in organ weight with age; these results are considered to indicate either a real reduction in organ weight with age, or to be due to a sampling variation. The former proposal is considered the more likely explanation.

Contributors: David C. Shaw and Jon A. Turton

References

1. Festing, M. F. W., ed. 1975. International Index of Laboratory Animals. Laboratory Animals Centre, Carshalton, Surrey, U.K.
2. Hoffman, R. A., et al., ed. 1968. The Golden Hamster: Its Biology and Use in Medical Research. Iowa State Univ., Ames.
3. Medical Research Council. 1974. The Accreditation and Recognition Schemes for Suppliers of Laboratory Animals. Laboratory Animals Centre, Carshalton, Surrey, U.K.
4. Parrott, R. F., and M. F. W. Festing. 1977. Standardized Laboratory Animals. Laboratory Animals Centre, Carshalton, Surrey, U.K.

100. STATISTICS OF AGING: HAMSTER

Inbred Strain	Mean Longevity d	Sex	Generations Inbred	Mean Body Weight at Death, g	Mean Heart Weight at Death, mg	Mean Liver Weight at Death, g	Mean Kidney Weight at Death, mg
BIO 1.26	476	♂	28.0	99	522	6.04	1,509
		♀	27.5	95	477	5.98	1,366
BIO 1.5	599	♂	11.2	97	437	5.26	1,210
		♀	11.8	98	495	6.13	1,497

continued

Inbred Strain	Mean Longevity d	Sex	Generations Inbred	Mean Body Weight at Death, g	Mean Heart Weight at Death, mg	Mean Liver Weight at Death, g	Mean Kidney Weight at Death, mg
BIO 2.4	532	♂	20.4	108	509	7.82	1,239
		♀	21.3	100	570	6.82	1,490
BIO 4.22	481	♂	31.9	103	609	7.29	1,487
		♀	33.4	92	527	6.94	1,436
BIO 4.24	589	♂	23.8	132	604	6.93	1,593
		♀	26.2	144	644	9.04	1,975
BIO 12.14	473	♂	12.0	94	439	4.91	1,098
		♀	12.3	98	471	6.51	1,354
BIO 45.5	562	♂	15.6	106	506	6.14	1,334
		♀	16.0	108	622	6.79	1,536
BIO 54.7	509	♂	12.3	100	457	4.81	1,157
		♀	11.8	103	534	6.44	1,745
BIO 82.73	502	♂	13.9	91	484	4.80	1,118
		♀	13.1	89	524	5.11	1,362
BIO 86.93	494	♂	6.4	102	513	5.37	1,304
		♀	7.1	109	575	6.48	1,557
BIO 87.20	690	♂	12.0	114	506	7.92	1,525
		♀	12.1	136	602	7.05	1,598
BIO X.3	527	♂	27.6	105	468	6.08	1,148
		♀	27.6	96	472	6.41	1,361
BIO X.68	531	♂	23.4	105	614	5.18	1,144
		♀	24.6	102	672	5.06	1,326

Contributors: Chai H. Yoon and J. Peterson

Reference: Haverland, L. H., et al. 1972. Prog. Exp. Tumor Res. 16:120-141.

101. MUTANTS FOR COAT COLOR AND OTHER COAT CHARACTERISTICS: HAMSTER

Some of the mutants listed below can be found—in mixed combinations—in pet shop stocks. Commercially available lines used in research are mostly agouti, acromelanic white (c^d/c^d), or non-extension of eumelanin ⟨cream⟩ (e/e). A majority of the mutants are held by Yoon and Peterson, or Robinson. Some are held by private breeders, and therefore are not generally available. As a result, a few mutants may have been lost entirely. For reviews of the data on hamster mutant factors, consult the General References.

Gene Symbol	Gene Name	Gene Effect		Inheritance & Linkage	Reference
		Primary on Coat	Other		
		Type	Description			
b[1]	Brown[1]	Color	Similar to pink-eyed dilution (p), but darker	....	Autosomal	1,50
Ba	White band	Pattern	White band in trunk region; band may be wider on ventrum than on dorsum	....	Autosomal; linkage with longhair (l)[2]	1,33,36, 42,45
c^d	Acromelanic albino	Color	White pelage	Eyes pink at weaning, turning to red at maturity; pinnae dark	Autosomal; linkage with pink-eyed dilution (p)	1,29,31, 41,50
dg	Dark gray	Color	Dark gray with less brown or yellow	....	Autosomal	1,18

[1] Formerly called rust (r). [2] In reference 45, original crossing-over frequency is amended.

continued

Gene Symbol	Gene Name	Gene Effect		Other	Inheritance & Linkage	Reference
		Primary on Coat				
		Type	Description			
Ds	Dominant spot	Pattern	Small irregular patches of white fur over the back & sides; ventral fur white	Lethal when homozygous	Autosomal	1,22
e	Non-extension of eumelanin[3]	Color	Rich creamy yellow	....	Autosomal; close linkage with hydrocephalus (*hy*)	1,15,28, 30,51, 52
f	Frost	Color	Coat mottled white; fur becoming lighter with age	Partial or complete absence of ear pigment. Occasional eye anomalies.	Autosomal	24,25,48
hr	Hairless	Absence of hair	Atrichosis; sparse hair that quickly falls out	....	Autosomal	17
J	Jute	Color	Creamy yellow	Lethal when homozygous	Autosomal; close linkage with seizure (*sz*)	26,53
l	Longhair	Texture	Long hair; ♂ have longer hair than ♀	....	Autosomal; linkage with white band (*Ba*)	42,46,47
Lg	Lethal gray	Color	Coat gray	Lethal when homozygous	Autosomal	1,18,21, 25
Mo	Mottled white	Pattern	Heterozygous ♀ have white patches	Lethal when homozygous (*Mo/Mo*) or hemizygous (*Mo/Y*)	X chromosome (sex-linked)	14,20
N	Naked	Absence of hair	Atrichosis; heterozygotes have sparse hair; homozygotes are devoid of hair except for a short down	....	Autosomal; semidominant	6
p[4]	Pink-eyed dilution[4]	Color	Eumelanin changed to brown	Eye dark red; rim of eyelid with little or no pigment; general reduction of skin pigment	Autosomal; linkage with acromelanic albino (*c^d*)	1,32,34, 41
pi	Pinto	Pattern	Large, random white patches on sides & dorsum	....	Autosomal	19
ru	Ruby eye	Color	Coat color dilution	Eyes ruby; size of animal reduced; ♂ invariably sterile	Autosomal	28-31
rx	Rex	Texture	Wavy hair	Vibrissae crooked & twisted throughout life	Autosomal	43,49
s	Piebald white spotting	Pattern	White patches	Reduced size of animal due in part to abnormal (light in weight) bones. Urogenital abnormalities prevalent.	Autosomal	1,5,7-10, 13,16, 23,30, 31
Sa	Satin	Texture	Hair has satiny sheen in heterozygotes, and is satiny thin & straggly in homozygotes	....	Autosomal; semidominant	40
T	Tawny	Color	Similar to agouti but lighter & paler	....	X chromosome (sex-linked); incompletely dominant	15,27

[3] Synonym: cream. [4] Formerly called brown (*b*); synonyms: cinnamon, amber.

continued

Gene Symbol	Gene Name	Gene Effect			Inheritance & Linkage	Reference
		Primary on Coat		Other		
		Type	Description			
To	Tortoiseshell	Color/pattern	Yellow in ♂ & homozygous ♀; yellow patches in heterozygous ♀	Clear interaction of *To*/+ genotype with *Ds*/+ and with *Ba*/−, causing agouti & yellow patches to be more discreet, as in the cat	X chromosome (sex-linked); semidominant	1,20,38, 39
U	Umbrous	Color	Coat suffused with melanic pigmentation	....	Autosomal	44
Wh	Anophthalmic white	Color/pattern	Agouti heterozygotes (*Wh*/+): Almost normal coat color on sides & dorsum; ventral fur totally white (termed "Imperial"). Homozygotes (*Wh*/*Wh*): Complete absence of pigment in coat.	Homozygotes: Complete absence of pigment in skin & eyes. Eyes usually reduced (microphthalmia), or apparently occasionally lacking (anophthalmia). Hearing may also be impaired.	Autosomal	1,4,11, 12,35, 37

Contributors: C. William Nixon; Roy Robinson; Chai H. Yoon and J. S. Peterson

General References
1. Nixon, C. W., et al. 1970. J. Hered. 61:221-228.
2. Robinson, R. 1968. In R. A. Hoffman, et al., ed. The Golden Hamster. Iowa State Univ., Ames. pp. 41-72.
3. Robinson, R. 1975. In R. C. King, ed. Handbook of Genetics. Plenum, New York. v. 4, pp. 261-274.

Specific References
4. Beher, M. E., and W. T. Beher. 1959. Am. Nat. 93: 201-203.
5. Bock, M. 1953. Z. Naturforsch. 8:669-672.
6. Festing, M. F. W., and M. K. Wright. 1972. Nature (London) 236:81-82.
7. Foote, C. L. 1949. J. Hered. 40:100-101.
8. Foote, C. L. 1955. Anat. Rec. 121:831-842.
9. Foote, C. L., and H. E. Bullock. 1949. Ibid. 105:608 (Abstr. 269).
10. Foote, C. L., and F. M. Foote. 1950. Trans. Ill. State Acad. Sci. 43:237-243.
11. Hughes, R. D., and W. J. Geeraets. 1962. Genetics 47: 962.
12. Knapp, B. H., and S. Polivanov. 1958. Am. Nat. 92: 317-318.
13. Koch, W. 1951. Berl. Muench. Tieraerztl. Wochenschr. 64:114.
14. Magalhaes, H. 1954. Anat. Rec. 120:752 (Abstr. 112).
15. Magalhaes, H. 1954. Ibid. 120:752 (Abstr. 113).
16. Magalhaes, H. 1959. Ibid. 134:604 (Abstr. 108).
17. Nixon, C. W. 1972. J. Hered. 63:215-216.
18. Nixon, C. W., and M. E. Connelly. 1967. Ibid. 58: 295-296.
19. Nixon, C. W., and M. E. Connelly. 1977. Ibid. 68(6): 399-402.
20. Nixon, C. W., and R. Robinson. 1973. Genetica (the Hague) 44:588-590.
21. Nixon, C. W., et al. 1969. J. Hered. 60:74.
22. Nixon, C. W., et al. 1969. Ibid. 60:299-300.
23. Orsini, M. W. 1952. Ibid. 43:37-40.

24. Peterson, J. S. 1975. Ibid. 66:102-103.
25. Peterson, J. S. Unpublished. Bio-Research Institute, Cambridge, MA, 1978.
26. Peterson, J. S., and C. H. Yoon. 1975. J. Hered. 66: 246-247.
27. Peterson, J. S., et al. 1977. Ibid. 68:131-132.
28. Robinson, R. 1955. Nature (London) 176:353-354.
29. Robinson, R. 1957. Ibid. 180:443-444.
30. Robinson, R. 1958. J. Genet. 56:1-18, 85-102.
31. Robinson, R. 1959. Heredity 13:165-177.
32. Robinson, R. 1960. Nature (London) 187:170-171.
33. Robinson, R. 1960. Ibid. 188:764-765.
34. Robinson, R. 1962. Genetica (the Hague) 33:81-87.
35. Robinson, R. 1962. Am. Nat. 96:183-185.
36. Robinson, R. 1962. Heredity 17:477-486.
37. Robinson, R. 1964. Genetica (the Hague) 35:241-250.
38. Robinson, R. 1966. Nature (London) 212:824-825.
39. Robinson, R. 1972. Genetica (the Hague) 43:239-243.
40. Robinson, R. 1972. J. Hered. 63:52.
41. Robinson, R. 1973. Ibid. 64:232.
42. Robinson, R. 1975. Ibid. 66:312.
43. Robinson, R. 1976. Heredity 36:181-184.
44. Robinson, R. 1977. J. Hered. 68:328.
45. Robinson, R., et al. 1978. Ibid. 69(3):199.
46. Schimke, D. J., et al. 1973. Ibid. 64:236-237.
47. Schimke, D. J., et al. 1974. Ibid. 65:57-58.
48. Whitney, R. 1963. In W. Lane-Petter, ed. Animals for Research. Academic, London. pp. 365-392.
49. Whitney, R., and C. W. Nixon. 1973. J. Hered. 64: 239.
50. Whitney, R., et al. 1964. Am. Nat. 98:121-122.
51. Yoon, C. H. 1973. J. Hered. 64:305-307.
52. Yoon, C. H., and J. S. Peterson. 1977. Ibid. 68:418.
53. Yoon, C. H., et al. Unpublished. Boston College, Dep. Biology, Chestnut Hill, MA, 1978.

102. DENTAL ANATOMY: HAMSTER

All material presented in this table is based on data from outbred Syrian hamsters. To date no work has been done on dental anatomy and disease using inbred strains of hamsters. Syrian hamsters are monophyodont, polybunodont, brachyodont, and heterodont [ref. 9, 17]. The dental formula for Syrian hamsters is $I\frac{1}{1}$, $C\frac{0}{0}$, $PM\frac{0}{0}$, $M\frac{3}{3}$ [ref. 9]. For information concerning dental caries of molars, consult references 1, 4, 7, 8, 10, and 17. For information concerning periodontal disease, consult references 2, 3, 5, 6, and 11-16.

Specification	Incisors	Calcification and Eruption of Teeth, d					
		1st Molar		2nd Molar		3rd Molar	
		Maxillary	Mandibular	Maxillary	Mandibular	Maxillary	Mandibular
Osseous crypt first visible	..	At birth	At birth	2	2	12	12
First evidence of calcification	..	2	2	6	5	20-22	18
Crown completely formed	..	8	8	13	12	30-34	29-30
First evidence of eruption	1	8	8	14	12	32-35	29-32
Complete eruption; teeth in occlusion	2	8-9	8-9	16-18	16-18	40-46	40-46
Roots completely calcified	..	35-40	25-30	42-46	36-38	90-100	75-85
Reference	9	9,17	9,17	9,17	9,17	9,17	9,17

Contributor: Peter J. Robinson

References

1. Arnold, F. A., Jr. 1942. Public Health Rep. 57:1599-1604.
2. Costich, E. R. 1954. Thesis. Univ. Rochester, School Medicine and Dentistry, NY.
3. Costich, E. R., et al. 1957. J. Am. Dent. Assoc. 55:617-619.
4. Dale, P. P., et al. 1944. J. Dent. Res. 23:209(Abstr. 49).
5. Gold, H. S., and P. H. Keyes. 1955. Oral Surg. Oral Med. Oral Pathol. 8:1060-1062.
6. Jordan, H. V., et al. 1972. J. Periodontal Res. 7:21-28.
7. Keyes, P. H. 1944. J. Dent. Res. 23:439-444.
8. Keyes, P. H. 1959. Ibid. 38:525-533.
9. Keyes, P. H., and P. P. Dale. 1944. Ibid. 23:427-438.
10. Keyes, P. H., and R. J. Fitzgerald. 1962. Arch. Oral Biol. 7:267-278.
11. Keyes, P. H., and H. S. Gold. 1955. Oral Surg. Oral Med. Oral Pathol. 8:492-499.
12. Keyes, P. H., and H. V. Jordan. 1964. Arch. Oral Biol. 9:377-400.
13. King, J. D. 1949. J. Pathol. Bacteriol. 61:413-425.
14. King, J. D., and A. P. Gimson. 1948-1949. Br. J. Nutr. 2:111-118.
15. Klingsberg, J., and E. O. Butcher. 1959. J. Dent. Res. 38:421.
16. Mitchell, D. F. 1954. J. Am. Dent. Assoc. 49:177-183.
17. Orland, F. J. 1946. J. Dent. Res. 25:445-453.

103. MYOPATHIC DYSTROPHIES: HAMSTER

Strain: All animals available from BIO. For full name, *see* list of HOLDERS at front of book.

Strain	Derivation	Coat Color	Coat Color Genes	Course of Disease[2]	Reference
BIO 1.50[1]	White LaCasse sire, brown Schwentker dam	Acromelanic white	c^d/c^d	Rapid	3
BIO 14.6	Schwentker, LaCasse	Acromelanic white	c^d/c^d	Moderate, death 280-350 d	1
BIO 40.54	Schwentker, LaCasse, Toolan, Gulf	Agouti	+/+	Rapid	2
BIO 53.58	Whitney	Acromelanic white	c^d/c^d	Rapid	2
BIO 82.62	Schwentker, LaCasse, Toolan, Gulf	Acromelanic white	c^d/c^d	Rapid	2

[1] Strain lost. [2] Cardiomyopathy and skeletal myopathy.

Contributor: Freddy Homburger

References

1. Gertz, E. W. 1972. Prog. Exp. Tumor Res. 16:242-260.
2. Handler, A. H., et al. 1975. Proc. Soc. Exp. Biol. Med. 148:573-577.
3. Homburger, F., et al. 1962. Med. Exp. 6:339-345.

Gene Symbol	Condition	Mode of Inheritance	Description	Reference
hy [1]	Hydrocephalus	Autosomal recessive	Distended brain ventricles & displacement of various brain structures	7
pa [2]	Hindleg paralysis	Sex-linked recessive	Hindlegs become paralyzed between 6 & 10 mo; penetrance in ♀ not complete	1,4
sz [1]	Spontaneous seizure	Autosomal recessive	Frequent seizures between the 3rd & 4th wk	8
Wh [2]	Anophthalmia	Autosomal semi-dominant	Homozygotes show amelanosis, anophthalmia, & anomalous optic nerve & hearing; heterozygotes have paler ventral hair	3,5,6
Fn [3]	Extreme microphthalmia	Autosomal recessive	Homozygotes have extremely small eyes or no eyes. Coat color, white. No allelic test with Anophthalmia (Wh) has been made.	2

[1] Maintained in non-inbred lines listed in Table 95. [2] Maintained in inbred lines listed in Table 94. [3] No gene symbol yet assigned.

Contributors: Chai H. Yoon and J. Peterson

References

1. Homburger, F., and E. Bajusz. 1970. J. Am. Med. Assoc. 212:604-610.
2. Hughes, R. D., and W. J. Geeraets. 1962. Genetics 47:962.
3. Knapp, B. H., and S. Polivanov. 1958. Am. Nat. 92: 317-318.
4. Nixon, C. W., and M. E. Connelly. 1968. J. Hered. 59: 276-278.
5. Robinson, R. 1964. Genetica (the Hague) 35:241-250.
6. Yoon, C. H. 1975. Invest. Ophthalmol. 14(4):321-325.
7. Yoon, C. H., and J. Slaney. 1972. J. Hered. 63:344-346.
8. Yoon, C. H., et al. 1976. Ibid. 67:115-116.

105. BEHAVIOR PATTERNS: HAMSTER

Part I. Development and Control

Figures in heavy brackets are reference numbers.

Description	Development	Sensory Control	Hormonal Control	Neural Control
Male Courtship				
Ultrasonic vocalization by ♂ facilitates lordosis and assists ♀ in short distance localization of ♂ [61, 62, 64]. ♂ licks ♀ vaginal area and consumes vaginal secretion [123]. ♂ display preference for conspecific ♀ over heterospecific ♀ [122, 128], for ♀ over ♂ [44, 92, 110, 123], but not for conspe-	Early experience with vaginal secretion is not required for adult attraction to vaginal secretion [72]. Sexual experience is not required for preference for conspecific ♀ or for vaginal secretion to be displayed [129]. Attraction to heterospecific ♀ increased by	♂ ultrasounds are elicited by ♀ odors [64]. Courtship & sexual preference are eliminated by olfactory impairment to main & accessory olfactory systems [45, 110, 127, 129, 130, 156]. Dimethyl disulfide is one of the components of vagi-	Castration abolishes preference for vaginal secretion [72]. Injections of estrogen & progesterone in ♂ may abolish ♂ preference for ♀ [87].	....

continued

Part I. Development and Control

Description	Development	Sensory Control	Hormonal Control	Neural Control
cific ♀ in different hormonal conditions [44, 110].	cross-fostering to heterospecific mothers [129]. Sexual preferences are established earlier in development than are copulatory patterns [87]. Taste aversion to vaginal secretion fails to modify mating behavior [59].	nal secretion which attracts ♂ [180].		

Female Courtship				
Ultrasounds serve as sexual advertisement to attract ♂ [61, 64]. ♀ "solicit" non-copulating ♂ [124, 127]. ♀ show preference for conspecific over heterospecific ♂ [122, 128], and for ♂ over ♀ [10].	♂ ultrasounds elicit ♀ ultrasound production [62]. Olfactory bulb removal eliminates ♀ soliciting of non-copulating ♂ [127]. Partial deafening eliminates preference for restricted ♂ (animals that ♀ can see & smell but not touch) over restricted ♀ [10].		Ultrasound production greater in estrous ♀ [64]. Attraction to ♂ greater in naturally estrous ♀ than in ♀ in induced estrus [10]. Castrated ♀ show no preference for ♂ hamsters, but estrogen & progesterone restore preference [87].	

Male Copulatory Behavior				
Copulation consists of series of 1-18 intromissions ending in ejaculations. Many more intromissions precede first ejaculation than precede subsequent ejaculations in one mating period. ♂ grooms penis following most intromissions. Refractory period of non-copulatory activity follows each ejaculation. May be 10 or more ejaculations before satiety is reached [23, 158]. Full recovery from sexual exhaustion takes ∿5 days of sexual inactivity [9]. Early intromissions accomplished by a single thrust into vagina and are 2-3 seconds long. Later in a copulatory period, following most of the ejaculations, a shift is made to intromissions with multiple intravaginal thrusting 5-30 seconds long. Such intromissions do not result in ejaculation. This is the most fundamental shift in copulatory pattern yet described for any species [23, 105]. Whereas rat requires only 1 ejaculation to achieve maximal probability of pregnancy in ♀, hamster requires more than 4 (but fewer than 7) ejaculations, to accomplish same result [49, 105]. Function of copulation past 7 ejaculations, including intromissions with multiple thrusts, is unknown [49, 105].	All components of adult mating behavior are displayed by 55 days of age [157], but form of mating behavior continues to change with mating experience [120, 123, 157]. Importance of neonatal hormones on development of ♂, ♀ or bisexual copulatory patterns has been extensively investigated [27, 30, 39, 57, 67, 86, 132, 137, 144, 189, 193, 204]. In general, ♂ require testosterone as neonates for ♂ patterns of behavior to develop normally.	Various techniques of impairing olfaction, including lesions of olfactory bulb [53, 110, 130, 205], lesions of lateral olfactory tract [45, 46, 115], nasal occlusion [47], or damaging or anesthetizing nasal mucosa [45, 52, 110], eliminate ♂ mating behavior in almost every case. Discussion continues on relative importance of main & accessory (vomeronasal) olfactory systems in controlling hamster mating [127, 155, 156]. Attention has focused on vaginal secretion as a crucial odor source in hamster mating [44, 59, 72, 88, 92, 110, 114, 123, 180]. Urine odors are apparently not important [88].	Castration eliminates ejaculation & intromissions, and reduces mounting attempts [8, 190, 200, 201]. Abortive attempts to mount survive much longer after castration in hamster than they do in rat [8]. Time course of this behavioral change is affected by amount & frequency of copulatory experience both before & after castration [20, 21]. Spontaneous seminal emission is eliminated by castration and restored by testosterone [7]. Treatment with androgens restores copulatory behavior in castrated ♂ [8, 34, 143, 190, 192, 193, 202]. A fairly high degree of ♀ copulatory behavior (lordosis) may be elicited from castrated ♂ hamsters after injections of estrogen, or estrogen & progesterone [31, 62, 99, 191].	Medial cortical lesions produce a temporary decrease in intromissions; lesions of dorsolateral cortex have no effect on mating [22]. Complete removal of olfactory bulb or sectioning lateral olfactory tract eliminates or severely disrupts copulatory behavior [45, 115, 130].

continued

Part I. Development and Control

Description	Development	Sensory Control	Hormonal Control	Neural Control
Female Copulatory Behavior				
Behavior consists of assuming a rigid, lordotic, receptive posture in response to ♂ attempting to mount. Rigid receptive posture facilitates intromission by ♂. Unlike ♀ rat, ♀ hamster does not break receptive posture between intromissions or even between ejaculations by ♂, and may hold posture for 30 minutes or longer [158, 190]. Unmated ♀ display a regular 4-day estrous cycle [2]. ♂ hamsters may elicit lordosis about 2 hours before lights-out on evening of ovulation [2]. Ovulation occurs about 7 hours after lights-out [2]. Lordosis may be elicited for a 14- to 16-hour period [2, 10, 36], unless mating occurs; even if fresh ♂ are introduced, receptivity is eliminated after 2 hours of copulation [29]. Mating has been known to occur during pregnancy, but not during postpartum or lactation [100].	Lordosis normally appears in its full adult form by 35 days of age; precocious lordosis may be stimulated in ♀ as young as 18 days by injections of estrogen & progesterone [50]. Exogenous hormone elicited lordosis in ♀ castrated at 1 or 43 days of age [67]. Neonatal injection, or implantation with testosterone, results in increased capacity to show ♂ patterns of copulatory behavior [30, 69, 134, 139, 204] and a decreased capacity to show ♀ patterns of sexual behavior [30, 66, 144].	Tactual (manual) stimulation alone can elicit lordosis from estrous ♀ [124, 132, 133]; non-tactual stimuli (e.g., odors) from conspecific ♂ facilitate display of lordosis [124, 131, 133]. Olfactory impairment does not affect sexual receptivity [26, 107, 127]. Partial deafening greatly reduces display of receptive behavior towards ♂ that ♀ can see & smell, but not touch [10]. It is tactual stimulation of mounting & intromitting ♂ that causes postcopulatory decline in sexual receptivity; ejaculation is not necessary [25].	♀ sexual receptivity induced by estrogen released on day before estrus, followed by progesterone released on day of estrus [38, 65, 68, 160]. Continued release of progesterone necessary for maintenance of receptivity, but eventually leads to a progesterone-insensitive period & termination of heat [35, 36]. Injections with estrogen alone for 15 days may elicit significant lordosis in response to a ♂, but even then, progesterone further increases duration of receptive behavior [31]. Neither ovaries nor adrenal glands are necessary for postcopulatory decline in sexual receptivity [24]. High levels of injected progesterone tend to prolong duration of postcopulatory sexual receptivity [28].	Anterior dorsal hypothalamus has been implicated as an estrogen-sensitive site controlling hormonal mediation of sexual receptivity [37]. Lesions of suprachiasmatic nucleus abolish estrous cycle, producing persistent estrus [184].
Aggressive Behavior				
Aggression & relationships of dominance & submission involve stereotyped postures & actions that have received considerable descriptive analysis [51, 63, 71, 82, 106, 109, 145]. Wild hamsters are solitary, and probably defend their home burrow & a small territory [51]. In laboratory, hamsters are usually individually housed to prevent injury from fights [51]. Such social isolation increases aggression when social encounters occur [16, 74, 150, 206]. Hamsters are most aggres-	Young littermates engage in play fighting [51]. Aggression increases with age up to at least 60 days old [203]. Brain of hamster is incompletely androgenized at birth. Neonatal injections of testosterone propionate into either ♂ or ♀ causes increased aggression in adults. Such neonatally androgenized animals are more sensitive to effects of castration (decreasing aggression) & to testosterone injections (increasing aggres-	♀ hamster vaginal secretion inhibits aggression of ♂ hamsters [123, 126]. Other progesterone-dependent ♀ odors may also inhibit ♂ aggression [147, 151]. Olfactory impairment greatly reduces aggression of ♂ [47, 79, 126, 130], but not of ♀ [79, 107]. Visually perceived postures & markings may be important signals indicating dominance or submission [70, 71, 93, 148]. Blind-	Importance of testosterone in controlling aggression in ♂ hamsters is not certain. ♂ aggression has been found to decrease after castration and increase after replacement with testosterone propionate [74, 141, 150, 194]. Size & pigmentation of androgen-dependent [195] flank gland and amount of testosterone propionate injected into castrated ♂ are positively correlated with social rank [55]. However, some workers found no decrease in	Bilateral lesions of either olfactory bulbs or amygdala cause decreases in social behavior & aggression in ♂ hamsters [19, 79, 126]. Lesions of septal region, however, increase social behavior & aggression [83, 183]. Unilateral, as well as bilateral, lesions of olfactory bulbs in 10-day-old ♀ hamsters greatly reduced the increased aggression that normally occurs during preg-

continued

Part I. Development and Control

Description	Development	Sensory Control	Hormonal Control	Neural Control
sive when defending their home cage from an intruder [126, 140]. ♀ are usually dominant over ♂ [145, 151]. Heavier animals are more likely to win fights and become dominant [54, 55, 194]. Once formed, dominant/ submissive relationships between 2 animals tend to remain stable [203]. An animal may suffer psychological effects of defeat for many weeks [51]. Thus, previous social experience is extremely important in studies of hamster aggression. Aggression towards conspecifics or defeat by conspecifics did not correlate with cannibalism of young pups [117, 129] or predatory behavior on locusts [154], respectively.	sion) than are normal animals of same sex. [27, 142, 149, 152]	ing increases aggression in ♂ [125].	aggression after castration, and have suggested that aggression of hamsters is less androgen-dependent than aggression of rats [190, 203]. Injections of progesterone [150], estrogen [194], or implantation of ovarian tissue [146] increase ♂ aggression. Aggression of ♂ is circadian, being highest just after onset of dark phase of light/dark cycle [103]. Adrenalectomy eliminates this rhythm [104]. Isolated (and consequently more aggressive) ♂ have heavier adrenal glands [16]; injections of hydrocortisone [L] greatly increase aggression [104]. Thus, adrenal hormones may be involved in controlling aggression in ♂ hamsters. ♀ hamsters are generally aggressive toward conspecifics of either sex at all times except when in heat [63, 97, 194]. Aggressiveness returns at end of heat or following mating, regardless of when mating occurs during estrus [25]. Aggression is highest during pregnancy & lactation [107, 206]. Castration abolishes cyclic nature of aggression and slightly decreases amount of aggression [97, 147, 151] (see also references 142 & 194). Estrogen injections alone may increase aggression [74, 97], but not always [194]. Progesterone injections may increase ♀ aggression towards ♂ [147, 151]. Estrogen followed by progesterone produces estrous behavior and inhibits aggression [97, 147, 194]. Flank gland size & pigmentation along with amount of injected testosterone are positively correlated with social rank [54] & fighting [74] (see also reference 194).	nancy & lactation [107]. This indicates a possible non-sensory role of the olfactory bulb in controlling ♀ hamster aggression [107]. Lesions of medial preoptic area reduce aggressiveness in ♀ hamsters, whereas lesions of anterior hypothalamus have opposite effect [78].

Scent Marking

Description	Development	Sensory Control	Hormonal Control	Neural Control
Both sexes deposit scent from bilaterally located sebaceous flank glands [51, 89]. ♀ flank mark at higher rates than do ♂ [190]. ♀ also deposit vaginal secretion by dragging their perineal area on substrate [51, 94]. Both flank & vaginal scent deposits may remain functional for as long as 25 days [94]. In ♂, flank marking rates are negatively correlated with sexual motivation [89]; in both sexes, flank marking is positively correlated with dominance [54, 55, 89, 90]. ♂ are relatively inhibited on entering an area which has been flank marked by another ♂ [1].	Amount of flank marking increases with age to 60 days of age [203].	In ♂, flank marking is strongly influenced by environmental odors. Flank marking greatly increases in cage of another ♂ [89, 121], probably because of odor of other ♂ flank gland secretion [91]. Flank marking is relatively inhibited in cage of an estrous ♀ [89]. Flank gland removal does not decrease flank marking rates indicating that olfactory feedback is not necessary for marking [91]. Olfactory impairment reduces flank marking in both sexes [79, 115, 129, 130], & vaginal marking in ♀ [107, 129].	Flank marking in ♀ is lowest on day of estrus [145, 190]. Castration in adulthood greatly decreases flank marking in both sexes; treatment with either testosterone or estrogen restores it to normal, or above normal, levels [142, 194]. Castration at puberty does not inhibit development of flank marking in ♂ [203]. An inverse correlation between flank marking & testosterone has been found in hamsters during mating or with recent mating opportunity [115, 196], perhaps reflecting inhibition of flank marking by estrous ♀ [89, 94]. ♀ vaginal marking is highest on day before behavioral estrus, but is inhibited during estrus, throughout pregnancy, & during early part of lactation [94, 107, 123].	

[L] Synonym: Cortisol.

continued

Part I. Development and Control

Description	Development	Sensory Control	Hormonal Control	Neural Control
Maternal Behavior				
Lactating ♀ care for young pups in nest by licking them and assuming nursing posture [42, 167, 169]. They retrieve displaced pups to nest by mouth, walking in a high-stepping maternal gait [42, 167, 169]. Maternal response is optimally elicited from lactating ♀ by pups 6-14 days old [167], which may relate to short gestation of hamster [43]. Pup retrieval stops, and family begins to break up, by time pups are 25 days old; mother may move	Maternal response is present by 19 days of age, long before conception is possible. By 29-47 days of age, ♀ start killing and eating young pups, and do so until they give birth to their own litter [168]. Exposure of non-lactating ♀ to newborn young, which are then killed, increases maternal responsiveness to 6-day-old pups presented 48 hours after initial kill [136].	It is presumed that ultrasonic cries of hamster pups are important in controlling maternal behavior of ♀ hamsters, but this has not been studied. Some anosmic ♀ show normal maternal behavior; however, many destroy or neglect their litters [107, 129].	Increase in nest building that normally occurs after pregnancy is eliminated by gonadectomy, and restored by implants of estrogen plus progesterone, but not by either hormone alone [165]. Progesterone injected day before parturition delays birth but not onset of maternal behavior [178]. Castrated, non-lactating ♀ still kill pups [117]. Progesterone does not increase pup killing by ♂ that had previously retrieved pups [117].	....

her nest away from pups' nest or become aggressive toward pups if she is confined with them [42, 169]. Both nulliparous & primiparous animals become maternal at ∿2-6 hours before parturition, demonstrating that experience of giving birth is not essential for maternal behavior [178].

Solitary living, non-lactating, adult ♀ usually kill and eat pups less than 6 days old [117, 136, 162, 163]. Group-housed ♀ are less likely to eat pups. Pups 6-10 days old elicit some maternal behavior from non-lactating ♀ [43]. ♂ are less likely to kill pups than are non-lactating ♀, and 60-100% of ♂ actually retrieve pups to nest [117, 129, 168]. Fostering of pups is possible [129, 167]. Nest building, hoarding, & digging begin to increase in frequency shortly after copulation, probably in preparation for increased needs of pregnant ♀ & litter [42, 107].

Description	Development	Sensory Control	Hormonal Control	Neural Control
Food Hoarding				
When given opportunity, hamsters will carry great quantities of food from a source to an area in home cage or burrow [181]. Food may be carried in mouth or in large cheek pouches. In	Hoarding is influenced by housing conditions & previous experience with hoarding [11]	Food deprivation does not increase hoarding [198]. Cold stimulates increase in hoarding [112].	Adrenalectomy depresses hoarding [182]	Amygdalectomy increases hoarding of food pellets in a social setting, but not when animal is alone [19]. Septal lesions cause great decrease in hoarding [83].

laboratory cage, hamsters tend to pile hoarded food in one corner [107]. Hamsters show much stronger hoarding tendencies than do rats [198]. Hoarding is much greater during dark phase of light/dark cycle [198]. Under cold conditions, act of hoarding facilitates onset of hibernation [112]. Distinct preferences are shown for hoarding of different food & even non-food objects [77].

continued

Part I. Development and Control

Description	Development	Sensory Control	Hormonal Control	Neural Control
Eating				
Voluntary wheel running results in weight gain [12, 13]. When opportunity to run is withdrawn, weight gain stops but weight is maintained at new, higher level [12, 13]. Unlike rats, when starved for a period of time, hamsters fail to show a post-fast increase in food intake, thus leading to substantial loss in body weight, & often, death [179]. Hamsters fed only once a day and provided with an exercise wheel are likely to develop ulcers (called activity-stress ulcers); control animals without wheels do not develop ulcers [196, 197].	....	....	There are striking differences between rats & hamsters with respect to hormonal regulation of eating, body weight, & taste preferences [209]. Gonadectomized hamsters eat more and gain weight rapidly when given 5 mg of progesterone daily; this effect is greater in ♀ than in ♂ [209]. Injections of testosterone decrease food intake in adult ♂ but not in adult ♀ [209]. Whereas hoarding increases during pregnancy [42, 107], food intake does not [209].	....
Drinking				
Hamsters will imbibe much higher concentrations of alcohol than will rats [3]. ♂ prefer higher concentration of alcohol than do ♀ [3]. Food restriction produces polydipsia in hamsters which does not decrease when additional salt is given [101]—unlike response of the rabbit.	....	....	Neither adrenalectomy nor treatment with deoxycorticosterone acetate affect salt consumption. In contrast to what has been observed in rats, sodium balance in hamster is relatively independent of adrenal hormones [170, 209]. Intake of saccharin solutions is decreased by ovariectomy in ♀, but unaffected by castration in ♂ [209].	....
Development of Olfactory Preferences				
By ∼8 days of age, pups display strong preference for odor of bedding from home cage over clean bedding [48, 73]. However, there is no evidence for a maternal pheromone in hamsters [73]. As early as 3 days old, pups display aversions to certain odors, such as cedar, garlic, & lemon [40, 48]. Either long- or short-term exposure to an aversive odor selectively reduces aversion to that odor [40, 41].	Avoidance of aversive odors is eliminated by bilateral olfactory bulb removal or bilateral sectioning of lateral olfactory tracts [40]	....	Bilateral lesions of superior colliculus resulted in only a transient deficit in orientation towards or away from odors [40]
Behavioral Thermoregulation				
Hamsters display strong preference for environmental temperature of 26°C when alternatives are 1, 6, 12, or 18°C. After a short hypothermic period, preferred temperature decreases temporarily [76]. Just before entering hibernation, hamsters show preferences for lowered temperatures [75].	Before 10 days old, hamsters are ectothermic. Litter conserves heat by burrowing together in nest. Pups are strongly thermotaxic until 8 days old [108].	....	....	Injecting chlorpromazine into anterior hypothalamus elicits immediate, dose-dependent hypothermia [159]

continued

Part I. Development and Control

Description	Development	Sensory Control	Hormonal Control	Neural Control
Hibernation				
Hibernation can often be induced by placement in cold room at ∿3°C [33, 60, 113]. Golden hamster does not fatten prior to hibernation, but is stimulated by cold to store food. This food hoard is used during periodic arousals during hibernation, and without it hamster would starve [112].	....	Prevention of opportunity to hoard food causes marked delay in entering hibernation [112]	....	Cerebral cortex is electrically quiescent during arousal from hibernation, but parts of limbic system are active [33]. Stimulation of sympathetic nervous system required for arousal from hibernation. Arousal from hibernation is blocked by inhibition of norepinephrine synthesis [60].
Activity Rhythms				
Hamsters display a circadian activity rhythm, most of their activity occurring in dark part of light/dark cycle [17, 58]. They will even self-select a 24-hour rhythm of light/dark [199]. Hamsters also have a lunar component to their activity, so that they are least active during full moon [17, 18, 98]. Cycling ♀ hamsters display 4-day activity rhythm, with activity being highest on day before & on day of heat [161, 164].	....	While onset & offset of light in light/dark cycle synchronize hamster's activity, an endogenous circadian rhythm persists under constant lighting conditions [4, 58] or blindness [166, 208]. Control of lunar periodicity is not by direct light but via some, as yet unknown, geophysical variation [18].	....	Septal lesions do not alter circadian rhythm, but do cause increase in activity during dark part of day [80]. Destruction of suprachiasmatic nuclei abolishes rhythms of locomotor activity, estrous cyclicity, & photoperiodic photosensitivity, suggesting that this brain area contains biological clock [184].
General Activity				
In open field, ♀ are about twice as active as ♂ [185] 186, 188]. Weanlings of both sexes are more active than adults [188]. Hamsters display higher rates of spontaneous alternation than rats [96]. Novel & complex stimuli evoke exploration in hamsters, and have reinforcing properties [176]. Even in a small laboratory cage, hamsters organize their environment by building a nest & food pile, and by having a special site for urination [51, 85, 121].	Sex differences in open field activity do not appear until puberty [187]. As adults, ♂ castrated before puberty tend to behave more like ♀ [185]. As adults, ♀ injected as neonates with either testosterone or estrogen act more like ♂ [186]. Rates of spontaneous alternation increase with age [96]. Handling neonates leads to increased activity as adults [187, 188]. Independent of handling, injections of neonates with large doses of hydrocortisone [1] lead to increased activity as adults [188].	Activity in open field is quite sensitive to previous testing experience [187]. Bilateral, but not unilateral, olfactory bulb removal results in a decrease in open field activity in both sexes. Whereas activity of ♀ returns to normal, or above normal, levels several weeks after surgery, activity of ♂ seems not to recover [79].	Sex-typical activity patterns in open field are not affected by gonadectomy or adrenalectomy after puberty [185, 187]. Activity in open field by ♀ is not affected by stage of estrous cycle [185]. Wheel-running activity tends to decrease during pregnancy [164].	Rats & hamsters differ in regard to effects of hippocampal lesions on open field activity [84]

[1] Synonym: Cortisol.

continued

Part I. Development and Control

Description	Development	Sensory Control	Hormonal Control	Neural Control
Learning & Conditioning				
Hamsters are superior to rats in learning avoidance conditioning in a Skinner box [153], but are much inferior to rats in avoidance conditioning involving a locomotor response as in a shuttle box [6, 118, 172, 173]. Hamsters acquire jumping response at slower rates than do rats [171], but are about equal to rats in maze learning [15]. Hamsters readily form taste/odor aversions to flavors paired with gastrointestinal illness [59, 81, 95, 207]. Food reinforcement can be used to modify occurrence of some behavior patterns (e.g., bar pressing, digging), but not others (e.g., grooming, scent marking) [177].	....	Blindness decreases ability of hamsters to learn two-way avoidance response but not that of rats [56]. Olfactory bulb removal disrupts acquisition of taste aversions [81].	....	Learning a two-way locomotor avoidance response is increased by bilateral septal lesions [118] & by injections of amphetamine [172, 173]. Lesions of visual cortex eliminate pattern discrimination; lesions of superior colliculus eliminate visual orientation [174, 175]; lesions of anterior olfactory bulb disrupt acquisition of taste aversions [80].

Contributor: Michael R. Murphy

References

1. Alderson, J., and R. E. Johnston. 1975. Behav. Biol. 15:505-510.
2. Alleva, J. J., et al. 1971. Endocrinology 88:1368-1379.
3. Arvola, A., and O. A. Forsander. 1963. Q. J. Stud. Alcohol 24:591-597.
4. Aschoff, J., et al. 1973. J. Comp. Physiol. Psychol. 85:20-28.
5. Asdell, S. A., and S. R. Joshi. 1976. Biol. Reprod. 14:478-480.
6. Babbini, M., and W. Davis. 1967. Psychonom. Sci. 9: 149-150.
7. Beach, F. A., and G. Eaton. 1969. Physiol. Behav. 4: 155-156.
8. Beach, F. A., and R. S. Pauker. 1949. Endocrinology 45:211-221.
9. Beach, F. A., and R. G. Rabedeau. 1959. J. Comp. Physiol. Psychol. 52:56-61.
10. Beach, F. A., et al. 1976. Behav. Biol. 18:473-487.
11. Bevan, W., and M. A. Grodsky. 1958. J. Comp. Physiol. Psychol. 51:342-345.
12. Borer, K. T. 1974. Physiol. Behav. 12:589-597.
13. Borer, K. T., and A. A. Kooi. 1975. Behav. Biol. 13: 301-310.
14. Borer, K. T., et al. 1974. J. Comp. Physiol. Psychol. 86:396-403.
15. Bowland, J. A., and R. H. Waters. 1955. Psychol. Rep. 1:437-440.
16. Brain, P. F. 1972. Behav. Biol. 7:349-357.
17. Brown, F. A., Jr. 1965. Proc. Soc. Exp. Biol. Med. 120:792-797.
18. Brown, F. A., Jr., and Y. H. Park. 1967. Ibid. 125: 712-715.
19. Bunnell, B. N. et al. 1970. Physiol. Behav. 5:153-161.
20. Bunnell, B. N., and C. K. Flesher. 1965. Psychonom. Sci. 3:181-182.
21. Bunnell, B. N., and M. E. Kimmel. 1965. Ibid. 3:179-180.
22. Bunnell, B. N., et al. 1966. J. Comp. Physiol. Psychol. 61:492-495.
23. Bunnell, B. N., et al. 1977. Behaviour 59:180-206.
24. Carter, C. S. 1972. Horm. Behav. 3:261-265.
25. Carter, C. S. 1973. Anim. Behav. 21:827-834.
26. Carter, C. S. 1973. Physiol. Behav. 10:47-51.
27. Carter, C. S., and M. R. Landauer. 1975. Ibid. 14:1-6.
28. Carter, C. S., and S. W. Porges. 1974. Horm. Behav. 5:303-315.
29. Carter, C. S., and M. W. Schein. 1971. Ibid. 2:191-200.
30. Carter, C. S., et al. 1972. Physiol. Behav. 9:89-95.
31. Carter, C. S., et al. 1973. Horm. Behav. 4:129-141.
32. Carter, C. S., et al. 1976. J. Comp. Physiol. Psychol. 90:839-850.
33. Chatfield, P. O., and C. P. Lyman. 1954. Electroencephalogr. Clin. Neurophysiol. 6:403-408.
34. Christensen, L. W., et al. 1973. Horm. Behav. 4:223-229.
35. Ciaccio, L. A., and R. D. Lisk. 1971. J. Endocrinol. 50:201-207.
36. Ciaccio, L. A., and R. D. Lisk. 1971. Am. J. Physiol. 221:936-942.

continued

Part I. Development and Control

37. Ciaccio, L. A., and R. D. Lisk. 1974. Neuroendocrinology 13:21-28.
38. Coniglio, L. P., et al. 1973. J. Endocrinol. 57:55-61.
39. Coniglio, L. P., et al. 1973. Physiol. Behav. 10:1087-1094.
40. Cornwell, C. A. 1975. Behav. Biol. 14:175-188.
41. Cornwell, C. A. 1976. Ibid. 17:131-139.
42. Daly, M. 1972. Z. Tierpsychol. 31:289-299.
43. Daly, M. 1976. Dev. Psychobiol. 9:315-323.
44. Darby, E. M., et al. 1975. J. Comp. Physiol. Psychol. 88:496-502.
45. Devor, M. 1973. Brain Res. 64:437-441.
46. Devor, M. 1975. Science 190:998-1000.
47. Devor, M., and M. Murphy. 1973. Behav. Biol. 9:31-42.
48. Devor, M., and G. E. Schneider. 1974. Ibid. 10:211-221.
49. Diamond, M. 1972. Biol. Reprod. 6:281-287.
50. Diamond, M., et al. 1974. Horm. Behav. 5:129-133.
51. Dieterlen, F. 1959. Z. Tierpsychol. 16:47-103.
52. Doty, R. L., and J. J. Anisko. 1973. Physiol. Behav. 10:395-397.
53. Doty, R. L., et al. 1971. Horm. Behav. 2:325-335.
54. Drickamer, L. C., and J. G. Vandenbergh. 1973. Anim. Behav. 21:564-570.
55. Drickamer, L. C., et al. 1973. Ibid. 21:557-563.
56. Dyer, R. S., et al. 1975. Physiol. Behav. 14:211-216.
57. Eaton, G. 1970. Endocrinology 87:934-940.
58. Elliott, J. A., et al. 1972. Science 178:771-773.
59. Emmerick, J. J., and C. T. Snowdon. 1976. J. Comp. Physiol. Psychol. 90:857-869.
60. Feist, D. D. 1970. Life Sci. 9:1117-1125.
61. Floody, O. R., and D. W. Pfaff. 1977. J. Comp. Physiol. Psychol. 91:794-806.
62. Floody, O. R., et al. 1977. Ibid. 91:807-819.
63. Floody, O. R., and D. W. Pfaff. 1977. Ibid. 91:443-464.
64. Floody, O. R., and D. W. Pfaff. 1977. Ibid. 91:820-829.
65. Frank, A. H., and R. M. Fraps. 1945. Endocrinology 37:357-361.
66. Gerall, A. A., et al. 1975. J. Endocrinol. 67:439-445.
67. Gerall, A. A., and A. R. Thiel. 1975. J. Comp. Physiol. Psychol. 89:580-589.
68. Goldman, B. D., and P. J. Sheridan. 1974. Physiol. Behav. 12:991-995.
69. Gottlieb, H., et al. 1974. Ibid. 12:61-68.
70. Grant, E. C., et al. 1970. Z. Tierpsychol. 27:73-77.
71. Grant, E. C., and J. H. Mackintosh. 1963. Behaviour 21:246-259.
72. Gregory, E., et al. 1975. J. Comp. Physiol. Psychol. 89:442-446.
73. Gregory, E. H., and A. Bishop. 1975. Physiol. Behav. 15:373-376.
74. Grelk, D. F., et al. 1974. Horm. Behav. 5:355-366.
75. Gumma, M. R., and F. E. South. 1970. Anim. Behav. 18:504-511.
76. Gumma, M. R., et al. 1967. Ibid. 15:534-537.
77. Hammer, L. R. 1972. Psychonom. Sci. 26:139-140.
78. Hammond, M. A., and F. A. Rowe. 1976. Physiol. Behav. 17:507-513.
79. Hilger, W. N., Jr., and F. A. Rowe. 1975. Physiol. Psychol. 3:162-168.
80. Hobbs, S. H., et al. 1972. Physiol. Behav. 9:349-352.
81. Hobbs, S. H., et al. 1976. Ibid. 17:235-238.
82. Huang, D., and B. A. Hazlett. 1974. Anim. Behav. 22:467-472.
83. Janzen, W. B., and B. N. Bunnell. 1976. Physiol. Behav. 16:445-452.
84. Jarrard, L. E., and B. N. Bunnell. 1968. J. Comp. Physiol. Psychol. 66:500-502.
85. Johnson, R. 1974. Z. Tierpsychol. 35:124-131.
86. Johnson, W. A. 1975. J. Comp. Physiol. Psychol. 89:433-441.
87. Johnson, W. A., and L. Tiefer. 1972. Physiol. Behav. 9:213-217.
88. Johnston, R. E. 1974. Behav. Biol. 12:111-117.
89. Johnston, R. E. 1975. Z. Tierpsychol. 37:75-98.
90. Johnston, R. E. 1975. Ibid. 37:138-144.
91. Johnston, R. E. 1975. Ibid. 37:213-221.
92. Johnston, R. E. 1975. Anim. Learn. Behav. 3:161-166.
93. Johnston, R. E. 1976. Behav. Biol. 17:161-176.
94. Johnston, R. E., and N. A. Lee. 1976. Ibid. 16:199-210.
95. Johnston, R. E., and D. M. Zahorik. 1975. Science 189:893-894.
96. Kirkby, R. J., and G. H. Lackey. 1968. Psychonom. Sci. 10:257-258.
97. Kislak, J. W., and F. A. Beach. 1955. Endocrinology 56:684-692.
98. Klinowska, M. 1972. J. Interdiscip. Cycle Res. 3:145-150.
99. Kow, L. M., et al. 1976. J. Comp. Physiol. Psychol. 90:26-40.
100. Krehbiel, R. H. 1952. Anat. Rec. 113:117-121.
101. Kutscher, C. L., et al. 1968. Psychonom. Sci. 11:243-244.
102. Kwan, M., and R. E. Johnston. Unpublished. Cornell Univ., Dep. Psychology, Ithaca, NY, 1978.
103. Landau, I. T. 1975. Physiol. Behav. 14:767-774.
104. Landau, I. T. 1975. Ibid. 14:775-780.
105. Lanier, D. L., et al. 1975. Ibid. 15:209-212.
106. Lawlor, M. M. 1963. Bull. Br. Psychol. Soc. 16:25-38.
107. Leonard, C. M. 1972. J. Comp. Physiol. Psychol. 80:208-215.
108. Leonard, C. M. 1974. Ibid. 86:458-469.
109. Lerwill, C. J., and P. Markings. 1971. Anim. Behav. 19:714-721.
110. Lisk, R. D., et al. 1972. J. Exp. Zool. 181:69-78.
111. Lisk, R. D., et al. 1974. Ibid. 189:1-6.
112. Lyman, C. P. 1954. J. Mammal. 35:545-552.
113. Lyman, C. P., and P. O. Chatfield. 1950. J. Exp. Zool. 114:491-515.
114. Macrides, F., et al. 1974. Neuroendocrinology 15:355-364.
115. Macrides, F., et al. 1976. Brain Res. 109:97-109.

continued

116. Macrides, F., et al. 1977. Behav. Biol. 20:377-386.
117. Marques, D. M., and E. S. Valenstein. 1976. J. Comp. Physiol. Psychol. 90:653-657.
118. Matalka, E. S., and B. N. Bunnell. 1968. Psychonom. Sci. 12:27-28.
119. Meyerson, B. J. 1970. Psychopharmacologia 18:50-57.
120. Miller, L. L., et al. 1977. J. Comp. Physiol. Psychol. 91:245-259.
121. Murphy, M. R. 1970. Proc. Am. Psychol. Assoc. 237-238.
122. Murphy, M. R. 1973. Am. Zool. 13:1260.
123. Murphy, M. R. 1973. Behav. Biol. 9:367-375.
124. Murphy, M. R. 1974. Ibid. 11:115-119.
125. Murphy, M. R. 1976. Ibid. 17:139-141.
126. Murphy, M. R. 1976. Brain Res. 113:95-110.
127. Murphy, M. R. 1976. In R. L. Doty, ed. Mammalian Olfaction, Reproductive Processes and Behavior. Academic, New York. pp. 95-117.
128. Murphy, M. R. 1977. J. Comp. Physiol. Psychol. 91:1337-1346.
129. Murphy, M. R. Unpublished. N.I.M.H., National Institutes of Health, Bethesda, MD, 1978.
130. Murphy, M. R., and G. E. Schneider. 1970. Science 167:302-304.
131. Noble, R. G. 1973. Physiol. Behav. 10:663-666.
132. Noble, R. G. 1973. Ibid. 10:973-975.
133. Noble, R. G. 1973. Horm. Behav. 4:45-52.
134. Noble, R. G. 1974. Ibid. 5:227-234.
135. Noble, R. G., and P. B. Alsum. 1975. Physiol. Behav. 14:567-574.
136. Noirot, E., and M. P. M. Richards. 1966. Anim. Behav. 14:7-10.
137. Nucci, L. P., and F. A. Beach. 1971. Endocrinology 88:1514-1515.
138. Orsini, M. W. 1961. Proc. Anim. Care Panel 11:193-206.
139. Paup, D. C., et al. 1974. Behav. Biol. 10:353-363.
140. Payne, A. P. 1973. Physiol. Behav. 10:629-631.
141. Payne, A. P. 1974. Ibid. 13:21-26.
142. Payne, A. P. 1974. J. Endocrinol. 63:497-506.
143. Payne, A. P., and N. K. Bennett. 1976. J. Reprod. Fertil. 47:239-244.
144. Payne, A. P. 1976. J. Endocrinol. 69:23-31.
145. Payne, A. P., and H. H. Swanson. 1970. Behaviour 36:259-269.
146. Payne, A. P., and H. H. Swanson. 1971. J. Endocrinol. 51:217-218.
147. Payne, A. P., and H. H. Swanson. 1971. Physiol. Behav. 6:355-357.
148. Payne, A. P., and H. H. Swanson. 1972. Behaviour 42:1-7.
149. Payne, A. P., and H. H. Swanson. 1972. Nature (London) 239:282-283.
150. Payne, A. P., and H. H. Swanson. 1972. Physiol. Behav. 8:687-691.
151. Payne, A. P., and H. H. Swanson. 1972. Anim. Behav. 20:782-787.
152. Payne, A. P., and H. H. Swanson. 1973. J. Endocrinol. 58:627-636.
153. Pearl, J. 1963. Psychol. Rep. 12:139-145.
154. Polsky, R. H. 1976. Ibid. 38:571-577.
155. Powers, J. B., and S. S. Winans. 1973. Physiol. Behav. 10:361-368.
156. Powers, J. B., and S. S. Winans. 1975. Science 187:961-963.
157. Rabedeau, R. G. 1963. Can. J. Psychol. 17:420-429.
158. Reed, C. A., and R. Reed. 1946. J. Comp. Physiol. Psychol. 39:7-12.
159. Reigle, T. G., and H. H. Wolf. 1971. Life Sci. 10:121-132.
160. Reuter, L. A., et al. 1970. Endocrinology 8:1287-1297.
161. Richards, M. P. M. 1964. Nature (London) 204:1327-1328.
162. Richards, M. P. M. 1966. Anim. Behav. 14:303-309.
163. Richards, M. P. M. 1966. Ibid. 14:310-313.
164. Richards, M. P. M. 1966. Ibid. 14:450-458.
165. Richards, M. P. M. 1969. Ibid. 17:356-361.
166. Richter, C. P. 1975. Johns Hopkins Med. J. 136:1-10.
167. Rowell, T. E. 1960. Proc. Zool. Soc. London 135:265-282.
168. Rowell, T. E. 1961. Anim. Behav. 9:11-15.
169. Rowell, T. E. 1961. Behaviour 17:81-94.
170. Salber, P., and I. Zucker. 1974. Behav. Biol. 10:295-311.
171. Sandler, B. E., and G. G. Karas. 1968. Psychonom. Sci. 10:191-192.
172. Sansone, M., and P. Renzi. 1970. Pharmacol. Res. Commun. 2:355-360.
173. Sansone, M., and P. Renzi. 1971. Ibid. 3:113-119.
174. Schneider, G. E. 1967. Psychol. Forsch. 31:52-62.
175. Schneider, G. E. 1970. Brain, Behav. Evol. 3:295-323.
176. Schneider, G. E., and C. Gross. 1965. J. Comp. Physiol. Psychol. 59:150-152.
177. Shettleworth, S. J. 1975. J. Exp. Psychol. 104:56-87.
178. Siegel, H. I., and G. S. Greenwald. 1975. Horm. Behav. 6:237-245.
179. Silverman, H. J., and I. Zucker. 1976. Physiol. Behav. 17:271-285.
180. Singer, A. G., et al. 1976. Science 191:948-950.
181. Smith, W. I., and S. Ross. 1950. J. Genet. Psychol. 77:211-215.
182. Smith, W. I., et al. 1954. J. Comp. Physiol. Psychol. 47:154-156.
183. Sodetz, F. J., and B. N. Bunnell. 1970. Physiol. Behav. 5:79-88.
184. Stetson, M. H., and M. Watson-Whitmyre. 1976. Science 191:197-199.
185. Swanson, H. H. 1966. Anim. Behav. 14:522-529.
186. Swanson, H. H. 1967. Ibid. 15:209-216.
187. Swanson, H. H. 1969. Ibid. 17:148-154.
188. Swanson, H. H. 1969. Horm. Behav. 1:1-5.
189. Swanson, H. H. 1970. J. Reprod. Fertil. 21:183-186.
190. Tiefer, L. 1970. Horm. Behav. 1:189-202.
191. Tiefer, L., and W. A. Johnson. 1971. J. Endocrinol. 51:615-620.

105. BEHAVIOR PATTERNS: HAMSTER

Part I. Development and Control

192. Tiefer, L., and W. A. Johnson. 1973. Horm. Behav. 4:359-364.
193. Tiefer, L., and W. A. Johnson. 1975. J. Comp. Physiol. Psychol. 88:239-247.
194. Vandenbergh, J. G. 1971. Anim. Behav. 19:589-594.
195. Vandenbergh, J. G. 1973. Horm. Res. 4:28-33.
196. Vincent, G. P., and W. P. Pare. 1976. Physiol. Psychol. 4:521-523.
197. Vincent, G. P., and W. P. Pare. 1976. Physiol. Behav. 16:557-560.
198. Waddell, D. 1951. J. Comp. Physiol. Psychol. 44: 383-388.
199. Warden, A. W., and B. D. Sachs. 1974. Ibid. 91:127-134.
200. Warren, R. P., and L. R. Aronson. 1956. Endocrinology 58:293-304.
201. Warren, R. P., and L. R. Aronson. 1957. J. Comp. Physiol. Psychol. 50:475-480.
202. Whalen, R. E., and J. F. DeBold. 1974. Endocrinology 95:1674-1679.
203. Whitsett, J. M. 1975. Horm. Behav. 6:47-57.
204. Whitsett, J. M., and J. G. Vandenbergh. 1975. J. Comp. Physiol. Psychol. 88:248-255.
205. Winans, S. S., and J. B. Powers. 1974. Behav. Biol. 10:461-471.
206. Wise, D. A. 1974. Horm. Behav. 5:235-250.
207. Zahorik, D., and R. E. Johnston. 1976. J. Comp. Physiol. Psychol. 90:57-66.
208. Zucker, I., and F. K. Stephan. 1973. Physiol. Behav. 11:239-250.
209. Zucker, I., et al. 1972. Ibid. 8:101-111.

Part II. Characteristics

Characteristics: FHVD = female hamster vaginal discharge; BOB = bilateral removal of main and accessory olfactory bulbs; UOB = unilateral removal of main and accessory olfactory bulbs. **Source:** OLS = Con Olson Co., Madison, Wisconsin—no longer in business; for full name of other sources, *see* list of HOLDERS at front of book. Data in brackets refer to the column heading in brackets.

Characteristics	Source [Strain]	Reference
Reproductive Behavior		
♀ have a regular 4-day cycle of receptivity. Most ♀ housed singly or in pairs are behaviorally receptive, as evidenced by lordotic response when tested at appropriate time in their cycle (evening of day 1). However, 60% of ♀ housed in groups (4-12/cage) fail to mate. This percentage can be reduced by pre-exposing ♀ to ♂ shortly before estrus.	....	111,138
Copulation reduces period of ♀ receptivity for several days. Rate at which receptivity wanes is proportional to amount of stimulation received from ♂.	ENG	29
Pregnancy is increasingly probable as number of ejaculations received by ♀ increases	LAK [Outbred Lak:LVG(SYR)]	105
Antisera to ovulatory gonadotropic hormones prevent both ovulation & lordotic behavior in ♀. Both responses restored by injections of luteinizing hormone ⟨LH⟩. Follicle-stimulating hormone ⟨FSH⟩ restores ovulation and, to a lesser extent, lordosis. Progesterone restores lordosis but not ovulation; estradiol benzoate has no effect on either.	LAK	68
Castrated ♀ are not receptive to ♂. Replacement therapy with estradiol benzoate restores receptivity.	....	147
Castrated ♀ receiving estradiol benzoate & progesterone may remain non-receptive for as long as 9 days	ENG	28, 32
Both isolated & group-housed ♀ show regular 4-day cycles of ovulation & vaginal discharge production	....	111
♀ have cyclic production of vaginal discharge. Peak production of vaginal discharge coincides with time of maximal receptivity.	....	138
♀ deposit vaginal discharge with characteristic anogenital drag known as vaginal marking. This marking behavior is relatively frequent on day 1 of cycle.	LAK	94
Lactating or castrated ♀ continue to produce vaginal discharge which is indistinguishable from that produced by an estrous ♀, in that the discharge continues to elicit attraction & ♂ sexual behavior	LAK	92,116
Odor of FHVD is sufficient to elicit approach & intense investigatory responses on part of ♂	....	44,123

continued

Part II.   Characteristics

Characteristics	Source [Strain]	Reference
Approach & intense investigatory response initiated by odor of FHVD occurs even if	....	88
♂ is sexually inexperienced	LAK	72,92,116
♀ lacking vaginas & presumably vaginal discharge are less attractive to ♂ than are normal, intact ♀. Once in contact with a ♂, both receive same amount of ♂ interest & mounting behavior.	LAK	102
When FHVD is applied to surrogates with increasing resemblance to an estrous ♀,	....	44,110,123
amount of overt sexual behavior increases on part of ♂	LAK	92,116
FHVD continues to elicit increased levels of sniffing & licking in ♂ 25 days after deposition	LAK	94
Odors of ♀ urine are not attractive	....	88
Dimethyl disulfide isolated from FHVD was identified as one of the compounds responsible for discharge's attractiveness to inexperienced ♂	LAK [Outbred Lak:LVG(SYR)]	180
In a two-bottle preference test, dimethyl disulfide odor was nearly as attractive to sexually experienced ♂ as was FHVD odor. Although attractive, dimethyl disulfide does not promote mating behavior when placed on a suitable surrogate.	LAK	116
Plasma testosterone levels are increased by a 30-min exposure to either a receptive ♀ or the odor of FHVD. Baseline levels of testosterone are positively correlated with amount of time spent investigating source of FHVD.	ENG	114
♂ can develop a conditioned aversion to FHVD	....	95,207
♂ can develop a conditioned aversion to a novel odor	SCH [Random-bred]	59
♂ that have developed an aversion to FHVD or a novel odor are slightly hesitant about	....	207
approaching a receptive ♀, or one scented with novel odor, but other aspects of ♂ sex behavior are unaltered. ♂ with conditioned aversion to receptive ♀ also have normal sex behavior.	SCH [Random-bred]	59
♂ sex behavior and sniffing & licking bouts usually elicited by FHVD are eliminated in both experienced & inexperienced ♂ by treating olfactory mucosa with procaine hydrochloride	SIM	52
Zinc sulfate treatments which spare vomeronasal system result in anosmic individuals with normal ♂ sex behavior	OLS	155,156
Combining zinc sulfate treatment with destruction of vomeronasal nerves completely eliminates ♂ sex behavior	OLS	156
UOB has no effect on ♂ sex behavior or exploratory sniffing	....	110,130
UOB coupled with contralateral nostril occlusion does eliminate ♂ sex behavior, as does destruction of olfactory mucosa with zinc sulfate	....	47,110
BOB ♂ show decrease in exploratory sniffing of receptive ♀, and a shift in attention from hindquarters to sides & head	....	110
BOB eliminates ♂ sex behavior regardless of sexual experience	....	45,47,110,130
	ENG	53
	OLS	14,205
Severing efferent fibers of main & accessory olfactory bulbs eliminates ♂ sex behavior	....	45
without changing levels of circulating testosterone	ENG	115
Testosterone propionate replacement therapy can restore normal ♂ sex behavior in castrated ♂ but not in BOB ♂	....	130
Normal ♂ can exhibit both ♂ & ♀ sex behavior; there is little correlation between their incidence	DEN, LAK	99
Tactile stimulation of flanks but not shoulder elicits lordosis in 80% of ♂, and in 100%	....	124
of ♀ on day 1 of cycle	DEN, LAK	99
Castrated ♂ exhibit normal amounts of ♀ sexual behavior	DEN, LAK	99
Castrated ♂ have reduced preferences for FHVD and depressed ♂ mating behavior.	....	130
Both behaviors can be restored by testosterone propionate replacement therapy.	DEN, LAK	99
	LAK	72
Administration of estradiol benzoate & progesterone to castrated ♂ enhances sensitivity to tactile stimulation and increases duration of lordotic responses to levels comparable to those seen in normal ♀	DEN, LAK	99

continued

Part II. Characteristics

Characteristics	Source [Strain]	Reference
Gonadectomized ♂ & ♀ treated with estradiol benzoate & progesterone respond with lordosis	ENG	27,28,135
	HSN [Inbred albino]	119
Lordotic response to estradiol benzoate & progesterone in gonadectomized ♂ & ♀ can be suppressed by neonatal treatment with testosterone propionate or with inhibitors of amine oxidase (flavin-containing) [L/]	ENG	27,86
	HSN [Inbred albino]	119
Neonatally androgenized ♂ & ♀ both mount receptive ♀ more than normal animals when administered either testosterone propionate or ovarian hormones	ENG	86
♂ sex behavior observed in neonatally androgenized ♀ is eliminated by BOB, but ♀ sex behavior normally seen in intact ♂ is unaffected by BOB	ENG	53
Aggressive & Territorial Behavior		
Grouped adult ♂ form stable dominance hierarchies within a few hours	....	55
	LAK [Outbred Lak:LVG(SYR)]	91
Dominant ♂ chase subordinates, move about freely, and maintain a large food hoard. Subordinate ♂ are chased, move cautiously, and have difficulty maintaining a hoard.	LAK [Outbred Lak:LVG(SYR)]	91
In stable dominance hierarchies, dominance is positively correlated with body weight and size & pigmentation of flank glands. For ♂ of equal weight, dominant animals have larger, darker flank glands.	....	55
	LAK [Outbred Lak:LVG(SYR)]	91
♂ flank gland is larger & more heavily pigmented than that of ♀. ♂ gland regresses with castration, and is restored with testosterone replacement therapy.	....	55
	PET	203
♂ scent marks usually deposited on places previously flank marked. Site for mark is usually explored with several bouts of sniffing before mark is applied.	LAK	94
	[Outbred Lak:LVG(SYR)]	90
Flank marks as old as 25 days still elicit more sniffing than clean areas	LAK	94
Surgical removal of flank gland does not change an animal's average marking rate. Flank marking in cage of castrated ♂ is intermediate between that seen in cage of a normal ♂ & a clean cage.	LAK [Outbred Lak:LVG(SYR)]	90
Bilateral transsection of lateral olfactory tract in 1- or 2-stage operation severely depresses ♂ scent marking without depressing circulating levels of testosterone. Testosterone levels are negatively correlated with rate of scent marking.	ENG	115
Dominant ♂ flank mark more than submissive ♂, especially after winning fights. All ♂ mark more often after a fight with a non-estrous ♀ regardless of who wins fight.	....	55
	LAK [Outbred Lak:LVG(SYR)]	89,91
In ♂—♂ encounters, distance at which a test ♂ shows submissive behaviors is longer if that ♂ has lived in isolation for several weeks prior to test. However, familiarity with test site reduces submissive distance. Dominant status in these encounters is negatively correlated with submissive distance.	....	82
Time required for test ♂ to enter territory of second ♂ is shortened if second ♂ has had his flank glands excised, but time is still longer than that of a test ♂ entering a clean, unscented territory	....	1
Aggression in ♂ encounters has endogenous rhythm with a peak shortly after dark (12:12, L/D cycle). Level of aggression independent of ambient light level. Aggression rhythm persists for more than a week under continuous illumination, and requires 2-4 weeks to reset after 12-hour phase shift.	ENG	103
Adrenalectomy eliminates nocturnal peak of endogenous rhythm without changing overall levels of aggression	ENG	104
Naive ♂ with larger, darker chest patches are more likely to win fights with other naive ♂ of comparable age & weight. Advantage is lost if encounter is staged in dark.	LAK	93
Blinded ♂ initiate fights with other ♂ as often as do normal ♂, but fights last twice as long	....	125

[L/] Synonym: Monoamine oxidase.

continued

Part II.   Characteristics

Characteristics	Source [Strain]	Reference
Levels of aggression in normal ♂, castrated ♂, or normal-castrated ♂ pairs are comparable	PET	203
Neonatally androgenized animals fight more than normal ♀ or neonatally castrated ♂	ENG	27
Fighting in ♂—♂ pairs is reduced if one of the animals is scented with FHVD	....	123
Amount of aggression found in ♂—♀ pairs increases as receptivity of ♀ decreases	ENG	29
	LAK [Outbred Lak:LVG(SYR)]	89
Although non-receptive ♀ is usually dominant over ♂, the castrated ♀ is submissive. Her dominance can be restored partially by hormone replacement with estradiol benzoate and to a large measure by supplements of progesterone. Testosterone propionate is without effect.	....	147
BOB reduces fighting in both ♂ & ♀ in single sex or ♂—♀ encounters. Aggressive deficit is more pronounced in ♂ than in ♀.	....	47,130
	SCH	79
Aggressive deficit can be mimicked by peripheral deafferentation with zinc sulfate or by UOB coupled with contralateral nostril occlusion	....	47
♂ BOB animals show transient increases in handling reactivity and longer lasting decreases in open field ambulation. ♀ BOB animals show large increases in handling reactivity and only slight depressions in open field behaviors.	SCH	79
Miscellaneous Behavior		
BOB briefly depresses food intake, body weight, locomotor activity, & intercranial self-stimulation of the median forebrain bundle, without affecting water consumption	ENG	53
	OLS	14
Severing lateral olfactory tract rostral to olfactory tubercle eliminates ability to find food by odor alone, and disrupts food hoarding behavior	....	45
	ENG	115
♂ learn to avoid saccharin, a normally preferred substance, when it is paired with compounds which produce gastrointestinal distress	SCH [Random-bred]	59
Conditioned aversions, like that produced with saccharin association, can also be demonstrated with carrot & cabbage juice	....	207
	DEN, LAK	99
Pups show clear cut odor preferences by day 3 or 4 of life. Continuous exposure to an adversive odor diminishes adverseness without affecting preferences for other odors. BOB eliminates both preferences & aversions.	....	40,48
Specific preference for home cage odors develops at 7-8 days of age, peaks on day 10-11, & disappears by day 19. In general, odor of home or another lactating ♀ with pups is preferred over odor of another ♀ or ♂, which are in turn preferred over a clean cage.	....	48,73
Virgin ♂ carry displaced pups; 50% of ♀ kill & cannibalize them	OLS	117
Propensity to kill pups sometimes seen in virgin ♀ is not associated with a concomitant increase in aggression towards adult ♂. This propensity is not dependent on circulating levels of ♀ hormone nor, in ♂, on elevated levels of progesterone.	OLS	117

Contributor: Robert J. O'Connell

References: *See* Part I.

106.   IMMUNOGENETICS: HAMSTER

Beginning in the early 1950's, the initial immunogenetic studies were performed on Syrian hamsters. These early studies were concerned with the ability of various outbred hamster populations to reject allogeneic and xenogeneic

continued

tissue. With the development of inbred lines, it was shown that hamsters could acutely reject some skin allografts, and that they possessed a strong histocompatibility ⟨H⟩ locus and relatively few minor H-loci. Other studies demonstrated the ability of hamsters to undergo patent graft-versus-host reactions and in vitro mixed lymphocyte responses, comparable in strength to the reactions observed in other laboratory animal models. Recent investigations indicate that the strong H-locus is most likely the major histocompatibility complex ⟨MHC⟩ equivalent in this species. The MHC in the Syrian hamster has been defined as *Hm-1*.

Part I. Major Histocompatibility Complex

Data are for inbred and outbred populations.

Strain	Haplotype
CB	*Hm-1*[b]
LAK (outbred)	*Hm-1*[a]

Strain	Haplotype
LHC	*Hm-1*[a]
LSH	*Hm-1*[a]

Strain	Haplotype
MHA	*Hm-1*[a]
PD4	*Hm-1*[a]

Contributor: William R. Duncan

General References

1. Duncan, W. R., and J. W. Streilein. 1977. J. Immunol. 118:832-839.
2. Duncan, W. R., and J. W. Streilein. 1977. Transplant. Proc. 9:571-573.
3. Duncan, W. R., and J. W. Streilein. 1978. Transplantation 25:12-16.

Part II. Immune Reactions in Various Strain Combinations

Acute SGR = acute skin graft rejection; + indicates all grafts rejected, with a median survival time of less than 15 days; ± indicates a graft survival time of greater than 15 days, with some grafts not rejected. **GVHR** = graft-versus-host response(s); + indicates a popliteal lymph node hypertrophy response greater than five times; ± indicates a popliteal lymph node hypertrophy response of three-to-five times; − indicates a popliteal lymph node hypertrophy response of less than three times. **MLR** = mixed lymphocyte reaction; + indicates a stimulation index of greater than 2.5; ± indicates an index of 2.0-2.5; − indicates an index of less than 2.0. **CML** = cell-mediated lympholysis; + indicates a net cytotoxicity greater than 10%; − indicates a net cytotoxicity less than 10%. **Alloantibody** = alloantibody response; − indicates the inability to detect cytotoxic antibody after immunization, using the indicated strain combinations.

Strain Combination	Acute SGR	GVHR	MLR	CML	Allo-antibody	Reference
CB ↔ LHC	+	+	+	..	−	1-4
CB ↔ LSH	+	+	+	+	−	1-4
CB ↔ MHA	+	+	+	+	−	1-4
CB ↔ PD4	+	+	+	..	−	1-4

Strain Combination	Acute SGR	GVHR	MLR	CML	Allo-antibody	Reference
MHA ↔ LHC	±	−	−	..	..	1,3,4
MHA ↔ LSH	±	±	±	..	..	1,3,4
MHA ↔ PD4	+	−	−	−	..	1,3,4

Contributor: William R. Duncan

References

1. Billingham, R. E., and W. H. Hildemann. 1958. Ann. N.Y. Acad. Sci. 73:676-686.
2. Billingham, R. E., and W. K. Silvers. 1964. Plast. Reconstr. Surg. 34:329-353.
3. Duncan, W. R., and J. W. Streilein. 1977. J. Immunol. 118:832-839.
4. Duncan, W. R., and J. W. Streilein. 1977. Transplant. Proc. 9:571-573.

continued

Part III. Number of Histocompatibility Loci

Involvement of H-Y antigens in graft rejection, using large-size skin grafts, has not been demonstrated. [ref. 1]

Size of Skin Graft	Number of H-loci Detected	Reference
1.5 cm	2-3	2
1.5 cm	2-3	3
3 mm X 3 mm	10-12	3

Contributor: William R. Duncan

References

1. Adams, R. A. 1958. Transplant. Bull. 5:24-26.
2. Billingham, R. E., et al. 1960. Proc. Natl. Acad. Sci. USA 46:1079-1090.
3. Silvers, W. K., et al. 1975. J. Immunol. 115:1309-1311.

Part IV. Immune Response Genes

Control of the antibody response to low doses of bovine serum albumin—0.1 and 1.0 μg—is the only evidence for genetic control of the immune response reported to exist in Syrian hamsters. No linkage has been found to any other known locus, including *Hm-1*.

Strain	Response
CB	High
LHC	Low
LSH	Low

Strain	Response
MHA	Low
PD4	Low

Contributor: William R. Duncan

Reference: Duncan, W. R., and J. W. Streilein. 1978. Transplantation 25:12-16.

107. IMMUNOGLOBULINS: HAMSTER

The listed immunoglobulins are for the Syrian hamster. *Symbols:* + = present; 0 = absent; ± = presence is infrequent and minimal. Values in parentheses are ranges, estimate "b" (*see* Introduction).

Characteristics	IgG$_2$	IgG$_1$	IgA	IgM	Reference
Size ($s_{20, w}$)	7.2	7.2	7 to $\sim$13	20.7	2-4
Electrophoretic mobility	Slow γ	γ	β	β	1,13
Biological half-life (hours)	91.1	75.2	20	26.5	12
Known monoclonal Ig	+	0	0	0	6
Complement fixation (classical pathway)	+	0	....	....	11
Cytophilic capacity					
Macrophages	+	+[1]	....	....	14
Mast cells[2]	+	0	+	0	16
Opsonizing capacity: macrophages	+[3]	+	....	....	14
Antibody synthesis to					
Egg albumin in saline	±	+	0	0	5,15
Egg albumin in adjuvant	+	+	+	+	5,15
Polyoma virus					10
V antigen					
Neonatal inoculation	+	0	0	0	
Adult inoculation	+	0	0	+	
T antigen					
Neonatal inoculation	+	+	0	0	
Adult inoculation	+	0	0	0	
Rabies virus	+	±	0	0	8
Membrane-bound Ig: % splenic lymphocytes with Ig class	5%	1%	5%	25%	9

[1] Greater than IgG$_2$. [2] As measured by histamine release. [3] Greater than IgG$_1$.

continued

Characteristics	IgG_2	IgG_1	IgA	IgM	Reference
Serum Ig levels, mg/ml: LAK outbred					7
Normal adult, ♂	5.3(3.8-6.8)	2.1(1.5-2.7)	0.24(0.20-0.28)	1.5(1.2-1.8)	
♀	6.1(5.1-7.1)	2.7(2.2-3.2)	0.43(0.30-0.56)	2.1(1.6-2.6)	
Immunized[4/] adult, ♂	7.9(5.33-10.47)	6.5(4.47-8.53)	0.53(0.31-0.75)	2.4(1.93-2.87)	
Presence in other fluids					13
Saliva	+	0	+	0	
Enteric contents	0	0	+	0	
Colostrum	+	+	+	0	
Urine	0	0	+	0	

[4/] 50-day post-injection of 5 μg hen egg albumin in complete Freund's adjuvant.

Contributor: John E. Coe

References

1. Bienenstock, J. 1970. J. Immunol. 104:1228-1235.
2. Bienenstock, J., and K. J. Bloch. 1970. Ibid. 104: 1220-1227.
3. Coe, J. E. 1968. Ibid. 100:507-515.
4. Coe, J. E. 1970. Immunology 18:223-236.
5. Coe, J. E. 1971. Ibid. 21:175-191.
6. Coe, J. E. 1976. Ibid. 31:495-502.
7. Coe, J. E. Unpublished. Rocky Mountain Laboratory, Hamilton, MT, 1978.
8. Coe, J. E., and J. F. Bell. 1977. Infect. Immun. 16: 915-919.
9. Coe, J. E., and I. Green. 1975. J. Natl. Cancer Inst. 54:269-270.
10. Coe, J. E., and K. K. Takemoto. 1972. Ibid. 49:39-44.
11. Coe, J. E., et al. 1971. J. Immunol. 107:76-82.
12. Converse, J., and J. E. Coe. 1972. Ph.D. Thesis. Univ. Montana, Missoula.
13. Haakenstad, A. O., and J. E. Coe. 1971. J. Immunol. 106:1026-1034.
14. Portis, J. L., and J. E. Coe. 1975. Ibid. 115:695-700.
15. Portis, J. L., and J. E. Coe. 1976. Ibid. 117:835-840.
16. Portis, J. L., and J. E. Coe. Unpublished. Rocky Mountain Laboratory, Hamilton, MT, 1978.

108. IN VITRO ASSAYS OF THE IMMUNE RESPONSE: HAMSTER

The hamster is used as an experimental source of lymphoid cells for evaluating the immune response, using in vitro assays. The cells are easily harvested from lymphoid tissues under the same conditions as for other species. There are additional lymph nodes occurring on the top of each cheek pouch. The lymphoid cells of the hamster, unlike those of other species, can be cultured for short periods of time (2-4 days) in the absence of serum—a distinct advantage for the investigator who wishes to evaluate the function of known substances. Hamster lymphoid cells appear to react to various mitogens at concentrations similar to other species, with the exception of phytohemagglutinin, which is mitogenic in doses ten times the doses necessary to stimulate lymphocytes from other species.

Response: (+) = positive response; (−) = negative response; (±) = variable response. Data in brackets refer to the column heading in brackets.

Assay ⟨Synonym⟩	Tissue Utilized	Response	Reference
Stimulants			
[³H]Thymidine incorporation			
Mitogens			
Anti-immunoglobulin	Spleen cells	−	11
	Thymus	−	
	Lymph node cells	+	

Assay ⟨Synonym⟩	Tissue Utilized	Response	Reference
Concanavalin A ⟨Con A⟩	Bone marrow cells	±	11,18, 19,24, 29
	Spleen cells	+	
	Thymus	+	
	Lymph node cells	+	
Dextran sulfate	Bone marrow cells	+	10,11, 24
	Spleen cells	+	
	Thymus	−	

continued

Assay ⟨Synonym⟩	Tissue Utilized	Response	Reference
Lipopolysaccharide	Lymph node cells	±	10,11, 24
	Bone marrow cells	±	
	Spleen cells	+	
	Thymus	−	
Phytohemagglutinin ⟨PHA⟩	Lymph node cells	+	4,11, 18,24
	Bone marrow cells	−	
	Spleen cells	+	
	Thymus	+	
	Lymph node cells	+	
Pokeweed mitogen ⟨PWM⟩	Spleen cells	+	11,25
Proteases	Bone marrow cells	±	8,10
	Spleen cells	+	
	Thymus	−	
	Lymph node cells	±	
ZnCl$_2$	Spleen cells	−	7
	Thymus	−	
	Lymph node cells	+	
Antigens			
Mixed lymphocyte reaction ⟨MLR⟩	Spleen cells	+	12,14, 21,24
Azophenylarsenate-tyrosine	Lymph node cells	−	26
Keyhole limpet hemocyanin ⟨KLH⟩; azophenylarsenate-KLH	Lymph node cells	+	26
Trinitrophenyl-bovine serum albumin ⟨TNP-BSA⟩	Lymph node cells	+	26
Antibody-forming cells			
In vivo immunization—in vitro assay			
Hen egg albumin ⟨HEA⟩	Spleen cells	+	16

Assay ⟨Synonym⟩	Tissue Utilized	Response	Reference
Sheep erythrocytes ⟨SRBC⟩	Spleen cells	+	1,2,28
In vitro primary response			
Horse erythrocytes	Spleen cells	+	26
	Lymph node cells	+	
Sheep erythrocytes ⟨SRBC⟩	Spleen cells	+	23,26, 27
	Lymph node cells	+	
Trinitrophenyl-Brucella ⟨TNP-Brucella⟩	Spleen cells	+	26
	Lymph node cells	+	
Trinitrophenyl-Ficoll ⟨TNP-Ficoll⟩	Spleen cells	+	26
	Lymph node cells	+	
Suppressants			
Protease inhibitors	Spleen cells	+	6,9,10
	Thymus	+	
	Lymph node cells	+	
Serum factors	Spleen cells	+	22,24, 25
	Lymph node cells	+	
T-suppressor cells	Spleen cells	−	12
	Thymus	−	
	Lymph node cells	−	
Other			
Culture conditions	Bone marrow cells	+	4,5,15, 24
	Spleen cells	+	
	Thymus	+	
	Lymph node cells	+	
Cell-mediated lympholysis	Spleen cells	+	3,13,20
	Lymph node cells	+	
Lymphokines	Lymph node cells	+	17

Contributors: Joan Stein-Streilein and David A. Hart

References

1. Blazkovec, A. A., and M. W. Orsini. 1976. Int. Arch. Allergy Appl. Immunol. 50:55-67.
2. Blazkovec, A. A., et al. 1973. Ibid. 44:274-293.
3. Duncan, W. R., and J. W. Streilein. 1977. Transplant. Proc. 9:571-573.
4. Fernald, G. W., and R. S. Metzgar. 1971. J. Immunol. 107:456-463.
5. Galton, M., and S. F. Holt. 1962. Proc. Soc. Exp. Biol. Med. 114:218-219.
6. Hart, D. A. 1977. Cell. Immunol. 32:146-159.
7. Hart, D. A. 1978. Infect. Immun. 19:457-461.
8. Hart, D. A., and J. S. Streilein. 1976. Exp. Cell Res. 102:246-252.
9. Hart, D. A., and J. S. Streilein. 1976. Ibid. 102:253-263.
10. Hart, D. A., and J. S. Streilein. 1977. Ibid. 107:434-440.
11. Hart, D. A., et al. 1978. Fed. Proc. Fed. Am. Soc. Exp. Biol. 37:2039-2041.
12. Lause, D., and J. W. Streilein. 1977. Transplant. Proc. 9:819-822.
13. Laush, R. N., et al. 1975. J. Immunol. 114:459-465.
14. Ling, N. R. 1973. Immunol. Commun. 2:119-127.
15. Miggiano, C. C., et al. 1975. Tissue Antigens 5:173-185.
16. Portis, J. L., and J. E. Coe. 1976. J. Immunol. 117:835-840.
17. Rees, R. C., et al. 1975. Eur. J. Cancer 11:79-86.
18. Ron, N., et al. 1973. Immunology 25:433-439.
19. Singh, S. B., and S. S. Tevethia. 1972. Infect. Immun. 5:339-345.
20. Singh, S. B., and S. S. Tevethia. 1973. Ibid. 7:46-52.
21. Singh, S. B., and S. S. Tevethia. 1973. Proc. Soc. Exp. Biol. Med. 142:443-445.

continued

22. Stein-Streilein, J., and D. A. Hart. 1978. Fed. Proc. Fed. Am. Soc. Exp. Biol. 37:2042-2044.
23. Stein-Streilein, J., et al. 1978. Ibid. 37(6):1489 (Abstr. 1206).
24. Streilein, J. S., and D. A. Hart. 1976. Infect. Immun. 14:463-470.
25. Streilein, J. S., and D. A. Hart. 1977. Fed. Proc. Fed. Am. Soc. Exp. Biol. 36(3):1270 (Abstr. 5306).
26. Streilein, J. S., and D. A. Hart. Unpublished. Southwestern Medical School, Dep. Microbiology, Dallas, 1978.
27. Streilein, J. W., and S. A. Thompson. Unpublished. Univ. Texas Health Science Center, Dep. Cell Biology and Internal Medicine, Dallas, 1978.
28. Streilein, J. W., et al. 1977. Transplant. Proc. 9:1229-1233.
29. Tevethia, S. S., and S. B. Singh. 1978. Fed. Proc. Fed. Am. Soc. Exp. Biol. 37:2037-2038.

109. IMMUNITY AND INFECTION: HAMSTER

Immunity: AR = antibody response; CI = cellular immunity; ++ = detailed information; + = incidental information (+) = inconclusive information. Data in brackets refer to the column heading in brackets.

Agent ⟨Synonym⟩	Acute Infection [Chronic Infection]	Immunity	Remarks	Reference
Viruses[1]				
Parvoviridae: *Parvovirus*	Survival ["Mongoloid" osteolytic cerebellar hypoplasia]	....	Newborn susceptible	140
Adenoviridae: Adenovirus type 2	Death	....	Newborn susceptible	25
	Survival	....	Adult susceptible	25
Herpetoviridae Equine rhinopneumonitis	Hepatitis; fatal in 2-5 d	AR: +; vaccine effective. CI: +; vaccine effective. Sterile immunity.	....	37,55,59
Herpes simplex	....	Latent infection with immunity	Implantation of non-permissive glial cells results in infection	125
	Adrenocortical necrosis; placental necrosis; death	....	Pregnant ♀ susceptible	45
	Hepatitis, adrenal necrosis; death [Sarcoma]	....	Fetus & newborn susceptible	105
	Death or survival	....	Hypercorticoid adult susceptible	21
Varicella zoster	....	....	Resistant	42
Poxviridae Vaccinia	....	....	Resistant	42
Variola	....	....	Resistant	42
Reoviridae[2] Colorado tick fever	Lymphocytic changes	....	....	12
Reovirus type 1	Aqueductal stenosis	....	Newborn susceptible	99
Togaviridae *Alphavirus* Eastern equine encephalomyelitis	Death	....	....	123

[1] For information on Papovaviridae, *see* Table 115. For information on Picornaviridae, consult reference 84 (encephalomyocarditis virus), reference 43 (foot-and-mouth disease virus), and reference 138 (poliovirus-2, strain MEF-1). For information on Rhabdoviridae (rabies virus), consult references 87, 118, and 136. [2] For information on reovirus type 3, consult reference 142.

continued

Agent ⟨Synonym⟩	Acute Infection [Chronic Infection]	Immunity	Remarks	Reference
Venezuelan equine encephalomyelitis	Hematopoietic, intestine, brain; death or survival	AR: +. Sterile immunity.	Treatment with interferon, or poly I:C modifies disease	77,78,143
Western equine encephalomyelitis	Death	AR: +; vaccine effective	....	23
Flavivirus Dengue	Survival	Protects against St. Louis & West Nile viruses	....	124
St. Louis	Death	....	....	124
West Nile	Death	AR: +; vaccine effective	....	74
Orthomyxoviridae: Influenza	....	Latent infection with immunity	....	79,89
Paramyxoviridae[3] Measles	Encephalitis; 100% fatal	....	Newborn susceptible	18,81,115
	Encephalitis; 90% fatal	....	Adults treated with antilymphocyte serum are susceptible	18,81,115
Mumps	Aqueductal stenosis, hydrocephalus	....	Newborn susceptible	82
Newcastle disease	Asymptomatic interferon inducer; survival	....	....	59
Parainfluenza 1 ⟨Sendai⟩	Pneumonia	....	Interferes with rubella infection	113,142
Parainfluenza 3	Tracheobronchitis	....	....	141
Respiratory syncytial	Tracheobronchitis	....	....	153
Retroviridae[4]: Oncovirus ⟨Oncornavirus⟩	....	AR: +	....	107
Arenaviridae Junin	[Urinary shedding]	AR: +. CI: +. Chronic infection with immunity	Infants susceptible	85
Lymphocytic choriomeningitis	Viremia lasts ∿4 wk; survival [Urinary shedding]	AR: +. CI: +. Chronic infection with immunity	....	5,130
	[Vasculitis, glomerulonephritis]	AR: +. Antigen-antibody complex disease.	Newborn susceptible	10,71
Machupo	[Urinary shedding]	AR: +. CI: +. Chronic infection with immunity.	Infants susceptible	85
Pichinde	Hamster strain LVG: fatal to 1- to 6-day-olds Hamster strain MHA: fatal to newborn & adults	AR: +. CI: +. No evident immunopathology.	Susceptibility varies with hamster strain; cyclophosphamide modifies susceptibility	16
Bunyaviridae[5] Arbovirus	....	AR: +	....	63,102
Oriboca; Ossa	Hepatitis; fatal in 4-6 d	AR: +; vaccine effective	....	59
Unclassified Borna	Survival [Asymptomatic]	Chronic infection with immunity	....	3
Marburg	Lesions in liver, spleen; neuronal necrosis	....	....	129,155

[3] For information on pneumonia virus of mice ⟨PVM⟩ and SV-5 virus, consult reference 142. [4] For additional information on Retroviridae, *see* Table 115, for C-particles and Bernhardt particles, consult reference 142. [5] For information on arbovirus C, consult reference 132.

continued

Agent ⟨Synonym⟩	Acute Infection [Chronic Infection]	Immunity	Remarks	Reference
Scrapie	Death [Neurological symptoms]	....	....	19,86,101
Rickettsias				
Chlamydiaceae: *Chlamydia* ⟨*Bedsonia*⟩	Pneumonia	....	....	111
Rickettsiaceae[6/]: *Rickettsia typhi* ⟨*R. mooseri*⟩	Scrotal reaction: 10 d old, fatal; 18 d old, survival	Chronic carriers for >4 wk	Nurslings susceptible	119
	Peritonitis; ∿100% fatal in 7-10 d [Recrudescence]	AR: +. CI: +. Chronic carriers for >4 wk.	Adult susceptible when treated with corticosteroids	150,151
Mycoplasmas				
Mycoplasma sp.	Reproductive failure	....	....	62
M. pneumoniae	....	....	Baby hamsters susceptible; not oncogenic	64
Intranasal	Bronchopneumonia; subsided after 3-4 wk	AR: high titers immunizing. Sterile immunity.	Prior passage through chick embryo required for manifest infection; not transferable hamster to hamster	41
Parenteral	....	AR: high titers not immunizing	Prior passage through chick embryo required for manifest infection; not transferable hamster to hamster	33,46
Bacteria [7/]				
Bacteroides sp.	[Intestinal flora; abscesses]	....	Hypercorticoid	66
Clostridium tetani	Tetanus; fatal	....	....	28
Coliforms	[Intestinal flora]	....	....	60,66
Eperythrozoon	....	....	Hamsters naturally resistant; passage through hamster may serve to eliminate this organism which becomes a contaminant to another organism during passage in mice	72
Francisella tularensis	Disseminated infection; often fatal	....	....	38,112
Haemobartonella	....	....	Hamsters naturally resistant; passage through hamster may serve to eliminate this organism which becomes a contaminant to another organism during passage in mice	72
Lactobacilli	[Intestinal flora]	....	....	66
Leptospira interrogans ⟨*L. icterohaemorrhagiae*⟩	Often fatal	AR: vaccine effective. CI: vaccine effective.	....	15
L. serotype ballum ⟨*L. ballum*⟩	Hemolysis, hepatitis, interstitial nephritis; often fatal in 4-6 d	AR: +; vaccine effective. Sterile immunity.	Chlortetracycline preventative	57
	Renal tubule degeneration, uremic encephalopathy; often fatal in 14-21 d	AR: +. Sterile immunity.	Sulfadiazine delays death	57

[6/] For information on *Coxiella burnetii,* consult reference 47. [7/] For information on dental flora, *see* Table 102; for *Mycobacterium leprae,* consult references 11 and 27.

continued

Agent ⟨Synonym⟩	Acute Infection [Chronic Infection]	Immunity	Remarks	Reference
L. serotype canicola ⟨*L. canicola*⟩	Often fatal [Urinary shedding]	AR: vaccine effective. CI: vaccine effective.	Penicillin suppressive	15
L. serotype pomona ⟨*L. interrogans* type Pomona⟩	[Urinary shedding]	....	....	103
⟨*L. pomona*⟩	Often fatal	AR: vaccine effective. CI: vaccine effective.		133
Leptospirosis	[Urinary shedding]	AR: vaccine effective. CI: vaccine effective.	Modified by treatment	6,73,103
Listeria monocytogenes	Rare abscesses	AR: +. CI: ++. Hypersensitivity: +. Sterile immunity.	....	59
Micrococci	[Intestinal flora, abscesses]	....	....	66
Mycobacterium bovis ⟨*M. tuberculosis* var. *bovis*⟩, strain BCG	Lesions in lungs, liver, spleen, lymph nodes [Schaumann bodies]	Hypersensitive to old tuberculin		17,40,80
M. kansasii	Lesions in lungs, liver, spleen, lymph nodes, bone marrow, & adrenals [Schaumann bodies]	....		51,57,116
M. paratuberculosis	....	....	Accentuated by aflatoxin	91
M. tuberculosis ⟨*M. tuberculosis* var. *humanum*⟩	Lesions in lungs, liver, spleen, & lymph nodes	CI: ++. Hypersensitive to old tuberculin.	Hibernation modifies disease	9,22,122
Neisseria gonorrhoeae	....	....	Grown in subcutaneous chamber	4
Pseudomonas pseudomallei ⟨*Malleomyces pseudomallei*⟩	Pneumonia	....		34,35
Salmonella sp.	Pulmonary thrombophlebitis	AR: ++. CI: +.	....	75
Staphylococcus sp. Cheek pouch	[Abscess]	....	Hematogenous spread	154
Skin	[Impetigo; abscesses]	....	Hematogenous & lymphogenous spread	30,128
Streptococci	[Intestinal flora]	....	....	83
Streptococcus sp. Skin	Impetigo	....	....	30-32
Repeat immunization	[Amyloidosis]	....	....	156
S. agalactiae	Mastitis [Mastitis]	....	....	61,88
S. pneumoniae	Pneumonia	....	Enhanced by mycoplasma infection	94
Treponema pallidum	....	....	Hibernation modifying influence	9
Vaccine: diphtheria, pertussis, tetanus	[Amyloidosis]	....	....	156
"Wet-tail"	Ulcerative enteritis; 30-100% fatal in 1-2 wk [Ileal hyperplasia]	....	Antibiotics may produce intestinal disease similar to "wet-tail"	76,139, 146,157- 159
Fungi[8]				
Histoplasma capsulatum	Lesions in lungs, liver, spleen, & lymph nodes; 10-100% fatal in 30-50 d [Conchoid Schaumann bodies]	AR: (+). CI: +. Hypersensitivity: +.	Adult susceptible	7,54,57, 108,109, 126

[8] For information on *Blastomyces dermatitidis,* consult reference 58; for *Coccidioides immitis,* reference 39; *Cryptococcus neoformans,* reference 68; *Nocardia asteroides* and *N. brasiliensis,* reference 97; *Paracoccidioides brasiliensis,* references 26 and 65; and *Sporothrix schenckii* ⟨*Sporotrichum schenckii*⟩, reference 100.

continued

Agent ⟨Synonym⟩	Acute Infection [Chronic Infection]	Immunity	Remarks	Reference
Protozoa					
Babesia microti	Hemolytic anemia	Carrier	Splenectomy renders hamster more susceptible	95,149
Besnoitia jellisoni	Pneumonia, encephalitis, retinochoroiditis, adrenalitis; 0-100% fatal in 6-365 d [Retinochoroiditis, adrenalitis; recrudescence]	AR: +. CI: ++. Hypersensitivity: +. Chronic infection with immunity.	Administration of corticoids accentuates infection	50,52,53, 55,69, 93,152
Chilomastix	Intestinal flora	Chronic infection with immunity	....	148
Encephalitozoon	Pancreatitis, nephritis, encephalitis; 10-50% fatal	Chronic infection with immunity	Hypercorticism accentuates infection	56,110
Entamoeba muris	Intestinal flora	Chronic infection with immunity	....	148
Giardia	Intestinal flora	Chronic infection with immunity	....	13,66
Hexamita	Intestinal flora	Chronic infection with immunity	....	147
Leishmania brasiliensis	Ulcerated superficial lesion	CI: +. Chronic infection with immunity.	"Stress" treatment applied	14,106
L. donovani	Disseminated infection [Amyloidosis of the kidney, liver, & spleen; Schaumann bodies]	CI: +. Chronic infection with immunity.	Dose-response effects discussed in reference	44,57,134
L. mexicana ⟨L. mexicanum⟩	Subcutaneous lesion; survival [Amyloidosis of the kidney, liver, & spleen; Schaumann bodies]	CI: +. Chronic infection with immunity.	....	58
⟨L. tropica⟩	Superficial lesion	CI: +. Chronic infection with immunity.	....	58
Plasmodium berghei	90% fatal in 10-40 d	....	....	96
Toxoplasma gondii	Pneumonia, hepatitis, encephalitis, retinochoroiditis; 0-100% fatal in 6-365 d [Encephalitis, retinochoroiditis; recrudescence]	AR: +. CI: ++. Hypersensitivity: +. Chronic infection with immunity.	Administration of corticoids accentuates infection	48,49,53, 93
Trichomonas	Intestinal flora	Chronic infection with immunity	....	66
Tritrichomonas foetus ⟨Trichomonas foetus⟩	Vaginitis; survival	....	Drug assay discussed in reference	1
Trypanosoma cruzi	Myocarditis; duration: 10-25 d	....	....	121
Helminths [2]					
Dipetalonema viteae	[Amyloidosis]	....	....	29

[2] For information on *Ancylostoma ceylanicum,* consult reference 117; for *Brugia pahangi,* references 67 and 98; *Dictyocaulus viviparus,* reference 145; *Hymenolepis nana,* references 20, 120, and 148; *Necator americanus,* reference 127; *Opisthorchis felineus,* reference 90; *Plagiorchis proximus,* reference 114; *Schistosoma haematobium,* references 104 and 137; *S. japonicum,* reference 104; *Syphacia mesocriceti,* references 36 and 92; *Taenia saginata* and *T. solium,* reference 144; *Trichinella spiralis,* references 8 and 24.

continued

Agent ⟨Synonym⟩	Acute Infection [Chronic Infection]	Immunity	Remarks	Reference
Hymenolepis diminuta	....	....	Enhanced with *Moniliformis*	70
Moniliformis dubius	....	....	Enhanced with *Hymenolepis*	70
Schistosoma mansoni	....	Chronic infection with immunity	WO strain develops immunity; LGN strain develops little or no immunity	2,104, 131,135

Contributor: J. K. Frenkel

References

1. Actor, P., et al. 1969. Science 164:438-440.
2. Akpom, C. A., et al. 1970. Am. J. Trop. Med. Hyg. 19:996-1000.
3. Anzil, A. P., et al. 1973. Arch. Gesamte Virusforsch. 40:52-57.
4. Arko, R. J. 1974. J. Infect. Dis. 129:451-455.
5. Armstrong, D., et al. 1969. J. Am. Med. Assoc. 209:265-267.
6. Baldwin, E. W., et al. 1972. Am. J. Vet. Res. 33:863-865.
7. Bauman, D. S., and E. W. Chick. 1969. Am. Rev. Respir. Dis. 100:79-81.
8. Bernard, G. R. 1961. J. Infect. Dis. 108:1-11.
9. Bessemans, A., et al. 1956. Rev. Belge Pathol. 25:491-497.
10. Biggar, R. J., et al. 1975. J. Am. Med. Assoc. 232:494-500.
11. Binford, C. H. 1959. Lab. Invest. 8:901-923.
12. Black, W. C., et al. 1947. Am. J. Pathol. 23:217-224.
13. Bockman, D. E., and W. B. Winborn. 1968. J. Protozool. 15:26-30.
14. Brazil, R. P., and B. Gilbert. 1976. Rev. Inst. Med. Trop. Sao Paulo 18:87-88.
15. Brunner, K. T., and K. F. Meyer. 1950. J. Immunol. 64:365-372.
16. Buchmeier, M. J., and W. E. Rawls. 1977. Infect. Immun. 16:413-421.
17. Bunch-Christensen, K., et al. 1970. Bull. WHO 43:65-70.
18. Byington, D. P., and K. P. Johnson. 1975. Lab. Invest. 32:91-97.
19. Chandler, R. L., and B. A. Turfrey. 1972. Res. Vet. Sci. 13:219-224.
20. Chesterman, F. C., and A. Pomerance. 1965. Br. J. Cancer 19:802-811.
21. Chinchilla, M., and J. K. Frenkel. 1978. Infect. Immun. 19(3):999-1012.
22. Chute, R. M., et al. 1954. Am. J. Clin. Pathol. 24:223-226.
23. Cole, F. E. 1969. Appl. Microbiol. 17:927-928.
24. Concannon, J., and A. L. Ritterson. 1965. J. Parasitol. 51:938-941.
25. Connor, J. D. 1970. Proc. Soc. Exp. Biol. Med. 133:655-661.
26. Conti-Diaz, I. A., and M. Furcolow. 1972. Mycopathol. Mycol. Appl. 47:73-79.
27. Convit, J. 1964. Int. J. Leprosy 32:310-321.
28. Cravetz, H., et al. 1951. Am. J. Pharm. 123:130.
29. Crowell, D. A., and C. L. Votava. 1975. Vet. Pathol. 12:178-185.
30. Cushing, A. H., and E. A. Mortimer. 1970. J. Infect. Dis. 122:1224-1226.
31. Dajani, A. S., and L. W. Wanamaker. 1970. Ibid. 122:196-204.
32. Dajani, A. S., and L. W. Wanamaker. 1971. J. Exp. Med. 134:588-599.
33. Dajani, A. S., et al. 1965. Ibid. 121:1071-1086.
34. Dannenberg, A. M., and E. M. Scott. 1958. Ibid. 107:153-166.
35. Dannenberg, A. M., and E. M. Scott. 1960. J. Immunol. 84:233-246.
36. Dick, T. A., et al. 1973. J. Parasitol. 59:256-259.
37. Doll, E. R., et al. 1954. Cornell Vet. 44:133-138.
38. Downs, C. M., et al. 1947. J. Immunol. 56:217-243.
39. Drouhet, E. 1961. Bull. Soc. Pathol. Exot. 54:1002-1007.
40. Dumont, A., and H. Sheldon. 1965. Lab. Invest. 14:2034-2055.
41. Eaton, M. D., et al. 1944. J. Exp. Med. 79:649-668.
42. Eddy, B. E. 1972. Prog. Exp. Tumor Res. 16:454-496.
43. Eunes, E. S. 1955. Bull. Off. Int. Epizoot. 43:756-760.
44. Farrell, J. P. 1976. Exp. Parasitol. 40:89-94.
45. Ferm, V. H., and R. J. Low. 1965. J. Pathol. Bacteriol. 89:295-300.
46. Fernald, G. W. 1969. J. Infect. Dis. 119:255-266.
47. Franti, C. E., et al. 1974. Lab. Anim. Sci. 24:656-665.
48. Frenkel, J. K. 1953. Am. J. Trop. Med. Hyg. 2:390-415.
49. Frenkel, J. K. 1955. Am. J. Ophthalmol. 39:203-225.
50. Frenkel, J. K. 1956. J. Exp. Med. 103:375-407.
51. Frenkel, J. K. 1958. Am. J. Pathol. 34:586-587.
52. Frenkel, J. K. 1960. Proc. Soc. Exp. Biol. Med. 130:552-555.
53. Frenkel, J. K. 1961. Surv. Ophthalmol. 6:799-825.
54. Frenkel, J. K. 1962. Lab. Invest. 11:1192-1208.

continued

55. Frenkel, J. K. 1967. J. Immunol. 98:1309-1319.
56. Frenkel, J. K. 1971. In R. A. Marcial-Rojas, ed. Pathology of Protozoal and Helminthic Diseases with Clinical Correlations. Williams and Wilkins, Baltimore. pp. 318-369.
57. Frenkel, J. K. 1972. Prog. Exp. Tumor Res. 16:326-367.
58. Frenkel, J. K. Unpublished. Univ. Kansas Medical Center, Dep. Pathology and Oncology, Kansas City, KS, 1979.
59. Frenkel, J. K., and S. A. Caldwell. 1975. J. Infect. Dis. 131:201-209.
60. Frisk, C. S., and J. E. Wagner. 1976. Meet. Am. Assoc. Lab. Anim. Sci. Abstr. 77.
61. Frisk, C. S., et al. 1976. Lab. Anim. Sci. 26:97.
62. Gabridge, M. G., and L. J. Cohen. 1976. Ibid. 26:206-210.
63. Galindo, P., and S. Srihongse. 1967. Am. J. Trop. Med. Hyg. 16:525-530.
64. Girardi, A. J., et al. 1965. Proc. Soc. Exp. Biol. Med. 118:173-179.
65. Guimaraes, F. N. 1951. Hospital (Rio de Janeiro) 40:515-550.
66. Hagen, C. A., et al. 1965. Lab. Anim. Care 15:185-193.
67. Harbut, C. L. 1974. Southeast Asian J. Trop. Med. Public Health 4:487-491.
68. Herrold, K. M. 1965. Fed. Proc. Fed. Am. Soc. Exp. Biol. 24:492.
69. Hoff, R. L., and J. K. Frenkel. 1974. J. Exp. Med. 139:560-580.
70. Holmes, J. C. 1962. J. Parasitol. 48:97-100.
71. Hotchin, J., et al. 1974. Science 185:1173-1174.
72. Hsu, D. Y. M., and Q. M. Geiman. 1952. Am. J. Trop. Med. Hyg. 1:747-749.
73. Huhn, R. G., et al. 1975. Am. J. Vet. Res. 36:71-74.
74. Imam, I., and W. M. Hammon. 1957. Proc. Soc. Exp. Biol. Med. 95:17-21.
75. Innes, J. R. M., et al. 1956. J. Infect. Dis. 98:133-141.
76. Jacoby, R. O., et al. 1975. Lab. Anim. Sci. 25:465-473.
77. Jahrling, P. B., and W. F. Scherer. 1973. Am. J. Pathol. 72:25-38.
78. Jahrling, P. B., et al. 1976. Arch. Virol. 51:23-35.
79. Jennings, R., et al. 1977. Med. Microbiol. Immunol. 162:217-238.
80. Jespersen, A., and M. W. Bentzon. 1964. Acta Tuberc. Pneumol. Scand. 44:222-249.
81. Johnson, K. P., and D. P. Byington. 1971. Exp. Mol. Pathol. 15:373-379.
82. Johnson, R. T., and K. P. Johnson. 1968. J. Neuropathol. Exp. Neurol. 27:591-606.
83. Jordan, H. V., and J. van Houte. 1972. Prog. Exp. Tumor Res. 16:539-556.
84. Jungeblut, C. W. 1958. Handbuch der Virusforschung. Springer-Verlag, Berlin.
85. Justines, G., and K. M. Johnson. 1968. Am. J. Trop. Med. Hyg. 17:788-790.
86. Kimberlin, R. H., et al. 1975. Lancet 2:1309-1310.
87. Koprowski, H., et al. 1954. J. Immunol. 72:94-106.
88. Kummeneje, K., et al. 1975. Acta Vet. Scand. 16:554-556.
89. Lacorte, J. G. 1974. Mem. Inst. Oswaldo Cruz 72:129-130.
90. Lämmler, G., et al. 1968. Z. Parasitenk. 31:166-202.
91. Larsen, A. B., et al. 1975. Am. J. Vet. Res. 36:1545-1547.
92. Levine, N. D. 1968. Nematode Parasites of Domestic Animals and Man. Burgess, Minneapolis.
93. Lindberg, R. E., and J. K. Frenkel. 1977. Infect. Immun. 15:855-862.
94. Liu, C., et al. 1970. Ann. N.Y. Acad. Sci. 174:828-834.
95. Lykins, J. D., et al. 1975. Exp. Parasitol. 37:388-397.
96. MacCallum, D. K. 1969. J. Reticuloendothel. Soc. 6:253-270.
97. Macotela-Ruiz, E., and F. Mariat. 1963. Bull. Soc. Pathol. Exot. 56:46-54.
98. Malone, J. B., and P. E. Thompson. 1975. Exp. Parasitol. 38:279-290.
99. Margolis, G., and L. Kilham. 1969. Lab. Invest. 21:189-198.
100. Mariat, F., and E. Drouhet. 1954. Ann. Inst. Pasteur 86:485-492.
101. Marsh, R. F., and R. P. Hanson. 1978. Fed. Proc. Fed. Am. Soc. Exp. Biol. 37(7):2076-2078.
102. McIntosh, B. M., et al. 1976. J. Med. Entomol. 12:641-644.
103. Miller, N. G. 1972. Med. Microbiol. Immunol. 158:1-8.
104. Mostofi, F. K. 1967. Bilharziasis. Springer-Verlag, New York.
105. Naib, Z., et al. 1970. Lab. Invest. 22:506.
106. Noble, G. A. 1971. Exp. Parasitol. 29:30-32.
107. Nowinski, R. C., et al. 1971. Nature (London) New Biol. 230:282-284.
108. O'Hern, E. M. 1965. J. Immunol. 94:592-602.
109. Okudaira, M., et al. 1961. Lab. Invest. 10:968-982.
110. Pakes, S. P., et al. 1975. J. Protozool. 22:481-488.
111. Pearson, H. E., and M. D. Eaton. 1940. Proc. Soc. Exp. Biol. Med. 45:677-679.
112. Perman, V., and M. E. Bergeland. 1967. Lab. Anim. Care 17:563-569.
113. Profeta, M. L., et al. 1969. Am. J. Epidemiol. 89:316-324.
114. Rachford, F. W. 1970. J. Parasitol. 56:1137.
115. Raine, C. S., et al. 1974. Lab. Invest. 31:355-368.
116. Rasmussen, P., and J. B. Caulfield. 1960. Ibid. 9:330-338.
117. Ray, D. K., and K. K. Bhopale. 1972. Experientia 28:359-361.
118. Reagan, R. L., et al. 1955. Proc. Soc. Exp. Biol. Med. 90:301-302.
119. Roger, F., and A. Roger. 1956. Bull. Soc. Pathol. Exot. 49:241-242.
120. Ronald, N. C., and J. E. Wagner. 1975. Lab. Anim. Sci. 25:219-220.
121. Rubio, M. 1959. Biologica 27:95-113.
122. Saenz, A. 1958. Ann. Inst. Pasteur 95:534-556.

continued

123. Sanmartin, C., et al. 1971. Am. J. Trop. Med. Hyg. 20:469-473.
124. Sather, G. E., and W. M. Hammon. 1970. Proc. Soc. Exp. Biol. Med. 135:573-578.
125. Schwartz, J., and T. S. Elizan. 1973. Arch. Neurol. (Chicago) 28:224-230.
126. Schwarz, J., et al. 1957. Lab. Invest. 6:547-550.
127. Sen, H. G. 1972. Exp. Parasitol. 32:26-32.
128. Shepro, D., et al. 1964. J. Immunol. 93:725-731.
129. Siegert, R. 1971. Marburg-Virus-Krankheit. Springer-Verlag, Berlin.
130. Smadel, J. E., and M. J. Wall. 1942. J. Exp. Med. 75:581-591.
131. Smith, M. A., and J. A. Clegg. 1976. Parasitology 73:47-52.
132. Srihongse, S., and K. M. Johnson. 1969. Am. J. Trop. Med. Hyg. 18:273-279.
133. Stalheim, O. H. 1968. Am. J. Vet. Res. 29:1463-1468.
134. Stauber, L. A. 1966. Exp. Parasitol. 18:1-11.
135. Stirewalt, M. A. 1963. Ibid. 13:18-44.
136. Sulkin, S., et al. 1959. J. Exp. Med. 110:369-388.
137. Taylor, M. G., and B. J. Andrews. 1973. J. Helminthol. 47:439-453.
138. Teodoru, C. V., and G. Shwartzman. 1954. J. Exp. Med. 100:563-574.
139. Thomlinson, J. R. 1975. Vet. Rec. 96:42.
140. Toolan, H. W. 1972. Prog. Exp. Tumor Res. 16:410-425.
141. Van Der Maaten, M. J. 1969. Can. J. Comp. Med. 33:134-140.
142. Van Hoosier, G. L., et al. 1970. Lab. Anim. Care 20:232-237.
143. Ventura, A. K., and N. J. Ehrenkranz. 1975. Am. J. Trop. Med. Hyg. 24:715-717.
144. Verster, A. 1974. Onderstepoort J. Vet. Res. 41:23-28.
145. Wade, A. E., et al. 1960. Am. J. Vet. Res. 21:753-757.
146. Wagner, J. E., et al. 1973. Ibid. 34:249-252.
147. Wagner, J. E., et al. 1974. Lab. Anim. Sci. 24:349-354.
148. Wantland, W. W. 1968. In R. A. Hoffman, et al., ed. The Golden Hamster. Iowa State Univ., Ames. pp. 171-184.
149. Western, K. A., et al. 1970. N. Engl. J. Med. 283:854-856.
150. Whitmire, C. E. 1957. J. Bacteriol. 74:417-424.
151. Whitmire, C. E., and C. M. Downs. 1957. Ibid. 74:425-431.
152. Wilson, H. R., and J. K. Frenkel. 1971. Infect. Immun. 3:756-761.
153. Wright, P. F., et al. 1970. J. Infect. Dis. 122:510-512.
154. Young, G. 1954. J. Exp. Med. 99:299-306.
155. Zlotnik, I., and D. I. H. Simpson. 1969. Br. J. Exp. Pathol. 50:393-399.
156. Zoltowska, A., and T. Wrzolkowa. 1973. J. Pathol. 109:93-99.
157. Browne, R. A., et al. 1977. Johns Hopkins Med. J. 141:183-192.
158. Chang, T.-W., et al. 1978. Infect. Immun. 20:526-529.
159. Small, J. D. 1968. Lab. Anim. Care 18:411-420.

110. SPONTANEOUS TUMOR DEVELOPMENT: HAMSTER

Classification of tumors is according to Stewart, et al. [ref. 22]. Included are all tumors reported in the literature as "malignant," or those reported by histological type and site. Excluded are tumors of unspecified site, or metastatic tumors with the primary site unknown. With the exception of the lymphomas reported in reference 1, most of the spontaneous tumors were observed after the animals were one year old. References 1, 4, 8, 9, 14, and 21 suggest the possibility of viral etiology of hamster lymphomas, skin papillomas, and melanomas. For detailed discussions of tumor development, consult references 18 and 28.

Part I. Benign Tumors

Relative Frequency gives the total number of tumors reported for the specified type and site.

Tissue & Group	Tumor Type	Site	Relative Frequency	Reference
Epithelial: I	Polyp	Stomach	<10	7
		Intestine	>100	5-7,13,20,23
		Uterus	<10	3,7
	Adenoma	Harderian gland	<10	3
		Nasal cavity	<10	3
		Bile duct	<10	3
		Pancreas	<10	7,13,26
		Ovary	<10	10
		Thyroid	30-100	13,15,27
		Parathyroid	10-30	7,13
		Adrenal cortex	>100	2,3,5,7,13,15,16,24,26,27

continued

Part I. Benign Tumors

Tissue & Group	Tumor Type	Site	Relative Frequency	Reference
	Adenomatosis	Lung	<10	13,20,27
	Papilloma	Skin	<10	11
		Pharynx	<10	3
		Palate	<10	3
		Stomach	30-100	3,7,15,17,20,26,27
	Keratoacanthoma	Skin	<10	13
		Vagina	<10	7,9,25
Connective: III	Hemangioma	Skin	<10	13
		Subcutis	<10	13
		Liver	10-30	3,7,13,17,23,26
		Spleen	30-100	3,6,7,13,23
	Lymphangioendothelioma	Mesentery	<10	13
	Cholangioma	Bile duct	10-30	13,20,24,26,27
	Thecoma	Ovary	10-30	5,7,13
	Fibroma	Face	<10	16
		Uterus	<10	22
	Leiomyoma	Prostate	<10	12
		Uterus	<10	3,12
Melanin-forming: IV	Cellular blue nevus	Skin	10-30	12,19
Neural: V	Pheochromocytoma	Adrenal	<10	27
	Ganglioneuroma	Adrenal	<10	12
	Schwannoma	Facial nerve	<10	25

Contributors: G. L. Van Hoosier, Jr., and John J. Trentin

References

1. Ambrose, K. R., and J. H. Coggin, Jr. 1975. J. Natl. Cancer Inst. 54(4):877-879.
2. Cox, C. B., et al. 1972. Appl. Microbiol. 23:675-678.
3. Dontenwill, W., et al. 1973. Z. Krebsforsch. 80:127-158.
4. Epstein, W. L., et al. 1968. Nature (London) 219:979-980.
5. Fortner, J. G. 1957. Cancer 10:1153-1156.
6. Fortner, J. G. 1958. Arch. Surg. (Chicago) 77:627-633.
7. Fortner, J. G. 1961. Cancer Res. 21:1491-1498.
8. Graffi, A., et al. 1968. Br. J. Cancer 22:577-581.
9. Graffi, A., et al. 1968. J. Natl. Cancer Inst. 40:867-868.
10. Heubner, R. J., et al. 1965. Proc. Natl. Acad. Sci. USA 54:381-388.
11. Horn, K. H., and R. Siewert. 1968. Acta Biol. Med. Ger. 20:103-110.
12. Kirkman, H. 1950. Anat. Rec. 106:227.
13. Kirkman, H., and F. T. Algard. 1968. In R. A. Hoffman, et al., ed. The Golden Hamster. Iowa State Univ., Ames. pp. 227-240.
14. Kistler, G. S. Unpublished. Univ. Zürich, Anatomisches Institut, Switzerland, 1975.
15. Lee, K. Y., et al. 1963. Proc. Soc. Exp. Biol. Med. 114:579-582.
16. Muto, M. 1974. Exp. Anim. 23:100-102.
17. Porta, G. D. 1961. Cancer Res. 21:575-579.
18. Pour, P., et al. 1976. J. Natl. Cancer Inst. 56:931-974.
19. Sherman, J. D., et al. 1963. Cancer Res. 23:1689-1693.
20. Shubik, P., et al. 1962. Henry Ford Hosp. Int. Symp. Biol. Interact. Norm. Neoplast. Growth, pp. 285-297.
21. Stenback, W. A., et al. 1966. Proc. Soc. Exp. Biol. Med. 122:1219-1223.
22. Stewart, H. L., et al. 1959. U.S. Armed Forces Inst. Pathol. Fasc. 40:378.
23. Stewart, S. E., and M. Irwin. 1960. Natl. Cancer Conf. Proc., 4th, pp. 539-557.
24. Tomatis, L., et al. 1961. Cancer Res. 21:1513-1517.
25. Toolan, H. W. 1967. Nature (London) 214:1036.
26. Toth, B. 1967. Cancer Res. 27:1430-1442.
27. Toth, B., et al. 1961. Ibid. 21:1537-1541.
28. Van Hoosier, G. L., Jr. 1979. Prog. Exp. Tumor Res. 23:1-12.

continued

Part II. Malignant Tumors

Of the laboratory rodents, it appears that the hamster, in common with the guinea pig [ref. 3], develops fewer spontaneous malignant tumors than the mouse [ref. 36] or the rat [ref. 21, 45]. Where the total number of hamsters observed was reported, the cumulative incidence of spontaneous malignant neoplasms approximated 3.7% (435 tumors in 11,792 animals). **Tumor:** The total number of tumors per site is given only when it differs from the sum of the tumors of each type at the specified site; when the difference occurs, it does so because some tumors were reported only as malignant, with histological type unspecified.

Tissue & Group	Site	Tumor		Reference
		Type	No.	
Epithelial IA	Salivary gland	Undifferentiated carcinoma	1	38,39,43
		Total no. of tumors	3	
	Stomach	Carcinoma	3	9,15
		Adenocarcinoma	3	
	Intestine	Adenocarcinoma	75	10,13-15,32,37,46
	Liver & intrahepatic bile duct	Adenocarcinoma	1	9,13,15,30,32,40,44,52
		Hepatocarcinoma	6	
		Cholangiocarcinoma	11	
	Extrahepatic bile duct	Adenocarcinoma	1	15
	Pancreas	Carcinoma	3	2,13,15
		Adenocarcinoma	2	
	Kidney	Carcinoma	1	10,13,15,22,33,52,54
		Adenocarcinoma	5	
		Nephroblastoma	2	
		Renal cell carcinoma	1	
	Epididymis	Adenocarcinoma	1	16
	Prostate	Adenocarcinoma	2	15
	Cowper's gland	Cystadenocarcinoma	7	15
	Ovary	Granulosa cell	9	10,33,41,52
		Total no. of tumors	11	
	Uterus	Carcinoma	2	9,10,15,33,47,52
		Adenocarcinoma	10	
		Adenoacanthoma	1	
	Cervix	Carcinoma	3	
	Mammary gland	Adenocarcinoma	4	10,11,18
	Thyroid	Spindle cell carcinoma	6	10,15,17,33,52
		Follicular cell carcinoma	5	
		Total no. of tumors	18	
	Parathyroid	Carcinoma	2	33
	Adrenal	Carcinoma	26	9,10,13,15,23,31,51,52
		Adenocarcinoma	4	
		Pheochromocytoma	1	
IB	Lower respiratory tract	Carcinoma	2	10,13,33,47
		Bronchogenic adenocarcinoma	1	
		Total no. of tumors	8	
IC	Skin	Squamous cell carcinoma	5	8,10,28,33
		Basal cell carcinoma	3	
	Esophagus	Squamous cell carcinoma	1	6,33
Lymphoid [L] IIA	Skin	Lymphosarcoma	3	55
	Small intestine	Lymphosarcoma	79	1

[L] Approximately 75% of lymphosarcomas reported resulted from an epizootic of horizontally transmitted lymphomas in one hamster colony [ref. 1].

continued

Part II. Malignant Tumors

Tissue & Group	Site	Tumor Type	No.	Reference
	Liver	Lymphosarcoma	20	1
	Spleen	Lymphosarcoma	12	1
	Lymph node	Lymphosarcoma	113	1,9,10,12,25,29,30,37,47,51,54
	Kidney	Lymphosarcoma	18	1
IIC	Lymph node	Reticulum cell sarcoma	121	5,10,13,15,23,27-29,39,47,48,50-55
IID	Extramedullary	Plasma cell tumor	13	9,10,12,15,20,28,39
Connective IIIA	Subcutis	Fibrosarcoma	1	7,33,34,54
		Leiomyosarcoma	1	
		Osteosarcoma	1	
		Undifferentiated sarcoma	1	
	Cheek pouch	Myxofibrosarcoma	2	19,20,50,54
		Myxoma	1	
		Myxoid liposarcoma	1	
		Hemangiopericytoma	1	
	Intestine	Leiomyosarcoma	4	13-15,23
		Angiosarcoma	1	
		Liposarcoma	1	
	Liver	Hemangioendothelioma	2	9
	Liver & spleen	Angiosarcoma	1	15
	Spleen	Hemangioendothelioma	3	9,31
	Urinary bladder	Leiomyosarcoma	1	51
	Testis	Fibrosarcoma	1	55
	Uterus	Leiomyosarcoma	4	15,33,52
	Internal chest wall	Hemangioendothelioma	1	55
	Rib	Osteosarcoma	1	18
	Humerus	Chondrosarcoma	1	49
	Femur	Osteosarcoma	2	10,55
	Tendon sheath	Giant cell tumor	2	42
IIIB	Subcutis	Sarcoma	4	10,35,53
	Pleura	Sarcoma	2	10,50
	Peritoneum	Endothelioma	1	10,33
		Sarcoma	1	
Melanin-forming: IV	Skin	....	30[2/]	4,13,15,16,24,26,33,51,52

[2/] Incidence was 0.4(0.1-2.76)%; occurrence by sex—male:female = 10:1.

Contributors: G. L. Van Hoosier, Jr., and John J. Trentin

References

1. Ambrose, K. R., and J. H. Coggin, Jr. 1975. J. Natl. Cancer Inst. 54(4):877-879.
2. Ashbel, R. 1945. Nature (London) 155:607.
3. Blumenthal, H. T., and J. B. Rogers. 1965. In W. E. Ribelin and J. R. McCoy, ed. The Pathology of Laboratory Animals. Thomas, Springfield, IL. pp. 183-209.
4. Bomirski, A., et al. 1962. Acta Unio Int. Contra Cancrum 18:178-180.
5. Brindley, D. C., and W. G. Banfield. 1961. J. Natl. Cancer Inst. 26:949-954.
6. Chesterman, F. C. 1963. 8th Int. Cancer Congr. 1962, p. 486.
7. Cox, C. B., et al. 1972. Appl. Microbiol. 23:675-678.
8. Crabb, E. D., and M. A. Kelsall. 1952. Cancer Res. 12:256.
9. Dontenwill, W., et al. 1973. Z. Krebsforsch. 80:127-158.
10. Dunham, L. J., and K. M. Herrold. 1962. J. Natl. Cancer Inst. 29:1047-1067.
11. Eddy, B. E., et al. 1958. Ibid. 20:747-762.

continued

Part II. Malignant Tumors

12. Finkel, M. P., et al. 1968. Proc. Natl. Acad. Sci. USA 60:1223-1230.
13. Fortner, J. G. 1957. Cancer 10:1153-1156.
14. Fortner, J. G. 1958. Arch. Surg. (Chicago) 77:627-633.
15. Fortner, J. G. 1961. Cancer Res. 21:1491-1498.
16. Fortner, J. G., and A. C. Allen. 1958. Ibid. 18:98-104.
17. Fortner, J. G., et al. 1960. Endocrinology 66:364-376.
18. Fortner, J. G., et al. 1961. Cancer Res. 21:199-229.
19. Friedell, G. H., et al. 1960. Transplant. Bull. 7:97-100.
20. Garcia, H., et al. 1961. J. Natl. Cancer Inst. 27:1323-1333.
21. Gilbert, C., and J. Gillman. 1958. S. Afr. J. Med. Sci. 23:257-272.
22. Girardi, A. J., et al. 1962. Proc. Soc. Exp. Biol. Med. 111:84-93.
23. Girardi, A. J., et al. 1964. Ibid. 115:1141-1150.
24. Greene, H. S. N. 1958. Cancer Res. 18:422-425.
25. Greene, H. S. N., and E. K. Harvey. 1960. Ibid. 20:1094-1100.
26. Gye, W. E., and L. Foulds. 1939. Am. J. Cancer 35:108.
27. Haemmerli, G., et al. 1966. Int. J. Cancer 1:599-612.
28. Handler, A. H. 1965. (Loc. cit. ref. 3). pp. 210-240.
29. Handler, A. H., et al. 1960. Acta Unio Int. Contra Cancrum 16:1175-1177.
30. Horn, K. H., and R. Siewert. 1968. Acta Biol. Med. Ger. 20:103-110.
31. Kesterson, J. W., and W. W. Carlton. 1970. Lab. Anim. Care 20:220-225.
32. Kirkman, H. 1950. Anat. Rec. 106:227.
33. Kirkman, H., and F. T. Algard. 1968. In R. A. Hoffman, et al., ed. The Golden Hamster. Iowa State Univ. Press, Ames. pp. 227-240.
34. Klein, M. 1961. J. Natl. Cancer Inst. 26:1381-1390.
35. Lee, K. Y., et al. 1963. Proc. Soc. Exp. Biol. Med. 114:579-582.
36. Murphy, E. D. 1966. In E. L. Green, ed. Biology of the Laboratory Mouse. Ed. 2. McGraw-Hill, New York. pp. 521-562.
37. Muto, M. 1974. Exp. Anim. 23:100-102.
38. Patterson, W. B. 1963. Acta Unio Int. Contra Cancrum 19:640-643.
39. Porta, G. D. 1961. Cancer Res. 21:575-579.
40. Porta, G. D., et al. 1959. J. Natl. Cancer Inst. 22:463-471.
41. Rolle, G. K., and H. A. Charipper. 1949. Anat. Rec. 105:281-297.
42. Ruffolo, P. R., and H. Kirkman. 1965. Br. J. Cancer 19:573-580.
43. Sherman, J. D., et al. 1963. Cancer Res. 23:1689-1693.
44. Shubik, P., et al. 1962. Henry Ford Hosp. Int. Symp. Biol. Interact, Norm. Neoplast. Growth, pp. 285-297.
45. Snell, K. C. 1965. (Loc. cit. ref. 3). pp. 241-302.
46. Stewart, H. L., et al. 1959. U.S. Armed Forces Inst. Pathol. Fasc. 40:378.
47. Stewart, S. E., and M. Irwin. 1960. Natl. Cancer Conf. Proc., 4th, pp. 539-557.
48. Strauli, V. P. 1962. Pathol. Microbiol. 25:301-305.
49. Taylor, D. O. N. 1968. Cancer Res. 28:2051-2055.
50. Tomatis, L., et al. 1961. Ibid. 21:1513-1517.
51. Toolan, H. W. 1967. Nature (London) 214:1036.
52. Toth, B. 1967. Cancer Res. 27:1430-1442.
53. Toth, B., et al. 1961. Ibid. 21:1537-1541.
54. Van Hoosier, G. L., Jr., et al. 1971. Defining Lab. Anim. Proc. 4th Symp. Int. Comm. Lab. Anim. Inst. Lab. Anim. Resour., pp. 450-473.
55. Yabe, Y., et al. 1972. Gann 63:329-336.

111. INDUCED TUMORS: HAMSTER

Part I. Viral Oncogenesis

Newborn hamsters are probably the most susceptible animals to the oncogenic viruses of other species. They are therefore the most sensitive in vivo test system for the oncogenic viruses of other mammalian species. Newborn hamsters injected with certain human viruses, such as reovirus types 1 and 2 and herpes simplex viruses, may undergo acute morbidity and mortality [ref. 21]. A transplanted hamster sarcoma became a carrier of lymphocytic choriomeningitis virus of mice and transmitted the infection to other hamsters and humans [ref. 11]. In addition, hamsters have relatively few indigenous viruses [ref. 17], and a low incidence of spontaneous tumors (see Table 110 and consult reference 25), making them ideal assay animals for oncogenic viruses. Although most hamster colonies harbor certain viruses "borrowed" from other species—such as pneumonia virus of mice, simian virus type 5, and parainfluenza 1 ⟨Sendai virus⟩—specific pathogen-free ⟨SPF⟩ hamsters uncontaminated by these viruses are available, both random-bred and inbred [ref. 24].

Virus Titer or Dose: $TCID_{50}$ = tissue culture infective dose, 50%; $MTCID_{100}$ = minimum tissue culture infective dose, 100%; GMK indicates assayed in GMK cell cultures; HeLa indicates assayed in HeLa cell cultures; HEK indicates

continued

Part I. Viral Oncogenesis

assayed in HEK cell cultures; CELD$_{50}$ = chicken egg lethal dose, 50%; PFU = plaque-forming units. **Route**: i.p. = intraperitoneal; i.v. = intravenous. **Hamster**: Tumor incidence of the concurrent controls is not given since in most cases it was zero; in some cases, where controls were kept beyond a year, they showed the low incidence of spontaneous late-arising tumors typical of untreated hamsters (*see* Table 110 and consult reference 25). *Abbreviations*: d = days; s.c. = subcutaneous; Fn = footnote. Values in parentheses are ranges, estimate "c" (*see* Introduction).

Virus Name, [Natural Host], & Modifying Factors	Virus Titer or Dose [Route]	Hamster		Tumor		Ref-er-ence
		Age at Injection d[1]	Tumorous/ Surviving No. [%]	Type & Site	Latent Period d[1]	
Papovaviruses						
JC virus [Man][2]	10^6 TCID$_{50}$ [Intracranial & s.c.]	<1	52/63 [83]	Multiple malignant brain tumors: glioblastomas (most), medulloblastomas, unclassified primitive tumors, papillary ependymomas (2 only). No s.c. tumors. No metastases.	4-6 mo	26
SV40 virus [Monkey] Effect of virus dose	32 TCID$_{50}$ [s.c.]	Newborn	0/25 [0]	....	....	5
	3200 TCID$_{50}$ [s.c.]	Newborn	5/28 [18]	Malignant s.c. sarcomas	344(262-416)	5
	320,000 TCID$_{50}$ [s.c.]	Newborn	52/54 [96]	Malignant s.c. sarcomas	201(115-403)	5
Effect of route of injection	10^7 TCID$_{50}$ [s.c.]	Newborn	17/22 [77]	Malignant s.c. sarcomas	....	5
	[i.p.]	Newborn	0/25 [0]	....	....	
	[Intrapulmonary]	Newborn	2/18 [11]	Malignant s.c. sarcomas	....	
	10^7 TCID$_{50}$[3] [Intra-cerebral]	<1	4/9 [44]	Ependymomas	(100-124)	9
	10^8 TCID$_{50}$ [i.v.]	(17-18)	90/95 [95]	Reticulum cell sarcomas, 78% Osteogenic sarcomas, 72% s.c. sarcomas, 6% Lymphosarcomas, 3% Malignant adrenal tumors, 3%	(3-6) mo	2
	10$^{8.5}$ TCID$_{50}$ [i.v.]	(21-22)	125/143 [87]	Reticulum cell sarcomas, 72% Osteogenic sarcomas, 55% s.c. sarcomas, 4% Lymphosarcomas, 4% Lymphocytic leukemia, 1%	(4-6) mo	2
Effect of hamster age	0.2 ml of 10$^{-5.75}$ titer (GMK) [s.c.]	Newborn	52/54 [96]	Malignant s.c. sarcomas	201(115-403)	5
	0.2 ml of 10$^{-5.5}$ titer (GMK) [s.c.]	7	24/40 [60]	Malignant s.c. sarcomas	314(178-487)	5
	0.2 ml of 10^{-6} titer (GMK) [s.c.]	30	6/26 [23]	Malignant s.c. sarcomas	360(188-494)	5
		90	0/35 [0]	....	....	5
Polyoma virus [Mouse]	0.2 ml unfiltered tissue culture fluid [s.c.]	<1	34/40 [85]	Sarcoma of kidney, s.c. tissue, heart, stomach, or intestines; hemangiomas of liver, ovaries, & lung[4]	(4-28) wk	3

[1] Days, unless otherwise specified. [2] Isolated from brain of a case of progressive multiple leukoencephalopathy (PML). [3] Stated as "0.02 ml of 18$^{8.7}$ TCID$_{50}$/ml" in reference. [4] Range of tumor types more limited than in mouse.

continued

Part I. Viral Oncogenesis

Virus Name, [Natural Host], & Modifying Factors	Virus Titer or Dose [Route]	Hamster		Tumor		Reference
		Age at Injection d	Tumorous/ Surviving No. [%]	Type & Site	Latent Period d	
Adenoviruses						
Human adenoviruses [5] [Man] Types 1, 3, 7, 8 (?), 11, 14, 16, 21, 24 (?)	....	<1	Fn [6]	Most were undifferentiated sarcomas at site of injection; some were lymphosarcomas at site of injection or remote site	....	4,7, 10, 20, 22
Types 12, 18, 31	....	<1	Fn [7]	Undifferentiated sarcomas at site of injection	....	6,15, 19
Type 12 Effect of virus dose	0.5 MTCID$_{100}$ (HeLa) [Intrapulmonary]	<1	1/5 [20]	Undifferentiated sarcomas at site of injection	73	27
	50 MTCID$_{100}$ (HeLa) [Intrapulmonary]	<1	16/19 [84]	Undifferentiated sarcomas at site of injection	(33-91)	27
	500 MTCID$_{100}$ (HeLa) [Intrapulmonary]	<1	26/27 [96]	Undifferentiated sarcomas at site of injection	59(35-157)	27
Effect of route of injection	50 MTCID$_{100}$ (HeLa) [i.p.]	<1	5/6 [83]	Undifferentiated sarcomas at site of injection and/or in liver	....	28
	500 MTCID$_{100}$ (HeLa) [s.c.]	<1	3/3 [100]	Undifferentiated sarcomas at site of injection and/or in liver	(39-98)	28
	[Intrapleural]	<1	6/6 [100]	Undifferentiated sarcomas at site of injection and/or in liver	(29-45)	
	[Intrapulmonary]	<1	4/5 [80]	Undifferentiated sarcomas at site of injection and/or in liver	(42-45)	
	[i.v.]	<1	2/3 [67]	Undifferentiated sarcomas at site of injection and/or in liver	(50, 70)	
	1000 MTCID$_{100}$ (HeLa) [i.v.]	<1	7/11 [64]	Undifferentiated sarcomas at site of injection and/or in liver	(36-103)	28
Effect of hamster age	500 MTCID$_{100}$ (HeLa) [Intrapulmonary]	<1	26/27 [96]	Undifferentiated sarcomas at site of injection	59(35-157)	27
		5	5/7 [71]	Undifferentiated sarcomas at site of injection	57(41-78)	
		8	2/9 [22]	Undifferentiated sarcomas at site of injection	86(70, 102)	
	1000 MTCID$_{100}$ (HeLa) [Intrapulmonary]	14	1/8 [12]	Undifferentiated sarcomas at site of injection	56	27
		(21-77)	0/20 [0]	....	....	

[5] Of the 31 human adenovirus serotypes, all those not listed were non-oncogenic in newborn hamsters, but some transform rat embryo cells or the NIL-2 hamster cell line in vitro [ref. 12, 20]. [6] Weakly oncogenic. [7] Strongly oncogenic.

continued

Part I. Viral Oncogenesis

Virus Name [Natural Host], & Modifying Factors	Virus Titer or Dose [Route]	Hamster		Tumor		Reference
		Age at Injection d[1]	Tumorous/ Surviving No. [%]	Type & Site	Latent Period d[1]	
Effect of sex: ♂	10^6 TCID$_{50}$ (HEK) [s.c.]	<1	19/71 [27]	....	≤120	29
♀	10^6 TCID$_{50}$ (HEK) [s.c.]	<1	47/82 [57]	....	≤120	29
Effect of hamster strain Non-inbred	10^6 TCID$_{50}$ (HEK) [s.c. or i.p.]	<1	26/29 [90]	....	61	23
Inbred: LSH	10^6 TCID$_{50}$ (HEK) [s.c. or i.p.]	<1	15/31 [48]	....	51	23
Simian adenoviruses[8] SA7 [*Cercopithecus* monkey]	0.05 ml undiluted virus[9] [s.c.]	<1	46/47 [98]	....	(28-48)	8
Effect of hamster strain Non-inbred	$10^{7.5}$ TCID$_{50}$ [s.c. or i.p.]	<1	21/23 [91]	....	43	23
Inbred: LSH	$10^{7.5}$ TCID$_{50}$ [s.c. or i.p.]	<1	32/34 [94]	....	49	23
[Rhesus or cynomolgus monkey] SV20	0.05 ml undiluted virus[9] [s.c.]	<1	54/141 [38]	....	(40-211)	8
SV33	0.05 ml undiluted virus[9] [s.c]	<1	2/25 [8]	....	(82, 229)	
SV34	0.05 ml undiluted virus[9] [s.c.]	<1	3/48 [6]	....	(110-330)	
SV37	0.05 ml undiluted virus[9] [s.c.]	<1	1/20 [5]	....	231	
SV38	0.05 ml undiluted virus[9]	<1	3/14 [21]	....	(154-280)	
Bovine adenovirus Types 1, 2, 4-10	0.2 ml virus[9] [s.c.]	Newborn	0/234 [0]	....	>1 yr[10]	13
Type 3	($10^{4.0}$-$10^{5.2}$) [s.c., i.p., intrathoracic, intracerebral]	<1	22/45 [49]	Firm or cystic undifferentiated sarcomas	(24-67)	1
	2.3×10^5 PFU [s.c.]	Newborn	17/19 [90]	....	48	14
Chicken adenovirus: CELO virus	10^6 CELD$_{50}$[11] [s.c.]	<1	23/69 [33]	Well-differentiated fibrosarcomas	(88-195)	16
	($10^{6.6}$-10^8) TCID$_{50}$ or PFU [s.c. or i.p. or intracerebral]	<1 [12]	130/277 [47]	Most were fibrosarcomas at site of injection; also 3 brain tumors (glioma, papilloma, & ependymoma), & 12 liver tumors (5 hepatocellular carcinomas, 5 hepatic adenocarcinomas, 2 hepatic sarcomas)	....	18

[1] Unless otherwise specified. [8] Twelve additional serotypes tested were non-oncogenic [ref. 8]. [9] Titer unspecified. [10] No tumors after 1 yr of observation. [11] Stated as "0.1 ml of 10^7 CELD$_{50}$/ml" in reference. [12] Both non-inbred & inbred LSH.

Contributor: John J. Trentin

continued

111. INDUCED TUMORS: HAMSTER

Part I. Viral Oncogenesis

References

1. Darbyshire, J. H. 1966. Nature (London) 211:102.
2. Diamondopoulos, G. T. 1973. J. Natl. Cancer Inst. 50:1347-1365.
3. Eddy, B. E., et al. 1958. Ibid. 20:747-756.
4. Fujinaga, K., and M. Green. 1967. J. Virol. 1:576-582.
5. Girardi, A. J., et al. 1963. Proc. Soc. Exp. Biol. Med. 112:662-667.
6. Huebner, R. J., et al. 1962. Proc. Natl. Acad. Sci. USA 48:2051-2058.
7. Huebner, R. J., et al. 1965. Ibid. 54:381-388.
8. Hull, R. N., et al. 1965. Science 150:1044-1046.
9. Kirchstein, R. L., and P. Gerber. 1962. Nature (London) 195:299-300.
10. Larson, V. M., et al. 1965. Proc. Soc. Exp. Biol. Med. 118:15-24.
11. Lewis, A. M., et al. 1965. Science 150:363-364.
12. McAllister, R. M., et al. 1969. J. Natl. Cancer Inst. 43:917-923.
13. Mohanty, S. B. 1971. Am. J. Vet. Res. 32:1899-1905.
14. Panigrahy, B., et al. 1975. J. Natl. Cancer Inst. 54:449-451.
15. Pereira, M. A., et al. 1965. Lancet 1:21-23.
16. Sarma, P. S., et al. 1965. Science 149:1108.
17. Stenback, W. A., et al. 1970. Bibl. Haematol. (Basal) 36:559-565.
18. Stenback, W. A., et al. 1973. J. Natl. Cancer Inst. 50:963-970.
19. Trentin, J. J., et al. 1962. Science 137:835-841.
20. Trentin, J. J., et al. 1968. Proc. Soc. Exp. Biol. Med. 127:683-689.
21. Trentin, J. J., et al. 1969. Ibid. 132:912-915.
22. Van Hoosier, G. L., Jr., et al. 1968. Ibid. 128:467-469.
23. Van Hoosier, G. L., Jr., et al. 1970. Ibid. 134:427-429.
24. Van Hoosier, G. L., Jr., et al. 1970. Lab. Anim. Care 20:232-237.
25. Van Hoosier, G. L., Jr., et al. 1971. Defining Lab. Anim. Proc. 4th Symp. Int. Comm. Lab. Anim. Inst. Lab. Anim. Resour., pp. 450-473.
26. Walker, D. L., et al. 1973. Science 181:674-676.
27. Yabe, Y., et al. 1962. Proc. Soc. Exp. Biol. Med. 111:343-344.
28. Yabe, Y., et al. 1963. Ibid. 113:221-224.
29. Yohn, D. S., et al. 1965. J. Natl. Cancer Inst. 35:617-624.

Part II. Survival and Tumor Incidence After Irradiation

The hamster is relatively resistant to radiation-induced tumors. **X-Radiation:** R = roentgen. **Hamsters:** Equal numbers of males and females were used. Values in parentheses are ranges, estimate "c" (*see* Introduction).

Dose Rate R/wk	Duration wk	Total R	Total at Beginning	Surviving Last Irradiation	Days Survival from First Irradiation	%	Total No.	Type & Site
20	10	200	10	10	(241-442)	0	0	....
	20	400	10	10	(206-423)	0	0	....
	30	600	20	20	(284-485)	5	1	Undifferentiated neoplasm of spleen & liver
40	10	400	10	10	(122-449)	10	1	Adenocarcinoma of liver
	20	800	20	19	(216-440)	0	0	....
	30	1200	20	19	(233-492)	0	0	....
80	10	800	10	10	(108-340)	0	0	....
	20	1600	15	15	(161-423)	13	1	Reticulum cell sarcoma of spleen & liver
							1	Melanoma of neck
	30	2400	25	24	(267-333)	13	1	Undifferentiated neoplasm of spleen
							1	Squamous cell carcinoma of lung
							1	Undiagnosed transplantable neoplasm of spleen
150	10	1500	15	15	(172-429)	13	2	Reticulum cell sarcoma of spleen
	20	3000	45	33	(149-269)	12	1	Small cell sarcoma of spleen
							1	Small cell sarcoma of spleen & liver
							2	Undifferentiated neoplasm of spleen & liver

Column header note: X-Radiation[1]; Tumors spans % / Total No. / Type & Site.

[1] 250 kVp X-irradiation, whole body, once a week.

Contributor: John J. Trentin

Reference: Stenback, W. A., et al. 1979. Prog. Exp. Tumor Res. 23:89-99.

Data are from Homburger, et al. [ref. 3], unless otherwise indicated. Data illustrate extremes of susceptibility and resistance to chemical carcinogens. There are strains of intermediate degrees of susceptibility and resistance which have not been included below. In all strains in both categories, incidence of spontaneous tumors during comparable lifetime was negligible. **Route:** s.c. = subcutaneous. **Dose:**

ppm = parts per million. **Strain:** R = resistant; S = susceptible. **Incidence:** percent of tumors among survivors. **Iball Index:** percent of tumors divided by average latent period in days × 100 [ref. 4]. Data in light brackets refer to the column heading in brackets. Figures in heavy brackets are reference numbers.

Target Organ	Carcinogen ⟨Synonym⟩	Route [Dose]	Strain	Incidence [Iball Index]
Subcutaneous tissue	Benzo[a]pyrene ⟨3,4-Benzpyrene⟩	s.c. [500 µg]	S: BIO 7.88; BIO 15.16; BIO 45.5; BIO 87.20	[15-35][1]
			R: BIO 1.5; BIO 54.7; BIO 82.73; BIO 86.93	[5-14][2]
	3-Methylcholanthrene ⟨20-Methylcholanthrene⟩	s.c. [500 µg]	S: BIO 7.88; BIO 15.16; BIO 45.5; BIO 87.20	[51-70][3]
			R: BIO 1.5; BIO 12.14; BIO 82.73	[15-37][4]
Stomach	3-Methylcholanthrene ⟨20-Methylcholanthrene⟩	Gavage [250 mg in 50 gavages during 7 wk]	S: BIO 15.16♀ BIO 72.29♂ BIO 87.20♂	.... 40% (40-45)%
			R: 20 strains	....
	N-Nitrosodiethylamine ⟨Diethylnitrosamine; DENA⟩; N-nitrosodimethylamine ⟨dimethylnitrosamine; DMNA⟩	Drinking water [1 ppm]	S: BIO 87.20	....
Small intestine	3-Methylcholanthrene ⟨20-Methylcholanthrene⟩	Gavage [250 mg in 50 gavages during 7 wk]	S: BIO 4.22 BIO 15.16 BIO 87.20	♂, 50%; ♀, 45%[5] ♂, 39%[5] ♂, 45%[5]
			R: BIO 82.73; BIO 86.93; random-bred	....
Large intestine	3-Methylcholanthrene ⟨20-Methylcholanthrene⟩	Gavage [250 mg in 50 gavages during 7 wk]	S: BIO 15.16 BIO 87.20	♂, 50% ♂, 65%; ♀, 53%
			R: BIO 4.22; BIO 82.73; random-bred	....
Bronchi	Alpha-radiation from polonium [5]	Instillation into trachea	BIO 2.4; BIO 4.22; BIO 15.16; BIO 87.20	(33-50)%[6]
Larynx	Cigarette smoke [1]	Inhalation	S: BIO 15.16	(20-60)%
			R: Random-bred [2]	10%
Urinary bladder	2-Naphthylamine ⟨β-Naphthylamine⟩	Feeding [1% of diet]	S: BIO 1.5♀ BIO 7.88♂ BIO 7.88♀ BIO 86.93♀ BIO 87.20♂	50% 40% 75% 60% 80%
			R: BIO 1.5♂ BIO 15.16♂ BIO 54.7♂ BIO 54.7♀ BIO 72.29♂ BIO 84.9♂ BIO 86.93♂ BIO PD4 ♂	0 0 0 0 0 0 0 0

[1] Latency: 21-34 wk. [2] Latency: 22-38 wk. [3] Latency: 20.4-33 wk. [4] Latency: 26-58 wk. [5] Higher incidence in males because females die of mammary cancer. [6] Lines listed had similar tumor incidences but different times of latency.

continued

489

Target Organ	Carcinogen ⟨Synonym⟩	Route [Dose]	Strain		Incidence [Iball Index]
				BIO XX.B ♂	0
				Random-bred ♂♀	0
Mammary gland	3-Methylcholanthrene ⟨20-Methylcholanthrene⟩	Gavage [250 mg in 50 gavages during 7 wk]	S:	BIO 15.16	86%
				BIO 54.7	91%
				BIO 87.20	87%
			R:	BIO 4.22	61%
				Random-bred	52% [14]

Contributor: Freddy Homburger

References

1. Bernfeld, P., et al. 1974. J. Natl. Cancer Inst. 53: 1141-1157.
2. Dontenwill, W., et al. 1973. Ibid. 51:1781-1832.
3. Homburger, F., et al. 1972. Cancer Res. 32:360-366.
4. Iball, J. 1939. Am. J. Cancer 35:188-190.
5. Little, J. B., et al. 1973. Eur. J. Cancer 9:825-828.

113. TUMOR IMMUNITY: HAMSTER

Abbreviation: SV40 = Simian virus 40.

Part I. Analysis and Detection of Tumors

Description	Reference
Transplantation immunity studies	15,47,48
Cellular immunity to SV40 tumor-specific transplantation antigen	1,2,8,9,11,61
Transplantation antigens & surface antigens	9,11,57
Effects of anti-hamster thymocyte serum	56
Spleen cell cytotoxicity	
To herpesvirus-transformed cells	40
To cytomegalovirus-transformed cells	44,45
Resistance to tumor challenge	27,36,49
Serum blocking activity	
Against SV40-transformed cells	7,11,26,41,55
Against Para-7 tumor cells	11,50
Immunosensitivity to tumor induction by various agents	
Polyoma virus	52
SV40 virus & SV40-transformed cells	4,7,11,16,34,58
BK & JC viruses	46,59
Simian adenovirus 7[1]: virus & tumor cells	6,53
Adenovirus proteins	19
Herpes type 2 tumor cells (333-8-9)	14
Human tumors in hamsters	24,25,51
Dimethylbenzanthracene & other chemical carcinogens	20,37,38
Analysis of virus-induced surface antigens	
Polyoma virus	
Immunofluorescent detection	33
Solubilization of antigens	3,8

[1] Synonym: SA7.

continued

Part I. Analysis and Detection of Tumors

Description	Reference
SV40	12,13
Mixed hemagglutination detection	31,32
Immunofluorescent detection	35
Solubilization of antigens	9,10,18
Adenovirus type 12	5
Cytomegalovirus	39
Fetal antigens on SV40 tumor cell surface	4,7,10,17,23
Analysis & detection of Forssman antigen on hamster tumor cells	28,54
Analysis of RNA type C oncovirus in hamster cells	
Passive hemagglutination detection	29
Detection in normal, and polyoma-, SV40-, or chemical-transformed cells	21,30
Analysis of solubilized antigens	8,11,42,43
Immunological maturation & sexual tumor sensitivity	22,60
Virus-induced or -transformed tumor cell lines	
Polyoma virus(es)	3,12,32
SV40	12,13,15,16,27,34,36,57
Adenovirus(es)	15,27,36
Herpes simplex virus(es)	14,40
Cytomegalovirus-transformed cells	39,44,45

Contributors: J. H. Coggin, Jr., and Donadee Heffron

References

1. Ambrose, K. R., et al. 1969. Proc. Soc. Exp. Biol. Med. 132:1013-1020.
2. Ambrose, K. R., et al. 1971. Embryonic and Fetal Antigens in Cancer. Oak Ridge National Laboratories, Oak Ridge, TN. pp. 281-289.
3. Barra, Y., et al. 1977. J. Natl. Cancer Inst. 58:721-726.
4. Becker, L. E., et al. 1977. J. Infect. Dis. 135:962-964.
5. Biron, K. K., and K. Raska, Jr. 1977. Virology 76:516-526.
6. Chen, T. T., et al. 1975. Cancer Res. 35:3566-3570.
7. Coggin, J. H., and N. G. Anderson. 1974. Adv. Cancer Res. 19:105-165.
8. Coggin, J. H., et al. 1967. Proc. Soc. Exp. Biol. Med. 124:774-781.
9. Coggin, J. H., et al. 1967. Ibid. 124:1295-1301.
10. Coggin, J. H., et al. 1971. J. Immunol. 107:226-230.
11. Coggin, J. H., et al. 1974. Cancer Res. 34:2092-2101.
12. Collins, J. J., and P. H. Black. 1973. J. Natl. Cancer Inst. 51:95-114.
13. Collins, J. J., and P. H. Black. 1973. Ibid. 51:115-134.
14. Copple, C. D., and J. K. McDougall. 1976. Int. J. Cancer 17:501-510.
15. Defendi, V. 1963. Proc. Soc. Exp. Biol. Med. 113:12-16.
16. Diamondopoulos, G. T. 1973. J. Natl. Cancer Inst. 50:1347-1365.
17. Dierlan, P., et al. 1971. (Loc. cit. ref. 2). pp. 203-215.
18. Drapkin, M. S., et al. 1974. J. Natl. Cancer Inst. 52:259-264.
19. Dreesman, G. R., et al. 1971. Proc. Soc. Exp. Biol. Med. 137:1337-1342.
20. Evans, C. H., and J. A. DiPaolo. 1976. Cancer Res. 36:128-131.
21. Freeman, A. E., et al. 1974. J. Natl. Cancer Inst. 52:1469-1476.
22. Friedman, H., and H. Goldner. 1970. Ibid. 44:809-817.
23. Girardi, A. J., et al. 1973. Proc. Natl. Acad. Sci. USA 70:183-186.
24. Goldenberg, D. M., and H. J. Hansen. 1972. Science 175:1117-1118.
25. Goldenberg, D. M., et al. 1967. Transplantation 4:760-763.
26. Goldrosen, M. H., and P. B. Dent. 1975. Br. J. Cancer 32:667-677.
27. Habel, K., and B. E. Eddy. 1963. Proc. Soc. Exp. Biol. Med. 113:1-4.
28. Hannon, W. H., et al. 1975. Ibid. 148:1075-1080.
29. Hatch, G. G., et al. 1973. J. Natl. Cancer Inst. 51:519-524.
30. Hatch, G. G., et al. 1975. Cancer Res. 35:3792-3797.
31. Häyry, P., and V. Defendi. 1968. Virology 36:317-321.
32. Häyry, P., and V. Defendi. 1970. Ibid. 41:22-29.
33. Irlin, I. S., et al. 1967. Ibid. 32:725-728.
34. Kaliev, Y. 1969. Neoplasma 16:285-291.
35. Kluchareva, T. E., et al. 1967. J. Natl. Cancer Inst. 39:825-828.

continued

Part I. Analysis and Detection of Tumors

36. Koch, M. A., and A. B. Sabin. 1963. Proc. Soc. Exp. Biol. Med. 113:4-12.
37. Lausch, R. N., and F. Rapp. 1971. Int. J. Cancer 7: 322-330.
38. Lausch, R. N., et al. 1969. Ibid. 4:226-231.
39. Lausch, R. N., et al. 1974. J. Immunol. 112:1680-1684.
40. Lausch, R. N., et al. 1975. Ibid. 114:459-465.
41. Lausch, R. N., et al. 1975. Ibid. 115:682-687.
42. Law, L. W., and E. Appella. 1973. Nature (London) 243:83-87.
43. Meltzer, M. S., et al. 1971. J. Natl. Cancer Inst. 47: 703-709.
44. Murasko, D. M., and R. N. Lausch. 1974. Int. J. Cancer 14:451-460.
45. Murasko, D. M., and R. N. Lausch. 1975. Ibid. 16:24-32.
46. Padgett, B. L., et al. 1977. Cancer Res. 37:718-720.
47. Panteleakis, P. N., et al. 1968. Proc. Soc. Exp. Biol. Med. 129:50-57.
48. Potter, C. W., et al. 1969. Arch. Gesamte Virusforsch. 27:73-86.
49. Potter, C. W., et al. 1969. Ibid. 27:87-93.
50. Prather, S. O., and R. N. Lausch. 1976. Int. J. Cancer 17:380-388.
51. Primus, F. J., et al. 1976. Cancer Res. 36:2176-2181.
52. Rabson, A. S., and R. L. Kirschstein. 1960. Arch. Pathol. 69:663-671.
53. Rapp, F., et al. 1969. Cancer Res. 29:1173-1178.
54. Shantz, G. D., and R. N. Lausch. 1974. J. Natl. Cancer Inst. 53:239-246.
55. Tevethia, S. S., et al. 1968. J. Immunol. 100:358-362.
56. Tevethia, S. S., et al. 1968. Ibid. 101:1105-1110.
57. Tevethia, S. S., et al. 1968. Ibid. 101:1192-1198.
58. Tevethia, S. S., et al. 1971. Ibid. 106:1295-1300.
59. Uchida, S., et al. 1976. Gann 67:857-865.
60. Yohn, D. S., et al. 1965. J. Natl. Cancer Inst. 35:617-624.
61. Zarling, J. M., and S. S. Tevethia. 1973. Ibid. 50:137-147.

Part II. Characteristics of Certain Virus-Transformed Cell Lines

Presence of Antigens: TAg—tumor antigen, intranuclear; SAg—tumor antigen, surface; TSTA—tumor specific transplantation antigen.

Tumor Line	Presence of Antigens			Virus-Free	Reference
	TAg	SAg	TSTA		
SV40-induced or -transformed tumor cell lines					4-7,10,13,14,19
F5-1	+	+	+	+	1,2,8,9,15,16,21
H-50	+	+	+	+	4,9,17-19
H-50, H-50IR, IS	+	+	+	+	20,21
H65/90B	+	...	+	+	11,12

Tumor Line	Presence of Antigens			Virus-Free	Reference
	TAg	SAg	TSTA		
HK-LLE	+	...	+	+	12
Adenovirus-induced or -transformed tumor cell lines					6,10,14
Adenovirus 7	+	...	+	+	1,8,15,21
Adenovirus 12[1/]	+	...	...	...	3
Adenovirus 31	+	...	+	+	1

[1/] Synonym: T637.

Contributors: J. H. Coggin, Jr., and Donadee Heffron

References

1. Ambrose, K. R., et al. 1969. Proc. Soc. Exp. Biol. Med. 132:1013-1020.
2. Ambrose, K. R., et al. 1971. In N. G. Anderson and J. H. Coggin, Jr., ed. Embryonic and Fetal Antigens in Cancer. Oak Ridge National Laboratories, Oak Ridge, TN. pp. 281-289.
3. Biron, K. K., and K. Raska, Jr. 1977. Virology 76: 516-526.
4. Collins, J. J., and P. H. Black. 1973. J. Natl. Cancer Inst. 51:95-114.
5. Collins, J. J., and P. H. Black. 1973. Ibid. 51:115-134.
6. Defendi, V. 1963. Proc. Soc. Exp. Biol. Med. 113: 12-16.
7. Diamondopoulos, G. T. 1973. J. Natl. Cancer Inst. 50:1347-1365.
8. Girardi, A. J., et al. 1973. Proc. Natl. Acad. Sci. USA 70:183-186.
9. Goldrosen, M. H., and P. B. Dent. 1975. Br. J. Cancer 32:667-677.
10. Habel, K., and B. E. Eddy. 1963. Proc. Soc. Exp. Biol. Med. 113:1-4.
11. Häyry, P., and V. Defendi. 1968. Virology 36:317-321.

continued

12. Häyry, P., and V. Defendi. 1970. Ibid. 41:22-29.
13. Kaliev, Y. 1969. Neoplasma 16:285-291.
14. Koch, M. A., and A. B. Sabin. 1963. Proc. Soc. Exp. Biol. Med. 113:4-12.
15. Panteleakis, P. N., et al. 1968. Ibid. 129:50-57.
16. Potter, C. W., et al. 1969. Arch. Gesamte Virusforsch. 27:73-86.

17. Tevethia, S. S., et al. 1968. J. Immunol. 100:358-362.
18. Tevethia, S. S., et al. 1968. Ibid. 101:1105-1110.
19. Tevethia, S. S., et al. 1968. Ibid. 101:1192-1198.
20. Tevethia, S. S., et al. 1971. Ibid. 106:1295-1300.
21. Zarling, J. M., and S. S. Tevethia. 1973. J. Natl. Cancer Inst. 50:137-147.

114. NATURALLY OCCURRING TUMORS: HAMSTER

Tumors: Incidence, %—It was not always possible to base percent on the total number of animals in the study, since in some of the references only a proportion of the animals may have had a particular organ system thoroughly examined. **Reference:** In the list of references appended to the table, the figure in brackets [no.] after each reference is the total number of animals studied; the figures in parentheses (%/no.) in most cases show the total percent and number of *animals* with tumors; however, in some references, they represent the total percent and number of *tumors*.

Site & Type	Incidence No.	Incidence %	Reference
Lymphomas	2	1.1	3
& leuke-	14	1.3	4
mias	19	5.3	5
	4	0.9	6
	7	3.1	7
	6	3.2	8
	36	1.5	9
	4	0.5	10
	2	2.0	12
	6[1]	2.7[1]	13
	7[2]	3.3[2]	13
	7	1.3	14
	2	1.8	15
	9	4.5	16
	2	0.2	17
	3[3]	0.2[3]	18
	6	3.8	19
	139[4]	2.1[5]	
Melanoma	3	1.3	7
	5	2.7	8
	7	0.1	10
	....	0.1	11
	2	1.8	15
	17[4]	0.4[5]	
Nevi	21	0.3	10
	....	0.2	11
	1[2]	1.2[2]	13

Site & Type	Incidence No.	Incidence %	Reference
	1	0.2	14
	1	0.5	16
	24[4]	0.9[5]	
Epithelial Tumors			
Adrenal	10	1.0	1
gland[6]	221	39.1	4
(includes	....	15-30[7]	5
5 pheo-	8	3.6	7
chromo-	65	35.8	8
cytomas)	583	8.1	10
	667	14.5	11
	4	4.0	12
	35[1]	13.1[1]	13
	12[2]	6.0[2]	13
	7	1.3	14
	31	28.7	15
	4	2.0	16
	1647[4]	8.7[5]	
Gastroin-	3	1.6	3
testinal	60	10.7	4
tract[6,8]	....	15-30[7]	5
	>14	>6.3	7
	89	48.1	8
	1	0.1	10
	2	....	11
	2	2.0	12

Site & Type	Incidence No.	Incidence %	Reference
	19[1]	6.7[1]	13
	25[2]	14.1[2]	13
	4	0.8	14
	8	7.4	15
	8	4.0	16
	235[4]	6.0[5]	
Harderian	5[1]	1.7[1]	13
gland[6]	2[2]	1.3[2]	13
	7[4]	0.2[5]	
Head &	6	1.1	4
neck[6,9]	2	0.1	9
	7[1]	2.5[1]	13
	5[2]	2.5[2]	13
	2	0.2	17
	22[4]	0.4[5]	
Kidney[6]	1	0.2	5
	1	0.5	7
	1	0.5	8
	1[1]	0.3[1]	13
	1	0.5	16
	1[3]	0.05[3]	18
	6[4]	0.1[5]	
Liver[10]			
Cholan-	33	0.6	2[11]
gioma	....	1-15[7]	5
(includes	20	11.0	8
all tumors	1	0.04	9

[1] Data from Eppley colony. [2] Data from Hannover colony. [3] Only malignant tumors were listed. [4] Total number. [5] Average percent; obtained by adding the percentages for each type of tumor and dividing by the total number of references, assuming that if there was no incidence for a particular type of tumor in the reference, none existed. [6] Tumors were predominantly benign. [7] Percentages of benign tumors in this reference are given within a range. [8] Adenomas of the stomach were most common, followed by adenomatous polyps of large and small intestine. [9] Include mostly papillomas and squamous cell carcinomas of upper respiratory and gastrointestinal tracts, as well as tumors of ears and skin. [10] Tumors are predominantly malignant. [11] All animals examined were males.

continued

493

Site & Type	Incidence No.	Incidence %	Reference
of the gallbladder & extrahepatic biliary tract)	6	0.09	10
	2	0.4	11
	1	1.0	12
	16[2]	7.9[2]	13
	10	1.9	14
	2	1.8	15
	4	2.0	16
	95[4]	1.8[5]	
Hepatocellular tumors	6	0.1	2[11]
	2	0.9	7
	1	0.5	8
	101	1.4	10
	1	0.2	11
	3[2]	1.5[2]	13
	114[4]	0.2[5]	
Lung[10]	1	0.2	5
	1	0.5	7
	8	0.11	10
	8	....	11
	1	1.0	12
	2[1]	0.6[1]	13
	2[2]	1.0[2]	13
	2	0.4	14
	25[4]	0.2[5]	
Pancreas[6] (includes both islet & acinar tumors)	1	0.1	1
	....	1-15[7]	5
	1	0.5	7
	11	6.1	8
	6	0.08	10
	....	1.4	11
	9[1]	4.2[1]	13
	9[2]	8.4[2]	13
	3	2.7	15
	40[4]	1.5[5]	
Parathyroid gland[6]	3	1.6	8
	6	0.08	10
	21	1.4	11
	8[1]	3.7[1]	13
	7[2]	4.5[2]	13
	3	2.7	15
	48[4]	0.8[5]	

Site & Type	Incidence No.	Incidence %	Reference
Salivary gland[6]	1	0.5	3
	3	0.04	10
	1	0.6	19
	5[4]	0.1[5]	
Testis, prostate, & epididymis[6]	9	4.8	8
	10	0.14	10
	1[1]	0.6[1]	13
	24	22.2	15
	44[4]	1.5[5]	
Thyroid gland[6]	2	0.4	4
	1	0.2	5
	2	1.1	8
	30	0.39	10
	38	2.6	11
	1	1.0	12
	20[1]	8.0[1]	13
	12[2]	6.5[2]	13
	1	0.2	14
	3	2.7	15
	2	1.0	16
	112[4]	1.4[5]	
Vagina, uterus, & uterine tubes[6]	9	1.7	4
	3	0.5	5
	4	1.8	7
	10	5.4	8
	3	0.04	10
	26[1]	20.0[1]	13
	3[2]	2.6[2]	13
	1	0.5	16
	59[4]	1.7[5]	
Others[12]	10	1.5	5
	2	0.5	6
	3	1.6	8
	3	0.04	10
	2[1]	0.6[1]	13
	1	0.1	17
	1[3]	0.05[3]	18
	22[4]	0.2[5]	
Mesenchymal Tumors			
Ovary: gran-	2	0.4	5

Site & Type	Incidence No.	Incidence %	Reference
ulosa cell tumor or thecoma	2	1.1	8
	2	0.03	10
	1[1]	0.9[1]	13
	4[2]	3.5[2]	13
	11[4]	0.3[5]	
Spleen & liver: hemangioma[6]	1	0.5	3
	9	1.8	4
	7	3.8	8
	8	0.11	10
	3	3.0	12
	6[1]	2.0[1]	13
	5[2]	2.5[2]	13
	2	0.4	14
	1	0.9	15
	2	1.0	16
	44[4]	0.9[5]	
Uterus & uterine tubes: leiomyoma[6]	2	0.4	4
	5	2.7	8
	3	0.1	11
	4[1]	3.1[1]	13
	1	0.5	16
	15[4]	0.4[5]	
Other soft tissue tumors[13]	2	0.2	1
	6	1.2	4
	3	0.6	5
	2	0.5	6
	1	0.5	7
	1	0.5	8
	10	0.14	10
	5	0.05	11
	1	1.0	12
	3[1]	4.3[1]	13
	2	1.8	15
	1	0.5	16
	2	0.2	17
	3[3]	0.2[3]	18
	2	1.2	19
	44[4]	0.7[5]	
Miscellaneous[11,14]			
Unspecified	4	0.06	2

[1] Data from Eppley colony. [2] Data from Hannover colony. [3] Only malignant tumors were listed. [4] Total number. [5] Average percent; obtained by adding the percentages for each type of tumor and dividing by the total number of references, assuming that if there was no incidence for a particular type of tumor in the reference, none existed. [6] Tumors were predominantly benign. [7] Percentages of benign tumors in this reference are given within a range. [10] Tumors are predominantly malignant. [11] All animals examined were males. [12] Tumors occurring too infrequently to be listed separately; they include an adrenal ganglioneuroma, a pituitary adenoma, a pituitary carcinoma, a seminoma, a thymic adenoma, 2 mesotheliomas, and a lacrimal gland adenoma. [13] Include 2 hemangiopericytomas, 2 neurofibroma/sarcomas, 1 hemangioma, 6 chondro- or osteo-sarcomas, 11 fibroma/sarcomas, 3 lipoma/sarcomas, 2 leiomyoma/sarcomas, 2 rhabdomyosarcomas, 3 synoviomas, and 10 undifferentiated sarcomas. [14] This miscellaneous category uncompasses all of the tumor types listed in the table, except those of the liver which are listed separately.

Contributor: Leonard D. Berman

continued

114. NATURALLY OCCURRING TUMORS: HAMSTER

References

1. Ashbel, R. 1945. Nature (London) 155:607. [1000] (1.3%/13)
2. Chesterman, F. C., and A. Pomerance. 1965. Br. J. Cancer 19:802-811. [5604]
3. Della Porta, G. 1961. Cancer Res. 21:575-579. [183] (3.4%/7)
4. Dontenwill, H. J. 1973. Z. Krebsforsch. 80:127-158. [1120]
5. Dunham, L. J., and K. M. Herrold. 1962. J. Natl. Cancer Inst. 29:1047-1067. [630]
6. Finkel, M. P. 1968. Proc. Natl. Acad. Sci. 60:1223-1230. [461] (1.9%/8)
7. Fortner, J. G. 1957. Cancer Res. 10:1153-1156. [223] (17%/40)
8. Fortner, J. G. 1961. Ibid. 21:1491-1498. [181] (73%/130)
9. Horn, K. H., and R. Siewert. 1968. Acta Biol. Med. Ger. 20:103-110. [2390] (1.7%/39)
10. Kirkman, H. 1962. Stanford Med. Bull. 20:163-166. [7200] (11.3%/814)
11. Kirkman, H., and T. F. Algard. 1968. In R. A. Hoffman, et al., ed. The Golden Hamster. Iowa State Univ., Ames. pp. 227-240. [Variable]
12. Lee, K. Y., et al. 1963. Proc. Soc. Exp. Biol. Med. 114:579-582. [101] (15%/15)
13. Pour, P., et al. 1976. J. Natl. Cancer Inst. 56:931-935, 937-948, 949-961, 963-974. [328] (32%/105) for Eppley colony; [203] (41%/83) for Hannover colony.
14. Shubick, P., et al. 1962. Henry Ford Hosp. Int. Symp. Biol. Interact. Norm. Neoplast. Growth, pp. 285-297. [549] (6.2%/34)
15. Sichuk, G., et al. 1966. Cancer Res. 26:2154-2164. [108] (75%/81)
16. Toth, B. 1967. Ibid. 27:1430-1442. [200] (17%/34)
17. Trentin, J. J., et al. 1968. Proc. Soc. Exp. Biol. Med. 127:683-689. [1322] (0.7%/7)
18. Van Hoosier, G. L., Jr., et al. 1971. In National Research Council, Institute of Laboratory Animal Resources, ed. Defining the Laboratory Animal. National Academy of Sciences, Washington, D. C. pp. 450-473. [1671] (0.5%/8)
19. Yabe, Y., et al. 1972. Gann 63:329-336. [156] (6%/9)

115. VIRUS SUSCEPTIBILITY: HAMSTER

Because of its relative lack of indigenous viruses, and its great susceptibility to heterologous agents, the hamster has proven to be of inestimable value to the virologist. Since it has been used as a laboratory animal for a relatively short period, the provenance of some of the viruses now associated with hamster tissues has not as yet been clarified. Many of them are derived obviously from animals housed in the same laboratory. New (and "old") viruses constantly are being tested for their viability in, and their effect on, the hamster. The data below, therefore, can only offer current information on the viruses which proliferate in the hamster or cell cultures thereof.

Method of Injection or Use: s.c. = subcutaneous; TC = tissue culture; i.c. = intracerebral; i.p. = intraperitoneal; i.n. = intranasal; i.m. = intramuscular. **Result:** CNS = central nervous system.

Virus ⟨Synonym⟩	Method of Injection or Use	Result	Reference
DNA Viruses			
Parvoviridae: *Parvovirus* H. Group H-1; H-3; HT; HB[1]	s.c.; TC	Mongoloid deformity or death; tissue culture displays cytopathic changes	76-78
Rat virus ⟨RV⟩	s.c.; TC	Mongoloid deformity or death; tissue culture displays cytopathic changes	32
Lu III	s.c.; TC	Death; cytopathic changes in tissue culture	72,79
MVM ⟨Minute virus of mice⟩	s.c.; TC	Mongolism?	33
		Death; no mongolism	79
TVX	s.c.	Slight illness	79
Papovaviridae *Papillomavirus*: Bovine papillomavirus	s.c.	Papillomas	67
Polyomavirus Polyoma (mouse)	s.c.	Oncogenic	18
BK & JC (human)	s.c.	Oncogenic	54,82,84
SV40 ⟨Simian vacuolating⟩	s.c.	Oncogenic	19,20

[1] H-1, H-3, HT, HB are probably of human origin.

continued

Virus (Synonym)	Method of Injection or Use	Result	Reference
Adenoviridae			
Mastadenovirus			
Human types 2, 5	s.c.	Illness, death	12,56
Human type 3	s.c., i.c.	Weakly oncogenic	28
Human type 5	TC	Intranuclear inclusions	74
Human type 7	s.c., i.c.	Oncogenic	41
Human types 11, 14, 21	s.c.	Weakly oncogenic	40
Human type 12	s.c., i.p., i.c.	Oncogenic	80,88
Human type 18	s.c.	Oncogenic	27
Human type 31	s.c.	Oncogenic	57
Simian SV 1, 11, 23, 25, 30	s.c.	Weakly oncogenic	10
Simian SV 7	i.c.	Oncogenic	59
Simian SV 20	s.c.	Oncogenic	17
Simian SV 33, 37, 38	s.c.	Oncogenic	17
Bovine adenovirus	s.c.; TC	Oncogenic	13
Canine adenovirus	s.c.	Weakly oncogenic	69
Aviadenovirus: CELO	s.c.	Oncogenic	68
	i.p.; TC	Oncogenic	45
Herpetoviridae			
Herpesvirus (Herpes simplex group)			
Human herpesvirus 1 (Herpes simplex encephalitis)	s.c., i.c.	CNS symptoms or death	89
Human herpesvirus 2 (Herpes simplex type 2)	s.c.; TC	Oncogenic	16,52
	Intravaginal	CNS symptoms or death	65
Herpetovirus of horse [2] (Equine herpes; equine influenza; equine abortion)	s.c.	Focal liver necrosis; liver damage or death	2,15
Poxviridae			
Orthopoxvirus: Vaccinia	TC	Cytopathic changes	4
Leporipoxvirus: Myxoma (rabbit)	TC	One report of viral propagation	11
RNA Viruses			
Picornaviridae			
Enterovirus			
Poliovirus (human)	i.c.	Some CNS symptoms & mortality	3,51,62
Coxsackie (human)	s.c.	Lesions in many organs	43
	TC	Cytopathic effects	4
Echoviruses 12, 17, 22, 23, 29 (human)	s.c.	Weakly oncogenic	81
Columbia SK group [3]	i.c., i.p.	Paralysis & death	30
Rhinovirus			
Rhinovirus, MR strain (human)	i.n.	Wheezing, cold symptoms	63
Foot-and-mouth disease	s.c.	Encephalitis & death	50
Reoviridae (Diplornaviruses)			
Reovirus			
Reovirus, type 1	i.c.	Hydrocephalus	46
Reovirus, type 3	s.c.	Weakly oncogenic	81
Orbivirus			
Blue-tongue (sheep)	i.c.	Death	9
Colorado tick fever	i.p.	Splenic changes	5
Togaviridae			
Alphavirus (Arbovirus group A)			
Eastern equine encephalomyelitis (Eastern encephalitis) & western equine encephalomyelitis (western encephalitis)	i.c.	Death	23,85

[2] Unclassified yet as to genus. [3] Primate virus adapted to hamsters via rats and mice.

continued

Virus ⟨Synonym⟩	Method of Injection or Use	Result	Reference
Venezuelan equine encephalomyelitis ⟨Venezuelan equine encephalitis⟩	TC	Lysis of culture	35
Flavivirus ⟨Arbovirus group B⟩			
Dengue, types 1 & 2	i.c., i.p., i.n., s.c.	CNS symptoms & death	14,26,48,64
Japanese encephalitis	i.c., i.p., or i.n.	Death	42
St. Louis ⟨St. Louis encephalitis⟩	i.c., i.p., or i.n.	Death	7,42
West Nile	i.c.	Death	37
Rubivirus: Rubella	Intratracheal	Persistence in lung	53
Orthomyxoviridae ⟨Myxoviruses⟩: *Influenzavirus*—Influenza virus (human)	i.c.	Convulsions with recovery	24
	i.n.	Antibody production	29
	TC	Viral propagation	4,21
Paramyxoviridae			
Paramyxovirus			
Newcastle disease	i.c.	Paralysis & death	4,60
Mumps	i.c.	Paralysis & death	34,47,87
Parainfluenza			
Sendai	i.n.	Pulmonary & renal pathology	6
SA	i.c.	Paralysis & death	70
SV5	TC	Viral propagation	36
Morbillivirus			
Measles	i.c.	CNS symptoms	83
		Chronic myoclonic tremors	86
	TC	Inclusions in dorsal root ganglia cultures	58
Canine distemper	i.c.	Death	8,22
Pneumovirus: Pneumonia virus of mice ⟨PVM⟩	i.n.	Pneumonia & death	25,55
	TC	Viral replication	75
Rhabdoviridae			
Vesiculovirus: Vesicular stomatitis	i.c., i.n.	Death	39
Lyssavirus: Rabies	i.c.	Death	38,61
Retroviridae ⟨Leukoviruses⟩: Type C oncoviruses			
Murine leukemia & lymphoma			
Maloney leukemia	s.c.	Tumors	49
Rauscher erythroleukemia ⟨Rauscher leukemia⟩	TC	Viral transformation	66
Bovine type C oncovirus ⟨Bovine leukemia⟩	s.c.	Wasting disease, some deaths	44
Chicken Rous sarcoma	s.c., i.m.	Oncogenic	1,73
Arenaviridae: *Arenavirus*			
Lymphocytic choriomeningitis	s.c.	Viremia with systemic lesions	71
Machupo & Junin [4/]	i.c.	CNS symptoms & death	31

[4/] Cause Bolivian and Argentine hemorrhagic fevers.

Contributor: Helene Wallace Toolan

Specific References

1. Ahlstrom, C. G., and N. Forsby. 1962. J. Exp. Med. 115:839-852.
2. Anderson, K., and E. Goodpasture. 1942. Am. J. Pathol. 18:555-559.
3. Aronson, S. M., and G. Schwartzman. 1953. Ibid. 29:381-399.
4. Barron, A. L., and D. T. Karzon. 1959. Proc. Soc. Exp. Biol. Med. 100:316-320.
5. Black, W. C., et al. 1947. Am. J. Pathol. 23:217-224.
6. Blanford, G., and D. Charlton. 1977. Am. Rev. Respir. Dis. 115:305-314.
7. Broun, G., et al. 1941. Proc. Soc. Exp. Biol. Med. 46:601-603.
8. Cabasso, V. J., et al. 1955. Ibid. 88:199-202.
9. Cabasso, V. J., et al. 1955. Ibid. 88:678-681.
10. Casto, B. C. 1969. J. Virol. 3:513-519.
11. Chaproniere, D. M., and C. H. Andrewes. 1957. Virology 4:351-365.

continued

12. Conner, J. D. 1970. Proc. Soc. Exp. Biol. Med. 133:655-661.
13. Darbyshire, J. H. 1966. Nature (London) 211:102.
14. Diercks, F. H., et al. 1961. Am. J. Hyg. 73:164-172.
15. Doll, E. R., et al. 1954. Cornell Vet. 44:133-138.
16. Duff, R., and F. Rapp. 1971. Nature (London) New Biol. 233:48-50.
17. Eddy, B. E. 1972. Prog. Exp. Tumor Res. 16:454-496.
18. Eddy, B. E., et al. 1958. J. Natl. Cancer Inst. 20:747-761.
19. Eddy, B. E., et al. 1962. Virology 17:65-75.
20. Girardi, A. J., et al. 1962. Proc. Soc. Exp. Biol. Med. 109:649-660.
21. Grossberg, S. E. 1964. Science 144:1246-1247.
22. Gutierrez, J. C., and J. R. Gorham. 1955. Am. J. Vet. Res. 16:325-330.
23. Havens, W. P., Jr., et al. 1943. J. Exp. Med. 77:139-153.
24. Henle, G., and W. Henle. 1946. Ibid. 84:623-637.
25. Horsfall, F. A., and E. C. Curnan. 1946. Ibid. 83:43-64.
26. Hotta, S., et al. 1961. Jpn. J. Microbiol. 5:77-88.
27. Huebner, R. J., et al. 1962. Proc. Soc. Exp. Biol. Med. 48:2051-2059.
28. Huebner, R. J., et al. 1965. Proc. Natl. Acad. Sci. USA 54:381-388.
29. Jennings, R., et al. 1976. Med. Microbiol. Immunol. 162:217-226.
30. Jungeblut, C. W. 1958. In C. Hallauer and K. F. Meyer, ed. Handbuch der Virusforschung. Springer-Verlag, Wien. v. 4, pp. 459-580.
31. Justines, G., and K. M. Johnson. 1968. Am. J. Trop. Med. Hyg. 17:788-790.
32. Kilham, L. 1961. Virology 13:141-143.
33. Kilham, L., and G. Margolis. 1970. Proc. Soc. Exp. Biol. Med. 133:1447-1452.
34. Kilham, L., and J. L. Overman. 1953. J. Immunol. 70:147-151.
35. Kissling, R. E. 1957. Proc. Soc. Exp. Biol. Med. 96:290-294.
36. Klenk, H. D., and P. W. Choppin. 1969. Virology 38:255-268.
37. Koprowski, H., and E. H. Lennette. 1946. J. Exp. Med. 84:181-190.
38. Koprowski, H., et al. 1954. J. Immunol. 72:94-106.
39. Kowalczyk, T., and C. A. Brandly. 1955. Am. J. Vet. Res. 15:98-101.
40. Lacy, S., and M. Green. 1967. J. Gen. Virol. 1:413-418.
41. Larson, V. M., et al. 1965. Proc. Soc. Exp. Biol. Med. 11:15-24.
42. Lennette, E. H. 1941. Ibid. 47:178-181.
43. Lou, T. Y., et al. 1961. Arch. Gesamte Virusforsch. 10:451-464.
44. Lussier, G., and V. Pavilanis. 1969. Can. J. Comp. Med. 33:81-83.
45. Mancini, I. O., et al. 1969. Nature (London) 220:190-191.
46. Margolis, G., and L. Kilham. 1969. Lab. Invest. 21:189-198.
47. Margolis, G., et al. 1974. J. Neuropathol. Exp. Neurol. 33:13-28.
48. Meiklejohn, G., et al. 1952. Am. J. Trop. Med. Hyg. 1:59-65.
49. Moloney, J. B. 1962. Fed. Proc. Fed. Am. Soc. Exp. Biol. 21:19-31.
50. Mowat, G. N., and W. G. Chapman. 1962. Nature (London) 194:253-255.
51. Moyer, A. W., et al. 1952. Proc. Soc. Exp. Biol. Med. 81:512-518.
52. Nahmias, A. J., et al. 1970. Ibid. 134:1065-1069.
53. Oxford, J. S., and G. C. Schild. 1966. Virology 28:780-782.
54. Padgett, B. L., et al. 1977. Cancer Res. 37:718-720.
55. Pearson, H. E., and M. D. Eaton. 1940. Proc. Soc. Exp. Biol. Med. 45:677-679.
56. Pereira, H. G., et al. 1962. Nature (London) 196:244-245.
57. Pereira, M. S., et al. 1965. Lancet 1:21-23.
58. Raine, C. S., et al. 1971. J. Virol. 8:318-329.
59. Rapp, F., et al. 1969. Cancer Res. 29:1173-1178.
60. Reagan, R. L., et al. 1948. Proc. Soc. Exp. Biol. Med. 68:293-294.
61. Reagan, R. L., et al. 1952. Am. J. Trop. Med. Hyg. 1:987-989.
62. Reagan, R. L., et al. 1954. Proc. Soc. Exp. Biol. Med. 87:581.
63. Reagan, R. L., et al. 1956. Arch. Pathol. 61:420-421.
64. Reagan, R. L., et al. 1956. Am. J. Trop. Med. Hyg. 5:809-811.
65. Renis, H. E. 1975. Proc. Soc. Exp. Biol. Med. 150:723-727.
66. Rhim, J. S., et al. 1970. Int. J. Cancer 5:28-38.
67. Robl, M. G., and C. Olson. 1968. Cancer Res. 28:1596-1604.
68. Sarma, P. S., et al. 1965. Science 149:1108.
69. Sarma, P. S., et al. 1967. Nature (London) 215:293-295.
70. Schultz, E. W., and K. Habel. 1959. J. Immunol. 82:274-278.
71. Smadel, J. E., and M. J. Ward. 1942. J. Exp. Med. 75:581-592.
72. Soike, K. F., et al. 1976. Arch. Virol. 51:235-241.
73. Svoboda, J., and V. Klement. 1963. Folia Biol. (Prague) 9:403-411.
74. Takahashi, M., et al. 1966. Proc. Soc. Exp. Biol. Med. 122:740-746.
75. Tennant, R. W., and T. G. Ward. 1962. Ibid. 111:395-398.
76. Toolan, H. W. 1960. Science 131:1446-1448.
77. Toolan, H. W. 1968. Int. Rev. Exp. Pathol. 6:135-180.
78. Toolan, H. W. 1972. Prog. Exp. Tumor Res. 16:410-425.
79. Toolan, H. W., and K. A. O. Ellem. 1979. CRC Handb. Ser. Clin. Lab. Sci., Sect. H, 1(2):3-15.
80. Trentin, J. J. 1962. Science 137:835-841.
81. Trentin, J. J., et al. 1969. Proc. Soc. Exp. Biol. Med. 132:912-915.
82. Uchida, S., et al. 1976. Gann 67:857-868.
83. Waksman, B. H., et al. 1962. J. Neuropathol. Exp. Neurol. 21:25-49.

continued

84. Walker, D. L., et al. 1973. Science 181:674-676.
85. Watson, D. W., and J. E. Smadel. 1943. Proc. Soc. Exp. Biol. Med. 52:101-104.
86. Wear, D., and F. Rapp. 1971. J. Immunol. 107:1593-1598.
87. Wolinsky, J. S., et al. 1976. J. Infect. Dis. 133:260-267.
88. Yabe, Y., et al. 1963. Proc. Soc. Exp. Biol. Med. 113:221-224.
89. Zarafonetis, C. J. D., et al. 1944. Am. J. Pathol. 20:429-445.

General References

90. Eddy, B. E. 1972. Prog. Exp. Tumor Res. 16:454-496.
91. Frenkel, J. K. 1972. Ibid. 16:326-367.
92. Handler, A. H., et al. 1968. In R. A. Hoffman, et al., ed. The Golden Hamster. Iowa State Univ., Ames. pp. 215-226.
93. Toolan, H. W. 1978. Fed. Proc. Fed. Am. Soc. Exp. Biol. 37:2065-2068.

116. MODELS OF SLOW VIRUS DISEASES: HAMSTER

Incubation Period: i.c. = intracerebral.

Disease ⟨Synonym⟩	Virus	Natural Host	Incubation Period	Pathobiologic Features	Reference
Progressive multifocal leukoencephalopathy ⟨PML⟩	JC (Polyoma virus)	Human	4-6 mo after i.c. inoculation of day-old animals	Produces high incidence of malignant brain tumors rather than the degenerative leukoencephalopathy seen in natural disease	11
Subacute sclerosing panencephalitis ⟨SSPE⟩	Measles (Paramyxovirus)	Human	Variable, depending on age at inoculation	Immune status of hamster is important regulator of viral replication & establishment of defective cell-associated infection	1,3, 4
Lymphocytic choriomeningitis ⟨LCM⟩	Lymphocytic choriomeningitis (Arenavirus)	Mouse, hamster	>3 mo	Usually non-pathogenic if inoculated into adults, but can produce late-onset vasculitis & glomerulonephritis with persisting viremia, viruria & complement fixing antibody if inoculated into newborns	2, 10
Scrapie	Unconventional	Sheep, goat	8 wk after i.c. inoculation with hamster-adapted scrapie agent from sheep brain	Shorter incubation periods & higher brain titers than mouse model	5,8, 12
Transmissible mink encephalopathy ⟨TME⟩	Scrapie-like	Mink	17 wk after i.c. inoculation with hamster-adapted TME agent from mink brain	Faster, more convenient bioassays than carnivore or primate models	8,9
Creutzfeldt-Jakob disease	Scrapie-like	Human	18 mo after i.c. inoculation with human brain	Produces spongiform encephalopathy similar to that seen in the natural human disease, and in TME & scrapie	6

Contributor: Richard F. Marsh

References

1. Byington, D. P., and K. P. Johnson. 1975. Lab. Invest. 32:91-97.
2. Igel, H. J., et al. 1969. Am. J. Pathol. 55(Abstr):12a-13a.
3. Johnson, K. P., and E. Norrby. 1974. Exp. Mol. Pathol. 21:166-171.
4. Johnson, K. P., et al. 1975. Infect. Immun. 12:1464-1469.

continued

5. Kimberlin, R. H., and C. Walker. 1977. J. Gen. Virol. 34:295-304.
6. Manuelidis, E. E., et al. 1977. Lancet 1:479.
7. Marsh, R. F., and R. P. Hanson. 1978. Fed. Proc. Fed. Am. Soc. Exp. Biol. 37:2076-2078.
8. Marsh, R. F., and R. H. Kimberlin. 1975. J. Infect. Dis. 131:104-110.
9. Marsh, R. F., et al. 1969. Ibid. 120:713-719.
10. Smadel, J. E., and M. G. Wall. 1942. J. Exp. Med. 75:581-592.
11. Walker, D. L., et al. 1973. Science 181:674-676.
12. Zlotnik, I. 1963. Lancet 2:1072.

117. TOXICOLOGY: HAMSTER

Target: CNS = central nervous system. **Strain:** S = susceptible; R = resistant. Data in brackets refer to the column heading in brackets.

Substance ⟨Synonym⟩	Route [Dose]	Target	Strain	Effect	Reference
Calcium cyclamate	Gavage [32 g/kg body wt for 6 d]	Heart	S: BIO 2.4[1/]	Calcification	2
			R: Colony of Eppley Institute (Omaha, Nebraska)	Calcification	1
Cigarette smoke	Inhalation	CNS	S: Random-bred[2/]	Death; mean survival time, 86 min	3
			R: BIO 15.16	Death; mean survival time, 244 min	3
Nicotine tartrate	Intraperitoneal	CNS	S: Random-bred[2/]	Death; LD_{50}, 125 mg/kg body wt	3
			R: BIO 15.16	Death; LD_{50}, 320 mg/kg body wt	3
Thalidomide ⟨2-(2,6-Dioxo-3-piperidinyl)-1H-isoindole-1,3(2H)-dione⟩	Feeding (not gavage) for life-time [0.6% of diet]	Fetal tissue	S: BIO 4.24, BIO 45.5, BIO X.3	Malformations	4
			R: BIO 4.22, BIO 12.14, BIO 87.20	Malformations	4
Trichlorofluoromethane ⟨Freon 11⟩	Inhalation	Heart	S: BIO 82.62	Increased susceptibility to cardiac arrhythmias	5
			R: Random-bred	Increased susceptibility to cardiac arrhythmias	5

[1/] Formerly LSH. [2/] Somewhat more susceptible than BIO strains.

Contributor: Freddy Homburger

References
1. Althoff, J., et al. 1975. Cancer Lett. 1:21-24.
2. Bajusz, E. 1969. Nature (London) 223:406-407.
3. Bernfeld, P., and F. Homburger. 1972. Toxicol. Appl. Pharmacol. 22:324-325(Abstr. 133).
4. Homburger, F., et al. 1965. Ibid. 7:686-693.
5. Taylor, G. J., and R. T. Drew. 1975. Ibid. 32:177-183.

118. CHINESE AND ARMENIAN HAMSTERS

Representative members from two (*barabensis* and *migratorius*) of the four subgroups of the genus *Cricetulus* (Old World dwarf hamsters) are (1) the Chinese or striped-back hamster, *Cricetulus barabensis griseus* [ref. 1, 2, 10, 11, 20],

continued

and (2) the Armenian or gray hamster, *Cricetulus migratorius migratorius (C. migratorius phaeus)* [ref. 10, 11].

The Chinese hamster was first introduced as a laboratory specimen in 1919 [ref. 15]. Subsequently, it was found to be highly susceptible to experimental leishmaniasis [ref. 14, 17, 28, 35], tubercle bacilli [ref. 19], pneumococcus [ref. 26], diphtheria [ref. 29], rabies [ref. 30], influenza [ref. 31], *Monilia* [ref. 19], encephalitis [ref. 5], and *Trichinella* [ref. 24]. Historical and cytogenetic relationships of all species of hamsters are documented in reference 34. Practical breeding procedures are outlined in references 3, 8, 21, 25, 27, 32, and 33. Pertinent references are also available for the following: growth and reproduction [ref. 4], the reproductive process [ref. 22], testicular development [ref. 6], sperm development [ref. 9], fertilization and early development [ref. 23], cheek pouch and microcirculation [ref. 7, 12], behavioral aspects [ref. 16], and breeding activity in simulated environments [ref. 13].

The historic and taxonomic relationships of dwarf hamsters to the Syrian hamster, *Mesocricetus auratus auratus,* that led to the introduction of the latter as a laboratory animal in studies pertaining to Mediterranean kala-azar (*Leishmania* spp.), are documented in reference 34.

References

1. Allen, G. M. 1938. The Mammals of China and Mongolia. American Museum of Natural History, New York. v. 11.
2. Argyropulo, A. Z. 1933. Z. Saeugetierkd 8:129-149.
3. Avery, T. L. 1968. Lab. Anim. Care 18:151-159.
4. Chang, C. Y., and H. Wu. 1938. Chin. J. Physiol. 13:109-118.
5. Chang, N., et al. 1951. Chin. Med. J. 69:420-426.
6. Chung, S. 1927. Ibid. 41:864-865.
7. Copley, A. L. 1962. Biorheology 1:3-14.
8. Derks, G. I. 1968. Biotechnik 7:89-98.
9. Douglas, L. T. 1965. Genetica 36:59-64.
10. Ellerman, J. R. 1941. The Families and Genera of Living Rodents. British Museum (Natural History), London. v. 2.
11. Ellerman, J. R., and T. C. S. Morrison-Scott. 1951. Checklist of Palaearctic and Indian Mammals, 1756-1946. British Museum (Natural History), London.
12. Fulton, G. P., et al. 1954. J. Lab. Clin. Med. 44:145-148.
13. Herter, K. 1956. Z. Saeugetierkd. 21:161-171.
14. Hindle, E., and W. S. Patton. 1926. Proc. R. Soc. London B100:374-379.
15. Hsieh, E. T. 1919. Natl. Med. J. China 5:20-24.
16. Jöchle, W. 1963. Z. Versuchstierkd. 3:30-33.
17. Kala-azar Prevention Conference, 1946. 1949. Chin. Med. J. 67:24-46.
18. Korns, J. H., and G. Y. C. Lu. 1927. Proc. Soc. Exp. Biol. Med. 24:807-809.
19. Kurotchkin, T. J., and C. E. Lim. 1930. Natl. Med. J. China 16:332-337.
20. Milne-Edwards, H., and A. Comte. 1836. Cahiers d'histoire naturelle, à l'usage des collèges et des écoles normales primaires. Ed. 2. Crochard, Paris. v. 2.
21. Moore, W. 1965. Lab. Anim. Care 15:94-101.
22. Parkes, A. S. 1931. Proc. R. Soc. London B108:138-147.
23. Pickworth, S., et al. 1968. Anat. Rec. 162:197-207.
24. Ritterson, A. L. 1967. J. Parasitol. 53:652-653.
25. Schwentker, V. 1957. In A. N. Worden and W. Lane-Petter, ed. The UFAW Handbook on the Care and Management of Laboratory Animals. Ed. 2. Universities Federation for Animal Welfare, London. pp. 176-181.
26. Sia, R. H. P. 1930. Natl. Med. J. China 16:65-67.
27. Smith, C. 1957. J. Anim. Tech. Assoc. 7:59-60.
28. Smyly, H. J., and C. W. Young. 1923. Proc. Soc. Exp. Biol. Med. 21:354-356.
29. Tung, T., and S. H. Zia. 1937. Ibid. 37:10-21.
30. Yen, A. C. H. 1936. Ibid. 34:315-318.
31. Yen, C. H. 1940. Chin. Med. J. (Suppl. 3):342-348.
32. Yerganian, G. 1958. J. Natl. Cancer Inst. 20:705-727.
33. Yerganian, G. 1967. In Universities Federation for Animal Welfare, ed. The UFAW Handbook on the Care and Management of Laboratory Animals. Ed. 3. Livingstone, Edinburgh. pp. 340-352.
34. Yerganian, G. 1972. Prog. Exp. Tumor Res. 16:2-41.
35. Young, C. W., et al. 1923. Proc. Soc. Exp. Biol. Med. 21:357-359.

Part I. Characteristics of Inbred Strains

Generations Inbred: Number of generations of brother x sister mating, as of March 1977. **Source:** For full name, *see* list of HOLDERS at front of book.

ABBREVIATIONS	
AI-p = autoimmune-prone	il = ileocecal lymphoma
AIL = angio-immunoblastic lymphadenopathy	ls = lymphosarcoma
bb = "brittle-bristle" (sex-limited (female) autoimmunity)	os = osteogenic sarcoma
dd = diabetes mellitus	sz = seizures
hep = hepatocarcinoma	tf = tumor-free
hl = histiocytic lymphoma	ut = uterine (adeno)carcinoma
IBS = immunoblastic sarcoma of B-cells	

continued

Part I. Characteristics of Inbred Strains

Strain	Generations Inbred	Source	Phenotypic Characteristics
Chinese Hamster			
A/GY	42	NU	bb, hep[L], ls[L], ut[L]
8Aa/GY	27	NU	bb, hep[L], ut[L]
B/GY	39	NU, UPJ	dd, ut[L]
C/GY	17	NU	os[L], sz

Strain	Generations Inbred	Source	Phenotypic Characteristics
Armenian Hamster			
IV/GY	29	NU	AI-p, AIL[L], IBS[L], hep[L]
IVa/GY	8	NU	AI-p, hep[L], hl[L]
VIII/GY	29	NU	AI-p, il
XVI/GY	18	NU	tf

[L] Cell and tumor lines (classic diploid & aneuploid) with these characteristics are retained in Cell Repository of Laboratories of Environmental Biomedical Sciences, Northeastern University (NU).

Contributor: George Yerganian

Part II. Meiosis and Mitosis

Diploid chromosome number for each—Chinese hamster and Armenian hamster—is 22, including sex chromosomes.

Specification	Reference
Chinese Hamster	
In situ	
Meiotic cycle (♂)	
General descriptions	43,57
Sex chromosomes	
DNA replication	39,53-55
Effect of bromodeoxyuridine	38
Effect of X rays	5
Localized chiasma	26
Nuclear rotation	56
Pairing mechanism	12,15,21,31-34, 40,53,57
Viable translocations	
Spontaneous	37
X-ray-induced	57
Mitotic cycle	
Bone marrow	52
Hydrocarbons	22
Strontium-90	6
X rays	2,5
Cheek pouch	45,46
Corneal epithelium	3
Regenerating liver	51
Thyroid	36
In vitro: Cultured cells	
Chromatid segregation	9
Chromosomal RNA	24
Chromosome non-disjunction	8

Specification	Reference
DNA replication	48,50
Endogenous (latent) cytomegalovirus	65
Heteromorphic X chromosomes	7,17,41,42,59, 68,69
Histone synthesis	16
Lactate dehydrogenase	23
Mitotic apparatus	4
Mitotic synchrony	1,49,67
Nucleolar association	20
Nucleolar extrusions	30
Retention of diploidy	19,60,61,63
RNA synthesis	10,13,14,44
Secondary constriction of X chromosome	11,18,63
Armenian Hamster	
In situ: Meiotic cycle (♂)	
General descriptions	28,32,35
Sex chromosomes	
Localized chiasma	28
Pairing mechanism	28
Translocations	25,29
In vitro: Cultured cells	60
Adenovirus type 12 transformation	58,64,65
DNA replication patterns of sex chromosomes	47
Immunoblastic sarcoma of B-cells	66
Karyotype	27,62

Contributor: George Yerganian

continued

118. CHINESE AND ARMENIAN HAMSTERS

Part II. Meiosis and Mitosis

References

1. Anderson, E. C., and D. F. Petersen. 1965. Exp. Cell Res. 36:423-426.
2. Bender, M. A., and P. C. Gooch. 1961. Int. J. Radiat. Biol. 4:175-184.
3. Brewen, J. G. 1964. Science 138:820-822.
4. Brinkley, B. R., et al. 1967. J. Ultrastruct. Res. 19:1-18.
5. Brooks, A. L., and L. F. W. Lengemann. 1967. Radiat. Res. 32:587-595.
6. Brooks, A. L., and R. O. McClellan. 1968. Nature (London) 219:761-763.
7. Corey, M. J., et al. 1967. Cytogenetics 6:314-320.
8. Cox, D. M., and T. T. Puck. 1969. Ibid. 8:158-169.
9. Deaven, L. L., and E. Stubblefield. 1968. Exp. Cell Res. 55:132-135.
10. Dewey, W. C., and H. H. Miller. 1969. Ibid. 57:63-70.
11. Dewey, W. C., et al. 1966. Science 152:519-521.
12. Eberle, P. 1964. Genetica 35:34-46.
13. Enger, M. D., and R. A. Tobey. 1969. J. Cell Biol. 42:308-315.
14. Enger, M. D., et al. 1968. Ibid. 36:583-593.
15. Fredga, K., and B. Santesson. 1964. Hereditas 52:36-48.
16. Gurley, L. R., and J. M. Hardin. 1968. Arch. Biochem. Biophys. 128:285-292.
17. Hsu, T. C. 1964. J. Cell Biol. 23:53-62.
18. Hsu, T. C., and C. E. Somers. 1961. Proc. Natl. Acad. Sci. USA 47:396-403.
19. Hsu, T. C., and M. T. Zenzes. 1964. J. Natl. Cancer Inst. 32:857-869.
20. Hsu, T. C., et al. 1965. J. Cell Biol. 26:539-553.
21. Husted, L., et al. 1957. Va. J. Sci. 8:121-127.
22. Kato, R., et al. 1969. Hereditas 61:1-8.
23. Klevecz, R. R. 1969. J. Cell Biol. 43:207-219.
24. Klevecz, R. R., and T. C. Hsu. 1964. Proc. Natl. Acad. Sci. USA 52:811-817.
25. Lavappa, K. S. 1974. Lab. Anim. Sci. 24:62-65.
26. Lavappa, K. S. 1974. Ibid. 24:817-819.
27. Lavappa, K. S. 1977. Cytologia 42:65-72.
28. Lavappa, K. S., and G. Yerganian. 1970. Exp. Cell Res. 61:159-172.
29. Lavappa, K. S., and G. Yerganian. 1971. Science 172:171-174.
30. Longwell, A. C., and G. Yerganian. 1965. J. Natl. Cancer Inst. 34:53-69.
31. Matthey, R. 1952. Chromosoma 5:113-118.
32. Matthey, R. 1953. Rev. Suisse Zool. 60:225-283.
33. Matthey, R. 1959. Ibid. 66:175-209.
34. Matthey, R. 1960. Caryologia 13:199-223.
35. Matthey, R. 1961. Rev. Suisse Zool. 68:41-61.
36. Moore, W., and M. Colvin. 1968. Int. J. Radiat. Biol. 14:161-167.
37. Moorthy, A. S., et al. 1976. Nucleus (Calcutta) 19:35-40.
38. Mukherjee, A. B. 1968. Mutat. Res. 6:173-174.
39. Muller, D., and F. Grehn. 1972. Beitr. Pathol. 146:63-78.
40. Ohno, S., and C. Weiler. 1962. Chromosoma 13:106-110.
41. Pflueger, O., and J. J. Yunis. 1966. Exp. Cell Res. 44:413-420.
42. Pflueger, O., and J. J. Yunis. 1966. Nature (London) 210:1074-1075.
43. Pontecorvo, G. 1943. Proc. R. Soc. Edinburgh B62:32-42.
44. Saponara, A. G., and M. D. Enger. 1966. Biochim. Biophys. Acta 119:492-500.
45. Sobkowski, F. J. 1964. J. Dent. Res. 45:762-763.
46. Sobkowski, F. J. 1964. Exp. Cell Res. 33:594-597.
47. Sonnenschein, C., and G. Yerganian. 1969. Ibid. 57:13-18.
48. Stubblefield, E. 1965. J. Cell Biol. 25:137-147.
49. Stubblefield, E., and R. R. Kelvecz. 1965. Exp. Cell Res. 40:660-664.
50. Taylor, J. H. 1960. J. Biophys. Biochem. Cytol. 7:455-464.
51. Tonomura, A., and G. Yerganian. 1956. Genetics 41:664-665.
52. Tonomura, A., and G. Yerganian. 1957. Anat. Rec. 127:377.
53. Utakoji, T. 1966. Chromosoma 18:449-454.
54. Utakoji, T. 1966. Exp. Cell Res. 42:585-596.
55. Utakoji, T., and T. C. Hsu. 1965. Cytogenetics 4:295-315.
56. Yao, K. T. S., and D. J. Ellingson. 1969. Exp. Cell Res. 55:39-42.
57. Yerganian, G. 1959. Cytologia 24:66-75.
58. Yerganian, G., and S. S. Cho. 1966. J. Cell Biol. 31:126A.
59. Yerganian, G., and L. A. Grodzins. 1962. J. Histochem. Cytochem. 10:665.
60. Yerganian, G., and K. S. Lavappa. 1971. Chemical Mutagens. Plenum, New York.
61. Yerganian, G., and M. J. Leonard. 1961. Science 133:1600-1601.
62. Yerganian, G., and S. A. Papoyan. 1965. Hereditas 52:307-319.
63. Yerganian, G., et al. 1964. Cytogenetics of Cells in Culture. Academic, New York.
64. Yerganian, G., et al. 1968. J. Cell Biol. 39:146A.
65. Yerganian, G., et al. 1968. Natl. Cancer Inst. Monogr. 29:241-268.
66. Yerganian, G., et al. 1978. Am. J. Pathol. 91:209-212.
67. Yu, C. K., and W. K. Sinclair. 1967. J. Natl. Cancer Inst. 39:619-632.
68. Zakharov, A. F., et al. 1964. Ibid. 33:935-956.
69. Zakharov, A. F., et al. 1966. Ibid. 36:215-232.

continued

Part III. Diabetes Mellitus

Specification	Reference
Aging & glomerulonephrosis	18
Blood glucose regulation	3
Cortisone & growth hormone	9
Fatty acid metabolism	8

Specification	Reference
Genetic aspects	7,28,29
Histometry of testicular tissue	26
Hypoglycemic therapy	23
Insulin secretion	25
Pancreatic adenocarcinoma	24
Pancreatic islets	1,2,4-6

Specification	Reference
Pathology, adult	21,25
newborn	22
Periodontia, dental caries	10,11,27
Renal lesions	20,25
Retinopathy	19
Serum proteins	13-17
Stress and glycosuria	12

Contributor: George Yerganian

References

1. Boquist, L. 1967. Acta Soc. Med. Ups. 72:331-344.
2. Boquist, L. 1967. Ibid. 72:345-357.
3. Boquist, L. 1967. Ibid. 72:358-375.
4. Boquist, L. 1968. Virchows Arch. B1:157-168.
5. Boquist, L. 1968. Ibid. B1:169-181.
6. Boquist, L. 1968. Z. Zellforsch. 89:519-532.
7. Butler, L. 1967. Diabetologia 3:124-129.
8. Campbell, J., and G. R. Green. 1966. Can. J. Physiol. Pharmacol. 44:47-57.
9. Campbell, J., et al. 1966. Endocrinology 79:749-756.
10. Cohen, M. M., et al. 1961. Am. J. Med. 31:864-867.
11. Cohen, M. M., et al. 1963. J. Oral Surg. 16:104-112.
12. Ehrentheil, O. F., et al. 1964. Diabetes 13:83-86.
13. Gerritsen, G. C., and W. E. Dulin. 1966. Ibid. 15:331-335.
14. Green, M. N., and G. Yerganian. 1963. Ibid. 12:369.
15. Green, M. N., and G. Yerganian. 1964. Excerpta Med. Int. Congr. Ser. 74:53(Abstr. 102).
16. Green, M. N., et al. 1960. Experientia 16:503-504.
17. Green, M. N., et al. 1963. Nature (London) 197:396.
18. Guttman, P. H., et al. 1960. Am. J. Pathol. 37:293-307.
19. Hausler, H. R., et al. 1963. Invest. Ophthalmol. 2:378-383.
20. Lawe, I. E. 1962. Arch. Pathol. 73:166-174.
21. Meier, H., and G. Yerganian. 1959. Proc. Soc. Exp. Biol. Med. 100:810-815.
22. Meier, H., and G. Yerganian. 1961. Diabetes 10:12-18.
23. Meier, H., and G. Yerganian. 1961. Ibid. 10:19-21.
24. Poel, W. E., and G. Yerganian. 1961. Am. J. Med. 31:861-863.
25. Renold, E. E., and E. W. Dulin. 1967. Diabetologia 3:63-286.
26. Schoffling, K., et al. 1967. Acta Endocrinol. 54:335-346.
27. Sklar, G., et al. 1962. J. Periodontol. 33:14-21.
28. Yerganian, G. 1964. Ciba Found. Colloq. Endocrinol. 15:25-41.
29. Yerganian, G. 1965. In B. S. Leibel and G. A. Wrenshall, ed. On the Nature and Treatment of Diabetes. Excerpta Medica Foundation, Amsterdam. pp. 612-626.

IV. GUINEA PIG

ORIGIN OF THE DOMESTIC GUINEA PIG AND OF INBRED STRAINS

The guinea pig (*Cavia porcellus*) became known to Europeans in the 16th century when the Spaniards invaded Peru and found the animals being bred by the natives for food. When the conquistadores returned to Europe, they took some of the guinea pigs with them as pets.

Guinea pigs are still bred for food by the Peruvian Indians. Castle, on a trip to Peru in 1913, discovered that the Indians kept as many as 40 on the floors of their adobe cabins. Escape was prevented by a high (38-cm) sill. Most of the animals were piebalds or tricolors of familiar colors. Some, however, were of unfamiliar colors—combinations with two mutant genes that seem to have been unknown in Europe or the United States. [ref. 1, 7]

The diversely colored guinea pigs bred by the Incas in the 16th century were obviously not merely caged wild animals. The closest wild species in Peru is the wild cavy, *C. cutleri*, an extremely agile little animal (weight ∿400 g). Its light, cream-tinged, gray coloring effectively aids concealment in dried grass. Animals of the species *C. porcellus* are much more sluggish. The adult males of diverse inbred strains vary in weight from 800 to 1000 g, the latter weight being roughly that of the typical random-bred strains [ref. 4]. Castle derived a strain from animals purchased from Peruvian Indians in which the males averaged ∿1200 g.

That *C. cutleri* actually was the wild ancestor is strongly indicated by the complete fertility of the hybrids of both sexes [ref. 1]. In contrast, crosses of *C. porcellus* with the wild cavy of Brazil, *C. rufescens*, resulted in fertile females but sterile males. In successive backcrosses of fertile females to males of *C. porcellus*, fertile males first appeared in the 7/8 bloods. Only gradually did the percentage frequency rise, the rate being close to that expected if male fertility depended on the shuffling off of eight independently segregating genes (or chromosomes) of *C. rufescens*. [ref. 2]

It is also interesting that while the agouti factor of *C. cutleri* was found to be indistinguishable from that of *C. porcellus* in segregants from backcrosses to recessive black guinea pigs, the agouti factor of the somewhat darker *C. rufescens* proved to have an effect intermediate between the agouti factor of *C. porcellus* and the recessive black. In later backcrosses to black guinea pigs, the agouti segregants were almost black at birth, developing later only slight yellow ticking on back and belly. However, the golden agoutis, in parallel experiments with *C. cutleri*, had strongly ticked backs and yellow bellies. A series of three alleles was demonstrated, with "A^r" of *C. rufescens* recessive to "A" of *C. porcellus* or of *C. cutleri* but dominant over black "a." Fertile, ticked-bellied agouti males were obtained, indicating that the A-locus was not among those that had to be shuf-

fled off to permit male fertility. The gene "A^r" was thus introduced into the guinea pig from a foreign species.

The most extensive inbreeding experiment with guinea pigs was started in 1906 by G. M. Rommel, chief of the Animal Husbandry Division, Bureau of Animal Industry, U.S. Department of Agriculture. The Bureau had maintained since 1894 a colony of ∿300 guinea pigs (at one time the colony was reduced to 54). In 1906, 24 females mated with a smaller number of males, all from the colony, became the founders of inbred families 1-24, while 12 other females from the colony were mated with males from outside to become the founders of families 31-42. All of the families but one (No. 4) were to be maintained exclusively by brother x sister mating; propagation for family 4 would be by parent x offspring mating. Seven of the first set and five of the second set were, however, lost by the second generation, and family 4 was never analyzed. This left 16 families of set 1 (traced back to only 4 founder males) and seven families of set 2 (traced back to 5 founder males) that persisted long enough (at least six years) to provide significant data.

In 1915, S. Wright took over the task of analyzing the recorded data from some 30,000 animals, and of continuing the experiments. By this time, five more families had become extinct, in spite of efforts to maintain them, leaving 18. In the next few years, these were reduced to the five most vigorous (families 2, 13, 32, 35, and 39), to obtain space for extensive crossbreeding experiments. All five families were traceable to different males. By late 1915, these families had averaged approximately 10.5 generations of sib mating, but because of the continual branching, there were only a few generations of common inbred ancestry in each family. This was remedied as rapidly as practicable by eliminating lagging branches. Thus, family 35 came to be descended from a single mating of generation 12 (11 of sib mating) by 1921. The other families lagged somewhat.

Data were published in 1922 [ref. 8, 9] on the average decline of each aspect of vigor (size and frequency of litters, percentages born alive and percentages weaned of those born alive, birth weight and gain to weaning at 33 days) from 1906 to 1920, relative to a fairly large control stock, and on the differentiation among the 23 inbred families in the periods 1900-10 and 1911-15. The separate averages for the five leading inbred families and for the others collectively—first crosses, two generations of renewed sib mating, second crosses bringing together three or four inbred families, and the controls—were compared in each case with the contemporary inbred average for 1916-19, which was based on the inbred averages for each three-month period, weighted by the number born in that period in the group

continued

505

under consideration. The rather extreme seasonal irregularities in this period made it necessary to insure, so far as practicable, contemporaneity in the paired comparisons [ref. 10].

The annual averages for the retained inbred families and for the controls were compared over the period 1916-24 by Wright and Eaton [ref. 13]. The same paper gives the history from 1906-24, with respect to the various characters, of each of the considerable number of branches into which the five leading families were divided.

For information on inbred families used in numerous studies of special traits (white-spotting, digit number, otocephaly, sizes and shapes of internal organs, resistance to tuberculosis, and transplantation responses), consult references 11

and 12. For the results of relatively recent studies in immunogenetics, and biochemical genetics in which the two still extant families (2 and 13) have been used, as well as the earlier studies, consult reference 3.

A less extensive inbreeding experiment with guinea pigs is reported in references 5 and 6. In that experiment, 14 strains were started in 1926 and maintained by brother x sister mating, producing a total of 9301 young. One strain was lost in the fourth generation and 10 more by 1953, leaving one that reached the 20th generation and two the 25th in 1953.

In recent years, a number of new lines, of various degrees of inbreeding, have been started (*see* Table 119).

Contributor: Sewall Wright

References
1. Castle, W. E. 1916. Carnegie Inst. Washington Publ. 241:3-55.
2. Detlefsen, J. A. 1914. Ibid. 205.
3. Festing, M. F. W. 1976. In J. E. Wagner and P. J. Manning, ed. The Biology of the Guinea Pig. Academic, New York. pp. 99-120.
4. McPhee, H. C., and O. N. Eaton. 1931. U.S. Dep. Agric. Tech. Bull. 222.
5. Mehner, A. 1950. Z. Tierz. Zuechtungsbiol. 58:339-350.
6. Mehner, A. 1956. Ibid. 66:149-172.
7. Wright, S. 1916. Carnegie Inst. Washington Publ. 241: 57-121.
8. Wright, S. 1922. U.S. Dep. Agric. Bull. 1090:1-36.
9. Wright, S. 1922. Ibid. 1090:37-63.
10. Wright, S. 1922. Ibid. 1121.
11. Wright, S. 1968. Evolution and the Genetics of Populations. Univ. of Chicago Press, Chicago. v. 1.
12. Wright, S. 1977. Ibid. v. 3.
13. Wright, S., and O. N. Eaton. 1929. U.S. Dep. Agric. Tech. Bull. 103.

The importance of the guinea pig to medical research is demonstrated by its synonymity in several languages with the term "experimental subject"—French (cobaye), German (Meerschweinchen), and, of course, English. Lavoisier is credited as being the first scientist to have used the guinea pig in research [ref. 32], in order to measure heat production. At the turn of this century, its widespread use for diagnosis and study of infections, such as tuberculosis [ref. 29], contributed to its popularity as a laboratory rodent.

Among small laboratory animals, the guinea pig most closely resembles man in hormonal balance [ref. 44], reproductive physiology [ref. 41], and immune response [ref. 4, 43]. (See Table 1 below for characteristics that could influence use of the guinea pig for research.) A number of factors, however, are responsible for the fact that at present guinea pigs account for less than 2% of the rodents used in research [ref. 56]. Among the unfavorable factors are the small size of the litters and the relatively long gestation time; the high degree of development at birth; the fastidiousness of the animals in their choice of diet, making nutritional changes difficult; the relatively high susceptibility to infections; and the high cost of maintenance as compared to that for smaller rodents. The rarity of naturally occurring tumors, and the difficulty with which tumors are induced with carcinogens, also limit the usefulness of the guinea pig in some aspects of experimental oncology [ref. 34].

Table 1. **Characteristics Which May Influence Use in Research**

Classification	Characteristics
Operational	Readily available & inexpensive to purchase
	Easy & relatively inexpensive to maintain
	Very amenable to handling (rarely bites)
	Body weight range between the rat & rabbit
	Relatively few inbred strains & mutants are available
	Specific-pathogen-free (SPF) stocks available
Breeding	Long gestation
	Young relatively mature at birth
	Small litter size
Anatomical	No large superficial blood vessel, making blood collection & i.v. injections difficult
	Ear anatomically convenient for study
	Skin physiologically similar to man [25]
Other features	Requirement for dietary ascorbic acid
	Immunologically sensitive—delayed hypersensitivity & anaphylaxis
	Blood a good source of complement
	Spontaneous tumors rare
	Relatively susceptible to many infections
	Distended colon in germ-free conditions prevents breeding

The main areas of medical and biological research for which the guinea pig has been used are described below. Since it is impossible to include all experimental studies in which the guinea pig was the model or test animal, the interested reader is referred to the most recent and very useful review by Wagner and Manning [ref. 58].

Physiology

The guinea pig has been used extensively in hematological studies [ref. 44], but there are few comparative data for the various strains. No significant differences in blood and bone marrow of unrelated Dunkin-Hartley and Bahndorf strains have been found [ref. 20]. The similarity of bone marrow physiology and hematopoiesis appears to be greater between man and the guinea pig than between man and the rat or mouse [ref. 13, 27, 33, 57]. Thymic physiology also resembles more closely the human condition [ref. 15]. The guinea pig, ferret, monkey, and man are considered to be "corticosteroid-resistant" species because treatment with steroids does not markedly affect thymic physiology or peripheral lymphocyte counts—in contrast to what occurs in rabbits, hamsters, and other rodents [ref. 7]. In studies of platelet functions [ref. 36] and blood coagulation [ref. 3, 47], however, a number of differences have been observed between the guinea pig and man.

Unlike other small laboratory rodents, the electrocardiogram of the guinea pig is very similar to human ECG tracings [ref. 39]. The newborn guinea pig also is commonly used in studies on closure of the ductus arteriosus [ref. 16, 44].

continued

The guinea pig is well-suited for studies in reproductive physiology because of all the small laboratory animals, its reproductive system most resembles that of man (long cycle, spontaneous ovulation, actively secreting corpus luteum) [ref. 19, 41]. It has therefore become a laboratory model for endocrine control of pregnancy [ref. 10], and was the first species, excluding man, in which it was shown that pregnancy could be normally completed in the absence of both ovaries [ref. 23]. The animal also is useful in the study of placental physiology since its placenta appears to have endocrine activity and some morphologic features in common with the human placenta. The gestation period is long enough to permit easy differentiation between various stages of development, and the fetuses are large enough in the last trimester for easy blood collection [ref. 24].

Immunology

The first "immune response gene" in guinea pigs—i.e., a gene governing the specific immune response to a given antigen ("polylysine gene")—was discovered in 1963 [ref. 5]. Since then a large number of immune response genes have been identified in these animals (see Tables 119, 132, and 133), as has been done in several other species. In principle, the guinea pig should be a particularly suitable model for the study of immune regulation since of the small laboratory animals, its natural balance between cellular and humoral immunity appears to be the closest to that of man. Delayed-type hypersensitivity reactions and manifestations of cellular immunity, such as contact dermatitis, appear immunologically and morphologically very similar to the corresponding human diseases. Accordingly, the guinea pig has been for a long time the animal of choice in the study of cellular immunity and the model for a number of autoimmune diseases, such as experimental allergic encephalomyelitis, thyroiditis and autoimmune orchitis (see Table 134). The guinea pig is also very well-suited for studies of immediate-type allergic diseases, e.g., bronchial asthma [ref. 38] and systemic anaphylaxis [ref. 46, 49]. The animal also develops a number of diseases resembling human conditions—polyarthritis [ref. 2], nephrosclerosis [ref. 48], and myopathy [ref. 53]—for which the immunological nature has not yet been ascertained.

Genetics

Studies of guinea pig genetics in the first part of this century were largely concerned with the analysis of visible characters—such as coat color and texture [ref. 42]—and with the effects of inbreeding [ref. 17, 55]. These studies yielded fundamental contributions to genetic theory, particularly to the theory of inbreeding, gene interaction, and the genetic basis of threshold characteristics. In recent years, the emphasis has been on the genetic analysis of biochemical, physiological, and immunological characteristics. More is known about the genetics of pigmentation in guinea pigs than in any other rodent species including the mouse [ref. 17]. Studies on transplantation antigens have uncovered equivalent loci to those found in man and other species (see Table 132). A number of immune response genes appear to be closely associated with histocompatibility antigens (see Tables 132 and 133). From a biochemical point of view, the major polymorphic systems studied in guinea pigs have been immunoglobulin allotypes [ref. 28], several complement deficiencies [ref. 1], isoenzymes such as carbonate dehydratase ⟨carbonic anhydrase⟩ [ref. 8], and phosphoglucomutase [ref. 9], hypocatalasemia [ref. 40], and the phenomenon of hydrocortisone ⟨cortisol⟩ hydroxylation [ref. 6]. A number of genetic abnormalities have been described—polydactyly [ref. 17], anphthalmia [ref. 31], and the "waltzing" or circling behavior [ref. 14].

Otology

The guinea pig has been frequently used in modern otologic research [ref. 21, 35], primarily because of the ease with which the animal can be handled and because of its convenient anatomical constitution for microsurgical purposes. It may also serve as a model for otitis studies [ref. 30].

Infectious Diseases

Because guinea pigs are very susceptible to human bacterial infections, they were used extensively at the end of the last and beginning of this century as a model for diagnosing and studying the course of human infectious diseases, especially tuberculosis.

The animals develop some infections of their own which may become endemic in guinea pig colonies—e.g., *Salmonella, Streptococcus, Yersinia pseudotuberculosis, Bordetella bronchiseptica, Klebsiella pneumoniae,* and others [ref. 18]. Guinea pigs have also been widely used for the study of viral infections: those occurring spontaneously (polioviruses, reovirus type 3, paramyxoviruses, leukoviruses, lymphocytic choriomeningitis, herpes viruses), chlamydiae of the psittacosis-lymphogranuloma-trachoma group, and many other experimental viral infections [ref. 51].

Mycoses

The guinea pig is frequently the animal model for studies on dermatomycoses, especially lesions due to *Trichophyton mentagrophytes.* Although susceptible to most of the systemic mycoses (coccidioidomycosis, histoplasmosis, blastomycosis), the guinea pig is less frequently used for the study of these diseases [ref. 45].

Parasites

The guinea pig may serve as a model for infections by several protozoa—leishmaniasis (*Leishmania enriettii*), toxoplasmosis (*Toxoplasma gondii*), trypanosomiasis (*Trypanosoma cruzi* and *T. brucei*), amebiasis (*Entamoeba histolytica*), balantidiasis, and trichomoniasis. It may also be used as host for numerous other parasites [ref. 52]. Due to the lack of spontaneous infections with helminths, it is a good model for experimental infections from *Trichinella*

continued

spiralis, Trichostrongylus colubriformis, various types of lung worms, ascarids, and *Fasciola hepatica* [ref. 54].

Nutrition

A marked requirement for exogenous input of ascorbic acid (vitamin C) places the guinea pig in a unique category, along with man and other primates. This makes the guinea pig a useful model for investigations related to ascorbic acid metabolism, and studies of collagen biosynthesis, skin and bone-healing, and atherosclerosis, as well as of adrenal-pituitary physiology and the influence of stress [ref. 37]. Difficulty in modifying the animal's eating habits causes some practical problems in most nutritional studies.

Oncology

The spontaneous incidence of tumors appears to be low in the guinea pig [ref. 12, 26], and a relative resistance to chemical carcinogens has frequently been assumed [ref. 12, 34]. It has also been observed that special factors, such as a serum factor, may be responsible for the relative resistance of the animal to tumor development [ref. 22]. While these characteristics may impede large-scale oncological studies, they may also make the guinea pig an interesting model for the investigation of factors causing tumor immunity [ref. 11].

Toxicology

The guinea pig has long been a good experimental model for the study of various types of toxic inhalants [ref. 25]. It is the animal of choice for the assessment of dermal toxicity and skin-sensitizing properties of topically applied drugs. It is also frequently used in oral toxicity studies, although results obtained with several antibiotics, especially penicillin, do not parallel those obtained in other species.

Teratology

The long gestation period with trimester characteristics, provides an opportunity for separation of toxic effects in the guinea pig embryo from those manifested in the fetus. It is also possible to investigate fetuses possessing a mature central nervous system prior to delivery. And since endocrine control of pregnancy appears to be quite similar to that in man, the guinea pig certainly deserves a place in teratological studies.

Table 2 below provides a classification by subject of 3,867 papers, published between 1970 and 1974, on investigations in which the guinea pig was used. Its relative importance to the different disciplines is apparent from the figures in the table.

Table 2. Estimate of Comparative Use in Different Disciplines

The data were compiled from papers published between 1970 and 1974 [ref. 50]. Values in parentheses are ranges over those years, estimate "c" (*see* Introduction).

Subject	No. of Papers	Percent
Anatomy, cytology, morphology	276	7.1(4.7-8.3)
Behavior	91	2.4(1.4-4.7)
Biochemistry, pharmacology & toxicology	1021	26.4(23.2-28.2)
Endocrinology	233	6.0(3.9-7.8)
Genetics	60	1.6(1.0-2.2)
Hearing (otology)	242	6.3(5.0-7.8)
Immunology	960	24.8(22.2-28.1)
Microbiology	330	8.5(7.3-9.5)
Nutrition & ascorbic acid metabolism	136	3.5(2.7-5.0)
Pathology & cancer	211	5.5(4.7-7.0)
Radiation	44	1.1(0.4-2.5)
Reproduction, growth, & development	133	3.4(1.7-5.0)
Techniques	75	1.9(1.0-2.6)
Miscellaneous	55	1.4(0.3-3.4)
Grand total	3867	....

In summary, the guinea pig is a very valuable animal for biological and medical investigations. The fact that other rodents, especially mice and rats, are presently being used in much larger numbers in medical research, apparently is due to economic considerations: maintenance costs and statistical requirements for large numbers of experimental animals. In genetic experiments, the small guinea pig litters and long gestation time also represent a definite drawback. On the basis of physiological considerations alone, however, the guinea pig would probably be more often the experimental animal of choice.

continued

Contributors: Alain L. de Weck; Michael F. W. Festing

Specific References

1. Alper, C. A., and F. S. Rosen. 1971. Adv. Immunol. 14:251-290.
2. Alspaugh, M. A., and G. L. Van Hoosier, Jr. 1973. Lab. Anim. Sci. 23:724-736.
3. Astrup, T., et al. 1970. Lab. Invest. 22:381-386.
4. Bellanti, J. A., et al. 1965. J. Immunol. 94:1-11.
5. Benacerraf, B., and H. O. McDevitt. 1972. Science 175:273-279.
6. Burstein, S. 1971. Endocrinology 89:928-931.
7. Calman, H. N. 1972. N. Engl. J. Med. 287:388-397.
8. Carter, N. D. 1972. Comp. Biochem. Physiol. 43:743-747.
9. Carter, N. D., et al. 1972. Biochem. Genet. 6:147-156.
10. Challis, J. R. G., et al. 1971. J. Endocrinol. 51:333-345.
11. Ellman, L., and I. Green. 1971. Cancer 28:645-654.
12. Epstein, M. A. 1972. J. Natl. Cancer Inst. 49:213-217.
13. Epstein, R. D., and E. H. Tompkins. 1943. Am. J. Med. Sci. 206:249-260.
14. Ernston, S. 1970. Acta Oto-Laryngol. 69:358-362.
15. Ernström, U. 1970. Ciba Found. Study Group 36:53-65.
16. Fay, F. S., and P. H. Cooke. 1972. Am. J. Physiol. 222:841-849.
17. Festing, M. F. W. 1976. In J. E. Wagner and P. J. Manning, ed. The Biology of the Guinea Pig. Academic, New York. pp. 99-120.
18. Ganaway, J. R. 1976. Ibid. pp. 121-135.
19. Goy, R. W., et al. 1957. Anat. Rec. 128:747-757.
20. Griffiths, D. A., and W. O. Rieke. 1969. Exp. Hematol. 18:36-39.
21. Hawkins, J. E., Jr. 1973. Adv. Oto-Rhino-Laryngol. 20:125-141.
22. Herbut, P. A., et al. 1961. Am. J. Pathol. 38:387-391.
23. Herrick, E. H. 1928. Anat. Rec. 39:193-200.
24. Hill, P. M. M., and M. Young. 1973. Br. J. Pharmacol. 47:655-656.
25. Hoar, R. M. 1976. (Loc. cit. ref. 17). pp. 269-280.
26. Hsiung, G. D., et al. 1973. Cancer Res. 33:1436-1442.
27. Innes, J., et al. 1949. J. Lab. Clin. Med. 34:883-901.
28. Kelus, A. S. 1969. Nature (London) 223:398-399.
29. Koch, R. 1891. Dtsch. Med. Wochenschr. 9:101.
30. Kohn, D. F. 1974. Lab. Anim. Sci. 24:823-825.
31. Komich, R. J. 1971. Am. J. Vet. Res. 32:2099-2105.
32. Lane-Petter, W., and G. Porter. 1963. Animals for Research. Academic, New York. pp. 287-291.
33. Lucarelli, G., and U. Butturini. 1967. Proc. R. Soc. Med. 60:1036-1037.
34. Manning, P. J. 1976. (Loc. cit. ref. 17). pp. 211-225.
35. McCormick, J. G., and A. L. Nutall. 1976. (Loc. cit. ref. 17). pp. 281-303.
36. Mills, D. C. B. 1970. Symp. Zool. Soc. London 27:99-107.
37. Navia, J. M., and C. E. Hunt. 1976. (Loc. cit. ref. 17). pp. 235-267.
38. Patterson, R., and J. F. Kelly. 1974. Annu. Rev. Med. 25:53-68.
39. Petelenz, T. 1971. Acta Physiol. Pol. 22:113-121.
40. Radev, T. 1960. J. Genet. 57:169-172.
41. Reed, M., and W. F. Hounslow. 1971. J. Endocrinol. 49:203-211.
42. Searle, A. G. 1968. Comparative Genetics of Coat Colour in Mammals. Academic, New York.
43. Shewell, J., and D. A. Long. 1956. J. Hyg. 54:452-460.
44. Sisk, D. B. 1976. (Loc. cit. ref. 17). pp. 63-98.
45. Sprouse, R. F. 1976. (Loc. cit. ref. 17). pp. 153-161.
46. Stone, S. H., et al. 1964. Science 146:1061-1062.
47. Takada, Y., et al. 1969. Thromb. Diath. Haemorrh. 21:594-603.
48. Takeda, T., and A. Grollman. 1970. Am. J. Pathol. 60:103-118.
49. Takino, Y., et al. 1971. J. Allergy 47:247-261.
50. Turton, J. 1976. Guinea Pig Newslett. 10:15-18.
51. Van Hoosier, G. L., and L. R. Robinette. 1976. (Loc. cit. ref. 17). pp. 137-152.
52. Vetterling, J. M. 1976. (Loc. cit. ref. 17). pp. 163-196.
53. Webb, J. N. 1970. J. Pathol. 100:155-159.
54. Wescott, R. B. 1976. (Loc. cit. ref. 17). pp. 197-200.
55. Wright, S. 1960. J. Cell. Comp. Physiol. 56:123-132.
56. Yager, R. H., and C. B. Frank, ed. 1972. ILAR News 16(1):i-xv.
57. Yoffey, J. M., and F. C. Courtice. 1970. Lymphatics, Lymph, and the Lymphomyeloid Complex. Academic, New York.

General Reference

58. Wagner, J. E., and P. J. Manning, ed. 1976. The Biology of the Guinea Pig. Academic, New York.

Degree of Inbreeding: Date refers to the most recent information available. Fx indicates the unknown number of generations that existed before a count was begun. **Genes Carried**: *see also* Table 132. For *GPLA* genes, consult references 5, 11, and 13. **Principal Holder**: For full name, *see* list of HOLDERS at front of book. Data in brackets refer to the column heading in brackets.

ABBREVIATIONS AND SYMBOLS	
Bf-F = properdin factor B fast	*Ir-DNP-GPA* = immune response to 2,4-dinitrophenyl-guinea pig albumin
Bf-S or S_1 = properdin factor B slow or slow 1	*Ir-GA* = immune response to poly(L-glutamic acid-L-alanine)
Ca-2ᵃ = carbonic anhydrase IIA	*Ir-GT* = immune response to poly(L-glutamic acid-L-tyrosine)
Ca-2ᵇ = carbonic anhydrase IIB	*Ir-HRP* = immune response to horseradish peroxidase
2C-A = complement factor C2 acidic	*Ir-HSA* = immune response to human serum albumin
2C-B = complement factor C2 basic	*Ir-PHEN* = immune response to phenetidine
4C-F = complement factor C4 fast	*Ir-PLL* = immune response to poly(L-lysine)
4C-S or S_1 = complement factor C4 slow or slow 1	*Ir-(TGAGly)ₙ* = immune response to poly(Tyr-Glu-Ala-Gly)
Ir-ASAN = immune response to aspirin anhydride	*Ir-TGAL* = immune response to poly(Tyr-Glu-Ala-Lys)
Ir-BPO-BGG = immune response to benzylpenicilloyl-bovine gammaglobulin	*Pgm-1* = phosphoglucomutase-1
Ir-BSA = immune response to bovine serum albumin	*Pgm-2* = phosphoglucomutase-2

Strain ⟨Synonym⟩	Origin	Degree of Inbreeding [Date]	Genes Carried	Main Characteristics	Principal Holder	Reference
2	US Dept. of Agriculture, 1906, to S. Wright, 1915, at F11; b x s mating for 33 generations to 1933, then random mating until 1940. To Heston, 1940, when b x s mating resumed. To NIH 1950; all sublines from that colony.	Fx + F26	*GPLA-B1, GPLA-S; Ia-2,4,5,6; Ir-PLL, Ir-GA, Ir-BSA, Ir-HSA; Bf-S; 4C-F; 2C-A*	Tricolor (black, red, white). Average breeders. Histocompatible within strain. Fairly resistant to tuberculosis.	NIH	1,2,5, 6,13, 14
13	Same as for strain 2	Fx + F26	*GPLA-B1, GPLA-S; Ia-1,3,5,6,7; Ir-GT, Ir-DNP-GPA, Ir-BPO-BGG, Ir-ASAN, Ir-TGAL, Ir-PHEN, Ir-(TGAGly)ₙ; Bf-S; 4C-F; 2C-A*	Tricolor (black, red, white). Average breeders. Less active sexual behavior & larger body size than strain 2. Histocompatible within strain. Less resistant to tuberculosis than strain 2.	NIH	1,2,5, 6,13, 14
B/Lac ⟨BE⟩	Selected by S. Lundberg, State Serum Inst. Copenhagen, for resistance to anaphylaxis to ovalbumin. To LAC 1967. To be considered as subline from IMM/R	F20	*GPLA-B3; Ia-1,6,7; Ir-GT; Ca-2ᵃ; Bf-F; 4C-S; 2C-B*	Albino. Almost entirely histocompatible within strain. Poor immune response to most antigens tested.	LAC	2,4,5, 8,13
BIOAC	Developed by A. de Weck, 1969, from colony of Himalayan spotted animals closed for 25 years, Biological Institute, Füllinsdorf, Switzerland	F11 [Sept. 1977]	*GPLA-B2; Ia-1,3,5,6,7; Bf-S; 4C-F; 2C-A*	White. Good breeding performance. Leukocytes histocompatible within strain.	WEK	1-5,10, 12,13

continued

Strain ⟨Synonym⟩	Origin	Degree of Inbreeding [Date]	Genes Carried	Main Characteristics	Principal Holder	Reference
BIOAD	Same as for BIOAC	F9 [Sept. 1977]	*GPLA-B3; Ia-1,3,5,6,7; Bf-F; 4C-S; 2C-B*	White. Poor breeding performance. Leukocytes histocompatible within strain.	WEK	1-5,10, 12,13
BIOB	Same as for BIOAC	F11 [Sept. 1977]	*GPLA-B1, GPLA-S; Ia-1,6; Ir-GT, Ir-TGAL; Ir-BPO-BGG, Ir-ASAN; Bf-F; 4C-S; 2C-B*	White. Good breeding performance. Leukocytes histocompatible within strain (no graft-versus-host reaction with lymphoid cell transfer).	WEK	1-5,10, 12,13
BIOC	Same as for BIOAC	F10 [Sept. 1977]	*GPLA-B2; Ia-1,6,7; Ir-GT, Ir-PHEN; Bf-S or Bf-F; 4C-F or 4C-S; 2C-A or 2C-B*	White. Medium breeding performance. Leukocytes histocompatible within strain.	WEK	1-5,10, 12,13
ICRF	From outbred stock by P. C. Williams, 1954	Fx + F28	....	Albino	?	2
IMM/R	Developed by S. Lundberg, 1958, for poor susceptibility to ovalbumin-induced respiratory anaphylaxis	F22	*GPLA-B3; Ia-2,4; Ir-GT*	Albino. Good breeding performance.	LUN	2,9,12
IMM/S	Origin same as for IMM/R. Selected for high susceptibility to ovalbumin-induced respiratory anaphylaxis	F22	*GPLA-B3; Ia-1,3; Ir-PLL, Ir-GA, Ir-BSA*	Albino. Good breeding performance.	LUN	2,9,12
JY-1	From one pair outbred stock from Rockland Farms (USA) 1949. To JNAH.	F35 [Sept. 1977]	*GPLA-B3*	Albino. Good breeding performance. Histocompatible within strain.	JNAH	2,8,10
OM3	Developed from outbred stock by J. B. Rogers, 1952. To LAC, 1965.	Fx + F15	*GPLA-B3; Ia-1,3,5,6,7; Ir-GT, Ir-DNP-GPA; Bf-F; 4C-S₁; 2C-B; Pgm-1; Ca-2ᵇ*	Albino. Good breeding performance. Not yet fully histocompatible within strain. No spontaneous tumors.	LAC	2,4,5, 8,13
PCA ⟨DHCBA⟩	Developed by D. H. Campbell, 1967, for superior passive cutaneous anaphylaxis ⟨PCA⟩ reactions	F21 [Sept. 1977]	*GPLA-B3; Ia-1,3,5,6,7; Ir-GT, Ir-DNP-GPA; Bf-F; 4C-S or 4C-S₁; 2C-B*	Albino. Good breeding performance. Superior PCA reactions & immune responses.	CIT	2,10
R9	Developed from outbred stock by J. B. Rogers, 1941. To LAC, 1965.	Fx + F14	*GPLA-B3; Ia-1,3,5,6,7; Ir-HRP; Bf-F, Bf-S₁; 4C-F, 4C-S₁; 2C-B; Pgm-2; Ca-2ᵇ*	Brown & white. Histocompatible within strain. 14% spontaneous tumor incidence in animals >3 yr old.	LAC	2,4,5, 8,13
WM ⟨Weiser-Maples⟩	Denver hospital to Weiser, 1954. Selected for coat color.	F15 [April 1969]	....	Buff coat color. Uniform response to experimental tuberculosis.	?	2,7

Contributors: Ethan M. Shevach; Michael F. W. Festing; Alain L. deWeck

References

1. Bitter-Suermann, D., et al. 1977. J. Immunol. 119: 2016-2018.

2. Festing, M. F. W. 1975. Guinea Pig Newslett. 9:3-8.

3. Geczy, A. F., et al. 1975. Eur. J. Immunol. 5:711-719.

continued

4. Geczy, A. F., et al. 1975. Immunology 28:331-342.
5. Geczy, A. F., et al. 1975. J. Immunol. 115:1704-1710.
6. Green, I. 1974. Immunogenetics 1:4-21.
7. Jones, L. D., and O. L. Weiser. 1969. Lab. Anim. 3: 69-70.
8. Kataoka, T., and T. Tokunaga. 1976. Gann 67:25-31.
9. Lundberg, S. Unpublished. Dep. Medical Microbiology, Rikshospitalet, Copenhagen, Denmark, 1978.
10. Shevach, E. M. Unpublished. N.I.A.I.D., National Institutes of Health, Bethesda, MD, 1978.
11. Shevach, E. M., et al. 1977. J. Exp. Med. 146:561-570.
12. Weck, A. L. de. Unpublished. Institute for Clinical Immunology, Inselspital, Bern, Switzerland, 1978.
13. Weck, A. L. de, et al. 1976. Transplantation 21:225-241.
14. Wright, S. 1922. U.S. Dep. Agric. Bull. 1090.

120. MUTANTS: GUINEA PIG

The genetics of visible traits such as coat color and texture was studied intensively between 1900 and approximately 1960—largely by Sewell Wright and his students—and many mutants affecting such characteristics were isolated. In the last few years some new mutants have been reported, but the only traits undergoing intensive genetic study at present are those associated with immune responses and histocompatibility.

The genetics of the guinea pig has recently been reviewed independently by Robinson [ref. 3] and Festing [ref. 2]; the list of mutants given in the table below was compiled from the lists prepared by these two authors. Further information on the characteristics and genetics of these mutants can be found in one or both of the above references.

It has not been possible to compile a definitive list of the location of these mutants. Many mutant genes are present in guinea pigs held by fanciers, but in some cases the expression of a coat color or texture mutation may require a number of generations of breeding. Some mutants are undoubtedly extinct. So far as can be ascertained, there is no institute in the world with a comprehensive collection of mutants of the guinea pig. Unfortunately, the loss of mutants could cause difficulties in the future in developing the linkage map for this species.

Robinson [ref. 3] has reviewed data on linkage. Only two cases of linkage among the classical mutants have been established. The first is between Px and R, with a recombination frequency of 45.7 ± 1.6 when all data are combined. The second is between m and si, with a crossover value of 21.7 ± 4.3.

Linkage has also been established between the major histocompatibility complex and the immune response genes [ref. 1]. Genetic studies of the major histocompatibility complex have only just commenced, and data on frequency of crossing over are not yet available. However, assuming that the major histocompatibility complex resembles that of other mammalian species, crossing over can also be expected within the complex.

General Gene Effect: 1 = pigmentation; 2 = hair texture and growth; 3 = skeleton; 5 = eye; 6 = ear and circling; 7 = neuromuscular; 8 = blood, endocrine, internal defects, dwarfs, sterility; 9 = biochemical; 10 = immunological. **Location:** Ex = believed to be extinct; F = probably carried by animals available from guinea pig fanciers; L = common in laboratory stocks; P = polymorphic, and therefore probably found in laboratory stocks. For full name of holders (LAC and N), *see* list of HOLDERS at front of book.

Symbol	Designation	General Gene Effect	Location
A	Light-bellied agouti	1	F, L
A^r	Ticked-bellied agouti	1	?
a	Non-agouti	1	F
b	Brown	1	F
c^k	Dark dilution	1	?
c^d	Light dilution	1	F
c^r	Red-eyed dilution	1	F
c^a	Acromelanic albino	1	F
ca	Catalase activity	9	?
$Ca-2$	Carbonic anhydrase	9	P

Symbol	Designation	General Gene Effect	Location
co	Cornea abnormality	5	Ex ?
$co-3$	Complement deficiency	9	Ex
$Co-4$	Complement deficiency	9	N, LAC
dm	Diminished	1	?
dw	Dwarf	8	Ex
e	Extension	1	F, L
e^p	Partial extension	1	F
$GPIr-1$ [1]	Immune response [2]	10	P
$GPLA$ [1]	Major histocompatibility locus [3]	10	P

[1] Complex loci which are under intensive study at present. Number of alleles and nomenclature system not yet worked out.
[2] Alleles include PLL, GT, GA, etc. [3] Several alleles.

continued

Symbol	Designation	General Gene Effect	Location
f	Fading yellow	1	?
Fz	Fuzzy	2	?
gr	Grizzled	1	?
l	Long hair	2	F
m	Rough modifier	2	F?
n	Congenital palsy	7	?
p^r	Ruby eye	1	?
p	Pink-eyed dilution	1	F
Pgi^a	Phosphoglucose isomerase[4]	9	?
Pgi^p	Phosphoglucose isomerase[5]	9	?
Pgm	Phosphoglucomutase	9	P
Px	Polydactyly	3	Ex ?
R	Rough	2	F

Symbol	Designation	General Gene Effect	Location
Rex	Rex or curly coat	2	LAC
Rs	Roan spotting & anophthalmos	1,5	F
s	White spotting[6]	1	F, L
S^{hy}	Serum factor-hypersensitivity	10	P
sh	Sexual hypogenesis	8	Ex ?
si	Silvering	1	F ?
sk	Sticky coat	2	Ex ?
sm	Salmon eye	1	?
St	Star	2	F
W	Whitish or white tipped	1	?
wtz[7]	Recessive waltzing	6	Ex ?
Wz	Dominant waltzing	6	N

[4] Aperea type. [5] Porcellus type. [6] Synonym: Piebald spotting. [7] Synonym: *wa*.

Contributor: Michael F. W. Festing

References

1. Bluestein, H. G., et al. 1971. J. Exp. Med. 134:1529-1537.
2. Festing, M. F. W. 1976. In J. E. Wagner and P. J. Manning, ed. The Biology of the Guinea Pig. Academic, New York. pp. 99-120.
3. Robinson, R. 1975. In R. C. King, ed. Handbook of Genetics. Plenum, New York and London. v. 4, pp. 275-307.

121. NON-INBRED COLONIES OF SPECIAL INTEREST: GUINEA PIG

Colonies of laboratory animals may be defined either by specific genetic characteristics—such as color, size, hair texture, or the presence of a genetic abnormality—or they may be defined operationally as the descendants of a particular closed colony. In the latter case, there may be no known set of characteristics that will always distinguish the stock from other stocks of similar appearance. It is highly probable that stocks of similar outward appearance have often become muddled in the past, and this may lead to difficulty in repeating some published work. The solution lies in better definition of common laboratory stocks so that they may be identified by their physical, biochemical, behavioral, or other characteristics. Such definition has not yet been attempted for the guinea pig; hence few characteristics are given in the table below for the various stocks. Figures in heavy brackets are reference numbers.

Breed	Characteristic
Abyssinian	Defined in terms of a rosette hair pattern, and carries the genes $R/- m/m$ (R stands for the mutant rough, and m is a modifier of rough). Typically, these animals have at least two rosettes (anterior & posterior) on the back, well-developed head rosettes, & rosettes or partings on the belly. Coat color is variable, and little is known as to how much this breed differs in terms of characteristics of potential interest to research from the other two breeds. Battisto, et al. [1], noted that animals of this breed reacted to dextran, whereas the reaction was less common in other breeds.
Peruvian	Defined by the presence of the long hair gene l, as well as a low grade of rosettes caused by R. Continued selection by fancy breeders has probably also fixed a large array of genetic modifiers of coat length & texture. Again, little is known of the extent to which animals of this breed (which vary in coat color) differ from the other two breeds in characteristics of biomedical interest.

continued

Breed	Characteristic
Short haired or English	Breed most commonly used in research. A number of different color varieties are recognized for show purposes. Most research colonies, however, are operationally defined.
Anophthalmia	Colony with a high incidence (>80%) of eye abnormalities, including anophthalmia & microphthalmia, has been described by Komich [6]. Exact mode of inheritance is not known.
Dunkin-Hartley	This synthetic albino (c^a/c^a e/e) was established at the National Institute for Medical Research, Mill Hill (U. K.) in 1926 by Drs. Dunkin & Hartley [3]. The original stock consisted of 12 ♂ & 20 ♀. Albino animals were chosen for immunological studies, as hypersensitivity reactions register better on white skin. Stock has been widely distributed internationally, and may almost be regarded as the standard laboratory guinea pig. A number of sublines have been recognized operationally rather than by any known characteristic. These include the Pirbright-Hartley, the Hartley, the Jap-Hartley, & the Camm-Hartley [7]. Genetic theory suggests that these colonies are likely to be genetically distinct, but the degree of genetic distinctiveness has never been quantified. Albino color may give a spurious impression of genetic uniformity.
NIH	Genetically heterogeneous colony, segregating for various coat color and other genes. Vigorous, with a high level of reproduction [5]. A spontaneous mutation causing C4 complement deficiency was located in this stock, and is maintained as a separate subline [4,5]. A mutation, "Waltzer," occurred in the stock in 1953. Mutation causes degeneration of elements in the organ of Corti, and has a dominant mode of inheritance, with variable expression. It is maintained as a separate subline [5].
White Himalayan spotted colony of Roche (BIO)	Maintained as a closed colony since approximately 1945, without any attempt at inbreeding. Of special interest because of the extensive studies of the histocompatibility antigens carried by the colony [2].

Contributor: Michael F. W. Festing

References
1. Battisto, J. R., et al. 1968. J. Immunol. 101:203-209.
2. de Weck, A. L., et al. 1971. Transplant. Proc. 3:192-194.
3. Dunkin, G. W., et al. 1930. J. Hyg. 30:311-330.
4. Ellman, L., et al. 1970. Science 170:74-75.
5. Hansen, C. T., et al. 1973. U.S. Dep. HEW Publ. (NIH) 74-606.
6. Komich, R. J. 1971. Am. J. Vet. Res. 32:2099-2105.
7. National Research Council, Institute of Laboratory Animal Resources. 1975. Animals for Research. Ed. 9. National Academy of Sciences, Washington, D.C.

122. KARYOLOGY: GUINEA PIG

The species of guinea pig commonly used in laboratories is *Cavia porcellus*. Strain 2 guinea pigs [ref. 2], an inbred line, are used for carrying L_2C leukemic cells for virologic, chemotherapeutic, and immunotherapeutic studies. Skin fibroblast cultures from these animals are easily established and quite stable in early passages in vitro. Accurate chromosome analysis, using careful comparisons of banding patterns, has demonstrated that there are some differences in the heterochromatic regions between Strain 2 and other *C. porcellus* strains, such as the Hartley outbred line.

Chromosome preparations

Direct: A bone marrow cell suspension was obtained by flushing the cavity of the femur with colchicine solution (0.02-0.2 μg/ml), or cell suspensions were prepared from fetal liver or spleen (aged 59-61 days, gestational period 62-69 days). After 30-45 minutes in colchicine (under a lamp, at ∿28°C), the cells were placed in a hypotonic solution (0.075 M KCl) for 10 minutes. A modified Carnoy's fixative (3:1 absolute ethanol to glacial acetic acid) was added to the hypotonic solution, and the cells were immersed for 5 minutes. They were then fixed for 10 minutes. After the final centrifugation, slides were prepared by the air-dry technique. [ref. 6]

Cultured cells—Short term: A few drops of whole blood, obtained by cardiac puncture, or a suspension of spleen cells were cultured with phytohemagglutinin ⟨PHA⟩, using the method of Moorhead, et al. [ref. 4]. After four days of culture, colchicine (0.2 μg/ml) was added. Two hours later, the cells were harvested by the method described above, under *Direct*, for bone marrow cells. *Long term*: Fibroblast cultures derived from ear clippings were treated with colchicine (0.02 μg/ml) for 1 hour before harvesting. After 20 minutes in a hypotonic solution (3:1 H_2O to culture medium), the cells were then fixed in Carnoy's solution. Slides were prepared by the air-dry technique.

continued

Giemsa Banding

One of two procedures was used; for both methods, slides which were one-to-two weeks old gave the best results. Method 1: The slides were dried for 4-5 hours, at 37°C, and immediately placed in trypsin solution at room temperature for 10-15 seconds while they were still warm, then rinsed in cold saline. Because of the unusual sensitivity of the chromosomes of the guinea pig to trypsin digestion, the concentration used was 0.025%. The slides were then placed for 30-40 minutes in Giemsa stain (Gurr's R66) diluted in buffer of pH 6.8. Method 2: The slides were dried for 1 week, at 65°C, then treated with trypsin (0.005%). The time varied from 0.5 to 2 minutes, depending on the age of the slide, the batch of trypsin, etc. If further treatment was necessary, the slides were briefly dipped in urea (6M in Sorensen's phosphate buffer). Urea dips were repeated until the desired banding pattern was obtained [ref. 5]. The slides were then stained in Giemsa.

Chromosome Analysis

The normal guinea pig has 64 chromosomes: 31 pairs of autosomes and one pair of sex chromosomes. Although Strain 2 (Figure 3) and the Hartley outbred strain (Figure 4) have similar banding patterns, some differences—now easily demonstrated using C-banding [ref. 1]—are seen in the short arms of chromosome pairs 17-25. In addition, the karyotype for Strain 2 reveals that chromosome pairs 1-16 have a definite short arm; pairs 17-31 are acrocentric; the X chromosome is third in size; and the Y chromosome is one of the smallest. The Hartley strain, on the other hand, has only seven pairs of acrocentric chromosomes (pairs 25-31), and chromosome 1 has a heterochromatic region on the tip of the short arm. (The deletion of this heterochromatic tip appears to be a common finding.) Because Strain 2 has less heterochromatin, its karyotype is used as a standard for the arrangement of the chromosomes of the genus *Cavia*.

STRAIN 2 (FEMALE)

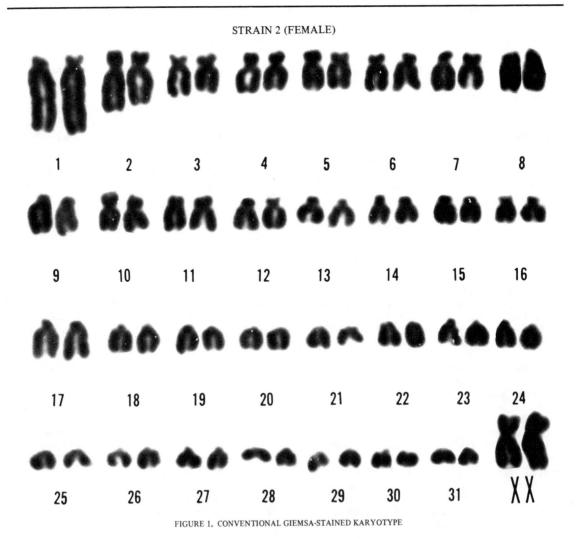

FIGURE 1. CONVENTIONAL GIEMSA-STAINED KARYOTYPE

continued

STRAIN 2 (MALE)

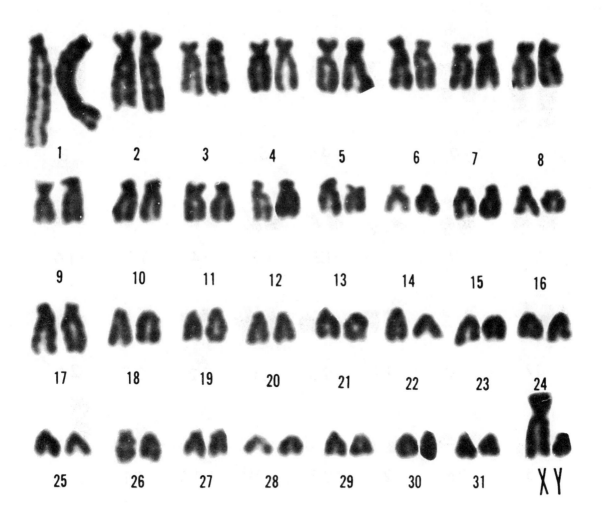

FIGURE 2. CONVENTIONAL GIEMSA-STAINED KARYOTYPE

continued

STRAIN 2 (MALE)

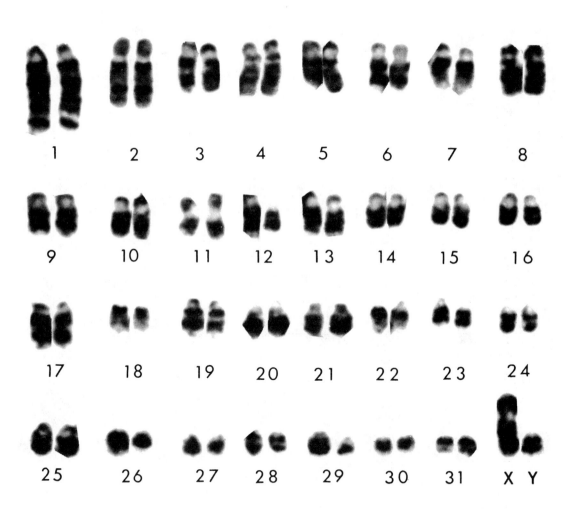

FIGURE 3. GIEMSA-TRYPSIN BANDING KARYOTYPE

continued

HARTLEY OUTBRED STRAIN

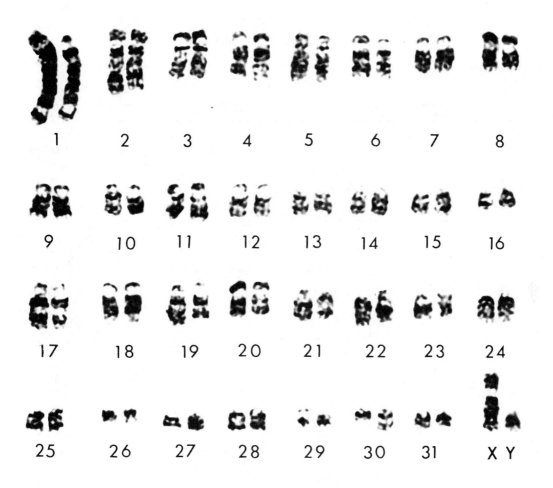

FIGURE 4. GIEMSA-BANDING KARYOTYPE

continued

122. KARYOLOGY: GUINEA PIG

Contributors: J. Whang-Peng, E. Lee, and H. R. Hubbell

References

1. Arrighi, F. E., and T. C. Hsu. 1971. Cytogenetics 10: 81-86.
2. Festing, M. F. W., ed. 1975. International Index of Laboratory Animals. Ed. 3. Medical Research Council, Laboratory Animals Centre, Carshalton, Surrey, U.K. pp. 52-53.
3. Hubbell, H. R., et al. 1976. Exp. Cell Res. 102:385-393.
4. Moorhead, P. S., et al. 1960. Ibid. 20:613-616.
5. Stock, A. D., et al. 1974. Cytogenet. Cell Genet. 13: 410-418.
6. Tjio, J. H., and J. Whang. 1962. Stain Technol. 37:17-20.
7. Whang-Peng, J., et al. 1976. J. Natl. Cancer Inst. 57: 897-905.

123. BREEDING AND REPRODUCTION: GUINEA PIG

Plus/minus (±) values are standard errors, unless otherwise indicated. Values in parentheses are ranges, estimate "c" (*see* Introduction).

Specification	Observation	Reference
Chromosome number, diploid	64	1
Age at puberty	♂: (10-19 wk)	15,34,38, 46
	♀: 67.8 ± 21.5[1] (33-134) d	
Breeding age (recommended)	(2.5-3) mo, or (450-600) g	13,31
Estrous cycle		
Type	Polyestrous, non-seasonal	36,42,44
Duration	16 d & 6 h (13-21.5) d	25,42,45, 46
Estrus[2]		
Onset	Correlated with light:dark sequence; most predominant at 1800-0600	8,10,45
Duration	8.21 ± 0.07 (1-18) h	10,21,25, 42,45
Postpartum		
Onset	2-10 h after parturition	5
Duration	3.5 h	6,12,28, 36,37
Vaginal membrane		
Age of initial rupture	58.2 (33-111) d	26,31,42
Opening during estrus: duration	2.3 ± 0.1 d	14,21,26, 42
Ovulation		
Spontaneous	10 h following onset of estrus, and usually within 1.5-2 h of the end of estrus	3,10,33, 42,45
Postpartum	12-15 h postpartum	28,37
Ova		
No. ovulated at once by mature ♀	3.34 ± 0.41 (1-5)	22,24
Fertilizable longevity in fallopian tube	(3-20) h	3,24,41
Transit time, ovary to uterus	72 h	24,41
Sperm		
Ejaculate volume	0.5(0.1-1.2) ml	16
No. per ejaculate	13.376 × 10^6	16
Transit time, vagina to fallopian tubes	15 min	29,40

[1] Plus/minus (±) value is standard deviation. [2] Synonym: Heat.

continued

Specification	Observation	Reference
Fertilizable longevity in ♀ reproductive tract	(18-24) h	41,44
Fertilization site	Fallopian tube	3,24,41
Implantation of fertilized ova	(6-7.5) d post-coitus	4,7
Placenta: type	Hemochorial, with fetal trophoblasts in direct contact with maternal blood	2,17,32, 39
Gestation: duration	68(59-72) d	18,27,28, 30,36,44
Birth canal: symphysis pubis		23,25,43
Separation	(5-7) d before parturition	
Closure	24 h postpartum	
Parturition		5
Duration	(10-30) min	
Interval between deliveries	7.4(1-16) min	
Litter size	3 or 4 (1-8)	6,9,11,19, 35
Weight at birth	Inversely proportional to litter size, and varies with strain characteristics	11,30
	♂: (82.4-130.1) g	
	♀: (80.8-128.2) g	
Abortion/stillbirth	Occurs 99.9% of the time in deliveries where length of gestation is 3 standard deviations above or below mean length for colony	18
Standard monthly reproductive index: obtained by dividing no. of young weaned per month by no. of ♀ breeders making up the colony; this value is used as a standard by which the reproductive efficiency of colonies is compared	Outbred: 1.0	13,20.
	Strain 2: 0.6	
	Strain 13: 0.4	

Contributor: Raymond D. Ediger

References

1. Awa, A. M., et al. 1959. Jpn. J. Zool. 12:257.
2. Bartels, H., et al. 1967. Respir. Physiol. 2:149-162.
3. Blandau, R. J. 1939. Am. Anat. 64:303-330.
4. Blandau, R. J. 1949. Anat. Rec. 103:19-47.
5. Boling, J. L., et al. 1939. Proc. Soc. Exp. Biol. Med. 42:128-132.
6. Bruce, H. M. 1948. J. Hyg. 46:434-437.
7. Deanesly, R. 1960. J. Reprod. Fertil. 1:242-248.
8. Dempsey, E. W., et al. 1934. Am. J. Physiol. 109: 307-311.
9. Dillard, E. U., et al. 1972. J. Anim. Sci. 34:193-194.
10. Donovan, B. T., et al. 1972. J. Endocrinol. 55:599-607.
11. Dunkin, G. W., et al. 1930. J. Hyg. 30:311-330.
12. Eaton, O. N. 1941. U.S. Dep. Agric. Tech. Bull. 765.
13. Ediger, R. D. 1976. In J. E. Wagner and P. J. Manning, ed. The Biology of the Guinea Pig. Academic, New York. pp. 5-12.
14. Ford, D. H., et al. 1953. Anat. Rec. 115:495-504.
15. Freund, M. 1962. Fertil. Steril. 13:190-201.
16. Freund, M. 1969. J. Reprod. Fertil. 19:393-403.
17. Fuchs, F. 1952. Acta Physiol. Scand. 20:162-171.
18. Goy, R. W., et al. 1957. Anat. Rec. 128:745-757.
19. Haines, G. 1931. J. Agric. Res. 42:123-164.
20. Hansen, C. T., et al. 1971. In National Research Council, Institute of Laboratory Animal Resources, ed. Defining the Laboratory Animal. National Academy of Sciences, Washington, D.C. pp. 179-202.
21. Harned, M. A. 1972. J. Mammal. 53:223-225.
22. Hermreck, A. S. 1964. Anat. Rec. 148:171-176.
23. Hisaw, F. L., et al. Endocrinology 34:122-134.
24. Hunter, R. H. F., et al. 1969. Anat. Rec. 165:411-430.
25. Ishii, O. 1920. Biol. Bull. 38:237-250.
26. Kelly, G. L., et al. 1927. Am. J. Anat. 40:387-411.
27. Kenneth, J. H. 1947. Imp. Bur. Anim. Breed. Genet. Tech. Commun. 5(Ed. 2):1-30.
28. Labhsetwar, A. P. 1970. Biol. Reprod. 2:53-57.
29. Martan, J., et al. 1973. Anat. Rec. 175:625-630.
30. McKeown, T. 1955. Endocrinology 13:195-200.
31. Mills, P. G., et al. 1971. J. Endocrinol. 50:329-337.
32. Moll, W., et al. 1973. Pfluegers Arch. 338:125-131.
33. Myers, H. I., et al. 1936. Anat. Rec. 65:381-402.
34. Reid, M. E. 1958. The Guinea Pig in Research. Human Factors Research Bureau, Washington, D.C.
35. Rogers, J. B. 1951. J. Gerontol. 6:13-16.

continued

36. Rowlands, I. W. 1949. J. Hyg. 47:281-287.
37. Rowlands, I. W. 1956. Ciba Found. Colloq. Ageing 2:69-85.
38. Sayles, E. D. 1939. Physiol. Zool. 12:256-267.
39. Shepard, J. T., et al. 1951. J. Physiol. (London) 115: 150-157.
40. Simeone, F. A., et al. 1931. J. Exp. Biol. 8:163-175.
41. Squier, R. R. 1932. Carnegie Inst. Washington Contrib. Embryol. 23:225-250.

42. Stockard, C. R., et al. 1917. Am. J. Anat. 22:225-283.
43. Todd, T. W. 1923. Ibid. 31:345-357.
44. Wright, S. 1960. J. Cell. Comp. Physiol. 56(Suppl. 1): 123-151.
45. Young, W. C., et al. 1935. J. Comp. Physiol. Psychol. 19:313-335.
46. Young, W. C., et al. 1939. Ibid. 27:49-68.

124.   REPRODUCTION AND GROWTH: GUINEA PIG

Part I.   Effect of Parity on Litter Size

Plus/minus (±) values are standard errors, unless otherwise indicated.

Strain or Stock	Parity	At Birth		At Weaning		Young Weaned per Sow per Year	Pre-weaning Mortality, %	Reference
		Litter Size	Total No. of Litters	Avg. Litter Size	Total No. of Litters			
Inbred								
2	..	....	....	2.48 ± 0.03	73	7.8 ± 2.86[1]	....	3
13	..	....	....	2.69 ± 0.06	62	5.2 ± 3.90[1]	....	3
B/Lac	1	2.29 ± 0.10	59					1,2
	2	3.36 ± 0.23	52					
	3	3.43 ± 0.23	44	2.5 ± 0.2	34	9.3	11	
	4	3.34 ± 0.27	38					
	5	3.06 ± 0.20	32					
	6	3.56 ± 0.59	16					
OM3	1	2.52 ± 0.11	69					1,2
	2	2.78 ± 0.15	59					
	3	2.84 ± 0.19	51	2.3 ± 0.1	52	5.6	14	
	4	2.49 ± 0.18	41					
	5	2.63 ± 0.20	27					
	6	2.76 ± 0.39	17					
R9	1	2.52 ± 0.13	63					1,2
	2	2.98 ± 0.16	45					
	3	3.31 ± 0.23	36	2.5 ± 0.2	44	7.0	16	
	4	2.70 ± 0.21	30					
	5	2.94 ± 0.39	16					
	6	2.50 ± 0.26	8					
Outbred								
Dunkin-Hartley	..	....	....	4.2	....	16.9	14	6
Dunkin-Hartley[2,3]	1	3.2	66					5
	2	4.3	63					
	3	4.7	61	....	....	16.8	15	
	4	4.3	58					
	5	3.6	57					
	6	3.6	54					
Lac:DHP[4]	..	4.4	297	3.7	....	13.9	10	4

[1] Plus/minus (±) value is standard deviation. [2] Presumed Dunkin-Hartley. [3] Average litter size at birth, all litters = 3.98 ± 0.07. [4] Specific pathogen-free.

continued

124. REPRODUCTION AND GROWTH: GUINEA PIG

Part I. Effect of Parity on Litter Size

Contributor: Michael F. W. Festing

References
1. Festing, M. F. W. 1971. Guinea-Pig News Lett. 4:19-20.
2. Festing, M. F. W. Unpublished. MRC Laboratory Animals Centre, Carshalton, Surrey, U.K., 1979.
3. Hansen, C. T., and W. J. McEleney. 1971. Defining Lab. Anim. Proc. 4th Symp. Int. Comm. Lab. Anim. Inst. Lab. Anim. Resour. 1969, pp. 179-202.
4. Lovell, D., et al. 1972. Guinea-Pig News Lett. 6:6-11.
5. Rowlands, I. W. 1949. J. Hyg. 47:281-287.
6. Wills, J. E., and S. D. Sutherland. 1970. J. Inst. Anim. Tech. 21:134-147.

Part II. Effect of Litter Size on Developmental Variables

Value: Plus/minus (±) values are standard deviations, unless otherwise indicated. **Number of Observations** = number of litters, unless otherwise indicated.

Specification	Strain or Stock	Litter Size	Value	Number of Observations	Reference
Frequency of litter size at birth	Average of several inbred strains	1	17.05%	Total: 11,945	4
		2	33.08%		
		3	30.92%		
		4	13.73%		
		5	4.05%		
		6	0.97%		
		7	0.16%		
		8	0.03%		
	Dunkin-Hartley	1	4.5%	Total: 404	2
		2	23.1%		
		3	45.5%		
		4	22.4%		
		5	4.0%		
		6	0.5%		
	Mill Hill Dunkin-Hartley	1	6%	Total: 324	1
		2	13%		
		3	26%		
		4	25%		
		5	17%		
		6	5%		
		7	7%		
		8	<1%		
	Outbred stock presumed to be Frant Dunkin-Hartley	1	4.18%	Total: 406	6
		2	10.10%		
		3	20.69%		
		4	32.51%		
		5	19.70%		
		6	9.36%		
		7	1.97%		
		8	0.98%		
		9	0.25%		
		10	0.25%		

continued

Part II. Effect of Litter Size on Developmental Variables

Specification	Strain or Stock	Litter Size	Value	Number of Observations	Reference
Litters aborted, no.	Genetically heterogeneous, plus strain 13	1 2 3 4 5	2 [11%] 5 [9%] 9 [8%] 8 [9%] 6 [17%]	277 ♀ of genetically heterogeneous stock, plus 53 ♀ of strain 13	3
Litters with stillborn, no.	Genetically heterogeneous, plus strain 13	1 2 3 4 5 6	10 [17%] 30 [12%] 80 [15%] 125 [35%] 53 [46%] 9 [90%]	1338 ♀	3
Mortality at birth	Average of several inbred strains	1 2 3 4 5 6 7 8	19.0% of young 13.2% of young 14.8% of young 22.7% of young 29.3% of young 38.1% of young 51.9% of young 29.1% of young	2037[1] 7904[1] 11079[1] 6564[1] 2420[1] 696[1] 133[1] 24[1]	4
	Outbred stock presumed to be Frant Dunkin-Hartley	1 2 3 4 5 6 7 8 9 10	0% of young 0% of young 1.2% of young 2.5% of young 4.8% of young 6.1% of young 5.4% of young 28.1% of young 44.6% of young 60.0% of young	17[1] 82[1] 252[1] 528[1] 400[1] 228[1] 56[1] 32[1] 9[1] 10[1]	6
Pre-weaning mortality (of animals alive at birth)	Average of several inbred strains	1 2 3 4 5 6 7 8	18.1% 16.0% 16.4% 19.8% 22.0% 29.7% 34.4% 11.8%	1650[2] 6861[2] 9439[2] 5074[2] 1711[2] 431[2] 64[2] 17[2]	4
	Outbred stock presumed to be Frant Dunkin-Hartley	1 2 3 4 5 6 7 8 9 10	11.8% 12.2% 13.7% 7.8% 11.5% 11.2% 17.0% 34.8% 40.0% 50.0%	17[2] 82[2] 249[2] 515[2] 381[2] 214[2] 53[2] 23[2] 5[2] 4[2]	6
Birth weight	Dunkin-Hartley	1 2	103 ± 3.9 g[3] 92 ± 1.1 g[3]	18[1] 186[1]	2

[1] Number of young born, including live and stillborn. [2] Number of young born alive. [3] Plus/minus (±) value is standard error.

continued

Part II. Effect of Litter Size on Developmental Variables

Specification	Strain or Stock	Litter Size	Value	Number of Observations	Reference
		3	84 ± 0.5 g [3]	551 [1]	
		4	74 ± 0.6 g [3]	362 [1]	
		5	70 ± 1.1 g [3]	80 [1]	
		6	73 ± 2.6 g [3]	12 [1]	
Birth weight of animals surviving to weaning	Average of several inbred strains	1	♂, 107 g; ♀, 106 g	1351 [4]	4
		2	♂, 92 g; ♀, 89 g	5763 [4]	
		3	♂, 79 g; ♀, 78 g	7891 [4]	
		4	♂, 72 g; ♀, 69 g	4069 [4]	
		5	♂, 67 g; ♀, 65 g	1335 [4]	
		6	♂, 63 g; ♀, 60 g	303 [4]	
		7	♂, 56 g; ♀, 56 g	42 [4]	
		8	♂, 56 g; ♀, 65 g	15 [4]	
Birth weight of animals alive at 28 days of age	Outbred stock presumed to be Frant Dunkin-Hartley	1	♂, 130 g; ♀, 128 g	6♂; 9♀	5
		2	♂, 113 g; ♀, 112 g	32♂; 40♀	
		3	♂, 101 g; ♀, 101 g	108♂; 86♀	
		4	♂, 96 g; ♀, 91 g	218♂; 172♀	
		5	♂, 90 g; ♀, 85 g	128♂; 112♀	
		6	♂, 82 g; ♀, 81 g	62♂; 52♀	
Age to reach 200 g	Mill Hill Dunkin-Hartley	1	11 d	Total: 324	1
		2	9 d		
		3	14 d		
		4	17 d		
		5	19 d		
		6	18 d		
		7	20 d		
		8	23 d		
Weaning weight	Average of several inbred strains	1	♂, 280 g; ♀, 273 g	1351 [4]	4
		2	♂, 251 g; ♀, 241 g	5763 [4]	
		3	♂, 221 g; ♀, 215 g	7891 [4]	
		4	♂, 204 g; ♀, 197 g	4069 [4]	
		5	♂, 199 g; ♀, 190 g	1335 [4]	
		6	♂, 193 g; ♀, 179 g	303 [4]	
		7	♂, 201 g; ♀, 179 g	42 [4]	
		8	♂, 145 g; ♀, 141 g	15 [4]	
28-day weight	Outbred stock presumed to be Frant Dunkin-Hartley	1	♂, 348 g; ♀, 316 g	6♂; 9♀	5
		2	♂, 299 g; ♀, 285 g	32♂; 40♀	
		3	♂, 283 g; ♀, 275 g	108♂; 86♀	
		4	♂, 281 g; ♀, 270 g	218♂; 172♀	
		5	♂, 279 g; ♀, 271 g	128♂; 112♀	
		6	♂, 274 g; ♀, 264 g	62♂; 52♀	
Mean duration of gestation	Outbred stock presumed to be Frant Dunkin-Hartley [5]	1 + 2	68.7 d	13	5
		3	68.2 d	15	
		4	67.1 d	37	
		5	67.4 d	38	
		≥6	66.6 d	34	
Mean duration of gestation of litters with ≥1 live young	Strain 13	1	69.9 ± 1.4 d	15	3
		2	69.7 ± 1.6 d	42	
		3	68.5 ± 1.6 d	73	
		4	67.6 ± 1.7 d	70	

[1] Number of young born, including live and stillborn. [3] Plus/minus (±) value is standard error. [4] Number of young surviving to weaning. [5] Data from females in second through fourth pregnancies only.

continued

Part II. Effect of Litter Size on Developmental Variables

Specification	Strain or Stock	Litter Size	Value	Number of Observations	Reference
		5	66.5 ± 1.3 d	36	
		6	65.3 ± 0.7 d	3	
	Genetically heterogeneous	1	70.5 ± 1.1 d	37	3
		2	69.5 ± 1.4 d	216	
		3	68.8 ± 1.6 d	427	
		4	68.2 ± 1.6 d	276	
		5	67.4 ± 1.7 d	63	
		6	66.8 ± 1.5 d	8	
Coefficient of regression of fetal weight on duration of gestation	Outbred stock presumed to be Frant Dunkin-Hartley	1	9.95	14	5
		2	5.81	24	
		3	2.60	51	
		4	1.23	87	
		5	3.69	62	
		6	−1.66	32	
		7	−0.02	6	

Contributor: Michael F. W. Festing

References

1. Bruce, H. M., and A. S. Parkes. 1948. J. Hyg. 46:434-437.
2. Dunkin, G. W., et al. 1930. Ibid. 30:311-330.
3. Goy, R. W., et al. 1957. Anat. Rec. 128:747-757.
4. Haines, G. 1931. J. Agric. Res. 42:123-164.
5. McKeown, T., and B. MacMahon. 1956. J. Endocrinol. 13:195-200.
6. Rowlands, I. W. 1949. J. Hyg. 47:281-287.

125. BODY AND ORGAN WEIGHTS: GUINEA PIG

Part I. Growth

Data are for males and females from the colonies of three inbred strains: B/Lac, OM3/Lac, and R9/Lac [ref. 1, 2]. Animals of all colonies were classified as having a two-star "conventional" status [ref. 3, 4], and were fed RGP diet and hay. The animal-room temperature was 21 ± 2°C, and the lighting cycle was 15 hours light:9 hours darkness. Adult animals were kept as monogamous pairs. Young animals were weaned at 21 days and paired at 13 weeks [ref. 5]. All unweaned and weaned animals, adult males, and non-pregnant and non-lactating adult females in the three colonies were weighed at weekly intervals for 7 months. Thus, all results are based on sample weighings and reflect ranges of variation in body weights for each colony. Values for animals 2-10 weeks old were calculated from body weights at each particular time period ± 3 days. Values for animals older than 10 weeks were computed from all observations available for each given time period. Data were previously unpublished. Values in parentheses are ranges, estimate "b" (see Introduction).

Age wk	B/Lac Body Weight g	No. of Observations	OM3/Lac Body Weight g	No. of Observations	R9/Lac Body Weight g	No. of Observations
			Male			
0 (birth)	100.6(82.2-119.0)	10	70.8(55.6-86.0)	6	96.3(80.6-112.0)	7
2	209.8(134.6-285.0)	19	142.3(87.9-196.7)	19	179.3(110.0-248.6)	15
4	315.7(232.6-398.8)	23	210.9(137.6-284.2)	20	267.0(176.6-357.4)	19

continued

Part I. Growth

Age wk	B/Lac Body Weight, g	No. of Observations	OM3/Lac Body Weight, g	No. of Observations	R9/Lac Body Weight, g	No. of Observations
6	414.6(334.3-494.9)	20	278.7(179.1-378.3)	11	371.2(278.9-463.5)	17
8	517.8(434.1-601.5)	16	358.1(260.0-456.2)	15	437.5(321.5-553.5)	12
10	594.9(536.9-652.9)	9	419.2(314.4-524.0)	11	520.6(342.1-699.1)	8
14-21	770.5(648.3-892.7)	35	595.1(488.8-701.4)	50	709.2(506.2-912.2)	43
21-28	857.2(781.5-932.9)	24	697.0(617.8-776.2)	39	841.1(697.9-984.3)	29
28-35	886.2(810.9-961.5)	20	752.4(677.8-827.0)	34	916.1(843.2-989.0)	21
35-42	910.5(752.6-1068.4)	26	778.1(724.0-832.2)	29	934.1(849.5-1018.7)	17
>42	988.6(820.5-1156.7)	91	844.4(721.9-966.9)	85	953.8(862.7-1044.9)	92
Female						
0 (birth)	103.7(89.0-118.4)	7	75.1(51.5-98.7)	9	88.8(68.3-109.3)	6
2	200.1(144.4-255.8)	18	137.4(73.9-200.9)	22	168.4(103.9-232.9)	10
4	299.3(245.5-353.1)	23	203.3(136.2-270.4)	20	253.2(171.7-334.7)	13
6	370.6(325.8-415.4)	15	278.5(190.0-367.0)	14	337.3(215.5-459.1)	9
8	429.1(375.8-482.4)	7	341.1(244.2-438.0)	15	389.6(272.8-506.4)	9
10	475.5(398.3-552.7)	6	402.7(281.1-524.3)	12	487.0(368.3-605.7)	4
14-21	644.6(511.3-777.9)	30	540.6(429.6-651.6)	29	638.0(509.3-766.7)	24
21-28	806.6(714.2-899.0)	13	638.8(515.9-761.7)	19	688.7(569.7-807.7)	15
28-35	846.4(819.5-873.3)	5	682.6(538.2-827.0)	15	745.8(653.8-837.8)	18
35-42	803.2(775.4-831.0)	10	687.2(525.1-849.3)	19	747.5(595.2-899.8)	14
>42	938.9(763.7-1114.1)	50	771.1(639.9-902.3)	74	828.7(688.6-968.8)	65

Contributors: Jon A. Turton and David C. Shaw

References

1. Festing, M. F. 1975. Guinea-Pig News Lett. 9:3-8.
2. Festing, M. F. W., ed. 1975. International Index of Laboratory Animals. Ed. 3. Medical Research Council Laboratory Animals Centre, Carshalton, Surrey, U.K.
3. Medical Research Council. 1974. The Accreditation and Recognition Schemes for Suppliers of Laboratory Animals. Laboratory Animals Centre, Carshalton, Surrey, U.K.
4. Turton, J. A. 1977. Guinea-Pig News Lett. 11:3-9.
5. Turton, J. A., et al. 1977. Ibid. 11:10-31.

Part II. Weight of Body Structures

Data are for males and females of three inbred strains: B/Lac, OM3/Lac, and R9/Lac [ref. 2, 3]; for comparative purposes, data have also been included for Lac:DHP [ref. 3, 5], a commonly used outbred stock. Animals of the inbred strains were classified as having a two-star "conventional" status; those of the Lac:DHP stock were of the four-star SPF category [ref. 4, 6]. All animals were ex-breeding stock. Generally, each breeding pair had had five litters before being culled, but some animals had produced more than five litters. All were fed the RGP diet and hay. (For further information on the status and husbandry of the colonies, consult references 7, 8.) Animals were killed with an overdose of diethyl ether, and the body weight and body length determined. Each animal was then dissected and the various organs removed and weighed (consult references 7 and 8 for details, 1 and 9 for anatomical descriptions). Values in parentheses are ranges, estimate "b" (see Introduction).

Specification	B/Lac	OM3/Lac	R9/Lac	Lac:DHP
Male				
No. of animals	9	10	8	9
Age, wk	62.2(52.6-71.8)	72.3(26.4-118.2)	86.2(33.6-138.8)	83.0(54.2-111.8)

continued

Part II. Weight of Body Structures

Specification	B/Lac	OM3/Lac	R9/Lac	Lac:DHP
Body weight, g	1054.6(904.3-1204.9)	894.9(790.6-999.2)	974.9(866.4-1083.4)	1219.2(1049.9-1388.5)
Body length, cm	31.3(30.0-32.6)	29.5(26.5-32.5)	31.0(26.5-35.5)	32.2(28.5-35.9)
Femur length, cm				
Left	4.599(4.507-4.691)	4.178(4.042-4.314)	4.519(4.265-4.773)	4.593(4.365-4.821)
Right	4.624(4.534-4.714)	4.184(4.046-4.322)	4.520(4.266-4.774)	4.608(4.394-4.822)
Mandible length, cm				
Left	5.392(5.206-5.578)	5.133(4.871-5.395)	5.450(5.282-5.618)	5.703(5.453-5.953)
Right	5.335(5.153-5.517)	5.109(4.925-5.293)	5.449(5.293-5.605)	5.667(5.449-5.885)
Weight of structure, g				
Brain	4.434(4.120-4.748)	4.565(4.059-5.071)	4.103(3.713-4.493)	4.652(4.226-5.078)
Eye, left	0.611(0.565-0.657)	0.624(0.484-0.764)	0.612(0.510-0.714)	0.625(0.521-0.729)
right	0.607(0.497-0.717)	0.610(0.478-0.742)	0.604(0.468-0.740)	0.627(0.499-0.755)
Stomach	3.421(1.949-4.893)	3.126(2.280-3.972)	3.409(2.193-4.625)	4.101(2.455-5.747)
Liver	31.113(25.359-36.867)	23.637(18.211-29.063)	30.717(24.153-37.281)	41.040(26.642-55.438)
Small intestine	6.656(3.668-9.644)	5.576(4.568-6.584)	6.325(3.803-8.847)	6.931(5.047-8.815)
Cecum	5.331(4.039-6.623)	4.666(3.290-6.042)	6.295(4.557-8.033)	7.068(5.206-8.930)
Abdominal fat, left	4.541(2.873-6.209)	3.365(1.461-5.269)	5.706(4.012-7.400)	5.039(3.619-6.459)
right	4.770(3.224-6.316)	3.604(1.642-5.566)	5.368(3.648-7.088)	5.016(3.816-6.216)
Lungs	4.938(3.612-6.264)	5.104(4.154-6.054)	5.077(4.063-6.091)	4.640(3.334-5.946)
Heart	2.236(1.838-2.634)	2.079(1.631-2.527)	2.447(2.089-2.805)	2.687(2.045-3.329)
Spleen	0.560(0.496-0.624)	0.740(0.556-0.924)	0.853(0.647-1.059)	0.840(0.556-1.124)
Thymus[1], left	0.321(0.197-0.445)	0.195(0.027-0.363)	0.258(0.084-0.432)	0.353(0.181-0.525)
right	0.309(0.181-0.437)	0.196(0.060-0.332)	0.246(0.068-0.424)	0.372(0.172-0.572)
Kidney, left	2.955(2.265-3.645)	2.137(1.303-2.971)	2.623(2.181-3.065)	3.347(2.787-3.907)
right	2.868(2.244-3.492)	2.057(1.465-2.649)	2.561(2.153-2.969)	3.306(2.654-3.958)
Bladder	0.469(0.337-0.601)	0.461(0.257-0.665)	0.508(0.402-0.614)	0.518(0.254-0.782)
Adrenal, left	0.254(0.162-0.346)	0.288(0.202-0.374)	0.402(0.202-0.602)	0.373(0.193-0.553)
right	0.251(0.175-0.327)	0.235(0.155-0.315)	0.330(0.116-0.544)	0.323(0.165-0.481)
Testis, left	1.609(1.291-1.927)	2.005(1.387-2.623)	1.613(0.901-2.325)	2.546(2.176-2.916)
right	1.597(1.309-1.885)	1.997(1.395-2.599)	1.619(0.837-2.401)	2.520(2.094-2.946)
Femur, left	2.031(1.917-2.145)	1.805(1.473-2.137)	1.966(1.672-2.260)	2.416(2.044-2.788)
right	2.049(1.903-2.195)	1.813(1.393-2.233)	1.949(1.649-2.249)	2.418(2.012-2.824)
Female				
No. of animals	11	12	8	14
Age, wk	76.8(37.6-116.0)	73.8(40.6-107.0)	86.8(39.4-134.2)	95.0(71.6-118.4)
Body weight, g	1026.8(850.6-1203.0)	823.3(667.7-978.9)	868.3(645.5-1091.1)	1060.0(761.0-1359.0)
Body length, cm	30.6(29.0-32.2)	29.4(27.6-31.2)	29.8(27.9-31.7)	32.3(28.8-35.8)
Femur length, cm				
Left	4.507(4.395-4.619)	4.102(3.956-4.248)	4.328(4.180-4.476)	4.535(4.405-4.665)
Right	4.508(4.410-4.606)	4.133(4.037-4.229)	4.330(4.134-4.526)	4.533(4.349-4.717)
Mandible length, cm				
Left	5.156(5.024-5.288)	5.030(4.868-5.192)	5.153(4.911-5.395)	5.510(5.134-5.886)
Right	5.186(5.062-5.310)	5.044(4.848-5.240)	5.200(4.982-5.418)	5.550(5.192-5.908)
Weight of structure, g				
Brain	4.191(3.881-4.501)	4.302(4.060-4.544)	3.831(3.231-4.431)	4.319(3.843-4.795)
Eye, left	0.624(0.528-0.720)	0.623(0.511-0.735)	0.607(0.465-0.749)	0.650(0.536-0.764)
right	0.625(0.565-0.685)	0.610(0.476-0.744)	0.622(0.528-0.716)	0.647(0.525-0.769)
Stomach	4.467(3.175-5.759)	3.975(2.473-5.477)	3.966(2.766-5.166)	5.037(3.379-6.695)
Liver	34.988(27.846-42.130)	30.349(19.299-41.399)	31.074(24.596-37.552)	44.719(22.641-66.797)
Small intestine	7.685(5.155-10.215)	6.512(3.926-9.098)	7.490(5.038-9.942)	9.912(6.560-13.264)

[1] Cervical thymus.

continued

125. BODY AND ORGAN WEIGHTS: GUINEA PIG

Part II. Weight of Body Structures

Specification	B/Lac	OM3/Lac	R9/Lac	Lac:DHP
Cecum	7.071(4.785-9.357)	5.300(4.282-6.318)	7.046(4.700-9.392)	7.527(5.337-9.717)
Abdominal fat, left	3.464(1.728-5.200)	2.147(0.567-3.727)	3.075(0.579-5.571)	3.069(0.000-7.333)
right	3.263(1.743-4.783)	2.117(0.691-3.543)	3.235(0.369-6.101)	2.947(0.000-6.815)
Lungs	5.314(3.684-6.944)	5.138(3.268-7.008)	5.028(3.576-6.480)	4.648(2.916-6.380)
Heart	2.573(2.069-3.077)	2.328(1.840-2.816)	2.344(2.140-2.548)	2.990(2.208-3.772)
Spleen	0.696(0.442-0.950)	1.018(0.610-1.426)	1.031(0.813-1.249)	0.991(0.493-1.489)
Thymus[1], left	0.350(0.190-0.510)	0.182(0.102-0.262)	0.217(0.077-0.357)	0.220(0.078-0.362)
right	0.355(0.205-0.505)	0.205(0.067-0.343)	0.211(0.055-0.367)	0.213(0.073-0.353)
Kidney, left	2.919(2.489-3.349)	2.124(1.710-2.538)	2.552(2.150-2.954)	3.109(2.267-3.951)
right	2.863(2.557-3.169)	2.014(1.600-2.428)	2.477(2.137-2.817)	2.884(2.176-3.592)
Bladder	0.735(0.407-1.063)	0.551(0.387-0.715)	0.596(0.288-0.904)	0.769(0.369-1.169)
Adrenal, left	0.531(0.295-0.767)	0.303(0.231-0.375)	0.397(0.215-0.579)	0.558(0.276-0.840)
right	0.455(0.283-0.627)	0.243(0.185-0.301)	0.293(0.191-0.395)	0.395(0.203-0.587)
Ovary, left	0.113(0.075-0.151)	0.097(0.017-0.177)	0.056(0.028-0.084)	0.169(0.000-0.607)
right	0.132(0.034-0.230)	0.103(0.015-0.191)	0.053(0.023-0.083)	0.150(0.000-0.488)
Uterine horn, left	1.514(0.922-2.106)	1.180(0.392-1.968)	0.922(0.268-1.576)	1.309(0.237-2.381)
right	1.458(0.804-2.112)	1.219(0.433-2.005)	0.922(0.066-1.778)	1.312(0.408-2.216)
Femur, left	1.804(1.640-1.968)	1.603(1.441-1.765)	1.676(1.500-1.852)	2.145(1.855-2.435)
right	1.803(1.609-1.997)	1.603(1.443-1.763)	1.671(1.503-1.839)	2.156(1.856-2.456)

[1] Cervical thymus.

Contributors: Jon A. Turton and David C. Shaw

References

1. Cooper, G., and A. L. Schiller. 1975. Anatomy of the Guinea Pig. Harvard Univ., Cambridge.
2. Festing, M. F. 1975. Guinea-Pig News Lett. 9:3-8.
3. Festing, M. F. W., ed. 1975. International Index of Laboratory Animals. Ed. 3. Medical Research Council Laboratory Animals Centre, Carshalton, Surrey, U.K.
4. Medical Research Council. 1974. The Accreditation and Recognition Schemes for Suppliers of Laboratory Animals. Laboratory Animals Centre, Carshalton, Surrey, U.K.
5. Parrott, R. F., and M. F. W. Festing. 1977. Standardised Laboratory Animals. Medical Research Council Laboratory Animals Centre, Carshalton, Surrey, U.K.
6. Turton, J. A. 1977. Guinea-Pig News Lett. 11:3-9.
7. Turton, J. A., et al. 1977. Ibid. 11:10-31.
8. Turton, J. A., et al. 1977. Ibid. 12:11-22.
9. Wagner, J. E., and P. J. Manning, ed. 1976. The Biology of the Guinea Pig. Academic, New York.

126. CONGENITAL ABNORMALITIES: GUINEA PIG

Abnormality	Mode of Inheritance	No. Observed	No. at Risk	Incidence, %	Reference
Exencephaly & hydrocephaly	Polygenic threshold (?)	25	76,000	0.03	15
Anophthalmia & microphthalmia	Highly inheritable, but exact mode not yet known	....	....	26[1]	1
				82[2]	4,7
Microphthalmia	Not known	145	76,000	0.19	15
Anophthalmia & roan spotting; absence of pigment in homozygotes	Autosomal dominant, with *Rs/Rs* anophthalmic	....	....	....	10

[1] In a partly inbred strain. [2] In matings of two affected animals.

continued

Abnormality	Mode of Inheritance	No. Observed	No. at Risk	Incidence, %	Reference
Otocephaly & cyclopia: varies from shortness of mandible to complete absence of mandible, maxilla, nose, eyes, all of brain in front of medulla oblongata, & most of the skull	Polygenic threshold (?)	500	76,000	0.04[3/]; 28.00[4/]	4,11, 15,16
Anotia: superficially resembles otocephaly, but eye defect is bilateral microphthalmia rather than cyclopia; complete absence of internal, middle, or external ears	Mutant with very low penetrance (?)	0 7	9,000 160	0.0[5/] 4.3[6/]	4,15 4,15
Waltzing Progressive atrophy of organ of Corti & cochlear neurons	Mendelian dominant, Wz	....	....	....	2,3
Behavior similar to that found in Japanese waltzing mice	Autosomal recessive, wtz	....	....	....	5,8
Harelip & missing or abnormal incisors	Not known	4	76,000 (?)	....	8
Cruciate double monsters: joined at chest with head, or heads, at right angles to the bodies	Polygenic threshold (?)	3	76,000	....	4,15
Polydactylous monster: vertebral (spinal) column C-shaped rather than S-shaped; excessive subcutaneous fat; shortening of limbs except upper foreleg; tibia missing, hindlimb rotated; feet double width, with 7-10 digits; many abnormalities of head region	Semi-dominant mutant, Px. Monsters are Px/Px, of which 89% die in utero.	....	....	....	4,9,14, 15
Chunky monster: body length only 2/3 of normal, but normal weight; leg abnormalities & flexure of feet	Polygenic threshold	26	76,000	0.03	4,15
Micromelia with dropsy; stillborn monsters, with body undersized & legs rudimentary	Mendelian recessive; low penetrance	5 4	120,000 76,000	....	15 15
Flexure of feet, sometimes associated with torsion of legs	Non-genetic (?)	50	76,000	0.07	4,15
Abnormal digits, including missing, distorted, fused, or double digits	Presumed polygenic	21	76,000	0.03	4,15
Atavistic polydactyly: presence of a fourth digit on hind feet	Polygenic threshold [7/]	Common	....	0-100[8/]	12
Spermatogenic hypoplasia: animals vigorous & healthy, but males subfertile or sterile; condition associated with chocolate or red coat color	Single gene	....	....	....	6
Anemia & sterility of silver-whites of genotype si/si dm/dm: high mortality; reduced hemoglobin; sterility	Interaction of two loci, only double homozygotes si/si dm/dm affected	....		....	13,15

[3/] Incidence in general colony. [4/] Incidence in some branches of strain 13. [5/] In main branch of strain 2. [6/] In a strain 2 subline. [7/] Genetic analysis of this characteristic by Wright (the classic example) demonstrates the polygenic threshold mode of inheritance. [8/] Zero incidence in strain 2 but 100% incidence in strain D (now extinct) selected for extra digit.

Contributor: Michael F. W. Festing

References
1. Eaton, O. N. 1937. J. Hered. 28:353-358.
2. Ernstson, S. 1971. Acta Oto-Laryngol. 71:469-482.
3. Ernstson, S. 1971. Ibid. 72:303-309.
4. Festing, M. F. W. 1976. In J. E. Wagner and P. J. Manning, ed. Biology of the Guinea Pig. Academic, New York. pp. 99-116.
5. Ibsen, H. L., and K. T. Risty. 1929. Anat. Rec. 44:294(Abstr.).
6. Jakway, J. S., and E. C. Young. 1958. Fertil. Steril. 9:533-544.
7. Komich, R. J. 1971. Am. J. Vet. Res. 32:2099-2105.
8. Lurie, M. H. 1941. Ann. Otol. 50:113-128.

continued

9. Scott, J. P. 1938. J. Morphol. 62:299-321.
10. Whiteway, C., and R. Robinson. 1975. Guinea-Pig News Lett. 9:13-16.
11. Wright, S. 1934. Cold Spring Harbor Symp. Quant. Biol. 2:137-147.
12. Wright, S. 1934. Genetics 19:537-551.
13. Wright, S. 1959. Ibid. 44:563-590.
14. Wright, S. 1934. J. Hered. 25:359-362.
15. Wright, S. 1960. J. Cell. Comp. Physiol. 56(Suppl.): 123-151.
16. Wright, S., and K. Wagner. 1934. Am. J. Anat. 54: 383-447.

127. COAT COLOR: GUINEA PIG

For reviews on the genetics of coat color in guinea pigs, consult references 1-3.

Part I. Loci Affecting Coat and Eye Color

Data summarize those loci known to affect coat and eye color. Brief descriptions of the various mutants are included. Further details can be found in the three reviews noted above which also give original source references.

Locus	Allele	Comment
A	...	Agouti locus. Controls amount & distribution of eumelanin (black or brown pigment) & phaeomelanin (yellow & reddish pigment), both in individual hairs & in the coat.
	A	Light-bellied agouti, analogous to A^w in mice. Agouti, but with light belly. This is the *Cavia porcellus* wild type.
	A^r	Ticked-bellied agouti. Found by Detlefsen in 1914 in wild *C. rufescens*. Variable expression, but probably homologous with the agouti wild type in mice.
	a	Non-agouti. Eliminates phaeomelanin from individual hairs; animals are therefore black.
B	...	Brown locus
	B	Wild type, with black eumelanin
	b	Brown. Changes eumelanin in hair, skin, & eyes from black to brown.
C	...	Color, or albino locus. This series of mutations reduce the amount of pigment and in some cases make it heat-labile. The effect is more severe on yellow phaeomelanin than on eumelanin. There is no true albino mutation homologous with c in mice. However, c^a interacts with the extension allele at the E locus to give a synthetic albino ($c^a/c^a\ e/e$).
	C	Wild type, with full pigmentation
	c^k	Dark dilution. Similar to c^d, but with slightly more black/brown pigment.
	c^d	Light dilution. Black is reduced to sepia-brown similar to human brown hair. Red is reduced to yellow or cream. Eye color remains black.
	c^r	Red-eyed dilution. Black pigment reduced to sepia brown, but yellow pigment eliminated altogether. Eyes glowing red.
	c^a	Acromelanic albino. Black reduced to patches on extremities (nose, feet, ears). Yellow eliminated completely. Eyes pink.
Dm	...	Diminished locus. The single mutant at this locus interacts with si to give an anemia syndrome which may be equivalent to that found in the black-eyed whites of the W & Sl mutants of the mouse.
	Dm	Full color
	dm	Causes extra dilution of the coat with the less dominant mutants at the albino locus, but has no phenotypic effect in the presence of C
E	...	Extension locus. Alleles at this locus control the amount of eumelanin/phaeomelanin in individual hairs, and the distribution of the two types of pigment.
	E	Wild type, having the usual agouti-banded hair
	e	Black pigment eliminated in favor of the yellow/red phaeomelanin. Animals have uniform reddish color.
	e^p	Partial extension. Homozygotes have a brindled or tortoiseshell pattern, with a mixture of black & yellow areas (black predominating). This allele interacts with the spotted mutation, s. In animals of the genotype $s/s\ e^p/e^p$, the areas of black & yellow separate to give tricolor pattern of black & red patches on a white background.

continued

127. COAT COLOR: GUINEA PIG

Part I. Loci Affecting Coat and Eye Color

Locus	Allele	Comment
F	...	Fading locus. The single mutation at this locus affects only phaeomelanin; its effects increase with age.
	F	Wild type, with full color
	f	Homozygotes have reduced phaeomelanin rather similar to the c^k mutation at the albino locus. The mutant interacts with p so that animals of the genotype $p/p \ f/f$ are pale cream.
Gr	...	Grizzled locus
	Gr	Full color, but incompletely dominant over gr
	gr	Causes a silvering which only appears after the first pelage and progresses with age
P	...	Pink-eyed dilution locus. Alleles at this locus alter the shape & distribution of pigment granules in the hair. It only affects eumelanin, and not phaeomelanin, in contrast with alleles at the C locus.
	P	Wild type, with full color
	p^r	Ruby-eye. Has little or no effect on hair pigmentation, but causes a reddish gleam in the eye.
	p	Homozygotes have a pink eye similar to albinos, & a marked dilution of the black/brown pigments, but the yellow/red pigment is unaffected.
Ro	...	Roan locus. A mutation has been described, but it is probably identical to si.
Rs	...	Roan spotting & anophthalmos locus. Mutation described by Whiteway & Robinson [ref. 4] may be homologous with the anophthalmic white found in the hamster, chinchilla, & mouse.
	Rs	Partially dominant mutation. Homozygotes are anophthalmic white. Heterozygotes have an uneven silvering, with white hairs on back, sides, & belly, & a white blaze & dark red eyes.
	rs	Full color
S	...	White spotting or piebald spotting locus. A single mutation at this locus is common in both fancy & laboratory stocks (including two inbred strains, 2 & 13), particularly in combination with partial extension e^p, which produces a tri-colored phenotype of black & red areas on a white background.
	S	Full color, but incompletely dominant so that heterozygotes have a reduced degree of spotting. In the presence of an extreme array of modifiers, even SS animals may have some white spots.
	s	Homozygotes have white spots which vary in size & shape from ⌄10-97% of the total body surface. The variable expression is controlled both by modifying genes & by chance environmental factors, so that even within an inbred strain the degree of spotting may vary from a trace of white to almost 100% white. ♀ have slightly more white than ♂.
Si	...	Silvering locus
	Si	Full color, but incompletely dominant
	si	Homozygotes vary enormously in expression of this gene. Commonly, the belly (thorax & abdomen) may be more or less uniformly silvered, or there may be irregular blotches of white within silvered areas. In higher grades, silvering may also occur on the back.
Sm	...	Salmon-eye. Locus mainly controls pigmentation of eye.
	Sm	Normal eye
	sm	Pigmentation of eye limited to circular region around pupillary margin of iris. This ring of pigmentation may vary widely in density & width.
W	...	Whitish, or white tipped (not to be confused with the W series in the mouse)
	W	An incompletely dominant gene that causes whitening or extreme paling of the hair several millimeters below the tip. Only expressed in the presence of C, and does not affect phaeomelanin; red animals ($e/e \ C/-$) therefore are unaffected.
	w	Full color

Contributor: Michael F. W. Festing

References

1. Festing, M. F. W. 1976. In J. E. Wagner and P. J. Manning, ed. The Biology of the Guinea Pig. Academic, New York and London. pp. 99-120.
2. Robinson, R. 1975. In R. C. King, ed. Handbook of Genetics. Plenum, New York and London. v. 4, pp. 275-307.
3. Searle, A. G. 1968. Comparative Genetics of Coat Colour in Mammals. Academic, New York and London.
4. Whiteway, C., and R. Robinson. 1975. Guinea-Pig News Lett. 9:13-16.

continued

127.   COAT COLOR: GUINEA PIG

Part II.   Genotypes of Fancy Varieties

Data summarize the coat color genotypes of fancy breeds. The names of the majority are surprisingly descriptive.

Where there is epistasis, it is possible for the variety to have several genotypes.

Variety	Genotype
Albino	$c^a\ e$
Beige	$a\ b\ p$
Black	a
Black-eyed white	$c^r\ e$
Brindle	$a\ e^p$
Chocolate	$a\ b$
Cinnamon agouti	$b\ c^r$

Variety	Genotype
Cream	$c^d\ e$
Dutch	$a\ s$
Golden agouti	$+$
Himalayan	$a\ c^a$
Lemon agouti	c^d or $b\ c^d$
Lilac	$a\ p$
Orange agouti	b

Variety	Genotype
Red	e
Roan	si or Rs
Salmon agouti	p or $b\ p$
Self golden	$e\ p$
Silver agouti	c^r
Tortoiseshell	$a\ e^p$
Tortoiseshell and white	$a\ e^p\ s$

Contributor: Michael F. W. Festing

Reference: Robinson, R. 1975. In R. C. King, ed. Handbook of Genetics. Plenum, New York and London. v. 4, pp. 275-307.

---

128.   BIOCHEMICAL POLYMORPHISMS AND VARIANTS: GUINEA PIG

Biochemical variation in the guinea pig has been described at very few loci, and for several of the described loci, no breeding has been done to confirm the single-locus mode of inheritance that is strictly required before a gene symbol is assigned [ref. 9]. This lack of data contrasts strongly with the mouse for which approximately 100 biochemical loci have been delineated [ref. 7]. It is virtually certain that many more polymorphic loci in the guinea pig could be discovered if a sufficiently wide range of stocks were to be surveyed at a reasonable number of potentially polymorphic loci. The Peruvian and Abyssinian breeds of *Cavia porcellus* maintained by fanciers may be a rich source of genetic variation which has not yet been studied by research scientists, and further studies of biochemical variation between *C. porcellus* and *C. aperea*, which hybridize to produce fertile offspring, may well be worthwhile. [ref. 6] Recent reviews of biochemical variation in guinea pigs include those of Lush [ref. 13, 14] and Festing [ref. 11]. Data in brackets refer to the column heading in brackets.

Type of Variation ⟨Synonym⟩	Locus Symbol	Description	Reference
Allotypic marker	$GP\gamma_2\text{-}1$ [1]	Immunoglobulin polymorphism described in a small sample of animals, without breeding tests	12
C2 polymorphism	$Co\text{-}2$ [1]	Polymorphism for isoelectric point of guinea pig C2 complement, but no breeding tests	8
C3 deficiency	$co\text{-}3$ [1]	Presumed deficiency of the 3rd component of complement. Mutant now extinct.	1
C4 deficiency	$Co\text{-}4$	Deficiency of the 4th component of complement. Mutant well characterized.	10
Carbonate dehydratase ⟨Carbonic anhydrase⟩	$Ca\text{-}2$	Strains OM3 & R9 homozygous for the b allele, and strain B/Lac homozygous for the a allele	4,5
Catalase	ca	Polymorphism for catalase activity in an unnamed stock. It is not known if this variation is common, or whether it is now extinct.	15
Glucosephosphate isomerase ⟨Phosphoglucose isomerase⟩	Pgi	Polymorphic between the species *Cavia porcellus* and *C. aperea*, which may be hybridized and produce fertile offspring of both sexes	6
Hydrocortisone ⟨Cortisol⟩ hydroxylation	Ch [1]	Controls ability to form hydroxylated derivatives of hydrocortisone ⟨cortisol⟩, with large differences between strains 2 & 13. May not be however, a single gene character.	2,3

[1] Provisional symbol. The mode of inheritance has not yet been confirmed by breeding tests.

continued

128. BIOCHEMICAL POLYMORPHISMS AND VARIANTS: GUINEA PIG

Type of Variation ⟨Synonym⟩	Locus Symbol	Description	Reference
Phosphoglucomutase	*Pgm*	Inbred strain OM3 homozygous for *Pgm¹*, and R9 homozygous for alternative allele *Pgm²*	5

Contributor: Michael F. W. Festing

References

1. Alper, C. A., and F. S. Rosen. 1971. Adv. Immunol. 14:251-290.
2. Burstein, S. 1971. Endocrinology 89:928-931.
3. Burstein, S., et al. 1965. Ibid. 76:753-761.
4. Carter, N. D. 1973. Comp. Biochem. Physiol. 46B: 387-393.
5. Carter, N. D., and M. F. W. Festing. 1972. Guinea-Pig News Lett. 6:12-16.
6. Carter, N. D., et al. 1972. Biochem. Genet. 6:147-156.
7. Chapman, V. M., et al. 1979. In P. L. Altman and D. D. Katz, ed. Inbred and Genetically Defined Strains of Laboratory Animals. Federation of American Societies for Experimental Biology, Bethesda, MD. pt. 1, pp. 77-95.
8. Colten, H. R., et al. 1970. Immunology 18:467-472.
9. Committee on Standardized Genetic Nomenclature for Mice. 1973. Biochem. Genet. 9:369-374.
10. Ellman, L., et al. 1970. Science 170:74-75.
11. Festing, M. F. W. 1976. In J. E. Wagner and P. J. Manning, ed. The Biology of the Guinea Pig. Academic, New York and London. pp. 99-120.
12. Kelus, A. S. 1969. Nature (London) 223:398-399.
13. Lush, I. E. 1966. The Biochemical Genetics of Vertebrates Except Man. North Holland, Amsterdam.
14. Lush, I. E. 1970. Symp. Zool. Soc. London 26:43-71.
15. Radev, T. 1960. J. Genet. 57:169-172.

129. BLOOD CHARACTERISTICS: GUINEA PIG

Data are for males and females of three inbred strains: B/Lac, OM3/Lac, and R9/Lac [ref. 1, 2]; Lac:DHP [ref. 2, 4], a commonly used outbred stock, was included for comparative purposes. Animals of the inbred strains were given two-star "conventional" status; those of the Lac:DHP stock were of the four-star SPF category [ref. 3, 5]. All animals were ex-breeding stock. Generally, each breeding pair had had five litters before being culled, but a few animals had produced more than five litters. All were fed an RGP diet and hay. For further information on the status and husbandry of the colonies, consult references 7 and 8. Particulars of the hematological techniques employed have been reported in detail in references 6-9. Values in parentheses are ranges, estimate "b" (*see* Introduction).

Part I. Blood Parameters

Specification: μl = microliter (10^{-6} liter); fl = femtoliter (10^{-15} liter); dl = deciliter (10^{-1} liter); pg = picogram.

Specification ⟨Synonym⟩	Value			
	B/Lac	**OM3/Lac**	**R9/Lac**	**Lac:DHP**
Male				
No. of animals	9	10	8	8
Age, wk	62.2(52.6-71.8)	72.3(26.4-118.2)	86.2(33.6-138.8)	82.2(67.0-97.3)
Body weight, g	1054.6(904.3-1204.9)	894.9(790.6-999.2)	974.9(866.4-1083.4)	1209.1(1040.1-1378.1)
Erythrocyte count, $10^6/\mu l$	4.98(4.49-5.46)	5.50(4.50-6.49)	4.61(3.81-5.40)	4.91(4.21-5.61)
Erythrocyte packed volume ⟨Hematocrit⟩, %	44.1(40.0-48.2)	47.8(39.8-55.8)	41.0(34.5-47.5)	45.4(39.3-51.5)

continued

Part I. Blood Parameters

Specification ⟨Synonym⟩	Value			
	B/Lac	OM3/Lac	R9/Lac	Lac:DHP
Erythrocyte volume, fl	88.9(79.9-97.9)	87.5(71.5-103.5)	89.4(78.8-100.0)	92.4(86.7-98.1)
Hemoglobin concentration				
In blood, g/dl	13.8(12.6-15.0)	14.4(12.4-16.4)	12.6(10.9-14.3)	13.9(12.3-15.5)
In erythrocytes, g/dl	31.3(29.3-33.3)	31.6(26.8-36.4)	31.9(29.2-34.6)	30.5(28.4-32.6)
Erythrocyte hemoglobin content, pg	27.9(25.8-30.0)	26.1(22.6-29.6)	27.2(24.4-30.0)	28.1(26.1-30.1)
Leukocyte count, $10^3/\mu l$	5.739(0.810-10.668)	8.785(4.024-13.546)	3.887(2.300-5.474)	6.106(2.622-9.590)
Plasma viscosity, centipoise	1.44(1.24-1.64)	1.45(1.27-1.63)	1.51(1.41-1.61)	1.51(1.23-1.79)
Female				
No. of animals	11	11	8	12
Age, wk	76.8(37.6-116.0)	71.6(41.2-102.0)	86.8(39.4-134.2)	96.2(71.7-120.7)
Body weight, g	1026.8(850.6-1203.0)	824.5(661.5-987.5)	868.3(645.5-1091.1)	1036.8(738.6-1335.0)
Erythrocyte count, $10^6/\mu l$	4.33(3.69-4.98)	4.86(4.17-5.55)	4.36(3.77-4.96)	4.57(3.74-5.40)
Erythrocyte packed volume ⟨Hemotocrit⟩, %	40.6(35.8-45.4)	43.3(37.2-49.4)	40.2(33.6-46.8)	42.7(38.0-47.4)
Erythrocyte volume, fl	93.2(84.5-101.9)	88.9(81.1-96.7)	92.4(82.5-102.3)	93.8(84.8-102.8)
Hemoglobin concentration				
In blood, g/dl	12.5(11.1-13.9)	12.9(11.1-14.7)	12.0(10.0-14.0)	13.1(11.0-15.2)
In erythrocytes, g/dl	32.1(29.2-35.0)	32.8(28.6-37.0)	31.9(27.2-36.6)	30.8(27.7-33.9)
Erythrocyte hemoglobin content, pg	28.9(26.3-31.5)	26.6(23.3-29.9)	27.5(25.1-29.9)	28.7(24.1-33.3)
Leukocyte count, $10^3/\mu l$	5.736(2.187-9.285)	8.182(1.358-15.006)	4.187(1.607-6.767)	8.217(0.00-17.077)
Plasma viscosity, centipoise	1.50(1.33-1.67)	1.46(1.18-1.74)	1.48(1.40-1.56)	1.59(1.33-1.85)

Contributors: Jon A. Turton and David C. Shaw

References

1. Festing, M. F. 1975. Guinea-Pig News Lett. 9:3-8.
2. Festing, M. F. W., ed. 1975. International Index of Laboratory Animals. Ed. 3. Medical Research Council Laboratory Animals Centre, Carshalton, Surrey, U.K.
3. Medical Research Council. 1974. The Accreditation and Recognition Schemes for Suppliers of Laboratory Animals. Laboratory Animals Centre, Carshalton, Surrey, U.K.
4. Parrott, R. F., and M. F. W. Festing. 1977. Standardised Laboratory Animals. Laboratory Animals Centre, Carshalton, Surrey, U.K.
5. Turton, J. A. 1977. Guinea-Pig News Lett. 11:3-9.
6. Turton, J. A., et al. 1975. Tropenmed. Parasitol. 26: 196-200.
7. Turton, J. A., et al. 1977. Guinea-Pig News Lett. 11: 10-31.
8. Turton, J. A., et al. 1977. Ibid. 12:11-12.
9. Turton, J. A., et al. 1978. Folia Primatol. 29:64-79.

Part II. Plasma Electrolytes and Osmotic Pressure

Specification: mM = millimolar; mosm = milliosmole.

Specification	Value			
	B/Lac	OM3/Lac	R9/Lac	Lac:DHP
Male				
No. of animals	8	9	8	9
Age, wk	62.2(57.0-67.4)	73.8(26.0-121.6)	86.2(33.6-138.8)	83.0(54.2-111.8)

continued

Part II. Plasma Electrolytes and Osmotic Pressure

Specification	Value			
	B/Lac	OM3/Lac	R9/Lac	Lac:DHP
Body weight, g	1055.5(894.9-1216.1)	901.7(689.7-1113.7)	974.9(866.4-1083.4)	1219.2(1049.9-1388.5)
Electrolytes				
Calcium, mM	2.35(0.53-4.17)	2.57(1.07-4.07)	2.43(0.99-3.87)	2.23(1.75-2.71)
Chloride, mM	108.9(101.3-116.5)	107.8(103.7-111.9)	114.9(103.7-126.1)	105.9(99.3-112.5)
Magnesium, mM	1.61(1.25-1.97)	1.57(1.31-1.83)	1.62(1.36-1.88)	1.23(0.91-1.55)
Potassium, mM	4.89(2.22-7.56)	4.74(2.69-6.79)	4.47(2.51-6.43)	4.15(3.04-5.26)
Sodium, mM	137.8(120.5-155.1)	138.2(124.5-151.9)	140.4(129.4-151.4)	130.0(119.4-140.6)
Osmotic pressure, mosm/kg water	280.1(254.6-305.6)	283.1(260.5-305.7)	286.9(269.8-304.0)	277.4(246.5-308.3)
Female				
No. of animals	10	11	8	13
Age, wk	77.4(36.0-118.8)	71.6(41.2-102.0)	86.8(39.4-134.2)	94.6(70.3-118.9)
Body weight, g	1036.4(863.0-1209.8)	824.5(661.5-987.5)	868.3(645.5-1091.1)	1063.5(753.5-1373.5)
Electrolytes				
Calcium, mM	2.42(1.22-3.62)	2.15(0.91-3.39)	2.38(0.83-3.93)	2.10(1.51-2.69)
Chloride, mM	109.6(100.3-118.9)	109.0(98.1-119.9)	112.7(104.7-120.7)	111.0(103.6-118.4)
Magnesium, mM	1.51(1.16-1.86)	1.32(1.18-1.46)	1.53(1.06-2.00)	1.21(0.93-1.49)
Potassium, mM	4.55(2.66-6.44)	3.88(2.31-5.45)	4.65(2.94-6.36)	4.27(2.25-6.29)
Sodium, mM	139.5(124.4-154.6)	137.7(116.8-158.6)	138.1(116.6-159.6)	127.4(117.6-137.2)
Osmotic pressure, mosm/kg water	279.5(254.8-304.2)	282.0(251.8-312.2)	277.4(247.3-307.5)	279.3(254.2-304.4)

Contributors: Jon A. Turton and David C. Shaw

References: *See* **Part I.**

130. PROPERTIES OF IMMUNOGLOBULINS: GUINEA PIG

Property	Immunoglobulin					Refer-ence
	IgG$_1$	IgG$_2$	IgA	IgM	IgE	
Physicochemical						
Molecular weight, daltons						19,32
Ultracentrifugation	165,000	161,000	....	970,000	....	
Gel filtration	150,000 ± 10,000	151,000 ± 10,000	....	930,000 ± 60,000	185,000	
Sedimentation coefficient, $s^0_{20,w}$, in Svedberg units	6.6-7.0	6.3-6.9	7-11	19.4	....	1,19,42
Electrophoretic mobility	γ_1	γ_2	β	....	....	1,42
Extinction coefficient, $E^{1\%}_{1cm, 280\ nm}$ [1]/	15.0-15.2	13.2-14.7	....	12.0	....	19,27
Segmental flexibility	Restricted	Freer	....	....	....	8,9

[1]/ Measured in 0.5% $(NH_4)_2 CO_3$ buffer.

continued

Property	Immunoglobulin					Reference
	IgG_1	IgG_2	IgA	IgM	IgE	
Valency	2	2	....	....	....	34
Carbohydrate content, %	2.9	2.8	....	10.5	....	19
Immunological						
Light chain						
Types	κ or λ	κ or λ	κ or λ	κ or λ	....	9,19,24
Molecular weight, daltons	22,000	22,000	22,000	22,000	....	19
Ratio of $\kappa:\lambda$						
Normal Ig	66:33	69:31	....	....	....	9,24
Anti-dinitrophenol Ig	99:1	99:1	....	....	....	9,25
Anti-trimethylammonium Ig	....	16:84	....	....	....	9
Heavy chain						19
Classes	γ_1	γ_2	α	μ	ϵ	
Molecular weight, daltons	52,000	53,000	....	70,000	....	
Structural						
Molecular formula	$2\gamma_1 2\kappa; 2\gamma_1 2\lambda$	$2\gamma_2 2\kappa; 2\gamma_2 2\lambda$	$(2\alpha 2\kappa)_{1\text{-}2};$ $(2\alpha 2\kappa)_2$[2/]; $(2\alpha 2\lambda)_{1\text{-}2};$ $(2\alpha 2\lambda)_2$ [2/]	$(2\mu 2\kappa)_5;$ $(2\mu 2\lambda)_5$	....	1,19,42
No. of S-S bonds						19
Heavy chain-light chain	1	1	....	1	....	
Heavy chain-heavy chain	4	3	....	5	....	
Intrachain, heavy	4	4	....	4	....	
light	2	2	....	....	....	
Biological						
Mean concentration, mg/100 ml						3,36,42
Serum						
Normal	263-700	700-1000	7.2	43.0	....	
Immune	800-1800	1000-1400	....	....	....	
Urine	0.95	1.9	0.14	0.16	....	
Saliva	0.60	1.0	0.48	0.10	....	
Bile	0.10	0.2	0.5	0.07	....	
Milk	13.75	49.5	75.75	11.0	....	
Tears	16.0	42.0	14.8	0.90	....	
Average half-life in plasma, d						18
Normal	7.1	5.1	....	....	....	
Immunized	6.0-8.8	4.1-8.0	....	....	....	
Present in ascitic fluids	+	+	....	....	....	45
Placental transfer	+	+	....	....	....	2
Membrane bound to						
B lymphocytes[3/]	....	....	....	+	....	13,14,39
Mast cells	....	....	....	....	+	44
Cytophilic to						
Basophils	+	−	....	....	....	44
Kurloff cells	−	+	....	....	....	44

2/ Secretory component. 3/ IgD is probably not bound, but this is not definite.

continued

Property	Immunoglobulin					Reference
	IgG$_1$	IgG$_2$	IgA	IgM	IgE	
Macrophages, homologous	+	+	....	+	....	1,2,16, 20,38
Mast cells	+	....	....	....	....	31
Chemotaxis for granulocytes	–	+	....	....	....	17
Homocytotrophic activity	+	....	....	....	+	6,11,26, 30,31, 40,41
Homocytotrophic properties						12,35
Heat & mercaptoethanol resistant	+	....	....	....	....	
Heat resistant & mercaptoethanol labile	+ (?)	....	....	....	....	
Heat & mercaptoethanol labile	....	....	....	....	+	
Complement binding						
Classical	–	+	....	+, –	....	4,21,29, 31
Alternative	+	+	....	....	....	37,43
Arthus reaction (both IgG$_1$ & IgG$_2$ required)	+	+	....	....	....	5,22
Tissue sensitization: skin						4,31,32
Homologous species	+	–	....	–	+	
Heterologous species	–	+	....	–	–	
Antibody synthesis to						
Arsenate-protein conjugates	+	+	....	....	....	7,8
Ascaris suum	....	....	....	....	+	10
Bordetella pertussis	....	....	....	....	+	23
DNP-*Escherichia coli*	–	+	....	....	....	15
DNP-protein conjugates	+	+	....	+	....	7,15
Lys$_{10}$-Lys (DNP)[4,5]	+	+	+	....	–	45
Picryl chloride	+	–	....	....	+	33
Trichinella spiralis	....	....	....	....	+	6
Trimethylammonium-protein conjugate	+	+	....	....	....	7,8
Induction of killer lymphocyte cell (K-cell)-mediated lysis	–	+	....	....	....	28
Induction of monocyte/macrophage-mediated phagocytosis	+	+	....	....	....	28

[4] Oligolysyl N^ϵ-2,4-dinitrophenyllysine. [5] Applies only to response in Wright Strain 2 guinea pigs.

Contributor: Manuel J. Ricardo, Jr.

References

1. Benacerraf, B., et al. 1963. J. Exp. Med. 117:937-949.
2. Berken, A., and B. Benacerraf. 1966. Ibid. 123:119-144.
3. Binaghi, R. A. 1966. J. Immunol. 97:159-164.
4. Bloch, K. J., et al. 1963. J. Exp. Med. 117:965-979.
5. Bloch, K. J., et al. 1963. Proc. Soc. Exp. Biol. Med. 114:52-56.
6. Catty, D. 1969. Monogr. Allergy 5.
7. Cebra, J. J., et al. 1974. Science 186:263-265.
8. Cebra, J. J., et al. 1974. Robert A. Welch Found. Proc. 18th Immunochem., pp. 67-117.
9. Cebra, J. J., et al. 1977. Prog. Immunol. III, pp. 269-277.
10. Dobson, C., et al. 1971. J. Immunol. 106:128-133.
11. Dobson, C., et al. 1971. Ibid. 107:1431-1439.

continued

12. Dwyer, R. St. C., et al. 1974. Int. Arch. Allergy Appl. Immunol. 46:910-924.
13. Finkelman, F. D., et al. 1976. J. Immunol. 116:1173-1181.
14. Forni, G., et al. 1976. J. Exp. Med. 143:1067-1081.
15. Furuichi, K., and J. Koyama. 1975. J. Biochem. (Tokyo) 77:689-694.
16. Guercio, P. del, et al. 1969. Immunology 16:361-371.
17. Keller, H. U., et al. 1968. Immunochemistry 5:293-295.
18. LeFever, J. D., and K. Ishizaka. 1972. J. Immunol. 108:1698-1703.
19. Leslie, R. G. Q., and S. Cohen. 1970. Biochem. J. 120:787-795.
20. Leslie, R. G. Q., and S. Cohen. 1976. Eur. J. Immunol. 6:848-855.
21. Linscott, W. D., and S. S. Hansen. 1969. J. Immunol. 103:423-428.
22. Maillard, J. L., and G. A. Voisin. 1970. Proc. Soc. Exp. Biol. Med. 133:1188-1194.
23. Mota, I., and A. Perini. 1970. Life Sci. 9(2):923-930.
24. Nussenzweig, V., and B. Benacerraf. 1966. J. Exp. Med. 124:787-803.
25. Nussenzweig, V., and B. Benacerraf. 1966. Ibid. 124:805-818.
26. Nussenzweig, V., et al. 1969. J. Immunol. 103:1152-1154.
27. Oettgen, H. F., et al. 1965. Proc. Soc. Exp. Biol. Med. 118:336-342.
28. Öhlander, C., et al. 1978. Scand. J. Immunol. 7:285-296.
29. Osler, A. G., et al. 1969. J. Immunol. 102:269-271.
30. Ovary, Z., and N. L. Warner. 1971. Ibid. 108:1055-1062.
31. Ovary, Z., et al. 1963. J. Exp. Med. 117:951-964.
32. Ovary, Z., et al. 1976. Int. Arch. Allergy Appl. Immunol. 51:416-428.
33. Parish, W. E. 1970. J. Immunol. 105:1296-1298.
34. Paul, W. E., et al. 1966. J. Exp. Med. 123:689-705.
35. Perini, A., and I. Mota. 1972. Immunology 22:915-923.
36. Reisfeld, R. A., and N. E. Hyslop. 1966. Proc. Soc. Exp. Biol. Med. 121:508-514.
37. Sandberg, A. L., et al. 1971. J. Immunol. 106:282-285.
38. Shinomiya, T., and J. Koyama. 1976. Immunology 30:267-275.
39. Stevenson, G. T., et al. 1975. Ibid. 28:807-820.
40. Strejan, G., and D. H. Campbell. 1967. J. Immunol. 99:347-356.
41. Strejan, G., and D. H. Campbell. 1968. Ibid. 100:1245-1254.
42. Vaerman, J. P., and J. F. Heremans. 1972. Ibid. 108:637-648.
43. Vuagnat, P. 1975. Ibid. 115:787-795.
44. Wilson, A. B., and R. R. A. Coombs. 1971. Int. Arch. Allergy Appl. Immunol. 40:19-46.
45. Yaron, A., et al. 1977. J. Immunol. 119:968-975.

131. COMPLEMENT FACTORS: GUINEA PIG

The guinea pig is the only species with a well-defined complement system comparable to that of man. This is true for the classical as well as for the alternative pathway of complement activation. The parallelism between both species with regard to biological functions, reaction sequence, and physicochemical data of the complement proteins is nearly complete. The general test system for all components of the classical pathway is the hemolytic system. Factors of the alternative pathway also can be tested by generating hemolytically active C3b and C5b fragments. Whereas promotion of lysis is measurable directly, it is also possible to measure lysis inhibition by activation of a complement component in the fluid phase, followed in most cases by a rapid decay of this component. This results in inactivation with regard to subsequent hemolysis. One should be careful not to overestimate the biological significance of the cytolytic reaction in comparision to other mediator functions, especially of C3 and C5.

Part I. Complement Sequence

The guinea pig complement system is naturally controlled and balanced by the C1s-inactivator [ref. 1], the C3b-inactivator, and β_1H-globulin $\langle\beta_1 H\rangle$ (well characterized in man, but not in guinea pigs). C3b-inactivator enzymatically cleaves C3b (fluid or cellbound) into C3c and C3d. Properdin protects C3b from this inactivation. β_1H binds to C3b and dissociates Bb from C3b, thereby circumventing the stabilizing effect of properdin. *Abbreviations*: Ag = antigen; Ab = anti-

continued

Part I. Complement Sequence

body; AS = activating substance (e.g. zymosan, inulin, bacterial lipopolysaccharide, dextran sulfate); B = factor B; D = factor D; P = properdin; a bar (⌒) over a component (e.g.,

$\overline{C1}$) indicates the activated enzyme; ‑ ‑ ‑➤ = acts on; ⟶ = gives rise to; ▭ = the main C3-cleaving enzymes.

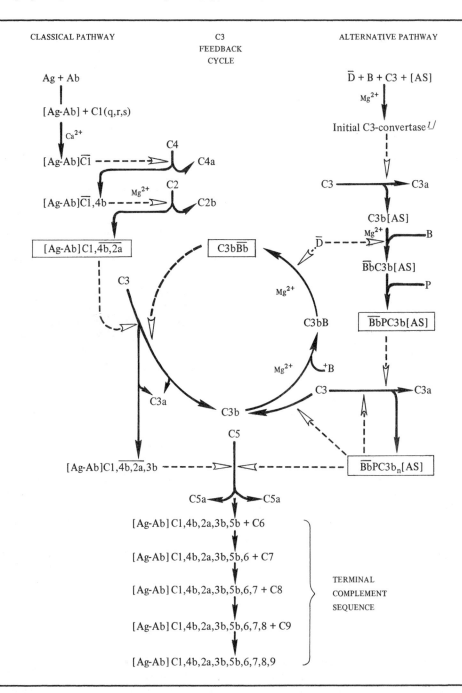

L/ Unknown molecular composition.

Contributor: D. Bitter-Suermann

Reference: 1. Loos, M., et al. 1970. Protides Biol. Fluids Proc. Colloq. 17:311-314.

continued

Part II. Proteins of the Complement System

All data are derived from studies with outbred guinea pigs, using pooled serum- or plasma-EDTA, stored at −70°C. At present, there is no reason to believe that the main physico-chemical, functional, and biological properties are significantly different in inbred strains. For information on the assay or purification of properdin, consult references 12, 24, and 35. *Abbreviations:* μ = ionic strength; S = Svedberg unit; MW = molecular weight; s = sedimentation coefficient; pI = isoelectric point. Figures in heavy brackets are reference numbers.

Protein	Properties	Cleavage Products & Their Biological Effects	Site of Synthesis	Assay/Purification Methods
C1	Subunits = C1q, C1r, C1s; Ca^{2+}-dependent macromolecular complex; at 0.065 μ, present as 19S macromolecules, at 0.6 μ, present as subunits [5,14,50]	....	Epithelial cells of the small intestine [13]	[5,14,34]
C4[1]	MW = 180,000 [6]	C4b, C4a	Mononuclear peritoneal cells [27,54]	[34,37]
C2[2]	MW = 130,000; s = 5.4-5.5S; pI = 5.6 & 5.2; heat labile (50°C) [15,50,52]	C2a, C2b [50]	Mononuclear peritoneal cells [54]	Mg^{2+} dependent [34,52]
C3	MW = 180,000; s = 7.4S [40]	C3b, C3a: immunoadherence [28, 32]; opsonization [44,53]; stimulation of cells [39,45]; anaphylatoxic activity [30]; platelet activation [1,2]; cytotoxic activity [19]	Mononuclear peritoneal cells [11,48]	[3,34,40,41,55]
C5	MW = 200,000; s = 7.6-8.3S; pI = 5.05-5.10 [26,31,33,42]	C5b: opsonization; C5a: anaphylatoxic/chemotactic activities [43,46,47]	....	[3,34]
C6	MW = 130,000; s = 5.5-5.6S; pI = 6.25-6.63 [26,33]	....	....	[23,34]
C7	MW = 150,000; s = 5.1-5.3S; pI = 5.78 [26,31,33]	....	....	[34]
C8	MW = 150,000; s = 7.8-8.5S; pI = 6.34-6.70 [26,31,33]	Membrane damage [49]	....	[34,49]
C9	MW = 80,000; s = 4.5-4.7S; pI = 4.95-5.18 [26,31,33]	Membrane damage [20]	....	[34,51]
Factor B[3]	MW = 100,000-106,000 for single subunit; pI = 6.3; heat labile (50°C) [7,25]	Bb, Ba: chemotactic (Ba) [25]	Mononuclear peritoneal cells [11]	Mg^{2+} dependent [7,25,36]
Factor D	MW = 22,000; s = 2.6S; pI = 9.35-9.50 [8,16]	....	Mononuclear peritoneal cells [11]	[8,9,16]

[1] For information on C4-deficient strain, consult references 17, 18, 21, 29, and 38. [2] For information on incompatibility with human complement components, consult reference 22. [3] For information on incompatibility with human C3b, and reaction with cobra venom factor, consult references 4 and 10.

Contributor: D. Bitter-Suermann

References

1. Becker, S., et al. 1978. Scand. J. Immunol. 7:173-180.
2. Becker, S., et al. 1978. Ibid. 8:551-555.
3. Bitter-Suermann, D., et al. 1970. Immunochemistry 7:955-965.
4. Bitter-Suermann, D., et al. 1972. Immunology 23:267-281.
5. Borsos, T., and H. J. Rapp. 1963. J. Immunol. 91:851-858.
6. Borsos, T., and H. J. Rapp. 1964. Ibid. 94:510-513.
7. Brade, V., et al. 1972. Ibid. 109:1174-1181.
8. Brade, V., et al. 1974. Ibid. 112:1845-1854.
9. Brade, V., et al. 1974. Ibid. 113:1735-1743.
10. Brade, V., et al. 1976. Immunology 30:171-179.
11. Brade, V., et al. 1977. Fed. Proc. Fed. Am. Soc. Exp. Biol. 36:1245.
12. Brade, V., et al. 1977. Z. Immunitaetsforsch. Immunobiol. 152:402-414.

continued

131. COMPLEMENT FACTORS: GUINEA PIG

Part II. Proteins of the Complement System

13. Colten, H. R., et al. 1968. J. Immunol. 100:788-792.
14. Colten, H. R., et al. 1969. Ibid. 103:862-865.
15. Colten, H. R., et al. 1970. Immunology 18:467-472.
16. Dierich, M. P., et al. 1974. Immunochemistry 11:527-532.
17. Ellman, L., et al. 1970. Science 170:74-75.
18. Ellman, L., et al. 1971. J. Exp. Med. 134:162-175.
19. Ferluga, J., et al. 1976. Br. J. Cancer 34:626-634.
20. Frank, M. M., et al. 1970. J. Immunol. 104:1502-1510.
21. Frank, M. M., et al. 1971. J. Exp. Med. 134:176-187.
22. Gigli, I., and K. F. Austen. 1971. Annu. Rev. Microbiol. 25:324-326.
23. Hadding, U., et al. 1969. Protides Biol. Fluids Proc. Colloq. 17:319-321.
24. Hadding, U., et al. 1973. J. Immunol. 111:286-287.
25. Hamura, J., et al. 1978. Ibid. 120:438-444.
26. König, W., et al. 1971. Eur. J. Immunol. 1:372-376.
27. Littleton, C., et al. 1970. Immunology 18:693-704.
28. May, J. E., et al. 1972. Proc. Soc. Exp. Biol. Med. 141:287-290.
29. May, J. E., et al. 1972. J. Immunol. 109:595-601.
30. Meuer, S., et al. 1978. Z. Immunitaetsforsch. Immunobiol. 154:135-146.
31. Mukojima, T., and T. Tachibana. 1969. J. Immunol. 102:1343.
32. Nelson, D. S. 1965. Ciba Found. Symp. Complement, pp. 222-241.
33. Nelson, R. A., Jr. 1967. Protides Biol. Fluids Proc. Colloq. 15:385-399.
34. Nelson, R. A., Jr., et al. 1966. Immunochemistry 3:111-135.
35. Nicholson, A., and K. F. Austen. 1977. J. Immunol. 118:103-108.
36. Nicholson, A., et al. 1975. Ibid. 115:1108-1113.
37. Röllinghoff, M., and R. Ringelmann. 1969. Protides Biol. Fluids Proc. Colloq. 17:315-318.
38. Root, R. K., et al. 1972. J. Immunol. 109:477-486.
39. Schorlemmer, H. U., et al. 1977. Immunology 32:929-940.
40. Shin, H. S., and M. M. Mayer. 1968. Biochemistry 7:2991-2996.
41. Shin, H. S., and M. M. Mayer. 1968. Ibid. 7:2997.
42. Shin, H. S., et al. 1968. J. Immunol. 101:813.
43. Shin, H. S., et al. 1968. Science 162:361-363.
44. Shin, H. S., et al. 1969. J. Exp. Med. 130:1229-1242.
45. Snyderman, R., and S. E. Mergenhagen. 1976. In D. S. Nelson, ed. Immunobiology of the Macrophage. Academic, New York. pp. 335.
46. Snyderman, R., et al. 1969. J. Immunol. 103:413-422.
47. Snyderman, R., et al. 1971. Proc. Soc. Exp. Biol. Med. 138:387-390.
48. Stecher, V. J., and G. J. Thorbecke. 1967. J. Immunol. 99:643-652.
49. Stolfi, R. L. 1968. Ibid. 100:46-54.
50. Stroud, R. M., et al. 1966. Immunochemistry 3:163-176.
51. Tamura, N., and A. Shimada. 1971. Immunology 20:415-425.
52. Wagner, H., and M. Röllinghoff. 1970. Immunochemistry 7:977-987.
53. Winkelstein, J. A., et al. 1972. J. Immunol. 108:1681-1689.
54. Wyatt, H. V., et al. 1972. Ibid. 108:1609-1614.
55. Yonemasu, K., and K. Inoue. 1968. Biken J. 11:169-180.

Part III. Bf, C4, and C2 Genotypes in Various Strains

GPLA = Guinea pig leukocyte antigens. **Alleles:** At the 7th International Complement Workshop at St. Petersburg, Florida, 20-22 November 1977, the Complement Nomenclature Committee designated the loci for complement components C4 and C2 as *4C* and *2C*, to be analogous to *Bf* for factor B. This was done mainly to avoid confusion with the *HLA-C* loci. *Bf* **Locus:** *F* = fast; *S* = slow. *4C* **Locus:** *F* = fast; *S* = slow; *O* = absent. *2C* **Locus:** isoelectric focusing— *A* = acidic; *B* = basic.

Strain	Alleles					
	GPLA-B Locus	*GPLA-S* Locus	*I* Region	*Bf* Locus	*4C* Locus	*2C* Locus
2	*B1*	*S1*	*Ia-2,4,5*	*SS*	*FF*	*A1A1*
13	*B1*	*S1*	*Ia-1,3,5*	*SS*	*FF*	*A1A1*
BIOAC	*B2*	*S1*	*Ia-1,3*	*SS*	*FF*	*A1A1*
BIOAD	*B3*	—	*Ia-1,3*	*FF*	*SS*	*AA*
BIOB	*B1*	—	*Ia-1,4*	*FF*	*SS*	*BB*
BIOC	*B2*	—	*Ia-1*	*SS, FS*	*FF, FS*	*A1A1, A1B*

continued

Part III. Bf, C4, and C2 Genotypes in Various Strains

Strain	Alleles					
	GPLA-B Locus	*GPLA-S* Locus	*I* Region	*Bf* Locus	*4C* Locus	*2C* Locus
B/Lac[1]/	*B3*	–	*Ia-1*	*FF*	*SS*	....
C4D	*B1*	–	*Ia-1,3,5*	*SS*	*OO*	*A1A1*
OM3	*B3*	–	*Ia-1,3*	*FF*	*S1S1*	*BB*
PCA	*B3*	–	*Ia-1,3*	*FF*	*SS, SS1, S1S1*	*BB*
R9	*B3*	–	*Ia-1,3*	*FF, FS, SS*	*FF, FS1, S1S1*	*A1A1, A1B, BB*
Reference	3,4,7	3,4,7	3,4,7	1,5,6	1,5,6	2

[1]/ Synonym: BE.

Contributor: D. Bitter-Suermann

References

1. Bitter-Suermann, D., et al. 1977. J. Immunol. 118: 1822-1826.
2. Bitter-Suermann, D., et al. 1978. Ibid. 120:1765 (Abstr.).
3. Geczy, A. F., and A. L. de Weck. 1977. Prog. Allergy 22:147-213.
4. Geczy, A. F., et al. 1975. J. Immunol. 115:1704-1710.
5. Krönke, M., et al. 1977. Ibid. 119:2016-2018.
6. Krönke, M., et al. 1977. Immunogenetics 5:461-466.
7. Shevach, E. M., et al. 1976. Ibid. 3:595-601.

132. HISTOCOMPATIBILITY ANTIGENS: GUINEA PIG

The two most widely used inbred guinea pig strains are Strains 2 and 13 which have been inbred since 1906. The proportion of parental strain grafts surviving in F_2 and backcross animals, and the proportion of F_2 animals retaining both parental strain grafts, indicate that at least six genes control the rejection of Strain 2 grafts, and at least four genes control the rejection of Strain 13 grafts [ref. 1]. In the early 1970's, it was demonstrated that some of the gene products responsible for skin graft rejection could be detected by serological techniques [ref. 2, 3, 5]. Analysis of these guinea pig histocompatibility antigens revealed that they were determined by genes in the guinea pig histocompatibility (*GPLA*) complex which were homologous to the *H-2K* and *H-2D* loci of mice, and the *HLA-A* and *HLA-B* loci of man. For historical reasons, the *GPLA* loci were termed *GPLA-B* and *GPLA-S* [ref. 4, 6, 14]. Strains 2 and 13 were found to share serologically detected antigens determined by the *GPLA-B.1* and *GPLA-S* alleles, but do differ by a number of other antigens which were shown to be determined by *GPLA* complex-linked genes in the three sub-regions of the *I* region [ref. 8, 9, 12, 13, 16]. Most of the *Ir* genes discovered in the guinea pig also map to the various sub-regions of the *I* region [ref. 16].

Part I. *GPLA* Loci Antigens

The GPLA-B and GPLA-S antigens are glycoproteins of 40,000 daltons associated with β_2-microglobulin [ref. 6, 10, 11], and have a wide tissue distribution [ref. 7, 14, 15].

GPLA Locus	Allele	Antigen	Strain or Stock
B	*B.1*	B.1	2; 13; BIOB
	B.2	B.2	BIOAC; BIOC
	B.3	B.3	B/Lac; BIOAD; OM3; PCA; R9
	B.4	B.4	Outbred
S	S	S	2; 13

Contributors: Benjamin D. Schwartz; A. F. Geczy

132. HISTOCOMPATIBILITY ANTIGENS: GUINEA PIG

Part I. *GPLA* Loci Antigens

References

1. Bauer, J. A. 1960. Ann. N.Y. Acad. Sci. 87:78-92.
2. Brummerstedt, E., and D. Franks. 1970. Transplantation 10:137-140.
3. de Weck, A. L., et al. 1971. Transplant. Proc. 3:192-194.
4. de Weck, A. L., et al. 1976. Transplantation 21:225-241.
5. Ellman, L., et al. 1971. J. Immunol. 107:382-388.
6. Finkelman, F. D., et al. 1975. J. Exp. Med. 141:27-41.
7. Forni, G., et al. 1975. J. Immunol. 115:204-210.
8. Geczy, A. F., et al. 1975. Ibid. 115:1704-1710.
9. Sato, W., and A. L. de Weck. 1972. Z. Immunitaetsforsch. Allerg. Klin. Immunol. 144:49-62.
10. Schwartz, B. D., et al. 1976. Transplant. Rev. 30:174-196.
11. Schwartz, B. D., et al. 1976. J. Exp. Med. 143:541-558.
12. Schwartz, B. D., et al. 1977. Ibid. 146:547-560.
13. Shevach, E. M., et al. 1972. Ibid. 136:1207-1221.
14. Shevach, E. M., et al. 1973. Transplantation 16:126-133.
15. Shevach, E. M., et al. 1975. Transplant. Proc. 7:141-147.
16. Shevach, E. M., et al. 1977. J. Exp. Med. 146:561-570.

Part II. *I* Region Antigens

The Ia antigens are borne by molecules consisting of two glycoprotein chains of 33,000 daltons and 25,000 daltons, respectively (either linked by disulfide bonds, or non-covalently associated), or in two cases are borne on a single glycoprotein chain of 26,000 daltons [ref. 1-3, 6]. They are not associated with β_2-microglobulin, and are represented predominantly on T lymphocytes, B lymphocytes, and macrophages [ref. 4, 5]. *Ir*-Gene Association: GT = poly(L-Glu,L-Tyr); GA = poly(L-Glu,L-Ala); GL = poly(L-Glu,L-Lys); PLL = poly(L-Lys); DNP-GPA = dinitrophenyl derivative of guinea pig albumin.

Antigen	Structure	*Ir*-Gene Association	Strain or Stock
Ia.1	Single chain, 26,000 daltons	Not tested	B/Lac; BIOAC; BIOAD; BIOB; BIOC; OM3; RA; R9
		Ir-GT	13
Ia.2	Two chains, 33,000 & 25,000 daltons, non-covalently associated	*Ir-Ga, Ir-GL, Ir-PLL*	2
Ia.3	Same as Ia.2	Not tested	BIOAC; BIOAD; OM3; PCA; R9
		Ir-DNP-GPA	13
Ia.4	Two chains, 33,000 & 25,000 daltons, disulfide-linked	None known	2
Ia.5	Same as Ia.3	Not tested	BIOAC; BIOAD; OM3; PCA; R9
	Same as Ia.3	*Ir-DNP-GPA*	13
	Same as Ia.4	None known	2
Ia.6	Unknown	None known	2
	Same as Ia.1	*Ir-GT*	13
Ia.7	Same as Ia.4	None known	13; B/Lac; BIOAC; BIOAD; OM3; PCA; R9

Contributors: Benjamin D. Schwartz; A. F. Geczy

References

1. Schwartz, B. D., et al. 1976. Transplant. Rev. 30:174-196.
2. Schwartz, B. D., et al. 1976. J. Exp. Med. 143:541-558.
3. Schwartz, B. D., et al. 1977. Ibid. 146:547-560.
4. Shevach, E. M., et al. 1973. Transplantation 16:126-133.
5. Shevach, E. M., et al. 1975. Transplant. Proc. 7:141-147.
6. Shevach, E. M., et al. 1977. J. Exp. Med. 146:561-570.

Mode of Immunization: CFA = complete Freund's adjuvant. **Type of Response:** DHSR = delayed hypersensitivity skin reaction; PCA = passive cutaneous anaphylaxis; DNP = 2,4-dinitrophenyl group. **Histocompatibility Linkage:** strains in which histocompatibility linkage occurs. *Abbreviation:* i.d. = intradermal. Data in brackets refer to the column heading in brackets.

Antigen ⟨Synonym⟩	Mode of Immunization	Type of Response	Histocompatibility Linkage	Reference
Proteins & Protein Conjugates			
Benzyl-penicilloyl bovine gamma globulin ⟨BPO-BGG⟩	Multiple i.d. injections without CFA	DHSR (i.d.)	Strain 13[1]; Strain B.1 [1]	16-18
Bovine serum albumin (low dose)	CFA	DHSR (i.d.); antibody production	Strain 2	20,24
Dinitrophenylated guinea pig skin protein conjugates	CFA	DHSR (i.d.); anti-DNP antibodies	Strain 13[2]	35
2,4-Dinitrophenyl guinea pig albumin	CFA	Antibody production	Strain 13	12,26
2,4-Dinitrophenyl protamine	CFA	DHSR (i.d.); antibody production	Strain 2	23
Human serum albumin (low dose)	CFA	DHSR (i.d.); antibody production	Strain 2	19,20
Insulin	Aluminum precipitate insulin[3] in CFA	Antibody production	Strain 2	1
A chain	CFA	Antibody response	Strain 2	2
B chain	CFA	Antibody response	Strain 13	2
Poly(L-lysyl) rabbit serum albumin	CFA	Antibody production	Strain 2	5
Synthetic Antigens			
2,4-Dinitrophenyl-poly(L-Arg) ⟨DNP-PLA⟩	CFA	DHSR (i.d.); antibody production	Strain 2	23
2,4-Dinitrophenyl-poly(L-Glu,L-Lys) ⟨DNP-GL⟩	CFA	DHSR (i.d.); antibody production	Strain 2	22,27
2,4-Dinitrophenyl-poly(L-Lys) ⟨DNP-PLL⟩	CFA	Arthus reaction, DHSR (i.d.); antibody production	Strain 2	3,13,15,21, 22,25,28-32,36
2,4-Dinitrophenyl-poly(L-Orn) ⟨DNP-PLO⟩	CFA	DHSR (i.d.); antibody production	Strain 2	23
Multichain copolymer: poly-(L-Tyr,L-Glu)-poly(DL-Ala)-poly(L-Lys) ⟨(T,G)-A—L⟩	CFA	Immediate & delayed hypersensitivity skin reaction (i.d.); PCA antibodies	Strain 2	5,6
	Multiple i.d. injections without CFA	DHSR (i.d.)	Strain 13[1]	16-18
Oligolysine-containing copolymers; poly(Glu,Ala) ⟨GA⟩; aggregate of poly(Glu) with methylated guinea pig plasma albumin ⟨G + MeGPA⟩	CFA	DHSR (i.d.); PCA antibodies	Strain 2	4
Poly(L-Glu,L-Ala) ⟨GA⟩	CFA	DHSR (i.d.); antibody production	Strain 2	4,7-9,20

[1] The responsiveness to these antigens is under polygenic control [ref. 16-18]. At least one gene required for the response is linked to the histocompatibility complex, while the other gene(s) also required for responsiveness segregate(s) independently. [2] Since no linkage studies were performed in these experiments, it is not clear whether the gene(s) governing the response to these compounds is (are) linked to the 2 or 13 major histocompatibility complex, or to some other closely associated chromosomal region in Strain 2 and Strain 13 guinea pigs. [3] Crystalline zinc insulin suspended in 1% aluminum ammonium sulfate and precipitated with sodium hydroxide.

continued

Antigen ⟨Synonym⟩	Mode of Immunization	Type of Response	Histocompatibility Linkage	Reference
Poly(L-Glu,L-Tyr) ⟨GT⟩	CFA	DHSR (i.d.); antibody production	Strain 13	7,9,10
Poly(L-Glu,L-Ala,L-Tyr) ⟨GAT⟩; aggregate of poly-(Glu,Tyr) with methylated bovine plasma albumin ⟨GT + MeBPA⟩	CFA	DHSR (i.d.); PCA antibodies	Strain 2; Strain 13	4
Poly(Tyr-Glu-Ala-Gly)	CFA	DHSR (i.d.); antibody production	Strain 13	33
Low Molecular Weight Chemical Sensitizers				
Aspirin anhydride	Multiple topical applications without CFA	DHSR (contact)	Strain 13 [1/]	16-18
Beryllium fluoride	Multiple topical applications without CFA	DHSR (contact)	Strain 2 [2/]	34
1-Chloro-2,4-dinitrobenzene ⟨2,4-dinitrochlorobenzene⟩	Epicutaneous	Contact sensitivity	?	11
Hydralazine	CFA	DHSR (i.d.); antibody production	Strain 13 [4/]	14
Mercuric chloride	Multiple topical applications without CFA	DHSR (contact)	Strain 13 [2/]	34
Phenetidine	Multiple i.d. injections without CFA	DHSR (contact)	Strain B.2 [1/]	16
Potassium dichromate	Initial sensitization with CFA, then multiple topical and i.d. applications without CFA	DHSR (contact)	Strain 2 [2/]	34

[1/] The responsiveness to these antigens is under polygenic control [ref. 16-18]. At least one gene required for the response is linked to the histocompatibility complex, while the other gene(s) also required for responsiveness segregate(s) independently. [2/] Since no linkage studies were performed in these experiments, it is not clear whether the gene(s) governing the response to these compounds is (are) linked to the 2 or 13 major histocompatibility complex, or to some other closely associated chromosomal region in Strain 2 and Strain 13 guinea pigs. [4/] Strain 13 guinea pigs respond to this drug more strongly than do Strain 2 animals, and breeding studies suggest that immune responsiveness is inherited in an autosomal dominant manner. However, the immune response to hydralazine appears not to be linked to the Strain 13 major histocompatibility complex.

Contributors: A. F. Geczy; Ira Green; L. Polak; Alain L. de Weck

References

1. Arquilla, E. R., and J. Finn. 1963. Science 142:400-401.
2. Barcinski, M. A., and A. S. Rosenthal. 1977. J. Exp. Med. 145:726-742.
3. Benacerraf, B., et al. 1967. Cold Spring Harbor Symp. Quant. Biol. 32:569-575.
4. Ben Efraim, S., and P. H. Maurer. 1966. J. Immunol. 97:577-586.
5. Ben Efraim, S., et al. 1966. Immunochemistry 3:491-493.
6. Ben Efraim, S., et al. 1967. Immunology 12:573-581.
7. Bluestein, H. G., et al. 1971. J. Exp. Med. 134:458-470.
8. Bluestein, H. G., et al. 1971. Ibid. 134:471-481.
9. Bluestein, H. G., et al. 1971. Ibid. 134:1529-1537.
10. Bluestein, H. G., et al. 1971. Ibid. 134:1538-1544.
11. Chase, M. W. 1941. Ibid. 73:711-726.
12. Davie, J. M., et al. 1972. J. Immunol. 109:193-200.
13. Ellman, L., et al. 1970. Proc. Natl. Acad. Sci. USA 66:322-328.
14. Ellman, L., et al. 1971. Clin. Exp. Immunol. 9:927-937.
15. Ellman, L., et al. 1971. J. Immunol. 107:382-388.
16. Geczy, A. F., and A. L. de Weck. 1975. Immunology 28:331-342.
17. Geczy, A. F., and A. L. de Weck. 1977. Prog. Allergy 22:147-213.
18. Geczy, A. F., et al. 1975. Eur. J. Immunol. 5:711-719.
19. Green, I. 1970. Guinea-Pig News Lett. 2:40-47.
20. Green, I. 1974. Immunogenetics 1:4-21.
21. Green, I., et al. 1966. J. Exp. Med. 123:859-879.
22. Green, I., et al. 1969. J. Immunol. 103:403-412.

continued

23. Green, I., et al. 1969. Proc. Natl. Acad. Sci. USA 64: 1095-1102.
24. Green, I., et al. 1970. Ibid. 66:1267-1274.
25. Green, I., et al. 1971. Cell. Interact. Immune Response 2nd Int. Convocat. Immunol., pp. 76-82.
26. Green, I., et al. 1972. J. Immunol. 109:457-463.
27. Kantor, F., et al. 1963. J. Exp. Med. 117:55-69.
28. Levine, B. B., and B. Benacerraf. 1964. Ibid. 120:955-965.
29. Levine, B. B., and B. Benacerraf. 1965. Science 147: 517-518.
30. Levine, B. B., et al. 1963. Nature (London) 200:544-546.
31. Levine, B. B., et al. 1963. J. Exp. Med. 118:953-957.
32. Martin, W. J., et al. 1970. Ibid. 132:1259-1266.
33. Maurer, P. H., et al. 1973. J. Immunol. 111:1018-1021.
34. Polak, L., et al. 1968. Immunology 14:707-711.
35. Polak, L., et al. 1974. Int. Arch. Allergy Appl. Immunol. 46:417-426.
36. Schlossman, S. F., et al. 1965. Biochemistry 4:1638-1645.

134. IMMUNE REACTIONS AND IMMUNOLOGICAL DISEASES: GUINEA PIG

Data in brackets refer to the column heading in brackets.

Disease ⟨Synonym⟩	Strain	Breeding	Genetic Basis	Characteristics	Assay	Reference
Experimental allergic encephalomyelitis	2	Inbred	....	Resistant, using basic encephalitogenic protein	Clinical signs, histology, antibody	5,6, 17
	2/He	Inbred	....	Low responder and resistant to encephalitogenic nonapeptide	Skin test	16
	2/N	Inbred	....	Resistant	Clinical signs	11
	13	Inbred	....	Susceptible	Skin test	5,6, 17
			Dominant in F_1	High responder and susceptible to encephalitogenic nonapeptide	Lymphocyte transformation	16
	13/N	Inbred	....	Susceptible	Clinical signs	11
	Hartley	Random-bred	....	Susceptible	Clinical signs	11
Experimental autoimmune uveitis	2/N	Inbred	Response dominant in (Hartley x 2)F_1	Low responder, no uveitis	Clinical signs, histology, skin test, antibody	9
	13/N	Inbred	....	Moderate responder, uveitis	Clinical signs, histology, skin test, antibody	9
	Hartley	Random-bred	Response dominant in (Hartley x 2)F_1	High responder, uveitis	Clinical signs, histology, skin test, antibody	9
	NIH	Random-bred	....	High responder, uveitis	Clinical signs, histology, skin test, antibody	9
	NIH:c4d	Random-bred	Deficient in C4	High responder, uveitis	Clinical signs, histology, skin test, antibody	9
Experimental autoimmune myasthenia ⟨EAM⟩	13	Inbred	....	Susceptible to transfer EAM with lymph node cells	Skin test, electromyograph	15
Experimental autoimmune thyroiditis	2	Inbred	Dominant in F_1; linked to major histocompatibility complex	High responder	Antibody, histology	1
	13	Inbred	....	Low responder	Antibody, histology	1,8
	Hartley	Random-bred	....	High responder	Antibody, histology	8

continued

Disease ⟨Synonym⟩	Strain	Breeding	Genetic Basis	Characteristics	Assay	Reference
Bronchial wall sensitivity to histamine & acetylcholine	"Sensitive line"	Partially inbred	....	Susceptible	Dyspnea, contraction of tracheobronchial strips	10, 13, 14
	"Non-sensitive line"	Partially inbred	....	Resistant	Dyspnea, contraction of tracheobronchial strips	10, 13, 14
Autoimmune tubulo-interstitial nephritis ⟨TN⟩	2	Inbred	....	Resistant	Histology of kidney lesions	3,4
	13	Inbred	*Ir* gene linked to major histocompatibility complex	Susceptible to induction of autoimmune TN by rabbit tubular basement membrane	Histology of kidney lesions	3,4
Experimental autoimmune orchitis	13	Inbred	....	Response to GP1 glycoprotein of sperm acrosome	Histology	2
Acute systemic anaphylaxis	2/N	Inbred	....	Resistant	Intensity of bronchospasm, amount of histamine release	12
	Hartley	Random-bred	....	Susceptible	Intensity of bronchospasm, amount of histamine release	12
Systemic anaphylaxis after inhalation challenge with egg albumin	IMM/R[1]	Partially inbred	....	Resistant	Dyspnea, systemic anaphylaxis	7
	IMM/S	Partially inbred	....	Susceptible	Dyspnea, systemic anaphylaxis	7

[1] B/Lac derived from this strain.

Contributors: Larry D. Bacon and Noel R. Rose; Robert P. Lisak; Alain L. deWeck

References

1. Braley-Mullen, H., et al. 1976. Immunogenetics 3: 205-208.
2. Carlo, D. J., et al. 1976. J. Immunol. 116:619-622.
3. Hyman, L. R., et al. 1976. Ibid. 116:327-335.
4. Hyman, L. R., et al. 1976. Ibid. 117:1894-1897.
5. Kies, M. W., et al. 1975. Ibid. 115:75-79.
6. Lisak, R. P., et al. 1975. Ibid. 114:546-549.
7. Lundberg, L. 1979. Acta Pathol. Microbiol. Scand. C87:55-66.
8. McMaster, P. R. B., et al. 1967. J. Immunol. 99:201-207.
9. McMaster, P. R. B., et al. 1976. Mod. Probl. Ophthalmol. 16:62-71.
10. Nakazawa, H., and R. Townley. 1976. Ann. Allergy 36:77-85.
11. Stone, S. H. 1962. Int. Arch. Allergy 20:193-202.
12. Stone, S. H. 1964. Science 146:1061-1062.
13. Takino, Y., et al. 1969. Tohoku J. Exp. Med. 97:399-400.
14. Takino, Y., et al. 1971. J. Allergy 41:247-261.
15. Tarrab-Hazdi, R., et al. 1975. J. Exp. Med. 142:785-789.
16. Teitelbaum, D., et al. 1977. Cell. Immunol. 29:265-271.
17. Webb, C., et al. 1973. Immunol. Commun. 2:185-192.

135. SUSCEPTIBILITY TO INFECTIOUS DISEASES: GUINEA PIG

Agent ⟨Synonym⟩ [Disease]	Reference
Viruses[1,2]	
DNA viruses Herpetoviruses Cytomegalovirus of guinea pig ⟨Salivary gland virus⟩	63,66,146,275

Agent ⟨Synonym⟩ [Disease]	Reference
Guinea pig herpes-like virus ⟨GPHLV⟩	22,30,75,173-175, 209,210,259
Poxviruses: Guinea pig pox-like virus ⟨GPPLV⟩	144
RNA viruses Picornaviruses: Enteroviruses—human poliovirus	306

[1] Naturally occurring infections. [2] For a review, consult reference 358.

continued

Agent ⟨Synonym⟩ [Disease]	Reference
Reoviruses: Human reovirus type 3	47,279,280
Paramyxoviruses	
Parainfluenza 1 ⟨Sendai⟩	279
Pneumonia virus of mice ⟨PVM⟩	279
Simian virus 5 ⟨SV5⟩	279,358,359
Retroviruses—Oncoviruses ⟨Leukoviruses⟩: Guinea pig type C [Leukemia]	64,111,137,178,188, 220,258,269-271, 313
Arenaviruses: Lymphocytic choriomeningitis	172,230,287
[Hepatoenteritis[3/]]	306
[Highly fatal disease[3/]]	352
[Myositis[3/]]	306,314,366
[Viral pneumonia[3/]]	26,208,306
[Wasting disease[3/]]	293
Viruses[4/]	
DNA viruses	
Papovaviruses: Polyomaviruses—polyoma virus (mouse)	110
Herpetoviruses	
Herpes simplex group	145
Cercopithecoid herpesvirus 1 ⟨B virus⟩	242
Porcine herpesvirus 1 ⟨Pseudorabies⟩	242
Others	
Equine rhinopneumonitis	242
Human herpesvirus 4 ⟨Epstein-Barr⟩	134
Poxviruses: Cowpox	104
RNA viruses	
Picornaviruses	
Enteroviruses	
Coxsackie	125
Encephalomyocarditis	76
Human poliovirus	312
Rhinoviruses: Foot-and-mouth disease	294
Reoviruses: African horsesickness	113
Togaviruses	
Alphaviruses	
Bebaru	177
Chikungunya	142,143,232,308
Eastern equine encephalomyelitis	130,351
Everglades	54
Middleburg	232,234,235
Ndumu	234
Semliki Forest	327
Venezuelan equine encephalomyelitis	21,197
Western equine encephalomyelitis	21,245

Agent ⟨Synonym⟩ [Disease]	Reference
Flaviviruses	
Absettarov	21
Banzi	233
Dakar bat	36
Japanese encephalitis	247,248
Kokobera	102
Kumlinge	267
Kunjin	102
Louping ill	389
Murray Valley encephalitis	122
Omsk hemorrhagic fever	57-59
Phnom Penh bat	21
Russian spring-summer encephalitis	60
Sepik	299
Spondweni	232,234,236
St. Louis ⟨St. Louis encephalitis⟩	242
Uganda	99
Usutu	238
Wesselsbron	242
West Nile	328
Zika	100
Orthomyxoviruses: Influenza A	242
Paramyxoviruses: Narina	355
Rhabdoviruses	
Cocal	185
Marburg[5/]	323,324
Mount Elgon bat	243
Piry	380
Rabies	330
Vesicular stomatitis	73,257,353
Arenaviruses	
Amapari	292
Junin	194,281
Tacaribe	72
Tamiami	21,182
Bunyaviruses	
Anopheles A	305
Bwamba	329
California encephalitis	141
Calovo	15,16
Chagres	231
Ganjam	32,85
Germiston	234,235
Ingwavuma	237
Manzanilla	12
Oropouche	13
Pacui	21
Patois	335
Pongola	232,234
Punta Toro	342
Restan	186
San Angelo	136
Silverwater	239
Simbu	232

[3/] Disease of possible viral etiology. [4/] Experimentally induced infections. [5/] Possible member of group.

continued

Agent ⟨Synonym⟩ [Disease]	Reference
Turlock	214
Uukuniemi	268
Witwatersrand	233,234
Arboviruses[6]	
Abu Hammad	21
Bandia	37
Hughes	61
Kao Shuan	21
Kasba	86
Lebombo	238
Nyamanini	238
Pathum Thani	21
Pretoria	21
Quaranfil	349,350
Triniti	331
Rickettsias[1,7]	
Chlamydias ⟨Bedsoniae; Psittacosis-LGV-Trachoma group⟩[2]: Guinea pig inclusion conjunctivitis virus ⟨GPIC⟩	133,191,256,340
Rickettsias[4]	
Chlamydias ⟨Bedsoniae; Psittacosis-LGV-Trachoma group⟩	
[Psittacosis]	303
[Trachoma]	181
Others	277
Mycoplasmas[1,7]	
Acholeplasma spp.	337
Mycoplasma caviae	162-166,337
M. pulmonis	187
Bacteria[1,7]	
Aeromonas punctata subsp. caviae ⟨Pseudomonas caviae⟩	315
Bordetella bronchiseptica	124,325
Clostridium perfringens	221
Corynebacterium kutscheri	357
C. pyogenes	250
Escherichia coli	274
Klebsiella pneumoniae	34,95,288
Leptospira interrogans ⟨L. ictero-hemorrhagiae⟩	229
Listeria monocytogenes	274
Pasteurella multocida	381
Pseudomonas aeruginosa	33
Salmonella amersfoort	124
S. blegdam	124
S. dublin	124

Agent ⟨Synonym⟩ [Disease]	Reference
S. enteritidis	118
S. glostrup	124
S. limete	124
S. moscow	124
S. nagoya	124
S. poona	124
S. typhimurium	338
S. weltevreden	124
Staphylococcus sp.	
Coagulase-positive	25,348
β-Hemolytic	227
S. aureus	140
Streptobacillus moniliformis	198,326
Streptococcus sp.	
Lancefield group A, α-hemolytic	139
Lancefield group C, β-hemolytic	120,190,282,283, 357
S. pneumoniae	169,171
S. zooepidemicus	91,301
Yersinia pseudotuberculosis	24,283
Bacteria[4,8]	
Brucella abortus	124,249,344
B. melitensis	124,249,344
B. suis	124,249,344
Mycobacterium tuberculosis	124
Salmonella typhimurium	192,346
Yersinia pestis	124
Fungi[1,9]	
Systemic mycoses	
Candida albicans	119
Cryptococcus neoformans	97
Histoplasma capsulatum	70
Pneumocystis carinii	48,53,93
Dermatophytic mycoses	
Microsporum audouinii	109,364
M. canis	109,128
M. cookei	109
M. distortum	109
M. gypseum	109
M. nanum	114
Trichophyton equinum	260
T. megninii	109
T. mentagrophytes	109
T. rubrum	334
T. violaceum	334
Fungi[4]	
Systemic mycoses	
Blastomyces dermatitidis	69,304

[1] Naturally occurring infections. [2] For a review, consult reference 358. [4] Experimentally induced infections. [6] Not already included in above groups. [7] For a review, consult reference 124. [8] In addition to the agents in this group, the bacteria and mycoplasmas listed in the previous group—those producing naturally occurring diseases—have also been used for experimental work in guinea pigs. [9] For a review, consult reference 334.

continued

Agent ⟨Synonym⟩ [Disease]	Reference
Candida albicans	302
Coccidioides immitis	129,307
Cryptococcus neoformans	121
Histoplasma capsulatum	212,333
Paracoccidioides brasiliensis	18,334
Dermatophytic mycoses	
Alternaria solani	127
Aspergillus sp.	39,262
Botrytis allii	127
Microsporum canis	126
Trichophyton mentagrophytes	11,126
T. verrucosum	126
Protozoa[1,10]	
Amoebas	
Endolimax caviae	115,152,266,368
Entamoeba caviae	56,115,170,266,365, 369,370
Ciliates	
Balantidium caviae	115,151,153,154, 201,202,261,266, 317,373
Cyathodinium chagasi	80,81
C. conicum	78,216,217
C. cunhai	147,148,216,217
C. piriforme	78,216,217
Enterophrya elongata	83,147,199
Kopperia intestinale	199,266
Protocaviella acuminata	78,199
Flagellates	
Caviomonas mobilis	266
Chilomastix intestinalis	84,206,265,266
C. wenrichi	265,266
Chilomitus caviae	84
C. conexus	266
Enteromonas caviae	219,266
Giardia caviae	149,266
Hexamastix caviae	266
H. robustus	266
Leishmania enriettii	4,240,241,255
Monocercomonas caviae	23,88,266
M. minuta	266
M. pistillum	266
Monocercomonoides caviae	82,266
M. exilis	266
M. quadrifunilis	266
M. wenrichi	266
Oikomonas termo	252,382
Proteromonas brevifilia	7
Retortamonas caviae	23,155,266,370
Selenomonas ruminantium	79,84
Sphaeromonas communis	84,382
Spiromonas augusta	115

Agent ⟨Synonym⟩ [Disease]	Reference
Tritrichomonas caviae ⟨*Trichomonas caviae; Trichomonas flagelliphora*⟩	88,150-152,266, 347,370
Trypanosoma brucei	244
T. cruzi ⟨*Schizotrypanum cruzi*⟩	17,53,98,116
Microsporidians: *Encephalitozoon cuniculi* ⟨*Nosema cuniculi*⟩	289,309
Sporozoa	
Cryptosporidium wrairi	183,362,363
Eimeria caviae	46,112,157,211,285, 320
Klossiella cobayae	28,29,71,167,203, 228,273,284,291, 318,339,370
Sarcocystis caviae	90
Toxoplasma gondii	20,27,49,92,96,123, 158,207,222,225, 226,246,251,263, 272,290,310,360
Protozoa[4]	
Babesia[11]	168
Balantidium coli	372,373
Eimeria[11]	286
Entamoeba histolytica	3,50,115,345,378, 379
Leishmania (human)	1,19,40,55,62,94, 156,374,383-388
L. enriettii	19,35,41-45,55,74, 87,94,105-108,132, 135,156,204,213, 223,254,276,298, 300,367,383,387, 388
Theileria[11]	138
Toxoplasma gondii	322
Trichomonas vaginalis	376,377
Tritrichomonas foetus	218,253,264
Trypanosoma spp.[12]	117,131,156,176, 180,189,224,356, 383-388
Helminths[1,13]	
Fasciola spp.	31,341,371
Paraspidodera uncinata	38,161,296,371
Helminths[4]	
Flukes	
Fasciola hepatica	31,89,354
Schistosoma haematobium	311
S. mansoni	2,6,316
Nematodes	
Ascaris suum	101,184,319

[1] Naturally occurring infections. [4] Experimentally induced infections. [10] For a review, consult reference 361.

[11] Unsuccessful. [12] 19 species. [13] For a review, consult reference 371.

continued

Agent ⟨Synonym⟩ [Disease]	Reference
Brugia pahangi	5
Bunostomum trigonocephalum	336
Dictyocaulus filaria	51,375
D. viviparus	67,68,103
Gongylonema pulchrum	215
Hyostrongylus rubidus	10
Metastrongylus apri	295
Necator americanus	316
Nippostrongylus brasiliensis	278
Obeliscoides cuniculi	8

Agent ⟨Synonym⟩ [Disease]	Reference
Oesophagostomum dentatum	9
Parelaphostrongylus tenuis ⟨*Pneumostrongylus tenuis*⟩	14,332
Strongyloides ratti	321
Toxocara canis	179,205,319
Trichinella spiralis	52,77,179,195,196, 200,319
Trichostrongylus colubriformis	65,159,160,297,343
Pentastomids: *Linguatula serrata*	193

Contributor: John M. Vetterling

References

1. Abboud, I. A., et al. 1970. Br. J. Ophthalmol. 54:256-262.
2. Abboud, I. A., et al. 1971. Ibid. 55:106-115.
3. Adams, A. R. D. 1937. Trans. R. Soc. Trop. Med. Hyg. 31:2.
4. Adler, S., and L. Halff. 1955. Ann. Trop. Med. Parasitol. 49:37-41.
5. Ahmed, S. S. 1968. J. Trop. Med. Hyg. 71:241-242.
6. Akpom, C. A., et al. 1970. Am. J. Trop. Med. Hyg. 19:996-1000.
7. Alexeieff, A. 1946. Arch. Zool. Exp. Gen. 84:150-151.
8. Alicata, J. E. 1932. J. Agric. Res. 44:401-419.
9. Alicata, J. E. 1933. J. Parasitol. 20:73.
10. Alicata, J. E. 1933. Ibid. 20:97.
11. Alteras, I., and R. Evolceanu. 1966. Derm. Venerol. 4:33-337.
12. Anderson, C. R., et al. 1960. Am. J. Trop. Med. Hyg. 9:78-80.
13. Anderson, C. R., et al. 1961. Ibid. 4:574-578.
14. Anderson, R. C., and U. R. Strelive. 1966. Can. J. Zool. 44:533-540.
15. Bardos, V., and E. Copkova. 1961. J. Hyg. Epidemiol. Microbiol. Immunol. 6:186.
16. Bardos, V., and V. Danielova. 1961. Cesk. Epidemiol. Mikrobiol. Imunol. 10:389-395.
17. Barretto, M. P., et al. 1966. Rev. Inst. Med. Trop. Sao Paulo 8:103-112.
18. Batista, A. C., et al. 1962. Publ. Inst. Micol. Univ. Recife (Braz.) 373:27.
19. Benex, J., and L. Lamy. 1967. Bull. Soc. Pathol. Exot. 60:506-510.
20. Berengo, A., et al. 1967. Minerva Med. 58:1947-1957.
21. Berge, T. O., ed. 1975. U.S. Dep. HEW Publ. (CDC) 75-8301.
22. Bhatt, P. N., et al. 1971. J. Infect. Dis. 123:178-189.
23. Bishop, A. 1932. Parasitology 24:233-237.
24. Bishop, L. M. 1932. Cornell Vet. 22:1-9.
25. Blackmore, D. K., and R. A. Francis. 1970. J. Comp. Pathol. 80:645-651.
26. Blanc, G. 1952. Sem. Hop. 28:3805-3810.
27. Boisseau, R., and L. Nodenot. 1936. Bull. Soc. Pathol. Exot. 29:135-141.
28. Bonciu, C., and M. Petrovici. 1966. Arch. Roum. Pathol. Exp. Microbiol. 25:523-532.
29. Bonciu, C., et al. 1957. Ibid. 16:131-143.
30. Booss, J., and G. D. Hsiung. 1971. J. Infect. Dis. 123:284-291.
31. Boray, J. C. 1969. Adv. Parasitol. 7:95-210.
32. Boshell, J., et al. 1970. Indian J. Med. Res. 58:561-562.
33. Bostrum, R. E., et al. 1969. J. Am. Vet. Med. Assoc. 155:1195-1199.
34. Branch, A. 1927. J. Infect. Dis. 40:533-548.
35. Bray, R. S., and V.C.L.C. Wilson. 1972. Trans. R. Soc. Trop. Med. Hyg. 66:955-956.
36. Bres, P., and L. Chambon. 1963. Ann. Inst. Pasteur Paris 104:705-711.
37. Bres, P., et al. 1967. Ibid. 113:739-747.
38. Breza, M., and V. Jurasek. 1965. Helminthol. Abstr. 34:238.
39. Brook, P. J. 1966. Annu. Rev. Phytopathol. 4:171-194.
40. Bryceson, A. D. M. 1970. Proc. R. Soc. Med. 63:1056-1060.
41. Bryceson, A. D. M., and J. L. Turk. 1971. J. Pathol. 104:153-165.
42. Bryceson, A. D. M., et al. 1970. Trans. R. Soc. Trop. Med. Hyg. 64:472.
43. Bryceson, A. D. M., et al. 1970. Clin. Exp. Immunol. 7:301-341.
44. Bryceson, A. D. M., et al. 1972. Ibid. 10:305-335.
45. Bryceson, A. D. M., et al. 1974. Ibid. 16:189-201.
46. Bugge, G., and P. Heinke. 1921. Dtsch. Tieraerztl. Wochenschr. 29:41-42.
47. Calisher, C. H., and W. P. Rowe. 1966. Natl. Cancer Inst. Monogr. 20:67-75.
48. Carini, A., and J. Maciel. 1915. Zentralbl. Bakteriol. Parasitenk. Infektionskr. Hyg. Abt. 1 Orig. 77:46-50.
49. Carini, A., and L. Migliano. 1916. Bull. Soc. Pathol. Exot. 9:435-436.

continued

50. Carrera, G. M., and E. C. Faust. 1949. Am. J. Trop. Med. 29:647-667.
51. Casarosa, L. 1969. Helminthol. Abstr. 38:200.
52. Castro, G. A., et al. 1967. J. Parasitol. 53:595-612.
53. Chagas, C. 1911. Mem. Inst. Oswaldo Cruz 3:219-275.
54. Chamberlain, R. W., et al. 1964. Science 145:272-274.
55. Chance, M. L. 1972. Trans. R. Soc. Trop. Med. Hyg. 66:352.
56. Chatton, E. 1917. Bull. Soc. Pathol. Exot. 10:794-799.
57. Chumakov, M. P. 1948. Ter. Arkh. 2:68.
58. Chumakov, M. P. 1948. Vestn. Akad. Med. Nauk SSSR 2:19-27.
59. Chumakov, M. P. 1949. Ibid. 3:21-27.
60. Chumakov, M. P., and N. A. Zeitlenok. 1939. Arkh. Biol. Nauk 56(11):112-120.
61. Clifford, C. M., et al. 1968. Am. J. Trop. Med. Hyg. 17:881-885.
62. Clinton, B. A., et al. 1972. J. Immunol. 108:1570-1577.
63. Cole, R., and A. G. Kuttner. 1926. J. Exp. Med. 44:855-874.
64. Congdon, C. C., and E. Lorenz. 1954. Am. J. Pathol. 30:337-359.
65. Connan, R. M. 1966. Parasitology 56:521-530.
66. Cook, J. E. 1958. J. Natl. Cancer Inst. 20:905-909.
67. Cornwell, R. L., and R. M. Jones. 1970. Res. Vet. Sci. 11:484-485.
68. Cornwell, R. L., and R. M. Jones. 1971. J. Comp. Pathol. 81:97-103.
69. Corrado, A. 1963. Nuova Vet. 39:162-166.
70. Correa, W. M., and A. C. Pacheco. 1967. Can. J. Comp. Med. 31:203-206.
71. Cossel, L. 1958. Schweiz. Z. Allg. Pathol. Bakteriol. 21:62-73.
72. Coto, C. E., et al. 1967. Arch. Gesamte Virusforsch. 20:81-86.
73. Cotton, W. E. 1926. J. Am. Vet. Med. Assoc. 69:313-332.
74. Coutinho, J. O. 1954. Folia Clin. Biol. 21:15-18.
75. Craft, J. L., and D. A. Hilding. 1968. Science 162:1485-1487.
76. Craighead, J. E. 1965. Nature (London) 207:1268-1269.
77. Cypess, R., et al. 1971. J. Parasitol. 57:103-106.
78. da Cunha, A. M. 1914. Mem. Inst. Oswaldo Cruz 6:212-216.
79. da Cunha, A. M. 1915. Braz. Med. 29:33.
80. da Cunha, A. M., and G. de Freitas. 1936. C. R. Soc. Biol. 123:436-438.
81. da Cunha, A. M., and G. de Freitas. 1936. Ibid. 123:711-713.
82. da Cunha, A. M., and J. Muniz. 1927. Ibid. 96:496-498.
83. da Cunha, A. M., and J. Muniz. 1927. Ibid. 97:825-827.
84. da Fonseca, O. O. R. 1916. Mem. Inst. Oswaldo Cruz 8(1):5-40.
85. Dandawate, C. N., and K. V. Shah. 1969. Indian J. Med. Res. 57:799-804.
86. Dandawate, C. N., et al. 1969. Ibid. 57:1420-1426.
87. Danforth, W. F. 1967. Res. Protozool. 1:201-306.
88. Davaine, C. 1875. Dict. Encycl. Sci. Med. [2] 9:115-130.
89. Dawes, B., and D. L. Hughes. 1964. Adv. Parasitol. 2:97-168.
90. de Almeida, F. P. 1928. An. Fac. Med. Univ. Sao Paulo 3:65-67.
91. Deibel, R. H., and H. W. Seeley, Jr. 1974. In R. E. Buchanan and N. E. Gibbons, ed. Bergey's Manual of Determinative Bacteriology. Ed. 8. Williams and Wilkins, Baltimore. pp. 490-498.
92. de la Barrera, J. M., and A. Riva. 1928. Rev. Inst. Bacteriol. Dep. Nacl. Hig. (Argent.) 5:470-490.
93. Delanoë, P., and C. Delanoë. 1912. C. R. Acad. Sci. 155:658-660.
94. Demina, N. A. 1963. Proc. 1st Int. Congr. Protozool. 1961, 1:545-548.
95. Dennig, H. K., and E. Eidmann. 1960. Berl. Tieraerztl. Wochenschr. 73:273-274.
96. de Rodaniche, E., and T. de Pinzon. 1949. J. Parasitol. 35:152-155.
97. Dezest, G. 1953. Ann. Inst. Pasteur Paris 85:131-133.
98. Dias, E. 1956. In E. Rosenwaldt, ed. Welt-Seuchen-Atlas. Falk, Hamburg. pt. 2, pp. 135-137.
99. Dick, G. W. A., and A. J. Haddow. 1952. Trans. R. Soc. Trop. Med. Hyg. 46:600-618.
100. Dick, G. W. A., et al. 1952. Ibid. 46:509-520.
101. Dobson, C., et al. 1971. J. Immunol. 106:128-133.
102. Doherty, R. L., et al. 1963. Aust. J. Exp. Biol. Med. Sci. 41:17-40.
103. Douvres, F. W., and J. T. Lucker. 1958. J. Parasitol. 44(4 Suppl.):28-29.
104. Downie, A. W. 1939. J. Pathol. Bacteriol. 48:361-379.
105. Doyle, J. J., et al. 1974. J. Exp. Med. 139:1061-1069.
106. du Buy, H. G., and F. L. Riley. 1967. Proc. Natl. Acad. Sci. USA 57:790-797.
107. du Buy, H. G., et al. 1965. Science 147:754-756.
108. du Buy, H. G., et al. 1966. Biochim. Biophys. Acta 123:298-305.
109. Dvorak, J., and M. Otcenasek. 1964. Mycopathol. Mycol. Appl. 23:294-296.
110. Eddy, B. E., et al. 1960. J. Infect. Dis. 107:361-368.
111. Ediger, R. D., and M. M. Rabstein. 1968. J. Am. Vet. Med. Assoc. 153:954-956.
112. Ellis, P. A., and A. E. Wright. 1961. J. Clin. Pathol. 14:394-396.
113. Erasmus, B. J. 1963. Onderstepoort J. Vet. Res. 30:11-21.

continued

114. Evolceanu, R., et al. 1963. Mycopathologia 19:24-36.

115. Faust, E. C. 1950. An. Inst. Biol. Univ. Nacl. Auton. Mex. 20:229-250.

116. Ferriolli Filho, F., and M. P. Barretto. 1966. Rev. Inst. Med. Trop. Sao Paulo 8:267-276.

117. Fink, E. H., et al. 1971. Z. Tropenmed. Parasitol. 22:343-350.

118. Fish, N. A., et al. 1968. Can. Med. Assoc. J. 99:418-420.

119. Flores, D. F., et al. 1948. Agric. Tec. (Santiago) 8:87-111.

120. Fraunfelter, F. C., et al. 1971. Lab. Anim. 5:1-13.

121. Freeman, W., and F. D. Weidman. 1923. Arch. Neurol. Psychiatr. 9:589-603.

122. French, E. L. 1952. Med. J. Aust. 1:100-103.

123. Frenkel, J. K. 1973. In D. M. Hammond and P. L. Long, ed. The Coccidia. Univ. Park, Baltimore. pp. 343-410.

124. Ganaway, J. R. 1976. In J. E. Wagner and P. J. Manning, ed. The Biology of the Guinea Pig. Academic, New York. pp. 121-135.

125. Gaudin, E. G., et al. 1971. Ann. Inst. Pasteur Paris 120:228-242.

126. Gentles, J. C. 1958. Nature (London) 182:476-477.

127. Gentles, J. C., et al. 1959. Ibid. 183:256-257.

128. Georg, L. K. 1960. U.S. Public Health Serv. Publ. 727.

129. Giltner, L. T. 1918. J. Agric. Res. 14:533-542.

130. Giltner, L. T., and M. S. Shahan. 1933. North Am. Vet. 14(11):25.

131. Glazunova, Z. I. 1964. Med. Parazitol. Parazit. Bolez. 33:643-650.

132. Gleiberman, S. E., and E. M. Belova. 1964. Ibid. 34:650-654.

133. Gordon, F. B., et al. 1966. J. Infect. Dis. 116:203-207.

134. Grace, J. T., Jr. 1970. Ann. N.Y. Acad. Sci. 174:946-966.

135. Greenblatt, C. L., and B. K. Wetzel. 1966. J. Protozool. 13:521-531.

136. Grimes, J. E., et al. 1962. Am. Soc. Trop. Med. Hyg. Annu. Meet. (Atlanta) 11.

137. Gross, L., and D. G. Feldman. 1970. Arch. Geschwulstforsch. 36:1-9.

138. Guilbride, P. D. 1963. Bull. Epizoot. Dis. Afr. 11:283-287.

139. Gupta, B. N., et al. 1970. Am. J. Vet. Res. 31:1703-1707.

140. Gupta, B. N., et al. 1972. Lab. Anim. Sci. 22:362-368.

141. Hammon, W. M., et al. 1952. J. Immunol. 69:493-510.

142. Hammon, W. M., et al. 1960. Trans. Assoc. Am. Physicians 73:140-155.

143. Hammon, W. M., et al. 1960. Science 131:1102-1103.

144. Hampton, E. G., et al. 1968. J. Gen. Virol. 2:205-206.

145. Harper, I. A., and R. G. Sommerville. 1965. Arch. Ophthalmol. 73:552-554.

146. Hartley, J. W., et al. 1957. Proc. Soc. Exp. Biol. Med. 96:281-285.

147. Hasselmann, G. 1918. Braz. Med. 32:81.

148. Hasselmann, G. 1924. Mem. Inst. Oswaldo Cruz 17:229-235.

149. Hegner, R. W. 1923. Am. J. Hyg. 3:345-349.

150. Hegner, R. W. 1924. Ibid. 4:143-151.

151. Hegner, R. W. 1926. Ibid. 6:593-601.

152. Hegner, R. W. 1926. J. Parasitol. 12:146-147.

153. Hegner, R. W. 1927. Host-Parasite Relations Between Man and His Intestinal Protozoa. Century, New York.

154. Hegner, R. W. 1934. Am. J. Hyg. 19:38-67.

155. Hegner, R. W., and E. Schumaker. 1928. J. Parasitol. 15:31-37.

156. Heisch, R. B., et al. 1970. Trans. R. Soc. Trop. Med. Hyg. 64:679-682.

157. Henry, D. P. 1932. Univ. Calif. Berkeley Publ. Zool. 37:211-268.

158. Henry, L., and J. K. Beverly. 1977. J. Comp. Pathol. 87:97-102.

159. Herlich, H. 1966. J. Parasitol. 52:871-874.

160. Herlich, H. 1969. Ibid. 55:88-93.

161. Herlich, H., and C. F. Dixon. 1965. Ibid. 51:300.

162. Hill, A. 1971. Br. Med. J. 2:711-712.

163. Hill, A. 1971. J. Gen. Microbiol. 65:109-113.

164. Hill, A. 1971. Nature (London) 232:560.

165. Hill, A. 1971. Vet. Rec. 89:225.

166. Hill, A., et al. 1969. Ibid. 85:291-292.

167. Hofmann, H., and T. Hänichen. 1970. Berl. Muench. Tieraerztl. Wochenschr. 83:151-153.

168. Holbrook, A. A., and W. M. Frerichs. 1970. J. Parasitol. 56:930-931.

169. Holman, W. L. 1916-1917. J. Med. Res. 35:151-185.

170. Holmes, F. O. 1923. J. Parasitol. 10:47-50.

171. Homburger, F., et al. 1945. Science 102:449-450.

172. Hotchin, J. 1971. Am. J. Pathol. 64:747-769.

173. Hsiung, G. D., and L. S. Kaplow. 1969. In R. M. Dutcher, ed. Comparative Leukemia Research 1969. Karger, Basel. pp. 578-583.

174. Hsiung, G. D., and L. S. Kaplow. 1969. J. Virol. 3:355-357.

175. Hsiung, G. D., et al. 1971. Am. J. Epidemiol. 93:298-307.

176. Hsu-Kuo, M. Y., et al. 1970. Chin. J. Microbiol. 3:148-149.

177. Institute for Medical Research. 1957. Annual Report. Kuala Lumpur, Malaysia. pp. 100-102.

178. Ioachim, H. L., and L. Berwick. 1969. (Loc. cit. ref. 173). pp. 566-573.

179. Ivey, M. H. 1964. J. Parasitol. 50(3 Suppl.):24-25.

180. Jadin, J. B., and M. Wery. 1963. Ann. Soc. Belg. Med. Trop. 43:831-842.

continued

181. Jawetz, E., and P. Thygeson. 1965. In F. L. Horsfall, Jr., and I. Tamm, ed. Viral and Rickettsial Infections of Man. Ed. 4. Lippincott, Philadelphia. pp. 1042-1058.

182. Jennings, W., et al. 1970. Am. J. Trop. Med. Hyg. 19:527-536.

183. Jervis, H. R., et al. 1966. Am. J. Vet. Res. 27:408-414.

184. Jeska, E. L., et al. 1969. Exp. Parasitol. 26:187-192.

185. Jonkers, A. H., et al. 1964. Am. J. Vet. Res. 25:236-242.

186. Jonkers, A. H., et al. 1967. Am. J. Trop. Med. Hyg. 16:74-78.

187. Juhr, N. C., and S. Obi. 1970. Z. Versuchstierk. 12:383-387.

188. Jungeblut, C. W., and H. Kodza. 1962. Arch. Gesamte Virusforsch. 12:537-551.

189. Kallinikova, V. D. 1974. Zh. Obshch. Biol. 35:228-235.

190. Karel, L., et al. 1941. J. Infect. Dis. 69:125-130.

191. Kazdan, J. J., et al. 1967. Am. J. Ophthalmol. 64:116-124.

192. Kent, T. H., et al. 1966. Arch. Pathol. 81:501-508.

193. Khalil, G. M., and J. F. Schacher. 1965. Am. J. Trop. Med. 14:736-746.

194. Kierszenbaum, F., et al. 1970. Arch. Gesamte Virusforsch. 30:217-223.

195. Kim, C. W. 1966. J. Parasitol. 52:722-726.

196. Kim, C. W., et al. 1970. J. Immunol. 105:175-186.

197. Kissling, R. E., and R. W. Chamberlain. 1967. Adv. Vet. Sci. 11:65-84.

198. Klineberger, E. 1939. J. Pathol. Bacteriol. 49:451-452.

199. Kopperi, A. J. 1935. Suom. Elaintietell. Julk. Vanamo 3:1-92.

200. Kozar, Z., et al. 1965. Acta Parasitol. Pol. 13:271-274.

201. Krascheninnikow, S. 1959. J. Protozool. 6:61-68.

202. Krascheninnikow, S., and D. H. Wenrich. 1958. Ibid. 5:196-202.

203. Krenn, E. 1936. Wien. Tieraerztl. Monatsschr. 23:699-700.

204. Kretschmar, W. 1965. Z. Tropenmed. Parasitol. 16:277-283.

205. Krupp, J. 1956. Exp. Parasitol. 5:421-426.

206. Kuczynski, M. H. 1914. Arch. Protistenk. 33:119-204.

207. Kulasiri, C. 1962. Ceylon J. Med. Sci. 11:11-14.

208. Kunz, L. L., and G. M. Hutton. 1971. Vet. Scope 16:12-20.

209. Lam, K. M., and G. D. Hsiung. 1971. Am. J. Epidemiol. 93:308-313.

210. Lam, K. M., and G. D. Hsiung. 1971. Proc. Soc. Exp. Biol. Med. 138:422-426.

211. Lapage, G. 1940. Vet. J. 96:144-154, 190-202, 242-254, 280-295.

212. Larsh, H. W. 1960. Ann. N.Y. Acad. Sci. 89:78-90.

213. Lemma, A., and P. Yau. 1973. Am. J. Trop. Med. Hyg. 22:477-481.

214. Lennette, E. H. 1957. Ibid. 6:1036-1046.

215. Lichtenfels, J. R. 1971. J. Parasitol. 57:348-355.

216. Lucas, M. S. 1932. Arch. Protistenk. 77:64-72.

217. Lucas, M. S. 1932. Ibid. 77:407-423.

218. Lwoff, A., and S. Nicolau. 1935. Bull. Soc. Pathol. Exot. 28:277-281.

219. Lynch, K. M. 1922. J. Parasitol. 9:29-32.

220. Ma, B. I., et al. 1969. Proc. Soc. Exp. Biol. Med. 130:586-590.

221. Madden, D. L., et al. 1970. Lab. Anim. Care 20:454-455.

222. Makstenieks, O., and J. D. Verlinde. 1957. Doc. Med. Geogr. Trop. 9:213-224.

223. Mancilla, R., et al. 1965. Nature (London) 206:27-28.

224. Marciacq, Y., and J. R. Seed. 1970. J. Infect. Dis. 121:653-655.

225. Mariani, G. 1941. Riv. Biol. Colon. 4:47-54.

226. Markham, F. S. 1937. Am. J. Hyg. 26:193-196.

227. Markham, N. P., and J. G. Markham. 1966. J. Comp. Pathol. 76:49-56.

228. Marzan, B. 1952. Vet. Arh. 22:187-193.

229. Mason, N. 1937. Lancet 232:564-565.

230. Maurer, F. D. 1964. Lab. Anim. Care 14:415-419.

231. McCloskey, R. V., and A. Shelokov. 1965. Am. J. Trop. Med. Hyg. 14:152-155.

232. McIntosh, B. M. 1961. Trans. R. Soc. Trop. Med. Hyg. 55:63-68.

233. McIntosh, B. M., et al. 1960. South Afr. J. Med. Sci. 25:33-37.

234. McIntosh, B. M., et al. 1962. Ibid. 27:77-86.

235. McIntosh, B. M., et al. 1962. Ibid. 27:87-94.

236. McIntosh, B. M., et al. 1962. Am. J. Trop. Med. Hyg. 11:685-686.

237. McIntosh, B. M., et al. 1965. South Afr. J. Med. Sci. 30:67-70.

238. McIntosh, B. M., et al. Unpublished. South African Institute for Medical Research, Arbovirus Unit, Johannesburg, 1964.

239. McLean, D. M., et al. 1966. Can. Med. Assoc. J. 94:532-536.

240. Medina, H. 1946. Arq. Biol. Tecnol. 1:39-74.

241. Medina, H. 1947. Ibid. 2:3-6.

242. Merchant, I. A., and R. A. Packer. 1967. Veterinary Bacteriology and Virology. Ed. 7. Iowa State Univ., Ames, pp. 610-731.

243. Metselaar, D., et al. 1969. Arch. Gesamte Virusforsch. 26:183-193.

244. Mettam, R. W. M. 1932. Rep. Vet. Dep. Uganda Prot. 1931, pp. 16-20.

245. Meyer, K. F., et al. 1931. Science 74:227-228.

246. Miller, L. T., and H. A. Feldman. 1953. J. Infect. Dis. 92:118-120.

247. Mitamura, T., et al. 1935. Kansai Iji 260:1-5.

continued

248. Mitamura, T., et al. 1936. Trans. Soc. Pathol. Jpn. 26:429-452.

249. Mitscherlich, E. 1958. In P. Cohrs, et al., ed. Pathologie der Laboratoriumstiere. Springer-Verlag, Berlin and New York. v. 2, pp. 240-249.

250. Mlinac, F., and M. Hajsig. 1958. Vet. Arh. 28:43-48.

251. Mooser, H. 1929. J. Infect. Dis. 44:186-193.

252. Morénas, L. 1938. Ann. Univ. Lyon Sci. Med. [3] 1:1-234.

253. Morgan, B. B. 1943. Proc. Helminthol. Soc. Wash. 10:26-29.

254. Mühlpfordt, H. 1964. Angew. Parasitol. 5:7-8.

255. Muniz, J., and H. Medina. 1948. Arq. Biol. Tecnol. 3:13-30.

256. Murray, E. S. 1964. J. Infect. Dis. 114:1-12.

257. Myers, M. L., and R. P. Hanson. 1962. Am. J. Vet. Res. 23:1078-1080.

258. Nadel, E., et al. 1967. J. Natl. Cancer Inst. 38:979-982.

259. Nayak, D. P. 1971. J. Virol. 8:579-588.

260. Negroni, D. 1932. Rev. Soc. Argent. Biol. 8:7-9.

261. Neiva, A., et al. 1914. Mem. Inst. Oswaldo Cruz 6:180-191.

262. Newberne, P. M., and W. H. Butler. 1969. Cancer Res. 29:236-250.

263. Nicolau, S. 1932. C. R. Soc. Biol. 100:676-678.

264. Nicolau, S., and A. Lwoff. 1935. Ann. Inst. Pasteur Paris 55:654-675.

265. Nie, D. 1948. J. Morphol. 82:287-329.

266. Nie, D. 1950. Ibid. 86:381-493.

267. Oker-Blom, N., et al. 1962. Biol. Viruses Tick-borne Encephalitis Complex Proc. Symp. Czech. Acad. Sci. (Smolenice) 1960, pp. 423-429.

268. Oker-Blom, N., et al. 1964. Ann. Med. Exp. Biol. Fenn. 42:109-112.

269. Opler, S. R. 1967. J. Natl. Cancer Inst. 38:797-800.

270. Opler, S. R. 1968. Proc. 3rd. Int. Symp. Comp. Leuk. Res. 1967, pp. 81-88.

271. Opler, S. R. 1971. Defining Lab. Anim. Proc. 4th Symp. Int. Comm. Lab. Anim. Inst. Lab. Anim. Resour., pp. 435-449.

272. Orio, J., et al. 1958. Bull. Soc. Pathol. Exot. 51:607-615.

273. Otto, H. 1957. Frankf. Z. Pathol. 68:41-48.

274. Pallaske, G., and R. Krahnert. 1958. (Loc. cit. ref. 249). v. 2, pp. 1-53.

275. Pappenheimer, A. M., and C. A. Slanetz. 1942. J. Exp. Med. 76:299-306.

276. Paraense, W. L. 1953. Trans. R. Soc. Trop. Med. Hyg. 47:556-560.

277. Parker, H. D., and R. L. Younger. 1963. Am. J. Vet. Res. 24:367-370.

278. Parker, J. C. 1961. Exp. Parasitol. 11:380-390.

279. Parker, J. C. Unpublished. Microbiological Associates, Bethesda, MD, 1972.

280. Parker, J. C., et al. 1966. Natl. Cancer Inst. Monogr. 20:25-36.

281. Parodi, A. S., et al. 1958. Dia Med. 30:2300.

282. Paterson, J. S. 1962. In R. J. C. Harris, ed. The Problems of Laboratory Animal Disease. Academic, New York. pp. 169-184.

283. Paterson, J. S. 1967. In Universities Federation for Animal Welfare, ed. UFAW Handbook on the Care and Management of Laboratory Animals. Ed. 3. Williams and Wilkins, Baltimore. pp. 241-287.

284. Pearce, L. 1916. J. Exp. Med. 23:431-442.

285. Pellérdy, L. P. 1965. Coccidia and Coccidiosis. Akadémiai Kiadó, Budapest.

286. Pellérdy, L. P., and U. Dürr. 1969. Acta Vet. (Budapest)19:253-268.

287. Pellissier, A., et al. 1950. Ann. Inst. Pasteur Paris 79:200-202.

288. Perkins, R. G. 1901. J. Exp. Med. 5:389-396.

289. Perrin, T. L. 1943. Arch. Pathol. 36:559-567.

290. Perrin, T. L. 1943. Ibid. 36:568-578.

291. Pianese, G. 1901. Z. Hyg. Infektionskr. 36:350-367.

292. Pinheiro, F. P., et al. 1966. Proc. Soc. Exp. Biol. Med. 122:531-535.

293. Pirtle, E. C., and A. P. McKee. 1951. Ibid. 77:425-429.

294. Platt, H. 1958. J. Pathol. Bacteriol. 76:119-131.

295. Porter, D. A. 1937. J. Parasitol. 23:73-82.

296. Porter, D. A., and G. F. Otto. 1934. Ibid. 20:323.

297. Poynter, D., and P. H. Silverman. 1962. Ibid. 48(2 Suppl.):52.

298. Preston, P. M., and D. C. Dumonde. 1971. Trans. R. Soc. Trop. Med. Hyg. 65:18-19.

299. Queensland Institute of Medical Research. 1973. Annual Report. Brisbane, Australia. p. 15.

300. Radwanski, Z. K., et al. 1974. Trans. R. Soc. Trop. Med. Hyg. 68:124-132.

301. Rae, M. V. 1936. J. Infect. Dis. 59:236-241.

302. Redaelli, P. 1924. J. Trop. Med. Hyg. 27:211-213.

303. Rivers, T. M., and G. P. Berry. 1931. J. Exp. Med. 54:119-128.

304. Robinson, V. B., and F. G. Schell. 1951. Am. Vet. 32:555-558.

305. Roca-Garcia, M. 1944. J. Infect. Dis. 75:160-169.

306. Röhrer, H., et al. 1958. (Loc. cit. ref. 249). v. 2, pp. 104-111.

307. Rosenthal, S. R., and F. H. Elmore. 1950. Am. Rev. Tuberc. 61:106-115.

308. Ross, R. W. 1956. J. Hyg. 54:177-191.

309. Ruge, H. 1951. Zentralb. Bakteriol. Parasitenk. Infektionskr. Hyg. Abt. 1 Orig. 156:543-544.

310. Sabin, A. B., and P. K. Olitsky. 1937. Science 85:336-338.

311. Sadun, E. H., and R. W. Gore. 1970. Exp. Parasitol. 28:435-449.

312. Sandrow, J. 1969. Zentralbl. Bakteriol. Parasitenk. Infektionskr. Hyg. Abt. 1 Orig. 209:389-406.

313. Sarma, P. S., et al. 1969. (Loc. cit. ref. 173). pp. 574-577.

314. Saunders, L. Z. 1958. J. Natl. Cancer Inst. 20:899-903.

continued

315. Scherago, M. 1936. J. Bacteriol. 31:83.
316. Schwartz, B., and J. E. Alicata. 1931. J. Parasitol. 18:54.
317. Scott, M. J. 1927. J. Morphol. 44:417-465.
318. Seidelin, H. 1914. Ann. Trop. Med. Parasitol. 8:553-564.
319. Sharp, A. D., and L. J. Olson. 1962. J. Parasitol. 48:362-367.
320. Sheather, A. L. 1924. J. Comp. Pathol. 37:243-246.
321. Sheldon, A. J., and G. F. Otto. 1937. J. Parasitol. 23:570-571.
322. Shevkunova, E. A., and T. P. Fedichkina. 1976. Med. Parazitol. Parazit. Bolez. 45:660-665.
323. Siegert, R. 1972. Virol. Monogr. 11:97-153.
324. Simpson, D. I. H., et al. 1968. Br. J. Exp. Pathol. 49:458-464.
325. Smith, T. 1913. J. Med. Res. 29:291-323.
326. Smith, W. 1941. J. Pathol. Bacteriol. 53:29-37.
327. Smithburn, K. C., and A. J. Haddow. 1944. J. Immunol. 49:141-157.
328. Smithburn, K. C., et al. 1940. Am. J. Trop. Med. 20:471-492.
329. Smithburn, K. C., et al. 1941. Ibid. 21:75-90.
330. Soave, O. A. 1964. Am. J. Vet. Res. 25:268-269.
331. Spence, L., et al. 1964. Am. J. Trop. Med. Hyg. 13:114-117.
332. Spratt, D. M., and R. C. Anderson. 1968. J. Helminthol. 42:139-155.
333. Sprouse, R. F. 1969. Am. Rev. Respir. Dis. 100:685-689.
334. Sprouse, R. F. 1976. (Loc. cit. ref. 124). pp. 153-161.
335. Srihongse, S., et al. 1966. Am. J. Trop. Med. Hyg. 15:379-384.
336. Srivastava, V. K., and G. Subramanian. 1969. J. Helminthol. 43:389-394.
337. Stalheim, O. H. V., and P. J. Matthews. 1975. Lab. Anim. Sci. 25:70-73.
338. Steele, J. H. 1969. In W. Hobsen, ed. The Theory and Practice of Public Health. Oxford Univ., London and New York. pp. 220-251.
339. Stojanov, D. P., and J. L. Cvetanov. 1965. Z. Parasitenk. 25:350-358.
340. Storz, J. 1964. Zentralbl. Bakteriol. Parasitenk. Infektionskr. Hyg. Abt. 1 Orig. 193:432-446.
341. Strauss, J. M., and D. Heyneman. 1966. J. Parasitol. 52:413.
342. Subcommittee for Information Exchange. 1970. Am. J. Trop. Med. Hyg. 19:1103-1104.
343. Symons, L. E. A. 1970. Gut 11:980.
344. Szukiewicz, Z., and Z. Prazmo. 1971. Med. Wet. 27:12-13.
345. Takeuchi, A., and B. P. Phillips. 1972. Am. J. Pathol. 66:29A-30A.
346. Takeuchi, A., and H. Sprinz. 1967. Ibid. 51:137-161.
347. Tanabe, M. 1925. J. Parasitol. 11:170-176.
348. Taylor, J. L., et al. 1971. Lab. Anim. Sci. 21:944-945.
349. Taylor, R. M., et al. 1966. Am. J. Trop. Med. Hyg. 15:76-86.
350. Taylor, R. M., et al. 1966. Ibid. 15:87-90.
351. Ten Broeck, C., and M. H. Merrill. 1933. Proc. Soc. Exp. Biol. Med. 31:217-220.
352. Ten Broeck, C., and J. B. Nelson. 1938. Ibid. 39:572-573.
353. Tesh, R. B., and K. M. Johnson. 1975. In W. T. Hubbert, et al., ed. Diseases Transmitted from Animals to Man. Ed. 6. Thomas, Springfield, IL. pp. 897-910.
354. Tewari, H. C. 1968. Ann. Trop. Med. Parasitol. 62:495-501.
355. Tikasingh, E. S., et al. 1966. Am. J. Trop. Med. Hyg. 15:235.
356. Turk, J. L., and A. D. M. Bryceson. 1971. Adv. Immunol. 13:209-266.
357. Vallée, A., et al. 1969. Bull. Acad. Vet. Fr. 42:797-800.
358. Van Hoosier, G. L., Jr., and L. R. Robinette. 1976. (Loc. cit. ref. 124). pp. 137-152.
359. Van Hoosier, G. L., Jr., et al. 1970. Lab. Anim. Care 20:232-237.
360. Varela, G., et al. 1953. Rev. Inst. Salubr. Enferm. Trop. Mexico City 13:217-222.
361. Vetterling, J. M. 1976. (Loc. cit. ref. 124). pp. 163-196.
362. Vetterling, J. M., et al. 1971. J. Protozool. 18:243-247.
363. Vetterling, J. M., et al. 1971. Ibid. 18:248-260.
364. Vogel, R. A., and A. Timpe. 1957. J. Invest. Dermatol. 28:311-312.
365. von Schuckmann, W. 1926. Arb. Reichsgesundheitsam. 57:801-820.
366. Webb, J. N. 1970. J. Pathol. 100:155-159.
367. Weissberger, H., et al. 1973. J. Protozool. 20:534-535.
368. Wenrich, D. H. 1935. Proc. Am. Phil. Soc. 75:605-650.
369. Wenrich, D. H. 1946. J. Parasitol. 32:40-53.
370. Wenyon, C. M. 1926. Protozoology. Baillière, Tindall and Cox, London. v. 1 and 2.
371. Wescott, R. B. 1976. (Loc. cit. ref. 124). pp. 197-200.
372. Westphal, A. 1957. Z. Tropenmed. Parasitol. 8:288-294.
373. Westphal, A. 1971. Ibid. 22:138-148.
374. Wetzel, J. C. 1972. Diss. Abstr. Int. B, 32:5549B.
375. Wieczorowski, S. 1965. Acta Parasitol. Pol. 13:81-92.
376. Wittfogel, H. 1935. Dtsch. Tieraerztl. Wochenschr. 43:310-312.
377. Wittfogel, H. 1935. Arch. Gynaekol. 159:612-617.

continued

378. Wittner, M., and R. M. Rosenbaum. 1970. Am. J. Trop. Med. Hyg. 19:755-761.

379. Wittner, M., et al. 1971. J. Parasitol. 57:44-45.

380. Woodall, J. P. 1967. Atas Simp. Biota Amazon. 6: 31-63.

381. Wright, J. 1936. J. Pathol. Bacteriol. 42:209-212.

382. Yakimov, V. L., et al. 1921. Bull. Soc. Pathol. Exot. 14:558-564.

383. Zeledón, R. 1959. J. Parasitol. 45(4 Suppl.):49.

384. Zeledón, R. 1960. Ibid. 46:541-551.

385. Zeledón, R. 1960. J. Protozool. 7:146-150.

386. Zeledón, R. 1960. Rev. Biol. Trop. 8:25-33.

387. Zeledón, R. 1960. Ibid. 8:181-195.

388. Zeledón, R. 1960. Rev. Bras. Biol. 20:409-414.

389. Zlotnik, I., et al. 1971. Br. J. Exp. Pathol. 52: 395.

136. SUSCEPTIBILITY TO VARIOUS DISEASES: GUINEA PIG

Part I. Infectious and Parasitic Diseases

Disease or Organ Affected	Agent	Reference
Viral Diseases[1]		
Hepatoenteritis	....	46,55
Pneumonia, viral	....	4,5,31
Myositis	....	46,49
Wasting disease	....	42,55
Bacterial Diseases[2]		
Generalized infections	Bordetella bronchiseptica	23,61
	Salmonella spp.	22,35, 36
	Streptococcus (Lancefield group)	20,44
	Yersinia pseudotuberculosis	3,38
Protozoan Diseases		
Generalized infections	Encephalitozoon cuniculi[3]	40,41
	Sarcocystis caviae	21,57
	Toxoplasma gondii	9,33, 34,48
Cutaneous infections	Leishmania enriettii	32,37, 57
Small intestine	Cryptosporidium wrairi	29
	Giardia caviae	24,45
	Tritrichomonas caviae	57,62
Lung	Pneumocystis carinii	8,10, 56
Blood	Trypanosoma cruzi	2,15, 19

Disease or Organ Affected	Agent	Reference
Kidney	Encephalitozoon cuniculi[3]	57
	Klossiella cobayae	26,39, 50,59
	Toxoplasma gondii	57
Helminthan Diseases		
Natural infections	Paraspidodera uncinata	7,43
Experimental infections	Ascaris suum	16,30
	Dictyocaulus viviparus	12,17
	Fasciola hepatica	6,54
	Nippostrongylus brasiliensis	60
	Trichinella spiralis	13,52
	Trichostrongylus colubriformis	11,25
Arthropod Diseases		
Cutaneous lesions	Arachnida: Acarina	
	Chirodiscoides caviae	14,58
	Demodex caviae	1
	Myocoptes musculinus	51
	Notoedris muris	53
	Insecta	
	Gliricola lindolphoi	27
	G. porcelli	18,27
	Gyropus ovalis	18,27
	Hectopsylla eskeyi	28
	Trimenopon hispidum	47

[1] Diseases of possible viral etiology. [2] Guinea pigs have been shown to be susceptible to a number of bacterial diseases. According to Ganaway [ref. 22], at least 19 genera of bacteria, mycoplasmas, and rickettsia-like agents have been recovered from laboratory guinea pigs with spontaneous disease. The most frequently reported are included here. [3] Synonym: *Nosema cuniculi*.

Contributor: A. F. Geczy

continued

Part I. Infectious and Parasitic Diseases

References

1. Bacigaluppi, J., and R. J. Roveda. 1954. Rev. Med. Vet. 36:149-153.
2. Barretto, M. P., et al. 1966. Rev. Inst. Med. Trop. Sao Paulo 8:103-112.
3. Bishop, L. M. 1932. Cornell Vet. 22:1-9.
4. Blanc, G. 1952. Sem. Hop. 28:3805-3810.
5. Blanc, G., et al. 1951. Bull. Acad. Natl. Med. Paris 135:520-528.
6. Boray, J. C. 1969. Adv. Parasitol. 7:95-210.
7. Breza, M., and V. Jurasek. 1965. Helminthol. Abstr. 34:238.
8. Campbell, W. G., Jr. 1972. Arch. Pathol. 93:312-324.
9. Carini, A., and L. Migliano. 1916. Bull. Soc. Pathol. Exot. 9:435-436.
10. Chagas, C. 1911. Mem. Inst. Oswaldo Cruz 3:219-275.
11. Connan, R. M. 1966. Parasitology 56:521-530.
12. Cornwell, R. L., and R. M. Jones. 1971. J. Comp. Pathol. 81:97-103.
13. Cypress, R., et al. 1971. J. Parasitol. 57:103-106.
14. Deoras, P. J., and K. K. Patel. 1960. Indian J. Entomol. 22:7-14.
15. Dias, E. 1956. In E. Rodenwaldt, ed. Welt-Seuchen-Atlas. Falk, Hamburg. pt. 2, pp. 135-137.
16. Dobson, C., et al. 1971. J. Immunol. 106:128-133.
17. Douvres, F. W., and J. T. Lucker. 1958. J. Parasitol. 44(Suppl. 28).
18. Ewing, H. G. 1924. Proc. U.S. Natl. Mus. 63(Artic. 20):1-42.
19. Ferriolli Filho, F., et al. 1966. Rev. Inst. Med. Trop. Sao Paulo 8:267-276.
20. Fraunfelter, F. C., et al. 1971. Lab. Anim. 5:1-13.
21. Frenkel, J. K. 1973. In D. H. Hammond and P. L. Long, ed. The Coccidia. Univ. Park, Baltimore. pp. 318-369.
22. Ganaway, J. R. 1976. In J. E. Wagner and P. J. Manning, ed. The Biology of the Guinea Pig. Academic, New York. pp. 121-135.
23. Ganaway, J. R., et al. 1965. Lab. Anim. Care 15:156-162.
24. Hegner, R. W. 1923. Am. J. Hyg. 3:345-349.
25. Herlich, H. 1966. J. Parasitol. 52:871-874.
26. Hofmann, H., and T. Hänichen. 1970. Berl. Muench. Tieraerztl. Wochenschr. 83:151-153.
27. Hopkins, G. H. E. 1949. Proc. Zool. Soc. London 119:387-604.
28. Hopkins, G. H. E., and M. Rothschild. 1953. An Illustrated Catalogue of the Rothschild Collection of Fleas (Siphonaptera) in the British Museum (Natural History). British Museum, London. v. 1, pp. 50, 63-65.
29. Jervis, H. R., et al. 1966. Am. J. Vet. Res. 27:408-414.
30. Jeska, E. L., et al. 1969. Exp. Parasitol. 26:187-192.
31. Lepine, F., et al. 1943. C. R. Soc. Biol. 137:317-318.
32. Medina, H. 1946. Arq. Biol. Tecnol. 1:39-74.
33. Mesnil, F. 1918. Bull. Inst. Pasteur 16:71.
34. Mooser, H. 1929. J. Infect. Dis. 44:186-193.
35. Nelson, J. B. 1927. J. Exp. Med. 46:541-548.
36. Nelson, J. B., and T. Smith. 1927. Ibid. 45:353-363.
37. Paraense, W. L. 1952. An. Acad. Bras. Cienc. 24:307-310.
38. Paterson, J. S., and R. Cook. 1963. J. Pathol. Bacteriol. 85:241-242.
39. Pearce, L. 1916. J. Exp. Med. 23:431-442.
40. Perrin, T. L. 1943. Arch. Pathol. 36:559-567.
41. Petri, M. 1966. Acta Pathol. Microbiol. Scand. 66:13-30.
42. Pirtle, E. C., and A. F. McKee. 1951. Proc. Soc. Exp. Biol. Med. 77:425-429.
43. Porter, D. A., and G. F. Otto. 1934. J. Parasitol. 20:323(Abstr. 1).
44. Rae, M. V. 1936. J. Infect. Dis. 59:236-241.
45. Ray, H., et al. 1961. Bull. Calcutta Sch. Trop. Med. 9:154-155.
46. Röhrer, H., et al. 1958. In P. Cohrs, et al., ed. Pathologie der Laboratoriumstiere. Springer-Verlag, Berlin. v. 2, pp. 104-111.
47. Ronald, N. C., and J. E. Wagner. 1976. (Loc. cit. ref. 22). pp. 201-209.
48. Sabin, A. B., and P. K. Olitsky. 1937. Science 85:336-338.
49. Saunders, L. Z. 1958. J. Natl. Cancer Inst. 20:899-903.
50. Seidelin, H. 1914. Ann. Trop. Med. Parasitol. 8:553-564.
51. Sengbusch, H. G. 1960. J. Econ. Entomol. 53:168.
52. Sharp, A. D., and L. J. Olson. 1962. J. Parasitol. 48:362-367.
53. Soerenson, B., et al. 1963. Biologico 29:232-234.
54. Tewari, H. C. 1968. Ann. Trop. Med. Parasitol. 62:495-501.
55. Van Hoosier, G. L., Jr., and L. R. Robinette. 1976. (Loc. cit. ref. 22). pp. 137-152.
56. Vavra, J., and K. Kučera. 1970. J. Protozool. 17:463-483.
57. Vetterling, J. M. 1976. (Loc. cit. ref. 22). pp. 163-196.
58. Wagner, J. E., et al. 1972. Lab. Anim. Sci. 22:750-752.
59. Wenyon, C. M. 1926. Protozoology. Wood, New York. v. 2, pp. 1076-1078.
60. Wescott, R. B. 1976. (Loc. cit. ref. 22). pp. 197-200.
61. Woode, G. N., and N. McLeod. 1967. Lab. Anim. 1:91-94.
62. Zasukhin, D. N., and E. M. Kheisin. 1957. Tr. Inst. Zool. Akad. Nauk Kaz. SSR 7:241-251.

continued

Part II. Other Miscellaneous Disease Conditions

System	Condition	Reference
Central nervous	Experimental allergic encephalo-myelitis[1]	7,14-16
Digestive	Malocclusion of lower premolars & anterior molars	11
	Gastric ulcers	21
	Focal coagulative necrosis of liver	5,6
	Cecitis	8,21
Respiratory	Bony spicules in lung	4,21
	Pulmonary perivascular lymphoid nodules	18
Urogenital	Chronic interstitial nephritis	13,17

System	Condition	Reference
	Cystic ovaries	12
	Experimental allergic orchitis	3,15,19, 20,22
	Obstruction of urethra; seminal vesiculitis	21
	Prepuce infections	21
Endocrine	Experimental autoimmune thy-roiditis[2]	1,2,9
	Diabetes mellitus	10
	Fatty ingrowth of pancreas	21
Muscular	Myopathy	21,23
	Diaphragmatic hernia	21

[1] Strain 2 guinea pigs more resistant than Strain 13 animals. [2] Strain 2 guinea pigs more susceptible than Strain 13 animals.

Contributor: A. F. Geczy

References

1. Braley-Mullen, H., et al. 1975. J. Immunol. 114:371-373.
2. Braley-Mullen, H., et al. 1976. Immunogenetics 3: 205-208.
3. Freund, J., et al. 1955. J. Exp. Med. 101:591-603.
4. Kaufmann, A. F. 1970. Lab. Anim. Care 20:1002-1003.
5. Latour, J. G., et al. 1974. Am. J. Pathol. 76:179-192.
6. Latour, J. G., et al. 1974. Ibid. 76:195-210.
7. Lisak, R. P., et al. 1975. J. Immunol. 114:546-549.
8. Madden, D. L., et al. 1970. Lab. Anim. Care 20:454-455.
9. McMaster, P. R. B., et al. 1974. Cell. Immunol. 14: 39-45.
10. Munger, B. L., and C. M. Lang. 1973. Lab. Invest. 29: 685-702.
11. Olson, G. A. 1971. Lab. Anim. Dig. 7:12-14.
12. Schoenbaum, M., and U. Klopfer. 1969. Refu. Vet. 26:118-121.
13. Steblay, R. W., and U. Rudofsky. 1971. J. Immunol. 107:1192-1196.
14. Stone, S. H., et al. 1968. Science 159:995-997.
15. Stone, S. H., et al. 1969. Proc. Soc. Exp. Biol. Med. 132:341-344.
16. Stone, S. H., et al. 1969. 1st Int. Convocat. Immunol., pp. 339-341.
17. Takeda, T., and A. Grollman. 1970. Am. J. Pathol. 60:103-118.
18. Thompson, D. J., et al. 1964. J. Nutr. 84:27-30.
19. Tung, K. S. K., et al. 1971. J. Immunol. 106:1453-1462.
20. Tung, K. S. K., et al. 1971. Ibid. 106:1463-1472.
21. Wagner, J. E. 1976. In J. E. Wagner and P. J. Manning, ed. The Biology of the Guinea Pig. Academic, New York. pp. 227-234.
22. Waksman, B. H. 1959. J. Exp. Med. 109:311-324.
23. Webb, J. N. 1970. J. Pathol. 100:155-158.

137. AUDITORY AND VESTIBULAR NEUROLOGICAL MUTANTS: GUINEA PIG

Linkage relationships have not been established for either of the genes described below. **Locus Symbols** are according to Festing [ref. 10]. **Holder**: For full name, *see* list of HOLDERS at front of book. *Abbreviation*: CNS = central nervous system. For additional information, consult **General References.** Data in light brackets refer to the column heading in brackets. Figures in heavy brackets are reference numbers.

Locus Symbol [Name]	Mode of Inheritance	Strain [Holder]	Clinical Characteristics		Pathology	
			Auditory	Vestibular	Auditory	Vestibular
Wz [Dominant waltzing]	Autosomal dominant [3, 7, 10];	"Waltzer" [N]	A few animals show normal hearing development up to	Tendency to whirl or waltz. Swimming performance &	Pathological changes in hair cells of organ of Corti are evident at	Although by light microscopy the vestibular end

continued

Locus Symbol [Name]	Mode of Inheritance	Strain [Holder]	Clinical Characteristics		Pathology	
			Auditory	Vestibular	Auditory	Vesitibular
	lethal in homozygous state		age 10-14 d, but most have sudden onsets of hearing impairment. Hearing loss first occurs in high frequency range, progressing to total loss before 42 d of age. [6, 7]	righting reflex abnormal, and are the same in young & old animals. No pre- or post-rotatory nystagmus observed at any age. Animals born with severe impairment of vestibular function; progresses to total loss of function in older animals. [5, 7]	birth. First the sensory hairs broaden and fuse into a bundle. Total hair cell loss proceeds from outer hair cells to inner hair cells. [7] Supporting cells in organ of Corti degenerate after hair cell degeneration. Evidence of ganglion cell involvement subsequent to loss of organ of Corti [4]. Rest of structures of inner ear, including the vasculature, remain normal [1]. In the CNS, cochlear nuclei show significant degeneration [16].	organ & Scarpa's ganglion appear normal, transmission electron microscopy reveals extensive degeneration of the neuroepithelium affecting both the cristae & maculae [5, 9]. Immediately post-natal the hair cell population is present, but with age the neuroepithelium is replaced with supporting cells. Hair cell defects occur even in newborns in the form of anoma-

lous cilia & cytoplasmic protrusions into the endolymphatic space. Type I hair cells have rod-shaped inclusion body. [7-9] Microcirculation is normal regardless of age [1], and the neural reflex arc of the vestibular system is normal in newborn [5].

Locus Symbol [Name]	Mode of Inheritance	Strain [Holder]	Auditory	Vestibular	Auditory	Vesitibular
wtz [Recessive waltzing]	Autosomal recessive [3, 7, 10, 12-15]	Recessive waltzer (believed to be extinct [11])	Animals exhibited deafness, which was principally studied electrophysiologically & histologically [4, 13, 15] (*see* **Pathology**)	Tendency to whirl or waltz, similar to behavior of the dominant waltzing strain. Vestibular tests disclosed absence of peripheral responses. Animals also exhibited head tremors, with head thrown backward. Righting reflexes normal, but based only on senses of touch & sight. [2]	Perinatal degeneration of organ of Corti occurs, with outer hair cells degenerating before inner hair cells. Cochlear nerve & spiral ganglia cells degenerated after degeneration of the organ of Corti. Some lesions found in parts of stria vascularis; did not correlate with loss of organ of Corti. [4, 13, 14]	As in the dominant waltzing strain, no end organ pathology found with light microscopy. This finding led workers to postulate a CNS lesion to explain the abnormal behavior. Interpeduncular nuclei were proposed as a possible site of the

lesion. Electron microscopy of this strain was not carried out. [13]

Contributor: James G. McCormick

Specific References

1. Axelsson, A., and S. Ernstson. 1972. Acta Oto-Laryngol. 74:172-182.
2. Cogan, D. G. 1940. Arch. Ophthalmol. 24:78-82.
3. Ernstson, S. 1970. Acta Oto-Laryngol. 69:358-362.
4. Ernstson, S. 1971. Ibid. 71:469-482.
5. Ernstson, S. 1971. Ibid. 72:303-309.
6. Ernstson, S. 1972. Ibid., Suppl. 297.
7. Ernstson, S. 1972. The Waltzing Guinea Pig. Thule, Stockholm. pp. 1-15.

continued

8. Ernstson, S., et al. 1969. Acta Oto-Laryngol. 67:521-534.

9. Ernstson, S., et al. 1970. In M. M. Paparella, ed. Biochemical Mechanisms in Hearing and Deafness. Thomas, Springfield, IL. pp. 193-197.

10. Festing, M. F. W. 1976. In J. E. Wagner and P. J. Manning, ed. The Biology of the Guinea Pig. Academic, New York. pp. 99-120.

11. Festing, M. F. W. Unpublished. MRC Laboratory Animals Centre, Carshalton, Surrey, U.K., 1979.

12. Ibsen, H. L., and K. T. Risty. 1929. Anat. Rec. 43:294.

13. Lurie, M. H. 1939. Laryngoscope 69:558-571.

14. Lurie, M. H. 1940. J. Acoust. Soc. Am. 11:420-426.

15. Lurie, M. H. 1941. Ann. Otol. Rhinol. Laryngol. 50:113-128.

16. Webster, M., and D. B. Webster. 1979. Abstr. 2nd Midwinter Res. Meet. Assoc. Res. Otolaryngol. (St. Petersburg Beach, FL), p. 26.

General References

17. Altmann, F. 1950. Arch. Otolaryngol. 51:852-890.

18. Festing, M. F. W. 1976. (Loc. cit. ref. 10).

19. McCormick, J. G., and A. L. Nuttall. 1976. (Loc. cit. ref. 10). pp. 281-303.

20. Nuttall, A. L. 1974. Acta Oto-Laryngol. 78:187-191.

138. BEHAVIORAL GENETICS: GUINEA PIG

Guinea pigs have been infrequent subjects in behavioral genetics investigations. In two studies using animals of strains 2 and 13, inheritance of components of mating behavior in males and females was investigated using hybridization techniques. For both sexes, components of such behavior were found not to be inherited as a unitary trait.

Sex of Hybrid	Type of Behavior	Type of Inheritance	Reference
♂	Circling, nuzzling, mounting	Strain 13 (lethargic) dominance	2
	Intromission, ejaculation	Strain 2 (vigorous) dominance	
♀	Latency to heat, duration of heat, per cent exhibiting heat[1/]	Strain 2 dominance	1
	Duration of maximum lordosis	Intermediate	
	Frequency of ♂-like mounting activity	Intermediate	

[1/] These three characteristics were intercorrelated.

Contributor: Gary K. Beauchamp

References

1. Goy, R. W., and J. S. Jackway. 1959. Anim. Behav. 7:142-149.

2. Jackway, J. S. 1959. Ibid. 7:150-162.

139. TRANSPLANTABLE TUMORS: GUINEA PIG

Carcinogen: B(a)P = benzo[a]pyrene; DEN = N-nitroso-diethylamine ⟨diethylnitrosamine⟩; Ki-MSV = Kirsten strain of murine sarcoma virus; MCA = 3-methylcholanthrene; MNNG = N-methyl-N'-nitro-N-nitrosoguanidine. **Ascites Form:** A = available; NA = not available. **Holder:** For full name, see list of HOLDERS at front of book.

Tumor Name	Guinea Pig Strain	Sex	Year of Origin	Carcinogen	Histology	Ascites Form	Immuno-genic	Metastases	Holder	Reference
Line 1	2	♂	1968	DEN	Adenocarcinoma of liver	A	Yes	Lungs, lymph nodes	NCI-LIB	9
Line 10	2	♂	1971	DEN	Hepatocarcinoma	A	Yes	Lymph nodes	NCI-LIB	12
L$_2$C[1/]	2	♀	1954	None	Leukemia	NA	Yes	Lymph nodes, liver, spleen	NIAID	1,4, 10

[1/] 5 sublines available.

continued

Tumor Name	Guinea Pig Strain	Sex	Year of Origin	Carcinogen	Histology	Ascites Form	Immuno-genic	Metastases	Holder	Reference
MCA-25	2	♀	1963	MCA	Osteogenic sarcoma	NA	Yes	Occasional	UCLA	5
MCA-A	2	♀	1966	MCA	Liposarcoma	NA	Yes	Rare	UCLA	5
MC-A	13	♀	1968	MCA	Sarcoma	NA	Yes	....	SKI	8
MC-D	13	♀	1968	MCA	Sarcoma	NA	Yes	....	SKI	8
MC-E	13	♀	1968	MCA	Sarcoma	NA	Yes	....	SKI	8
104-C1	2	♀	1975	B(a)P	Fibrosarcoma	NA	No	None	NCI-BB	2
HM4C1	2	♀	1975	MNNG	Fibrosarcoma	NA	....	None	NCI-BB	2
J$_4$	JY-1	..	1974	MCA	Fibrosarcoma	NA	....	None	DT	6,7
H10	Hartley F	..	1974	MCA	Liposarcoma	NA	....	None	DT	6,7
1301	13	♂	1974	MCA	Fibrosarcoma	NA	No	Lymph nodes, lung	NCI-LIB	11
13/C	13	♂	1974	DEN	Hepatocarcinoma	NA	No	Lymph nodes, lung	NCI-LIB	11
Sarcoma 543	13	..	1974	K1-MSV	Sarcoma	NA	No	....	NIAID	3
Sarcoma 880	2	♀	1974	K1-MSV	Sarcoma	NA	No	....	NIAID	3

Contributors: Berton Zbar; Ira Green

References

1. Congdon, C. C., and E. Lorenz. 1954. Am. J. Pathol. 30:337-359.
2. Evans, C. H., and J. A. DiPaolo. 1975. Cancer Res. 35:1035-1044.
3. Forni, G., et al. 1975. J. Immunol. 115:204-210.
4. Forni, G., et al. 1976. J. Exp. Med. 143:1067-1081.
5. Holmes, E. C., et al. 1970. Cancer 25:373-379.
6. Kataoka, T., and T. Tokunaga. 1975. Gann 67:25-31.
7. Kataoka, T., et al. 1977. J. Natl. Cancer Inst. 58:803-808.
8. Oettgen, H. F., et al. 1968. Nature (London) 220:295-297.
9. Rapp, H. J., et al. 1968. J. Natl. Cancer Inst. 41:1-11.
10. Whang-Peng, J., et al. 1976. J. Natl. Cancer Inst. 57:879-905.
11. Zbar, B. Unpublished. National Cancer Institute, Bethesda, MD, 1979.
12. Zbar, B., et al. 1971. J. Natl. Cancer Inst. 46:831-839.

V. RABBIT

RABBIT INBREEDING

Inbreeding is a mating system which leads to genetic homozygosis and the reduction of genetic diversity in a population. In experimental laboratory animals, inbreeding is a highly desirable feature, despite some disadvantages for the animals. For example, genetic diversity provides animals with the ability to adapt to the environment and, consequently, any reduction in genetic diversity lowers their adaptability. Two favorable genetic features which are simultaneously abolished by inbreeding are gene dominance (often covering the undesirable recessives), and over-dominance (the basis of heterosis). Therefore, the total effect of inbreeding converts a flexible and homeostatic genetic system into a rigid and less-flexible system.

Inbred depression, represented by a decline in reproductive performance and survival ability, has been witnessed by breeders of many different animal species. Interestingly enough, the depression is less severe in rodents than in other mammalian species or birds. The rabbit, however, is a species that is severely affected, resulting in a marked reduction in breeding performance: a small percentage of animals that mate; a small percentage of fertilized eggs, with resultant small litters; litters that do not survive; or infertility or failure to complete pregnancy. The Figure and Table below show, respectively, the reduction in litter size as a result of inbreeding, and the high frequency of malformations in certain generations of inbreeding. The reduction in breeding performance possibly represents a loss of heterosis (an expression of segregational genetic load), and the production of malformed animals may indicate deleterious recessive or lethal genes (mutational load).

Decline of Litter Size Accompanying Inbreeding Progression [ref. 2].

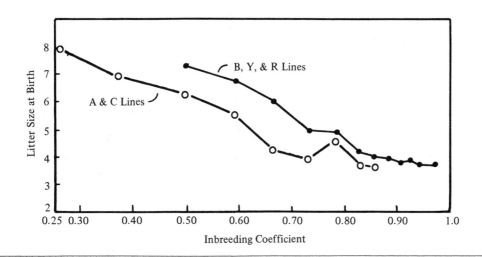

Percentage of Newborn with Skeletal Malformations [ref. 3]

Data are for B, R, and Y lines as a group, and for A and C lines as a group.

Group	No. of Generations	No. Examined	Head Malformation, %	Hydrocephaly %	Jaw Reduced or Absent, %	Vertebral Column Malformation, %
BRY	9-11	167	1.8	3.8	2.4	22.2
	12-19	385	1.0	3.1	0.5	3.4
AC	3-5	185	1.1	0	0.5	25.8
	8-11	253	0	0.8	0.8	0.8

continued

Continuous inbreeding by mating closely related relatives may be viewed as a type of selection to remove deleterious genes since the homozygotes will die, leaving no progeny. Thus, these genes will be eliminated automatically from the genetic system. Such elimination would appear to be beneficial to the line. There is, however, a hidden disadvantage: Depending on the number of recessive lethals relative to the size of the inbred population, the line may face a problem of survival. For example, if the number of recessive lethals carried by the parental generation is so large that by one generation of inbreeding each individual in the next generation will have at least one lethal at the homozygous state, the line will be facing extinction. Because of this circumstance, one must start with a large number of breeders, and maintain a large number of lines with a large number of breeders in each line. Consequently, in all generations of inbreeding, there will always be survivors free from severe deleterious genes. This, however, cannot be predetermined.

The reduction in heterosis resulting from elimination of heterozygosity is a necessary consequence of inbreeding—and there is no escape. Nevertheless, another genetic device, epistasis or non-allelic gene interaction, can be employed to counterbalance the loss of such favorable allelic interactions. That is, the decline in fitness resulting from homozygosis per se for a specific locus may be balanced by the presence of a specific gene in another locus or loci. This compensatory factor must actually be in operation in certain continuous inbreeding systems. Again, the larger the number of breeders, the greater the chance of obtaining animals carrying such specific gene combinations.

Another alternative is less-intensive inbreeding, so that the occurrence of homozygous lethals and the reduction of heterosis will be at a lower rate and, by reducing selection intensity, will not jeopardize survival of the line. It must be kept in mind that when there is an inbreeding depression, there is a simultaneous selection for heterozygosity. Therefore, the calculated inbreeding coefficient is an over-estimation of the actual inbreeding attained.

Contributor: C. K. Chai

References
1. Chai, C. K. 1968. Transplantation 6:689-693.
2. Chai, C. K. 1969. J. Hered. 60:64-70.
3. Chai, C. K. 1970. Ibid. 61:1-8.

Rabbit inbreeding was initiated at the Jackson Laboratory 25 years ago. Carl Cohen obtained a pair of rabbits of the ACCR stock from Paul Sawin and started a rabbit colony by inbreeding. At 6 or 7 generations of inbreeding in most families, C. K. Chai took over the management of this colony, and has continued the inbreeding, resulting in the establishment of the B inbred strain [ref. 1, 2]. The B strain, consisting of various families, is at the 27th and 28th generation of inbreeding, and has been distributed to research workers for breeding as well as for experimentation. Chai [ref. 2] in the meantime started (from the zero generation) additional lines from which an inbred line C has been developed. This line is at approximately 20 generations of inbreeding at the time of this writing. There are additional lines at the Jackson Laboratory which were initiated by Sawin and are maintained now by Richard Fox. Some of them are approaching 20 inbred generations.

Other sources known to maintain rabbits by inbreeding are at the Universiteit Utrecht, Netherlands, and University of Illinois College of Medicine, Chicago. At Universiteit Utrecht, W. K. Hirschfeld started a colony in 1937, but pedigreed records for inbreeding are available only since 1949. The calculated inbreeding coefficient since then is 0.92, corresponding to 12 generations of sib-mating [ref. 4]. At the University of Illinois College of Medicine, Tissot and Cohen [ref. 5] have reported a number of lines, with inbreeding coefficients ranging from 0.59 to 0.91.

Inbreeding, as generally practiced for laboratory animals, is essentially a selection for well-balanced gene systems at the homozygous state. Inbreds definitely decline in fitness, but with a balanced gene system they can survive in a controlled laboratory environment, and their genetic uniformity is a most useful tool for experimentation. In the future, any interesting new mutations occurring in an inbred animal can be tested in animals with the same genetic background.

4. Kremer, A. K. Unpublished. Rijksuniv. Utrecht, Vakgroep Zootechniek, Netherlands, 1977.
5. Tissot, R. G., and C. Cohen. 1972. Tissue Antigens 2:267-279.

Part I. Characteristics

The characteristics listed below were existent as of 1 January 1979. For additional information on **Origin** of the strains, *see* Part II of this table. **Coefficient of Inbreeding** is the maximum coefficient in the strain computed according to Cruden's method of calculating Wright's Inbreeding Coefficient [ref. 7]; inbreeding was by sib-mating or as close to sib-mating as possible consonant with maintenance of specific lethal or semilethal genes and an optimal reproductive capacity and viability. **Genes Carried:** For explanation of gene symbols, *see* lists of mutants and polymorphisms in the tables that follow in this Section. **Source:** For full name, *see* list of HOLDERS at front of book. *Abbreviations:* $\sim$ = approximately; Fn = footnote.

Strain [Mature Wt, g]	Origin	Coefficient of Inbreeding	Color	Genes Carried	Genes Segregating ⟨Synonym⟩	Immunoglobulin Genes	Source	Reference
AC/J [2400]	Dutch[1]	0.85	Black, recessive white marking	a, ac[2], du^d	du^w, ha[2], sb[2], y	$Aa^3/Aa^3 Ab^5/Ab^5$ Ac^7, Ac^{21}	JAX	4
ACEP/J [2400]	Dutch[1]	0.96	Blue-eyed white	ep, v	hg	$Aa^3/Aa^3 Ab^4/Ab^4$ Ac^{21}/Ac^{21}	JAX	4
AX/J [3500]	Outcross of Chinchilla race V to strains III & X	0.88	Chinchilla	ax[2], w	b, bu, c^{chd} ⟨c^{ch3}⟩, c^{chm} ⟨c^{ch2}⟩, c, du^w, Fn[3,4]	$Aa^3/Aa^3 Ab^4/Ab^4$	JAX	4
AXBU/J [3500]	AX strain	0.83	Albino	bu, c	b, c^{chd} ⟨c^{ch3}⟩, c^{chm} ⟨c^{ch2}⟩	$Aa^1/Aa^3 Ab^4/Ab^4$ Ac^7/Ac^7	JAX	4
B/J[5] [2400]	Dutch[1]	Inbred	Albino	c, du^d, sa	....	$Aa^3/Aa^3 Ab^5/Ab^5$ Ac^7/Ac^7	JAX	2,4
III/J[6] [3800]	New Zealand White; Castle, 1932	$\sim$1.0 (inbred)	Albino	as, c, E^D	l, rc, Fn[7,4]	$Aa^1/Aa^1 Ab^4/Ab^4$ Ac^7/Ac^7	JAX	4
III/cdJ [3800]	III/J	0.97	Albino	cd[2]	....	$Aa^1/Aa^1 Ab^4/Ab^4$ Ac^7/Ac^7	JAX	4
III/DwJ [3800]	III/J	0.95	Albino	Dw[2,8]	....	$Aa^1/Aa^1 Ab^4/Ab^4$ Ac^7/Ac^7	JAX	4
IIIEP/J [3800]	III/J	0.98	Albino	ep	....	$Aa^1/Aa^1 Ab^4/Ab^4$ Ac^7/Ac^7	JAX	4
IIIVO/J [3800]	III/J	0.98	Albino	....	rc	$Aa^1/Aa^3 Ab^4/Ab^4$ Ac^7/Ac^7	JAX	4
IIIVO/ahJ [3800]	III/J	0.97	Albino	ah[2]	rc	$Aa^1/Aa^3 Ab^4/Ab^4$ Ac^7/Ac^7	JAX	4
IIIVO/vptJ [3800]	III/J	0.97	Albino	$vpt-1, vpt-2$[2]	....	$Ab^4/Ab^4 Ac^7/Ac^7$	JAX	4

[1] Sublines of the same Dutch stock obtained from Rockefeller Institute in 1948. [2] Maintained in this strain by progeny testing of prospective parents; homozygous transmitters of this gene are obtainable from the same test. [3] Hypospadias also associated with this strain. [4] The genetic basis of this pathological trait is unclear—whether it is due to a single gene of incomplete penetrance or to more than one gene still segregating. [5] Previously referred to as ACCR(B). The first well-established inbred strain of rabbits, F_1's were produced by Carl Cohen in 1952 [ref. 5]. Transferred to C. K. Chai about F_7 [ref. 1], and maintained to 27 and 28 generations to date. Skin grafts were accepted within strain at 18th generation [ref. 2]. Blood group genotype is Hg^F/Hg^F. [6] Formerly called either strain III or strain IIImo. Developed by P. B. Sawin from Castle's NZW stock in 1932 for use in growth studies. This is a 13-ribbed albino stock selected in its early years for its presacral growth center in the lumbar region. It has been generally a high antibody-producing strain. Preliminary data showed skin grafts were accepted between sexually compatible sibs, i.e., males accept grafts of both males and females, but females accept only grafts of females. Very docile strain. There have been seven additional strains and substrains derived from this parent stock. For additional information on III/J and its related strains, consult references 3 and 4. [7] Scoliosis also associated with this strain. [8] Formerly symbolized dw, then recognized in the heterozygote [ref. 8] and the symbol changed to Dw to represent a semidominant.

continued

Part I. Characteristics

Strain [Mature Wt, g]	Origin	Coefficient of Inbreeding	Color	Genes Carried	Genes Segregating ⟨Synonym⟩	Immunoglobulin Genes	Source	Reference
IIIC/J [4000]	Outcross of strain III	0.96	Albino	c, E^D, mp	Fn [9,4]	$Aa^3/Aa^3\ Ab^4/Ab^4$ Ac^7/Ac^7	JAX	4
OS/J [3200]	Dutch; Rockefeller Institute, 1948	0.90	Black, minimal recessive white marking	a, du^d, E^D, os [2]	Fn [10,4]	$Aa^2/Aa^2\ Ab^4/Ab^4$ Ac^7/Ac^7	JAX	4
T [11] [2000]	"Small Silver race"; W. K. Hirschfeld, Holland, 1937	0.92 [12]	Albino	$Est\text{-}1^s$, $Est\text{-}2^{f'}$, $Est\text{-}3^d$	....	....	UTR	6
WH/J [2300]	Rockefeller Institute, 1949. Crossed with strains X, III, etc.	0.85	Agouti	Wh, ha [2]	c, e, $r\text{-}2$ ⟨$r2$⟩, wh	$Aa^1/Aa^1\ Ab^4/Ab^4$ Ac^7/Ac^7	JAX	4
X/J [2200]	Castle's small race	0.91	Sooty yellow	a, As, b, e, ha [2]	as, C, c^{chm} ⟨c^{ch2}⟩, Fn [13,4]	$Aa^3/Aa^3\ Ab^4/Ab^4$ Ac^7, Ac^{21}	JAX	4
Y-1/J [2400]	Dutch, cross of B/J & Y/J	0.86	Albino	c, sa	....	$Aa^3/Aa^3\ Ab^4/Ab^5$ Ac^7, Ac^{21}	JAX	4

[2] Maintained in this strain by progeny testing of prospective parents; homozygous transmitters of this gene are obtainable from the same test. [4] The genetic basis of this pathological trait is unclear—whether it is due to a single gene of incomplete penetrance or to more than one gene still segregating. [9] Hydrouterus also associated with this strain. [10] Hydrocephaly also associated with this strain. [11] Synonym: Klein Wit. [12] Inbreeding coefficient shown is based on period from 1949 to date; actual inbreeding coefficient is higher (*see* Part II). [13] Narrow axis also associated with this strain.

Contributors: C. K. Chai; A. K. Kremer; Richard R. Fox

References

1. Chai, C. K. 1968. Transplantation 6:689-693.
2. Chai, C. K. 1969. J. Hered. 60:64-70.
3. Fox, R. R. 1974. In S. H. Weisbroth, et al., ed. The Biology of the Laboratory Rabbit. Academic, New York. pp. 1-22.
4. Fox, R. R., ed. 1975. Handbook on Genetically Standardized JAX Rabbits. Jackson Laboratory, Bar Harbor, ME. pp. 1-12.
5. Fox, R. R. 1978. J. Hered. 69:269-270.
6. Kremer, A. K. Unpublished. Rijksuniv. Utrecht, vakgroep Zootechniek, Netherlands, 1977.
7. Li, F. H. F., and T. H. Roderick. 1970. J. Hered. 61: 37-38.
8. Sawin, P. B. 1955. Adv. Genet. 7:183-226.

Part II. Genealogy

The genealogy chart presented below is based on the version included in the reference and on additional information obtained through personal communication. The rabbit lines shown in the chart were developed from five independent origins: New Zealand White ⟨NZW⟩, Polish A-race, Chinchilla ⟨Chin⟩ IIb, Rockefeller stock, and Small Silver. The NZW III and Polish A-race were started by W. E. Castle. In 1932, Paul Sawin obtained rabbits from these stocks and subsequently developed a number of sublines from NZW III. He maintained the Polish A-race as a single line but

introduced genes into it from a number of other stocks. Sawin, who had had Chin IIb since 1929, obtained the rabbits for this stock from a rabbitry and brought them with him to the Bussey Institute. Later, in the 1940's, he was able to acquire some breeding pairs of the Rockefeller Institute stock maintained by Louis Pearce. (The Rockefeller stock was of comparatively recent development; information concerning its original source has not been found.) From these rabbits various sublines were developed, including the oldest inbred strain B/J. The origin of the T line

continued

140. INBRED AND PARTIALLY INBRED STRAINS: RABBIT

Part II. Genealogy

was the Small Silver stock maintained at Utrecht by W. K. Hirschfeld since 1937. It is the only known rabbit strain with a relatively long breeding history and a considerably high inbreeding coefficient that is maintained outside of the United States. It should be noted that mating records for the development of the T line were not kept until 1949. It is known, however, that before 1949 no animals from other stocks were introduced into the colony. The actual inbreeding coefficient attained by this line is therefore higher than that shown in Part I, which is based on the period from 1949 to date.

Since rabbit inbreeding is time consuming and lines frequently become extinct in the course of their development, several of the lines shown on this chart have subsequently been lost. It should be noted that, in the course of breeding, genes from different stocks have been introduced into many lines, as indicated by the short in-branching lines in the chart. This was done for the purpose of increasing vigor, introduction of specific genes, or other experimental purposes. For example, the dachs ⟨Da⟩ gene was introduced

into III by crossing with a rabbit from a California rabbitry which carried the gene. In a sib-mating system, whenever a cross-breeding occurred, the amount of inbreeding previously accumulated would be nullified. The effect would be smaller when non-sib matings were used, or when the offspring from the cross were not used as the sole breeders for continuing the line. Therefore the inbreeding program, initiated by Paul Sawin in 1932, was slowed down at times by his introductions of rabbits from other stocks. The problem with the introductions explains in part why rabbit breeding has a long history without many inbred lines having been established. Later, individual inbred lines were developed at The Jackson Laboratory by C. Cohen and C. K. Chai. Besides continuing the lines of Sawin, R. R. Fox also developed additional lines.

Symbols: Bx′ represents a backcrossing to III from an original cross of X x III; Bx″ = a backcrossing to V from an original cross of III x V; Bx‴ = a backcrossing to DA from an original cross of X x AV x DA.

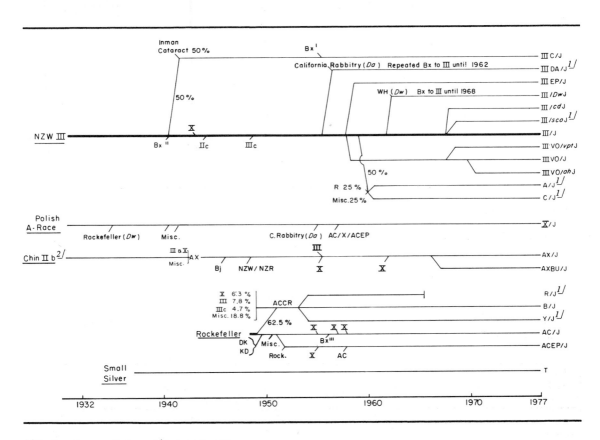

[1] Strain subsequently lost. [2] Later called V.

Contributors: C. K. Chai; Richard R. Fox

Reference: Fox, R. R., ed. 1975. Handbook on Genetically Standardized JAX Rabbits. Jackson Laboratory, Bar Harbor, ME. p. 13.

Part I. Map

For gene names and references, *see* Part II. Distances are given in centimorgans and represent percent recombination frequency between pairs of loci. Dotted lines indicate genes for which the exact position is not known.

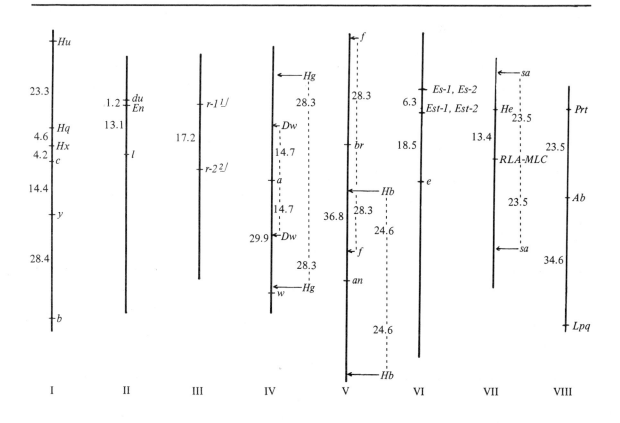

I   II   III   IV   V   VI   VII   VIII

[1/] Synonym: *r¹*. [2/] Synonym: *r²*.

Contributors: Richard R. Fox and Dorcas D. Crary; Carl Cohen

Part II. Gene Names

The gene *pt* ⟨paralytic tremor⟩, not included below, has been shown to be sex-linked [ref. 12]. For additional information, consult reference 14.

Gene Symbol ⟨Synonym⟩	Gene Name ⟨Synonym⟩	Reference
Linkage Group I[1/]		
Hu	Hu blood group	8,18
Hq	Hq blood group	8,18

Gene Symbol ⟨Synonym⟩	Gene Name ⟨Synonym⟩	Reference
Hx	Hemopexin	8,11,18
c	Albino	3,4,7
y	Yellow fat	5,13
b	Brown	5,17

[1/] It was formerly believed that the *bu* gene was 16 map units from the *c* locus [ref. 1]; however, more complete data suggest that if linkage is present, it is a loose linkage of about 41 map units [ref. 2].

continued

Part II. Gene Names

Gene Symbol (Synonym)	Gene Name (Synonym)	Reference
	Linkage Group II	
du	Recessive white spotting (Dutch pattern)	5,17
En	Dominant white spotting (English marking)	3,7
l	Angora	3
	Linkage Group III	
r-1 (r¹)	Rex-1	5,17
r-2 (r²)	Rex-2	4,6
	Linkage Group IV	
a	Non-agouti	17
Dw	Dwarf	7,9
Hg	Hg blood group	8
w	Wide-band agouti	15
	Linkage Group V	
br	Brachydactyly	17

Gene Symbol (Synonym)	Gene Name (Synonym)	Reference
f	Furless	7,9
an	A-antigen (Anti-human A cell)	17
Hb	Hb blood group	8,18
	Linkage Group VI	
Es-1	Esterase (erythrocyte)	10,16,22
Es-2	Esterase (platelet)	10,16,22
Est-1	Cocaine esterase	10,16,22
Est-2	Atropine esterase	10,16,22
e	Extension	10,17
	Linkage Group VII	
He	He blood group	8,18,19
RLA-MLC	Major histocompatibility complex	18
sa	Satin	18
	Linkage Group VIII	
Prt	Serum protein	20
Ab	Immunoglobulin kappa light chain	20,21
Lpq	Low-density lipoprotein	21

Contributors: Carl Cohen; Richard R. Fox and Dorcas D. Crary

References

1. Bauer, E. J., and J. Bennett. 1964. Genetics 50:234.
2. Bennett, J., et al. 1973. J. Hered. 64:363-364.
3. Castle, W. E. 1926. Carnegie Inst. Washington Publ. 337:1-47.
4. Castle, W. E. 1936. Proc. Natl. Acad. Sci. USA 22:222-225.
5. Castle, W. E. 1940. Mammalian Genetics. Harvard Univ., Cambridge.
6. Castle, W. E., and H. Nachtsheim. 1933. Proc. Natl. Acad. Sci. USA 19:1006-1011.
7. Castle, W. E., and P. B. Sawin. 1941. Ibid. 27:519-523.
8. Cohen, C., et al. Unpublished. N.I.A.I.D., National Institutes of Health, Bethesda, MD, 1977.
9. Fox, R. R. 1974. In S. H. Weisbroth, et al., ed. The Biology of the Laboratory Rabbit. Academic, New York. pp. 1-22.
10. Fox, R. R., and L. F. M. van Zutphen. 1979. Genetics 92:(in press).
11. Hagen, K. L., et al. Anim. Blood Groups Biochem. Genet. 9:151-159.
12. Osetowska, E. 1967. Acta Neuropathol. 8:331-344.
13. Pease, M. S. 1930. Verh. Int. Kaninchenzuchter-Kongr. (Leipzig) 1:91-95.
14. Robinson, R. 1958. Bibliogr. Genet. 17:229-588.
15. Sawin, P. B. 1934. J. Hered. 25:477-481.
16. Sawin, P. B., and D. Glick. 1943. Proc. Natl. Acad. Sci. USA 29:55-59.
17. Sawin, P. B., et al. 1944. Ibid. 30:217-221.
18. Tissot, R. G. Unpublished. Univ. Illinois, College Medicine, Chicago, 1978-1979.
19. Tissot, R. G., and C. Cohen. 1974. Transplantation 18:142-149.
20. Usher, D. C., et al. 1978. J. Immunol. 120:1832-1835.
21. Usher, D. C., et al. 1978. Immunogenetics 7:117-124.
22. van Zutphen, L. F. M., et al. 1977. Biochem. Genet. 15:989-1000.

142. KARYOLOGY: RABBIT

The rabbit (*Oryctolagus cuniculus*) has a chromosomal complement of 2n = 44 chromosomes, with all chromosome types represented. The sex chromosomes can be defined unequivocally by means of radiography and banding stains. With normal staining techniques, a determination of X chromosomes presents difficulties because they show a great deal of variability in relative arm lengths. With the aid of banding stains, all autosomes, as well as the sex chromosomes, can be differentiated from one another. Thus an exact assignment of homologous chromosomes is possible, and structural deviations can be recognized that cannot be demonstrated with normal staining techniques.

The precise number of rabbit chromosomes (44) was first discovered by Painter [ref. 16] in spermatogonia. Makino [ref. 13] published the first chromosomal atlas, and assigned 44 as the number of rabbit chromosomes in agreement with Painter. The diploid chromosome number (2n) in the

continued

rabbit, therefore, was found 12 years ahead of similar findings in man in spite of difficulties in the preparation of chromosomes.

The arrangement of chromosomes in the karyotype given by Hsu and Benirschke [ref. 11] in the "Atlas of Mammalian Chromosomes" (Folio 8) is simple and logical, and is used as a standard in this presentation. The following order is strictly based on the centromere position and chromosome size: the largest metacentric to the smallest metacentric chromosome, group A 1-6 (no. 1-6 in Figure below);

the largest sub-metacentric to the smallest sub-metacentric chromosome, group B 1-5 (no. 7-11 in Figure); the largest acrocentric to the smallest acrocentric chromosome, group C 1-6 (no. 12-17 in Figure); the four smallest telocentric to acrocentric chromosomes, group D 1-4 (no. 18-21 in Figure); and the two sex chromosomes. In the heterogametic sex, the X chromosome resembles chromosomes A4 and B2 in size and shape. The Y chromosome is usually the smallest chromosome of the karyotype in the submeta- to metacentric range.

Banding Karyotype [ref. 4]

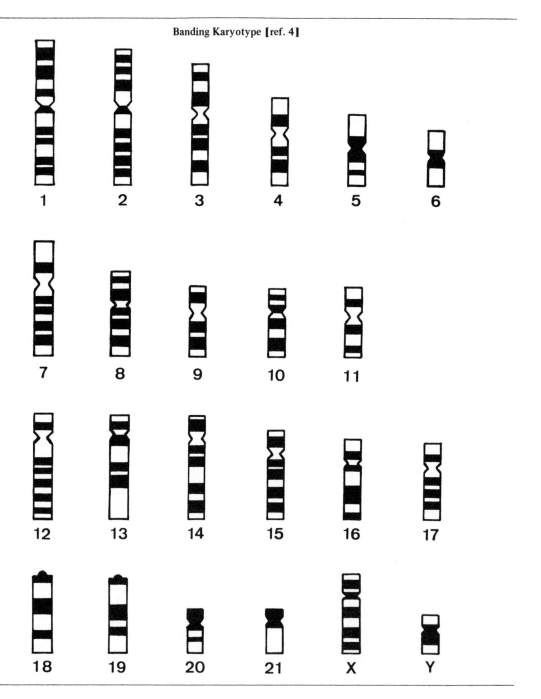

continued

Comparison of chromosomes on the basis of banding stains (G-bands), for the purpose of standardization, was first made at the Reading Karyotype Conference [ref. 4]; it was based on publications of band karyotypes by Echard [ref. 2], Stranzinger and Fechheimer [ref. 22, 23], Stranzinger [ref. 21] and unpublished karyograms by Hansen [ref. 7] and Gustavsson [ref. 6].

Summary of Chromosomal Aberrations

Aberration	Tissue	Treatment	Reference
Chromosome length	Blastocysts	Sperm aging, superovulation, deep freezing	17,25
Haploidy, heteroploidy	Blastocysts	Sperm aging	24
Haploidy, mosaics	Blastocysts	Spontaneous	8,9
Heteroploidy	Blastocysts	Different inbred lines	3
Heteroploidy	Blastocysts	Late fertilization	19
Hyperdiploidy	Germ cells	Aging	1
Hyperploidy	Blastocysts	Radiation of meiotic oocytes	12
Hyperploidy, mosaics	Blastocysts	Spontaneous	10
Miniature Y chromosome	Blastocysts, leukocytes	Spontaneous	15
Mitotic index	Blastocysts, leukocytes	Human chorionic gonadotropin	5
Mixoploidy	Blastocysts	Late fertilization	20
Mosaics, chimeras	Blastocysts	Sperm aging	14
Mosaics	Blastocysts	Pentobarbital sodium	18
Mosaics, X chromosome deletion	Leukocytes	Spontaneous	22
Mosaics, triploidy	Blastocysts	Estrogen, progesterone	26
Mosaics, triploidy, trisomy	Blastocysts in toto, embryo organ cells [1/], adult leukocytes	Culture, radiation	21
Trisomy	8-cell embryo	Culture	23

[1/] 16-day embryo heart, spleen, brain, and liver cells.

Contributor: Gerald Stranzinger

References

1. Austin, C. R. 1967. Nature (London) 11:1819.
2. Echard, G. 1973. Ann. Genet. Sel. Anim. 5(4):425-434.
3. Fechheimer, N. S., and R. A. Beatty. 1974. J. Reprod. Fertil. 37:331-342.
4. Ford, C. E., ed. 1978. Proc. 1st Int. Conf. Stand. Banded Karyotypes Domest. Anim., Reading, Engl., 1976.
5. Fujimoto, S., et al. 1975. Cytologia 40:307-311.
6. Gustavsson, I. Unpublished. Royal Veterinary College, Dep. Animal Genetics, Nutrition and Hygiene, Uppsala, Sweden, 1978.
7. Hansen, K. M. Unpublished. Dep. Obstetrics and Gynaecology. Bülowsvej 13, Copenhagen, Denmark, 1978.
8. Hansen-Melander, E., and Y. Melander. 1970. Hereditas 65:237-240.
9. Hansen-Melander, E., and Y. Melander. 1970. Ibid. 67:83-88.
10. Hofsass, F. R., and T. N. Meacham. 1971. J. Exp. Zool. 177:9-11.
11. Hsu, T. C., and K. Benirschke. 1967. An Atlas of Mammalian Chromosomes. Springer-Verlag, New York. v. 1(8).
12. Kuhlmann, W. 1964. Akad. Wiss. Lit. Mainz Abh. Math. Naturwiss. Kl. (6):301-307.
13. Makino, S. 1944. Dobutsugaku Zasshi 56:8-15.
14. Martin, P. A., and E. L. Shaver. 1972. Dev. Biol. 28:480-486.
15. Martin, P. A., and E. L. Shaver. 1972. J. Exp. Zool. 181:87-99.
16. Painter, T. S. 1926. J. Morphol. Physiol. 43:1-43.
17. Paufler, S., et al. 1975. Zentralbl. Veterinaermed. A22:414-426.
18. Shaver, E. L. 1975. Experientia 31(10):1212-1213.
19. Shaver, E. L., and D. H. Carr. 1967. J. Reprod. Fertil. 14:415-420.
20. Shaver, E. L., and D. H. Carr. 1969. Can. J. Genet. Cytol. 11:287-293.
21. Stranzinger, G. F. 1976. Thesis. Technische Univ. München, Freising-Weihenstephan, W. Germany. pp. 1-208.
22. Stranzinger, G. F., and N. S. Fechheimer. 1974. Zuchthygiene 1:15-19.
23. Stranzinger, G. F., and N. S. Fechheimer. 1974. Ibid. 9:163-169.
24. Stranzinger, G. F., and J. R. Lodge. 1974. Z. Tierz. Zuechtungsbiol. 91:125-130.
25. Stranzinger, G. F., et al. 1975. Zuchthygiene 10:152-158.
26. Widmeyer, M. A., and E. L. Shaver. 1972. Teratology 6:207-214.

Alleles are listed in order of dominance. Data in brackets refer to the column heading in brackets.

Locus ⟨Synonym⟩	Allele ⟨Synonym⟩	Description	Linkage Group	Reference
Agouti	A	Gray with white underside	IV	7
	a^t	Black and tan	IV	13
	a	Black (non-agouti)	IV	7
Angora	L	Hair length normal	II	1
	l	Hair long	II	14
Brown	B	Black	I	27
	b	Brown (chocolate)	I	9
Colored	C	Fully colored	I	2
	c^{chd} ⟨c^{ch3}⟩	Dark chinchilla; yellow absent, blue eyes	I	4
	c^{chm} ⟨c^{ch2}⟩	Medium chinchilla; black diluted, brown eyes, pigment thermolabile	I	32
	c^{chl} ⟨c^{ch1}⟩	Light chinchilla; further dilution of black to pale brown, brown eyes, pupil pinkish	I	6
	c^H	Himalayan albinism; pigment thermolabile and restricted to extremities	I	2,35
	c	Albino; lack of pigment all over, eyes pink	I	2
Dilution	D	Black & yellow intense	..	12
	d	Dilution of black to blue, and red to yellow	..	9
Dominant white spotting	En	English marking: black herringbone on white background in heterozygous animals	II	3
	en	Self-colored	II	30
Extension	E^D	Extension of black to underside obscures agouti	VI	27
	E^S	Weaker form of E^D; produces steel coat color	VI	31
	E	Normal gray	VI	27
	e^J	Japanese: mosaic distribution of black & yellow	VI	5
	e	Coat yellow, white underside	VI	9
Furless	F	Normal	V	8
	f	Furless	V	24
Naked	N	Normal	..	17
	n	Naked	..	16
Pelt-loss-1	$Ps-1$	Normal	..	22
	$ps-1$	Absence of wool hairs	..	24
Pelt-loss-2	$Ps-2$	Normal	..	23
	$ps-2$	Absence of underwool hair	..	24
Recessive white spotting	Du	Self-colored	II	28
	du^d	Dark Dutch; minimal amounts of white spotting on nose, forehead, & extremities	II	9
	du^w	Extensive white spotting	II	9
Red eye	Re	Normal	..	19
	re	Red pupil & red iris	..	20
Rex-1 ⟨French rex⟩	$R-1$ ⟨R^1⟩	Hair length normal	III	18
	$r-1$ ⟨r^1⟩	Hair & vibrissae short & curled	III	18
Rex-2 ⟨German rex⟩	$R-2$ ⟨R^2⟩	Hair length normal	III	11
	$r-2$ ⟨r^2⟩	Hair & vibrissae short & curled	III	11
Rex-3 ⟨Normandy rex⟩	$R-3$ ⟨R^3⟩	Hair length normal	..	11
	$r-3$ ⟨r^3⟩	Hair & vibrissae short & curled	..	9
Satin	Sa	Normal	VII	10
	sa	Absence of medulla of hair; silky sheen to the coat	VII	34
Silvering	Si	Normal	..	21
	si	Silver	..	29
Vienna white	V	Self-colored	..	25
	v	White, blue-eyed	..	9
Waved	Wa	Normal	..	26
	wa	Hair waved in rex rabbits only	..	26

continued

143. COAT AND EYE COLOR MUTANTS: RABBIT

Locus ⟨Synonym⟩	Allele ⟨Synonym⟩	Description	Linkage Group	Reference
Wide band	W	Normal agouti band	IV	32
	w	Subterminal agouti band double in width	IV	36
Wirehair	Wh	Absence of wool hair, leaving mainly coarse guard hairs	..	33
	wh	Normal	..	33
Wuzzy	Wu	Normal	..	33
	wu	Hair sticky & matted	..	15

Contributors: W. H. Spendlove; Richard R. Fox and Dorcas D. Crary; Roy Robinson

1. Castle, W. E. 1903. Science 18:760-761.
2. Castle, W. E. 1905. Carnegie Inst. Washington Publ. 23:1-78.
3. Castle, W. E. 1919. Ibid. 288:4-28.
4. Castle, W. E. 1921. Science 53:387-388.
5. Castle, W. E. 1924. J. Genet. 14:225-229.
6. Castle, W. E. 1926. Carnegie Inst. Washington Publ. 337:1-47.
7. Castle, W. E. 1930. The Genetics of Domestic Rabbits. Harvard Univ., Cambridge.
8. Castle, W. E. 1933. J. Hered. 24:81-86.
9. Castle, W. E. 1940. Mammalian Genetics. Harvard Univ., Cambridge.
10. Castle, W. E., and L. W. Law. 1936. J. Hered. 27:235-240.
11. Castle, W. E., and H. Nachtsheim. 1933. Proc. Natl. Acad. Sci. USA 19:1006-1011.
12. Castle, W. E., et al. 1909. Carnegie Inst. Washington Publ. 114:1-70.
13. Cleffmann, G. 1953. Z. Indukt. Abstamm. Vererbungsl. 85:137-162.
14. Crary, D. D., and P. B. Sawin. 1953. J. Exp. Zool. 124:31-62.
15. Crary, D. D., and P. B. Sawin. 1959. J. Hered. 50:31-34.
16. David, L. T. 1932. Z. Zellforsch. Mikrosk. Anat. 14:616-719.
17. Kislovsky, D. A. 1928. J. Hered. 19:438-439.
18. Lienhart, R. 1927. C. R. Soc. Biol. 97:386-388.
19. Magnussen, K. 1952. Z. Morphol. Anthropol. 44:127-135.
20. Magnussen, K. 1954. Ibid. 46:24-29.
21. Marchlewski, T. 1942. Bull. Int. Acad. Pol. Sci. Lett. Cl. Sci. Math. Nat. Ser., pp. 697-714.
22. Nachtsheim, H. 1937. Erbarzt 4:25-30, 50-55.
23. Nachtsheim, H. 1954. Proc. 9th Int. Congr. Genet. 1953, pp. 139-154.
24. Nachtsheim, H. 1958. In P. Cohrs, et al., ed. Pathologie der Laboratoriumstiere. Springer-Verlag, Berlin and New York. pp. 310-452.
25. Pap, E. 1921. Z. Indukt. Abstamm. Vererbungsl. 26:185-270.
26. Pickard, J. N. 1941. J. Genet. 42:215-222.
27. Punnett, R. C. 1912. Ibid. 2:221-238.
28. Punnett, R. C., and M. S. Pease. 1925. Ibid. 15:375-412.
29. Quevedo, W. C., Jr., and H. B. Chase. 1957. Anat. Rec. 129:87-95.
30. Robinson, R. 1955. J. Hered. 46:266.
31. Robinson, R. 1958. Bibliogr. Genet. 17:229-558.
32. Sawin, P. B. 1932. Carnegie Inst. Washington Publ. 427:15-50.
33. Sawin, P. B. 1955. Adv. Genet. 7:183-226.
34. Spendlove, W. H., and R. Robinson. 1970. Genetica 41:635-637.
35. Voloss-Mialhe, C. 1950. C. R. Soc. Biol. 144:19-20.
36. Wilson, W. K., and F. J. Dudley. 1946. J. Genet. 47:290-294.

144. ANATOMIC AND PHYSIOLOGIC MUTANTS: RABBIT

The data below do not include serum-associated traits; for these, *see* Table 147. **Source:** For full name, *see* list of HOLDERS at front of book.

Site	Locus	Allele	Description	Source	Reference
Ocular	Buphthalmia	Bu	Normal	JAX	2,16,27
		bu	Buphthalmos		
	Cataract 1	Cat-1	Normal	....	22,23
		cat-1	Cataract of lens		

continued

Site	Locus	Allele	Description	Source	Reference
	Cataract 2	*Cat-2*	Cataract of lens	....	4,22
		cat-2	Normal		
	Cyclopia	*Cy*	Normal	....	17,22
		cy	Cyclopia		
Oral cavity	Absent incisors	*I²*	Absence of secondary incisors	....	19,22
		i²	Normal		
	Mandibular prognathism	*Mp*	Normal	JAX, ROST	5,15,22
		mp	Overgrown incisors due to malocclusion		
	Supernumerary incisors	*Isup*	Normal	....	18,24
		isup	Extra secondary incisors		
Hematologic	Hemolytic anemia	*Ha*	Normal	JAX	1,9,10,12
		ha	Hemolytic anemia; lymphosarcoma		
	Hydrops fetalis	*Hd*	Hydrops of newborn[1]	....	14,20
		hd	Normal		
	Pelger	*Pg*	Abnormal leukocytes; chondrodystrophy	GAR	13,21,28
		pg	Normal		
Urogenital	Hypogonadia	*Hg*	Normal	JAX	6,26
		hg	Absence of germ cells		
	Renal agenesis	*Na*	Normal	JAX	25
		na	Renal agenesis		
	Renal cysts	*Rc*	Normal	JAX	11
		rc	Renal cysts in the cortex		
Other	Adrenal hyperplasia	*Ah*	Normal	JAX	8
		ah	Hyperplasia of the adrenal		
	Diaphragmatic hernia-1	*Dh-1*	Normal	JAX	7
		dh-1	Hernia of the diaphragm[2]		
	Diaphragmatic hernia-2	*Dh-2*	Normal	JAX	7
		dh-2	Hernia of the diaphragm[2]		
	Vestigial pulmonary-1	*Vpt-1*	Normal	JAX	3
		vpt-1	Vestigial pulmonary arterial trunk[3]		
	Vestigial pulmonary-2	*Vpt-2*	Normal	JAX	3
		vpt-2	Vestigial pulmonary arterial trunk[3]		
	Yellow fat[4]	*Y*	Normal color fat	....	29
		y	Yellow fat		

[1] *See also* Table 148, locus *Hg*. [2] *dh-1* and *dh-2* must both be homozygous for mutant phenotype to appear. [3] *vpt-1* and *vpt-2* must both be homozygous for mutant phenotype to appear. [4] In linkage group I.

Contributors: Richard R. Fox and Dorcas D. Crary; W. H. Spendlove

References

1. Bedigian, H. G., et al. 1976. Cancer Res. 36:4691-4696.
2. Brown, J. L., and W. J. Geeraets. 1972. Acta Ophthalmol. 50:486-494.
3. Crary, D. D., and R. R. Fox. 1975. J. Hered. 66:50-55.
4. Ehling, U. 1957. Z. Konstitutionsl. 34:77-104.
5. Fox, R. R., and D. D. Crary. 1971. J. Hered. 62:23-27.
6. Fox, R. R., and D. D. Crary. 1971. Ibid. 62:163-169.
7. Fox, R. R., and D. D. Crary. 1973. Ibid. 64:333-336.
8. Fox, R. R., and D. D. Crary. 1978. Ibid. 69:251-254.
9. Fox, R. R., and H. Meier. 1976. Ibid. 67:99-102.
10. Fox, R. R., et al. 1970. J. Natl. Cancer Inst. 45:719-729.
11. Fox, R. R., et al. 1971. J. Hered. 62:105-109.
12. Fox, R. R., et al. 1971. Oncology 25:372-382.
13. Harm, H. 1955. Blut 1:3-25.
14. Helmbold, W. 1956. Ibid. 2:9-31.
15. Kalinowski, T., and W. Rudolph. 1974. Wiss. Z. Univ. Rostock Math. Naturwiss. Reihe 23(1/2):131-135.
16. Lam, K.-W., et al. 1976. Arch. Ophthalmol. 94:1565-1567.
17. Menschow, G. B. 1934. Riv. Coniglicolt. 6:8-9.
18. Nachtsheim, H. 1936. Zuechtungskunde 11:273-287.
19. Nachtsheim, H. 1938. Fortschr. Erbpathol. 2:58-104.
20. Nachtsheim, H. 1947. Klin. Wochenschr. 24/25:590-592.
21. Nachtsheim, H. 1950. J. Hered. 41:131-137.

continued

22. Nachtsheim, H. 1958. In P. Cohrs, et al., ed. Pathologie der Laboratoriumstiere. Springer-Verlag, Berlin and New York. pp. 310-452.
23. Nachtsheim, H., and H. Gürich. 1939. Z. Konstitutionsl. 23:463-483.
24. Rohloff, R. 1945. Inaugural Dissertation. Univ. Berlin, Germany.
25. Rosa, F. M. da. 1943. Rev. Med. Vet. (Lisboa) 38: 349-363.
26. Sawin, P. B., and D. D. Crary. 1962. Anat. Rec. 142: 325(Abstr.).
27. Sheppard, L. B., et al. 1971. Ophthalmol. Res. 2:116-125.
28. Undritz, E. 1939. Schweiz. Med. Wochenschr. 69: 1177-1186.
29. Wilson, W. K., and F. J. Dudley. 1946. J. Genet. 47: 290-294.

145. NEUROLOGICAL AND BEHAVIORAL MUTANTS: RABBIT

Source: For full name, *see* list of HOLDERS at front of book.

Locus ⟨Synonym⟩	Allele	Description	Source	Reference
Acrobat	*Ak*	Normal	...	3,8,14
	ak	Walks on forelegs only		
Ataxia	*Ax*	Normal	JAX	10,13,17
	ax	Loss of coordination		
Epilepsy ⟨Audiogenic seizures⟩	*Ep*	Normal	JAX	1,6,9
	ep	Epileptic		
Hydrocephalus	*Hy*	Normal	...	7,15
	hy	High cranial vault; excess fluid in brain ventricles		
Lethal muscle contracture	*Mc*	Normal	...	7,16
	mc	Muscle contracture		
Paralytic tremor[1/]	*Pt*	Normal	...	4,11
	pt	Resembles Parkinson's trembling		
Shaking palsy	*Tr*	Normal	...	5,8
	tr	Continuous trembling & convulsions		
Spina bifida	*Sb*	Normal	JAX	2
	sb	Spina bifida occulta totalis		
Syringomyelia	*Sy*	Normal	...	8,12
	sy	Asymmetrical spastic paralysis		

[1/] Sex-linked.

Contributors: W. H. Spendlove; Richard R. Fox and Dorcas D. Crary; Roy Robinson

References
1. Antonitis, J. J., et al. 1954. J. Hered. 45:279-284.
2. Crary, D. D., et al. 1966. Ibid. 57:236-243.
3. Letard, E. 1935. Bull. Acad. Vet. Fr. 8:608-610.
4. Lindsey, J. R., and R. R. Fox. 1974. In S. H. Weisbroth, et al., ed. The Biology of the Laboratory Rabbit. Academic, New York. pp. 377-402.
5. Nachtsheim, H. 1934. Erbarzt 1:36-38.
6. Nachtsheim, H. 1937. Z. Indukt. Abstamm. Vererbungsl. 73:463-466.
7. Nachtsheim, H. 1939. In K. H. Bauer, et al., ed. Handbuch der Erbbiologie des Menschen. Springer-Verlag, Berlin and New York. pp. 1-58.
8. Nachtsheim, H. 1958. In P. Cohrs, et al., ed. Pathologie der Laboratoriumstiere. Springer-Verlag, Berlin and New York. pp. 310-452.
9. Nellhaus, G. 1965. Proc. Soc. Exp. Biol. Med. 120: 259-260.
10. O'Leary, J. L., et al. 1974. Acta Neuropathol. 30:11-24.
11. Osetowska, E. 1967. Ibid. 8:331-344.
12. Ostertag, B. 1930. Verh. Dtsch. Pathol. Ges. 25:166-174.
13. Robinson, N. 1970. Acta Neuropathol. 14:326-337.
14. Robinson, R. 1958. Bibliogr. Genet. 17:229-558.
15. Rosa, F. M. da. 1946. Rev. Med. Vet. (Lisboa) 41: 1-55.
16. Sawin, P. B. 1955. Adv. Genet. 7:183-226.
17. Sawin, P. B., et al. 1942. Proc. Natl. Acad. Sci. USA 28:123-127.

Source: For full name, *see* list of HOLDERS in front of book.

Locus	Allele	Description	Source	Reference
Achondro-plasia	Ac ac	Normal Achondroplastic	JAX	1,20
Brachy-dactyly [1]	Br br	Normal Absence of nails, digits, limbs	LPC	7,9, 16
Chondro-dystro-phy	Cd cd	Normal Disproportionate dwarf	JAX	5
Congenital luxation	Lu lu	Normal Luxation of the hip	...	17
Dachs	Da da	Viable chondroplastic dwarf Normal	JAX	2,18
Distal fore-leg curva-ture	Fc fc	Normal Distal foreleg curvature	...	4,14

Locus	Allele	Description	Source	Reference
Dwarf[2]	Dw dw	Proportionate (pituitary) dwarf Normal	JAX	8,11
Hypopla-sia pelvis	Hyp hyp	Normal Hypoplasia of ischium	...	12, 13
Nanosomia	Nan nan	Normal Proportionate dwarf	...	10, 19, 21
Osteope-trosis	Os os	Normal Abnormal bones & teeth	JAX	15, 22
Scoliosis	Sco sco	Normal Scoliosis	...	6
Zwerg-wuchs	Zw zw	Normal Proportionate dwarf	...	3

[1] In linkage group V. [2] In linkage group IV.

Contributors: Richard R. Fox and Dorcas D. Crary

References

1. Brown, W. H., and L. Pearce. 1945. J. Exp. Med. 82: 241-260.
2. Crary, D. D., and P. B. Sawin. 1952. J. Hered. 43:254-259.
3. Degenhardt, K.-H. 1960. Akad. Wiss. Lit. Mainz Abh. Math. Naturwiss. Kl. 12:919-988.
4. Fox, R. R. 1974. In S. H. Weisbroth, et al., ed. The Biology of the Laboratory Rabbit. Academic, New York. pp. 1-22.
5. Fox, R. R., and D. D. Crary. 1975. J. Hered. 66:271-276.
6. Fox, R. R., and D. D. Crary. 1975. Teratology 11(2): 18A.
7. Greene, H. S. N. 1935. Science 81:405-407.
8. Greene, H. S. N., et al. 1934. Ibid. 79:487-488.
9. Inman, O. R. 1941. Anat. Rec. 79:483-505.
10. Kröning, F. 1939. Biol. Zentralbl. 59:148-160.
11. Latimer, H. B., and P. B. Sawin. 1963. Anat. Rec. 146:85-92.
12. Nachtsheim, H. 1936. Dtsch. Tieraerztl. Wochenschr. 44:742-746.
13. Nachtsheim, H. 1958. In P. Cohrs, et al., ed. Pathologie der Laboratoriumstiere. Springer-Verlag, Berlin and New York. pp. 310-452.
14. Pearce, L. 1960. J. Exp. Med. 111:801-830.
15. Pearce, L., and W. H. Brown. 1948. Ibid. 88:579-596.
16. Petter, C., et al. 1973. C. R. Acad. Sci. 277:801-803.
17. Rosa, F. M. da. 1945. Rev. Med. Vet. (Lisboa) 40:1-23.
18. Sawin, P. B., and M. Hamlet. 1970. J. Morphol. 130: 397-420.
19. Schnecke, C. 1941. Z. Konstitutionsl. 25:427-457.
20. Shepard, T. H., and G. L. Bass. 1971. J. Embryol. Exp. Morphol. 25:347-363.
21. Suchalla, H. 1943. Z. Morphol. Anthropol. 40:274-333.
22. Walker, D. G. 1973. Clin. Orthop. Relat. Res. 97:158-174.

147. ENZYMES AND OTHER PROTEINS IN SERUM AND TISSUES: RABBIT

Data have not been included for the following serum or other tissue enzymes for which no variants were detectable by electrophoretic mobility or by activity differences: acid phosphatase [ref. 5], adenine phosphoribosyltransferase [ref. 81], alanine aminotransferase (glutamic pyruvic transaminase) [ref. 81], aspartate aminotransferase (glutamic oxalacetic transaminase) [ref. 81], 2,3-diphosphoglycerate mutase [ref. 81], enolase (phosphopyruvate hydratase)

continued

[ref. 81], glucose-6-phosphate dehydrogenase [ref. 81, 84, 129], hypoxanthine phosphoribosyltransferase ⟨hypoxanthine-guanine phosphoribosyltransferase⟩ [ref. 81], isocitrate dehydrogenase [ref. 81], organophosphate phosphorylphosphatase [ref. 140], phosphoglycerate kinase [ref. 81], purine-nucleoside phosphorylase [ref. 81], and superoxide dismutase [ref. 81]. Suggestions of variants of benzoylcholine esterase [37, 38, 126], lactate dehydrogenase [ref. 32, 81, 129], monoacetylmorphine esterase [ref. 38, 137, 138], and peptidase A [ref. 81] need additional study. A preliminary study of ferroxidase ⟨ceruloplasmin⟩ variation has been reported [ref. 15, 32]. Variants of transferrin [ref. 15] and group-specific protein ⟨Gc⟩ [ref. 104] have not been found in the rabbit.

E. C. No. = Enzyme Commission Number; for source, *see* Introduction. **Identification Method:** SGE = starch gel electrophoresis. **Characteristics & Remarks:** CNS = central nervous system. **Inheritance:** Ig = immunoglobulin. **Strain, Stock, or Colony:** ALU = Alaskan; CH = Chinchilla; FG = Flemish Giant; NZW = New Zealand White; VW = Vienna White. **Holder:** For full name, *see* list of HOLDERS at front of book. **Reference** gives the general reference for information other than that pertaining to **Proposed Genetic Control.** *Abbreviations:* At = atropine; Cc = cocaine; HDL = high-density lipoprotein; LDL = low-density lipoprotein; αNA = α-naphthyl acetate; αNB = α-naphthyl butyrate; PAGE = polyacrylamide gel electrophoresis; RBC = erythrocytes; WBC = leukocytes. Figures in heavy brackets are reference numbers. Data in light brackets refer to the column heading in brackets.

Protein ⟨Synonym⟩ [E. C. No.]	Identification Method	Characteristics & Remarks	Proposed Genetic Control		Strain, Stock, or Colony [Holder]	Ref- er- ence
			Locus ⟨Synonym⟩ [Inheritance]	Allele ⟨Synonym⟩		
Serum						
Esterases α₁-Arylesterase	Antigens in serum identified by means of precipitating alloantisera in gel diffusion studies. 3 phenotypes identified by family studies.	Phenotypes show differential activity for αNA: Ess1 hydrolyzes At, Ess2 does not. Possibly same as atropine esterase system. Radial immunodiffusion assay detected similar amounts of α₁-arylesterase in all phenotypes. Purified enzyme exhibits 2 post-albumin isozyme bands with PAGE at pH 8.9-9.4.	*Ess* [Autosomal, codominant alleles; not closely linked to Ig heavy chain loci, Ig light chain κb, haptoglobin *Hph*, HDL *Lhj*, LDL *Lpq*, or α₂-macroglobulin *Mtz* loci] [4, 71]	*Ess¹; Ess²*	....	6
Carboxylesterase [3.1.1.1] Atropine esterase	Manometric method to detect hydrolysis of At by serum samples.	Phenotypes show differential activity for substrate At: As—serum hydrolyzes At; as—enzyme is inactive or absent. Activity absent in neonates; generally higher in adult ♀. In As rabbits, activity also present in liver, gut mucosa, & some other tissues.	*As* [Autosomal; reported linkage to *E* (coat color extension) of linkage group VI, with recombination frequency of 26%. Incomplete functional dominance of *As* (gene dosage effect on activity).] [76, 105]	*As; as*	....	79,80

continued

Protein ⟨Synonym⟩ [E. C. No.]	Identification Method	Characteristics & Remarks	Proposed Genetic Control		Strain, Stock, or Colony [Holder]	Reference
			Locus ⟨Synonym⟩ [Inheritance]	Allele ⟨Synonym⟩		
Atropine esterase-cocaine esterase system						
Considered as a single-locus, multi-allelic system	SGE at pH 6.8; zymograms developed with αNA. 6 phenotypes distinguished by prominent prealbumin multiple-zone isozyme patterns in αNA: phenotype A has 1S, 1A, & 1F zones; phenotype AF has 1S, 1A, & 2F zones; phenotype F has 1S & 2F zones; phenotype M has 2F zones; phenotype P has 1S & 1F zones; phenotype S has 1S zone. Relative mobilities of isozyme zones are F > A > S.	Differential activities of serum for substrates At & Cc distinguish some phenotypes: phenotypes A & AF hydrolyze both At & Cc; phenotypes F, P, & S hydrolyze only Cc; and phenotype M hydrolyzes neither. Family studies show that genotypes As^A/As^A, As^A/As^M, As^A/As^P, & As^A/As^S yield phenotype A; genotypes As^F/As^F, As^F/As^M, As^F/As^P, & As^F/As^S yield phenotype F; and genotypes As^P/As^P, As^P/As^M, As^P/As^S, & As^M/As^S yield phenotype P.	As [Autosomal; appears to be linked to $Es-1$ of RBC esterase system & $Es-2$ of platelet carboxylesterase system] [116, 117, 119]	As^A As^F As^M As^P As^S	AC; WH [JAX][1] .... IIIc [JAX][1] III; IIIVO [JAX][1] AC; AX; AXBU; IIIc [JAX][1]	79,80
Considered as a multiple-locus system						
Atropine esterase	SGE at pH 6.2; zymograms developed with various substrates, including αNA & At. Phenotypes distinguished by isozyme bands found in medium fast prealbumin zone: F has 3 bands, f′ has 1 faint band, F′ has 1 band, & "?" has none.	Phenotypes show differential activity for αNA & At: F hydrolyzes both αNA & At; f′ hydrolyzes only At weakly; F′ hydrolyzes only αNA; & "?" phenotype shows no activity	$Est-2$ [Autosomal; close linkage with $Est-1$ [2]. Gene dosage effect on activity.] [126-128, 143]	.... $Est-2^F$ $Est-2^{f'}$ $Est-2^{F'}$ $Est-2^?$	15 JAX strains characterized for $Est-2$ alleles (1977). Cpb:ALU; Cpb:CH; Cpb:VW [CPB] Cpb:ALU; Cpb:CH; Cpb:VW [CPB] Cpb:VW [CPB] NZW[3]	125
Cocaine esterase	SGE at pH 6.2; zymograms developed with various substrates, including αNA & Cc. Isozyme bands found in slow prealbumin zone: phenotype S has 3 bands; phetype s has none.	Phenotypes show differential activity for αNA & Cc: S hydrolyzes both αNA & Cc, while s hydrolyzes neither ($Est-1^s$ product is functionally silent or absent)	$Est-1$ [Autosomal; close linkage with $Est-2$ [2]. Gene dosage effect on activity.] [126-128, 143]	$Est-1^S$; $Est-1^s$	Stocks surveyed (Cpb:ALU, Cpb:CH, & Cpb:VW [CPB]) each carried both alleles, but gene frequencies varied among stocks. 15 JAX strains characterized for $Est-1$ alleles (1977).	125

[1] These allele-strain associations were suggested by a *limited* survey of various JAX strains in 1969. [2] $Est-1$—$Est-2$ haplotypes SF, Sf', sf', & SF' were identified from genetic studies. Haplotypes sF & sF' are inferred from rare zymotypes of random samples [125-128]. [3] The "?" phenotype was found in a NZW stock and was not confirmed by genetic studies.

continued

Protein ⟨Synonym⟩ [E. C. No.]	Identification Method	Characteristics & Remarks	Proposed Genetic Control		Strain, Stock, or Colony [Holder]	Reference
			Locus ⟨Synonym⟩ [Inheritance]	Allele ⟨Synonym⟩		
"Dependent" prealbumin carboxylesterase	SGE at pH 6.2; zymograms developed with αNA, At, & Cc. Single isozyme band, when expressed, found in very fast prealbumin zone.	Phenotype D has strong αNA activity, which is dependent on presence of Est-2^F, and weak activity for At or Cc, which is independent of alleles of Est-2 locus. Phenotype d has weak αNA activity, which is dependent on presence of Est-2^F allele.	Est-3 [Autosomal; segregates independently from Est-1—Est-2, but gene interaction with Est-2 was found] [126-128, 143]	Est-3^D; Est-3^d	Stocks surveyed (Cpb:ALU, Cpb:CH, & Cpb:VW [CPB]) each carried both alleles, but gene frequencies varied among stocks. 15 JAX strains characterized for Est-3 alleles (1977); only Est-3^d found.	125
Other proteins A-antigen ⟨Digestive group A alloantigen; DG-A alloantigen⟩	Presence or absence of the A-antigen in serum by a complement fixation test, or of the DG-A alloantigen in digestive tract mucosa by a fluorescent antibody technique. Conversely, the absence or presence of naturally occurring A-substance agglutinins in rabbit serum defines the An and an phenotypes, respectively.	A-antigen not found on rabbit RBC's, but is cross-reactive with the human blood group A antigen. No alternative antigenic specificity identified in rabbits lacking the A antigenic specificity which is borne by a glycoprotein in the digestive mucosa. A-antigen system appears to be related to the bovine J and porcine I systems.	An [Autosomal; deficiency of A-antigen a recessive trait. An is on linkage group V, 36.8 map units from the Br locus.] [106, 118, 136, 141]	An; an	....	90, 142
Complement, 6th component ⟨C'6⟩	Various hemolytic assays, both qualitative & quantitative; also reactivity of serum samples with anti-C6 antibody. Radial immunodiffusion for quantitation.	C'6-deficient rabbits lack serum hemolytic activity. Antibody to C'6 detects no related protein counterpart in deficient rabbits. Heterozygotes are hemolytically competent, but express C'6 at a reduced level.	$C'6$ [Autosomal; $C'6$ is functionally dominant. Serum levels indicate a gene dosage effect. Not closely linked to heavy or light chain Ig loci, or to $Hb\alpha$ locus. No apparent association with hair color or skin thickness.] [16, 75, 101, 102, 121]	$C'6$ $C'6^{-4/}$	.... [UIGC$^{5/}$]	17, 85, 95, 103

$^{4/}$ Silent allele. $^{5/}$ Derived from animals from NIH colony.

continued

Protein ⟨Synonym⟩ [E. C. No.]	Identification Method	Characteristics & Remarks	Proposed Genetic Control		Strain, Stock, or Colony [Holder]	Reference
			Locus ⟨Synonym⟩ [Inheritance]	Allele ⟨Synonym⟩		
Haptoglobin	Reaction of serum samples with precipitating alloantisera, anti-Hph-1 & anti-Hph-2, in gel diffusion studies. 3 phenotypes identified: h1, h2, & h1,2.	h1 & h2 phenotypes express different alloantigens; heterozygote expresses both. Differences in electrophoretic mobility not noted for rabbit haptoglobin. Not known whether the antigenic variation occurs in the α chain or β chain of haptoglobin, or in both.	Hph [Autosomal, codominant alleles. Not closely linked to the Ig heavy chain loci, Ig light chain κb locus, Ess, Lpq, or Mtz loci.] [30]	Hph^1; Hph^2	....	74, 77, 78
Hemopexin ⟨Heme-binding protein; Hbp⟩	SGE at pH 7.5, or PAGE at pH 8.9, of serum mixed with heated RBC lysates or heme. Hemopexin zones (β region) visualized by peroxidase activity. 6 phenotypes identified: Hx 1-1 has a + c zones; Hx 2-2 has b + d zones; Hx 3-3 has c + e zones; and heterozygous phenotypes show a combination of the zones. Relative anodal mobilities of SGE peroxidase zones are a > b > c > d > e. Hx 1F mobility is greater than that of any other Hx type.	....	Hx ⟨Hbp⟩ [Autosomal, codominant alleles. Hx has been mapped to linkage group I, and is situated between the Hq blood group locus & the color locus c.] [56-58, 62]	Hx^1; Hx^2; Hx^3; Hx^{1F}	....	66, 69, 83, 113
Lipoproteins High-density lipoprotein ⟨HDL⟩	H1 1 (+) antigen in serum identified by a precipitating alloantiserum in gel diffusion studies. Absence of a reaction = H1 1 (−). Only 2 phenotypes identified.	H1 1 antigen has α region mobility. H1 1 (+) phenotype presumably includes homozygous & heterozygous genotypes. The H1 1 specificity is an isotypic specificity in man & some other species, and may identify a "new" lipoprotein family since the H1 1 (+) polypeptide has no sequence homology with other known HDL polypeptides.	Hl [Autosomal. Not closely linked to HDL $R67$, RBC blood group Hg, Ig heavy-chain loci, or Ig light-chain κb locus.] [7, 8, 18, 20, 21, 24-26]	Hl^1; Hl^{-} [4,6]	....	19, 23, 68
	Lhj1 & Lhj2 antigens in serum identified by means of precipitating alloantisera in gel diffusion studies. 3 phenotypes identified.	Lhj antigen has α region mobility. Immunoelectrophoretic precipitin arcs developed with alloantisera demonstrate esterase activity for αNA. No comparative studies of H1 1 & R67 with Lhj.	Lhj ⟨Lpj⟩ [Autosomal; codominant alleles. Not closely linked to Lpq.] [51]	Lhj^1; Lhj^2	....	68

[4] Silent allele. [6] Indicated by family studies.

continued

Protein ⟨Synonym⟩ [E. C. No.]	Identification Method	Characteristics & Remarks	Proposed Genetic Control		Strain, Stock, or Colony [Holder]	Reference
			Locus ⟨Synonym⟩ [Inheritance]	Allele ⟨Synonym⟩		
	R67(+) antigen in serum identified by means of a precipitating alloantiserum in gel diffusion studies. Absence of a reaction = R67(−). Only 2 phenotypes identified.	R67 antigen has α region mobility; found in apoA-I-containing HDL particles [7]. Comparison of H11 & R67 indicated that these 2 allotypic specificities reside on separate subpopulations of HDL in same rabbit.	R67 [Autosomal; R67(+) dominant. Not closely linked to HDL Hl, RBC blood group Hg, Ig heavy-chain loci, or Ig light-chain κb locus.] [18, 20-22, 24-26]	R67(+); R67(−) [4,6]	....	19, 23, 68
Low-density lipoprotein ⟨LDL⟩	Lp1 allotype in serum identified by means of a precipitating alloantiserum in gel diffusion studies. Only 2 phenotypes identified.	Lp antigen has β region electrophoretic mobility; possibly the same as one of the Lpq antigens, but no comparative studies made. Lp1(+) phenotype presumably includes both homozygous & heterozygous genotypes.	Lp [Autosomal] [70]	Lp^1; Lp^- [4,6]	....	68
	Lpq allotypes in serum identified by means of precipitating alloantisera in gel diffusion studies veloped with Lpq alloantisera react with lipid stains. Allelic exclusion was found for molecules controlled by Lpq: In a heterozygote, allotypic specificities controlled by one haplotype reside on same molecule, but specificities controlled by other haplotype reside on different molecules. Comparison of reagents between investigators indicated correspondence of the following specificities: Lpq1 = Af-A; Lpq2 = Af-B.	Lpq antigen has β region electrophoretic mobility. Precipitin arcs on immunoelectropherograms de	Lpq ⟨Af⟩ [Autosomal; Lpq^1 & Lpq^2 behave as codominant alleles; Lpq^3 & Lpq^4 behave as codominant alleles. Locus (or sublocus) controlling Lpq1 & Lpq2 closely linked to locus (or sublocus) controlling Lpq3 & Lpq 4. Only 3 haplotypes found: Lpq^1Lpq^3, Lpq^2Lpq^3, & Lpq^2Lpq^4. Lpq locus belongs to linkage group VIII, which includes the κb & Prt loci. Lpq locus not closely linked to Ig heavy-chain loci, arylesterase Ess, or α_2-macroglobulin Mtz.] [1-3, 33, 61, 122, 123]	Lpq^1 ⟨Af^A⟩; Lpq^2 ⟨Af^B⟩; Lpq^3; Lpq^4	[UIGC]	68
α_2-Macroglobulin ⟨α_2-M⟩	Mtz allotypes in serum identified by means of precipitating alloantisera in gel diffusion studies Mtz3 & Mtz4 specificities) are on major portion of same α_2-M molecules from a heterozygous rabbit. All four specificities can be present on same molecule, but it is not known whether the Mtz1/Mtz2 pair are markers for the same or different cistrons as the Mtz3/	Lack of allelic exclusion found for molecules controlled by Mtz: Mtz1 & Mtz2	Mtz ⟨Am⟩ [Autosomal; Mtz^1 & Mtz^2 behave as codominant alleles; Mtz^3 & Mtz^4 behave as codominant alleles. Locus (or sublocus) controlling Mtz1 & Mtz2 is closely linked to locus (or sublocus) controlling Mtz3 & Mtz4. 3 haplotypes iden	Mtz^1 ⟨Am^A⟩; Mtz^2 ⟨Am^B⟩; Mtz^3 ⟨Mty^3⟩; Mtz^4 ⟨Mty^4⟩	Mtz^1Mtz^3 & Mtz^2Mtz^3 haplotypes found in closed colony of NZW/FG [UIMC]. Mtz^1Mtz^4 haplotype introduced into this colony by an AX strain [JAX] rabbit in 1969. Survey of other rabbits from the AX strain indicated this strain also carried Mtz^1-	10, 53, 54, 82, 89, 94

[4] Silent allele. [6] Indicated by family studies. [7] Human HDL is composed of 2 major peptides—apo-A-I and apo-A-II; rabbit HDL is composed of only 1, analogous to human apo-A-I [19].

continued

Protein ⟨Synonym⟩ [E. C. No.]	Identification Method	Characteristics & Remarks	Proposed Genetic Control		Strain, Stock, or Colony [Holder]	Reference
			Locus ⟨Synonym⟩ [Inheritance]	Allele ⟨Synonym⟩		
	Mtz4 pair. Comparison of reagents between investigators indicated correspondence of the following specificities: Mtz1 = Am-A; Mtz2 = Am-B. Rabbit α_2-M is not homologous to human α_2-M; rabbit α_1-M is homologous to human α_2-M.		tified: Mtz^1Mtz^3, Mtz^1Mtz^4, & Mtz^2-Mtz^3. Mtz not closely linked to Ig heavy-chain loci, Ig light-chain κb locus, Ess, or Lpq.] [9, 11, 12, 33, 61, 72, 73]		Mtz^3 haplotype. Survey of random samples from other colonies suggested existence of Mtz^2-Mtz^4 haplotype.	
Pretransferrin ⟨Prt⟩	Presence or absence of a serum protein migrating ahead of transferrin in discontinuous PAGE, in alkaline pH. Only 2 phenotypes recognized; heterozygotes not distinguished by assay employed.	Serum protein of unknown function or structure.	Prt [Autosomal; deficiency of Prt is a recessive trait. Prt locus linked to Ig κb locus, with a recombination frequency of 23.5%, and present on Lpq-κb-Prt linkage group.] [122, 123]	prt^+; prt^-	....	122, 123

Erythrocytes

Protein ⟨Synonym⟩ [E. C. No.]	Identification Method	Characteristics & Remarks	Locus ⟨Synonym⟩ [Inheritance]	Allele ⟨Synonym⟩	Strain, Stock, or Colony [Holder]	Reference
Esterases Carboxylesterase [3.1.1.1] Carboxylesterase-1 ⟨Es-1⟩	SGE at pH 7.3; zymograms developed with αNB & various other substrates. All Es-1 isozymes migrate in a region just slightly anodal to the origin. 3 phenotypes identified by isozyme mobility patterns: A has 2 or 3 bands, most anodal; B has 2 bands, least anodal; AB has 5 or 6 bands—A + B bands & an additional "hybrid" band of intermediate mobility.	Classified as an ali-esterase. Es-1 activity present in CNS tissue also.	Es-1 [Autosomal, codominant alleles; closely linked to Es-2 [8]. Also appears to be linked to serum atropine esterase locus Est-2.] [59, 60, 109, 111, 119]	$Es-1^A$; $Es-1^B$	Both alleles found in AC [JAX] (1967)	108, 110
Carboxylesterase-3 ⟨Es-3⟩	SGE at pH 7.3; zymograms developed with αNB & various other substrates. 4 phenotypes identified: A has 2 strong & 1 weak bands; B has 2 bands; AB has A + B bands; AC has A bands & & C zone. Relative mobilities: A > B > C. [9]	Classified as a true propionyl esterase. Es-3 activity not present in CNS tissue.	Es-3 [Autosomal, codominant alleles. Segregates independently from Es-1—Es-2.] [59, 60, 109, 111, 119]	$Es-3^A$ $Es-3^B$ $Es-3^C$	AC [JAX] (1967) AC [JAX] (1967) Rare in populations surveyed; found at ≤2% frequency in NZW stocks from various USA vendors	108, 110
Esterase D [10] ⟨Es-D⟩	SGE; zymograms developed with 4-methylumbelliferyl esters (fluorogenic substrates). [11]	One variant isozyme pattern out of 40 samples. 2 samples lacked Es-D activity in group of Australian rabbits surveyed.	Es-D [32, 81]	....	....	65

[8] Reported test crosses indicate that all 4 possible haplotypes for the Es-1—Es-2 linkage group exist. [9] Es-3 iso- zyme system is more anodal than Es-2. [10] Preliminary report. [11] Es-D mobility region between Es-1 & Es-2 regions.

continued

Protein ⟨Synonym⟩ [E. C. No.]	Identification Method	Characteristics & Remarks	Proposed Genetic Control Locus ⟨Synonym⟩ [Inheritance]	Allele ⟨Synonym⟩	Strain, Stock, or Colony [Holder]	Reference
Other enzymes Adenosine de-aminase ⟨ADA⟩ [3.5.4.4]	SGE; zymograms. 6 phenotypes observed. Relative mobilities of ADA phenotypes: ADA2 > ADA1 >> ADA3.	....	*ADA* [Autosomal, codominant alleles] [29, 32, 61, 81]	ADA^1; ADA^2; ADA^3	....	64, 124
Adenylate kinase [2.7.4.3][10/]	SGE; zymograms	2 phenotypes reported: AK1-1 & AK1-2	*AK* [32, 81, 129]	....	....	27, 41
Carbonate dehydratase ⟨Carbonic anhydrase⟩ [4.2.1.1][10/]	SGE; zymograms	In most mammals, including rabbits, there exist 2 separate forms of RBC carbonate dehydratase—CAI & CAII— coded for by separate but linked loci. Preliminary reports suggest genetic variants for both loci in the rabbit.	*CAI*; *CAII* [Autosomal, codominant alleles] [13, 46, 120]	....	....	39, 40, 120
Cytochrome b_5 reductase ⟨NADH diaphorase⟩ [1.6.2.2][10/]	SGE at pH 8.6; zymograms. 3 phenotypes observed as variant isozyme patterns.	....	*Dia* [29, 81, 129]	....	....	42
Phosphoglucomutase [2.7.5.1]	SGE; zymograms. 3 phenotypes observed: A has 2 fast bands; B has 2 slow bands; AB has A + B bands	....	PGM_1 [Codominant alleles] [5, 32, 81, 129]	PGM_1^A; PGM_1^B	....	35, 36, 139
	Zymogram	Preliminary report of 1 variant with an extra slow isozyme band in addition to normal 3-band pattern	PGM_2[12/] [81]	....	....	93
Phosphogluconate dehydrogenase (decarboxylating) [1.1.1.44]	Cellulose acetate gel electrophoresis at pH 7.5, or SGE at pH 7.0; zymograms. 3 phenotypes observed: PGD1 ⟨PGDF⟩ has 1 fast band; PGD2 ⟨PGDS⟩ has 1 slow band; PGD1-2 ⟨PGDFS⟩ has F band + S band plus additional "hybrid" band.	....	*PGD* [Codominant alleles] [5, 31, 32, 81, 129]	PGD^1 ⟨PGD^F⟩; PGD^2 ⟨PGD^S⟩	....	92
Phosphohexose isomerase ⟨PHI⟩ [5.3.1.9]	SGE at pH 6.5; zymograms. 3 phenotypes identified. PHI migrates cathodally. B9 variant-type enzyme has a higher cathodal mobility than wild type.	Triplet-banding pattern of heterozygotes better visualized with WBC preparations than with RBC preparations	*PHI* [Autosomal; codominant alleles by zymogram patterns, but wild type appears to be functionally dominant by activity levels] [5, 81, 135]	Wild type / B9 variant type	.... / NZW stock [13/]	88

[10/] Preliminary report. [12/] PGM_1 & PGM_2 are not closely linked in man. [13/] No other variants found in a survey of Australian wild rabbits or in a limited survey of some JAX strains.

continued

585

Protein ⟨Synonym⟩ [E. C. No.]	Identification Method	Characteristics & Remarks	Proposed Genetic Control		Strain, Stock, or Colony [Holder]	Ref-er-ence
			Locus ⟨Synonym⟩ [Inheritance]	Allele ⟨Synonym⟩		
Other proteins: Hemoglobin ⟨Hb⟩ α-Chain	Amino acid composition studies of Hbα peptides and sequencing of Hbα chain	Variant at position 29—either Val or Leu	Hbα [Quantitative studies of peptides showed that individual rabbits had either 100% Leu, 50% Val & 50% Leu, or 100% Val at position 29] [107]	2 alleles	Random-bred [UIGC]	107
		Variants at 3 positions: 29, Val (allele I) or Leu (allele II); 48, Phe (I) or Leu (II); 49, Thr (I) or Ser (II). Position 70 always Val; positions 76 & 80 always Leu.	Hbα [Family studies showed simple Mendelian segregation of position 29 marker] [67]	I; II	....	67,99
		Variants at several positions: 29, Val or Leu; 48, Leu or Phe; 49, Ser or Thr; 70, Val or Thr; 76, Leu or Val; 80, Ser or Leu. Concluded this was due to either translational ambiguities or multiple alleles.	Hbα [Autosomal, codominant] [130]	Multiple alleles?	....	130
β-Chain	Amino acid sequence & composition studies of peptides	First report of variability in rabbit β-chain. 14 amino acid differences compared to human hemoglobin.	Hbβ	....	Mixed races of rabbits	14
		Variants found at 3 positions: 52, Asn (allele I) or His (allele II); 56, Asn (I) or Ser (II); 76, Ser (I) or Asn (II). Variants not found to be strain-specific. In a family with 10 offspring, 2 exceptions to sets I & II found. One variant set (His-Ser-Ser) explained by intra-cistronic crossover.	Hbβ	I; II	....	47,48
		Variant found at position 112: either Ile or Val	Hbβ [Controlled by Mendelian co-dominant alleles] [28, 49, 50, 114]	....	....	28, 49, 50, 99, 114
			Platelets			
Enzyme: Carboxylesterase [3.1.1.1] — Carboxylesterase-2 ⟨Es-2⟩	SGE at pH 7.3; zymograms developed with αNB & various other substrates. 3 phenotypes identified by isozyme mobility patterns (Es-2 isozymes have medium fast mobil-	Classified as a propionyl esterase. Es-2 activity also present in CNS tissue.	Es-2 [Autosomal, codominant alleles; closely linked to Es-1 8/. Also appears to be linked to atropine esterase locus, Est-2.] [59, 60, 109, 111, 119]	Es-2^A; Es-2^B	Both alleles found in strains AC, AX, & IIIc [JAX] (1967)	108, 110

8/ Reported test crosses indicate that all 4 possible haplotypes for the Es-1—Es-2 linkage group exist.

continued

586

Protein ⟨Synonym⟩ [E. C. No.]	Identification Method	Characteristics & Remarks	Proposed Genetic Control		Strain, Stock, or Colony [Holder]	Ref-er-ence
			Locus ⟨Synonym⟩ [Inheritance]	Allele ⟨Synonym⟩		
	ity): A has 3 bands; B has 3 bands; AB has 6 bands—A + B bands. Each of the A bands is more anodal than the corresponding B band.					
Blood						
Enzyme: *p*-Aminoben-zoic acid *N*-acetyl-transferase ⟨PABA-NAT⟩	In vitro assay: time/activity curve of blood for *p*-amino-benzoic acid ⟨PABA⟩ acetylation	Phenotype RR shows rapid acetylation, Rr shows interme-diate, and rr shows slow acetylation of PABA. Absolute ac-tivity of blood PABA-NAT within a family showed close correlation with genotype. Pre-diction of genotype in random samples less reliable, suggesting additional regulatory fac-tors or multiple alleles.	*PABA-NAT* [Auto-somal. Possible linkage with *INH-NAT.*] [133, 134]	*PABA-NAT^R; PABA-NAT^r*	....	63
Liver						
Enzyme: Iso-niazid *N*-acetyltrans-ferase	In vivo assay: serum half-life of unacetyl-ated drugs—iso-niazid ⟨INH⟩, sulfa-diazine ⟨SD⟩, or sul-famethazine ⟨SM⟩. In vitro assay: time/activity curve of liver homogenate for drug acetylation.	Phenotype R shows rapid acetylation of INH, SD, SM, & some other drugs; phenotype r shows slow acet-ylation of INH, SD, or SM. In vivo assay cannot distinguish be-tween phenotypes RR & Rr due to interference by extra-hepatic acet-ylating activities. Heterozygous trait Rr (intermediate rate of acetyla-tion) can be detected with in vitro assay when SD used for substrate. This enzyme activity also found in gut mucosa.	*INH-NAT* [Auto-somal; *INH-NAT^R* is considered func-tionally dominant. There is a gene dos-age effect detect-able by in vitro as-say.] [44, 45, 52, 134]	*INH-NAT^R; INH-NAT^r*	Both alleles have been found in various ran-dom outbred stocks & in NZW	55, 131-133
Kidney						
Enzymes Malate dehy-drogenase (decarbox-ylating) (NADP⁺) ⟨NADP mal-ic enzyme⟩ [1.1.1.40]	Cellulose acetate elec-trophoresis at pH 8.1; zymograms	Catalyzes NADP⁺-dependent decar-boxylation of malate to pyr-uvate	....	....	....	86,96
Soluble or cytoplas-mic form	3 phenotypes ob-served. Relative anodal mobilities of isozymes: A > B	....	*Mod-1* [Autosomal, codominant al-leles] [115]	*Mod-1^a; Mod-1^b*	....	
Mitochon-drial form	3 phenotypes ob-served. Relative cathodal mobilities of isozymes: A > B	....	*Mod-2* [Autosomal, codominant al-leles] [115]	*Mod-2^a; Mod-2^b*	....	

continued

Protein ⟨Synonym⟩ [E. C. No.]	Identification Method	Characteristics & Remarks	Proposed Genetic Control		Strain, Stock, or Colony [Holder]	Reference
			Locus ⟨Synonym⟩ [Inheritance]	Allele ⟨Synonym⟩		
Mannosephosphate isomerase ⟨Mannose-6-phosphate isomerase⟩ [5.3.1.8]	Cellulose acetate electrophoresis at pH 8.1; zymograms. 6 phenotypes observed. Relative anodal mobilities of isozyme bands: A > B > C.	Catalyzes reversible conversion of mannose 6-phosphate to fructose 6-phosphate	$Mpi\text{-}1$ [Autosomal, codominant alleles] [29, 115]	$Mpi\text{-}1^a$; $Mpi\text{-}1^b$; $Mpi\text{-}1^c$	Various JAX strains of rabbits have been characterized for $Mpi\text{-}1$ alleles. Heterozygosity at this locus higher than expected for strains with high coefficients of inbreeding.	87
Adipose Tissue						
Enzyme: Alkaline lipolytic activity	SGE at pH 7.0 of aqueous extracts of adipose tissue; zymograms developed with αNB. Isozyme patterns distinguish 3 phenotypes, although FF & Ff are very similar.	Family studies involving 3 generations reported	ALA [Autosomal; incomplete dominance of ALA^F. Gene dosage effect on activity.] [34, 112]	ALA^F; ALA^f	....	100
Miscellaneous Tissues						
Enzyme: Lysozyme [3.2.1.17]	Measurement of zone of lysis caused by tears or tissue extracts applied to plates of *Micrococcus luteus* [14] in agar; or determination of presence or absence of lysis of *M. luteus* [14] surrounding heterophiles & monocytes in blood-bacterial smears. Only 2 phenotypes, Ld & ld, observed. Heterozygotes not distinguishable by assays used.	Phenotype ld rabbits have either very low levels or absence of lysozyme activity in most tissues, with the exception of the thymus, where normal levels are found	Ld [Autosomal; deficiency of lysozyme activity is a recessive trait] [43, 97, 98]	Ld; ld	....	91

[14] Synonym: *M. lysodeikticus*.

Contributors: Alice Gilman-Sachs and W. Carey Hanly

References
1. Albers, J. J., and S. Dray. 1968. Biochem. Genet. 2: 25-35.
2. Albers, J. J., and S. Dray. 1969. J. Immunol. 103: 155-162.
3. Albers, J. J., and S. Dray. 1969. Ibid. 103:163-169.
4. Albers, L. V., et al. 1969. Biochemistry 8:4416-4424.
5. Amano, T., et al. 1974. Anim. Blood Groups Biochem. Genet. 5(Suppl. 1):21.
6. Augustinsson, K.-B. 1961. Ann. N.Y. Acad. Sci. 94: 844-860.
7. Berg, K., et al. 1971. Proc. Natl. Acad. Sci. USA 68: 905-908.
8. Berg, K., et al. 1975. J. Immunogenet. 2:79-85.
9. Berne, B. H., et al. 1970. J. Immunol. 105:856-864.
10. Berne, B. H., et al. 1971. Proc. Soc. Exp. Biol. Med. 138:531-535.
11. Berne, B. H., et al. 1972. Biochem. Genet. 7:95-110.
12. Berne, B. H., et al. 1973. Ibid. 8:175-186.
13. Bernoco, D. 1969. Atti Assoc. Genet. Ital. 15:226-227.
14. Best, J. S., et al. 1969. Hoppe-Seylers Z. Physiol. Chem. 350:563-580.
15. Binette, J. P., et al. 1965. Biochem. J. 94:143-149.
16. Biro, C. E., and G. Garcia. 1965. Immunology 8:411-419.
17. Biro, C. E., and M. L. Ortega. 1966. Arch. Inst. Cardiol. Mex. 36:166-168.
18. Boman, H., et al. 1972. Clin. Exp. Immunol. 11:297-303.
19. Børresen, A.-L. 1976. J. Immunogenet. 3:73-81.
20. Børresen, A.-L. 1976. Ibid. 3:83-89.
21. Børresen, A.-L. 1976. Ibid. 3:91-103.

continued

22. Børresen, A.-L. 1977. Ibid. 4:149-158.
23. Børresen, A.-L. 1978. Ibid. 5:13-23.
24. Børresen, A.-L., and T. J. Kindt. 1978. Ibid. 5:5-12.
25. Børresen, A.-L., et al. 1977. Ibid. 4:81-95.
26. Børresen, A.-L., et al. 1978. Ibid. 5:71-86.
27. Bowman, J. E., et al. 1967. Nature (London) 214: 1156-1158.
28. Bricker, J., and M. D. Garrick. 1974. Biochim. Biophys. Acta 351:437-441.
29. Carleer, J. Unpublished. Faculté de Medicine Veterinaire, Brussels, Belgium, 1978.
30. Chiao, J. W., and S. Dray. 1969. Biochem. Genet. 3: 1-13.
31. Coggan, M., et al. 1974. Aust. J. Biol. Sci. 27:671-675.
32. Coggan, M., et al. 1974. Anim. Blood Groups Biochem. Genet. 5(Suppl. 1):27.
33. Cohen, C., et al. 1968. Fed. Proc. Fed. Am. Soc. Exp. Biol. 27:275.
34. Cortner, J. A., and J. D. Schnatz. 1970. Biochem. Genet. 4:529-537.
35. Dawson, D. M., and S. Jaegar. 1970. Ibid. 4:1-9.
36. Duckworth, H. W., and B. D. Sanwal. 1972. Biochemistry 11:3182-3188.
37. Ellis, S. 1947. J. Pharmacol. Exp. Ther. 91:370-378.
38. Ellis, S. 1948. Ibid. 94:130-135.
39. Ferrell, R. E., et al. 1976. Fed. Proc. Fed. Am. Soc. Exp. Biol. 35:1659.
40. Ferrell, R. E., et al. 1978. Biochim. Biophys. Acta 533:1-11.
41. Fildes, R. A., and H. Harris. 1966. Nature (London) 209:261-263.
42. Fisher, R. A., et al. 1977. Ann. Hum. Genet. 41:139-149.
43. Fox, R. R. 1975. In R. C. King, ed. Handbook of Genetics. Plenum, New York. v. 4, pp. 309-328.
44. Frymoyer, J. W., and R. F. Jacox. 1963. J. Lab. Clin. Med. 62:891-904.
45. Frymoyer, J. W., and R. F. Jacox. 1963. Ibid. 62:905-909.
46. Funakoshi, S., and H. F. Deutsch. 1971. Comp. Biochem. Physiol. 39B:489-498.
47. Galizzi, A. 1970. Eur. J. Biochem. 17:49-55.
48. Galizzi, A. 1971. Nature (London) New Biol. 229: 142-143.
49. Garrick, M. D., et al. 1974. Genetics 76:99-108.
50. Garrick, M. D., et al. 1974. Ann. N.Y. Acad. Sci. 241: 436-438.
51. Gilman-Sachs, A., and K. L. Knight. 1972. Biochem. Genet. 7:177-191.
52. Gordon, G. R., et al. 1973. Xenobiotica 3:133-150.
53. Got, R., et al. 1965. Biochim. Biophys. Acta 107: 278-285.
54. Got, R., et al. 1967. Ibid. 136:320-330.
55. Grovier, W. C. 1965. J. Pharmacol. Exp. Ther. 150: 305-308.
56. Grunder, A. A. 1966. Genetics 54:1085-1093.
57. Grunder, A. A. 1968. Vox Sang. 14:218-223.
58. Grunder, A. A. 1968. Ibid. 14:236-240.
59. Grunder, A. A., et al. 1965. Genetics 52:1345-1353.
60. Grunder, A. A., et al. 1968. Anim. Prod. 10:221-222.

61. Hagen, K. L., and C. Cohen. Unpublished. Univ. Illinois Medical Center, Chicago, 1979.
62. Hagen, K. L., et al. 1978. Anim. Blood Groups Biochem. Genet. 9:151-159.
63. Hearse, D. J., and W. W. Weber. 1973. Biochem. J. 132:519-526.
64. Hirschhorn, R. 1977. Fed. Proc. Fed. Am. Soc. Exp. Biol. 36:2166-2170.
65. Hopkinson, D. A., et al. 1973. Ann. Hum. Genet. 37: 119-137.
66. Hrkal, Z., and U. Muller-Eberhárd. 1971. Biochemistry 10:1746-1750.
67. Hunter, T., and M. Munro. 1969. Nature (London) 223:1270-1272.
68. Johansson, M., and B. W. Karlsson. 1976. Comp. Biochem. Physiol. 54B:495-500.
69. Jones, N., et al. 1961. Biochem. J. 79:220-223.
70. Kelus, A. S. 1968. Nature (London) 218:595-596.
71. Knight, K. L. Unpublished. Univ. Illinois Medical Center, Chicago, 1979.
72. Knight, K. L., and S. Dray. 1968. Biochemistry 7: 1165-1171.
73. Knight, K. L., and S. Dray. 1968. Ibid. 7:3830-3835.
74. Kurosky, A., et al. 1975. Protides Biol. Fluids Proc. Colloq. 22:597-602.
75. Lachman, P. J. 1970. Ibid. 17:301-309.
76. Levy, J. 1946. C. R. Soc. Biol. 140:823-825.
77. Lombart, C., et al. 1965. Biochim. Biophys. Acta 97: 262-269.
78. Lombart, C., et al. 1965. Ibid. 97:270-274.
79. Margolis, F., and P. Feigelson. 1963. J. Biol. Chem. 238:2620-2627.
80. Margolis, F., and P. Feigelson. 1964. Biochim. Biophys. Acta 90:117-125.
81. McDermid, E. M., et al. 1975. Anim. Blood Groups Biochem. Genet. 6:127-174.
82. Mouray, H., et al. 1965. Biochim. Biophys. Acta 107: 286-293.
83. Muller-Eberhard, U., and H. H. Liem. 1974. In A. C. Allison, ed. Structure and Function of Plasma Proteins. Plenum, New York. v. 1, pp. 35-53.
84. Naik, S. N., and A. J. Baxi. 1970. 11th Eur. Conf. Anim. Blood Groups Biochem. Polymorphism Warsaw 1968, pp. 217-221.
85. Nelson, R. A., and C. E. Biro. 1968. Immunology 14: 527-540.
86. Nichols, E. A., and F. H. Ruddle. 1973. J. Histochem. Cytochem. 21:1066-1081.
87. Nichols, E. A., et al. 1973. Biochem. Genet. 8:47-53.
88. Noltman, E. A. 1964. J. Biol. Chem. 239:1545-1550.
89. Nomoto, S., et al. 1971. Biochemistry 10:1647-1651.
90. Oriol, R., and A. M. Dalix. 1977. Immunology 33:91-99.
91. Osserman, E. F., et al. 1975. Lysozyme. Academic, New York.
92. Parr, C. W., and L. Fitch. 1967. Ann. Hum. Genet. 30:339-353.
93. Parrington, J. M., et al. 1968. Ibid. 32:27-32.
94. Picard, J. J., et al. 1965. Protides Biol. Fluids Proc. Colloq. 12:353-362.

continued

95. Podack, E. R., et al. 1976. J. Immunol. 116:263-269.
96. Povey, S., et al. 1975. Ann. Hum. Genet. 39:203-212.
97. Prieur, D. J., et al. 1974. Fed. Proc. Fed. Am. Soc. Exp. Biol. 33:598.
98. Prieur, D. L., et al. 1974. Am. J. Pathol. 77:283-298.
99. Ramos, S. J. L., et al. 1972. 12th Eur. Conf. Anim. Blood Groups Biochem. Polymorphism Budapest 1970, pp. 657-660.
100. Rivello, R. C., et al. 1969. Proc. Soc. Exp. Biol. Med. 130:232-235.
101. Rother, K., et al. 1966. J. Exp. Med. 124:773-785.
102. Rother, U., and K. Rother. 1961. Z. Immunitaetsforsch. Exp. Ther. 121:224-232.
103. Rother, U., et al. 1967. J. Exp. Med. 126:565-579.
104. Ruoslahti, E., and I. J. T. Seppälä. 1970. Ann. Med. Exp. Biol. Fenn. 48:221-225.
105. Sawin, P. B., and D. Glick. 1943. Proc. Natl. Acad. Sci. USA 29:55-59.
106. Sawin, P. B., et al. 1944. Ibid. 30:217-221.
107. Schapira, G., et al. 1969. Biochim. Biophys. Acta 188:216-221.
108. Schiff, R. 1970. J. Histochem. Cytochem. 18:709-721.
109. Schiff, R. 1975. Proc. 3rd Int. Conf. Isozymes 1974, 3:775-797.
110. Schiff, R., and S. Jacobson. 1970. Genetics 64:s56-s57.
111. Schiff, R., and C. Stormont. 1970. Biochem. Genet. 4:11-23.
112. Schnatz, J. D., and J. A. Cortner. 1968. Biochim. Biophys. Acta 167:367-372.
113. Seery, V. L., et al. 1972. Arch. Biochem. Biophys. 150:269-272.
114. Shamsuddin, M., et al. 1973. Ibid. 158:922-924.
115. Skow, L. C., et al. 1978. J. Hered. 69:165-168.
116. Stormont, C., and Y. Suzuki. 1970. Science 167:200-202.
117. Stormont, C., and Y. Suzuki. 1975. Proc. 3rd Int. Conf. Isozymes 1974, 3:699-712.
118. Stuart, C. A., et al. 1936. J. Immunol. 31:25-30.
119. Suzuki, Y., and C. Stormont. 1972. 12th Eur. Conf. Anim. Blood Groups Biochem. Polymorphism Budapest 1970, pp. 653-655.
120. Tashian, R. E., and N. D. Carter. 1976. Adv. Hum. Genet. 7:1-56.
121. Tedesco, F., and P. J. Lachman. 1971. Clin. Exp. Immunol. 9:359-370.
122. Usher, D. C., et al. 1978. J. Immunol. 120:1832-1835.
123. Usher, D. C., et al. 1978. Immunogenetics 7:117-123.
124. Van der Weyden, M. B., and W. N. Kelley. 1977. Life Sci. 20:1645-1650.
125. van Zutphen, L. F. M. 1972. Enzymologia 42:201-208.
126. van Zutphen, L. F. M. 1974. Biochem. Genet. 12:309-326.
127. van Zutphen, L. F. M. 1974. Ibid. 12:327-343.
128. van Zutphen, L. F. M., and M. G. den Bieman. 1975. Ibid. 13:19-28.
129. Vergnes, H., et al. 1974. Anim. Blood Groups Biochem. Genet. 5:181-188.
130. von Ehrenstein, G. 1966. Cold Spring Harbor Symp. Quant. Biol. 31:705-714.
131. Weber, W. W. 1973. In W. H. Fishman, ed. Metabolic Conjugation and Metabolic Hydrolysis. Academic, New York. pp. 249-296.
132. Weber, W. W., et al. 1968. Ann. N.Y. Acad. Sci. 151:734-741.
133. Weber, W. W., et al. 1975. Proc. 3rd Int. Conf. Isozymes 1974, 4:813-828.
134. Weber, W. W., et al. 1976. Drug Metab. Dispos. 4:94-101.
135. Welch, S. G., et al. 1970. Biochem. J. 117:525-531.
136. Wheeler, K. M., et al. 1939. J. Immunol. 36:349-359.
137. Wright, C. I. 1941. J. Pharmacol. Exp. Ther. 71:164-177.
138. Wright, C. I. 1942. Ibid. 75:328-337.
139. Yankeelov, J. A., et al. 1974. Biochemistry 3:349-355.
140. Zech, R., and K. Zürcher. 1974. Comp. Biochem. Physiol. 48B:427-433.
141. Zweibaum, A., and E. Bouhou. 1973. Transplantation 15:291-293.
142. Zweibaum, A., and E. Bouhou. 1973. Biomedicine 19:544-546.
143. Fox, R. R., and L. F. M. van Zutphen. 1977. J. Hered. 68:227-230.

148. BLOOD GROUP SYSTEMS: RABBIT

Part I. Loci, Alleles, and Associated Typing Reagents

For further information on *Hg* locus, *see* Parts II and III of this table. Data in brackets refer to the column heading in brackets.

Locus	Alelles	Typing Reagents [Total No.]	No. of Phenotypes
Hg	Hg^A, Hg^D, Hg^F, Hg^N	Anti-A, anti-D, anti-F, anti-I, anti-J, anti-K, anti-N, anti-P, anti-R, anti-T, anti-V, anti-W [12]	10

continued

148. BLOOD GROUP SYSTEMS: RABBIT

Part I. Loci, Alleles, and Associated Typing Reagents

Locus	Alleles	Typing Reagents [Total No.]	No. of Phenotypes
Hb	Hb^B, Hb^M	Anti-B, anti-M [2]	3
Hc	Hc^C, Hc^L	Anti-C, anti-L [2]	3
He	He, he	Anti-E [1]	2
Hh	Hh, hh	Anti-H [1]	2
Hq	Hq^Q, Hq^S	Anti-Q, anti-S [2]	3
Hu	Hu^U, Hu^Y	Anti-U, anti-Y [2]	3

Contributor: Carl Cohen

Reference: Cohen, C., and R. G. Tissot. 1974. In S. H. Weisbroth, et al., ed. The Biology of the Laboratory Rabbit. Academic, New York. pp. 167-176.

Part II. Typing Results for Hg Blood Group System

Phenotype is equivalent to blood type.

Genotype	Reactions with Typing Sera												Phenotype
	Anti-A	Anti-D	Anti-F	Anti-I	Anti-J	Anti-K	Anti-N	Anti-P	Anti-R	Anti-T	Anti-V	Anti-W	
Hg^A/Hg^A	+	−	−	−	−	−	−	+	+	−	−	+[1]	A,P,R,W
Hg^A/Hg^D	+	+	−	+[1]	+	+	+	+	+	+[1]	+[1]	−	A,D,I,J,K,N,P,R,T,V
Hg^A/Hg^F	+	−	+	−	+[1]	+	−	+	+	+[1]	−	−	A,F,J,K,P,R,T
Hg^A/Hg^N	+	−	−	+[1]	+	+	+	+	+	+[1]	+[1]	−	A,I,J,K,N,P,R,T,V
Hg^D/Hg^D	−	+	−	−	+	+	+	−	+	−	−	−	D,J,K,N,R[2]
Hg^D/Hg^F	−	+	+	−	+	+	+	+	+	−	+[1]	−	D,F,J,K,N,P,R,V
Hg^D/Hg^N	−	+	−	−	+	+	+	−	+	−	−	−	D,J,K,N,R[2]
Hg^F/Hg^F	−	−	+	−	−	+	−	+	−	−	−	−	F,K,P
Hg^F/Hg^N	−	−	+	−	+	+	+	+	+	−	+[1]	−	F,J,K,N,P,R,V
Hg^N/Hg^N	−	−	−	−	+	+	+	−	+	−	−	−	J,K,N,R

[1] Interaction antigens. [2] Hg^D/Hg^D and Hg^D/Hg^N are not distinguishable by typing test.

Contributor: Carl Cohen

Reference: Cohen, C., et al. Unpublished. N.I.A.I.D., National Institutes of Health, Bethesda, MD, 1977.

Part III. Former Nomenclatures for Hg Blood Group System

Prior to 1962, the A, D, F, AD, AF, and DF phenotypes had other designations. They are shown below.

Genotype	Blood Type	Designation According to								
		Castle	Fischer	Marcussen	Kellner	Anderson	Joysey	Heard	Dahr	Ivanyi
Hg^A/Hg^A	A	H_2	K_1	Kb	g	A	B	Y	r_1	Hcsch
Hg^A/Hg^D [1]	ADI	H_2	K_1	.....	...	A	BC	YW	r_1	......

[1] "Gene interaction" antigen I found in this type of heterozygote.

continued

Part III. Former Nomenclatures for Hg Blood Group System

Genotype	Blood Type	Designation According to								
		Castle	Fischer	Marcussen	Kellner	Anderson	Joysey	Heard	Dahr	Ivanyi
Hg^A/Hg^F [2]	AFJ	H_1H_2	K_1K_2	KaKb	Gg	AB	AB	YZ	R_1r_1	Hc
Hg^D/Hg^D	D	O	O	Fn [3]	Fn [3]	O	C	W	O	......
Hg^D/Hg^F	DF	H_1	K_2	.....	...	B	AC	WZ	R_1	......
Hg^F/Hg^F	F	H_1	K_2	Ka	G	B	A	Z	R_1	HcN

[2] "Gene interaction" antigen J found in this type of heterozygote. [3] No O types reported.

Contributor: Carl Cohen

Reference: Cohen, C. 1962. Ann. N.Y. Acad. Sci. 97:26-36.

149. MAJOR HISTOCOMPATIBILITY COMPLEX: RABBIT

RLA Haplotypes 14-17 are reserved for the four haplotypes maintained in the East Grinstead Colony; haplotypes 18-20 are reserved for the three haplotypes maintained by the Polish Academy of Science. **Alleles:** *RLA-A* is a serologi-cally defined locus; *RLA-D* is a locus defined by the mixed leukocyte culture ⟨MLC⟩ test. **Source:** For full name, *see* list of HOLDERS at front of book.

RLA Haplo-type	Alleles		Strain	Source	Refer-ence
	RLA-A	*RLA-D*			
1	*RLA-A1*	*RLA-D1*	Fa5a [1], HIA [1]	UIGC	3-5
			Y1 [1]	FOX	2
2	*RLA-A2*	*RLA-D2*	Fa5a	UIGC	3-5
3	*RLA-A3*	*RLA-D3*	HIA, Sh9	UIGC	3-5
4	*RLA-A4*	*RLA-D2*	Non-inbred	UIGC	3-5
5	*RLA-A5*	*RLA-D4*	Sh1c	UIGC	3-5
6	*RLA-A6*	*RLA-D3*	Non-inbred	UIGC	3-5

RLA Haplo-type	Alleles		Strain	Source	Refer-ence
	RLA-A	*RLA-D*			
7	*RLA-A7*	*RLA-D4*	Sh5b, Sh5c	UIGC	3-5
8	*RLA-A8*	*RLA-D3*	Non-inbred	UIGC	3-5
9	*RLA-A9*	*RLA-D3*	Fa5a	UIGC	3-5
10	*RLA-A10*	*RLA-D2*	Sh16a	UIGC	1
11	*RLA-A11*	*RLA-D3*	B/J	FOX	2
12	*RLA-A12*	*RLA-D5*	Sh16a	UIGC	1
13	*RLA-A13*	*RLA-D4*	Non-inbred	UIGC	1

[1] This strain also carries *RLA-B1* allele. The *RLA-B* locus has been serologically defined for haplotype 1 only.

Contributors: Robert G. Tissot and David W. Lancki

References
1. Cohen, C. Unpublished. University Illinois, College Medicine, Chicago, 1976.
2. Fox, R. R. Unpublished. Jackson Laboratory, Bar Harbor, ME, 1979.
3. Lancki, D. W., et al. 1976. Fed. Proc. Fed. Am. Soc. Exp. Biol. 35:353.
4. Tissot, R. G., and C. Cohen. 1972. Tissue Antigens 2:267-279.
5. Tissot, R. G., and C. Cohen. 1974. Transplantation 18:142-149.

150. IMMUNOGLOBULIN ALLOTYPES: RABBIT

For additional information on rabbit immunoglobulin allo-types, consult references 27, 58, 63, 69, 83, 86, and 103.

At the present time, there is no single standardized system of nomenclature for rabbit immunoglobulin allotypes and

continued

corresponding genes. In this table, symbols for most of the loci are given in two forms. The first symbol listed will be either the symbol derived from the rules proposed at a workshop in 1962 [ref. 22], or the symbol used by the researchers in their original publication. The second symbol listed will be an alternate form of notation designed to convey information about the localization of the genetic markers on the polypeptide chains, when such information is available. For example, by the rules of the 1962 workshop, the symbols Aa^1, Aa^2, and Aa^3 designate alleles at the Aa locus, and the symbols, Aa1, Aa2, and Aa3 represent the corresponding allotypic specificities. For the alternate form of notation, the locus symbol would be V_Ha, the prefix V_H indicating that this locus controls synthesis of the variable region of the heavy chains.

In recent years, the prefix A, an abbreviation for allotypic specificity, or the prefix V_H has often been deleted from symbols and the short forms such as a1, a2, and a3 have been more frequently used. In interest of space, the symbols for alleles and allotypic specificities used in this table will most often be given in the short form; a prefix will be used in those instances where the short form notation might be confusing.

Identification Method: PEG = polyethylene glycol. **Strains, Stocks, or Colonies:** NZW = New Zealand White; NZW/FG = a closed colony derived from New Zealand White and Flemish Giant rabbits; PFG = Park Farm Grey, from Oxford University Farm, Northmoor, Oxon, U.K. **Holder:** For full name, *see* list of HOLDERS at front of book. *Abbreviations:* V = variable; C = constant; Ig = immunoglobulin; AA = amino acid; Fab = antigen-binding fragment; Fc = crystallizable fragment. Data in brackets refer to the column heading in brackets.

Proposed Genetic Control		Identification Method	Characteristics & Remarks	Strain, Stock, or Colony [Holder]	Reference
Locus & Alleles ⟨Synonym⟩ [Specificity]	Inheritance				
Heavy-Chain Variable Region					
Aa or V_Ha Considered as a simple locus: alleles a^1; a^2; a^3	Autosomal; classically behave as codominant alleles, with quantitative imbalance of expression in heterozygotes. Exceptions to allelic behavior have been noted with implications of complex loci & regulatory mechanisms controlling expression (*see* below). The V_Ha locus is part of the Ig heavy-chain chromosomal region (*see* Table 151).	Antigens in serum are most often identified by means of precipitating alloantisera in gel diffusion tests. Inhibition-of-hemagglutination or inhibition-of-precipitation type of assays are also used. More than one allotypic determinant constitutes a V_Ha allotypic specificity, and whereas a2 anti-a1, a3 anti-a1, & a2a3 anti-a1 each precipitate a1 molecules, the specificities of these antisera are not identical (*see* below).	The V_Ha allotypic specificities are present on the majority (70-90%) of IgG, IgA, & IgM molecules, as well as on IgE molecules, and are known to reside in the V-region of the heavy chains. The structural correlates of the serological specificities have not been positively identified, but 2 probable determinant sites are in the regions of residues 15-17 & 80-94. Several lines of evidence suggest a minimum of 2 determinant sites; the maximum is not known, but multiple AA differences exist between any 1 & the other 2 allotypes.	With rare exceptions, all domestic & laboratory rabbits tested have 1 or 2 of these 3 V_Ha allotypic specificities. The following allele-strain associations have been found in JAX strains: a^1 in C, IIIEP, IIIVO/*vpt*, & WH; a^2 in OS; a^3 in AC, ACEP, AX, B, & X. A geographic distribution of the a^1, a^2, & a^3 alleles has been noted in a study of Australian wild rabbits (*Oryctolagus*).	11, 20, 22, 23, 31, 32, 35, 36, 65, 75, 98, 101, 102, 111, 123, 133
Considered as a complex locus with respect to "framework" region only					
Alleles $a^1a^2a^3$; a^1a^2; a^1a^3; a^2a^3 [L/]	Proposed inheritance of a complex "V_Ha-locus" chromosomal region in all rabbits, with a normal mode of selected expres-	Precipitating alloantisera in gel diffusion studies identified relatively high levels of a1, a2, & a3 molecules in a single hyperimmunized rab-	The expression of low levels of "unexpected" or "latent" V_Ha allotypes was found in ∿50% of rabbits tested, and appeared to be an	....	96, 99, 115, 117, 118, 135,

L/ Individual genes of the hypothetical tandem-gene complexes are pseudoalleles for which expression is controlled by a system of regulator genes.

continued

Proposed Genetic Control		Identification Method	Characteristics & Remarks	Strain, Stock, or Colony [Holder]	Reference
Locus & Alleles ⟨Synonym⟩ [Specificity]	Inheritance				
	sion of only 1 V_Ha allotype per chromosome, and with expression controlled by another (regulator) locus with multiple alleles	bit. In addition, a sensitive inhibition-of-binding assay was used to detect very low levels of "unexpected" V_Ha allotypes.	intermittent phenomenon. From these studies, it appears that most rabbits carry genes for a1, a2, & a3, but that expression is regulated so that the apparent genotype, with regard to the V_Ha locus, actually reflects the genotype at a regulatory locus.		136
Alleles $a^1Ba^1Ca^1D;$ $a^2Ba^2Ca^2D;$ $a^3Ba^3Ca^3D$	Proposed inheritance in all rabbits of a complex "V_Ha locus" comprised of a family of related genes	Subpopulations of IgG bearing less than the full complement of alloantigenic specificities carried by unfractionated IgG of a particular V_Ha allotype have been identified by several experimental approaches: i) antibodies of restricted heterogeneity which are antigenically deficient have been used to fractionate alloantisera which thereafter discriminate among subpopulations; ii) soluble polymers of allo-antibodies used in gel diffusion studies form multiple precipitin bands with IgG of a single V_Ha allotype; iii) a2 anti-a3 cross-reacts with a subpopulation of a1 molecules, etc.; iv) AA sequencing studies of homogeneous antibodies & of IgG from a1, a2, or a3 rabbits suggest a complex "V_Ha locus."	Multiple lines of evidence have clearly identified subpopulations of a1, as well as a2 & a3, molecules. In at least some cases, the subpopulations have common as well as unique determinants. No comparative studies have yet been done among the various laboratories attempting with serologic methods to sort out and characterize the various subpopulations. Results of AA sequencing studies also strongly support the existence of families of a1, of a2, & of a3 molecules, but no comprehensive studies have yet been done to compare serologic behaviors of the various sequenced homogeneous antibodies with antisera directed against specific subpopulations of the V_Ha allotypes. These AA studies favor multiple V_Ha genes, but do not eliminate other mechanisms for superimposing variation within the framework regions of the V_H region. It should be noted that a complex locus need not be of the same size or composition in all members of a species.	The types of studies described have not progressed far enough to put major emphasis on associations of proposed gene complexes with strains of rabbits. However, it does appear that wild European rabbits have or express some different V_H gene complexes from those of domestic rabbits, and that these gene complexes may bridge the wide divergencies noted among the a^1, a^2, & a^3 families of genes. (See a^{100}.)	8,9, 53, 68, 92, 129
Alleles $a^{100};$ a^{101}	Data suggest control of a100 & a101 specificities by alleles a^{100} & a^{101} at the V_Ha locus alloantisera reacted by precipitation with some, but not all, serum samples of wild rabbits in gel diffusion studies, or interfacial (ring) precipitin tests in liquid media.	IgG samples from wild European rabbits, typed a1⁻, a2⁻, & a3⁻, were used to raise several alloantisera in domestic rabbits. Each of the	The a100 & a101 specificities have been localized to the V_H domain. Cross-reactions among a100, a1, & a3 molecules have been noted. Similar studies showed an absence of cross-reactivity of a101 with a1, a2, or a3.	The a100 specificity has been found in wild rabbits *Oryctolagus cuniculus cuniculus* & *O. cuniculus algirus,* whereas the a101 specificity has been found only in *O. cuniculus cuniculus* thus far. These specificities have not been identified in domestic rabbits.	9,10, 12- 14

continued

Proposed Genetic Control		Identification Method	Characteristics & Remarks	Strain, Stock, or Colony [Holder]	Reference
Locus & Alleles ⟨Synonym⟩ [Specificity]	Inheritance				
[A102, A103, A104]	Preliminary data from population surveys suggest that these 3 recently identified allotypic specificities are controlled by additional alleles at the V_Ha locus. Such studies have also suggested a complex nature of the V_Ha locus.	Alloantisera react with serum or IgG by precipitation with samples from European wild rabbits (*Oryctolagus cuniculus algirus*)	Whereas cross-reactions among the V_Ha-subgroup allotypes are not usually observed in assay systems dependent on direct precipitation with alloantisera, cross-reactions are observed when assessed by more sensitive binding assays. These newly identified V_Ha-subgroup allotypes in wild rabbits are reported to cross-react with a1 and/or a3 of domestic rabbits.	Studies on European wild rabbits	9,10
[Ts4-1 peptide; Ts4-3 peptide]	In family studies of 38 rabbits, these Ts4 peptides behaved as though controlled by alleles. Results were concordant with a1 & a3 serotypes; i.e., Ts4-1 from a1 IgG & Ts4-3 from a3 IgG.	Peptide mapping of Cys-radiolabeled CNBr-tryptic peptides to achieve differential mobilities of the Ts4 peptides (residues 80-94) derived from a1 & a3 molecules	The relationship of these structural variants to the serological specificities a1 & a3 is not entirely clear, since a2 & a3 molecules have the same sequence in the region studied	Studies on a family of rabbits descended from an a^1/a^1 NZW ♂ & 2 a^3/a^3 PFG ♀. (The PFG rabbits [OXF] are highly inbred.)	97
[A31]	....	An a^1/a^1 C/J strain rabbit immunized with V_Ha-negative IgG molecules (obtained from an a^2/a^2 rabbit suppressed in utero with a1 anti-a2) produced antiserum which precipitated a portion of Ig of some, but not all, rabbits	The anti-A31 reacted with serum samples to produce 0, 1, 2, or 3 precipitin bands in agar gel, depending on the sample tested. Two of the specificities in this antiserum were later identified as x32 & y33 (*see* below).	NZW/FG [UIMC] used for production of V_Ha-negative IgG	70
Ax or V_Hx: alleles x^{32}; x^-	Autosomal. Family studies were consistent with the existence of an x^- allele, although only x^{32} has been identified directly. V_Hx locus is closely linked to, but distinct from, the V_Ha locus.	Antigen in serum identified by means of precipitating alloantiserum in gel diffusion studies. Immunogen used to elicit the antiserum was from a V_Ha-immunosuppressed rabbit which expressed V_Ha-negative IgG in high concentrations.	V_Hx locus is believed to control one of the minor V_H subgroups of the rabbit. The x32 specificity is found on a minor subpopulation of IgG molecules distinct from subpopulations bearing V_Ha or V_Hy specificities. It has also been found on IgM & IgA molecules, and allotypic determinants are presumed to reside in the V_H region.	Studies on NZW/FG colony [UIMC], but the x32 specificity has also been observed in random samples from other sources	61,62

continued

Proposed Genetic Control		Identification Method	Characteristics & Remarks	Strain, Stock, or Colony [Holder]	Ref-er-ence
Locus & Alleles ⟨Synonym⟩ [Specificity]	Inheritance				
Ay or $V_H y$: alleles y^{33}; y^-	Autosomal. Family studies are consistent with the existence of a y^- allele, although only y^{33} has been identified directly. The $V_H y$ locus is closely linked to the $V_H a$ locus.	Antigen in serum (or cells) identified by means of precipitating alloantiserum in gel diffusion studies (or by immunofluorescent studies)	$V_H y$ locus is believed to control one of the minor V_H subgroups of the rabbit. The specificities representative of the 3 serologically identified subgroups ($V_H a$, $V_H x$, & $V_H y$) are found on separate subpopulations of molecules; the $V_H x$ & $V_H y$ subpopulations are members of the so-called $V_H a$-negative molecules.	Studies on NZW/FG colony [UIMC]. y33 specificity has also been observed in random samples from other sources.	61, 62, 74
[A50]	Limited family & population studies are consistent with control by a single locus different from $V_H a$, κb, & λc	An a^3/a^3 rabbit immunized with $V_H a$-negative IgG (obtained from an a^2/a^2 rabbit suppressed in utero with a1 anti-a2) produced antiserum which precipitated a portion of Ig of some, but not all, rabbits	The anti-A50 antiserum reacted with all 35 a^1/a^1 samples & with all 34 a^1/a^2 or a^1/a^3 heterozygotes, but reacted with only 18-27% of a^2/a^2, a^3/a^3, or a^2/a^3 samples. This antiserum may identify a minor V_H subgroup. No comparative studies of A50 with x32 or y33 have been done.	....	131
IgG: γ-Chain Constant Region					
Ad or $C_\gamma d$ [2/]: alleles d^{11}; d^{12}	Autosomal, codominant homoalleles. Part of the Ig heavy-chain chromosomal region, which includes V_H loci & other C_H loci.	Erythrocytes coated with d11 or d12 antigen react by agglutination with complementary alloantisera. Inhibition of this agglutination by serum or IgG is used to type rabbits. Anti-$C_\gamma d$ alloantisera do not usually form precipitating complexes with the complementary IgG antigens.	The d11 & d12 specificities correlate with a single AA interchange (Met/Thr) at position N-225 [3/] of the γ-chain hinge region. The $C_\gamma d$ specificities require an intact heavy-chain—heavy-chain disulfide bond for expression. The d11 & d12 have each been found in association with a1, a2, & a3 in various populations of rabbits, although $V_H a$ & $C_\gamma d$ are closely linked. $C_\gamma d$ specificities are also associated with $V_H a$-negative IgG molecules. Two germ-line recombinations between the $V_H a$ & $C_\gamma d$ loci have been reported.	The d^{11} & d^{12} alleles both occur in many breeds of rabbits, including wild *Oryctolagus* of Australia & central France. However, the $a^2 d^{11}$ haplotype does not appear to be common to many colonies in the USA.	1,48, 64, 66, 89-91, 94, 95, 107, 119, 139
Ae or $C_\gamma e$ [2/]: alleles e^{14}; e^{15}	Autosomal, codominant homoalleles. Part of the Ig heavy-chain chromosomal region.	A hemagglutination-inhibition assay, similar to that used for detection of d11 & d12 specificities, is most often used for typing e14 & e15. Typing can also be done by double diffusion in agar gel containing PEG. An assay uti-	An AA interchange (Thr/Ala) at position N-309 [3/] of the $C_H 2$ domain correlates with the e14 & e15 specificities. However, the actual determinants appear to be more complex, since in some other lago-	The e^{14} & e^{15} alleles both occur in many breeds of rabbits, although the e^{15} allele appears to be more frequent in many colonies. In a survey of a random-bred (panmictic) population in Ontario, Canada, all $V_H a$-	4,15, 16, 25-29, 33, 78, 85, 119, 120, 124

[2/] A sublocus. [3/] Numbering system based on residue numbers of human myeloma protein EU [ref. 21].

continued

Proposed Genetic Control		Identification Method	Characteristics & Remarks	Strain, Stock, or Colony [Holder]	Reference
Locus & Alleles ⟨Synonym⟩ [Specificity]	Inheritance				
	lizing cross-linked allo-antisera has been used for quantitation.	morph species, the e15 specificity can be divided into "i" & "j" subspecificities. e14 & e15 have each been found in association with a1, a2, & a3 (& e15 with V_Ha-negative) in various populations of rabbits, although V_Ha & $C_\gamma e$ are closely linked. A germ-line recombinant between the V_Ha & $C_\gamma e$ loci has been reported.	$C_\gamma e$ haplotypes except a^3e^{14} were found, but this haplotype has been found in the colony of IPP. The a^1e^{14} haplotype appears to be more frequent than the a^2e^{14}; however, the latter haplotype occurred anew in the described V_Ha—$C_\gamma e$ recombinant.	
Ade or *$C_\gamma de$*: alleles $de^{11,15}$; $de^{12,14}$; $de^{12,15}$	The $C_\gamma d$ & $C_\gamma e$ "subloci" are both within the $C_\gamma de$ locus for the constant region of the γ-chain. Only 3 of the 4 possible haplotypes have been documented in laboratory rabbits.	The $C_\gamma d$ & $C_\gamma e$ specificities are usually identified individually. It is possible to raise antisera directed against both d11 & e15 (or both d12 & e14), and these doubly specific antisera should be distinguished from monospecific antisera.	Each individual IgG molecule has 1 of the $C_\gamma d$ & 1 of the $C_\gamma e$ specificities	Each of the 3 documented $C_\gamma de$ haplotypes has been found in a number of breeds & colonies in the USA [e.g., NIHR, UIMC, UTA] & in Europe. Preliminary evidence for the $d^{11}e^{14}$ haplotype has been found in 1 population of Australian wild rabbits (*Oryctolagus*).	15,48
[A8]	The A8 specificity is controlled by a locus closely linked to the V_Ha locus; it has been found primarily in association with the a1 allotype	A8 was detected by an extra antibody specificity in some "anti-a1" antisera. These anti-a1 + anti-A8 antisera reacted (gel double diffusion) with some a1 serum samples to give 2 precipitin bands.	A8 may be identical to e14. Anti-A8 (prepared from anti-a1 + anti-A8 antiserum by immunosorption) binds to the Fc portion of A8 IgG molecules, but does not usually form precipitating complexes unless other antibodies also react with the same IgG molecules to convert the soluble complexes to precipitating complexes.	....	43-47, 88
[A10]	The A10 specificity is controlled by a locus closely linked to the V_Ha locus	A10 was detected by an extra antibody specificity in some "anti-a" antisera. The detection system used was similar to that for A8.	A10 may be identical to d11	....	44,88
xg or *$C_\gamma xg$*: alleles xg^+; xg^-	The $C_\gamma xg$ specificity behaves as a marker for a locus linked to the V_Ha locus. The xg^+ allele may be found in coupling with a^1, a^2, or a^3 in various rabbit families.	Originally, antisera to the $C_\gamma xg$ specificity were made by injecting a3b4 IgG mixed with somatic antigen of *Salmonella typhi* or *S. enteritidis*[4/] into other a3b4 rabbits. The xg+ serum samples give a	The xg+ specificity is found in all e14 rabbits tested, and only in e14 rabbits, but the specificity appears to be comprised of an additional determinant, in or near the hinge region (on F(ab')₂),	[IPP]	81, 82, 104

[4/] Synonym: *S. abortus-equi.*

continued

Proposed Genetic Control		Identification Method	Characteristics & Remarks	Strain, Stock, or Colony [Holder]	Reference
Locus & Alleles ⟨Synonym⟩ [Specificity]	Inheritance				
		reaction of precipitation at the interface of liquid media with such alloantisera.	which appears to be of a carbohydrate nature since carbohydrate can inhibit the reaction. Precipitating reactions of different anti-xg antisera may be inhibited by different polysaccharides, which may or may not be the polysaccharide used as the adjuvant.		

IgG: γ-Chain Constant Region Carbohydrate

$A90$ [A90]	Inheritance of genetic units controlling the A90 specificity appears to follow a simple Mendelian pattern. The $A90$ locus is not closely linked to the Ig heavy-chain chromosomal region or to κb.	Anti-A90 alloantiserum reacted by precipitation with soluble aggregates of IgG, as observed in gelled media or at the interface of liquid media	2 phenotypes of rabbits have been identified: A90+ & A90−; heterozygotes cannot be distinguished. The A90 specificity appears to be carried by the carbohydrate moiety attached to the $C_\gamma 1$ domain of IgG. This specificity has also been found in IgG samples from some other species. The proportion of rabbit IgG bearing A90 is at a maximum in young rabbits 1-4 mo of age.		109

IgA: α-Chain Constant Region

$Af\underline{5/}$ or $C_\alpha f$: alleles f^{69}; f^{70}; f^{71}; f^{72}; f^{73}	Autosomal, codominant alleles. The $C_\alpha f$ locus is part of the Ig heavy-chain chromosomal region.	Antigens in serum or secretions identified by means of precipitating alloantisera in gel diffusion studies	The IgA-f subclass is resistant to proteolytic cleavage. Each $C_\alpha f$ allotype has multiple alloantigenic determinants, some of which may be common to other $C_\alpha f$ allotypes; consequently, alloantisera prepared in rabbits with different genetic backgrounds behave differently.	Each of these $C_\alpha f$ & $C_\alpha g$ allotypes have been identified in rabbits obtained from a number of sources, including commercial breeders, and all are present in the breeding colony at UIMC. The f^{73} allele is generally rare in the populations surveyed, and was not found in any of 15 JAX strains in a 1977 survey of 4-6 rabbits of each strain. For more information, see Table 151.	18, 19, 24, 49, 50, 69, 71, 73, 76, 77, 87, 106, 125
$Ag\underline{5/}$ or $C_\alpha g$: alleles g^{74}; g^{75}; g^{76}; g^{77}	Autosomal, codominant alleles. The $C_\alpha g$ locus is part of the Ig heavy-chain chromosomal region.	Antigens in serum or secretions identified by means of precipitating alloantisera in gel diffusion studies	The IgA-g subclass is cleaved by papain, trypsin, & elastase into $Fc_{2\alpha}$ & $Fab_{2\alpha}$ fragments. Each $C_\alpha g$ allotype has multiple alloantigenic determinants, some of which may be common to other $C_\alpha g$ allotypes. The g74 & g75 specificities have been divided into subspecificities g74.1, g74.2, and g75.1, g75.2. The .1 & .2 subspecificities reside in the $C_\alpha 1$ domain and $Fc_{2\alpha}$ region, respectively.		
[c1]	....	Antigen in serum or whey identified by means of precipitating alloantiserum in gel diffusion studies	Limited study. Marker associated with a2 IgA molecules & with a3 and/or a1 IgA molecules. Not on Fab portion of papain-digested IgA molecules. No comparative studies of this marker & the $C_\alpha f$ & $C_\alpha g$ markers have been done.	....	93

$\underline{5/}$ In early reports, the Ag or $C_\alpha g$ locus was not distinguished from the Af or $C_\alpha f$ locus.

continued

Proposed Genetic Control		Identification Method	Characteristics & Remarks	Strain, Stock, or Colony [Holder]	Reference
Locus & Alleles ⟨Synonym⟩ [Specificity]	Inheritance				
Secretory IgA: Secretory Component					
t: alleles t^{61}; t^{62}	Autosomal; behave as codominant alleles. With limited studies, no close linkage to the Ig heavy-chain chromosomal region or to the κb locus was apparent.	Antigens in tears or milk identified by alloantisera in gel diffusion studies. Weak precipitin bands were enhanced with an anti-rabbit IgG reagent.	Alloantisera react with complementary antigens, either secretory IgA or free secretory component. Contribution of polypeptide chain & carbohydrate to antigenic determinants is not clear.	Limited study on NZW/ FG colony [UIMC]	72
IgM: μ-Chain Constant Region					
An [6] or $C_\mu n$ [7]: alleles n^{80}; n^{81} (also n^{82}, n^{83}, & n^{84} [8])	Autosomal, codominant alleles. This locus is part of the Ig heavy-chain chromosomal region.	Alloantigens in serum are identified by means of precipitating alloantisera in gel diffusion studies. PEG incorporated into the gel enhances precipitation of immune complexes.	A total of 7 alloantigenic specificities associated with rabbit IgM have been identified. The n80 & n81 are major specificities, and the corresponding alleles, n^{80} & n^{81}, have each been found in coupling with each of the 3 major $V_H a$ locus alleles, a^1, a^2, & a^3, in different rabbit families. Each of 5 additional $C_\mu n$ specificities identified—n82, n83, n84, n85, & n86—have been found in association with only 1 of the 3 major $V_H a$ allotypes. These latter specificities appear to relate to the conformational specificities of the Ms series. Comparison of reagents between investigators indicated that n80 ≅ Ms17, n81 ≅ Ms16, n82 ≅ Ms25, n83 ≅ Ms24, n85 ≅ Ms23, & n86 ≅ Ms26 (see Table 151).	(See Table 151)	38-40, 83
Ms or $C_\mu Ms$ [9]: alleles Ms^{16}; Ms^{17} [Ms21; Ms23; Ms24; Ms25 [10]]	Autosomal, codominant alleles	Alloantigens in serum identified by means of precipitating antisera in gel diffusion studies, or by radioimmunoassay	The Ms^{16} & Ms^{17} alleles have each been found in coupling with each of the 3 major $V_H a$ locus alleles, a^1, a^2, & a^3, in different rabbit families. Each of the specificities Ms21, Ms23, Ms24, & Ms25 is restricted in its association with $V_H a$ specificities; they are considered to be conformational specificities resulting from the following combinations of $V_H a$ & Ms allotypic specificities: a1 + Ms16 = Ms21; a2 + Ms16 = Ms22 [11]; a3 + Ms16 = Ms23; a1 + Ms17 = Ms24; a2 + Ms17 = Ms25; and a3 + Ms17 = Ms26 [11];	(See Table 151)	83, 100
[Ms1]	All Ms1(+) rabbits are a3(+), but not all a3(+) rabbits are Ms1(+). Limited	Antigen in serum identified by means of precipitating alloantiserum in gel diffusion studies,	Anti-Ms1 antiserum, raised in an a3b4b5 recipient in response to injection of a3b4	Of 305 samples from BII colony, 19% carried the Ms1 marker (1971)	57,59

[6] The symbol An used here to denote a locus controlling the synthesis of the constant region of an Ig μ-chain bears no relationship to the An locus of the A-antigen system listed on p. 581 of Table 147. [7] Probably identical to the $C_\mu Ms$ locus identified by a different group of investigators (see next entry). [8] n^{82}, n^{83}, and n^{84} have been described as alleles at the $C_\mu n$ locus, but more recent data suggest alternate interpretations (see column 4). [9] Probably identical to the $C_\mu n$ locus identified by a different group of investigators (see preceding entry). [10] Related specificities. [11] Postulated but not yet identified by alloantisera.

continued

Proposed Genetic Control		Identification Method	Characteristics & Remarks	Strain, Stock, or Colony [Holder]	Reference
Locus & Alleles ⟨Synonym⟩ [Specificity]	Inheritance				
	family studies are consistent with linkage of the locus controlling the Ms1 specificity to the V_Ha locus.	but low concentration of IgM in serum gives some false negatives	anti-*Proteus* antibody, reacts with IgM only. Ms1 marker may be on the constant region of the μ-chain, but is possibly a conformational variant of the a3 imposed by the C_μ region.		
[Ms2]	....	Antigen in serum identified by means of precipitating alloantiserum in gel diffusion studies	Ms2 is found only on IgM molecules, and appears to be different from Ms1, Ms3 [12], Ms4, & Ms5	Of BII colony rabbits tested, 20% carried the Ms2 marker (1971)	59, 110
[Ms4]	Possible linkage of the implied locus to V_Ha locus, but no documentation of inheritance. Apparent association of Ms4 with a3 allotype only.	Antigen in serum identified by means of precipitating alloantiserum in gel diffusion studies. Antigen associated with cells identified by immunofluorescence. Gel diffusion tests probably result in many false negatives.	Ms4 marker was associated with a3(+) IgM cells in an a^2/a^3 heterozygote. Isolated μ-chains adsorb out anti-Ms4 activity; light chains do not.	[BII]	59, 105
[Ms5]	....	....	May be very similar to Ms4; Ms4 & Ms5 not distinguished by limited immunofluorescent antibody studies on cells	[BII]	59
[Ms6]	Possible linkage of implied locus to V_Ha locus, but no documentation of inheritance	Antigen in serum identified by means of precipitating alloantiserum in gel diffusion studies. Antigen associated with cells identified by immunofluorescence.	Limited studies. Ms6 shown to be different from Ms3 [12], Ms4, & Ms5; presumed to be different from Ms1 since Ms6 was found associated with either a1 or a3. Isolated μ-chains adsorb out anti-Ms6 activity; light chains do not.	....	59, 105

κ Light Chains: Constant Region

Proposed Genetic Control		Identification Method	Characteristics & Remarks	Strain, Stock, or Colony [Holder]	Reference
Ab or *κb*, considered as a simple locus [13]; Alleles b^{4-1} [14]; b^{4-2} [14]	b^{4-1} & b^{4-2} behave as alleles at the *κb* locus	Alloantisera elicited by b4 IgM in other b4 rabbits react with IgM from some, but not all, b4 rabbits in gel diffusion studies	The preliminary report of these 2 different "b^4" alleles suggests that anti-Ms3 (now b4-1) & anti-Ms11 (now b4-2) actually distinguish inherited differences of κ-chains rather than μ-chains, since the anti-Ms3 also distinguishes between b4-1 & b4-2 types of IgG in a competitive binding assay	Study on colony rabbits [VUB]	128

[12] Now listed under Ig κ light chains κb locus, allele b^{4-1}.
[13] The κb locus belongs to linkage group VIII, and maps between the *Lpq* locus and the *Prt* locus (*see* p. 570) [ref. 126, 127]. [14] Subtle differences have been detected among b4 κ-chains, suggesting that the classical "b^4 allele" may be one of several closely related alleles [ref. 114, 128].

continued

Proposed Genetic Control		Identification Method	Characteristics & Remarks	Strain, Stock, or Colony [Holder]	Reference
Locus & Alleles ⟨Synonym⟩ [Specificity]	Inheritance				
[Ms3]	Appears to be genetically linked to κb locus by association of b4 & Ms3, but not all b4 rabbits are Ms3(+)	Antigen in serum identified by means of precipitating alloantiserum in gel diffusion studies. Antigen associated with cells identified by immunofluorescence.	Ms3 is present only on IgM molecules as detected by immunodiffusion studies, and present in IgM plasma cells. Ms3 is always associated with b4 type IgM. Ms3 is found in a1, a2, or a3 rabbits. Ms3 appears to be specified by a conformational determinant of the b4-1 allotype light chain, imposed by association of b4-1 light chains & μ-chains.	Among b4(+) rabbits, Ms3(+) rabbits greatly exceed Ms3(−) rabbits [BII]	59, 128
Alleles $b^{4\text{-}prototype}$[14]; $b^{4\text{-}var}$[14]	Inheritance pattern is consistent with autosomal codominant alleles _____ inherited sequence variations involving residues 121 & 124: prototype = Ala—Gln; var = Ser—Leu. The b4-prototype & b4-var can also be distinguished by a radioimmunoassay with selected antisera.	AA sequence studies of the C-region of b4 κ_B chains from some members of an 8-generation rabbit family identified	The serologic differences between b4-prototype & b4-var are detected only when the light chains are combined with heavy chains (IgG). The b4-prototype & b4-variant may correspond to b4-1 & b4-2, respectively.	....	5,17, 112-114, 116

κ Light Chains: Constant Region, or Constant and Variable Regions					
Ab or κb, considered as a simple locus[13] Alleles b^4[14]; b^5; b^6; b^9	Autosomal, codominant alleles, with quantitative imbalance of expression in heterozygotes. No apparent close linkage to Ig heavy-chain chromosomal region, light-chain λc locus, *Hph*, or *Mtz*. Exceptions to allelic behavior have been noted (*see* below).	Antigens in serum most often identified by means of precipitating alloantisera in gel diffusion studies. Assays utilizing inhibition of hemagglutination or inhibition of antibody binding are also used.	The κ chains are the major type of light chain expressed in the rabbit (70-90%). Each κb allotype has multiple alloantigenic determinants, some of which may be common to other κb allotypes; consequently, alloantisera prepared in rabbits with different genetic backgrounds may behave differently. At least some, if not all, of the determinants appear to be located in the constant region, but some data suggest V-region allotype-related residues as well. Structural correlates of the serologically detected allotypic determinants are not yet clear.	The b^6 allele, identified in European laboratory rabbits, was not common in American laboratory rabbit colonies until its purposeful introduction & expansion in the mid-1960's. The b^9 allele, originally identified in Toronto, is rare in European rabbit colonies, but more common in European wild rabbits. This allele is now carried in a number of rabbit colonies in the USA. Neither b^6 nor b^9 is carried by any of the JAX strains. Wild rabbits of Australia lack b^6, and there is a skewed geographic distribution of b^9.	3,5, 10, 12, 17, 20, 22, 23, 30-32, 37, 42, 67, 79, 101, 102, 116

[13] The κb locus belongs to linkage group VIII, and maps between the *Lpq* locus and the *Prt* locus (*see* p. 570) [ref. 126, 127]. [14] Subtle differences have been detected among b4 κ-chains, suggesting that the classical "b^4 allele" may be one of several closely related alleles [ref. 114, 128].

continued

Proposed Genetic Control		Identification Method	Characteristics & Remarks	Strain, Stock, or Colony [Holder]	Reference
Locus & Alleles ⟨Synonym⟩ [Specificity]	Inheritance				
[A93; A94; A95; A96]	Only A95 has been studied sufficiently to determine inheritance pattern. This specificity is under control of an allele at the κb locus.	Antisera raised against classical κb allotypes show unusual patterns of cross-reactivity with IgG from wild European rabbits. Cross-reactions are visualized by double diffusion in gelled or liquid media, or by binding assays.	These "new" allotypic specificities of the κb series were discovered in a population of wild rabbits *Oryctolagus cuniculus algirus* from an island in Tunisia	....	10
κ Light Chains: Constant and Variable Regions					
Ab or κb, considered as a complex locus Alleles $b^4b^5b^6b^9$; $b^4b^5b^6$; $b^4b^5b^9$; b^4b^5, etc. [L/]	Proposed inheritance of a complex "κb-locus" chromosomal region in all rabbits, with a normal mode of selected expression of only 1 κb allotype per chromosome (expression controlled by another locus with multiple alleles)	Precipitating alloantisera used in Ouchterlony analyses & radial diffusion tests identified the simultaneous presence of b4, b5, & b6 in multiple serum samples from a hyperimmunized rabbit	In the original study, ... unexpected b6 allotype in a hyperimmunized rabbit was expressed intermittently, but often in significant quantity ($\sim$12% of IgG). The b4 & b5 were expressed continuously. The C regions of b4 & b9 κ chains show only $\sim$65% homology, suggesting a complexity greater than that of alleles in the conventional sense. It should be noted that a complex locus does not have to be of the same size or composition in all members of a species. Low levels of latent or unexpected κb allotypes have been found in many rabbits by several investigators. In some, but not all, cases, "Lepore"-type κb chains could be responsible for reactions presumed due to expression of latent allotypes.		34, 52, 80, 96, 117, 134, 136, 137
κ_A & κ_B as isotypes	All rabbits appear to have both κ_A & κ_B light chains, irrespective of κb allotype, although the ratio $\kappa_A{:}\kappa_B$ (here designated ρ) varies with the κb allotype: $\rho_{b9} >>> \rho_{b6} \geqslant \rho_{b5} \geqslant \rho_{b4}$	Molecular sieving of mildly reduced & alkylated IgG in a dissociating medium separates κ_A & κ_B chains. Most notable among AA composition differences is that κ_A contains 5 Cys and κ_B contains 7 Cys.	Information on κ_A chains is limited, but both κ_A & κ_B seem to bear the same κb allotypic specificities. The κ chains appear to be controlled by a complex locus since one of the extra Cys residues in κ_B chains is in the V region and one is in the C region, and since κ chains with 6 Cys do not appear to exist, implying regulation of V-C joining to match $V\kappa_A$ to $C\kappa_A$ & $V\kappa_B$ to $C\kappa_B$.	....	108, 122, 138
κ Light Chains: Variable Region					
V_κ, considered as a complex locus with regard to "framework" regions only	Proposed inheritance of a family of V-region genes, with the implication of allelic sets, and with the further implica-	AA sequence studies of κ chains from homogeneous antibodies and from IgG of defined κb allotypic specificities have shown multi-	Comparisons of sequences obtained thus far show patterns of similarities & differences which indicate subgroups and imply	....	6,7, 51, 52, 54-56, 67,

L/ Individual genes of the hypothetical tandem-gene complexes are pseudoalleles for which expression is controlled by a system of regulator genes.

continued

Proposed Genetic Control		Identification Method	Characteristics & Remarks	Strain, Stock, or Colony [Holder]	Reference
Locus & Alleles ⟨Synonym⟩ [Specificity]	Inheritance				
	tion that a distinct allelic set is inherited with each different κb allele; i.e., close linkage of V_K & C_K, with a limited number of haplotypes	ple possible sequences for the V-region framework	multiple V-region genes. Different subgroups of κ chains differ in length at the N-terminus and/or at specific framework residues. A further complexity is that allotype-related residues appear to exist in the V region. Selective breeding appears to narrow variability in framework residues of antibodies elicited with streptococcal polysaccharides, which is consistent with inheritance of allelic sets of V-region genes.		121, 122, 132
λ Light Chains					
Ac or λc: alleles c^7; c^{21}; or c^7, c^{21}	Autosomal; c^7 & c^{21} behave as codominant alleles in some families, & as pseudoalleles in other families. Available data suggest that at least some rabbits have a complex λc locus.	Antigens in serum identified by means of precipitating alloantisera in gel diffusion studies. It is not known whether the antisera identify V_λ^- and/or C_λ^- region markers.	The λ chains comprise a small percentage (5-30%) of the light chains in most rabbits; thus Ig used as immunogen to elicit anti-λc is often obtained from κ-chain-"suppressed" rabbits. Quantitative data on percentages of molecules bearing the various specificities are insufficient to describe the nature of the λc locus, but c7 & c21 specificities are found on separate populations of Ig in the rabbits tested.	A limited survey of some JAX strains suggested the following allele-strain associations: c^7 in AC, B, C, OS, WH, & X; c^{21} in in ACEP; & c^7c^{21} in AX, AXBU, IIIVO/ah, & IIIVO/vpt. All 3 haplotypes defined thus far are present in the UIMC colony. A new strain, Bas [BII], expressing primarily λ light chains has recently been described.	2,23, 41, 60, 84, 130

Contributors: W. Carey Hanly and Alice Gilman-Sachs

References

1. Aggarawal, S. J., and W. J. Mandy. 1976. Immunochemistry 13:215-220.
2. Appella, E., et al. 1968. Proc. Natl. Acad. Sci. USA 60:975-981.
3. Appella, E., et al. 1969. J. Mol. Biol. 41:473-477.
4. Appella, E., et al. 1971. Proc. Natl. Acad. Sci. USA 68:1341-1345.
5. Appella, E., et al. 1973. Biochem. Biophys. Res. Commun. 53:1122-1129.
6. Braun, D. G., and J.-C. Jaton. 1973. Immunochemistry 10:387-395.
7. Braun, D. G., et al. 1976. Eur. J. Immunol. 6:570-578.
8. Brézin, C., and P.-A. Cazenave. 1975. Immunochemistry 12:241-247.
9. Brézin, C., and P.-A. Cazenave. 1976. Ann. Immunol. (Inst. Pasteur) 127C:333-346.
10. Brézin, C., et al. 1979. Ibid. 130C:167-178.
11. Cannon, L. E., et al. 1977. Immunogenetics 4:422.
12. Cazenave, P.-A., and C. Brézin. 1976. Eur. J. Immunol. 6:262-269.
13. Cazenave, P.-A., and J. Roland. 1976. Ann. Immunol. (Inst. Pasteur) 127C:317-332.
14. Cazenave, P.-A., et al. 1974. Biochem. Biophys. Res. Commun. 61:664-670.
15. Cazenave, P.-A., et al. 1977. Immunogenetics 4:489-498.
16. Cazenave, P.-A., et al. 1977. Ann. Immunol. (Inst. Pasteur) 128C:323-327.
17. Chen, K. C. S., et al. 1974. Proc. Natl. Acad. Sci. USA 71:1995-1998.
18. Conway, T. P., et al. 1969. J. Immunol. 102:544-554.
19. Conway, T. P., et al. 1969. Ibid. 103:662-667.

continued

20. Curtain, C. C., et al. 1973. Anim. Blood Groups Biochem. Genet. 4:101-109.
21. Dayhoff, M. O. 1972. Atlas of Protein Sequence and Structure. National Biomedical Research Foundation, Silver Spring, MD. v. 5, p. D-264.
22. Dray, S., et al. 1962. Nature (London) 195:785-786.
23. Dray, S., et al. 1963. J. Immunol. 91:403-415.
24. Dray, S., et al. 1970. Protides Biol. Fluids Proc. Colloq. 17:131-136.
25. Dubiski, S. 1969. J. Immunol. 103:120-128.
26. Dubiski, S. 1970. Protides Biol. Fluids Proc. Colloq. 17:117-124.
27. Dubiski, S. 1972. Med. Clin. North Am. 56:557-575.
28. Dubiski, S., and P. W. Good, Jr. 1972. Proc. Soc. Exp. Biol. Med. 141:486-489.
29. Dubiski, S., and P. W. Good, Jr. 1974. Ann. Immunol. (Inst. Pasteur) 125C:53-56.
30. Dubiski, S., and P. J. Muller. 1967. Nature (London) 214:696-697.
31. Dubiski, S., et al. 1961. Immunology 4:236-243.
32. Dubiski, S., et al. 1962. Acta Genet. 12:136-155.
33. Eby, W. C., et al. 1973. Immunochemistry 10:417-418.
34. Farnsworth, V., et al. 1976. Proc. Natl. Acad. Sci. USA 73:1293-1296.
35. Feinstein, A. 1963. Nature (London) 199:1197-1199.
36. Fox, R. R. Unpublished. Jackson Laboratory, Bar Harbor, ME, 1977.
37. Frangione, B. 1969. FEBS Lett. 3:341-342.
38. Gilman-Sachs, A. Unpublished. Univ. Illinois Medical Center, Chicago, 1979.
39. Gilman-Sachs, A., and S. Dray. 1972. Eur. J. Immunol. 2:505-509.
40. Gilman-Sachs, A., and S. Dray. 1977. J. Immunol. 118:1580-1585.
41. Gilman-Sachs, A., et al. 1969. Ibid. 103:1159-1167.
42. Goodfliesh, R. M. 1975. Ibid. 114:910-912.
43. Hamers, R., and C. Hamers-Casterman. 1965. J. Mol. Biol. 14:288-289.
44. Hamers, R., and C. Hamers-Casterman. 1967. Cold Spring Harbor Symp. Quant. Biol. 32:129-132.
45. Hamers, R., et al. 1965. Arch. Int. Physiol. Biochim. 73:147-148.
46. Hamers, R., et al. 1966. Immunology 10:399-408.
47. Hamers, R., et al. 1975. Z. Immunitaetsforsch. Exp. Klin. Immunol. 149:187-192.
48. Hamers-Casterman, C., and R. Hamers. 1975. Immunogenetics 2:597-603.
49. Hanly, W. C., et al. 1972. J. Immunol. 108:1723-1725.
50. Hanly, W. C., et al. 1973. Biochemistry 12:733-741.
51. Hood, L., et al. 1971. Ann. N.Y. Acad. Sci. 190:26-36.
52. Hood, L., et al. 1975. Annu. Rev. Genet. 9:305-353.
53. Horng, W. J., et al. 1976. J. Immunol. 116:117-125.
54. Jaton, J.-C. 1974. Biochem. J. 141:1-25.
55. Jaton, J.-C. 1975. Ibid. 147:235-247.
56. Jaton, J.-C., et al. 1973. J. Immunol. 111:1838-1843.
57. Kelus, A. S., and P. G. H. Gell. 1965. Nature (London) 206:313-314.
58. Kelus, A. S., and P. G. H. Gell. 1967. Prog. Allergy 11:141-184.
59. Kelus, A. S., and B. Pernis. 1971. Eur. J. Immunol. 1:123-132.
60. Kelus, A. S., and S. Weiss. 1977. Nature (London) 265:156-158.
61. Kim, B. S., and S. Dray. 1972. Eur. J. Immunol. 2:509-514.
62. Kim, B. S., and S. Dray. 1973. J. Immunol. 111:750-760.
63. Kindt, T. J. 1975. Adv. Immunol. 21:35-86.
64. Kindt, T. J., and W. J. Mandy. 1972. J. Immunol. 108:1110-1113.
65. Kindt, T. J., and C. W. Todd. 1969. J. Exp. Med. 130:859-866.
66. Kindt, T. J., et al. 1970. Immunochemistry 7:467-477.
67. Kindt, T. J., et al. 1972. J. Immunol. 109:735-741.
68. Kindt, T. J., et al. 1973. J. Exp. Med. 138:33-40.
69. Knight, K. L., and W. C. Hanly. 1975. Contemp. Top. Mol. Immunol. 4:55-88.
70. Knight, K. L., et al. 1971. J. Immunol. 106:761-767.
71. Knight, K. L., et al. 1973. Biochemistry 12:3197-3203.
72. Knight, K. L., et al. 1974. J. Immunol. 112:877-882.
73. Knight, K. L., et al. 1974. Proc. Natl. Acad. Sci. USA 71:1169-1173.
74. Knight, K. L., et al. 1979. Eur. J. Immunol. 9:36-39.
75. Koshland, M. E., et al. 1968. Immunochemistry 5:471-483.
76. Lammert, J. M. 1975. Ph.D. Thesis. Univ. Illinois Medical Center, Chicago.
77. Lammert, J. M., et al. 1977. J. Immunol. 118:1397-1402.
78. Landucci-Tosi, S., et al. 1972. Ibid. 108:264-267.
79. Landucci-Tosi, S., et al. 1975. Immunochemistry 12:865-872.
80. Landucci-Tosi, S., et al. 1976. J. Immunol. 117:679-685.
81. Le Guern, C. 1974. C. R. Acad. Sci. D279:1947-1950.
82. Le Guern, C., and J. Oudin. 1974. Biochem. Biophys. Res. Commun. 60:958-963.
83. Mage, R. G. 1979. Ann. Immunol. (Inst. Pasteur) 130C:105-114.
84. Mage, R. G., et al. 1968. J. Immunol. 101:617-620.
85. Mage, R. G., et al. 1971. Nature (London) New Biol. 230:63-64.
86. Mage, R. G., et al. 1973. The Antigens. Academic, New York. v. 1, pp. 299-376.
87. Malek, T. R., et al. 1974. Eur. J. Immunol. 4:692-697.
88. Mandy, W. J. Unpublished. Univ. Texas, Dep. Microbiol., Austin, 1977.
89. Mandy, W. J., and C. W. Todd. 1968. Vox Sang. 14:264-270.
90. Mandy, W. J., and C. W. Todd. 1969. Immunochemistry 6:811-823.
91. Mandy, W. J., and C. W. Todd. 1970. Biochem. Genet. 4:59-71.
92. Mariamé, B., et al. 1977. Ann. Immunol. (Inst. Pasteur) 128C:355-359.
93. Masuda, T., et al. 1969. J. Immunol. 102:1156-1162.
94. McBurnette, S. K., and W. J. Mandy. 1974. Immunochemistry 11:255-260.

continued

95. McBurnette, S. K., and W. J. Mandy. 1975. Ibid. 12: 861-864.
96. McCartney-Francis, N., and W. J. Mandy. 1979. Ann. Immunol. (Inst. Pasteur) 130C:115-131.
97. Mole, L. E. 1975. Biochem. J. 151:351-359.
98. Mole, L. E., et al. 1975. J. Immunol. 114:1442-1448.
99. Mudgett, M., et al. 1975. J. Exp. Med. 141:1448-1452.
100. Naessens, J., et al. 1978. Immunogenetics 6:17-27.
101. Oudin, J. 1960. J. Exp. Med. 112:107-124.
102. Oudin, J. 1960. C. R. Acad. Sci. D250:770-772.
103. Oudin, J. 1977. Ann. Immunol. (Inst. Pasteur) 128C: 371-384.
104. Oudin, J., and M. Michel. 1970. C. R. Acad. Sci. D271:2448-2451.
105. Pernis, B., et al. 1973. Immunochemistry 10:281-285.
106. Peterson, B. E. 1977. M.S. Thesis. Univ. Illinois Medical Center, Chicago.
107. Prahl, J. W., et al. 1969. Biochemistry 8:4935-4940.
108. Rejnek, J., et al. 1969. Ibid. 8:2712-2718.
109. Roland, J., and P.-A. Cazenave. 1976. Ann. Immunol. (Inst. Pasteur) 127C:317-332.
110. Sell, S. 1966. Science 153:641-643.
111. Seto, A. 1973. Immunochemistry 10:529-534.
112. Smith, L., et al. 1979. Eur. J. Immunol. 9:27-31.
113. Sogn, J. A., and T. J. Kindt. 1976. J. Exp. Med. 143:1475-1482.
114. Sogn, J. A., and T. J. Kindt. 1978. Immunogenetics 7:141-147.
115. Strosberg, A. D. 1977. Ibid. 4:499-513.
116. Strosberg, A. D., et al. 1972. Biochemistry 11:4978-4985.
117. Strosberg, A. D., et al. 1974. J. Immunol. 113:1313-1318.
118. Strosberg, A. D., et al. 1979. Ann. Immunol. (Inst. Pasteur) 130C:157-166.
119. Tack, B. F., et al. 1973. Biochemistry 12:5172-5180.
120. Teherani, J., and W. J. Mandy. 1976. Immunochemistry 13:401-406.
121. Thunberg, A. L., and T. J. Kindt. 1975. Scand. J. Immunol. 4:197-201.
122. Thunberg, A. L., et al. 1973. J. Immunol. 111:1755-1764.
123. Todd, C. W. 1963. Biochem. Biophys. Res. Commun. 11:170-175.
124. Tosi, R., and S. Landucci-Tosi. 1973. Contemp. Top. Mol. Immunol. 2:79-97.
125. Tseng, J. 1974. Ph.D. Thesis. Univ. Illinois Medical Center, Chicago.
126. Usher, D. C., et al. 1978. Immunogenetics 7:117-123.
127. Usher, D. C., et al. 1978. J. Immunol. 120:1832-1835.
128. Van der Loo, W., et al. 1975. Arch. Int. Physiol. Biochim. 83:203-204.
129. Van der Loo, W., et al. 1977. Eur. J. Immunol. 7: 15-22.
130. Vice, J. L., et al. 1970. J. Immunol. 104:38-44.
131. Vice, J. L., et al. 1972. Vox Sang. 23:190-196.
132. Waterfield, M., et al. 1973. J. Immunol. 110:227-232.
133. Wilkinson, J. M. 1969. Biochem. J. 112:173-185.
134. Yarmush, M. L., and T. J. Kindt. 1978. J. Exp. Med. 148:522-533.
135. Yarmush, M. L., et al. 1977. Ibid. 145:916-930.
136. Yarmush, M. L., et al. 1979. Ann. Immunol. (Inst. Pasteur) 130C:143-156.
137. Zeeuws, R., and A. D. Strosberg. 1975. Arch. Int. Physiol. Biochim. 83:205-206.
138. Zikan, J., et al. 1967. Folia Microbiol. 12:162-174.
139. Zullo, D. M., et al. 1968. Proc. Can. Fed. Biol. Soc. 11:111.

151. ALLOGROUPS OF THE IG HEAVY-CHAIN CHROMOSOMAL REGION: RABBIT

The allogroups or haplotypes listed below have been identified in laboratory rabbits. **Source:** For full name, *see* list of HOLDERS at front of book. *Symbol:* Older notations are given in parentheses. Data in brackets refer to the column heading in brackets.

V_H Region	Haplotype				Conformational Specificities C_μ-V_H	Source [Strain]
	C_H Region					
	γ	α_f	α_g	μ		
$a^1 x^- y^-$	$de^{12,15}$	f^{70}	g^{76}	$Ms^{16}(n^{81})$	Ms21	NIHK, UIMC, VUB, JAX [C, IIIEP, IIIVO/vpt][1/]
$a^1 x^- y^-$	$de^{12,15}$	f^{73}	g^{74}	$Ms^{16}(n^{81})$	....	UIMC, NIHK, NIHR
$a^1 x^- y^{33}$	$de^{11,15}$	f^{72}	g^{74}	$Ms^{17}(n^{80})$	Ms24 (n83)	UIMC, COH, VUB
$a^1 x^- y^{33}$	$de^{12,14}$	f^{69}[2/]	g^{77}[2/]	$Ms^{17}(n^{80})$	Ms24 (n83)	NIHR, VUB

[1/] Assignment of JAX strains to a particular allogroup is based on serotyping of a small number of rabbits for the $V_H a$, $C_\alpha f$, $C_\alpha g$, and $C_\mu n$ loci only. [2/] It is not yet certain that the f69 and g77 specificities are identical in all $f^{69} g^{77}$ haplotypes listed.

continued

| V_H Region | Haplotype | | | | Conformational Specificities C_μ-V_H | Source [Strain] |
| | C_H Region | | | | | |
	γ	α_f	α_g	μ		
$a^1\ x^-\ y^{33}$	$de^{12,15}$	f^{71}	g^{75}	$Ms^{17}(n^{80})$	Ms24 (n83)	UIMC, VUB
$a^1\ x^{32}\ y^{33}$	$de^{12,15}$	f^{71}	g^{75}	$Ms^{17}(n^{80})$	Ms24 (n83)	UIMC, VUB
a^1 ? ?	$de^{12,14}$	f^{69} 2/	g^{77} 2/	$Ms^{16}(n^{81})$	Ms21	VUB
a^1 ? ?	$de^{12,15}$	f^{69} 2/	g^{77} 2/	$Ms^{17}(n^{80})$	Ms24 (n83)	VUB
$a^2\ x^{32}\ y^{33}$	$de^{12,14}$	f^{69} 2/	g^{77} 2/	$Ms^{17}(n^{80})$ 3/	Ms25 (n82)	NIHR
$a^2\ x^{32}\ y^{33}$	$de^{12,15}$	f^{69} 2/	g^{77} 2/	$Ms^{17}\ (n^{80})$	Ms25	NIHK, NIHR, UIMC, VUB, JAX [OS]1/
$a^2\ x^{32}\ y^{33}$	$de^{12,15}$	f^{71}	g^{75}	$Ms^{17}(n^{80})$	Ms25 (n82)	UIMC, VUB
a^2 ? ?	$de^{11,?}$	?	?	? ?	....	IUMS
a^2 ? ?	$de^{12,14}$	f^{69} 2/	g^{77} 2/	$Ms^{16}(n^{81})$	Ms22	VUB
a^2 ? ?	$de^{12,15}$	f^{73}	g^{74}	$Ms^{16}(n^{81})$	Ms22	BII, NYU, VUB, UIMC
$a^3\ x^{32}\ y^-$	$de^{11,15}$	f^{72}	g^{74}	$Ms^{16}(n^{81})$	Ms23 (n84, n85)	UIMC, NIHK, VUB, JAX [AX, X]1/
$a^3\ x^{32}\ y^-$	$de^{12,15}$	f^{69} 2/	g^{77} 2/	? ?4/	....	NIHK, UTA
$a^3\ x^{32}\ y^-$	$de^{12,15}$	f^{71}	g^{75}	$Ms^{17}(n^{80})$	Ms26 (n84, n86)	UIMC, NIHK, VUB, JAX [AC, ACEP, B]1/
a^3 ? ?	$de^{12,15}$	f^{73}	g^{74}	$Ms^{16}(n^{81})$	Ms23	VUB
a^3 ? ?	$de^{?,14}$	?	?	? ?	....	IPP

1/ Assignment of JAX strains to a particular allogroup is based on serotyping of a small number of rabbits for the $V_H a$, $C_\alpha f$, $C_\alpha g$, and $C_\mu n$ loci only. 2/ It is not yet certain that the f69 and g77 specificities are identical in all $f^{69} g^{77}$ haplotypes listed. 3/ This haplotype (columns 1-5) was derived from apparent recombination between $a^1 x^- y^{33}$ $de^{12,14} f^{69} g^{77} Ms^{17}$ and $a^2 x^{32} y^{33} de^{12,15} f^{69} g^{77} Ms^{17}$.

4/ This haplotype (columns 1-5) was derived from apparent recombination between $a^2 x^{32} y^{33} de^{12,15} f^{69} g^{77} Ms^{17}$ and $a^3 x^{32} y^- de^{11,15} f^{72} g^{74} Ms^{16}$. The α-chain allotypes of the recombinant reported here differ from those in the original report; development of additional alloantisera clarified problematic typing due to cross-reactions.

Contributors: W. Carey Hanly and Alice Gilman-Sachs

General References

1. Dray, S., et al. 1974. Ann. Immunol. (Inst. Pasteur) 125C:41-47.
2. Knight, K. L., and W. C. Hanly. 1975. Contemp. Top. Mol. Immunol. 4:55-88.
3. Lammert, J. M., et al. 1977. J. Immunol. 118:1397-1402.
4. Mage, R. G. 1977. Prog. Immunol. Proc. 3rd Int. Congr. Immunol. Sydney, pp. 289-297.
5. Naessens, J., and R. Hamers. Unpublished. Laboratorium Algemene Biologie-Instituut voor Moleculaire Biologie Vrije Universiteit Brussel, 1978.

VI. CHICKEN

ORIGIN OF INBRED AND GENETICALLY DEFINED STRAINS OF CHICKENS

Breeds of chickens were well-established and described by the time Mendel's laws were redefined at the turn of the century [ref. 1]. In 1902, chickens were used by Bateson to demonstrate that animals conform to the Mendelian laws of inheritance [ref. 3]. The wide assortment of breeds available today [ref. 2, 12] are more likely due to fanciers' interest in maintaining birds of unique characteristics than to the fact that domesticated fowl are an important food source for the world. Nevertheless, the latter aspect has led to a well-developed husbandry and to a large accumulation of data on the physiology of the chicken, *Gallus gallus* ⟨*G. domesticus*⟩, and of the turkey, *Meleagris gallopavo*. This collective expertise may now be adapted for use with other genera of birds that are possibly better suited to laboratory conditions, such as the Japanese quail, *Coturnix coturnix japonica*.

The strains of chickens most valuable for initiating a study on the inheritance of a trait are those that have been either (i) inbred, or (ii) selected for a particular trait. Lerner [ref. 8] has briefly documented the work of early poultry breeders. In some cases, strains have been selected and inbred at the same time. However, selection during inbreeding is primarily for fitness (directly or indirectly), and secondarily for other parameters. There are many examples of inbred and/or selected strains given in the tables that follow in this Section. Data on genetic stocks—maintained by fanciers for various reasons—that do not fall in either of the above categories have not been included.

Inbred strains of chickens were first studied at the poultry science departments of land grant colleges in the United States. Shortly thereafter, investigation of inbred strains spread to agricultural research stations in the United States and England, and to private industry. The foundation stocks generally were obtained from the best commercially available, egg-laying strains of the White Leghorn or Rhode Island Red breeds. Although it is customary and desirable to note the origin and country of each inbred strain [ref. 7], there is a strong probability that within breeds a common ancestry was present, regardless of location, in many of the commercial stocks used for the development of inbred strains. Thus, the greatest dissimilarities among inbred strains will probably be noted among those of different breeds. This is not to say that common genes will not be found in all breeds [ref. 6]. Interestingly, the White Leghorn breed has displayed less inbreeding depression than other egg-production or heavy meat-production breeds, possibly due to a smaller genetic load [ref. 9, 10]. Most of the inbred lines which exist in the world today, with a few valiant exceptions, were developed from the best, rather widely distributed, White Leghorn strains, and it may be expected that they represent only a limited number of the alleles existing in *G. gallus* for a given locus.

Existing inbred lines do provide a useful array of strains. Several of these could be selected for the development of congenic lines that would differ for a portion of a chromosome which could be derived from any other chicken strain. In chickens, 29 of the 39 chromosome pairs are microchromosomes. If an autosomal trait is determined by a locus on one of these microchromosomes, then development of congenic lines that differ with respect to the microchromosome, but are essentially identical for most of the DNA located in the major chromosomes [ref. 1], could be facilitated. The important *B*-complex ⟨MHC⟩ appears to be carried on a microchromosome [ref. 1, 4, 11].

Development of specialized selected strains is relatively easy when simply inherited Mendelian traits are under study. Quantitative traits, however, require a genetically broad-based population, formed from a number of research-defined, and/or commercial, flocks prior to starting the selection program [ref. 5]. The general practice in poultry husbandry is to reproduce the flock once each year. This makes the development of selected strains, and particularly of highly inbred strains, a long-term study. Great care should therefore be taken in the choice of foundation stocks.

Contributor: Larry D. Bacon

References

1. Abbott, U., and G. W. Yee. 1975. In R. C. King, ed. Handbook of Genetics. Plenum, New York. v. 4, pp. 151-200.
2. American Poultry Association. 1953. Standard of Perfection for Domesticated Land and Water Fowl. Atlanta, GA.
3. Bateson, W. 1902. Exp. Stud. Physiol. Hered. Rep. Evol. Comm. R. Soc. London 21(1):87-124.
4. Bloom, S. E., et al. 1978. Poult. Sci. 57:1119(Abstr.).
5. Cole, R. K. 1968. Avian Dis. 12:9-28.
6. Craig, J. V., and E. M. McDermid. 1963. Transplantation 1:191-200.
7. Festing, M. F. W. 1979. Inbred Strains in Biomedical Research. Macmillan, London and New York. pp. 323-338.
8. Lerner, I. M. 1958. The Genetic Basis of Selection. Wiley, New York.
9. McGibbon, W. H. Unpublished. Univ. Wisconsin, Madison, 1978.
10. Nordskog, A. W. 1966. World's Poult. Sci. J. 22:207-216.
11. Pazderka, F., et al. 1975. Immunogenetics 2:101-130.
12. Somes, R. G., Jr. 1978. Conn. Agric. Exp. Stn. Storrs Bull. 446.

INVESTIGATIONS FOR WHICH THE CHICKEN IS WELL-SUITED

Birds are a particularly rich source of animal models for biomedical research. The chicken models presented below were selected, with slight modifications, from the list prepared by U. K. Abbott and G. W. Yee [ref. 4]. The first section lists general problems for which the chicken has a particular advantage; the second section includes a variety of diseases for which useful chicken models exist. Several mutants are grouped that produce the same type of abnormality, or which are useful in studies of a particular system. References to each system or condition are not intended to be complete.

Investigation	Reference
General Problems	
Hemoglobin synthesis and its control	13,28,34
Immunology	52
Immunoglobulin synthesis and its control	6,9,22, 23,35, 36,44, 45,54
Cellular antigens	11
Isogenicity: inbred lines	5
Pattern formation, especially pigmentation	12,30,48
Sex determination, differentiation, & reversal	4
Teratogenesis: screening various drugs, anticancer agents, pesticides, etc.	40,41
Tissue interactions	
Limb differentiation	24,43
Skin & integument	33,48-51
Virology: DNA viruses, viral resistance, tumor induction, etc.	10,46
Specific Conditions	
Integumental	
Ichthyosis	3

Investigation	Reference
Nakedness (partial & complete)	1,27,29, 51
Metabolic	
Diabetes (polydipsia & polyuria)	25
Gout	18,20,47
Liver disease	17,19
Obesity	16,35
Riboflavinuria (during embryonic development)	14,55
Neurological	
Epilepsy	21
Paroxysm	15
Muscular	
Muscle hypoplasia	7,41
Muscular dystrophy	32,42,47
Skeletal	
Achondroplasia & micromelia	37-39
Dwarfing (proportionate & disproportionate)	8,31
Hypodactyly	2,29,37, 39
Polydactyly	26
Scoliosis	53

Contributor: Raymond A. McBride

References

1. Abbott, U. K. 1967. In F. H. Wilt and N. K. Wessells, ed. Methods in Developmental Biology. Crowell, New York. pp. 13-52.
2. Abbott, U. K., and J. A. MacCabe. 1966. J. Hered. 57: 207-212.
3. Abbott, U. K., and R. H. Sawyer. 1974. Poult. Sci. 53:1897.
4. Abbott, U. K., and G. W. Yee. 1975. In R. C. King, ed. Handbook of Genetics. Plenum, New York. v. 4, pp. 185-200.
5. Abplanalp, H. 1974. World's Congr. Genet. Appl. Livestock Prod. 1st, 1:897-908.
6. Albini, B., and G. Wick. 1974. Nature (London) 249: 653-654.
7. Allenspach, A. L. 1970. J. Morphol. 131:89-102.
8. Bernier, P. E., and G. H. Arscott. 1972. Ann. Genet. Sel. Anim. 4:183-215.
9. Bienenstock, J., et al. 1973. J. Immunol. 111:1112-1118.
10. Bower, R. K., et al. 1965. Genetics 51:739-746.
11. Briles, W. E. 1964. Z. Tierz. Zuechtungsbiol. 79:371-391.
12. Brumbaugh, J. A., et al. 1972. J. Hered. 63:19-25.
13. Bruns, G. A. P., and V. M. Ingram. 1973. Phil. Trans. R. Soc. London B266:225-305.
14. Buss, E. G. 1969. In T. C. Carter and B. M. Freeman, ed. The Fertility and Hatchability of the Hen's Egg. Oliver and Boyd, Edinburgh. pp. 109-116.
15. Cole, R. K. 1961. J. Hered. 52:46-52.
16. Cole, R. K. 1966. Genetics 53:1021-1033.
17. Cole, R. K. 1969. (Loc. cit. ref. 14). pp. 57-69.
18. Cole, R. K., and R. E. Austic. 1971. Poult. Sci. 50: 1565-1566.
19. Cole, R. K., and D. G. Jones. 1972. Ibid. 51:1795.
20. Cole, R. K., et al. 1969. Ibid. 48:1796.
21. Crawford, R. D. 1970. J. Hered. 61:185-188.
22. David, C. S. 1972. Genetics 71:649-651.
23. David, C. S., et al. 1969. Biochem. Genet. 3:197-206.
24. Dhouailly, D., and M. Kieny. 1972. Dev. Biol. 28: 162-175.

continued

25. Dunson, W. A., et al. 1972. Am. J. Physiol. 222:1167-1176.
26. Fraser, R. A., and U. K. Abbott. 1971. J. Exp. Zool. 176:219-236.
27. Goetinck, P. F., and U. K. Abbott. 1963. Ibid. 154:1-19.
28. Hagopian, H. K., et al. 1972. J. Cell Biol. 54:98-106.
29. Hutt, F. B. 1949. Genetics of the Fowl. McGraw-Hill, New York.
30. Hutt, F. B. 1964. J. Hered. 55:200-206.
31. Jaap, R. G. 1971. World's Poult. Sci. J. 27:281-282.
32. Julian, L. M. 1973. Am. J. Pathol. 70:273-276.
33. Kato, Y. 1969. J. Exp. Zool. 170:229-252.
34. Keane, R. W., et al. 1974. Dev. Biol. 38:229-236.
35. Kite, J. H., Jr., et al. 1969. J. Immunol. 103:1331-1341.
36. Kramer, T. T. 1973. Avian Dis. 17:208-213.
37. Landauer, W. 1967. Conn. Agric. Exp. Stn. Storrs Monogr. 1(rev.).
38. Landauer, W. 1969. In C. A. Swinyard, ed. Limb Development and Deformity. Thomas, Springfield, IL. pp. 540-621.
39. Landauer, W. 1973. Conn. Agric. Exp. Stn. Storrs Monogr. 1(Suppl.).
40. Landauer, W., and N. Salam. 1973. Acta Embryol. Exp. 2:179-197.
41. Landauer, W., and N. Salam. 1974. Ibid. 1:51-66.
42. Linkhart, T. A., et al. 1975. Science 187:549-551.
43. MacCabe, J. A., et al. 1974. Dev. Biol. 39:69-82.
44. Moore, M. A. S., and J. J. T. Owen. 1966. Ibid. 14:40-51.
45. Moore, M. A. S., and J. J. T. Owen. 1967. Science 215:1081-1082.
46. Motta, J. V., and L. B. Crittenden. 1973. Poult. Sci. 52:2067.
47. Peterson, D. W., et al. 1971. J. Nutr. 101:347-354.
48. Rawles, M. E. 1959. J. Morphol. 105:33-48.
49. Rawles, M. E. 1965. In A. G. Lyne and B. F. Short, ed. Biology of the Skin and Hair Growth. Angus and Robertson, Sydney, Australia. pp. 105-128.
50. Rawles, M. E. 1972. Proc. Natl. Acad. Sci. USA 69:1136-1140.
51. Sawyer, R. H., and U. K. Abbott. 1972. J. Exp. Zool. 181:99-110.
52. Solomon, J. B. 1971. Front. Biol. 20.
53. Taylor, L. W. 1971. Avian Dis. 15:376-390.
54. Wick, G., and R. Steiner. 1972. J. Immunol. 109:471-476.
55. Winter, W. P., et al. 1967. Comp. Biochem. Physiol. 22:889-906.

The usefulness of inbred lines of chickens in the study of immunogenetics and in other areas of research has long been recognized. Recent advances in mapping the major histocompatibility system of mammalian species has, however, emphasized the need for lines that are nearly isogenic as well as highly inbred. Only a relatively small number of lines today meet this need.

The formation of homozygous lines of chickens is a slow and expensive process. With brother x sister matings every generation and allowing one year per generation, 11 years are necessary to achieve inbreeding coefficients exceeding 90%. The actual inbreeding of a line, as measured by the loss of heterozygosity relative to a base population, differs from the calculated inbreeding coefficients since chance or natural selection may favor the heterozygotes or either homozygote.

Evidence of persistent heterozygosity of red blood cell antigens in partially inbred lines has been demonstrated by Briles, et al. [ref. 3] and Gilmour [ref. 6]. It must be assumed that calculated inbreeding coefficients for inbred lines of chickens generally overestimate the actual levels of homozygosity attained by genes affecting the viability of birds. This is certainly true for the major histocompatibility complex and probably for other genes affecting viability and reproduction.

In the case of chickens, there are also other factors which tend to reduce actual inbreeding below the levels of neutral genes. Perhaps the most important and least documented are pedigree errors. Unlike mice and other laboratory animals, a hen under modern management does not raise its own young. In so-called floor management, several hens are mated to one male. The hens are then lured into individual trapnests where they lay their eggs. The latter are marked with the hen's leg or wing band number (often a four-digit number in larger breeding operations) and saved for collection 1-2 weeks later. For artificial incubation, the eggs are sorted by hen and set accordingly. To hatch the chicks, all eggs from a given hen are placed in a separate, closed-wire basket where the chicks emerge from the marked eggs and can be identified as a family by individual wing banding. Where hens are kept in single cages, artificial insemination is used.

Although the above processes generally result in accurate identification, there is more possibility of clerical errors and mixups than, for instance, in the typical mouse breeding program. Among the more serious pedigree errors are mismarking and misreading of the egg's identity, banding errors, and paternity errors connected with the use of artificial insemination—especially when males die and need to be replaced. Faulty trapnests or the misreading of the hen's identification are typical floor management hazards. On the positive side, it is possible to identify chicks genetically from plumage color for lines not carrying the dominant white gene (*I*) typical of the White Leghorn breed. Egg size and shape can also be characteristic of a given line once it has attained two or three generations of full-sib matings.

Considering these factors and the need for identifying each individual egg and offspring rather than entire litters, the likelihood of errors may exceed that for rodents by a ratio of approximately 10:1. Thus, at the laboratory of the University of California at Davis, where some 4,000 chicks are hatched each spring and later identified genetically by blood typing, one or two errors per year are not uncommon.

Pedigree errors between lines lead to a reduction—by half—in inbreeding in the affected line. Furthermore, offspring from such inadvertent crosses have better viability and tend to outproduce truly inbred offspring within the line, resulting in the further propagation of pedigree errors.

Another factor affecting heterozygosity beyond the level expected for neutral genes is the practice of subdividing a given line into several families in an attempt to ensure its survival. With full-sib mating of chickens, reserve matings of each generation are almost mandatory and can then be followed by elimination of the small families. In this way, natural selection between, as well as within, families is practiced, and the opportunity to eliminate homozygotes is greater. If sublines are retained for more than one generation and occasional matings between them occur, the level of inbreeding is reduced to that existing at the time the sublines branched from one another.

Blood typing of inbred lines by means of red blood cell antigens perhaps should be the most important tool for monitoring lines for possible genetic contamination. Since mating systems involving brother x sister matings, or parent x offspring matings, should lead to homozygosity of all but the most extremely heterotic loci within approximately 10 generations, one would expect long-established, highly inbred lines to reflect this in their blood types (*see* Table 161). The actual blood types shown in Table 161 may serve as an important indication of the lines' inbreeding status, as well as being a step in the establishment of an international standard for blood types.

Listings of existing inbred chicken lines have been compiled recently by Hala and also appear in Somes' *Registry of Poultry Genetic Stocks* [ref. 15]. Selection of lines for the following summaries was restricted to those that are highly inbred and for which there is recorded biological evidence of their breeding status. Most of the lines can be found in the above listings.

CSIRO Lines: Thirteen White Leghorn and four Australorp lines are currently maintained by Dr. B. Sheldon at the Genetics Research Laboratories of the Commonwealth

continued

Scientific and Industrial Research Organization, North Ryde, N.S.W., Australia. These lines were initiated by Dr. F. Skaller at the Werribee Poultry Research Centre, and propagated primarily by sib mating for 17 to 28 generations. One of the White Leghorn (WL) lines, designated as B_1 by Burnet and Burnet [ref. 4], was subdivided by these investigators into three sublines carrying different alleles of the major histocompatibility locus (*AA*, *BB*, *CC*, respectively), and used as genetic material in the study of graft-versus-host reactions in fowl.

IU Lines: An extensive inbreeding program was started in 1925 at Iowa State College, resulting in a number of lines that were described by Waters and Lambert [ref. 19]. Three of them, IU-8, IU-9, and IU-19, are still maintained at Iowa State University. Although a few generations of full-sib matings were used initially, these lines were later maintained as larger flocks and have only recently undergone renewed close inbreeding. Other inbred lines maintained at Iowa State University since 1953 were started from commercial White Leghorn (WL) flocks, imported Egyptian Fayoumi, and the Black Spanish fowl. Close inbreeding by full-sib and half-sib mating in these populations has been in force for the last nine generations. Segregation, however, of three or four *B* alleles in Lines IU-19, IU-GH, and IU-HN has been reported [ref. 18].

PR Lines: Three sets of syngeneic lines—based on Reaseheath Lines RH-C, RH-I, and RH-W, respectively—were established by Hašek and co-workers at the Prague Institute of Molecular Genetics in Czechoslovakia [ref. 7-10]. The initial lines were brought to Prague in the early 1960's and found to segregate for several blood group systems. Sublines PR-CA and PR-CB, differing in blood group system 404 (Prague nomenclature), were derived from RH-C; a third subline, PR-CC, differs from PR-CB at the major histocompatibility complex (B blood group system). Lines PR-WA and PR-WB, derived from the RH-W line, also differ from each other in the B system; and Lines PR-IA, PR-IB, and PR-IC are based on RH-I. They differ from each other in haplotypes of the closely linked A-E blood group systems. Two additional inbred lines were developed from local Black Minorca and Silkie-Leghorn flocks, respectively. In the latter lines, full-sib matings were initially practiced. Currently, the lines are maintained by about 3 males and 20 females each.

Recently, a recombinant of the MHC haplotypes of Lines PR-CB and PR-CC has been discovered. However, no separate subline based on the recombinant haplotype B^{RI} has so far been established.

PRC-R Line: This Brown Leghorn line was one of several developed at the Poultry Research Centre, Edinburgh, Scot-

land, during the 1930's. Line R was initiated from a closed flock in 1939 and inbred mostly by half-sib matings. For each generation, 1 or 2 males and as many as 20 hens were maintained to reproduce the line. Inbreeding in 1959 was calculated at 74% [ref. 2].

RH Lines: Four lines were developed at the National Poultry Institute, Northern Breeding Station, Reaseheath, Cheshire, England. Three (Lines RH-C, RH-W, RH-R) were initiated from commercial sources, and one (Line RH-I) was obtained in 1936 from Dr. Waters at Iowa State University after the line had already undergone at least 10 generations of close inbreeding (probably the Line 1 described by Waters and Lambert) [ref. 19]. According to Pease and Dudley [ref. 12], reproduction was by full-sib matings. However, the pedigree diagram described by Pease and Dudley for Line RH-C shows crossing of sublines in 1936, suggesting that exceptions to strict, full-sib matings may have occurred. A high degree of variability in blood group systems tested by Gilmour [ref. 6] also suggests heterozygosity in excess of what might be expected under strict, full-sib matings over many generations.

RPRL Lines: Inbred lines for the study of genetic resistance to the avian leukosis complex were developed by Waters at the Regional Poultry Disease Research Laboratory, East Lansing, Michigan. Of 15 lines initiated from 9 different commercial flocks, 4 (Lines RPRL-6, RPRL-7, RPRL-15, and RPRL-15I) are still in use. Of these, Line 15I, a subline of Line 15, was set up by Waters in 1942 in an isolated house so that the line could be maintained free of leukosis; genetically, it is thus quite distinct from Line 15. Lines were reproduced by 3-4 sires and approximately 10 dams. In 1962, each of the above lines was divided into two or three sublines, and sib mating was initiated as the predominant mode of reproduction. Sublining within each subline, however, was also practiced to maintain sufficient numbers for experimentation.

In 1962, a new line, RPRL-100, was initiated by crossing Lines 6 and 7, followed by four backcrosses to Line 7 while maintaining segregation for resistance to the A and B subgroups of the lymphoid leukosis virus. At the same time, susceptibility to the neural form of leukosis (now known as Marek's disease), typical of Line 7, was established.

Further separation of sublines occurred in 1965 when birds from most lines were introduced into specific-pathogen-free conditions. These and other aspects of the East Lansing program have been reviewed by Stone [ref. 16].

A summary of genetic resistance to lymphoid leukosis virus and the five subgroups of Rous sarcoma virus, as well as to Marek's disease virus of the RPRL lines, is given in Table 157.

continued

A summary of their blood types appears in Table 161. It appears that some of the RPRL lines still show segregation at several loci despite the fact that their calculated inbreeding coefficient exceeds 98%.

UCD Lines: In 1956-1958 at the University of California at Davis, a total of 240 full-sib families were started to produce inbred lines by strict full-sib matings. Until 1960, approximately half of the lines were discarded each year, and in 1966 only 12 were left. In 1969, five of the eight original lines were discarded for lack of space, leaving Lines UCD-02, UCD-03, and UCD-07 as the only survivors.

Additional lines were produced by crossing original inbreds, making a first backcross of the F_1 to one of the parent lines, and re-inbreeding the new line by full-sib matings. Line UCD-22 is of this type. Additional lines of the latter type are kept at Davis but are not listed because they are difficult to reproduce. All four lines accept skin grafts and are homozygous for the known blood group systems (see Table 161).

Other Lines: A number of less inbred lines have been used successfully in immunological research. One of them, Line NY-GB$_1$ of Schiermann, et al. [ref. 13], was derived from Line IU-GH. Using blood typing for several of the known systems to match experimental animals, Schiermann and associates have been able to use this partially inbred line with good success, as have others in the field of immunogenetics.

Two sublines of White Leghorns—developed by McDermid from commercial stock of Thornber Brothers, Mythelmrroyd, Yorkshire, England—were later moved to the Charles Salt Research Centre, Oswestry. One line, OS-B2, is homozygous for the B^2 haplotype; the second line, OS-B14, for the B^{14} haplotype. These lines subsequently have been found to segregate for serum globulin allotypes [ref. 5].

Several partially inbred lines, differing in resistance to Marek's disease, were developed at the Animal Research Institute, Ottawa, Canada, by Gowe and co-workers. In addition, a number of lines at the Institute are under development by full-sib matings. These are likely to become more prominent as they are further defined genetically and immunologically.

Increased interest in experimentally useful lines may soon add new ones to this list. Many of them may already be in existence, such as several of the CSIRO lines, as well as lines currently being developed at the University of California at Davis, the Animal Research Institute at Ottawa, Iowa State University, the University of Wisconsin, and probably at other research centers.

Place of Origin: With few exceptions, inbred lines of chickens have been maintained at the location of their origin. Matings—Type: FS = full-sib; HS = half-sib. Holder: For full name, see list of HOLDERS at front of book. Data in brackets refer to the column heading in brackets.

Line [Derivation]	Place of Origin	Year Initiated	Breed of Origin	Matings		Holder	Reference
				Type	No. of Years		
Highly Inbred							
CSIRO-Q0	Werribee	1948	Australorp	FS	18-20	AGS	14
CSIRO-R0	Werribee	1948	Australorp	FS	18-20	AGS	14
CSIRO-R1	Werribee	1948	Australorp	FS	18-20	AGS	14
CSIRO-R2	Werribee	1948	Australorp	FS	18-20	AGS	14
CSIRO-WL[1]	Werribee	1948	Leghorn	FS	17-28	AGS	4,14
IU-GH	Ames	1953	White Leghorn	FS/HS	9	IUA	11,17
IU-HN	Ames	1953	White Leghorn	FS/HS	9	IUA	11,17
IU-M	Ames	1953	Pencilled Fayoumi	FS/HS	9	IUA	11,17
IU-SP	Ames	1953	Black Spanish, Barred Spanish	FS/HS	9	IUA	11,17
IU-8	Ames	1940	Leghorn[2]	FS/HS	9+	IUA	11,17,20
IU-9	Ames	1940	Leghorn[3]	FS/HS	9+	IUA	11,17,20
IU-19	Ames	1953	White Leghorn	FS/HS	9+	IUA	11,17,20
PR-CA [From RH-C]	Prague	1964	White Leghorn	FS	20+	PH	7,9,10
PR-CB [From RH-C]	Prague	1964	White Leghorn	FS	20+	PH	7,9,10
PR-CC [From RH-C]	Prague	1964	White Leghorn	FS	20+	PH	7,9,10
PR-F	Prague	1963	Silkie-Leghorn	FS	7	PH	8
PR-IA [From RH-I]	Prague	1964	White Leghorn	FS	20+	PH	7,10
PR-IB [From RH-I]	Prague	1964	White Leghorn	FS	20+	PH	7,10
PR-IC [From RH-I]	Prague	1964	White Leghorn	FS	20+	PH	7,10
PR-M	Prague	1958	Black Minorca	FS	12	PH	7,10

[1] 13 lines. [2] Segregates for barring. [3] Segregates for dominant white.

continued

Line [Derivation]	Place of Origin	Year Initiated	Breed of Origin	Matings Type	Matings No. of Years	Holder	Reference
PR-WA [From RH-W]	Prague	1962	Cuckoo Leghorn	FS	20+	PH	7,10
PR-WB [From RH-W]	Prague	1962	Cuckoo Leghorn	FS	20+	PH	7,10
PRC-R	Edinburgh	1939	Brown Leghorn	HS	20+	PRC	2
RH-C	Reaseheath	1932	White Leghorn	FS	20+	HPRS	12
RH-I	Reaseheath	1936	White Leghorn	FS	20+	HPRS	12
RH-R	Reaseheath	1940	White Leghorn	FS	20+	HPRS	12
RH-W	Reaseheath	1937	Cuckoo Leghorn	FS	20+	HPRS	12
RPRL-6$_1$ [From RPRL-6]	East Lansing	1939[4/]	White Leghorn	FS	15+	RPRL	16,19
RPRL-6$_3$ [From RPRL-6]	East Lansing	1939[4/]	White Leghorn	FS	15+	RPRL	16,19
RPRL-7$_1$ [From RPRL-7]	East Lansing	1939[4/]	White Leghorn	FS	15+	RPRL	16,19
RPRL-7$_2$ [From RPRL-7]	East Lansing	1939[4/]	White Leghorn	FS	15+	RPRL	16,19
RPRL-15$_1$	East Lansing	1939[4/]	White Leghorn	FS	15+	RPRL	16,19
RPRL-15I$_4$ [From RPRL-15]	East Lansing	1941[4/]	White Leghorn[5/]	FS	15+	RPRL	16,19
RPRL-15I$_5$ [From RPRL-15]	East Lansing	1941[4/]	White Leghorn[5/]	FS	15+	RPRL	16,19
RPRL-100	East Lansing	1962	White Leghorn[6/]	......	.....	RPRL	16,19
UCD-02	Davis	1956	White Leghorn	FS	20+	UCD	1
UCD-03	Davis	1957	White Leghorn	FS	20+	UCD	1
UCD-07	Davis	1957	White Leghorn	FS	20+	UCD	1
UCD-11 [From inbred cross]	Davis	1966	White Leghorn	FS	12+	UCD	1
UCD-22 [From inbred cross]	Davis	1966	White Leghorn	FS	12+	UCD	1
Partially Inbred							
NY-GB$_1$ [From IU-GH]	Ames	1964	White Leghorn	......	.....	UGAS	11,13
NY-GB$_2$ [From IU-GH]	Ames	1964	White Leghorn	......	.....	UGAS	11,13

[4/] Year original line initiated; subline started in 1962. [5/] Isolated lymphoid-leukosis free. [6/] Congenic to RPRL-7 (four backcrosses); four sublines exist.

Contributor: Hans Abplanalp

References

1. Benedict, A. A., et al. 1975. Immunogenetics 2:313-324.
2. Blyth, J. S. S., and J. H. Sang. 1960. Genet. Res. 1:408-421.
3. Briles, W. E., et al. 1957. Genetics 42:631-648.
4. Burnet, D., and F. M. Burnet. 1961. Aust. J. Exp. Biol. Med. Sci. 39:101-110.
5. French, V. I. 1975. J. Immunogenet. 2:171-178.
6. Gilmour, D. G. 1959. Genetics 44:14-33.
7. Hala, K., et al. 1966. Folia Biol. (Prague) 12:407-421.
8. Hala, K., et al. 1974. Ibid. 20:378-385.
9. Hala, K., et al. 1976. Immunogenetics 3:97-103.
10. Hasek, M., et al. 1966. Folia Biol. (Prague) 12:335-353.
11. Maragu, J. P., and A. W. Nordskog. 1974. Theor. Appl. Genet. 45:215-221.

12. Pease, M., and F. Dudley. 1954. Rep. Worlds Poult. Congr. 10:45-49.
13. Schiermann, L. W., and A. W. Nordskog. 1964. Ann. N.Y. Acad. Sci. 120:348-355.
14. Sheldon, B. L. Unpublished. C.S.I.R.O., Division of Animal Production, Epping, New South Wales, Australia, 1977.
15. Somes, R. G., Jr. 1978. Conn. Agric. Exp. Stn. Storrs Bull. 446.
16. Stone, H. A. 1975. U.S. Dep. Agric. Tech. Bull. 1514.
17. Trowbridge, C. L., et al. 1977. Poult. Sci. 56:1763.
18. Warner, N. L. 1964. Br. J. Exp. Pathol. 45:459-466.
19. Waters, N. F., and C. O. Prickett. 1944. Poult. Sci. 23:321-333.
20. Waters, N. R., and W. V. Lambert. 1936. Iowa Agric. Res. Stn. Res. Bull. 202.

Data are for crossbred strains. For full name of holder (MIN), *see* list of HOLDERS at front of book. Data in brackets refer to the column heading in brackets.

Line	Linkage Group	Gene[1]/ [Gene Name]	Characteristic
1	V	*B* [Sex-linked barring] *S* [Silver]	Homozygous
2	I	*Cp* [Creeper] *R* [Rose comb] *U* [Uropygial]	Homozygous, except for *Cp* which is semi-lethal
3	II	*Cr* [Crest] *I* [Dominant white] *F* [Frizzling]	Segregates for *F*
4	IV	*D* [Duplex comb] *M* [Multiple spurs] *Po* [Polydactyly]	Homozygous

Line	Linkage Group	Gene[1]/ [Gene Name]	Characteristic
5	III	*O* [Blue egg] *P* [Pea comb] *Na* [Naked neck]	Homozygous
6	Independent	*E* [Extended black] E^R [Birchen]	Segregates for E, E^R
7	Independent	*W* [White skin]	Homozygous
8	Independent	*Mb* [Muffs & beard]	Homozygous
9	Independent	*Fs* [Feathered shanks]	Homozygous
10	....	Heterozygous gene pool	Segregates for all traits

[1]/ Unless otherwise specified.

Contributor: R. N. Shoffner

General References

1. Hutt, F. B. 1949. Genetics of the Fowl. McGraw-Hill, New York.
2. Somes, R. G., Jr. 1973. J. Hered. 64:217-221.
3. Somes, R. G., Jr. 1978. Conn. Agric. Exp. Stn. Storrs Bull. 446.

154. CHROMOSOME REARRANGEMENT STRAINS: CHICKEN

Data are for crossbred strains. **Mutagen:** EMS = ethyl methanesulfonate; TEM = triethylenemelamine. **Holder:** For full name, *see* list of HOLDERS at front of book.

Line	Mutagen	Chromosome Rearrangement	Characteristic	Holder	Reference
1-T1,m	TEM	t(1p−;m+)	Homozygous	MIN	1-3
3-Mn.T1,Z	TEM	t(1q−;Zq+)	Homozygous	MIN	1-4
4-N.M.T1,Z	X ray	t(1q−;Zq+)	Homozygous	MIN, NMS	3,5
5-T1,4	TEM	t(1q−;4q+)	Homozygous	MIN	1-4
6-Inversion	EMS	inv.(1p−;1q+)	Heterozygous only; homozygote not viable	MIN	1-4
7-O.S.U.T2,m	X ray	t(2p−;m+)	Homozygous	MIN, OSU	3
8-T2,m#1	TEM	t(2q−;m+)	Homozygous	MIN	1-3
9-T2,m#2	TEM	t(2q−;m+)	Heterozygous; homozygous ♂ are sterile	MIN	1-3
10-T3,Z	EMS	t(3q−;Zq+)	Homozygous	MIN	1-4
11-T3,m	TEM	t(3q−;m+)	Heterozygous	MIN	1-3
12-T4,m	EMS	t(4q−;m+)	Homozygous	MIN	1-3

Contributor: R. N. Shoffner

References

1. Shoffner, R. N. 1972. Poult. Sci. 51:1865.
2. Shoffner, R. N. 1972-1976. Annu. Rep. North Cent. Poult. Breed. Proj. NC-89.
3. Somes, R. G., Jr. 1978. Conn. Agric. Exp. Stn. Storrs Bull. 446.
4. Wang, N., and R. N. Shoffner. 1974. Chromosoma 47: 61-69.
5. Zartman, D. L. 1973. Poult. Sci. 52:1455-1462.

Genotype includes only pertinent genotypic variation from wild type. **Source**: For full name, *see* list of HOLDERS at front of book. Data in brackets refer to the column heading in brackets.

Tester Usage—Locus or Allele Symbol [Locus or Allele Name]	Breed or Line	Genotype	Source	Reference
Co [Columbian]	Light Brown Leghorn [1]	e^+/e^+	MAS	12
Db [Columbian-like restriction[2]]	Brown	e^b/e^b	MAS	7
	Buttercup[3]	e^{bc}/e^{bc}	MAS	11
E-locus	Dominant white e^+	$I/i\ e^+/e^{+}$[4]	MAS	4,10
	Dominant white e^b	$I/i\ e^b/e^b$	MAS	4,10
E [Extended black] & e^{Wh} [dominant wheaten]	Light Brown Leghorn	e^+/e^+	MAS	1,8
E [Extended black], e^{Wh} [dominant wheaten], & e^+ [wild type]	Brown	e^b/e^b	MAS	1,8
E [Extended black], e^{Wh} [dominant wheaten], e^+ [wild type], & e^b [brown]	Buttercup	e^{bc}/e^{bc}	MAS	1
	Recessive wheaten	e^y/e^y	MAS, NEB	1
E [Extended black], & e^+ [wild type] or e^b [brown]	Dominant wheaten	e^{Wh}/e^{Wh}	MAS	1,8
Id [Dermal melanin inhibitor] & id^+ [dermal melanin]	Dermal melanin[5]	id^+/id^+	MAS	3
Lg [Lacing]	Buff Brahma	$e^b/e^b\ Co/Co\ s^+/s^+$	MAS	6
Mh [Mahogany]	Light Brown Leghorn	e^+/e^+	MAS	2
Ml [Melanotic]	Brown	e^b/e^b	MAS	5
	Buff Brahma	$e^b/e^b\ Co/Co\ s^+/s^+$	MAS	6
	Light Brown Leghorn	e^+/e^+	MAS	5
S-locus In dominant white lines	Buff Brahma	$e^b/e^b\ Co/Co\ s^+/s^+$	MAS	4,12
	New Hampshire	$e^{Wh}/e^{Wh}\ Co/Co\ s^+/s^+$	MAS	4,9
S [Silver] & s^+ [gold] expression in presence of heterozygous dominant white (I/i^+)	Dominant white e^+	$I/i\ e^+/e^{+}$[4]	MAS	4,10
	Dominant white e^b	$I/i\ e^b/e^b$	MAS	4,10

[1] Best *Co* tester. [2] Formerly dark brown. [3] Best *Db* tester. [4] Maintained as heterozygote by backcrossing to Light Brown Leghorn. [5] Also segregates at *E*, *I*, *Co*, *Ml*, and *S* loci.

Contributor: J. Robert Smyth, Jr.

References

1. Brumbaugh, J. A., and W. F. Hollander. 1965. Iowa State J. Sci. 40:51-64.
2. Brumbaugh, J. A., and W. F. Hollander. 1966. Poult. Sci. 45:451-457.
3. Dunn, L. C. 1925. Anat. Rec. 31:343-344.
4. Malone, G. W., and J. R. Smyth, Jr. 1979. Poult. Sci. 58:489-497.
5. Moore, J. W., and J. R. Smyth, Jr. 1971. J. Hered. 62:214-219.
6. Moore, J. W., and J. R. Smyth, Jr. 1972. Ibid. 63:179-184.
7. Moore, J. W., and J. R. Smyth, Jr. 1972. Poult. Sci. 51:1149-1156.
8. Smyth, J. R., Jr. 1965. Ibid. 44:89-98.
9. Smyth, J. R., Jr. 1970. J. Hered. 61:280-283.
10. Smyth, J. R., Jr. 1976. Proc. 25th Annu. Poult. Breed. Roundtable (Kansas City, MO), pp. 69-86.
11. Smyth, J. R., Jr. Unpublished. Univ. Massachusetts, Dep. Veterinary and Animal Sciences, Amherst, 1979.
12. Smyth, J. R., Jr., and R. G. Somes. 1965. J. Hered. 56:151-156.

156. RANDOM-BRED CONTROL STRAINS: CHICKEN

For the theory pertaining to poultry control populations, consult references 6, 7, 23, and 33 through 35. **Holder**: For full name, *see* list of HOLDERS at front of book. **Size of Breeding Flock** gives latest known population size.

Origin of Stock: Year gives the date the strain was formed, unless otherwise indicated. Figures in heavy brackets are reference numbers.

continued

Strain Name ⟨Synonym⟩	Holder	Size of Breeding Flock		Origin of Stock		Traits
		No. ♂	No. ♀	Year	Source & Breed	
Egg Production Stocks						
Australorp Control Strain	7HILL	20	120	1959; 1972[1/]	A synthetic of 2 Australorp stocks; genetic contributions were unequal [2, 48]	Egg production [2, 48] Egg weight [48] Livability [2, 48] Feed intake and/or efficiency [48] Sexual maturity [2, 48] Body weight [2]
North Central Random-bred ⟨NCR⟩	NCRPBL	60	360	1972	A synthetic of 6 commercial layer stocks [13]	Egg production [14] Egg weight [14] Sexual maturity [14]
Ottawa Strain 5 Control ⟨Ottawa Control⟩	ARI	80	240	1950	A closed flock of White Leghorns [22]	Fertility and/or hatchability [1, 3, 4, 20] Egg production [1, 7, 12, 18, 20-22, 29, 34, 46, 53] Egg weight [7, 12, 20-22, 46, 49, 50] Egg quality traits [12, 20, 21, 24, 25, 34, 46, 49] Livability [1, 7, 16, 18-22, 27, 34, 53] Sexual maturity [1, 5, 20-22, 34, 46] Body weight [11, 20-22, 29, 34] Body measurements [11, 20] Resistance to specific diseases [10, 16-19, 27, 51-53] Behavior [11, 20]
Ottawa Strain 7 Control ⟨Kentville Control⟩	ARI	80	250	1958	A synthetic of 4 commercial White Leghorn stocks [21]	Fertility and/or hatchability [20] Egg production [8, 12, 15, 18, 20, 21, 30, 31, 34, 46, 50, 53] Egg weight [12, 15, 20, 21, 28, 30, 31, 34, 46, 49, 50, 53] Egg quality traits [12, 15, 20, 21, 28, 30, 31, 46, 49, 50] Livability [8, 15, 16, 18, 20, 21, 27, 30, 31, 34, 50, 53] Feed intake and/or efficiency [30, 31] Sexual maturity [15, 21, 34, 46, 50] Body weight [15, 20, 21, 30, 31, 34, 50] Blood composition [31] Resistance to specific diseases [10, 15, 16, 18, 27, 53] Behavior [9]

[1/] Date from which this strain has been maintained as an unselected control strain.

continued

Strain Name ⟨Synonym⟩	Holder	Size of Breeding Flock No. ♂	Size of Breeding Flock No. ♀	Origin of Stock Year	Origin of Stock Source & Breed	Traits
Ottawa Strain 10 Control	ARI	80	240	1972	A synthetic of 4 commercial White Leghorn stocks [18]	Egg production [18, 29, 30] Egg weight [29, 30] Egg quality traits [29, 30] Livability [16, 18, 30] Feed intake and/or efficiency [30] Body weight [29, 30] Resistance to specific diseases [16, 18]
Unselected Control Line	CSIRO	60	60	∿1970	Crossbred synthetic from Australorp x Strain Cross White Leghorn [47]	Egg production [47] Livability [47]
White Leghorn Control Strain	7HILL	20	120	1959; 1973[1]	A synthetic of 4 White Leghorn stocks; 2 stocks were related, and genetic contributions were unequal [2, 48]	Egg production [2, 48] Egg weight [48] Livability [2, 48] Feed intake and/or efficiency [48] Sexual maturity [2, 48] Body weight [2]
Meat Production Stocks						
Athens Canadian Control ⟨ACC⟩	SRPGL	60	300	1958	Ottawa Strain K Meat Control[2] [32]	Fertility and/or hatchability [39, 55] Egg production [37, 39, 55] Egg weight [37, 39] Egg quality traits [39, 40, 55] Livability [37, 39, 55] Feed intake and/or efficiency [40] Sexual maturity [37, 39] Body weight [37-39] Body measurements [39] Simply inherited morphological traits [37, 39] Body composition [38] Blood composition [55]
Athens Random-bred Control ⟨ARC⟩	SRPGL	64	384	1956	A synthetic of 8 commercial strain-cross meat stocks, mostly of meat breeds with reasonable egg production [32]	Fertility and/or hatchability [36, 55] Egg production [36, 55] Egg weight [36] Egg quality traits [55] Livability [36, 55] Sexual maturity [36] Body weight [36] Simply inherited morphological traits [36] Blood composition [55]

[1] Date from which this strain has been maintained as an unselected control strain. [2] Formerly Ottawa Meat Control.

continued

Strain Name ⟨Synonym⟩	Holder	Size of Breeding Flock		Origin of Stock		Traits
		No. ♂	No. ♀	Year	Source & Breed	
Ottawa Strain K Meat Control ⟨Ottawa Meat Control⟩	ARI	60	200	1955	A synthetic of 2 commercial meat stocks, 1 experimental meat strain, & 1 strain of White Wyandottes, in which all stocks were dominant white [43]	Fertility and/or hatchability [43, 45] Egg production [37, 42] Egg weight [37, 42, 43, 54] Egg quality traits [24] Livability [16, 27, 37, 43] Sexual maturity [37, 42, 43] Body weight [34, 37, 41-44] Body measurements [34, 41-44] Simply inherited morphological traits [37, 43] Isozymes [26] Resistance to specific diseases [16, 27]

Contributors: R. S. Gowe and R. W. Fairfull

References

1. Adams, A. W., et al. 1978. Poult. Sci. 57:48-53.
2. Beilharz, R. G., and M. W. McDonald. 1961. Aust. J. Agric. Res. 12:539-546.
3. Bhagwat, A. L., and J. V. Craig. 1975. Poult. Sci. 54:222-227.
4. Bhagwat, A. L., and J. V. Craig. 1975. Ibid. 54:228-233.
5. Bhagwat, A. L., and J. V. Craig. 1978. Ibid. 57:883-891.
6. Bowman, J. C., and J. C. Powell. 1971. Br. Poult. Sci. 12:511-528.
7. Clayton, G. A. 1968. World's Poult. Sci. J. 24:37-57.
8. Clayton, G. A. 1972. Ann. Genet. Sel. Anim. 4:561-568.
9. Craig, J. V., and A. L. Bhagwat. 1974. Appl. Anim. Ethol. 1:57-65.
10. Crittenden, L. B., et al. 1979. J. Avian Pathol. 8:125-131.
11. Frankham, R., and G. M. Weiss. 1969. Poult. Sci. 48:1691-1694.
12. Friars, G. W., et al. 1978. 16th World's Poult. Congr. 9:1612-1617.
13. Garwood, V. A. Unpublished. Purdue Univ., Dep. Animal Husbandry, West Lafayette, IN, 1977.
14. Garwood, V. A., et al. 1979. Theor. Appl. Genet. 55: (in press).
15. Gavora, J. S., et al. 1974. Poult. Sci. 53:889-897.
16. Gavora, J. S., et al. 1975. Br. Poult. Sci. 16:375-388.
17. Gavora, J. S., et al. 1977. Poult. Sci. 56:590-600.
18. Gavora, J. S., et al. 1977. Ibid. 56:846-853.
19. Gavora, J. S., et al. 1978. 16th World's Poult. Congr. 6:834-839.
20. Gowe, R. S. 1977. Proc. 26th Natl. Poult. Br. Roundtable, pp. 68-91.
21. Gowe, R. S., et al. 1959. 4th Eur. Poult. Conf. London, pp. 225-245.
22. Gowe, R. S., et al. 1959. Poult. Sci. 38:443-462.
23. Gowe, R. S., et al. 1959. Ibid. 38:462-471.
24. Gowe, R. S., et al. 1965. Ibid. 44:264-270.
25. Grunder, A. A., and K. G. Hollands. 1976. Ibid. 55:2255-2261.
26. Grunder, A. A., and E. S. Merritt. 1977. Can. J. Genet. Cytol. 19:645-650.
27. Grunder, A. A., et al. 1972. Can. J. Anim. Sci. 52:1-10.
28. Hamilton, R. M. G. 1978. Poult. Sci. 57:1192-1197.
29. Hamilton, R. M. G. 1978. Ibid. 57:1355-1364.
30. Hamilton, R. M. G., and I. R. Sibbald. 1979. Ibid. 58: (in press).
31. Hamilton, R. M. G., and B. K. Thompson. 1979. Ibid. 58:(in press).
32. Hess, C. W. 1962. Ibid. 18:147-152.
33. Hill, W. G. 1972. Anim. Breed. Abstr. 40:1-15.
34. Hill, W. G. 1972. Ibid. 40:193-213.
35. Latter, B. D. 1959. Aust. J. Biol. Sci. 12:500-505.
36. Marks, H. L. 1971. Poult. Sci. 50:1505-1507.
37. Marks, H. L. 1971. Ibid. 50:1507-1509.
38. Marks, H. L., and W. M. Britton. 1978. Ibid. 57:10-16.
39. Marks, H. L., and P. B. Siegel. 1971. Ibid. 50:1405-1411.
40. Marks, H. L., and K. W. Washburn. 1977. Br. Poult. Sci. 18:179-188.
41. Merritt, E. S. 1966. Poult. Sci. 45:118-125.
42. Merritt, E. S. 1968. Ibid. 47:190-198.

continued

43. Merritt, E. S., and R. S. Gowe. 1972. 12th World's Poult. Congr., pp. 66-70.
44. Merritt, E. S., et al. 1962. Can. J. Anim. Sci. 52:203-210.
45. Mitchell, R. L., and R. B. Buckland. 1976. Poult. Sci. 55:2195-2200.
46. Rodda, D. D., et al. 1977. Br. Poult. Sci. 18:459-473.
47. Sheldon, B. L., et al. 1978. 16th World's Poult. Congr. 9:1602-1611.
48. Sheridan, A. K., and M. C. Randall. 1977. Br. Poult. Sci. 18:69-77.
49. Sibbald, I. R. 1979. Poult. Sci. 58:404-409.
50. Sibbald, I. R., and R. S. Gowe. 1977. Br. Poult. Sci. 18:433-442.
51. Spencer, J. L., et al. 1974. Avian Dis. 18:33-44.
52. Spencer, J. L., et al. 1976. Ibid. 20:268-285.
53. Spencer, J. L., et al. 1979. Poult. Sci. 58:279-284.
54. Van Tijen, W. F., and A. R. Kuit. 1970. Arch. Gefluegelk. 6:201-210.
55. Washburn, K. W., and D. F. Nix. 1974. Poult. Sci. 53:109-115.

157. DISEASE PATTERNS: CHICKEN

Part I. Disease Resistance and Histocompatibility

LL = lymphoid leukosis. **RAV-0** refers to Rous-associated virus-0; to date this has not been shown to be pathogenic, but it has genetic material integrated into the host genome. **Chf** refers to chick helper factor, and is functional in virus replication. **GS** refers to the group-specific antigen of the leukosis-sarcoma viruses. **Histocompatible** refers to histocompatibility within families, unless otherwise indicated. *Abbreviations*: R = resistant; S = susceptible; Seg = segregating, i.e., presence of both S and R individuals within the line.

Line	Leukosis-Sarcoma Virus Subgroup					LL Tumor Development	Marek's Disease	Positive Response to Antigen, % of animals			Histocompatible
	A	B	C	D	E			RAV-0	Chf	GS	
Cornell JM-N	S	Seg	...	..	...	S	R	11.6	76.8	62.3	.....
Cornell JM-P	S	Seg	...	..	...	S	S	9.1	47.4	50.0	.....
RPRL-6₁	S	S	S	S	R	R	R	0.0	100.0	100.0	Yes[1]
RPRL-6₃	S	S	S	S	R	R	R	2.7	100.0	100.0	Yes
RPRL-7₁	R	S	...	..	R	S	S	100.0	100.0	.....	Yes
RPRL-7₂	R	R	S	S	R	S	S	100.0	50.0	.....	Yes
RPRL-15₁	Seg	S	Seg	S	R	S	S	33.0	100.0	99.2	Yes
RPRL-15₄	Seg	S	Seg	S	Seg	S	S	.....	.....	.....	.....
RPRL-15_B[2]	S	S	R	S	S	S	S	.....	.....	.....	.....
RPRL-15I₄	Seg	S	Seg	S	Seg	S	S	100.0	100.0	.....	Yes
RPRL-15I₅	S	S	R	S	R	S	S	20.4	100.0	0.0	Yes
RPRL-100	Seg	Seg	S	S	Seg	S	S	98.4	100.0	.....	85%
RPRL-100_B[2]	Seg	Seg	S	S	Seg	S	S	.....	.....	.....	.....

[1] Apparently histocompatible across the four families of the subline. [2] B subscript refers to lines which were developed at East Lansing, moved to Beltsville with L. B. Crittenden in 1967, and relocated at East Lansing in 1975.

Contributors: Howard A. Stone; Hans Abplanalp

General References

1. Crittenden, L. B. Unpublished. U.S. Dep. of Agriculture, Regional Poultry Research Laboratory, East Lansing, MI, 1978.
2. Stone, H. A. 1975. U.S. Dep. Agric. Tech. Bull. 1514.
3. Stone, H. A. Unpublished. 1827 Lyndhurst Way, Haslett, MI, 1978.

Part II. Inherited Muscular Dystrophy

Inherited muscular dystrophy in the chicken was first described by Asmundson and Julian [ref. 4] at the University of California at Davis. All dystrophic lines are characterized by progressive muscle atrophy. The disorder is expressed in "fast twitch" (alpha-white) muscle fibers [ref. 1, 6]. The fibers are rounded, variable in diameter, and

continued

Part II. Inherited Muscular Dystrophy

exhibit phagocytosis and necrosis [ref. 8]. Histochemical localization of cholinesterase is distinctive, the enzyme activity being found outside the motor end plates in high activity [ref. 12, 18]. There is evidence that the defect is expressed in muscle and not in nerve after 3½ days of incubation [ref. 10]. However, there is also evidence that dystrophic neural tube transplantation into normal host induces high thymidine kinase activity characteristic of dystrophic muscle [ref. 15]. There are some data which indicate that the gene causes a generalized membrane abnormality [ref. 16]. The primary lesion is unknown.

Birds with dystrophy were first described as homozygous for an autosomal gene recessive to normal, but heterozygotes invariably show some expression of the disorder. Flocks homozygous for the gene are maintained at CAL, CONG, and TUE. (For full name, *see* list of HOLDERS at front of book.) The gene is present in New Hampshire and White Leghorn breeds. For a current review of dystrophic mutants, consult reference 19.

Component refers to characteristics of dystrophic chicken pectoralis muscle.

Component	Reference
Increased from Normal	
Acetylcholinesterase (embryonic form)	18
Amino acids, free	14
Cathepsins	17
Cystathionine	13
Lactate dehydrogenase (H form)	9
Myoglobin	2
Serine ethanolamine phosphate	14
Succinate dehydrogenase	6

Component	Reference
Taurine	14
Triglycerides	7
Decreased from Normal	
Alkaline phosphatase, capillary	3
Anserine	14
Carnosine	14
Glyceraldehyde 3-phosphate dehydrogenase	11
Non-collagen protein nitrogen	17
Proteins, sarcoplasmic	5

Contributors: Daniel W. Peterson and Barry W. Wilson

References

1. Ashmore, C. R., and L. Doerr. 1971. Exp. Neurol. 30:431-446.
2. Ashmore, C. R., et al. 1966. Proc. Soc. Exp. Biol. Med. 122:1104-1107.
3. Ashmore, C. R., et al. 1968. Science 160:319-320.
4. Asmundson, V. S., and L. M. Julian. 1956. J. Hered. 47:248-252.
5. Barany, M., et al. 1966. Ann. N.Y. Acad. Sci. 138:360-366.
6. Cosmos, E., and J. Butler. 1967. Excerpta Med. Int. Congr. Ser. 147:197-204.
7. Jordan, J. P., et al. 1964. Proc. Soc. Exp. Biol. Med. 116:243-246.
8. Julian, L. M., and V. S. Asmundson. 1963. In G. H. Bourne and M. N. Golarz, ed. Muscular Dystrophy in Man and Animals. Hafner, New York. pp. 458-498.
9. Kaplan, N. O., and R. D. Cahn. 1962. Proc. Natl. Acad. Sci. USA 48:2123-2130.
10. Linkhart, T. A., et al. 1976. Dev. Biol. 48:447-457.
11. Patnode, R. E., et al. 1976. J. Biol. Chem. 251:4468.
12. Patterson, G. T., and B. W. Wilson. 1976. Exp. Neurol. 52:250-262.
13. Peterson, D. W., and A. L. Lilyblade. 1968. Proc. Soc. Exp. Biol. Med. 127:576-578.
14. Peterson, D. W., et al. 1963. Ibid. 113:798-802.
15. Rathbone, M. P., et al. 1975. Science 189:1106-1107.
16. Sha'afi, R. I., et al. 1975. Nature (London) 254:525-526.
17. Weinstock, I. M., and M. Lukacs. 1965. Enzymol. Biol. Clin. 5:103-112.
18. Wilson, B. W., et al. 1970. J. Exp. Zool. 174:39-54.
19. Wilson, B. W., et al. 1979. Ann. N.Y. Acad. Sci. 317:224-246.

158. LINKAGE RELATIONSHIPS: CHICKEN

The diploid complement of *Gallus gallus* ⟨*G. domesticus*⟩ contains about 78 chromosomes, ranging in size from around 8 μm to barely visible by light microscopy [ref. 1, 8-10, 16, 18]. The first five pairs are large (macrochromosomes), and are distinctive enough to permit rapid identification and detection of aberrations without the aid of a

photokaryotype [ref. 2, 5, 6]. Chromosome pairs 6-10 can be identified in photomicrographs. The remaining 29 pairs of smaller chromosomes (microchromosomes) are arranged in decreasing size order in the karyotype without numerical assignments. Since there is only a gradual decrease in size from one chromosome to the next, the terms macro- and

continued

microchromosome are used somewhat arbitrarily. The W sex chromosome, present only in females, is similar in size and shape to the chromosomes of pair 9. However, C-banding results in differential staining of the W chromosome at metaphase [ref. 3, 12]. The sex-determining mechanism is ZZ = ♂, ZW = ♀; the Z chromosome is the fifth largest in the karyotype [ref. 1, 3, 15]. The following techniques have been successfully applied to chick chromosomes: Giemsa-

⟨G-⟩ banding [ref. 14, 17], C-banding (stain for constitutive heterochromatin) [ref. 12], ammoniacal silver staining ⟨Ag-AS-banding⟩ of the nucleolar organizer region [ref. 4], and banding by incorporation of 5-bromodeoxyuridine ⟨BrdUrd-banding⟩ [ref. 5]. Also, studies on DNA replication [ref. 7, 11] and repetitive DNA sequences [ref. 13] have been performed.

Contributor: Stephen E. Bloom

References

1. Bloom, S. E. 1969. J. Hered. 60:217-220.
2. Bloom, S. E. 1970. Avian Dis. 14:478-490.
3. Bloom, S. E. 1974. BioScience 24:340-344.
4. Bloom, S. E., and C. Goodpasture. 1976. Hum. Genet. 34:199-206.
5. Bloom, S. E., and T. C. Hsu. 1975. Chromosoma 51:261-267.
6. Cormier, J. M., and S. E. Bloom. 1973. Mutat. Res. 20:77-85.
7. Donnelly, G. M., and E. H. Newcomer. 1963. Exp. Cell Res. 30:363-368.
8. Krishan, A., and R. N. Shoffner. 1966. Cytogenetics 5:53-63.
9. Ohno, S. 1961. Chromosoma 11:484-498.
10. Owen, J. J. T. 1965. Ibid. 16:601-608.
11. Schmid, W. 1962. Cytogenetics 1:344-352.
12. Stefos, K., and F. E. Arrighi. 1971. Exp. Cell Res. 68:228-231.
13. Stefos, K., and F. E. Arrighi. 1974. Ibid. 83:9-14.
14. Stock, A. D., et al. 1974. Cytogenet. Cell Genet. 13:410-418.
15. Suzuki, K. 1930. Dobutsugaku Zasshi 42:358.
16. van Brink, L. M., and G. A. Ubbels. 1956. Experientia 12:162-164.
17. Wang, N., and R. N. Shoffner. 1974. Chromosoma 47:61-69.
18. Yamashina, Y. 1944. Cytologia 13:270-296.

Part I.   Genes and Linkage Groups Assigned to Specific Chromosomes

Of the five largest chromosome pairs, only two have been assigned genes; pairs 2, 3, and 4 are as yet unmapped. Chromosome Morphology & Staining Properties: Arm ratio = length of long arm divided by length of short arm.

Linkage Group	Linked Genes ⟨Gene Symbol⟩	Chromosome Assignment	Chromosome Morphology & Staining Properties	Reference
III	Blue egg ⟨O⟩ Pea comb ⟨P⟩ Marbled down ⟨ma⟩ Naked neck ⟨Na⟩ Silkiness ⟨h⟩ Flightless ⟨Fl⟩	No. 1	Submetacentric; arm ratio = 1.6	6
V	Head streak ⟨ko⟩ Sex-linked barring ⟨B⟩ Dermal melanin inhibitor ⟨Id⟩ Brown eye ⟨br⟩ Light down ⟨Li⟩ Silver ⟨S⟩ Late feathering ⟨K⟩ Wing spot ⟨ws⟩ Prenatal lethal ⟨pn⟩ Sex-linked dwarfism ⟨dw⟩	No. 5 (Z sex chromosome)	Metacentric; arm ratio = 1.1. C-band at telomere.	3

continued

Part I.   Genes and Linkage Groups Assigned to Specific Chromosomes

Linkage Group	Linked Genes ⟨Gene Symbol⟩	Chromosome Assignment	Chromosome Morphology & Staining Properties	Reference
	Sex-linked lethal liver necrosis ⟨ln⟩ Paroxysm ⟨px⟩ Naked ⟨n⟩ Shaker ⟨sh⟩			
VI	W-linked histoantigen ⟨H-W⟩	No. 5 (W sex chromosome)	Submetacentric; arm ratio = 2.0. Entire chromosome is C-band positive.	2
VII	Adenine synthesis A ⟨Ade-A⟩	No. 7[1]	Submetacentric; arm ratio = 2.5	4
VIII	Adenine synthesis B ⟨Ade-B⟩	No. 8[1]	Acrocentric	4
IX	Cytosol thymidine kinase F ⟨Tk-F⟩	Microchromosome[2]	Acrocentric	5
X	B blood group ⟨Ea-B⟩ Nucleolar organizer region ⟨NOR⟩	Microchromosome[3]	Acrocentric. Stains with Ag-AS banding.	1

[1] The authors of reference 4 labeled these chromosomes as 6 and 7 since the Z chromosome was not given a numerical assignment; present convention, however, is to include the Z and W as pair number 5, so that chromosomes associated with Ade-A and Ade-B are 7 and 8, respectively. [2] Smaller than number 8. [3] In the size range of numbers 15-18.

Contributor: Stephen E. Bloom

References

1. Bloom, S. E., et al. 1978. Genetics 88(Suppl.):s13.
2. Gilmour, D. G. 1967. Transplantation 5:699-706.
3. Hutt, F. B. 1949. Genetics of the Fowl. McGraw-Hill, New York. pp. 486-498.
4. Kao, F. 1973. Proc. Natl. Acad. Sci. USA 70:2893-2898.
5. Leung, W. C., et al. 1975. Exp. Cell Res. 95:320-326.
6. Zartman, D. L. 1973. Poult. Sci. 52:1455-1462.

Part II.   Mapped and Unmapped Linkage Relationships

For additional information, consult reference 72.

Linked Gene Symbols	Linked Trait Names	Linkage Distance	Reference
Linkage Group I			
Cp—R	Creeper—rose comb	0.4	41,42,76
lav—R	Lavender—rose comb	32.5	12
Mp—R	Ametapodia—rose comb	16.0	16
R—U	Rose comb—uropygial	29.6	32
Linkage Group II			
Cr—F	Crest—frizzling	29.0	75,83

continued

Part II. Mapped and Unmapped Linkage Relationships

Linked Gene Symbols	Linked Trait Names	Linkage Distance	Reference
Cr—fr	Crest—fray	46.0	79
Cr—I	Crest—dominant white	12.5	83
F—I	Frizzling—dominant white	17.0	31,83
Linkage Group III[1,2]			
Ab—Db[3]	Autosomal barring—Columbian-like restriction	17.0	53
Db[3]*—P*	Columbian-like restriction—pea comb	28.0	66,84
Ea-A—Ea-E	A blood group—E blood group	0.5	9
Ea-A—Ea-J	A blood group—J blood group	45.0	8,20
Ea-C—Ea-J	C blood group—J blood group	44.5	8,20
Ea-H—Mb	H blood group—muffs and beard	44.3	10
Ea-H—w	H blood group—yellow skin	22.1	10
Ea-J—P	J blood group—pea comb	40.7	10
Ea-J—w	J blood group—yellow skin	45.1	10
Ea-P—Na	P blood group—naked neck	29.1	10
Fl—h	Flightless—silkiness	11.6	78,80
Fl—Na	Flightless—naked neck	46.2	82
h—Na	Silkiness—naked neck	43.3	82
ma—Na	Marbled down—naked neck	45.6	28
ma—P	Marbled down—pea comb	32.8	28
O—P	Blue egg—pea comb	5.0	11
P—se	Pea comb—sleepy-eye	45.1	67
P—t	Pea comb—tardy feather growth	41.0	20
pe—se	Perosis—sleepy-eye	27.0	68
se—w	Sleepy-eye—yellow skin	43.3	67
Linkage Group IV			
D—M	Duplex comb—multiple spurs	27.8	33
D—Po	Duplex comb—polydactyly	42.0	36,81
M—Po	Multiple spurs—polydactyly	33.5	36,81
Po—Po[d]	Polydactyly—duplicate polydactyly	0.0	81
Linkage Group V[4]			
B—B[Sd]	Sex-linked barring—dilution	0.0	20,35,77
B—Id	Sex-linked barring—dermal melanin inhibitor	9.3	60,64
B—j	Sex-linked barring—jittery	51.3	24
B—ko	Sex-linked barring—head streak	13.0	27,60
B—Li	Sex-linked barring—light down	40.0	29,60
B—S	Sex-linked barring—silver	48.0	3,26,60
B—xl	Sex-linked barring—sex-linked lethal	52.0	25
br—Id	Brown eye—dermal melanin inhibitor	27.0	44,60

[1] Linkage group III has been identified as being located on the largest autosome, chromosome 1 [ref. 86]. [2] The letters "*Ea*" (erythrocyte alloantigen) have been prefixed to the original letters assigned to the blood group loci, to eliminate confusion with previously assigned symbols.

[3] Formerly *fpi*, "partial feather achromatosis," which has recently been shown to be equivalent to *Db* [ref. 66]. [4] Linkage group V has been identified with the Z or sex chromosome.

continued

Part II. Mapped and Unmapped Linkage Relationships

Linked Gene Symbols	Linked Trait Names	Linkage Distance	Reference
br—K	Brown eye—late feathering	42.0	44,60
br—S	Brown eye—silver	44.0	44,60
cd[5]—	Cerebellar degeneration	....	46
chz—	Sex-linked chondrodystrophy	....	45
cm[6]—	Sex-linked coloboma	....	2
dp-4—	Diplopodia-4	....	1
dw—dw[B]	Sex-linked dwarfism—Bantam dwarfism	0.0	19,30
dw—dw[M]	Sex-linked dwarfism—MacDonald dwarfism	0.0	30
dw—K	Sex-linked dwarfism—late feathering	6.6	34,35
dw—S	Sex-linked dwarfism—silver	7.0	34,35
ga—	Gasper	....	59
H-Z[5]—	Z-linked histoantigen	....	4
Id—id[a]	Dermal melanin inhibitor—green spotting	0.0	51
Id—id[c]	Dermal melanin inhibitor—green shank [7]	0.0	48
Id—K	Dermal melanin inhibitor—late feathering	46.0	44,60
Id—Li	Dermal melanin inhibitor—light down	30.0	29,60
Id—ro	Dermal melanin inhibitor—restricted ovulator	42.0	50
Id—S	Dermal melanin inhibitor—silver	47.0	44,57
j—K	Jittery—late feathering	48.7	24
K—K[n]	Late feathering—extremely slow feathering	0.0	70
K—K[s]	Late feathering—slow feathering	0.0	49
K—ko	Late feathering—head streak	47.0	27,60
K—Li	Late feathering—light down	24.0	29,60
K—lk	Late feathering—ladykiller	5.9	65
K—n	Late feathering—naked	17.6	35
K—pn	Late feathering—prenatal lethal	3.0	69,70,73
K—ro	Late feathering—restricted ovulator	36.3	50
K—S	Late feathering—silver	1.1	35,70
K—sh	Late feathering—shaker	26.4	35,54
K—wl[6]	Late feathering—sex-linked wingless	1.3	40
ko—Li	Head streak—light down	47.0	27,60
Li—S	Light down—silver	16.0	29,60
ln—n	Sex-linked lethal liver necrosis—naked	10.6	18
ln—S	Sex-linked lethal liver necrosis—silver	8.5	18
n—px	Naked—paroxysm	6.0	15
n—S	Naked—silver	21.4	35
n—sh	Naked—shaker	13.3	35
pn—S	Prenatal lethal—silver	4.0	69,73
px—S	Paroxysm—silver	10.5	15
rg—	Recessive sex-linked dwarf	....	23
S—s[al]	Silver—imperfect albinism	0.0	17,85
S—sh	Silver—shaker	35.3	35,54
S—wl[6]	Silver—sex-linked wingless	4.7	40

[5] No gene symbol previously assigned; provisional gene symbol proposed. [6] Gene symbol changed as previous symbol refers to a different locus. [7] Synonym: dermal melanin-Cornell.

continued

Part II. Mapped and Unmapped Linkage Relationships

Linked Gene Symbols	Linked Trait Names	Linkage Distance	Reference
sex [5]/—	Sex-linked lethal-Bernier	....	71
sln [5]/—	Sex-linked nervous disorder	....	38
_Z_—	Dominant sex-linked dwarf	....	47
Linkage Group VI			
_H-W_ [5]/	W-linked histoantigen	....	5,22
Linkage Group VII[8]/			
Ade-A	Adenine synthesis A	....	37
Linkage Group VIII[8]/			
Ade-B	Adenine synthesis B	....	37
Linkage Group IX[9]/			
_Tk-F_ [5]/	Cytosol thymidine kinase F	....	43
Linkage Group X[2,10]/			
_B-F—B-G—B-L_	Major histocompatibility complex loci	Close	58
_B-F, B-G, & B-L—R-Rs-1_	Major histocompatibility complex loci—Rous sarcoma regression	Close	63
Ea-B—NOR	B blood group—nucleolar organizer region	....	6,7
Linkage Group Unknown[2]/			
_Ea-M—Ea-Q_	M blood group—Q blood group	5.4	62
_Ea-O—Ea-S_	O blood group—S blood group	2.6	62
_Es-1—Es-2_	Esterase-1—esterase-2	0.04	39
G_3—_Ov_	Ovoglobulin G_3—ovalbumin	0.8	13,14,74
_gs—Tv-E_	Group-specific antigen—tumor virus subgroup E	Close	56
IgG-1 [11]/—_IgM-1_ [12]/	7S-1 immunoglobulin heavy chain—immunoglobulin M	Close	57
_Lg—Ml_	Lacing—melanotic	10.3	52
_Ly-4—Th-1_	Lymphocyte antigen-4—thymocyte antigen-1	32.0	21
_Tv-A—Tv-C_	Tumor virus subgroup A—tumor virus subgroup C	0.17	55
_Tv-B—Tv-E_	Tumor virus subgroup B—tumor virus subgroup E	Close	61

[2]/ The letters "_Ea_" (erythrocyte alloantigen) have been prefixed to the original letters assigned to the blood group loci, to eliminate confusion with previously assigned symbols. [5]/ No gene symbol previously assigned; provisional gene symbol proposed. [8]/ Linkage groups VII and VIII have been identified as being located on chromosomes 7 and 8, respectively. The author in reference 37 labeled these chromosomes as 6 and 7 because he failed to include the Z chromosome as number 5 which is the present avian karyologic convention. [9]/ Linkage group IX has been identified as being located on a microchromosome smaller than number 8 [ref. 43]. [10]/ Linkage group X has been identified as being located on a microchromosome in the size range of numbers 15-18 [ref. 6, 7]. [11]/ Formerly _Cs-1_. [12]/ Formerly _Cm-1_.

Contributor: Ralph G. Somes, Jr.

References

1. Abbott, U. K., and M. Kieny. 1961. C. R. Acad. Sci. 242:1863-1865.
2. Abbott, U.K., et al. 1970. J. Hered. 61:95-102.
3. Agar, W. E. 1924. J. Genet. 14:265-272.
4. Bacon, L. D. 1970. Transplantation 10:126-129.
5. Bacon, L. D., and J. V. Craig. 1969. Ibid. 7:387-393.

continued

Part II. Mapped and Unmapped Linkage Relationships

6. Bloom, S. E., and R. K. Cole. 1978. Poult. Sci. 57: 1119.

7. Bloom, S. E., et al. 1978. Genetics 88(Suppl.):s13.

8. Briles, W. E. 1964. Z. Tierz. Zuechtungsbiol. 79:371-391.

9. Briles, W. E. 1968. Genetics 60:164.

10. Briles, W. E., et al. 1967. Poult. Sci. 46:1238.

11. Bruckner, J. H., and F. B. Hutt. 1939. Science 90:88-89.

12. Brumbaugh, J. A., et al. 1972. J. Hered. 63:19-25.

13. Buvanendran, V. 1964. Genet. Res. 5:330-332.

14. Buvanendran, V. 1967. Br. Poult. Sci. 8:9-12.

15. Cole, R. K. 1958. Poult. Sci. 37:1194-1195.

16. Cole, R. K. 1967. J. Hered. 58:141-146.

17. Cole, R. K., and T. K. Jeffers. 1963. Nature (London) 200:1238-1239.

18. Cole, R. K., and D. G. Jones. 1972. Poult. Sci. 51: 1795.

19. Custodio, R. W. S., and R. G. Jaap. 1973. Poult. Sci. 52:204-210.

20. Etches, R. J., and R. O. Hawes. 1973. Can. J. Genet. Cytol. 15:553-570.

21. Fredericksen, T. L., et al. 1977. Immunogenetics 5: 535-552.

22. Gilmour, D. G. 1967. Transplantation 5:699-706.

23. Godfrey, E. F. 1953. Poult. Sci. 32:248-259.

24. Godfrey, E. F., et al. 1953. J. Hered. 44:108-112.

25. Goodwin, K., et al. 1950. Science 112:460-461.

26. Haldane, J. B. S. 1921. Ibid. 54:663.

27. Hertwig, P. 1930. Biol. Zentralbl. 50:333-341.

28. Hertwig, P. 1933. Verhandl. Dtsch. Zool. Ges., pp. 112-118.

29. Hertwig, P., and T. Rittershaus. 1929. Z. Indukt. Abstamm. Vererbungsl. 51:354-372.

30. Hsu, P. L., et al. 1975. Poult. Sci. 54:1315-1319.

31. Hutt, F. B. 1933. Genetics 18:82-94.

32. Hutt, F. B. 1936. Neue Forsch. Tierz. Abstammungsl. (Festschr.):105-112.

33. Hutt, F. B. 1941. J. Hered. 32:356-364.

34. Hutt, F. B. 1959. Ibid. 50:209-221.

35. Hutt, F. B. 1960. Heredity 15:97-110.

36. Hutt, F. B., and C. D. Mueller. 1943. Am. Nat. 77: 70-78.

37. Kao, F. 1973. Proc. Natl. Acad. Sci. USA 70:2893-2898.

38. Kawahara, T. 1955. Annu. Rep. Natl. Inst. Genet. Jpn. 5:26-27.

39. Kimura, M., and N. Kameyama. 1970. Jpn. Poult. Sci. 7:39-41.

40. Lancaster, F. M. 1968. Heredity 23:257-262.

41. Landauer, W. 1932. J. Genet. 26:285-290.

42. Landauer, W. 1933. Nature (London) 132:606.

43. Leung, W. C., et al. 1975. Exp. Cell Res. 95:320-326.

44. MacArthur, J. W. 1933. Genetics 18:210-220.

45. Mann, G. E. 1963. NAAS Poult. Sect. Q. J. 69:1-2.

46. Markson, L. M. 1959. J. Comp. Pathol. 69:223-229.

47. Maw, A. J. G. 1935. Sci. Agric. 16:85-112.

48. McGibbon, W. H. 1974. Poult. Sci. 53:1251-1253.

49. McGibbon, W. H. 1977. Ibid. 56:872-875.

50. McGibbon, W. H. 1977. Genetics 86(Suppl.):s43-s44.

51. McGibbon, W. H. 1978. J. Hered. 69:97-100.

52. Moore, J. W., and J. R. Smyth, Jr. 1972. Ibid. 63: 179-184.

53. Moore, J. W., and J. R. Smyth, Jr. 1972. Poult. Sci. 51:1149-1156.

54. Mueller, C. D. 1952. Ibid. 31:1105-1106.

55. Pani, P. K. 1974. Nature (London) 248:592-594.

56. Pani, P. K. 1977. J. Gen. Virol. 38:61-74.

57. Pink, J. R. L., and J. Ivanyi. 1975. Eur. J. Immunol. 5:506-507.

58. Pink, J. R. L., et al. 1977. Immunogenetics 5:203-216.

59. Price, D. J., et al. 1966. Poult. Sci. 45:423-424.

60. Punnett, R. C. 1940. J. Genet. 39:335-342.

61. Robinson, H. L., and W. F. Lamoreux. 1976. Virology 69:50-62.

62. Scheinberg, S. L. 1956. Genetics 41:834-844.

63. Schierman, L. W. 1977. Immunogenetics 5:325-332.

64. Serebrovsky, A. S., and S. G. Petrov. 1930. J. Exp. Biol. 6:157-179.

65. Sheridan, A. K. 1964. Proc. Aust. Poult. Sci. Conv. 1:87-90.

66. Smyth, J. R., Jr., and G. W. Malone. 1979. Poult. Sci. 58:1108-1109.

67. Somes, R. G., Jr. 1968. J. Hered. 59:375-378.

68. Somes, R. G., Jr. 1969. Ibid. 60:163-166.

69. Somes, R. G., Jr. 1969. Ibid. 60:185-186.

70. Somes, R. G., Jr. 1969. Ibid. 60:281-286.

71. Somes, R. G., Jr. 1971. Conn. Agric. Exp. Stn. Storrs Bull. 420.

72. Somes, R. G., Jr. 1973. J. Hered. 64:217-221.

73. Somes, R. G., Jr., and J. R. Smyth, Jr. 1967. Ibid. 58:25-29.

74. Stratil, A. 1970. Anim. Blood Groups Biochem. Genet. 1:83-88.

75. Suttle, A. D., and G. R. Sipe. 1932. J. Hered. 23:135-142.

76. Taylor, L. W. 1934. Ibid. 25:205-206.

77. van Albada, M., and A. R. Kuit. 1960. Genen Phaenen 5:1-9.

78. Warren, D. C. 1935. Am. Nat. 69:82.

79. Warren, D. C. 1938. Genetics 23:174.

80. Warren, D. C. 1940. Am. Nat. 74:93-95.

81. Warren, D. C. 1944. Genetics 29:217-231.

82. Warren, D. C. 1949. Ibid. 34:333-349.

83. Warren, D. C., and F. B. Hutt. 1936. Am. Nat. 70: 379-394.

84. Washburn, K. W., and J. R. Smyth, Jr. 1967. J. Hered. 58:131-134.

85. Werret, W. F., et al. 1959. Nature (London) 184:480.

86. Zartman, D. L. 1973. Poult. Sci. 52:1455-1462.

continued

158. LINKAGE RELATIONSHIPS: CHICKEN

Part III. Linkage Map

Map is slight modification of one in reference 5.

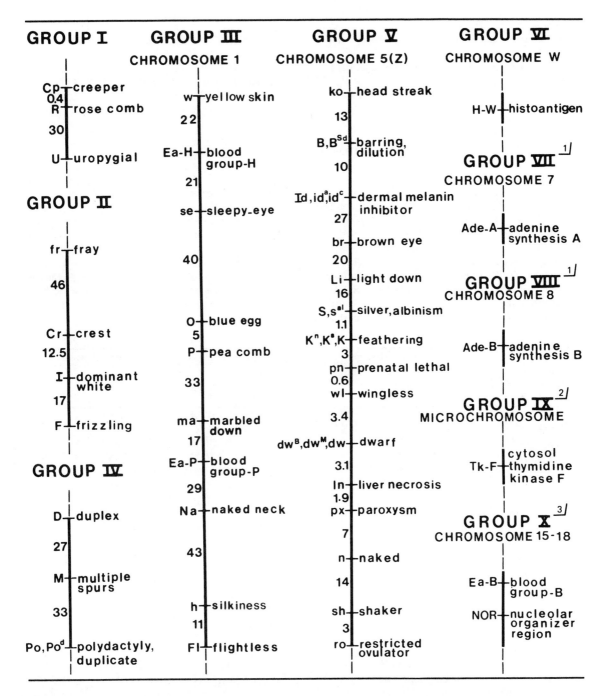

[1] Linkage groups VII and VIII have been identified as being located on chromosomes 7 and 8, respectively [ref. 3]. The author labeled these chromosomes as 6 and 7 because he failed to include the Z chromosome as number 5 which is the present avian karyologic convention. [2] Linkage group IX has been identified as being located on a microchromosome smaller than number 8 [ref. 4]. [3] Linkage group X has been identified as being located on a microchromosome in the size range of numbers 15-18 [ref. 1, 2].

continued

158. LINKAGE RELATIONSHIPS: CHICKEN

Part III. Linkage Map

Contributor: Ralph G. Somes, Jr.

References
1. Bloom, S. E., and R. K. Cole. 1978. Poult. Sci. 57: 1119.
2. Bloom, S. E., et al. 1978. Genetics 88(Suppl.):s13.
3. Kao, F. 1973. Proc. Natl. Acad. Sci. USA 70:2893-2898.
4. Leung, W. C., et al. 1975. Exp. Cell Res. 95:320-326.
5. Somes, R. G., Jr. 1978. J. Hered. 69:401-403.

Part IV. Genes Demonstrating Independent Segregation

The table below is a summary of investigations that demonstrated independent segregation. The first summary of linkage data showing independent segregation was published by Warren [ref. 9]. Since that time, similar reports have been published by Etches and Hawes [ref. 2] and Abbott and Yee [ref. 1]. Although the chicken contains 39 pairs of chromosomes, only 5 or 6 major linkage groups have been found. Of the 39 pairs, the 10 macrochromosomes probably contain at least 95% of the structural genes [ref. 1]. It seems likely, therefore, that the task of mapping the multitude of single-gene mutants in the chicken should not be formidable. The various summaries of linkage data showing independent segregation should be of assistance to those engaged in this area of research. The letters Ea (erythrocyte alloantigen) have been prefixed to the original letters assigned to the blood group loci to eliminate confusion with previously assigned symbols for other loci. For further information on this tentative nomenclature change, consult reference 8. Data in parentheses refer to the column heading in parentheses. Data in broken brackets are synonyms.

Marker Gene Symbol (Name)	Segregates Independently with Gene		Reference
	Symbol	Name	
a (Autosomal albinism)	*Cr*	Crest	9
	D	Duplex comb	9
	F [1/]	Frizzling	9
	Fl	Flightless	9
	Mb	Muffs and beard	9
	Na	Naked neck	9
	P	Pea comb	9
	Po	Polydactyly	9
	R	Rose comb	9
	Rp	Rumplessness, dominant	9
	w	Yellow skin	9
Acp-2 (Acid phosphatase)	*Akp 2/*	Alkaline phosphatase	2
	c	Recessive white	2
	Ea-A ⟨*CA*⟩ & *Ea-E* ⟨*CE*⟩	Blood groups A & E	2
	Ea-B ⟨*CB*⟩	Blood group B	2
	Ea-D ⟨*CD*⟩	Blood group D	2
Akp 2/ (Alkaline phosphatase)	*Acp-2*	Acid phosphatase	2
	c	Recessive white	2
	Ea-A ⟨*CA*⟩ & *Ea-E* ⟨*CE*⟩	Blood groups A & E	2
	Ea-B ⟨*CB*⟩	Blood group B	2
	Ea-D ⟨*CD*⟩	Blood group D	2
	Es-1	Plasma esterase	4

Marker Gene Symbol (Name)	Segregates Independently with Gene		Reference
	Symbol	Name	
Alb (Serum albumin)	*Ea-A* ⟨*CA*⟩ & *Ea-E* ⟨*CE*⟩	Blood groups A & E	3
	Ea-B ⟨*CB*⟩	Blood group B	2,3
	Ea-C ⟨*CC*⟩	Blood group C	3
	Ea-D ⟨*CD*⟩	Blood group D	3
	G₂	Ovoglobulin G_2	2
	G₃	Ovoglobulin G_3	2
	I	Dominant white	2
	IgM-1 ⟨*M1*⟩	Immunoglobulin M1	6
	Mr-1	Mitogen response-1	5
	P	Pea comb	2
	Pa	Prealbumin	2
	Tf	Transferrin-conalbumin	2
	w	Yellow skin	2
am (Muscular dystrophy)	*Cr*	Crest	1
	D	Duplex comb	1
	F	Frizzling	1
	I	Dominant white	1
	Mb	Muffs and beard	1
	Na	Naked neck	1
	P	Pea comb	1
	Po	Polydactyly	1
	R	Rose comb	1
	w	Yellow skin	1

[1/] Possible linkage. [2/] Formerly designated *Ap*, which symbol now refers to a different gene.

continued

Part IV. Genes Demonstrating Independent Segregation

Marker Gene Symbol (Name)	Segregates Independently with Gene		Reference
	Symbol	Name	
As (Auxiliary spurs)	*Db* [3]	Columbian-like restriction ⟨Feather achromatosis⟩	2
	P	Pea comb	2
Bl (Blue plumage)	*Cr*	Crest	9
	D	Duplex comb	9
	F	Frizzling	9
	Fl	Flightless	9
	fr	Fray	9
	h	Hookless ⟨Silkiness⟩	9
	Mb	Muffs and beard	9
	Na [1]	Naked neck	9
	P	Pea comb	9
	Po	Polydactyly	9
	R [1]	Rose comb	9
	ropy	Ropy	9
	Rp	Rumplessness, dominant	9
	w	Yellow skin	9
c (Recessive white)	*Acp-2*	Acid phosphatase	2
	Akp [2]	Alkaline phosphatase	2
	Cr	Crest	9
	D	Duplex comb	9
	F	Frizzling	9
	Fl	Flightless	9
	Mb	Muffs and beard	9
	Na	Naked neck	9
	P	Pea comb	9
	pk	Pink eye	9
	Po	Polydactyly	9
	R	Rose comb	9
	Rp	Rumplessness, dominant	9
	U	Uropygial	9
	w	Yellow skin	9
Cp (Creeper)	*Cr*	Crest	9
	D	Duplex comb	9
	F	Frizzling	9
	I	Dominant white	9
	Mb	Muffs and beard	9
	P	Pea comb	9
	Po	Polydactyly	9
	Rp	Rumplessness, dominant	9
	se	Sleepy-eye	2
	w	Yellow skin	9
Cr (Crest)	*a*	Autosomal albinism	9
	am	Muscular dystrophy	1
	Bl	Blue plumage	9
	c	Recessive white	9
	Cp	Creeper	9

Marker Gene Symbol (Name)	Segregates Independently with Gene		Reference
	Symbol	Name	
	D	Duplex comb	9
	Ea-A ⟨*CA*⟩ & *Ea-E* ⟨*CE*⟩	Blood groups A & E	2
	Ea-B ⟨*CB*⟩	Blood group B	2
	Ea-C ⟨*CC*⟩	Blood group C	2
	Ea-D ⟨*CD*⟩	Blood group D	2
	Ea-H ⟨*CH*⟩	Blood group H	2
	Ea-I ⟨*CI*⟩	Blood group I	2
	Ea-J ⟨*CJ*⟩	Blood group J	2
	Ea-K ⟨*CK*⟩	Blood group K	2
	Ea-L ⟨*CL*⟩	Blood group L	2
	Ea-P ⟨*CP*⟩	Blood group P	2
	epi	Epileptiform seizures	2
	Fl	Flightless	9
	M	Multiple spurs	9
	Mb	Muffs and beard	9
	mo	Mottling	9
	Na	Naked neck	9
	P	Pea comb	9
	pk	Pink eye	9
	Po	Polydactyly	9
	R	Rose comb	9
	ropy	Ropy	9
	Rp	Rumplessness, dominant	9
	sc	Scaleless	1
	se	Sleepy-eye	2
	sn	Sunsuit	2
	sw	Snow-white down	2
	t	Tardy feathering	9
	w	Yellow skin	9
D (Duplex comb)	*a*	Autosomal albinism	9
	am	Muscular dystrophy	1
	Bl	Blue plumage	9
	c	Recessive white	9
	Cp	Creeper	9
	Cr	Crest	9
	E	Extended black	9
	F	Frizzling	9
	Fl	Flightless	9
	fr	Fray	9
	I	Dominant white	9
	Mb	Muffs and beard	9
	mo	Mottling	9
	Mp	Ametapodia	2
	Na	Naked neck	9
	P [1]	Pea comb	9
	pk	Pink eye	9

[1] Possible linkage. [2] Formerly designated *Ap*, which symbol now refers to a different gene. [3] Formerly *mi* (feather achromatosis), but *mi* had already been assigned to micro-phthalmia. Recently, it was shown that feather achromatosis was the same as Columbian-like restriction ⟨*Db*⟩ [ref. 7].

continued

Part IV. Genes Demonstrating Independent Segregation

Marker Gene Symbol (Name)	Segregates Independently with Gene		Reference
	Symbol	Name	
	Po [1]	Polydactyly	9
	R	Rose comb	9
	ropy	Ropy	9
	Rp	Rumplessness, dominant	9
	se	Sleepy-eye	2
	sn	Sunsuit	2
	sw	Snow-white down	2
	t	Tardy feathering	9
	w [1]	Yellow skin	9
Db [3] (Columbian-like restriction ⟨Feather achromatosis⟩)	As	Auxiliary spurs	2
dehy (Ichthyosis)	dp-1	Diplopodia-1	1
	eu	Eudiplopodia	1
	sc	Scaleless	1
dp-1 (Diplopodia-1)	dehy	Ichthyosis	1
	dp-2	Diplopodia-2	2
	dp-3	Diplopodia-3	1
	eu	Eudiplopodia	1
	ta-2	Talpid-2	2
dp-2 (Diplopodia-2)	dp-1	Diplopodia-1	2
dp-3 (Diplopodia-3)	dp-1	Diplopodia-1	1
E (Extended black)	D	Duplex comb	9
	Ea-A ⟨CA⟩ & Ea-E ⟨CE⟩	Blood groups A & E	3
	Ea-B ⟨CB⟩	Blood group B	3
	Ea-C ⟨CC⟩	Blood group C	3
	Ea-D ⟨CD⟩	Blood group D	3
	P	Pea comb	2
	Po	Polydactyly	9
	se	Sleepy-eye	2
Ea-A ⟨CA⟩ & Ea-E ⟨CE⟩ (Blood groups A & E)	Acp-2	Acid phosphatase	2
	Akp [2]	Alkaline phosphatase	2
	Alb	Serum albumin	3
	Cr	Crest	2
	E	Extended black	3
	Ea-B ⟨CB⟩	Blood group B	2
	Ea-C ⟨CC⟩	Blood group C	2
	Ea-D ⟨CD⟩	Blood group D	2
	Ea-H ⟨CH⟩	Blood group H	2
	Ea-I ⟨CI⟩	Blood group I	2
	Ea-J ⟨CJ⟩ [1]	Blood group J	2
	Ea-K ⟨CK⟩	Blood group K	2
	Ea-L ⟨CL⟩	Blood group L	2
	Ea-P ⟨CP⟩	Blood group P	2

Marker Gene Symbol (Name)	Segregates Independently with Gene		Reference
	Symbol	Name	
	G₂	Ovoglobulin G₂	2,3
	G₃	Ovoglobulin G₃	2,3
	I	Dominant white	2
	Mb	Muffs and beard	2
	Na	Naked neck	2
	Ov	Ovalbumin	2,3
	P	Pea comb	2
	Po	Polydactyly	2
	R	Rose comb	2
	w	Yellow skin	2
Ea-B ⟨CB⟩ (Blood group B)	Acp-2	Acid phosphatase	2
	Akp [2]	Alkaline phosphatase	2
	Alb	Serum albumin	2,3
	Cr	Crest	2
	E	Extended black	3
	Ea-A ⟨CA⟩ & Ea-E ⟨CE⟩	Blood groups A & E	2
	Ea-C ⟨CC⟩	Blood group C	2
	Ea-D ⟨CD⟩	Blood group D	2
	Ea-H ⟨CH⟩	Blood group H	2
	Ea-I ⟨CI⟩	Blood group I	2
	Ea-J ⟨CJ⟩	Blood group J	2
	Ea-K ⟨CK⟩	Blood group K	2
	Ea-L ⟨CL⟩	Blood group L	2
	Ea-P ⟨CP⟩	Blood group P	2
	G₂	Ovoglobulin G₂	2,3
	G₃	Ovoglobulin G₃	2,3
	I	Dominant white	2,3
	IgM-1 ⟨M1⟩	Immunoglobulin M1	6
	Mb	Muffs and beard	2
	Mr-1	Mitogen response-1	5
	Na	Naked neck	2
	Ov	Ovalbumin	3
	P	Pea comb	2
	Po [1]	Polydactyly	2
	R	Rose comb	2
	w	Yellow skin	2
Ea-C ⟨CC⟩ (Blood group C)	Alb	Serum albumin	3
	Cr	Crest	2
	E	Extended black	3
	Ea-A ⟨CA⟩ & Ea-E ⟨CE⟩	Blood groups A & E	2
	Ea-B ⟨CB⟩	Blood group B	2
	Ea-D ⟨CD⟩	Blood group D	2
	Ea-H ⟨CH⟩	Blood group H	2
	Ea-I ⟨CI⟩	Blood group I	2
	Ea-J ⟨CJ⟩ [1]	Blood group J	2

[1] Possible linkage. [2] Formerly designated *Ap*, which symbol now refers to a different gene. [3] Formerly *mi* (feather achromatosis), but *mi* had already been assigned to microphthalmia. Recently, it was shown that feather achromatosis was the same as Columbian-like restriction ⟨*Db*⟩ [ref. 7].

continued

Part IV. Genes Demonstrating Independent Segregation

Marker Gene Symbol (Name)	Segregates Independently with Gene		Reference
	Symbol	Name	
	Ea-K ⟨*CK*⟩	Blood group K	2
	Ea-L ⟨*CL*⟩	Blood group L	2
	Ea-P ⟨*CP*⟩	Blood group P	2
	G_2	Ovoglobulin G_2	3
	G_3	Ovoglobulin G_3	3
	I	Dominant white	2
	Mb	Muffs and beard	2
	Mr-1	Mitogen response-1	5
	Na	Naked neck	2
	Ov	Ovalbumin	3
	P	Pea comb	2
	Po	Polydactyly	2
	R	Rose comb	2
	w	Yellow skin	2
Ea-D ⟨*CD*⟩ (Blood group D)	*Acp-2*	Acid phosphatase	2
	Akp [2]	Alkaline phosphatase	2
	Alb	Serum albumin	3
	Cr	Crest	2
	E	Extended black	3
	Ea-A ⟨*CA*⟩ & *Ea-E* ⟨*CE*⟩	Blood groups A & E	2
	Ea-B ⟨*CB*⟩	Blood group B	2
	Ea-C ⟨*CC*⟩	Blood group C	2
	Ea-H ⟨*CH*⟩	Blood group H	2
	Ea-I ⟨*CI*⟩	Blood group I	2
	Ea-J ⟨*CJ*⟩	Blood group J	2
	Ea-K ⟨*CK*⟩	Blood group K	2
	Ea-L ⟨*CL*⟩	Blood group L	2
	Ea-P ⟨*CP*⟩	Blood group P	2
	G_2	Ovoglobulin G_2	3
	G_3	Ovoglobulin G_3	3
	Mb	Muffs and beard	2
	Na	Naked neck	2
	Ov	Ovalbumin	3
	P	Pea comb	2
	Po	Polydactyly	2
	R	Rose comb	2
	w	Yellow skin	2
Ea-E ⟨*CE*⟩ (Blood group E) [4]	*Mr-1*	Mitogen response-1	5
Ea-H ⟨*CH*⟩ (Blood group H)	*Cr*	Crest	2
	Ea-A ⟨*CA*⟩ & *Ea-E* ⟨*CE*⟩	Blood groups A & E	2
	Ea-B ⟨*CB*⟩	Blood group B	2
	Ea-C ⟨*CC*⟩	Blood group C	2
	Ea-D ⟨*CD*⟩	Blood group D	2
	Ea-I ⟨*CI*⟩	Blood group I	2
	Ea-J ⟨*CJ*⟩	Blood group J	2

Marker Gene Symbol (Name)	Segregates Independently with Gene		Reference
	Symbol	Name	
	Ea-K ⟨*CK*⟩	Blood group K	2
	Ea-L ⟨*CL*⟩	Blood group L	2
	Ea-P ⟨*CP*⟩	Blood group P	2
	Mb [1]	Muffs and beard	2
	Na	Naked neck	2
	P [1]	Pea comb	2
	Po	Polydactyly	2
	R	Rose comb	2
Ea-I ⟨*CI*⟩ (Blood group I)	*Cr*	Crest	2
	Ea-A ⟨*CA*⟩ & *Ea-E* ⟨*CE*⟩	Blood groups A & E	2
	Ea-B ⟨*CB*⟩	Blood group B	2
	Ea-C ⟨*CC*⟩	Blood group C	2
	Ea-D ⟨*CD*⟩	Blood group D	2
	Ea-H ⟨*CH*⟩	Blood group H	2
	Ea-J ⟨*CJ*⟩	Blood group J	2
	Ea-K ⟨*CK*⟩	Blood group K	2
	Ea-L ⟨*CL*⟩	Blood group L	2
	Ea-P ⟨*CP*⟩	Blood group P	2
	Mb	Muffs and beard	2
	Na	Naked neck	2
	P	Pea comb	2
	Po	Polydactyly	2
	R	Rose comb	2
	w	Yellow skin	2
Ea-J ⟨*CJ*⟩ (Blood group J)	*Cr*	Crest	2
	Ea-A ⟨*CA*⟩ & *Ea-E* ⟨*CE*⟩ [1]	Blood groups A & E	2
	Ea-B ⟨*CB*⟩	Blood group B	2
	Ea-C ⟨*CC*⟩ [1]	Blood group C	2
	Ea-D ⟨*CD*⟩	Blood group D	2
	Ea-H ⟨*CH*⟩	Blood group H	2
	Ea-I ⟨*CI*⟩	Blood group I	2
	Ea-K ⟨*CK*⟩	Blood group K	2
	Ea-L ⟨*CL*⟩	Blood group L	2
	Ea-P ⟨*CP*⟩	Blood group P	2
	Mb	Muffs and beard	2
	Na	Naked neck	2
	P [1]	Pea comb	2
	Po	Polydactyly	2
	R	Rose comb	2
	w	Yellow skin	2
Ea-K ⟨*CK*⟩ (Blood group K)	*Cr*	Crest	2
	Ea-A ⟨*CA*⟩ & *Ea-E* ⟨*CE*⟩	Blood groups A & E	2
	Ea-B ⟨*CB*⟩	Blood group B	2
	Ea-C ⟨*CC*⟩	Blood group C	2
	Ea-D ⟨*CD*⟩	Blood group D	2
	Ea-H ⟨*CH*⟩	Blood group H	2

[1] Possible linkage. [2] Formerly designated *Ap*, which symbol now refers to a different gene. [4] See also *Ea-A*.

continued

Part IV. Genes Demonstrating Independent Segregation

Marker Gene Symbol (Name)	Segregates Independently with Gene		Reference	Marker Gene Symbol (Name)	Segregates Independently with Gene		Reference
	Symbol	Name			Symbol	Name	
	Ea-I ⟨CI⟩	Blood group I	2		Na	Naked neck	2
	Ea-J ⟨CJ⟩	Blood group J	2		P	Pea comb	2
	Ea-L ⟨CL⟩	Blood group L	2		Po	Polydactyly	2
	Ea-P ⟨CP⟩	Blood group P	2		R	Rose comb	2
	Mb	Muffs and beard	2	Er (Erminette)	R	Rose comb	2
	Na	Naked neck	2	Es-1 (Plasma esterase)	Akp [2/]	Alkaline phosphatase	4
	P	Pea comb	2	eu (Eudiplopodia)	dehy	Ichthyosis	1
	Po	Polydactyly	2		dp-1	Diplopodia-1	1
	R	Rose comb	2	F (Frizzling)	a [1/]	Autosomal albinism	9
	w	Yellow skin	2		am	Muscular dystrophy	1
Ea-L ⟨CL⟩ (Blood group L)	Cr	Crest	2		Bl	Blue plumage	9
	Ea-A ⟨CA⟩ & Ea-E ⟨CE⟩	Blood groups A & E	2		c	Recessive white	9
	Ea-B ⟨CB⟩	Blood group B	2		Cp	Creeper	9
	Ea-C ⟨CC⟩	Blood group C	2		D	Duplex comb	9
	Ea-D ⟨CD⟩	Blood group D	2		epi	Epileptiform seizures	2
	Ea-H ⟨CH⟩	Blood group H	2		Fl	Flightless	9
	Ea-I ⟨CI⟩	Blood group I	2		fr	Fray	9
	Ea-J ⟨CJ⟩	Blood group J	2		lav	Lavender	1
	Ea-K ⟨CK⟩	Blood group K	2		M	Multiple spurs	9
	Ea-P ⟨CP⟩	Blood group P	2		Mb	Muffs and beard	9
	Mb	Muffs and beard	2		Na	Naked neck	9
	Na	Naked neck	2		pk	Pink eye	9
	P	Pea comb	2		Po	Polydactyly	9
	Po	Polydactyly	2		R	Rose comb	9
	R	Rose comb	2		ropy	Ropy	9
	w [1/]	Yellow skin	2		Rp [1/]	Rumplessness, dominant	9
Ea-P ⟨CP⟩ (Blood group P)	Cr	Crest	2		se	Sleepy-eye	2
	Ea-A ⟨CA⟩ & Ea-E ⟨CE⟩	Blood groups A & E	2		sw	Snow-white down	2
	Ea-B ⟨CB⟩	Blood group B	2		w	Yellow skin	9
	Ea-C ⟨CC⟩	Blood group C	2	Fl (Flightless)	a	Autosomal albinism	9
	Ea-D ⟨CD⟩	Blood group D	2		Bl	Blue plumage	9
	Ea-H ⟨CH⟩	Blood group H	2		c	Recessive white	9
	Ea-I ⟨CI⟩	Blood group I	2		Cr	Crest	9
	Ea-J ⟨CJ⟩	Blood group J	2		D	Duplex comb	9
	Ea-K ⟨CK⟩	Blood group K	2		F	Frizzling	9
	Ea-L ⟨CL⟩	Blood group L	2		I	Dominant white	9
	Mb	Muffs and beard	2		M	Multiple spurs	9
	P	Pea comb	2		Mb	Muffs and beard	9
	Po	Polydactyly	2		mo	Mottling	9
	R	Rose comb	2		Na [1/]	Naked neck	9
	w [1/]	Yellow skin	2		P [1/]	Pea comb	9
ec (Ectrodactyly)	sc	Scaleless	2		pk	Pink eye	9
	ta-2	Talpid-2	1		Po	Polydactyly	9
epi (Epileptiform seizures)	Cr	Crest	2		R	Rose comb	9
	F	Frizzling	2		Rp	Rumplessness, dominant	9
	I	Dominant white	2		t	Tardy feathering	9

[1/] Possible linkage. [2/] Formerly designated *Ap*, which symbol now refers to a different gene.

continued

Part IV. Genes Demonstrating Independent Segregation

Marker Gene Symbol (Name)	Segregates Independently with Gene		Reference
	Symbol	Name	
	w	Yellow skin	9
Fm (Fibro-melanosis)	sc	Scaleless	1
fr (Fray)	*Bl*	Blue plumage	9
	D	Duplex comb	9
	F	Frizzling	9
	I [1]	Dominant white	9
	Mb	Muffs and beard	9
	Na	Naked neck	9
	P	Pea comb	9
	Po	Polydactyly	9
	R	Rose comb	9
	Rp	Rumplessness, dominant	9
	w	Yellow skin	9
G₂ (Ovo-globulin G₂)	*Alb*	Serum albumin	2
	Ea-A ⟨CA⟩ & *Ea-E* ⟨CE⟩	Blood groups A & E	2,3
	Ea-B ⟨CB⟩	Blood group B	2,3
	Ea-C ⟨CC⟩	Blood group C	3
	Ea-D ⟨CD⟩	Blood group D	3
	G₃	Ovoglobulin G₃	2
	P	Pea comb	2
	Pa	Prealbumin	2
	Tf	Transferrin-conalbumin	2
	w	Yellow skin	2
G₃ (Ovo-globulin G₃)	*Alb*	Serum albumin	2
	Ea-A ⟨CA⟩ & *Ea-E* ⟨CE⟩	Blood groups A & E	2,3
	Ea-B ⟨CB⟩	Blood group B	2,3
	Ea-C ⟨CC⟩	Blood group C	3
	Ea-D ⟨CD⟩	Blood group D	3
	G₂	Ovoglobulin G₂	2
	P	Pea comb	2
	Pa	Prealbumin	2
	Tf	Transferrin-conalbumin	2
	w	Yellow skin	2
h (Hookless ⟨Silkiness⟩)	*Bl*	Blue plumage	9
	I	Dominant white	9
	Mb	Muffs and beard	9
	P	Pea comb	9
	Po	Polydactyly	9
	R	Rose comb	9
	Rp	Rumplessness, dominant	9
	w	Yellow skin	9
I (Dominant white)	*Alb*	Serum albumin	2
	am	Muscular dystrophy	1
	Cp	Creeper	9
	D	Duplex comb	9

Marker Gene Symbol (Name)	Segregates Independently with Gene		Reference
	Symbol	Name	
	Ea-A ⟨CA⟩ & *Ea-E* ⟨CE⟩	Blood groups A & E	2
	Ea-B ⟨CB⟩	Blood group B	2,3
	Ea-C ⟨CC⟩	Blood group C	2
	epi	Epileptiform seizures	2
	Fl	Flightless	9
	fr [1]	Fray	9
	h	Hookless ⟨Silkiness⟩	9
	IgM-1 ⟨M1⟩	Immunoglobulin M1	6
	M	Multiple spurs	9
	Mb	Muffs and beard	9
	Mp	Ametapodia	2
	Na	Naked neck	9
	P	Pea comb	9
	pk	Pink eye	9
	Po	Polydactyly	9
	R	Rose comb	9
	Rp	Rumplessness, dominant	9
	se	Sleepy-eye	2
	sn	Sunsuit	2
	sw	Snow-white down	2
	t	Tardy feathering	9
	Tf	Transferrin-conalbumin	2
	w	Yellow skin	9
IgG-1 (Immunoglobulin-1)	*IgG-2*	Immunoglobulin-2	2
	IgG-3	Immunoglobulin-3	2
IgG-2 (Immunoglobulin-2)	*IgG-1*	Immunoglobulin-1	2
	IgG-3	Immunoglobulin-3	2
IgG-3 (Immunoglobulin-3)	*IgG-1*	Immunoglobulin-1	2
	IgG-2	Immunoglobulin-2	2
IgM-1 ⟨M1⟩ (Immunoglobulin M1)	*Alb*	Serum albumin	6
	Ea-B ⟨CB⟩	Blood group B	6
	I	Dominant white	6
	Mr-1	Mitogen response-1	5
lav (Lavender)	*F*	Frizzling	1
	Mb	Muffs and beard	1
M (Multiple spurs)	*Cr*	Crest	9
	F	Frizzling	9
	Fl	Flightless	9
	I	Dominant white	9
	Mb	Muffs and beard	9
	mo	Mottling	9
	P	Pea comb	9
	pk	Pink eye	9
	R	Rose comb	9

[1] Possible linkage.

continued

Part IV. Genes Demonstrating Independent Segregation

Marker Gene Symbol (Name)	Segregates Independently with Gene		Reference
	Symbol	Name	
	ropy	Ropy	9
	sw	Snow-white down	2
	w	Yellow skin	9
ma (Marbled down)	*Na*	Naked neck	9
Mb (Muffs and beard)	*a*	Autosomal albinism	9
	am	Muscular dystrophy	1
	Bl	Blue plumage	9
	c	Recessive white	9
	Cp	Creeper	9
	Cr	Crest	9
	D	Duplex comb	9
	Ea-A ⟨*CA*⟩ & *Ea-E* ⟨*CE*⟩	Blood groups A & E	2
	Ea-B ⟨*CB*⟩	Blood group B	2
	Ea-C ⟨*CC*⟩	Blood group C	2
	Ea-D ⟨*CD*⟩	Blood group D	2
	Ea-H ⟨*CH*⟩[1]	Blood group H	2
	Ea-I ⟨*CI*⟩	Blood group I	2
	Ea-J ⟨*CJ*⟩	Blood group J	2
	Ea-K ⟨*CK*⟩	Blood group K	2
	Ea-L ⟨*CL*⟩	Blood group L	2
	Ea-P ⟨*CP*⟩	Blood group P	2
	F	Frizzling	9
	Fl	Flightless	9
	fr	Fray	9
	h	Hookless ⟨Silkiness⟩	9
	I	Dominant white	9
	lav	Lavender	1
	M	Multiple spurs	9
	mo	Mottling	9
	Na	Naked neck	9
	P	Pea comb	9
	pk	Pink eye	9
	Po	Polydactyly	9
	R	Rose comb	9
	ropy	Ropy	9
	Rp	Rumplessness, dominant	9
	se	Sleepy-eye	2
	sw	Snow-white down	2
	t	Tardy feathering	9
	w	Yellow skin	9
mo (Mottling)	*Cr*	Crest	9
	D	Duplex comb	9
	Fl	Flightless	9
	M	Multiple spurs	9
	Mb	Muffs and beard	9
	Po	Polydactyly	9

Marker Gene Symbol (Name)	Segregates Independently with Gene		Reference
	Symbol	Name	
Mp (Ametapodia)	*D*	Duplex comb	2
	I	Dominant white	2
	P	Pea comb	2
Mr-1 (Mitogen response-1)	*Alb*	Serum albumin	5
	Ea-B ⟨*CB*⟩	Blood group B	5
	Ea-C ⟨*CC*⟩	Blood group C	5
	Ea-E ⟨*CE*⟩	Blood group E	5
	IgM-1 ⟨*M1*⟩	Immunoglobulin M1	5
Na (Naked neck)	*a*	Autosomal albinism	9
	am	Muscular dystrophy	1
	Bl[1]	Blue plumage	9
	c	Recessive white	9
	Cr	Crest	9
	D	Duplex comb	9
	Ea-A ⟨*CA*⟩ & *Ea-E* ⟨*CE*⟩	Blood groups A & E	2
	Ea-B ⟨*CB*⟩	Blood group B	2
	Ea-C ⟨*CC*⟩	Blood group C	2
	Ea-D ⟨*CD*⟩	Blood group D	2
	Ea-H ⟨*CH*⟩	Blood group H	2
	Ea-I ⟨*CI*⟩	Blood group I	2
	Ea-J ⟨*CJ*⟩	Blood group J	2
	Ea-K ⟨*CK*⟩	Blood group K	2
	Ea-L ⟨*CL*⟩	Blood group L	2
	epi	Epileptiform seizures	2
	F	Frizzling	9
	Fl[1]	Flightless	9
	fr	Fray	9
	I	Dominant white	9
	ma	Marbled down	9
	Mb	Muffs and beard	9
	P	Pea comb	9
	pk	Pink eye	9
	Po	Polydactyly	9
	R	Rose comb	9
	ropy	Ropy	9
	Rp[1]	Rumplessness, dominant	9
	t	Tardy feathering	9
	w	Yellow skin	9
nk (Ottawa naked)	*sc*	Scaleless	2
Ov (Ovalbumin)	*Ea-A* ⟨*CA*⟩ & *Ea-E* ⟨*CE*⟩	Blood groups A & E	2,3
	Ea-B ⟨*CB*⟩	Blood group B	3
	Ea-C ⟨*CC*⟩	Blood group C	3
	Ea-D ⟨*CD*⟩	Blood group D	3
P (Pea comb)	*a*	Autosomal albinism	9
	Alb	Serum albumin	2

[1] Possible linkage.

continued

Part IV. Genes Demonstrating Independent Segregation

| Marker Gene Symbol (Name) | Segregates Independently with Gene | | Reference |
	Symbol	Name	
	am	Muscular dystrophy	1
	As	Auxiliary spurs	2
	Bl	Blue plumage	9
	c	Recessive white	9
	Cp	Creeper	9
	Cr	Crest	9
	D [1]	Duplex comb	9
	E	Extended black	2
	Ea-A ⟨CA⟩ & Ea-E ⟨CE⟩	Blood groups A & E	2
	Ea-B ⟨CB⟩	Blood group B	2
	Ea-C ⟨CC⟩	Blood group C	2
	Ea-D ⟨CD⟩	Blood group D	2
	Ea-H ⟨CH⟩ [1]	Blood group H	2
	Ea-I ⟨CI⟩	Blood group I	2
	Ea-J ⟨CJ⟩ [1]	Blood group J	2
	Ea-K ⟨CK⟩	Blood group K	2
	Ea-L ⟨CL⟩	Blood group L	2
	Ea-P ⟨CP⟩	Blood group P	2
	epi	Epileptiform seizures	2
	Fl [1]	Flightless	9
	fr	Fray	9
	G₂	Ovoglobulin G₂	2
	G₃	Ovoglobulin G₃	2
	h	Hookless ⟨Silkiness⟩	9
	I	Dominant white	9
	M	Multiple spurs	9
	Mb	Muffs and beard	9
	Mp	Ametapodia	2
	Na	Naked neck	9
	Pa	Prealbumin	2
	pk	Pink eye	9
	Po	Polydactyly	9
	R	Rose comb	9
	ropy	Ropy	9
	Rp	Rumplessness, dominant	9
	sw	Snow-white down	2
	t [1]	Tardy feathering	9
	Tf	Transferrin-conalbumin	2
	w	Yellow skin	9
Pa (Prealbumin)	Alb	Serum albumin	2
	G₂	Ovoglobulin G₂	2
	G₃	Ovoglobulin G₃	2
	P	Pea comb	2
	w	Yellow skin	2
pk (Pink eye)	c	Recessive white	9
	Cr	Crest	9
	D	Duplex comb	9
	F	Frizzling	9
	Fl	Flightless	9

| Marker Gene Symbol (Name) | Segregates Independently with Gene | | Reference |
	Symbol	Name	
	I	Dominant white	9
	M	Multiple spurs	9
	Mb	Muffs and beard	9
	Na	Naked neck	9
	P	Pea comb	9
	Po	Polydactyly	9
	R	Rose comb	9
	Rp	Rumplessness, dominant	9
	w	Yellow skin	9
Po (Polydactyly)	a	Autosomal albinism	9
	am	Muscular dystrophy	1
	Bl	Blue plumage	9
	c	Recessive white	9
	Cp	Creeper	9
	Cr	Crest	9
	D [1]	Duplex comb	9
	E	Extended black	9
	Ea-A ⟨CA⟩ & Ea-E ⟨CE⟩	Blood groups A & E	2
	Ea-B ⟨CB⟩ [1]	Blood group B	2
	Ea-C ⟨CC⟩	Blood group C	2
	Ea-D ⟨CD⟩	Blood group D	2
	Ea-H ⟨CH⟩	Blood group H	2
	Ea-I ⟨CI⟩	Blood group I	2
	Ea-J ⟨CJ⟩	Blood group J	2
	Ea-K ⟨CK⟩	Blood group K	2
	Ea-L ⟨CL⟩	Blood group L	2
	Ea-P ⟨CP⟩	Blood group P	2
	epi	Epileptiform seizures	2
	F	Frizzling	9
	Fl	Flightless	9
	fr	Fray	9
	h	Hookless ⟨Silkiness⟩	9
	I	Dominant white	9
	Mb	Muffs and beard	9
	mo	Mottling	9
	Na	Naked neck	9
	P	Pea comb	9
	pk	Pink eye	9
	R	Rose comb	9
	ropy	Ropy	9
	Rp	Rumplessness, dominant	9
	sc	Scaleless	1
	se	Sleepy-eye	2
	sw	Snow-white down	2
	t	Tardy feathering	9
	w	Yellow skin	9
R (Rose comb)	a	Autosomal albinism	9
	am	Muscular dystrophy	1
	Bl [1]	Blue plumage	9

[1] Possible linkage.

continued

Part IV. Genes Demonstrating Independent Segregation

Marker Gene Symbol (Name)	Segregates Independently with Gene		Reference
	Symbol	Name	
	c	Recessive white	9
	Cr	Crest	9
	D	Duplex comb	9
	Ea-A ⟨CA⟩ & Ea-E ⟨CE⟩	Blood groups A & E	2
	Ea-B ⟨CB⟩	Blood group B	2
	Ea-C ⟨CC⟩	Blood group C	2
	Ea-D ⟨CD⟩	Blood group D	2
	Ea-H ⟨CH⟩	Blood group H	2
	Ea-I ⟨CI⟩	Blood group I	2
	Ea-J ⟨CJ⟩	Blood group J	2
	Ea-K ⟨CK⟩	Blood group K	2
	Ea-L ⟨CL⟩	Blood group L	2
	Ea-P ⟨CP⟩	Blood group P	2
	epi	Epileptiform seizures	2
	Er	Erminette	2
	F	Frizzling	9
	Fl	Flightless	9
	fr	Fray	9
	h	Hookless ⟨Silkiness⟩	9
	I	Dominant white	9
	M	Multiple spurs	9
	Mb	Muffs and beard	9
	Na	Naked neck	9
	P	Pea comb	9
	pk	Pink eye	9
	Po	Polydactyly	9
	ropy	Ropy	9
	Rp	Rumplessness, dominant	9
	sc	Scaleless	1
	se	Sleepy-eye	2
	sw	Snow-white down	2
	t	Tardy feathering	9
	w	Yellow skin	9
ropy (Ropy)	Bl	Blue plumage	9
	Cr	Crest	9
	D	Duplex comb	9
	F	Frizzling	9
	M	Multiple spurs	9
	Mb	Muffs and beard	9
	Na	Naked neck	9
	P	Pea comb	9
	Po	Polydactyly	9
	R	Rose comb	9
	Rp	Rumplessness, dominant	9

Marker Gene Symbol (Name)	Segregates Independently with Gene		Reference
	Symbol	Name	
Rp (Rumplessness, dominant)	a	Autosomal albinism	9
	Bl	Blue plumage	9
	c	Recessive white	9
	Cp	Creeper	9
	Cr	Crest	9
	D	Duplex comb	9
	F [1]	Frizzling	9
	Fl	Flightless	9
	fr	Fray	9
	h	Hookless ⟨Silkiness⟩	9
	I	Dominant white	9
	Mb	Muffs and beard	9
	Na [1]	Naked neck	9
	P	Pea comb	9
	pk	Pink eye	9
	Po	Polydactyly	9
	R	Rose comb	9
	ropy	Ropy	9
	t	Tardy feathering	9
	w	Yellow skin	9
sc (Scaleless)	Cr	Crest	1
	dehy	Ichthyosis	1
	ec	Ectrodactyly	2
	Fm	Fibromelanosis	1
	nk	Ottawa naked	2
	Po	Polydactyly	1
	R	Rose comb	1
se (Sleepy-eye)	Cp	Creeper	2
	Cr	Crest	2
	D	Duplex comb	2
	E	Extended black	2
	F	Frizzling	2
	I	Dominant white	2
	Mb	Muffs and beard	2
	Po	Polydactyly	2
	R	Rose comb	2
sn (Sun-suit)	Cr	Crest	2
	D	Duplex comb	2
	I	Dominant white	2
sw (Snow-white down)	Cr	Crest	2
	D	Duplex comb	2
	F	Frizzling	2
	I	Dominant white	2
	M	Multiple spurs	2
	Mb	Muffs and beard	2

[1] Possible linkage.

continued

Part IV. Genes Demonstrating Independent Segregation

Marker Gene Symbol (Name)	Segregates Independently with Gene		Reference
	Symbol	Name	
	P	Pea comb	2
	Po	Polydactyly	2
	R	Rose comb	2
t (Tardy feathering)	*Cr*	Crest	9
	D	Duplex comb	9
	Fl	Flightless	9
	I	Dominant white	9
	Mb	Muffs and beard	9
	Na	Naked neck	9
	P[1/]	Pea comb	9
	Po	Polydactyly	9
	R	Rose comb	9
	Rp	Rumplessness, dominant	9
	w	Yellow skin	9
ta-2 (Talpid-2)	*dp-1*	Diplopodia-1	2
	ec	Ectrodactyly	1
Tf (Transferrin-conalbumin)	*Alb*	Serum albumin	2
	G₂	Ovoglobulin G_2	2
	G₃	Ovoglobulin G_3	2
	I	Dominant white	2
	P	Pea comb	2
	w	Yellow skin	2
U (Uropygial)	*c*	Recessive white	9
w (Yellow skin)	*a*	Autosomal albinism	9
	Alb	Serum albumin	2
	am	Muscular dystrophy	1
	Bl	Blue plumage	9
	c	Recessive white	9
	Cp	Creeper	9

Marker Gene Symbol (Name)	Segregates Independently with Gene		Reference
	Symbol	Name	
	Cr	Crest	9
	D[1/]	Duplex comb	9
	Ea-A ⟨*CA*⟩ & *Ea-E* ⟨*CE*⟩	Blood groups A & E	2
	Ea-B ⟨*CB*⟩	Blood group B	2
	Ea-C ⟨*CC*⟩	Blood group C	2
	Ea-D ⟨*CD*⟩	Blood group D	2
	Ea-I ⟨*CI*⟩	Blood group I	2
	Ea-J ⟨*CJ*⟩	Blood group J	2
	Ea-K ⟨*CK*⟩	Blood group K	2
	Ea-L ⟨*CL*⟩[1/]	Blood group L	2
	Ea-P ⟨*CP*⟩[1/]	Blood group P	2
	F	Frizzling	9
	Fl	Flightless	9
	fr	Fray	9
	G₂	Ovoglobulin G_2	2
	G₃	Ovoglobulin G_3	2
	h	Hookless ⟨Silkiness⟩	9
	I	Dominant white	9
	M	Multiple spurs	9
	Mb	Muffs and beard	9
	Na	Naked neck	9
	P	Pea comb	9
	Pa	Prealbumin	2
	pk	Pink eye	9
	Po	Polydactyly	9
	R	Rose comb	9
	Rp	Rumplessness, dominant	9
	t	Tardy feathering	9
	Tf	Transferrin-conalbumin	2

[1/] Possible linkage.

Contributors: R. J. Etches and R. O. Hawes

References

1. Abbott, U. K., and G. W. Yee. 1975. In R. C. King, ed. Handbook of Genetics. Plenum, New York. v. 4, pp. 151-200.
2. Etches, R. J., and R. O. Hawes. 1973. Can. J. Genet. Cytol. 15:553-570.
3. Gintout, V. E., et al. 1976. Genetika 12(11):60-71.
4. Kimura, M., et al. 1972. Jpn. J. Zootech. Sci. 43:104-105.
5. Miggiano, V., et al. 1976. Nature (London) 263:61-63.
6. Pink, J. R. L. 1974. Eur. J. Immunol. 4:679-681.
7. Smyth, J. R., Jr., and G. W. Malone. 1979. Poult. Sci. 58:(in press).
8. Somes, R. G., Jr. 1978. J. Hered. 69:401-403.
9. Warren, D. C. 1949. Genetics 34:333-350.

Part I. Spontaneous Abnormalities

Chromosome Abnormality: Type—N = haploid, 2N − 1 = monosomic, 2N + 1 = trisomic, 3N = triploid, 4N = tetraploid; mosaic = abnormality combining two or more cell lines, e.g., haploid and diploid; **Frequency**—Where more than one type of chromosome abnormality is specified, the overall frequency is given.

Strain, Line, or Breed	Chromosome Abnormality		Reference
	Type	Frequency %	
Embryo			
PR-C & PR-W inbred lines	3N	....	5
AG-1 rapid growth	N, 2N + 1	0.83	6
Obese strain	3N, 2N + 1	0.9	2,7
Cornell K-resistant strain	N, 2N + 1	1.0	4
Riboflavin-deficient (*rd*) line	3N, 4N, 2N + 1	1.4	3
White Leghorn	Deletion, N, 3N, 2N − 1, mosaic	1.4	8
Naked (*n*) line	N, 2N + 1	1.9	3
Diabetes insipidus line	N, 3N	2.6	4
Araucana	N	2.7	3
Jungle Fowl	3N	2.8	3
Commercial egg-type	3N	3.3	4
Cornell C-resistant strain	N, 3N	3.5	4
Commercial inbred	N, 3N, 4N, deletion	5.4	4
Cornell low fecundity line	N, 3N, 2N + 1	5.7	3
Virginia LWS (low body weight strain)	N, 2N ± 1, mosaic	6.2	11
Cornell S-susceptible strain	N, 3N	7.1	3
Broiler stock	N, 3N, 4N, 2N ± 1, mosaic	11.9	9
Virginia HWS (high body weight strain)	N, 2N ± 1, mosaic	14.5	11
Adult			
Rhode Island Red	3N	....	10
Single Comb White Leghorn	Translocation between no. 2 & no. 3	....	12
Commercial egg-producing hybrids	3N	♀, 0.05	1

Contributor: Stephen E. Bloom

References

1. Abdel-Hameed, F., and R. N. Shoffner. 1971. Science 172:962-964.
2. Bloom, S. E. 1971. J. Hered. 62:186-188.
3. Bloom, S. E. 1972. Chromosoma 37:309-326.
4. Bloom, S. E. 1974. Proc. 15th World's Poult. Congr., pp. 316-321.
5. Donner, L., et al. 1969. J. Hered. 60:113-115.
6. Fechheimer, N. S., et al. 1968. J. Reprod. Fertil. 17: 215-217.
7. Korf, B. R., and S. E. Bloom. 1974. J. Hered. 65:219-222.
8. Lodge, J. R., et al. 1973. Poult. Sci. 52:397-399.
9. Miller, R. C., et al. 1976. Biol. Reprod. 14:549-560.
10. Ohno, S., et al. 1963. Cytogenetics 2:42-49.
11. Reddy, P. R. K., and P. B. Siegel. 1977. J. Hered. 68: 253-256.
12. Ryan, W. C., and P. E. Bernier. 1968. Experientia 24: 623-624.

Part II. Induced Aberrations

Agent & Dose: R = roentgen. **Method:** i.p. = intraperitoneal.

Agent & Dose	Method	Strain, Line, or Breed	Type of Aberration ⟨Synonym⟩	Reference
Chemical mutagens Ethyl methanesulfonate or methyl methanesulfonate	Expose embryos to chemicals	Cornell K-resistant & S-susceptible strains	Sister chromatid exchanges, breaks, gaps, rearrangements	2

continued

Part II.   Induced Aberrations

Agent & Dose	Method	Strain, Line, or Breed	Type of Aberration ⟨Synonym⟩	Reference
Ethyl methanesulfonate or triethylenemelamine	Inject ♂ i.p.	Rhode Island Red; Minnesota marker males; Minnesota rearrangement strains	Inversion in no. 1; translocations involving no. 1, 2, 3, 4, & 5 ⟨Z sex chromosome⟩	5,6
X radiation 50-250 R	Irradiate embryos	Araucana	Breaks, gaps	3
300-500 R	Irradiate semen	Dark Cornish; Single Comb White Leghorn	Translocation between no. 1 & no. 5 ⟨Z sex chromosome⟩	9
1000 R	Irradiate semen	Single Comb White Leghorn	Translocation between no. 1 & no. 2	4
1200 R	Irradiate semen	Ohio translocation strains	Translocations of autosomes, Z-chromosome, & microchromosomes	6,8
		White Leghorn	Translocation between no. 5 ⟨Z sex chromosome⟩ & a microchromosome	7
Marek's disease virus, strain JM	Inoculate chicks	Cornell C-resistant, K-resistant, & S-susceptible strains	Tetraploidy	1

Contributor: Stephen E. Bloom

References

1. Bloom, S. E. 1970. Avian Dis. 14:478-490.
2. Bloom, S. E. 1978. In A. Hollaender, ed. Chemical Mutagens. Plenum, New York. v. 5.
3. Cormier, J. M., and S. E. Bloom. 1973. Mutat. Res. 20:77-85.
4. Newcomer, E. H. 1959. Science 130:390-391.
5. Shoffner, R. N. 1972. Poult. Sci. 51:1865.
6. Somes, R. G., Jr. 1974. Conn. Agric. Exp. Stn. Storrs Bull. 437.
7. Telloni, R. V., et al. 1976. Poult. Sci. 55:1886-1896.
8. Wooster, W. E., et al. 1973. Ibid. 52:2104.
9. Zartman, D. L. 1973. Ibid. 52:1455-1462.

160.   GENETIC TRAITS: CHICKEN

Gene Symbol: (MF) indicates trait inherited as a multiple factorial trait; (UNK) indicates basis of inheritance unknown. **Holder:** For full name, *see* list of HOLDERS at front of book. Data in brackets refer to the column heading in brackets. Underlined names indicate varieties.

Gene Symbol	Trait Name ⟨Synonym⟩	Holder [Breed or Variety]	Reference
		Biochemical	
Acp	Acid phosphatase	....	249
acp⁰	Acid phosphatase null	....	249
Acp-2^A	Acid phosphatase-2A	....	194
Acp-2^B	Acid phosphatase-2B	....	194
Ade-A$^{1/}$	Adenine synthesis A	....	120
Ade-B$^{2/}$	Adenine synthesis B	....	120
Akp^F	Alkaline phosphatase fast	....	247,290
akp^S	Alkaline phosphatase slow	....	247,290
Akp-2⁰	Alkaline phosphatase-2 null	....	79
akp-2^a	Alkaline phosphatase-2a	....	79

[1/] Linkage group VII, chromosome 7. [2/] Linkage group VIII, chromosome 8.

continued

Gene Symbol	Trait Name ⟨Synonym⟩	Holder [Breed or Variety]	Reference
Alb^C	Albumin C	....	19,242
$Alb^{C'}$	Albumin C'	....	19,242
Alb^F	Albumin F	....	19,175
Alb^S	Albumin S	....	19,175
$Amy\text{-}1^A$	Amylase-1A	....	87
$Amy\text{-}1^B$	Amylase-1B	....	87
$Amy\text{-}1^C$	Amylase-1C	....	250
$Amy\text{-}2^A$	Amylase-2A	....	154
$Amy\text{-}2^B$	Amylase-2B	....	154
$Amy\text{-}2^C$	Amylase-2C	....	154
$Ca\text{-}1^A$	Carbonate dehydratase A ⟨Carbonic anhydrase A⟩	....	39
$Ca\text{-}1^B$	Carbonate dehydratase B ⟨Carbonic anhydrase B⟩	....	39
$Ca\text{-}1^C$	Carbonate dehydratase C ⟨Carbonic anhydrase C⟩	....	39
Ct^A	Catalase normal activity	....	215
ct^B	Hypocatalasemia	....	215
$Es\text{-}1^A$	Esterase-1A	....	55,82
$Es\text{-}1^B$	Esterase-1B	....	55,82
$Es\text{-}1^C$	Esterase-1C	....	83
$Es\text{-}2^A$	Esterase-2A	....	129
$es\text{-}2^{B}$ [3]	Esterase-2B	....	129
$Es\text{-}3^0$	Esterase-3 null	....	195
$Es\text{-}3^A$	Esterase-3A	....	195
$Es\text{-}3^B$	Esterase-3B	....	195
$Es\text{-}4^0$	Esterase-4 null	....	248
$Es\text{-}4^A$	Esterase-4A	....	248
$Es\text{-}4^B$	Esterase-4B	....	248
$Es\text{-}5^A$	Esterase-5A	....	193
$Es\text{-}5^B$	Esterase-5B	....	193
$Es\text{-}6^A$	Esterase-6A	....	248
$Es\text{-}6^B$	Esterase-6B	....	248
$Es\text{-}7^0$	Esterase-7 null	....	9
$Es\text{-}7^A$	Esterase-7A	....	9
$Es\text{-}8^A$	Esterase-8A	....	88,219
$Es\text{-}8^B$	Esterase-8B	....	88,219
$Es\text{-}9^A$	Esterase-9A	....	258
$es\text{-}9^0$	Esterase-9 null	....	258
$Es\text{-}10^A$	Esterase-10A	....	131
$Es\text{-}10^B$	Esterase-10B	....	131
G_1^F	Lysozyme G_1 fast	....	19
G_1^S	Lysozyme G_1 slow	....	19
G_2^A	Ovoglobulin G_2A	MLGF	19,159
G_2^B	Ovoglobulin G_2B	MLGF	19,159
G_2^L	Ovoglobulin G_2L	....	19
G_3^A	Ovoglobulin G_3A	MLGF	19,159
G_3^B	Ovoglobulin G_3B	MLGF	19,159
G_3^J	Ovoglobulin G_3J	....	17,19
G_3^M	Ovoglobulin G_3M	....	19,53
Gdr [4]	Glucose-6-phosphate dehydrogenase	....	24
Hp^F	Haptoglobin fast	....	216
Hp^S	Haptoglobin slow	....	216

[3] Previously assigned allele symbol "*a*" was changed to "*B*" to prevent confusion and to follow convention. [4] No gene symbol previously assigned; provisional gene symbol proposed.

continued

Gene Symbol	Trait Name ⟨Synonym⟩	Holder [Breed or Variety]	Reference
Lap^A	Aminopeptidase (cytosol) A ⟨Leucine aminopeptidase A⟩	....	56
$lap^{B3/}$	Aminopeptidase (cytosol) B ⟨Leucine aminopeptidase B⟩	....	56
Oc^b	Ornithine carbamoyltransferase b ⟨Ornithine transcarbamylase b⟩	....	257
Oc^g	Ornithine carbamoyltransferase g ⟨Ornithine transcarbamylase g⟩	....	257
Ov^A	Ovalbumin A	MLGF	19,159
Ov^B	Ovalbumin B	MLGF	19,159
Pa^A	Prealbumin A	....	243
Pa^B	Prealbumin B	....	243
$Pas\text{-}A$	Postalbumin A fast	....	134
$pas\text{-}A$	Postalbumin A null	....	134
Pgd^{ch}	Phosphogluconate dehydrogenase	....	155
Pgk^F	Phosphoglycerate kinase fast	....	34
Pgk^S	Phosphoglycerate kinase slow	....	34
Pgm^A	Phosphoglucomutase A	....	130
Pgm^B	Phosphoglucomutase B	....	130
Tf^A	Transferrin-conalbumin A	MLGF	19,192
Tf^B	Transferrin-conalbumin B	MLGF	19,192
Tf^{BW}	Transferrin-conalbumin BW	....	18,19
Tf^C	Transferrin-conalbumin C	....	19,54
$Tk\text{-}F^{4,5/}$	Cytosol thymidine kinase F	....	156

Metabolic

Gene Symbol	Trait Name ⟨Synonym⟩	Holder [Breed or Variety]	Reference
am	Muscular dystrophy	CONG, SAS, UCD	14,35
$Aro^{4/}$	Atresia of reproductive organs	....	70
$bf^{4/}$	Short down-blistered foot lethal	....	233
$bli^{4/}$	Blindness	....	99,102
$cla^{4/}$	Congenital leg anomaly	....	184
$coc^{4/}$	Congenital crippling	....	233
$cop^{4/}$	Congenital perosis	....	25
$deh^{4/}$	Dehydration	....	150,256
di	Diabetes insipidus	PEN	67,68
$ga^{6/}$	Gasper	NSA, SAS	198
$Gc^{F4/}$	Gamma globin chain fast	....	33
$Gc^{S4/}$	Gamma globin chain slow	....	33
$go^{4/}$	Gout, diet-induced	....	197
$Hb^{I4/}$	Hemoglobin type I	GEO	281,282
$Hb^{II4/}$	Hemoglobin type II	GEO	281,282
$Hgh^{4/}$	Hereditary gonad hyperplasia	....	158
Hi	"Hi" agglutinogen	MLGF	212
$Mi\text{-}2^{4/}$	Dominant microphthalmia	....	288
$mi\text{-}3^{7/}$	Microphthalmia-3	....	71
$pe^{8/}$	Perosis	....	229
rc	Induced retinal mutation	MIN	38
rd	Riboflavinuria	PEN	86,165
$ro^{6/}$	Restricted ovulator	WIS	115,172
$Tsh^{4/}$	Thyrotropin ⟨TSH⟩ sensitivity	....	75

[3/] Previously assigned allele symbol "a" was changed to "B" to prevent confusion and to follow convention. [4/] No gene symbol previously assigned; provisional gene symbol proposed. [5/] Linkage group IX—identified as being located on a microchromosome smaller than number 8. [6/] Linkage group V, chromosome Z. [7/] Gene symbol changed; previous symbol refers to a different locus. [8/] Linkage group III, chromosome 1.

continued

Gene Symbol	Trait Name ⟨Synonym⟩	Holder [Breed or Variety]	Reference
(MF)	Abnormal tibial-metatarsal joints	....	214
(MF)	Coloboma of the iris	....	289
(MF)	Cornish muscular dystrophy	....	261
(MF)	Crippling anomaly	....	183
(MF)	Double oviduct	SDA	186
(MF)	Encephaly	....	176
(MF)	Hereditary autoimmune thyroiditis	COR	42,47
(MF)	Hereditary uricemia and articular gout	COR	16
(MF)	Inherited anemia	....	284
Neurological			
cd [4,6]	Cerebellar degeneration	....	163
ce [4]	Cerebellar hypoplasia	....	291
cy	Crazy	WIS	168
epi	Epileptiform seizures	SAS	50,52
j [6]	Jittery	....	81
lo	Congenital loco	....	102,132
pir	Pirouette	WIS	169
px [6]	Paroxysm	COR, SAS	41
sh [6]	Shaker	....	213
sh-2	Shaker-2	WIS	235
sln [4,6]	Sex-linked nervous disorder	....	121
tip	Tipsy	MCD, SAS	89
xl [6]	Sex-linked lethal	....	82
(MF)	Arched neck	....	48
(MF)	Ataxia	....	23
(MF)	Congenital tremor	....	106,221
(UNK)	Bowing	ORE	25
Embryonic Lethal			
ch	Chondrodystrophy	CONG	137,150
chz [6]	Sex-linked chondrodystrophy	....	161
Cl	Cornish lethal	....	140,150
cm [6,7]	Coloboma	....	8,151
cn	Crooked-neck dwarf	CONG	13,150
dck	Duck beak	....	27,150
dd-2	Donald duck	....	4
dd-3	Donald duck-3	WIS	167
dl [4]	Dorking lethal	....	147,150
dp-1	Diplopodia-1	MCD	150,255
dp-2	Diplopodia-2	....	145,150
dp-3	Diplopodia-3	....	253,254
dp-4 [6]	Diplopodia-4	....	3
ec	Ectrodactyly	....	5,150
eu	Eudiplopodia	....	150,209
l	Recessive white lethal	....	63,150
lk [6]	Ladykiller	PAK	217
ln [6]	Sex-linked lethal liver necrosis	COR	47,151
md	Missing mandible	....	150,162
mi	Bilateral microphthalmia	....	111
mm-A [7]	Micromelia - California	CONG	149

[4] No gene symbol previously assigned; provisional gene symbol proposed. [6] Linkage group V, chromosome Z.

[7] Gene symbol changed; previous symbol refers to a different locus.

continued

Gene Symbol	Trait Name ⟨Synonym⟩	Holder [Breed or Variety]	Reference
mm-H [7]	Micromelia - Hays	CONG	91,150
mm-K [4]	Micromelia - Kawahara		122,150
mm-VII [4]	Micromelia VII		21,150
mx	Missing maxillae		11,150
nm	Nanomelia	CONG	148,150
obs [4]	Open breast syndrome		72,151
per [4]	Perocephaly	CONG	146,150
pn [6]	Prenatal lethal	CONS	230,241
sex [4,6]	Sex-linked lethal - Bernier		234
sf	Splitfoot		2,150
sm	Short mandible		102,166
stu [4]	Stumpy		7,150
su	Short upper beak		142,150
sy	Stickiness		32,150
ta-1	Talpid-1		40,150
ta-2	Talpid-2		6,150
ta-3	Talpid-3		69,151
wg	Wingless		150,287
wg-2	Wingless-2	CONG	151,292
(MF)	Micromelia - Asmundson		12,150

		Musculoskeletal	
By	Brachydactyly		102,272
Cp [9]	Creeper	[Japanese Bantam]	150,153
crn [4]	Crooked neck		102,117
Mp [9]	Ametapodia	CONS, COR	43,150
Po [10]	Polydactyly	[Dorking; Houdan; Salmon Faverolle; Silkie; Sultan]	144,275
Po^d [10]	Duplicate polydactyly		274,275
psp	Polydactyly-syndactyly-ptilopody (multiple trait, semi-lethal)	WIS	174
pt [7]	Palatal pits		119
Rp	Dominant rumplessness	CONG [Araucana]	66,102
rp-2	Recessive rumplessness	CONG	102,143
sno	Snub nose	MAS	235
Syn [4]	Syndactyly		278
wg-3 [4]	Autosomal wingless		151
wl [6,7]	Sex-linked wingless		138,196
(MF)	Cleft palate		118,208
(MF)	Crooked beak		102,141
(MF)	Crooked keel		102,269
(MF)	Crooked toes		94
(MF)	Kyphoscoliosis		252
(MF)	Malformed skeleton		58
(MF)	Tibial dyschondroplasia		218
(MF)	Ungual osteodystrophy		102,280
(MF)	Web-foot		95

		Body Size	
adw	Autosomal dwarfism	COR, FSIPR	44
dw [6]	Sex-linked dwarfism	BSRA, COR, GUE, MLGF, OHI, ORE, PSAM, RSAM	104
dw^B [6]	Bantam dwarfism	[Sebright]	57

[4] No gene symbol previously assigned; provisional gene symbol proposed. [6] Linkage group V, chromosome Z. [7] Gene symbol changed; previous symbol refers to a different locus. [9] Linkage group I. [10] Linkage group IV.

continued

Gene Symbol	Trait Name (Synonym)	Holder [Breed or Variety]	Reference
$dw^{M6/}$	MacDonald dwarfism	MCD	96
$rg^{6/}$	Recessive sex-linked dwarfism	....	80
td	Recessive dwarfism		139,259
$Z^{6/}$	Dominant sex-linked dwarfism		102,164
		Skin Structure	
As	Auxiliary spurs	....	285
Bd^+	Single comb	[All breeds except Breda]	20,102
bd	Breda comb	[Breda]	20,102
$D^{10/}$	Duplex or buttercup comb	[Buttercup; Crevecoeur; Houdan; LaFleche; Polish; Sultan]	59,102
$dac^{4/}$	Dactylolysis		102,220
$dpg^{4/}$	Double oil gland papillae		23
$Ds^{4/}$	Double spurs		102,276
Et	Ear-tuft	[Araucana]	236
He^+	Rugged rose-combed	MLGF	36,37
he^l	Smooth rose-combed	MLGF	36,37
$M^{10/}$	Multiple spurs	MIN [Sumatra]	101,102
$P^{8/}$	Pea comb	[Araucana; Aseel; Brahma; Cornish; Shamo; Yokohama]	102,189
$P^{8/} + R^{9/}$	Walnut, cushion, or strawberry comb	[Malay; Orloff; Silkie]	49
$R^{9/}$	Rose comb	[Ancona; Dominique; Dorking; Hamburg; Sebright; Wyandotte]	51
$sb^{4/}$	Spike blade comb		102,271
$se^{8/}$	Sleepy-eye	CONS, MAS	228
sl	Spurlessness		102,133
$U^{9/}$	Uropygial	MIN	98,124
(MF)	Comb side sprigs		10,102
(MF)	Self dubbing	ORE	22
(UNK)	Enlarged earlobes	[White-faced Black Spanish]	102
		Skin Color	
Fm	Fibromelanosis	[Silkie]	65,102
g	Yellow head	RSAM	62,206
$Id^{6/}$	Dermal melanin inhibitor	[Leghorn; Minorca; New Hampshire; Orpington; Plymouth Rock; Rhode Island Red]	64,102
$id^{c6/}$	Green shank (Dermal melanin - Cornell)	WIS	170
$id^{a6/}$	Green spotting	WIS	173
$id^{+6/}$	Dermal melanin	[Andalusian; Campine; Hamburg; Polish; Red Jungle Fowl; Silkie]	64,102
$W^{+8/}$	White skin	[Andalusian; Australorp; Hamburg; Orpington; Red Jungle Fowl; Sussex]	102,135
$w^{8/}$	Yellow skin	[Cornish; Leghorn; New Hampshire; Plymouth Rock; Rhode Island Red; Wyandotte]	102,135
(MF)	Red earlobes	[Brahma; Cochin; Cornish; New Hampshire; Plymouth Rock; Rhode Island Red]	102,263
(MF)	White earlobes	[Andalusian; Leghorn; Minorca; Polish; Red Jungle Fowl]	102,263
		Eye Color	
$br^{6/}$	Brown eye	[Campine; Langshan; Minorca; Orpington; Sebright; Sumatra]	26,160
(UNK)	Pearl eye	[Aseel; Cornish; Malay; Shamo]	26,190
(UNK)	Red eye	[American Game; LaFleche; Lakenvelder; Marans]	190

[4] No gene symbol previously assigned; provisional gene symbol proposed. [6] Linkage group V, chromosome Z.   [8] Linkage group III, chromosome 1. [9] Linkage group I. [10] Linkage group IV.

continued

Gene Symbol	Trait Name ⟨Synonym⟩	Holder [Breed or Variety]	Reference
		Feather Distribution	
Ap	Apterylosis	....	245,246
ba	Congenital baldness	CONS	110,244
n [6]	Naked	COR	102,108
Na [8]	Naked neck	[Naked neck; Turken]	61,267
nk	Ottawa naked	SAS	235
sc	Scaleless	CONG, CONS	1,211
(MF)	Ptilopody ⟨Feathered shanks⟩	[Booted Bantam; Brahma; Cochin; Langshan; Salmon Faverolle; Silkie]	102,136
(MF)	Stubs	....	90,102
		Feather Growth Rate	
K^n [6]	Extremely slow feathering	CONS	231
K^s [6]	Slow feathering	WIS	171
K [6]	Late feathering	[Brahma; Cochin; Cornish; Plymouth Rock; Rhode Island Red; Wyandotte]	205,262
k^+ [6]	Rapid feathering	[Ancona; Leghorn; Minorca]	205,262
t [8]	Tardy feather growth	WIS	102,113
t^s [8]	Retarded feather growth	....	113,266
(MF)	Modified slow feathering	MAS	225
		Feather Length	
Cr [11]	Crest	[Crevecoeur; Houdan; Polish; Silkie; Spitzhauben; Sultan]	74,279
Gt	Non-limited growth ⟨Long tail⟩	[Phoenix; Yokohama]	102,210
Lf	Long filoplumes	WIS	235
Mb [8]	Muffs and beard	[Crevecoeur; Houdan; Orloff; Salmon Faverolle; Silkie; Sultan]	59,102
mt	Non-molt	[Phoenix; Yokohama]	210
v	Vulture hocks	[Belgian Bearded d'Uccle; Booted Bantam; Sultan]	102,117
		Feather Structure	
F [11]	Frizzling	[Frizzle]	97,152
Fl [8]	Flightless	MCD	263,268
fr [11]	Fray	....	102,270
h [8]	Silkiness	[Silkie]	102,116
Hf	Hen feathering	[Campine; Sebright]	102,200
mf	Frizzle modifier	....	100,102
pc	Porcupine	....	286
ropy [4]	Ropy	....	277
rw [4]	Ragged wing	....	102,109
sn	Sunsuit	....	107
st [4]	Stringy	....	123
st-2 [4]	Stringy-2	....	31
wi [4]	Wiry syndrome	GUE	73
wo	Woolly	....	114
(MF)	Plastered down	....	78
		Feather Color or Pattern [12]	
a	Autosomal albinism	CONS, MAS	102,265

[4] No gene symbol previously assigned; provisional gene symbol proposed. [6] Linkage group V, chromosome Z. [8] Linkage group III, chromosome 1. [11] Linkage group II. [12] Other traits for feather pattern or color which have not been adequately studied include: Double lacing (present in Double Laced Barnevelder and Dark Cornish breeds); Quail pattern (present in Quail varieties); and White Crest (present in White-crested Black Polish and White-crested Blue Polish breeds).

continued

Gene Symbol	Trait Name ⟨Synonym⟩	Holder [Breed or Variety]	Reference
Ab	Autosomal barring	[Barred Fayoumi; Campine; Penciled Hamburg]	179
B [6/]	Sex-linked barring	[Barred; Cuckoo; Delaware; Dominique]	102,191
B^Sd [6/]	Sex-linked dilution	....	188,260
Bl	Blue	[Blue; Blue-splashed White]	102,157
c	Recessive white	[Cochin; Japanese Bantam; Langshan; Orpington; Plymouth Rock; Wyandotte]	102,204
Cb	Champagne blond	....	29
Co	Columbian restriction	[Buff Brahma; Columbian; Laced Wyandotte; Light Brahma; Light Sussex]	223,227
Db [8/]	Columbian-like restriction	CONS, MAS [Barred Fayoumi]	179,226, 283
Dil [7/]	Dilute	[Buff Leghorn; Buff Minorca]	29
E	Extended black	[Black; Blue]	28,222
E^R	Birchen	[Birchen; Brown-Red]	178
e^Wh	Dominant wheaten	[New Hampshire; Salmon Faverolle; Wheaten]	28,223
e^+	Wild type	[Black-breasted Red; Golden Leghorn; Light Brown Leghorn; Red Jungle Fowl; Silver Gray Dorking; Silver Leghorn]	28,222
e^b	Brown	[Columbian; Dark Brahma; Dark Brown Leghorn; Light Sussex; Partridge; Penciled]	28,222
e^s	Speckled head	....	28,182
e^bc	Buttercup	[Buttercup]	28
e^y	Recessive wheaten	[Buff Minorca; Rhode Island Red; Speckled Sussex]	181,182
Er	Erminette	[Erminette]	105
Gr	Ginger	[New Hampshire; Orpington; Rhode Island Red]	29
Hs [4/]	Head-spot	....	232
I [11/]	Dominant white	[Hamburg; Leghorn; Minorca; Modern Game; Polish]	84,102
ig	Cream	MLGF	102,201
ko [6/]	Head streak	[Golden Spangled Hamburg]	102,207
lav [9/]	Lavender	[Porcelain; Self-Blue]	30
lb [4/]	Light bar	....	185
Lg	Lacing	[Cornish; Laced Cochin; Laced Wyandotte; Sebright; Silver or Golden Polish]	180
Li [6/]	Light down	....	93,102
ma [8/]	Marbled down	[Silver Spangled Hamburg; Spitzhauben]	92,102
Mh	Mahogany	[New Hampshire; Orpington; Rhode Island Red]	29
Ml	Melanotic	[Black Minorca; Laced Cochin; Laced Wyandotte; White-crested Black Polish]	177
mo	Mottling ⟨Mille Fleur; Speckling⟩	[Mille Fleur; Mottled; Porcelain; Spangled Old English Game; Speckled Sussex]	15,238
Pg	Penciling	[Dark Brahma; Partridge; Penciled]	127,128
pi	Pied plumage	[Exchequer Leghorn]	102,202
pk	Pink eye	NEB	102,273
rs	Red-splashed white	....	102,203
S [6/]	Silver	[Silver]	60,102
s^+ [6/]	Gold	[Brown, Buff, Golden, or Red]	60,102
s^al [6/]	Imperfect albinism ⟨Sex-linked albinism⟩	CONS, COR, MAS	45,187
Sg^+	Stippling	[Black-breasted Red; Light Brown Leghorn; Red Jungle Fowl]	125,126
sg	Non-stippling	....	125,126
Sp	Spangling	[Silver Spangled Hamburg; Spitzhauben]	102,251
sw	Snow-white down	....	103
ws	Wing-spot	....	112
Ww	White-wing lethal	CONS	237
(MF)	Delayed amelanosis	MAS	224

4/ No gene symbol previously assigned; provisional gene symbol proposed. 6/ Linkage group V, chromosome Z. 7/ Gene symbol changed; previous symbol refers to a different locus. 8/ Linkage group III, chromosome 1. 9/ Linkage group I. 11/ Linkage group II.

continued

Gene Symbol	Trait Name ⟨Synonym⟩	Holder [Breed or Variety]	Reference
(MF)	Red-brown complex	[New Hampshire; Rhode Island Red]	239,240
(MF)	White Leghorn headspot	....	76,77
	Egg Shell Color		
O[8/]	Blue egg shell	[Araucana]	102,199
(MF)	Brown egg shell	[Brahma; Cornish; New Hampshire; Orpington; Plymouth Rock; Rhode Island Red]	85,102
(MF)	White egg shell	[Ancona; Campine; Hamburg; Houdan; Leghorn; Minorca]	85,102

[8/] Linkage group III, chromosome 1.

Contributor: Ralph G. Somes, Jr.

References

1. Abbott, U. K., and V. S. Asmundson. 1957. J. Hered. 48:63-70.
2. Abbott, U. K., and P. F. Goetinck. 1960. Ibid. 51:161-166.
3. Abbott, U. K., and M. Kieny. 1961. C. R. Acad. Sci. 252:1863-1865.
4. Abbott, U. K., and F. H. Lantz. 1967. J. Hered. 58:240-242.
5. Abbott, U. K., and J. A. MacCabe. 1966. Ibid. 57:207-211.
6. Abbott, U. K., et al. 1960. Ibid. 51:194-202.
7. Abbott, U. K., et al. 1966. Abstr. Pap. 6th Annu. Meet. Teratol. Soc., p. 1.
8. Abbott, U. K., et al. 1970. J. Hered. 61:95-102.
9. Asanoma, M., and Y. Tanabe. 1974. Jpn. Poult. Sci. 11:6-9.
10. Asmundson, V. S. 1926. J. Hered. 17:280-284.
11. Asmundson, V. S. 1936. Ibid. 27:401-404.
12. Asmundson, V. S. 1942. Ibid. 33:328-330.
13. Asmundson, V. S. 1945. Ibid. 36:173-176.
14. Asmundson, V. S., and L. M. Julian. 1952. Ibid. 47:248-252.
15. Asmundson, V. S., and H. I. Milne. 1930. Sci. Agric. 10:293-304.
16. Austic, R. E., and R. K. Cole. 1972. Am. J. Physiol. 223:525-530.
17. Baker, C. M. A. 1964. Comp. Biochem. Physiol. 12:389-403.
18. Baker, C. M. A. 1968. Genetics 58:211-226.
19. Baker, C. M. A., et al. 1970. Adv. Genet. 15:147-174.
20. Bateson, W., and R. C. Punnett. 1908. Rep. Evol. Comm. R. Soc. 4:18-35.
21. Bernier, P. E. 1951. Genet. Rec. 20:89.
22. Bernier, P. E. 1961. Poult. Sci. 40:1378.
23. Bernier, P. E., et al. 1975. Ibid. 54:1733.
24. Bhatnagar, M. K. 1969. Biochem. Genet. 3:85-90.
25. Bohren, B. B. 1952. In M. A. Jull. Poultry Breeding. Ed. 3. Wiley, New York. p. 214.
26. Bond, C. J. 1919. J. Genet. 9:69-81.
27. Broekhuizen, E. G., and I. M. van Albada. 1953. Genetica (the Hague) 26:415-429.
28. Brumbaugh, J. A., and W. F. Hollander. 1965. Iowa State J. Sci. 40:51-64.
29. Brumbaugh, J. A., and W. F. Hollander. 1966. Poult. Sci. 45:451-457.
30. Brumbaugh, J. A., et al. 1972. J. Hered. 63:19-25.
31. Buss, E. G., et al. 1950. Ibid. 41:143-144.
32. Byerly, T. C., and M. A. Jull. 1932. J. Exp. Zool. 62:489-498.
33. Callegarini, C., et al. 1969. Experientia 25:537-538.
34. Cam, A. E., and D. W. Cooper. 1978. Biochem. Genet. 16:261-270.
35. Cardinet, G. H., III, et al. 1972. Am. J. Vet. Res. 33:1671-1684.
36. Cavalie, A., and P. Merat. 1965. Ann. Biol. Anim. Biochim. Biophys. 5:451-468.
37. Cavalie, A., and P. Merat. 1967. Ibid. 7:205-207.
38. Cheng, K. M., and R. N. Shoffner. 1978. Poult. Sci. 57:1127.
39. Chopra, A. K., and M. R. Ahuja. Unpublished. 14th Int. Conf. Anim. Blood Groups Biochem. Polymorphism (Davis) 1974.
40. Cole, R. K. 1942. J. Hered. 33:83-86.
41. Cole, R. K. 1961. Ibid. 52:47-52.
42. Cole, R. K. 1966. Genetics 53:1021-1033.
43. Cole, R. K. 1967. J. Hered. 58:141-146.
44. Cole, R. K. 1973. Poult. Sci. 52:2012-2013.
45. Cole, R. K., and T. K. Jeffers. 1963. Nature (London) 200:1238-1239.
46. Cole, R. K., and D. G. Jones. 1972. Poult. Sci. 51:1795.
47. Cole, R. K., et al. 1968. Science 160:1357-1358.
48. Conner, M. H., and C. H. Shaffner. 1953. J. Hered. 44:223-224.
49. Crawford, R. D. 1964. Can. J. Anim. Sci. 44:184-186.
50. Crawford, R. D. 1970. J. Hered. 61:185-188.
51. Crawford, R. D. 1971. Poult. Sci. 50:867-869.
52. Crichlow, E. C., and R. D. Crawford. 1974. Can. J. Physiol. Pharmacol. 52:424-429.
53. Croizier, G. 1966. Ann. Biol. Anim. Biochim. Biophys. 6:379-388.

continued

54. Croizier, G. 1967. Ibid. 7:173-182.
55. Csuka, J., and E. Petrovsky. 1968. Folia Biol. (Prague) 14:165-167.
56. Csuka, J., and E. Petrovsky. 1972. Proc. 12th Eur. Conf. Anim. Blood Groups Biochem. Polymorphism (Budapest) 1970, pp. 459-465.
57. Custodia, R. W. S., and R. G. Jaap. 1973. Poult. Sci. 52:204-210.
58. Czaja, M. 1939. Proc. 7th World's Poult. Congr. (Cleveland), p. 55.
59. Davenport, C. B. 1906. Carnegie Inst. Washington Publ. 52.
60. Davenport, C. B. 1912. J. Exp. Zool. 13:1-26.
61. Davenport, C. B. 1914. J. Hered. 5:374.
62. Deakin, A., and G. Robertson. 1935. Am. Nat. 69:378-380.
63. Dunn, L. C. 1923. Ibid. 57:345-349.
64. Dunn, L. C. 1925. Anat. Rec. 31:343-344.
65. Dunn, L. C., and M. A. Jull. 1927. J. Genet. 19:27-63.
66. Dunn, L. C., and W. Landauer. 1934. Ibid. 29:217-243.
67. Dunson, W. A., and E. G. Buss. 1968. Science 161:167-169.
68. Dunson, W. A., et al. 1972. Am. J. Physiol. 222:1167-1176.
69. Ede, D. A., and W. A. Kelly. 1964. J. Embryol. Exp. Morphol. 12:161-182.
70. Finne, I., and N. Vike. 1949. Tidsskr. Nor. Landbruk 56:60-76.
71. Finzi, A., and I. Romboli. 1978. Proc. 16th World's Poult. Congr. 10:1823-1828.
72. Fiser, P. S., et al. 1972. Poult. Sci. 51:2006-2009.
73. Fiser, P. S., et al. 1973. Ibid. 52:121-126.
74. Fisher, R. A. 1934. Science 80:288-289.
75. Fodor, A., and G. Pethes. 1974. Gen. Comp. Endocrinol. 24:140-151.
76. Gleichauf, R. 1958. Arch. Gefluegelk. 22:157-169.
77. Gleichauf, R. 1964. Ibid. 23:201-206.
78. Gleichauf, R. 1965. Ibid. 29:107-134.
79. Goda, Y., et al. 1971. Abst. Pap. 1971 Meet. Jpn. Poult. Sci. Assoc., p. 11.
80. Godfrey, E. F. 1953. Poult. Sci. 32:248-259.
81. Godfrey, E. F., et al. 1953. J. Hered. 44:108-112.
82. Goodwin, K., et al. 1950. Science 112:460-461.
83. Grunder, A. A. 1971. Anim. Blood Groups Biochem. Genet. 2:189-194.
84. Hadley, P. B. 1915. J. Hered. 6:147-151.
85. Hall, G. O. 1944. Poult. Sci. 23:259-265.
86. Hammer, C. H., et al. 1973. Ibid. 52:520-530.
87. Hashiguchi, T., et al. 1970. Jpn. J. Genet. 45:341-349.
88. Hashiguchi, T., et al. 1979. Jpn. Poult. Sci. 16:(in press).
89. Hawes, R. O., et al. 1973. J. Hered. 64:310-311.
90. Hays, F. A. 1943. Am. Nat. 77:471-475.
91. Hays, F. A. 1944. Ibid. 78:54-58.
92. Hertwig, P. 1933. Verh. Dtsch. Zool. Ges. 6:112-118.
93. Hertwig, P., and T. Rittershaus. 1929. Z. Indukt. Abstamm. Vererbungsl. 51:354-372.
94. Hicks, A. F., and I. M. Lerner. 1949. Poult. Sci. 28:625-626.
95. Hollander, W. F., and J. A. Brumbaugh. 1969. Ibid. 48:1408-1413.
96. Hsu, P. L., et al. 1975. Ibid. 54:1315-1319.
97. Hutt, F. B. 1930. J. Genet. 22:109-127.
98. Hutt, F. B. 1932. Proc. 6th Int. Congr. Genet. 2:96-97.
99. Hutt, F. B. 1935. Poult. Sci. 14:297.
100. Hutt, F. B. 1936. J. Genet. 32:277-285.
101. Hutt, F. B. 1941. J. Hered. 32:356-364.
102. Hutt, F. B. 1949. Genetics of the Fowl. McGraw-Hill, New York.
103. Hutt, F. B. 1951. J. Hered. 42:117-120.
104. Hutt, F. B. 1959. Ibid. 50:209-221.
105. Hutt, F. B. 1964. Ibid. 55:200-206.
106. Hutt, F. B., and B. P. Child. 1934. Ibid. 24:341-350.
107. Hutt, F. B., and J. Long. 1950. Ibid. 41:145-150.
108. Hutt, F. B., and P. D. Sturkie. 1938. Ibid. 29:370-379.
109. Hutt, F. B., et al. 1944. Ibid. 35:27-32.
110. Jaap, R. G. 1937. Proc. Okla. Acad. Sci. 17:41-43.
111. Jeffrey, F. P. 1941. J. Hered. 32:310-312.
112. Jerome, F. N., and J. E. Bergey. 1953. Poult. Sci. 32:412-414.
113. Jones, D. G., and F. B. Hutt. 1946. J. Hered. 37:197-205.
114. Jones, D. G., and W. Morgan. 1956. Ibid. 47:137-141.
115. Jones, D. G., et al. 1975. Poult. Sci. 54:1780.
116. Jones, S. V. H. 1921. J. Hered. 12:117-128.
117. Jull, M. A., and J. P. Quinn. 1931. Ibid. 22:147-154.
118. Juriloff, D. M., and C. W. Roberts. 1973. Poult. Sci. 54:334-346.
119. Juriloff, D. M., and C. W. Roberts. 1977. Ibid. 56:386-388.
120. Kao, F. 1973. Proc. Natl. Acad. Sci. USA 70:2893-2898.
121. Kawahara, T. 1955. Annu. Rep. Natl. Inst. Genet. Jpn. 5:26-27.
122. Kawahara, T. 1956. Ibid. 6:15-16.
123. Kessel, E. L. 1945. Wasmann Collect. 6:82-84.
124. Kessel, E. L. 1945. Ibid. 6:84-87.
125. Kimball, E. 1951. Am. Nat. 85:265-266.
126. Kimball, E. 1952. J. Hered. 43:129-132.
127. Kimball, E. 1960. Poult. Sci. 39:232-233.
128. Kimball, E. 1960. Ibid. 39:233-234.
129. Kimura, M. 1969. Jpn. J. Genet. 44:107-108.
130. Kimura, M. 1974. Ibid. 49:435-438.
131. Kimura, M. 1975. Ibid. 50:169-171.
132. Knowlton, F. L. 1929. Oreg. Agric. Exp. Stn. Bull. 253:15.
133. Kozelka, A. W. 1933. J. Hered. 24:71-78.
134. Kuryl, J., and J. Gasparska. 1976. Anim. Blood Groups Biochem. Genet. 7:241-246.
135. Lambert, W. V., and C. W. Knox. 1927. Poult. Sci. 7:24-30.
136. Lambert, W. V., and C. W. Knox. 1929. Ibid. 9:51-64.
137. Lamoreux, W. F. 1942. J. Hered. 33:275-283.
138. Lancaster, F. M. 1968. Heredity 23:257-262.
139. Landauer, W. 1929. Am. J. Anat. 43:1-43.
140. Landauer, W. 1935. J. Genet. 31:237-242.

continued

141. Landauer, W. 1938. Ibid. 37:51-68.
142. Landauer, W. 1941. Genetics 26:426-439.
143. Landauer, W. 1945. Ibid. 30:403-428.
144. Landauer, W. 1948. Ibid. 33:133-157.
145. Landauer, W. 1956. J. Hered. 47:57-63.
146. Landauer, W. 1956. J. Genet. 54:219-235.
147. Landauer, W. 1959. J. Hered. 50:137-139.
148. Landauer, W. 1965. Ibid. 56:131-138.
149. Landauer, W. 1965. J. Exp. Zool. 160:345-354.
150. Landauer, W. 1967. Conn. Agric. Exp. Stn. Storrs Monogr. 1 (Rev.).
151. Landauer, W. 1973. Ibid. 1 (Rev.), Suppl.
152. Landauer, W., and L. C. Dunn. 1930. J. Hered. 21: 290-305.
153. Landauer, W., and L. C. Dunn. 1930. J. Genet. 23: 397-413.
154. Lehrner, L. M., and G. M. Malacinski. 1975. Biochem. Genet. 13:145-173.
155. Leung, E. S., and E. Haley. 1974. Ibid. 11:221-230.
156. Leung, W. C., et al. 1975. Exp. Cell Res. 95:320-326.
157. Lippincott, W. A. 1921. Am. Nat. 55:289-327.
158. Lojda, L., and P. Hovorka. 1968. Vet. Med. (Prague) 13:287-293.
159. Lush, I. E. 1961. Nature (London) 189:981-984.
160. MacArthur, J. W. 1933. Genetics 18:210-220.
161. Mann, G. E. 1963. NAAS Poult. Sect. Q. J. 69:1-2.
162. Marble, D. R., et al. 1944. Poult. Sci. 23:114-117.
163. Markson, L. M. 1959. J. Comp. Pathol. 69:223-229.
164. Maw, A. J. G. 1935. Sci. Agric. 16:85-112.
165. Maw, A. J. G. 1954. Poult. Sci. 33:216-217.
166. McGibbon, W. H. 1946. Ibid. 25:406.
167. McGibbon, W. H. 1973. J. Hered. 64:46-47.
168. McGibbon, W. H. 1973. Ibid. 64:91-94.
169. McGibbon, W. H. 1974. Ibid. 65:124-126.
170. McGibbon, W. H. 1974. Poult. Sci. 53:1251-1253.
171. McGibbon, W. H. 1977. Ibid. 56:872-875.
172. McGibbon, W. H. 1977. Genetics 86(Suppl.):43-44.
173. McGibbon, W. H. 1978. J. Hered. 69:97-100.
174. McGibbon, W. H., and R. M. Shackelford. 1972. Ibid. 63:209-211.
175. McIndoe, W. M. 1962. Nature (London) 195:353-354.
176. Mellen, W. J. 1959. J. Hered. 50:127-130.
177. Moore, J. W., and J. R. Smyth, Jr. 1971. Ibid. 62: 215-219.
178. Moore, J. W., and J. R. Smyth, Jr. 1972. Poult. Sci. 51:214-222.
179. Moore, J. W., and J. R. Smyth, Jr. 1972. Ibid. 51: 1149-1156.
180. Moore, J. W., and J. R. Smyth, Jr. 1972. J. Hered. 63:179-184.
181. Morejohn, G. V. 1953. Ibid. 44:46-52.
182. Morejohn, G. V. 1955. Genetics 40:519-530.
183. Morejohn, G. V. 1955. Poult. Sci. 34:64-67.
184. Morgan, W. 1963. J. Hered. 54:116-120.
185. Morgan, W., and D. Jones. 1956. Poult. Sci. 35:1160.
186. Morgan, W., and R. J. Greb. 1959. Ibid. 38:1456-1462.
187. Mueller, C. D., and F. B. Hutt. 1941. J. Hered. 32: 71-80.
188. Munro, S. S. 1946. Poult. Sci. 25:408.
189. Munro, S. S., and I. L. Kosin. 1940. Am. Nat. 74: 382-384.
190. Nelson, N. M. 1947. Poult. Sci. 26:61-66.
191. Nickerson, M. 1944. J. Exp. Zool. 95:361-397.
192. Ogden, A. L., et al. 1962. Nature (London) 195: 1026-1028.
193. Okada, I. 1973. Anim. Blood Groups Biochem. Genet. 4:115-118.
194. Okada, I., and Y. Hachinohe. 1968. Jpn. J. Genet. 43:243-248.
195. Okada, I., and S. Sasaki. 1970. Anim. Blood Groups Biochem. Genet. 1:181-188.
196. Pease, M. S. 1962. J. Hered. 53:109-110.
197. Peterson, D. W., et al. 1971. J. Nutr. 101:347-354.
198. Price, D. J., et al. 1966. Poult. Sci. 45:423-424.
199. Punnett, R. C. 1933. J. Genet. 27:465-470.
200. Punnett, R. C. 1937. Ibid. 35:129-140.
201. Punnett, R. C. 1948. Ibid. 48:327-332.
202. Punnett, R. C., and M. S. Pease. 1927. Ibid. 18:207-218.
203. Quinn, J. P. 1934. Ibid. 29:75-83.
204. Quinn, J. P. 1936. Poult. Sci. 15:169-178.
205. Ram, T., and F. B. Hutt. 1956. Ibid. 35:614-616.
206. Ricard, R. H. 1969. Ann. Genet. Sel. Anim. 1:33-37.
207. Rittershaus, T. 1930. Zuechter 2:324-330.
208. Roberts, C. W., et al. 1974. Poult. Sci. 53:700-713.
209. Rosenblatt, L. S., et al. 1959. Ibid. 38:1242.
210. Sasaki, K., and T. Yamaguchi. 1970. World's Poult. Sci. J. 26:562-568.
211. Sawyer, R. H., and U. K. Abbott. 1972. J. Exp. Zool. 181:99-110.
212. Scheinberg, S. L., and R. P. Reckel. 1962. Ann. N.Y. Acad. Sci. 97:194-204.
213. Scott, H. M., et al. 1959. J. Hered. 41:254-257.
214. Serfontein, P. J., and L. F. Payne. 1934. Poult. Sci. 13:61-63.
215. Shabalina, A. T. 1970. Genetika 6(5):48-52.
216. Shabalina, A. T. 1977. Anim. Blood Groups Biochem. Genet. 8(Suppl. 1):23.
217. Sheridan, A. K. 1964. Proc. Aust. Poult. Sci. Conv. 1:87-90.
218. Sheridan, A. K., et al. 1974. Proc. 15th World's Poult. Congr. New Orleans, pp. 34-35.
219. Shiihara, K., et al. 1974. Jpn. J. Zootech. Sci. 45 (Suppl.):109.
220. Shoffner, R. N. 1945. J. Hered. 36:375-378.
221. Sittmann, K. 1967. Genet. Res. 10:229-233.
222. Smyth, J. R., Jr. 1965. Poult. Sci. 44:89-98.
223. Smyth, J. R., Jr. 1970. J. Hered. 61:280-283.
224. Smyth, J. R., Jr. 1977. Poult. Sci. 56:1758.
225. Smyth, J. R., Jr., and H. L. Classen. 1976. Ibid. 55: 2094.
226. Smyth, J. R., Jr., and G. W. Malone. 1979. Ibid. 58: 1108-1109
227. Smyth, J. R., Jr., and R. G. Somes, Jr. 1965. J. Hered. 56:150-156.
228. Somes, R. G., Jr. 1968. Ibid. 59:375-378.
229. Somes, R. G., Jr. 1969. Ibid. 60:163-166.
230. Somes, R. G., Jr. 1969. Ibid. 60:185-186.
231. Somes, R. G., Jr. 1969. Ibid. 60:281-286.

continued

232. Somes, R. G., Jr. 1969. Ibid. 60:353-356.
233. Somes, R. G., Jr. 1970. Poult. Sci. 49:1172-1176.
234. Somes, R. G., Jr. 1971. Conn. Agric. Exp. Stn. Storrs Bull. 420.
235. Somes, R. G., Jr. 1978. Ibid. 446.
236. Somes, R. G., Jr. 1978. J. Hered. 69:91-96.
237. Somes, R. G., Jr. 1979. Ibid. 70:(in press).
238. Somes, R. G., Jr. 1979. Poult. Sci. 58:(in press).
239. Somes, R. G., Jr., and J. R. Smyth, Jr. 1965. Ibid. 54:47-52.
240. Somes, R. G., Jr., and J. R. Smyth, Jr. 1965. Ibid. 54:276-282.
241. Somes, R. G., Jr., and J. R. Smyth, Jr. 1967. J. Hered. 58:25-29.
242. Stratil, A. 1968. Comp. Biochem. Physiol. 24:113-121.
243. Stratil, A. 1970. Anim. Blood Groups Biochem. Genet. 1:15-22.
244. Sturkie, P. D. 1941. J. Morphol. 69:517-535.
245. Sturkie, P. D. 1942. J. Hered. 33:202-208.
246. Sturkie, P. D. 1950. Am. Nat. 84:179-182.
247. Tamaki, Y., and Y. Tanabe. 1970. Poult. Sci. 49:798-804.
248. Tanabe, Y., and T. Ise. 1972. Jpn. J. Genet. 47:257-263.
249. Tanabe, Y., and Y. Tamaki. 1966. Abst. Pap. 1966 Meet. Jpn. Poult. Sci. Assoc., p. 22.
250. Tanabe, Y., et al. 1977. Jpn. Poult. Sci. 14:173-178.
251. Taylor, L. W. 1932. J. Genet. 26:385-394.
252. Taylor, L. W. 1971. Avian Dis. 15:376-390.
253. Taylor, L. W. 1972. Can. J. Genet. Cytol. 14:417-422.
254. Taylor, L. W. 1974. Ibid. 16:121-135.
255. Taylor, L. W., and C. A. Gunns. 1947. J. Hered. 38:66-76.
256. Taylor, L. W., and V. M. Stinnett. 1957. Poult. Sci. 36:1162-1163.
257. Tsuji, S., and T. Fukushima. 1976. Biochem. Genet. 14:507-515.
258. Ueda, J., and Y. Hachinohe. 1973. Anim. Blood Groups Biochem. Genet. 4:221-226.
259. Upp, C. W. 1934. Poult. Sci. 13:157-165.
260. van Albada, I. M., and A. R. Kuit. 1960. Genen Phaenen 5:1-9.
261. Wagner, W. D., and R. A. Peterson. 1970. Am. J. Vet. Res. 31:331-338.
262. Warren, D. C. 1925. J. Hered. 16:13-18.
263. Warren, D. C. 1928. Genetics 13:470-487.
264. Warren, D. C. 1932. J. Hered. 23:449-452.
265. Warren, D. C. 1933. Ibid. 24:379-383.
266. Warren, D. C. 1933. Ibid. 24:430-434.
267. Warren, D. C. 1933. Genetics 18:68-81.
268. Warren, D. C. 1937. J. Hered. 28:16-18.
269. Warren, D. C. 1937. Kansas State Agric. Exp. Stn. Tech. Bull. 44.
270. Warren, D. C. 1938. J. Hered. 29:91-93.
271. Warren, D. C. 1939. Ibid. 30:257-260.
272. Warren, D. C. 1940. Ibid. 31:141-144.
273. Warren, D. C. 1940. Ibid. 31:291-292.
274. Warren, D. C. 1941. Ibid. 32:2-5.
275. Warren, D. C. 1944. Genetics 29:217-231.
276. Warren, D. C. 1946. J. Hered. 37:323-324.
277. Warren, D. C. 1949. Ibid. 40:267.
278. Warren, D. C. 1950. Ibid. 41:31-34.
279. Warren, D. C., and F. B. Hutt. 1936. Am. Nat. 70:379-394.
280. Warren, D. C., et al. 1944. J. Hered. 35:354-358.
281. Washburn, K. W. 1968. Poult. Sci. 47:561-564.
282. Washburn, K. W. 1976. Ibid. 55:436-438.
283. Washburn, K. W., and J. R. Smyth, Jr. 1967. J. Hered. 58:130-134.
284. Washburn, K. W., and J. R. Smyth, Jr. 1968. Poult. Sci. 47:1406-1411.
285. Washburn, K. W., and J. R. Smyth, Jr. 1971. Ibid. 50:385-388.
286. Waters, N. F. 1967. J. Hered. 58:163-164.
287. Waters, N. F., and J. H. Bywaters. 1943. Ibid. 34:213-217.
288. Wight, P. A. L., and J. G. Carr. 1965. J. Pathol. Bacteriol. 89:681-689.
289. Wilcox, F. H. 1958. J. Hered. 49:107-110.
290. Wilcox, F. H. 1966. Genetics 53:799-805.
291. Winterfield, R. W. 1953. J. Am. Vet. Med. Assoc. 123:136-138.
292. Zwilling, E. 1956. J. Exp. Zool. 132:241-251.

161. BLOOD GROUP SYSTEMS: CHICKEN

Part I. Erythrocyte Alloantigen Characteristics

Except where noted otherwise, the loci are autosomal, independent of each other so far as is known, and have co-dominant expression. **Linked Genes:** Only confirmed genetic linkages are listed. **Main Reference** provides the

continued

Part I. Erythrocyte Alloantigen Characteristics

original reference, and is the citation for all quoted material except that specifically cited separately. Figures in heavy brackets are additional reference numbers. Data in light brackets refer to the column heading in brackets.

Gene Symbol	Alleles	Linked Genes [Recombination Fraction]	Remarks	Main Reference
Ea-A	A^{1-7} [4, 5, 9, 27]	Ea-E [0.005] [8, 42]; consult also references 5, 7, & 19	Also expressed on lymphocytes [43]; consult also reference 40	16,28
Ea-B [1]	B^{1-30} [4, 9, 12, 17, 27, 37] [2]	Nucleolar organizer region (see Table VIII-9); consult also references 7 & 19	Present on lymphocytes (see Table 167), also on most tissues because associated with major histocompatibility [37-39]. Other associated traits: hatchability [1, 13, 31, 36]; mortality [1, 2, 13, 29]; Marek's disease [11, 20, 21, 33]; immune response [3, 32]; complex cross-reactive antigens [28]; complement levels [23]; male fertility [28, 35]; egg production [1, 2, 13].	16,28, 38
Ea-C	C^{1-8} [9, 18]	Consult references 7 & 19	Present on lymphocytes [40], also on most tissues because associated with minor histocompatibility [41]	18,27
Ea-D	D^{1-5} [4, 9, 12, 18]	Consult references 7 & 19	Associated with egg weight [10]	4,18
Ea-E	E^{1-11} [4, 5, 9]	Ea-A [0.005] [8, 42]; consult also references 5, 7, & 19	With Ea-A, forms very numerous combined pseudoallelic antigens [7]	4,5,28
Ea-H	H^{1-3} [6, 9]	w ⟨yellow skin⟩ [0.15] [19, 42]; consult also references 7 & 26	....	6
Ea-I	I^{1-8} [6, 9]	Consult references 7 & 19	....	6
Ea-J	$J^{1,2}$ [6, 9]	Consult references 7 & 19	....	6
Ea-K	K^{1-4} [9, 14]	Consult references 7 & 19	Associated with vaccinia virus [6, 22, 30]. vh (recessive inagglutinability by vaccinia virus & phospholipids [28, 30]) is identical with K [6, 14, 22], and also with Ka [34].	6,30
Ea-L	$L^{1,2}$ [9, 27]	Consult references 7 & 19	Identical with Ea-F [6]	27
Ea-N	$N^{1,2}$ [27]	....	Consult reference 7	27
Ea-P	P^{1-10} [6, 9]	Na ⟨naked neck⟩ [0.30] [19, 42]; consult also reference 7	....	6
Ea-R	$R^{1,2}$ [15, 24]	....	Associated with susceptibility to a leukosis-sarcoma virus [11, 24]. R^1 is associated with $Tv-B^{s1}$ ⟨susceptibility to subgroup B of avian type C oncoviruses⟩ [24, 25].	15,24

[1] Alleles at this locus are markers for haplotypes of the *B* complex ⟨major histocompatibility complex⟩, with sublocus *B-F* determining antigens common to erythrocytes, leukocytes, and probably most tissues; sublocus *B-L* determining antigens on B lymphocytes and some monocytes & macrophages; and sublocus *B-G* determining antigens unique to erythrocytes (see Table 167). [2] This number of alleles is a minimal estimate, based on proven differences in antigenic specificity [12]. Considering the nature of these differences and the number of alleles under study in various laboratories known to us, the number of alleles is likely to be much larger, probably well over one hundred.

Contributors: W. E. Briles; Douglas G. Gilmour

References

1. Allen, C. P. 1962. Ann. N.Y. Acad. Sci. 97:184-193.
2. Allen, C. P., and D. G. Gilmour. 1962. Genetics 47: 1711-1718.
3. Benedict, A. A., et al. 1975. Immunogenetics 2:313-324.
4. Briles, C. O., et al. 1959. Genetics 44:955-965.
5. Briles, W. E. 1958. Poult. Sci. 37:1189.
6. Briles, W. E. 1962. Ann. N.Y. Acad. Sci. 97:173-183.
7. Briles, W. E. 1964. Z. Tierz. Zuechtungsbiol. 79:371-391.
8. Briles, W. E. 1968. Genetics 60:164(Abstr.).
9. Briles, W. E. 1972. 12th Eur. Conf. Anim. Blood Groups Biochem. Polymorphism 1970, pp. 415-418.
10. Briles, W. E. 1972. Poult. Sci. 51:1788.
11. Briles, W. E. 1974. 1st World Congr. Genet. Appl. Livestock Prod. 1:299-306.

continued

161. BLOOD GROUP SYSTEMS: CHICKEN

Part I. Erythrocyte Alloantigen Characteristics

12. Briles, W. E. Unpublished. Northern Illinois Univ., Dep. Biological Sciences, DeKalb, 1979.
13. Briles, W. E., and C. P. Allen. 1961. Genetics 46:1273-1293.
14. Briles, W. E., and R. W. Briles. 1972. Anim. Blood Groups Biochem. Genet. Suppl. 1:82-83(Abstr.).
15. Briles, W. E., and L. B. Crittenden. 1971. Poult. Sci. 50:1558.
16. Briles, W. E., et al. 1950. Genetics 35:633-652.
17. Briles, W. E., et al. 1957. Ibid. 42:631-648.
18. Briles, W. E., et al. 1963. Poult. Sci. 42:1096-1103.
19. Briles, W. E., et al. 1967. Ibid. 46:1238(Abstr.).
20. Briles, W. E., et al. 1975. Ibid. 54:1738-1739.
21. Briles, W. E., et al. 1977. Science 195:193-195.
22. Brown, K. S., et al. 1973. Proc. Soc. Exp. Biol. Med. 142:16-18.
23. Chanh, T. C., et al. 1976. J. Exp. Med. 144:555-561.
24. Crittenden, L. B., et al. 1970. Science 169:1324-1325.
25. Crittenden, L. B., et al. 1973. Virology 52:373-384.
26. Etches, R. J., and R. O. Hawes. 1973. Can. J. Genet. Cytol. 15:553-570.
27. Gilmour, D. G. 1959. Genetics 44:14-33.
28. Gilmour, D. G. 1960. Br. Poult. Sci. 1:75-100.
29. Gilmour, D. G. 1962. Ann. N.Y. Acad. Sci. 97:166-172.
30. Gilmour, D. G., and A. C. Allison. 1969. Virology 37:237-242.
31. Gilmour, D. G., and J. R. Morton. 1970. Genet. Res. 15:265-284.
32. Gunther, E., et al. 1974. Eur. J. Immunol. 4:548-553.
33. Longenecker, B. M., et al. 1976. Immunogenetics 3:401-407.
34. McPhee, C. P. 1971. Br. Poult. Sci. 12:439-449.
35. Morton, J. R., and D. G. Gilmour. 1972. Theoret. Appl. Genet. 42:111-118.
36. Morton, J. R., et al. 1965. Genetics 51:97-107.
37. Pazderka, F., et al. 1975. Immunogenetics 2:93-100.
38. Pazderka, F., et al. 1975. Ibid. 2:101-130.
39. Schierman, L. W., and A. W. Nordskog. 1961. Science 134:1008.
40. Schierman, L. W., and A. W. Nordskog. 1962. Ibid. 137:620.
41. Schierman, L. W., and A. W. Nordskog. 1965. Transplantation 3:44-48.
42. Somes, R. G., Jr. 1973. J. Hered. 64:217-221.
43. Wong, S. Y., et al. 1972. Immunol. Commun. 1:597-613.

Part II. Distribution of Types in Certain Lines

Data are for the blood group genotypes present in 13 inbred lines. The erythrocyte alloantigens in these lines were detected by hemagglutination with reagents prepared from alloantisera [ref. 1]. In general, relatively few reagents, developed primarily in populations other than those presented below, were used in typing these lines. Any conclusions regarding the possible identity of alleles between lines must be limited to the agglutinations obtained with the limited spectrum of reagents used. This applies particularly when comparisons are made between lines of different origin (i.e., UCD vs. RPRL vs. Reaseheath). $Ea\text{-}B^2$ and $Ea\text{-}B^{15}$ in the RPRL lines are synonymous with similarly designated alleles having corresponding designations in Table 3 of reference 2 [ref. 3]. Other $Ea\text{-}B$ homologies between some of these lines and other populations are given in reference 3. A project determining possible $Ea\text{-}B$ homologies across these and several other experimental lines is nearing completion, and will be reported in due time [ref. 1]. Of these systems, $Ea\text{-}A$ and $Ea\text{-}E$ are closely linked, while all others are independent from one another. For another classification, by L. Warren Johnson of Auburn University, Auburn, Alabama, see Table 17 in reference 4.

Line: For a description of the lines, see Table 152. **Erythrocyte Alloantigen Loci:** A numeral gives the code number of the allele present in a given line. Single numerals represent genotypes, i.e., "8" in column $Ea\text{-}E$ stands for E^8E^8. More than one numeral in a given entry indicates that the corresponding alleles segregate within the line. Numerals in parentheses refer to alleles whose presence is not ruled out by typing of the given line.

Line	Erythrocyte Alloantigen Loci											
	Ea-A	Ea-B	Ea-C	Ea-D	Ea-E	Ea-H	Ea-I	Ea-J	Ea-K	Ea-L	Ea-P	Ea-R
RH-C (Reaseheath line C)	4	12	4	3	7	2	4	2	3	1	10 (2)	2
RPRL-6$_1$	4	2	5	3	7	2	2	2	3	1	7	2
RPRL-6$_3$	4	2	5	3,4	7	2	2	2	2	1	7	2
RPRL-7$_1$	4	2	2	1	5	2	3,2	2	2	1	4	1 (2)
RPRL-7$_2$	4	2	5	1	5	2	3	2	3	1,2	4	2
RPRL-15$_1$	4	5	5	4	7	2	8	2	2	1	4	1 (2)

continued

Part II. Distribution of Types in Certain Lines

Line	Erythrocyte Alloantigen Loci											
	Ea-A	Ea-B	Ea-C	Ea-D	Ea-E	Ea-H	Ea-I	Ea-J	Ea-K	Ea-L	Ea-P	Ea-R
RPRL-15I$_4$	4	5,15	2,5	2,3	1,5	2	3,8	2	2	1	3,4,7	1 (2)
RPRL-15I$_5$	4	15	5	2,3	5	2	8	2	2	1	3,4,7	1 (2)
RPRL-100	4	2	2,5	1	5	2	2,3	2	2,3	1,2	4	1,2
UCD-02	4	6	2	3	8	1	2	..	2	1	10	2
UCD-03	4	2	2	3	7	2	4	..	3	1	3	2
UCD-07	4	4	2	1	7	2	2	..	2	1	3	1
UCD-22	4	2	3	3	8	1	4	..	2	1	3	....

Contributors: Hans Abplanalp; W. E. Briles; Howard Stone

References
1. Briles, W. E. Unpublished. Northern Illinois Univ., Dep. Biological Sciences, DeKalb, 1979.
2. Briles, W. E., et al. 1957. Genetics 42:631-648.
3. Pazderka, F., et al. 1975. Immunogenetics 2:93-100.
4. Stone, H. A. 1975. U.S. Dep. Agric. Tech. Bull. 1514.

162. HISTOCOMPATIBILITY ANTIGENS: CHICKEN

Genetic System	Description	Related Traits	Reference
B-complex	Major histocompatibility complex	Allograft rejection	7,8,9,11,16
		Graft-versus-host reactions	8,9,13,18
		Mixed leukocyte reaction	14
		Lymphocyte antigens	17
		Blood group system	5
		Genetic recombinants	12,15
		Chemical properties	20
C blood group-histocompatibility locus	Minor histocompatibility system	Allograft rejection	19
		Lymphocyte antigens	17
		Blood group system	6
W-chromosome linked[1/]	Comparable to Y-linked histocompatibility system in mice	Allograft rejection	2,4,10
Z-chromosome linked[1/]	Comparable to X-linked histocompatibility system in mice	Allograft rejection	1,3

[1/] In chickens the sex chromosomes are labeled W and Z. The female is the heterogametic sex and is designated WZ; the male is designated ZZ.

Contributor: Louis W. Schierman

References
1. Bacon, L. D. 1970. Transplantation 10:126-129.
2. Bacon, L. D., and J. V. Craig. 1966. Poult. Sci. 45: 1066-1067(Abstr.).
3. Bacon, L. D., and J. V. Craig. 1967. Ibid. 46:1230 (Abstr.).
4. Bacon, L. D., and J. V. Craig. 1969. Transplantation 7:387-393.
5. Briles, W. E., et al. 1950. Genetics 35:633-652.
6. Briles, W. E., et al. 1950. Poult. Sci. 29:750(Abstr.).
7. Craig, J. V., and E. M. McDermid. 1963. Transplantation 1:191-200.
8. Crittenden, L. B., et al. 1964. Ibid. 2:362-374.
9. Gilmour, D. G. 1963. Heredity 18:123-124(Abstr.).
10. Gilmour, D. G. 1967. Transplantation 5:699-706.

continued

11. Gleason, R. E., and R. C. Fanguy. 1964. Ibid. 2:509-514.

12. Hala, K., et al. 1976. Immunogenetics 3:97-103.

13. Jaffe, W. P., and E. M. McDermid. 1962. Science 137:984.

14. Miggiano, V. C., et al. 1974. Eur. J. Immunol. 4:397-401.

15. Schierman, L. W., and R. A. McBride. 1969. Transplantation 8:515-516.

16. Schierman, L. W., and A. W. Nordskog. 1961. Science 134:1008-1009.

17. Schierman, L. W., and A. W. Nordskog. 1962. Ibid. 137:620-621.

18. Schierman, L. W., and A. W. Nordskog. 1963. Nature (London) 197:511-512.

19. Schierman, L. W., and A. W. Nordskog. 1965. Transplantation 3:44-48.

20. Ziegler, A., and R. Pink. 1976. J. Biol. Chem. 251:5391-5396.

163. GENETIC CONTROL OF IMMUNE RESPONSES: CHICKEN

Line: All lines are of the Leghorn breed. **Holder:** For full name, *see* list of HOLDERS at front of book. **Ea-B Locus Blood Group Genotype:** The B blood group locus, *Ea-B*, is a serological marker of the major histocompatibility complex in the chicken, corresponding to *H-2* in the mouse. However, the nomenclature for *B* alleles in chickens has not yet been standardized. Consequently, designation of *B* alleles is unique to each laboratory, i.e., the B^2 allele in the PR-CC line is not necessarily identical with the B^2 allele of the UG-G line. **Immune Response:** Description as high, intermediate, or low is relative and should be considered only within a specific system. Responses to DNP-CGG, GAT^{10}, GT, HSA, SP, (T, G)-A-L, thyroglobulin, and TUB have been found to be associated with the *B* complex. Data in brackets refer to the column heading in brackets.

ABBREVIATIONS & SYMBOLS

Antigen

ARS-CGG = arsanilic acid conjugate of chicken gamma globulin

DNP-CGG = dinitrophenyl conjugate of chicken gamma globulin

FITC-CGG = fluorescein isothiocyanate conjugate of chicken gamma globulin

GA = linear random copolymer: poly(Glu^{60}Ala^{40})

GAT^4 = linear random copolymer: poly(Glu^{58}Ala^{38}Tyr^4)

GAT^{10} = linear random copolymer: poly(Glu^{60}Ala^{30}Tyr^{10})

GT = linear random copolymer: poly(Glu^{50}Tyr^{50})

HSA = human serum albumin

PAB-CGG = *p*-aminobenzoic acid conjugate of chicken gamma globulin

SP = Salmonella pullorum bacterin

S-III = type III pneumococcal polysaccharide

(T,G)-A-L = branched synthetic polypeptide: poly(L-Tyr, L-Glu)-poly(DL-Ala)-poly(L-Lys)

TUB = tuberculin

Immunization Method

aq. sol. = aqueous solution

CFA = complete Freund's adjuvant

inj. = injection

Assay Method

ABC = antigen-binding capacity

AGG = tube agglutination

HA = hemagglutination

PHA = passive hemagglutination

REC = radioelectrocomplexing

WT = wattle thickness

Line [Holder]	*Ea-B* Locus Blood Group Genotype	Antigen	Immunization Method	Assay Method	Immune Response	Reference
Cornell C-resistant [1]; Cornell OS [COR]	B^1B^1	Thyroglobulin	Naturally occurring antibodies	PHA	Intermediate	13
	B^2B^2	Thyroglobulin	Naturally occurring antibodies	PHA	Low	13
	B^3B^3	Thyroglobulin	Naturally occurring antibodies	PHA	High	13
	B^4B^4	Thyroglobulin	Naturally occurring antibodies	PHA	Low	13

[1]/ Synonym: Cornell CS.

continued

Line [Holder]	Ea-B Locus Blood Group Genotype	Antigen	Immunization Method	Assay Method	Immune Response	Reference
IU-S1 [IUA]	B^1B^1	GAT^{10}	First inj. of antigen in CFA, booster inj. in aq. sol.	ABC	Low	12
		HSA	First & booster inj. of antigen in aq. sol.	PHA, ABC	Low	11
		(T,G)-A-L	First inj. of antigen in CFA, booster inj. in aq. sol.	PHA, ABC	Low	11
		SP	Single inj. of antigen in aq. sol.	AGG	Low	10
	Non-B^1B^1	SP	Single inj. of antigen in aq. sol.	AGG	High	10
	B^1B^1 - high	GAT^{10}	First inj. of antigen in CFA, booster inj. in aq. sol.	ABC	High	12
	B^1B^1 - low	GAT^{10}	First inj. of antigen in CFA, booster inj. in aq. sol.	ABC	Low	12
	B^2B^2	GAT^{10}	First inj. of antigen in CFA, booster inj. in aq. sol.	ABC	Intermediate-high	12
		HSA	First & booster inj. of antigen in aq. sol.	PHA, ABC	Low	11
		(T,G)-A-L	First inj. of antigen in CFA, booster inj. in aq. sol.	PHA, ABC	Intermediate-high	11
	$B^{19}B^{19}$	GAT^{10}	First inj. of antigen in CFA, booster inj. in aq. sol.	ABC	High	12
		HSA	First & booster inj. of antigen in aq. sol.	PHA, ABC	High	11
		(T,G)-A-L	First inj. of antigen in CFA, booster inj. in aq. sol.	PHA, ABC	High	11
	$B^{19}B^{19}$ - high	GAT^{10}	First inj. of antigen in CFA, booster inj. in aq. sol.	ABC	High	12
	$B^{19}B^{19}$ - low	GAT^{10}	First inj. of antigen in CFA, booster inj. in aq. sol.	ABC	Low	12
PR-CA [CZ]	B^1B^1	DNP-CGG	Single inj. of antigen in aq. sol.	PHA	High	1
		FITC-CGG	Single inj. of antigen in aq. sol.	PHA	High	2
		HSA	Single inj. of antigen in aq. sol.	PHA	High	2
		TUB	First inj. of antigen in CFA, booster inj. in aq. sol.	WT	Intermediate	8
PR-CB [CZ]	B^1B^1	ARS-CGG	Single inj. of antigen in aq. sol.	PHA	High	2
		DNP-CGG	Single inj. of antigen in aq. sol.	PHA	High	1,4
		FITC-CGG	Single inj. of antigen in aq. sol.	PHA	High	2
		HSA	Single inj. of antigen in aq. sol.	PHA	High	2
		PAB-CGG	Single inj. of antigen in aq. sol.	PHA	High	2
		S-III	Single inj. of antigen in aq. sol.	HA	Intermediate	3
		(T,G)-A-L	First inj. of antigen in CFA, booster inj. in aq. sol.	ABC	Intermediate	7
		TUB	First inj. of antigen in CFA, booster inj. in aq. sol.	WT	Intermediate	8
PR-CC [CZ]	B^2B^2	ARS-CGG	Single inj. of antigen in aq. sol.	PHA	Intermediate	2
		DNP-CGG	Single inj. of antigen in aq. sol.	PHA	Intermediate	1
		FITC-CGG	Single inj. of antigen in aq. sol.	PHA	Intermediate	2
		HSA	Single inj. of antigen in aq. sol.	PHA	Intermediate	2
		PAB-CGG	Single inj. of antigen in aq. sol.	PHA	High	2
		S-III	Single inj. of antigen in aq. sol.	HA	Intermediate	3
		TUB	First inj. of antigen in CFA, booster inj. in aq. sol.	WT	Intermediate	8
PR-I [CZ]	$B^{13}B^{13}$	DNP-CGG	Single inj. of antigen in aq. sol.	PHA	Intermediate	1
		HSA	Single inj. of antigen in aq. sol.	PHA	Intermediate	2
		(T,G)-A-L	First inj. of antigen in CFA, booster inj. in aq. sol.	ABC	Low	7
		TUB	First inj. of antigen in CFA, booster inj. in aq. sol.	WT	High	8

continued

Line [Holder]	*Ea-B* Locus Blood Group Genotype	Antigen	Immunization Method	Assay Method	Immune Response	Reference
PR-M [CZ]	B^6B^6	ARS-CGG	Single inj. of antigen in aq. sol.	PHA	High	2
		DNP-CGG	Single inj. of antigen in aq. sol.	PHA	High	1
		FITC-CGG	Single inj. of antigen in aq. sol.	PHA	Low	2
		HSA	Single inj. of antigen in aq. sol.	PHA	High	2
		S-III	Single inj. of antigen in aq. sol.	HA	High	3
		(T,G)-A-L	First inj. of antigen in CFA, booster inj. in aq. sol.	ABC	High	7
PR-WA [CZ]	B^9B^9	ARS-CGG	Single inj. of antigen in aq. sol.	PHA	Low	2
		DNP-CGG	Single inj. of antigen in aq. sol.	PHA	Low	1
		FITC-CGG	Single inj. of antigen in aq. sol.	PHA	Low	2
		HSA	Single inj. of antigen in aq. sol.	PHA	Low	2
		(T,G)-A-L	First inj. of antigen in CFA, booster inj. in aq. sol.	ABC	Intermediate	7
		TUB	First inj. of antigen in CFA, booster inj. in aq. sol.	WT	Low	8
PR-WB [CZ]	$B^{10}B^{10}$	ARS-CGG	Single inj. of antigen in aq. sol.	PHA	Low	2
		DNP-CGG	Single inj. of antigen in aq. sol.	PHA	Low	1,4
		FITC-CGG	Single inj. of antigen in aq. sol.	PHA	Low	2
		HSA	Single inj. of antigen in aq. sol.	PHA	Low	2
		PAB-CGG	Single inj. of antigen in aq. sol.	PHA	Low	2
		S-III	Single inj. of antigen in aq. sol.	HA	Intermediate	3
		(T,G)-A-L	First inj. of antigen in CFA, booster inj. in aq. sol.	ABC	Intermediate	7
		TUB	First inj. of antigen in CFA, booster inj. in aq. sol.	WT	Low	8
UCD-02 [UCD]	B^6B^6	GA	First & booster inj. of antigen in CFA	REC	High	5
		GAT^4	First & booster inj. of antigen in CFA	REC, WT	High	6
		GAT^{10}	First & booster inj. of antigen in CFA	REC	High	5
UCD-03 [UCD]	B^2B^2	GA	First & booster inj. of antigen in CFA	REC	High	5
		GAT^{10}	First & booster inj. of antigen in CFA	REC	High	5
UCD-07 [UCD]	B^4B^4	GA	First & booster inj. of antigen in CFA	REC	Low	5
		GAT^4	First & booster inj. of antigen in CFA	REC, WT	Low	6
		GAT^{10}	First & booster inj. of antigen in CFA	REC	Low	5
UCD-11 [UCD]	Segregating	GA	First & booster inj. of antigen in CFA	REC	High	5
		GAT^{10}	First & booster inj. of antigen in CFA	REC	High	5
UCD-13 [UCD]	Segregating	GA	First & booster inj. of antigen in CFA	REC	High	5
		GAT^{10}	First & booster inj. of antigen in CFA	REC	High	5
UCD-22 [UCD]	B^2B^2	GA	First & booster inj. of antigen in CFA	REC	High	5
		GAT^{10}	First & booster inj. of antigen in CFA	REC	High	5
UG-G [IUA, UGAS]	B^1B^1	GT	First inj. of antigen in CFA, booster inj. in aq. sol.	ABC	Low	9
		(T,G)-A-L	First inj. of antigen in CFA, booster inj. in aq. sol.	ABC	Low	9
	B^2B^2	GT	First inj. of antigen in CFA, booster inj. in aq. sol.	ABC	High	9
		(T,G)-A-L	First inj. of antigen in CFA, booster inj. in aq. sol.	ABC	High	9

Contributors: I. Y. Pevzner and A. W. Nordskog

References

1. Balcarova, J., et al. 1973. Folia Biol. (Prague) 19:19-24.
2. Balcarova, J., et al. 1973. Ibid. 19:329-336.
3. Balcarova, J., et al. 1974. Ibid. 20:221-224.

continued

4. Balcarova, J., et al. 1974. Ibid. 20:346-349.

5. Benedict, A. A., et al. 1975. Immunogenetics 2:313-324.

6. Benedict, A. A., et al. 1977. Ibid. 4:199-204.

7. Gunther, E., et al. 1974. Eur. J. Immunol. 4:548-553.

8. Karakoz, I., et al. 1974. Ibid. 4:545-548.

9. Koch, C., and M. Simmonsen. 1977. Immunogenetics 5:161-170.

10. Pevzner, I., et al. 1975. Genetics 80:753-759.

11. Pevzner, I. Y., et al. 1977. Fed. Proc. Fed. Am. Soc. Exp. Biol. 36:1225(Abstr.).

12. Pevzner, I. Y., et al. 1978. Immunogenetics 7:25-33.

13. Rose, N. R., et al. 1976. Transplant. Rev. 31:264-285.

164. IMMUNOLOGICAL DISEASES: CHICKEN

Part I. Spontaneous Autoimmune Thyroiditis

The Cornell Obese strain ⟨OS⟩ was developed by selective breeding of individual birds that exhibited phenotypic signs of hypothyroidism [ref. 3, 7]: (i) an excess of subcutaneous fat; (ii) a skeletal structure somewhat smaller than normal; (iii) long, silky feathers; and (iv) poor laying ability. Chickens with these characteristics were first observed in <1% of the Cornell C-resistant ⟨CS⟩ strain, a closed flock of normal White Leghorn chickens. By selective breeding, the incidence of hypothyroidism was increased from <1% to >90%. Characterization of this disease as spontaneous autoimmune thyroiditis was made after histological examination of the thyroid of OS chickens and demonstration of serum autoantibodies to thyroglobulin [ref. 4, 5, 10]. Bursa-derived lymphocytes are essential for the production of thyroiditis since surgical or chemical bursectomy will severely reduce or prevent the disease [ref. 4, 8]. A role for suppressor T cells has been indicated by an enhanced severity of thyroiditis after surgical thymectomy [ref. 9]. The major histocompatibility complex ⟨MHC; B-complex⟩ appears to be an important factor in determining the severity of the disease. Factors that may be mediated through the MHC and which may influence the development of thyroiditis include virus susceptibility and a defect in the thyroid gland, either by alterations in cell membranes or by disturbances in endocrine metabolism of the organ.

In OS birds that spontaneously develop autoimmune thyroiditis, two alleles, B^1 and B^4, were identified with equal gene frequency [ref. 1]. A third allele, B^3, was identified and observed only rarely (r = 0.04, where r is frequency of allele in those birds with disease). Matings of OS B^1B^4 heterozygotes resulted in the segregation of offspring into the expected genotypic ratio of $1B^1B^1:2B^1B^4:1B^4B^4$. Only one of the frequent alleles of the OS chicks, B^1, was identified in the parent strain, CS. The B^2 and B^3 alleles were present in moderate frequency in CS. In hybrids of OS x CS, the majority of the birds with the B^3 allele developed significant disease. On the assumption that immune response genes are responsible for susceptibility to thyroiditis, it has been proposed that the B^3 allele determines high, B^1 moderate, and B^2 and B^4 low or no response to an antigenic determinant on thyroglobulin [ref. 6]. The following data show that alleles at the Ea-B locus or genes directly linked to it influence the immune response in spontaneous autoimmune thyroiditis.

Thyroid Pathology: Values were obtained by measuring the percentage of normal tissue invaded by lymphoid cells, using a range of 0 (no infiltration) to 4 (complete replacement of the gland by lymphoid cells), so that 0.2 unit corresponds to each 5% increment of infiltration [ref. 2]. **Thyroglobulin Antibody Titer** is given in terms of logarithm on the base 2. Plus/minus (±) values are standard error of the mean.

Strain or Hybrid ⟨Synonym⟩	Genotype	Thyroid Pathology	Thyroglobulin Antibody Titer	Reference
Cornell Obese ⟨OS⟩[1]	B^1B^1	3.2	5.2	2
	B^1B^4	2.6	2.9	
	B^4B^4[2]	1.6	0.1	
(Cornell Obese ⟨OS⟩ x Cornell C-resistant ⟨CS⟩)F₁[3]	B^3B^3	2.0 ± 0.5	5.5 ± 1.4	6
	B^3B^4	1.9 ± 0.3	5.5 ± 1.0	
	B^2B^3	1.6 ± 0.3	6.6 ± 1.1	
	B^1B^3	1.4 ± 0.2	4.6 ± 0.7	

Strain or Hybrid ⟨Synonym⟩	Genotype	Thyroid Pathology	Thyroglobulin Antibody Titer	Reference
	B^1B^4	1.0 ± 0.2	2.8 ± 0.7	
	B^1B^1	0.5 ± 0.1	2.5 ± 0.7	
	B^1B^2	0.2 ± 0.0	0.8 ± 0.2	
	B^2B^4	0.2 ± 0.0	0.6 ± 0.3	

[1] Killed at 6 wk of age. [2] B^4B^4 from homozygous matings of a partially inbred line showed greater thyroiditis than B^4B^4 from heterozygous matings [ref. 6]. [3] Killed at 7 wk of age.

continued

164. IMMUNOLOGICAL DISEASES: CHICKEN

Part I. Spontaneous Autoimmune Thyroiditis

Contributor: Joseph H. Kite, Jr.

References

1. Bacon, L. D., et al. 1973. Transplantation 16:591-598.
2. Bacon, L. D., et al. 1974. Science 186:274-275.
3. Cole, R. K. 1966. Genetics 53:1021-1033.
4. Cole, R. K., et al. 1968. Science 160:1357-1358.
5. Kite, J. H., et al. 1969. J. Immunol. 103:1331-1341.

6. Rose, N. R., et al. 1976. Transplant. Rev. 31:264-285.
7. van Tiehoven, A., and R. K. Cole. 1962. Anat. Rec. 142:111-122.
8. Wick, G., et al. 1970. J. Immunol. 104:45-53.
9. Wick, G., et al. 1970. Ibid. 104:54-62.
10. Witebsky, E., et al. 1969. Ibid. 103:708-715.

Part II. Experimentally Induced Diseases

Injected Material: CFA = complete Freund's adjuvant.

Disease	Injected Material	Breed	Reference
Allergic encephalomyelitis[1]	Homologous spinal cord + CFA	Rhode Island Red	3
	Bovine spinal cord + CFA	White Leghorn	2,5,7
Allergic parathyroiditis	Homologous thyroid extract + CFA	White Leghorn	4
Allergic thyroiditis[2]	Homologous thyroid extract + CFA	White Leghorn	4,6
Serum sickness glomerulonephritis	Bovine serum albumin	White Leghorn	1

[1] Allergic encephalomyelitis could be produced in normal, bursectomized, or agammaglobulinemic chickens, indicating that antibodies are not necessary for development of the disease. Thymectomy inhibited the development of the disease. [2] Experimental thyroiditis was suppressed in birds thymectomized at hatching, but appeared unaffected following bursectomy.

Contributor: Joseph H. Kite, Jr.

References

1. Albini, B., et al. 1979. Immunopathology Proc. 6th Int. Conv. Immunol. (Basel), pp. 207-211.
2. Blaw, M. E., et al. 1967. Science 158:1198-1200.
3. Jankovic, B. D., and M. Isvaneski. 1963. Int. Arch. Allergy 23:188-206.
4. Jankovic, B. D., et al. 1965. Ibid. 26:18-33.

5. Wick, G. 1973. Adv. Exp. Med. Biol. 29:603-609.
6. Wick, G., and H. Burger. 1971. Z. Immunitaetsforsch. 142:54-70.
7. Wick, G., and R. Steiner. 1972. J. Immunol. 109:471-476.

165. IMMUNOGLOBULIN CHARACTERISTICS: CHICKEN

Immunoglobulin G is also known as low molecular weight immunoglobulin, or 7S immunoglobulin. **Immunoglobulin M** is also known as high molecular weight immunoglobulin, or 17S immunoglobulin, or 19S immunoglobulin. **Immunoglobulin A** is also known as secretory immunoglobulin.

Abbreviations: Ig = immunoglobulin; Fab = antigen-binding fragment(s); Fc = crystallizable fragment; BSA = bovine serum albumin. Figures in heavy brackets are reference numbers. Values in parentheses are ranges, estimate "c" (*see* Introduction), unless otherwise indicated.

Property	Immunoglobulin G	Immunoglobulin M	Immunoglobulin A	
			Source	Value
Subclasses	If present, <4% of Ig [42]	....	....	....

continued

Property	Immunoglobulin G	Immunoglobulin M	Immunoglobulin A	
			Source	Value
Molecular Weight				
Ig	$(165\text{-}180) \times 10^3$ [11, 14, 26, 31]	$(880\text{-}890) \times 10^3$ [3, 26]	Serum	$(170\text{-}{>}200) \times 10^3$ [28, 34]
			Intestine	$(300\text{-}500) \times 10^3$ [43]
			Bile	$(350\text{-}900) \times 10^3$ [6, 28, 34, 43]
In 1.5 M NaCl	550×10^3 [13]	....	....	....
Heavy chains	$(60.5\text{-}68) \times 10^3$ [19, 26]	$(62.6\text{-}70) \times 10^3$ [3, 26]	....	....
Light chains	$(22\text{-}23) \times 10^3$ [19, 26]	$(22\text{-}23.9) \times 10^3$ [3, 26]	....	....
Fab	55.7×10^3 [19]	....	....	....
Fc	56.9×10^3 [19]	....	....	....
Partial specific volume $\langle \bar{v} \rangle$, ml/g	0.728 [11]	....	....	....
Sedimentation coefficient $\langle s_{20,w} \rangle$, Svedberg units	$(7.3\text{-}7.4)$ [3, 11]	16.5, 28.5 [2]	Serum	$(7\text{-}15)$[1] [28, 34]
			Intestine	$(9\text{-}16)$[1] [34, 43]
			Bile	$(15\text{-}16)$[1] [6, 43]
In 1.5M NaCl	14 [13]	....	....	....
Diffusion coefficient $\langle D_{20,w} \rangle$, cm²/s	3.6×10^{-7} [32]; 3.68×10^{-7} [11]	....	....	....
Extinction coefficient $\langle E_{1cm}^{1\%} \rangle$				
In 5M guanidine	12.74 [26]	11.11 [26]	....	....
In 0.3M KCl	13.18 [26]	12.72 [26]	....	....
In 0.1M NaOH	14.4 [26]	....	....	....
At 290 nm	24.6 [31]	....	....	....
pH, 8.0; at 278 nm	15.1 [11]	....	....	....
pH, 7.0; at 280 nm	17.7 [31]	....	....	....
Isoelectric point	5.0, 5.6, 6.6 [12, 38]	....	....	....
Carbohydrate content, %				
Total	$(5.5\text{-}6.0)$ [1, 18]	6.6 [1]	....	....
Mannose	$(2.7\text{-}2.9)$ [1, 18]	2.18 [1]	....	....
Galactose	$(0.2\text{-}0.61)$ [1, 18]	1.41 [1]	....	....
Fucose	0.19 [1]	0.17 [1]	....	....
Glucosamine	$(1.7\text{-}2.8)$ [1, 18]	2.21 [1]	....	....
Sialic acid(s)	0.23 [1]	0.63 [1]	....	....
N-Terminal amino acids				
Heavy chains[2]	1 2 3 4 5 6 Ala-Val-Thr-Leu-Asp-Glu- 7 8 9 10 11 12 Ser-Gly-Gly-Gly-Leu-Gln- 13 14 15 16 17 18 Thr-Pro-Gly-Gly-——-Leu- 19 20 21 22 ——-Leu-Val-Cys[3] [23]	....		
Light chains[4]	1 2 3 4 5 [ ]-[ ]-Ala-Leu-Thr- 6 7 8 9 10 11 Gln-[ ]-Pro-Ala-Ser-Val- 12 13 14 15 16 17 Ser-Ala-Gln-Leu-Gly-Glu- 18 19 20 21 22 23 Thr-Val-Ser-Leu-Thr-Cys-[5] [17,22]	....		

[1] Estimated. [2] Resembles $V_{H III}$ subgroup. [3] The dashes in positions 17 and 19 indicate unknown amino acids. [4] Mostly unblocked λ chains. [5] The sequence has been aligned with known mammalian λ light chains, and the brackets in positions 1, 2, and 7 indicate that no amino acid is present at these positions.

continued

Property	Immunoglobulin G	Immunoglobulin M	Immunoglobulin A	
			Source	Value
Binding Site Valence	2 binding sites [4, 11] Binding exceeds 2 moles of ligand per antibody molecule [15, 16]	....	....	....
Residues	Tryptophan [41] Iodinatable (tyrosine) [4]	....	....	....
Enzymatic hydrolysis By papain	Fab; Fc [10] Fc crystals [21]	....	....	....
By pepsin	Fab' (major) [25] F(ab')$_2$ [41]	....	....	....
Reductive dissociation, in absence of dissociating agent	Light chains released [9]	Light chains released; 7S subunits [2]	Serum	Monomeric subunits produced [6]
Dissociation in guanidine or urea, in absence of reducing agent	....	....	Serum	Light chain monomers & dimers released [39]
Concentration in "normal" serum, mg/ml	(5-7)[6] [24, 30, 35, 40]	(1-2.5)[6] [24, 30, 35]	Serum Intestine Bile	(0.3-0.6)[6] [24, 28] 1.6 [24] 3.15 [24]
Metabolic half-life, d Neonatal	3.0 [33]	....	....	....
Adult	(1.5-4.3) [27, 44]	1.7 [27]	....	....
Complement ⟨C⟩ fixation: C1 activation Chicken C	Yes [7, 36, 37]	....	....	....
Guinea pig C	No [5, 7, 36, 37]	....	....	....
Hypersensitivity Amount of chicken anti-BSA nitrogen to give a minimal passive reaction in young birds				
Passive cutaneous anaphylaxis ⟨PCA⟩	0.28 µg [20]	....	....	....
Arthus reaction	0.12 mg [29]	....	....	....
Characteristics Passive cutaneous anaphylaxis ⟨PCA⟩	Homocytotropic; sensitizes young birds optimally [8, 20]	....	....	....
Arthus reaction	Sensitizes young birds optimally; guinea pig poorly sensitized [29]	....	....	....

[6] Range of mean values.

Contributor: Albert A. Benedict

References

1. Acton, R. T., et al. 1972. J. Immunol. 109:371-381.
2. Benedict, A. A. 1967. 7th Int. Congr. Biochem. (Tokyo) 5:979 (Abstr. J-131).
3. Benedict, A. A., and K. Yamaga. 1976. In J. J. Marchalonis, ed. Comparative Immunology. Blackwell Scientific, Oxford. pp. 335-375b.
4. Benedict, A. A., et al. 1972. Immunol. Commun. 1: 279-287.
5. Benson, H. N., et al. 1961. J. Immunol. 87:616-622.
6. Bienenstock, J., et al. 1973. Ibid. 110:524-533.
7. Bushnell, L. D., and C. B. Hudson. 1927. J. Infect. Dis. 41:388-394.
8. Celada, F., and A. Ramos. 1961. Proc. Soc. Exp. Biol. Med. 108:129-133.
9. Dreesman, G. R., and A. A. Benedict. 1965. Proc. Natl. Acad. Sci. USA 54:822-830.
10. Dreesman, G. R., and A. A. Benedict. 1965. J. Immunol. 95:855-866.
11. Gallagher, J. S., and E. W. Voss, Jr. 1969. Immunochemistry 6:199-206.
12. Gallagher, J. S., and E. W. Voss, Jr. 1970. Ibid. 7:771-785.
13. Hersh, R. T., and A. A. Benedict. 1966. Biochim. Biophys. Acta 115:242-244.

continued

14. Hersh, R. T., et al. 1969. Immunochemistry 6:762-765.
15. Hoffmeister, M. J., and E. W. Voss, Jr. 1974. Ibid. 11:641-650.
16. Hoffmeister, M. J., and E. W. Voss, Jr. 1975. Ibid. 12:745-749.
17. Hood, L., et al. 1970. Dev. Aspects Antibody Form. Struct. Proc. Symp. 1969 (Prague and Slapy) 1:283-309.
18. Howell, H. M., et al. 1973. Immunochemistry 10:761-766.
19. Kubo, R. T. 1970. Ph.D. Thesis. Univ. Hawaii, Honolulu.
20. Kubo, R. T., and A. A. Benedict. 1968. Proc. Soc. Exp. Biol. Med. 129:256-260.
21. Kubo, R. T., and A. A. Benedict. 1969. J. Immunol. 102:1523-1525.
22. Kubo, R. T., et al. 1970. Ibid. 105:534-536.
23. Kubo, R. T., et al. 1971. Ibid. 107:1781-1784.
24. Lebacq-Verheyden, A.-M., et al. 1974. Immunology 27:683-692.
25. Leslie, G. A., and A. A. Benedict. 1970. J. Immunol. 104:810-817.
26. Leslie, G. A., and L. W. Clem. 1969. J. Exp. Med. 130:1337-1352.
27. Leslie, G. A., and L. W. Clem. 1970. Proc. Soc. Exp. Biol. Med. 134:195-198.
28. Leslie, G. A., and L. N. Martin. 1973. J. Immunol. 110:1-9.
29. Luoma, B., and A. A. Benedict. 1977. Dev. Comp. Immunol. 1:33-39.
30. Martin, L. N., and G. A. Leslie. 1973. Proc. Soc. Exp. Biol. Med. 143:241-243.
31. Orlans, E. 1968. Immunology 14:61-67.
32. Orlans, E., et al. 1961. Ibid. 4:262-277.
33. Patterson, R., et al. 1962. J. Immunol. 89:272-278.
34. Porter, P., and S. H. Parry. 1976. Immunology 31:407-415.
35. Qualtiere, L. F., and P. Meyers. 1976. J. Immunol. 117:1127-1131.
36. Rice, C. E. 1947. Can. J. Comp. Med. 11:236-241.
37. Rose, M. E., and E. Orlans. 1962. Immunology 5:642-648.
38. Tenenhouse, H. S., and H. F. Deutsch. 1966. Immunochemistry 3:11-20.
39. Vaerman, J. P., et al. 1974. Immunol. Commun. 3:239-247.
40. Van Meter, R., et al. 1968. J. Immunol. 102:370-374.
41. Voss, E. W., Jr., and H. N. Eisen. 1972. Ibid. 109:944-950.
42. Wakeland, E. K., et al. 1977. Ibid. 118:401-404.
43. Watanabe, H., and K. Kobayashi. 1974. Ibid. 113:1405-1409.
44. Wostmann, B. S., and G. B. Olson. 1969. Immunology 17:199-206.

166. IMMUNOGLOBULIN ALLOTYPES: CHICKEN

Abbreviation: Ig = Immunoglobulin.

Part I. Specificities and Location

Symbols: Fd = piece of heavy chain in antigen-binding fragment ⟨Fab⟩.

Immunoglobulin Chain & Region	Locus ⟨Synonym⟩	Specificity	Structural Location	Reference
IgG[1] heavy chain constant region	IgG-1 ⟨G-1⟩	G-1.1	Fd fragment	3,6-9
		G-1.2	Fd fragment	
		G-1.3	Papain sensitive	
		G-1.4	Papain sensitive	
		G-1.5	Papain sensitive	
		G-1.6	Fd fragment	
		G-1.7	Papain sensitive	
		G-1.8	....	
		G-1.9	....	
		G-1.10	Fd fragment	
		G-1.11	....	

Immunoglobulin Chain & Region	Locus ⟨Synonym⟩	Specificity	Structural Location	Reference
		G-1.12	....	
		G-1.13	....	
IgM[2] heavy chain constant region	IgM-1 ⟨M-1⟩	M-1.1	....	1,3-5
		M-1.2	....	
		M-1.3	....	
		M-1.4	....	
		M-1.5	....	
Light chain constant region for both IgG and IgM	IgL-1 ⟨L-1⟩	L-1.1	....	2

[1] Also known as low molecular weight Ig or 7S Ig. [2] Also known as high molecular weight Ig or 17S Ig or 19S Ig.

continued

166. IMMUNOGLOBULIN ALLOTYPES: CHICKEN

Part I. Specificities and Location

Contributor: Albert A. Benedict

References

1. Foppoli, J. M., and A. A. Benedict. 1977. Adv. Exp. Med. Biol. 88:381-390.
2. Foppoli, J. M., and A. A. Benedict. 1979. J. Immunol. 122:1681-1685.
3. Foppoli, J. M., et al. 1979. Immunogenetics 8:(in press).
4. Ivanyi, J. 1975. Ibid. 2:69-75.
5. Pink, J. R. L. 1974. Eur. J. Immunol. 4:679-681.
6. Wakeland, E. K., and A. A. Benedict. 1975. Immunogenetics 2:531-541.
7. Wakeland, E. K., and A. A. Benedict. 1976. J. Immunol. 117:2185-2190.
8. Wakeland, E. K., et al. 1977. Ibid. 118:401-404.
9. Wakeland, E. K., et al. 1977. Ibid. 119:1218-1222.

Part II. Specificities and Line Distribution of Alleles of *IgG-1*

Allele: Each *IgG-1* ⟨*G-1*⟩ allele is defined by a unique phenogroup of immunoglobulin G ⟨IgG, 7S Ig⟩ specificities, and is designated by a lower case superscript. **Prototype Line:** Each line produces heavy chains which, by definition, are the products of the *G-1* allele assigned to that line. **Source:** For full name, *see* list of HOLDERS at front of book. All data are taken from references 1 and 5.

Allele	Allotypic Specificities													Prototype Line	Other Lines Homozygous for the Allele	Source
	1	2	3	4	5	6	7	8	9	10	11	12	13			
G-1ᵃ	+	−	−	+	−	−	−	−	−	−	−	−	+	UCD-02	UCD-11, UCD-13 / RPRL-7₁, RPRL-15I₅, RPRL-100 / OS-B14B [1/]; CHB [2,3/] / PR-WB [4,3,5/]	UCD / RPRL / WRL / CAS
G-1ᵇ	+	−	+	−	−	−	−	+	−	−	−	−	−	UCD-03	UCD-22 / PR-IA [6,3,5/]	UCD / CAS
G-1ᶜ	−	+	−	−	−	−	−	−	−	−	−	−	−	UCD-07	....	UCD
G-1ᵈ	+	−	−	+	−	−	+	−	−	−	−	−	−	UCD-50	UCD-58, UCD-72 / PRC-R [7/] / PR-F [8,9/]	UCD / WSM / CAS
G-1ᵉ	+	−	−	+	−	+	+	−	−	−	−	−	−	RPRL-6₁	RPRL-6₃	RPRL
G-1ᶠ	−	−	+	−	−	+	−	−	−	+	−	−	−	RPRL-15I₄	RPRL-15₁	RPRL
G-1ᵍ	−	−	+	−	−	−	−	−	−	+	−	−	−	OS-B14A [1/]	OS-B14D [1,10/]; CHA [2,3/] / RH-C [3/] / PR-CC [2,3,5/]	WRL / RPRL / CAS
G-1ʰ	−	−	−	−	−	+	+	−	+	−	−	−	−	PR-M [9,11/]	....	CAS
G-1ⁱ	−	−	−	+	−	−	−	−	−	−	+	−	−	OS-B14C [1/]	....	WRL

[1/] OS-B14 line was produced from flocks established by Thornber Brothers, Yorkshire, England; later moved to the Charles Salt Research Centre, Oswestry, England. [2/] Originally obtained from inbred line RH-C. [3/] Lines RH-C, RH-I, and RH-W were produced at the Northern Poultry Breeding Station, Reaseheath, Cheshire, England. Origin of these inbred lines has been described by Pease and Dudley [ref. 4]. [4/] Originally obtained from inbred line RH-W. [5/] Production of sublines has been described by Hašek, et al. [ref. 2]. [6/] Originally obtained from inbred line RH-I. [7/] Brown Leghorn line originally bred in Edinburgh and maintained at Wayne State University. [8/] From frizzle variety. [9/] Developed at Institute of Experimental Biology and Genetics, Czechoslovak Academy of Science, Prague. [10/] An Ig recombinant line [ref. 3]. [11/] From Minorca breed.

Contributor: Albert A. Benedict

References

1. Foppoli, J. M., et al. 1979. Immunogenetics 8:(in press).
2. Hašek, M., et al. 1966. Folia Biol. (Prague) 12:335-341.

continued

Part II. Specificities and Line Distribution of Alleles of *IgG-1*

3. Ivanyi, J. 1978. Nature (London) 272:166-167.
4. Pease, M., and F. Dudley. 1954. 10th World's Poult. Congr. (Edinburgh), pp. 45-49.

5. Wakeland, E. K., et al. 1977. J. Immunol. 119:1218-1222.

Part III. Specificities and Line Distribution of Alleles of *IgM-1*

Allele: Each *IgM-1* ⟨*M-1*⟩ allele is defined by a unique phenogroup of immunoglobulin M ⟨IgM, 17S Ig, 19S Ig⟩ specificities. **Prototype Line:** Each line produces heavy chains which, by definition, are the products of the *M-1* allele assigned to that line. **Source:** For full name, *see* list of HOLDERS at front of book. All data are taken from reference 1.

Allele	Allotypic Specificities					Prototype Line	Other Lines Homozygous for the Allele	Source
	1	2	3	4	5			
M-1ᵃ	+	+	−	−	−	UCD-02	UCD-03, UCD-07, UCD-11, UCD-13, UCD-22, UCD-50, UCD-56, UCD-58, UCD-60, UCD-71, UCD-72, UCD-74, UCD-79, UCD-80	UCD
							RPRL-6[1], RPRL-6[3], RPRL-7[1], RPRL-15[1], RPRL-15I[4], RPRL-15I[5], RPRL-100; RH-C[1]	RPRL
							PRC-R[2]	WSM
							OS-B14A[3], OS-B14B[3]; CHA[4,1], CHB[4,1]	WRL
							PR-CC[4,1,5]; PR-F[6,7]	CAS
M-1ᵇ	−	−	+	+	−	OS-B14C[3]	OS-B14D[3,8]	WRL
M-1ᶜ	−	−	−	+	−	PR-WB[9,1,5]	....	CAS
M-1ᵈ	−	+	−	+	+	PR-M[7,10]	PR-IA[11,1,5]	CAS

[1] Lines RH-C, RH-I, and RH-W were developed at the Northern Poultry Breeding Station, Reaseheath, Cheshire, England. Origin of these inbred lines has been described by Pease and Dudley [ref. 4]. [2] Brown Leghorn line originally bred in Edinburgh and maintained at Wayne State University. [3] OS-B14 line was produced from flocks established by Thornber Brothers, Yorkshire, England; later moved to the Charles Salt Research Centre, Oswestry, England. [4] Originally obtained from inbred line RH-C. [5] Production of sublines has been described by Hašek, et al. [ref. 2]. [6] From frizzle variety. [7] Developed at Institute of Experimental Biology and Genetics, Czechoslovak Academy of Science, Prague. [8] An Ig recombinant line [ref. 3]. [9] Originally obtained from inbred line RH-W. [10] From Minorca breed. [11] Originally obtained from inbred line RH-I.

Contributor: Albert A. Benedict

References
1. Foppoli, J. M., et al. 1979. Immunogenetics 8:(in press).
2. Hašek, M., et al. 1966. Folia Biol. (Prague) 12:335-341.

3. Ivanyi, J. 1978. Nature (London) 272:166-167.
4. Pease, M., and F. Dudley. 1954. 10th World's Poult. Congr. (Edinburgh), pp. 45-49.

Part IV. Specificities and Line Distribution of Alleles of *IgL-1*

Source: For full name, *see* list of HOLDERS at front of book. All data were adapted from reference 1.

Allele	Allotypic Specificity 1	Lines Homozygous for the Allele	Source
L-1ᵃ	+	UCD-03, UCD-07, UCD-22	UCD
		RPRL-6[1], RPRL-6[3], RPRL-15I[4]; RH-C[1]	RPRL

[1] Lines RH-C, RH-I, and RH-W were developed at the Northern Poultry Breeding Station, Reaseheath, Cheshire, England. Origin of these inbred lines has been described by Pease and Dudley [ref. 3].

continued

166. IMMUNOGLOBULIN ALLOTYPES: CHICKEN

Part IV. Specificities and Line Distribution of Alleles of *IgL-1*

Allele	Allotypic Specificity 1	Lines Homozygous for the Allele	Source
		OS-B14A[2], OS-B14C[2]	WRL
		PR-CC[3,1,4], PR-IA[5,1,4], PR-WB[6,1,4]; PR-F[7,8]	CAS
L-1[b]	–	UCD-02, UCD-13	UCD
		RPRL-7[2], RPRL-100	RPRL
		PR-M[8,9]	CAS

[1] Lines RH-C, RH-I, and RH-W were developed at the Northern Poultry Breeding Station, Reaseheath, Cheshire, England. Origin of these inbred lines has been described by Pease and Dudley [ref. 3]. [2] OS-B14 line was produced from flocks established by Thornber Brothers, Yorkshire, England; later moved to the Charles Salt Research Centre, Oswestry, England. [3] Originally obtained from inbred line RH-C. [4] Production of sublines has been described by Hašek, et al. [ref. 2]. [5] Originally obtained from inbred line RH-I. [6] Originally obtained from inbred line RH-W. [7] From frizzle variety. [8] Developed at Institute of Experimental Biology and Genetics, Czechoslovak Academy of Science, Prague. [9] From Minorca breed.

Contributor: Albert A. Benedict

References

1. Foppoli, J. M., and A. A. Benedict. 1979. J. Immunol. 122:1681-1685.
2. Hašek, M., et al. 1966. Folia Biol. (Prague) 12:335-341.
3. Pease, M., and F. Dudley. 1954. 10th World's Poult. Congr. (Edinburgh), pp. 45-49.

167. LYMPHOCYTE ALLOANTIGENS: CHICKEN

The loci are autosomal and have codominant expression. Unless otherwise stated, they are independent of each other, so far as is known. **Gene Symbol:** *Ea* refers to erythrocyte alloantigens (*see* Table 161). **Alleles:** "Very numerous" is of the order of 100; "several" is of the order of 10. The **Main Reference** includes all information not specifically cited separately. Figures in heavy brackets are additional reference numbers.

Gene Symbol	Alleles	Description	Detection	Tissue Distribution	Main Reference
B-F	Very numerous[1]	Sublocus of *B* major histocompatibility complex [8, 11, 12, 16] which also has *B-G* sublocus determining antigens unique to erythrocytes. Antigen on peripheral blood leukocytes & erythrocytes is composed of 2 polypeptide chains with mol wt of 40,000-43,000 & 11,000-12,000 [9, 19].	Immunoprecipitation by specific *Ea-B* alloantisera	All lymphocytes & erythrocytes; probably most tissues because associated with major histocompatibility [11, 13, 16]	18
B-L	Very numerous[1]	Sublocus of *B* major histocompatibility complex [8, 11, 12, 16] which also has *B-G* sublocus determining antigens unique to erythrocytes. Antigen on peripheral blood leukocytes is composed of 2 unequal polypeptide chains with mol wt of ∼30,000 [10].	Immunoprecipitation by some *Ea-B* alloantisera absorbed with erythrocytes; immunofluorescence by alloantisera to bursocytes (*Ia*-like antigen [2])	Most bursocytes, peripheral B lymphocytes, & plasma cells; some monocytes & macrophages	2,18

[1] For alleles, *see* Table 161, Part I.

continued

Gene Symbol	Alleles	Description	Detection	Tissue Distribution	Main Reference
Bu-1	3	Antigen on bursocytes is composed of 1 polypeptide chain with mol wt of ∼70,000 [1]	Cytotoxicity, or immunofluorescence [6], by alloantisera to bursocytes	Most bursocytes & peripheral B lymphocytes [3]	7
CA1	....	Autosomal locus inferred but not established	Immunofluorescence by alloantisera to lymphocytes (spleen & thymus)	CA1-T on thymocytes & T lymphocytes; CA1-B on peripheral B lymphocytes	5
Ea-A	Several[1]	....	Immunoadherence by specific Ea-A alloantisera	Most peripheral lymphocytes & erythrocytes	17
Ea-C	Several[1]	....	Agglutination by specific Ea-C alloantisera	Most tissues because associated with minor histocompatibility [15]	14
Ly-4	2	....	Splenomegaly inhibition, or immunofluorescence [3], by alloantisera to whole blood or peripheral leukocytes	Some thymocytes, most peripheral T lymphocytes [3]	4
Th-1	Several	....	Cytotoxicity, or immunofluorescence [3], by alloantisera to thymocytes	Most thymocytes, some peripheral T lymphocytes [3]	7

[1] For alleles, *see* Table 161, Part I.

Contributor: Douglas G. Gilmour

References

1. Cunningham-Rundles, C., and D. G. Gilmour. Unpublished. New York University Medical Center, New York, 1979.
2. Ewert, D. L., and M. D. Cooper. 1978. Immunogenetics 7:521-535.
3. Fredericksen, T. L., and D. G. Gilmour. Unpublished. New York University Medical Center, New York, 1979.
4. Fredericksen, T. L., et al. 1977. Immunogenetics 5:535-552.
5. Galton, J., and J. Ivanyi. 1977. Eur. J. Immunol. 7:241-246.
6. Gilmour, D. G., and J. Galton. Unpublished. New York University Medical Center, New York, 1979.
7. Gilmour, D. G., et al. Immunogenetics 3:549-563.
8. Hala, K., et al. 1976. Ibid. 3:97-103.
9. Kubo, R. T., et al. 1977. Adv. Exp. Med. Biol. 88:209-220.
10. Kvist, S., et al. 1978. Scand. J. Immunol. 7:447-452.
11. Pazderka, F., et al. 1975. Immunogenetics 2:101-130.
12. Pink, J. R. L., et al. 1977. Ibid. 5:203-216.
13. Schierman, L. W., and A. W. Nordskog. 1961. Science 134:1008-1009.
14. Schierman, L. W., and A. W. Nordskog. 1962. Ibid. 137:620-621.
15. Schierman, L. W., and A. W. Nordskog. 1965. Transplantation 3:44-48.
16. Vilhelmova, M., et al. 1977. Eur. J. Immunol. 7:674-679.
17. Wong, S. Y., et al. 1972. Immunol. Commun. 1:597-613.
18. Ziegler, A., and R. Pink. 1976. J. Biol. Chem. 251:5391-5396.
19. Ziegler, A., and R. Pink. 1978. Immunochemistry 15:515-516.

168. PROPERTIES OF AVIAN SARCOMA VIRUS AND AVIAN LEUKOSIS VIRUS STRAINS: CHICKEN

Subgroup: The virus subgroup—which is defined by host range, interference specificity, and antigenicity of the virus—has been used as a convenient marker for classification of the viruses [Part I, ref. 25, 52, 53]. However, it is known now that the subgroup of the virus can be changed by recombination with another virus [Part I, ref. 27, 51].

Therefore, the subgroup specificity of the viruses available today could have been fortuitously determined by natural recombinational events. Various viruses, including mutants, with subgroups different from that of the original virus have been prepared in the laboratory by recombination with other viruses, mostly with Rous associated viruses

continued

⟨RAV's⟩. Recombination is known to occur in all regions of the genome, and the above comments are thus applicable to viral functions other than the subgroup determinant. Some strains of Rous sarcoma virus ⟨RSV⟩ are defective in replication. For those that are defective in the synthesis of glycoprotein, which determines subgroup specificity of the virus, the virus subgroup(s) cannot be assigned. Figures in heavy brackets are reference numbers.

Part I. Avian Sarcoma Viruses

Non-conditional Mutants: It has been known that transformation-defective ⟨td⟩ virus spontaneously segregates from non-defective sarcoma virus by the deletion of a gene essential for sarcomagenic cell transformation [27, 50]. The td virus thus formed is essentially the same in its physical and biological properties as leukosis viruses such as RAV. Because this deletion mutation occurs with most, if not all, non-defective RSV, these mutants are not listed. Also, it seems reasonable to assume that some of the RAV (such as RAV-50) isolated earlier from stocks of non-defective strains of RSV are derived by this type of mutation. It should also be pointed out that some sarcoma and leukemia viruses listed as "defective in replication" are similar in properties to non-conditional mutants of non-defective sarcoma viruses. **Conditional Mutants** have been numbered according to published convention [54]. Class T (transformation) mutants have a mutation only in the transforming function; class R (replication) have a mutation in some function essential for replication; and class C (coordinated) have mutations affecting both transformation and replication. This last class includes two types of mutants: those containing a single mutation in an early step of virus infection essential for both T and R functions, or those containing mutations in both replicative and transformative functions.

Virus Strain	Abbreviation	Subgroup	Non-conditional Mutants	Conditional Mutants	Remarks
Avian sarcoma virus Bratislava 77 [47]	B-77	C [13]	rdPH2 [36]; rdPH10 [36]; rdPH11 [36]	Class T: tsOS260 [49] Class R: tsLA3342 [24] Class C: tsLA336m [48]; tsLA339m [16]	Non-defective. Infectious for mammalian cells [22].
Bryan high titer strain RSV [9, 37]	BH-RSV	Envelope negative	rdα [18, 19]	Class T: tsBE1 [4]; tsRO1-137 [5]	Defective in replication [20].[1/] Pseudotypes are widely used.
Bryan standard strain RSV [9, 45]	BS-RSV	A [52]; probably pseudotype	morph[r] [45]; morph[f] [45]	....	Defective in replication [46]
Carr-Zilber strain RSV [58]	CZ-RSV	D [13]	....	....	Infectious for mammalian cells [58]
Fujinami strain avian sarcoma virus [15]	Fu-ASV	A [52]	....	....	....
Harris strain RSV [41]	HA-RSV	Envelope negative	....	....	Defective in replication [38]
Mill Hill strain RSV [2]	MH-RSV	A [25]	....	....	....
Prague strain RSV [43]	PR-RSV	A; B; C [13]	rdPH9 [36]; rdPH18 [36]; cdSE21Q1b [31]; rdUV3-B1 [34]; rdUV3-B3 [34]; rdUV3-B5 [34]	Class T: tsLA22-29 [56]; tsLA31-35 [56]; tsLA30m [44, 56]; tsGI201-205 [6]; tsGI251-253 [6] Class R: tsLA672 [14]; tsPH734 [35] Class C: tsLA335 [56]; tsLA337 [30]; tsLA338m [23, 56]; tsLA343m [57]; tsLA351-377 [3]	Non-defective. Subgroup C was used for derivation of rat XC cells [42].

[1/] BH-RSV is known to contain a deletion in the gene which codes for the envelope glycoprotein [12, 21, 39]. The defective RSV can be obtained in an infectious form by coinfection with non-defective virus, which provides the envelope glycoprotein. These infectious derivatives are called pseudotypes of BH-RSV; the RAV-1 pseudotype virus ⟨BH-RSV (RAV-1)⟩ has the subgroup A specificity of RAV-1.

continued

Part I. Avian Sarcoma Viruses

Virus Strain	Abbreviation	Subgroup	Non-conditional Mutants	Conditional Mutants	Remarks
Schmidt-Ruppin strain RSV [40]	SR-RSV	A; B; D [13, 52]	rdNY8 [28]; rdNY8α [28]; rdLA7365 [55]	Class T: tsBK1 [32]; tsBK5 [33]; tsMI100 [8]; tsNY10 [29]; tsNY19 [29]; tsNY68 [26]; tsOS122 [49]; tsOS538 [49]; tsPA1 [7]; tsPA2 [11]; tsPA3-16 [10]	Non-defective. Subgroup D is infectious for mammalian cells [1, 17].

Contributor: Hidesaburo Hanafusa

References

1. Ahlström, C. G., and N. Forsby. 1962. J. Exp. Med. 115:839-852.
2. Ahlström, C. G., and N. Jonsson. 1962. Acta Pathol. Microbiol. Scand. 54:136-144.
3. Alevy, M. C., and P. K. Vogt. 1978. Virology 87:21-33.
4. Bader, J. P. 1972. J. Virol. 10:267-276.
5. Balduzzi, P. 1976. Ibid. 18:332-343.
6. Becker, D., et al. 1977. Ibid. 21:1042-1055.
7. Biquard, J. M., and P. Vigier. 1970. C. R. Acad. Sci. 271:2430-2433.
8. Bookout, J. B., and M. M. Sigel. 1975. Virology 67:474-486.
9. Bryan, W. R. 1959. Acta Unio Int. Contra Cancrum 15:764-767.
10. Calothy, G. Unpublished. Fondation Curie, Institut du Radium, Orsay, France, 1979.
11. Calothy, G., and B. Pessac. 1976. Virology 71:336-345.
12. Duesberg, P. H., et al. 1975. Proc. Natl. Acad. Sci. USA 72:1569-1573.
13. Duff, R. G., and P. K. Vogt. 1969. Virology 39:18-30.
14. Friis, R. R., and E. Hunter. 1973. Ibid. 53:479-483.
15. Fujinami, A., and K. Inamoto. 1914. Z. Krebsforsch. 14:94-119.
16. Graf, T., and R. R. Friis. 1973. Virology 56:360-374.
17. Hanafusa, H., and T. Hanafusa. 1966. Proc. Natl. Acad. Sci. USA 55:532-538.
18. Hanafusa, H., and T. Hanafusa. 1968. Virology 34:630-636.
19. Hanafusa, H., and T. Hanafusa. 1971. Ibid. 43:313-316.
20. Hanafusa, H., et al. 1963. Proc. Natl. Acad. Sci. USA 49:572-580.
21. Hanafusa, H., et al. 1964. Ibid. 51:41-48.
22. Hlayova, E., et al. 1964. Folia Biol. (Prague) 10:301-306.
23. Hunter, E., and P. K. Vogt. 1976. Virology 69:23-34.
24. Hunter, E., et al. 1976. Ibid. 69:35-49.
25. Ishizaki, R., and P. K. Vogt. 1966. Ibid. 30:375-387.
26. Kawai, S., and H. Hanafusa. 1971. Ibid. 46:470-479.
27. Kawai, S., and H. Hanafusa. 1972. Ibid. 49:37-44.
28. Kawai, S., and H. Hanafusa. 1973. Proc. Natl. Acad. Sci. USA 70:3493-3497.
29. Kawai, S., et al. 1972. Virology 49:302-304.
30. Linial, M., and W. S. Mason. 1973. Ibid. 53:258-273.
31. Linial, M., et al. 1978. Cell 15:1371-1382.
32. Martin, G. S. 1970. Nature (London) 227:1021-1023.
33. Martin, G. S. 1971. In L. G. Silvestri, ed. The Biology of Oncogenic Viruses. North Holland, Amsterdam, pp. 320-325.
34. Martin, G. S., et al. 1979. Virology 96:530-546.
35. Mason, W. S., and C. Yeater. 1977. Ibid. 77:443-456.
36. Mason, W. S., et al. 1979. J. Virol. 30:132-140.
37. Prince, A. M. 1960. Ibid. 11:371-399.
38. Reamer, R. H., and W. Okazaki. 1970. J. Natl. Cancer Inst. 44:763-767.
39. Scheele, C. M., and H. Hanafusa. 1971. Virology 45:401-410.
40. Schmidt-Ruppin, K. H. 1964. Oncologia (Basel) 17:247-272.
41. Simons, P. J., and R. M. Dougherty. 1963. J. Natl. Cancer Inst. 31:1275-1283.
42. Svoboda, J. 1960. Nature (London) 186:980-981.
43. Svoboda, J., and J. Grozdanovic. 1959. Folia Biol. (Prague) 5:46-50.
44. Tato, F., et al. 1978. Virology 88:71-81.
45. Temin, H. M. 1960. Ibid. 10:182-197.
46. Temin, H. M. 1963. Ibid. 20:235-245.
47. Thurzo, V., et al. 1963. Acta Unio Int. Contra Cancrum 19:304-305.
48. Toyoshima, K., and P. K. Vogt. 1969. Virology 39:930-931.
49. Toyoshima, K., et al. 1973. Biken J. 16:103-110.
50. Vogt, P. K. 1971. Virology 46:939-946.
51. Vogt, P. K. 1971. Ibid. 46:947-952.
52. Vogt, P. K., and R. Ishizaki. 1965. Ibid. 26:664-672.
53. Vogt, P. K., and R. Ishizaki. 1966. Ibid. 30:368-374.
54. Vogt, P. K., et al. 1974. J. Virol. 13:551-554.
55. Vogt, P. K., et al. 1979. Virology 92:285-290.
56. Wyke, J. A. 1973. Ibid. 52:587-590.
57. Wyke, J. A., and M. Linial. 1973. Ibid. 53:152-161.
58. Zilber, L. A. 1961. J. Natl. Cancer Inst. 26:1295-1309.

continued

Part II. Avian Leukosis Viruses

Virus Strain	Abbrevia-tion	Subgroup	Remarks
Avian Leukemia Viruses			
Avian erythroblastosis virus, strains ES4 & R [9]	AEV-ES4; AEV-R	B [13, 24], may be pseudotype	Defective in replication [13, 20, 24]. Original stocks (both strains) contain subgroup B helper viruses [13, 24].
Avian myeloblastosis virus, strain BAI [2]	AMV-BAI	A; B [42]; may be pseudotypes	Original stocks appear to be mixtures of AMV & myeloblastosis associated virus (MAV) of two subgroups [30, 42]. Probably defective in replication [31].
Avian myelocytomatosis virus, strain MC29 [27]	MC29	A; B [26]; may be pseudotypes	Defective in replication [4, 26]. Stocks contain both subgroup A & B helper viruses [11, 26].
Avian leukemia virus, strain CMII [29]	CMII	B or D [14]; may be pseudo-types	Defective in replication [14]. Apparently myeloid leukemia virus similar to MC29 [12, 14].
Avian leukemia virus, strain MH2 [3, 32]	MH2	A; C [23]; may be pseudo-types	Defective in replication [22, 23]. Mainly causes carcinomas [1, 12].
Avian leukemia virus, strain OK10 [33]	OK10	A [33]; probably pseudotype	Possibly defective in replication [12, 34]. Similar to MH2 in pathogenicity [12, 34].
Avian Lymphoid Leukosis Viruses			
Another Rous contaminant [7]	ARC	D	Isolated from a stock of SR-RSV-D[1/]
Avian erythroblastosis associated virus AEV-R associated virus [13]	REAV	B	Isolated from a stock of AEV-strain R
AEV-ES4 associated virus [13]	ES4AV	B	Isolated from a stock of AEV-strain ES4
Avian lymphomatosis virus, strain RPL-12 [5]	ALV-RPL12	A	A field isolate of avian leukosis virus
Avian myeloblastosis associated virus Myeloblastosis associated virus-1 [30]	MAV-1	A	Isolated from a stock of AMV
Myeloblastosis associated virus-2 [30]	MAV-2	B	Isolated from a stock of AMV
Avian myelocytomatosis associated virus MC29 associated virus-A [26]	MC29-AV-A	A	Isolated from a stock of MC29A
MC29 associated virus-B [11]	MC29-AV-B	B	Isolated from a stock of MC29-B
Resistance inducing factor-1 [36]	RIF-1	A	Field isolate of avian leukosis virus found in congenitally infected chicken embryos
Resistance inducing factor-2 [42]	RIF-2	B	Field isolate of avian leukosis virus found in congenitally infected chicken embryos
Rous associated virus-0 [40]	RAV-0	E	Found in cultures of certain lines of chickens, and considered to be a chicken endogenous virus produced spontaneously [6, 40]
Rous associated virus-1 [37]	RAV-1	A	Isolated from a stock of BH-RSV[1/]
Rous associated virus-2 [15, 39]	RAV-2	B	Isolated from stocks of BH-RSV[1/]
Rous associated virus-3 [41]	RAV-3	A	Isolated from stock of BH-RSV[1/]. Immunologically distinct from RAV-1 [25].
Rous associated virus-4 [42]	RAV-4	A	Isolated from a stock of BS-RSV[1/]

[1/] For full name of virus, see Part I.

continued

Part II. Avian Leukosis Viruses

Virus Strain	Abbreviation	Subgroup	Remarks
Rous associated virus-5 [42]	RAV-5	A	Isolated from a stock of BS-RSV[1]. Immunologically distinguishable from RAV-4 [25].
Rous associated virus-6 [35]	RAV-6	B	Isolated from a stock of HA-RSV[1]
Rous associated virus-7 [8]	RAV-7	C	Isolated from a stock of BH-RSV[1]
Rous associated virus-49 [8]	RAV-49	C	Isolated from a stock of RAV-50
Rous associated virus-50 [16]	RAV-50	D	Isolated from a stock of SR-RSV-D[1]. BH-RSV (RAV-50) is infectious for mammalian cells [16].
Rous associated virus-60 [19]	RAV-60	E	Isolated as recombinants between RSV or RAV & endogenous viral genes within chicken cells [21]. Different isolates may be genetically non-identical.
Rous associated virus-61 [18]	RAV-61	F	Isolated from a stock of BH-RSV[1] growing in ring-necked pheasant cells. Apparently a recombinant between BH-RSV & endogenous virus genes in the pheasant cell [38].[2]
Rous associated virus-62 [17]	RAV-62	H	Isolated from a stock of BH-RSV[1] grown in Hungarian partridge cells

[1] For full name of virus, *see* Part I. [2] Ring-necked pheasant virus ⟨RPV⟩ [10] and W8-1-1b ⟨RAV-F⟩ [28] were isolated by essentially the same method, and have the same properties as RAV-61.

Contributor: Hidesaburo Hanafusa

References

1. Alexander, R. W., et al. 1979. J. Natl. Cancer Inst. 62:359-366.
2. Beard, J. W. 1956. Poult. Sci. 35:203-223.
3. Begg, A. M. 1927. Lancet 1:912-915.
4. Bister, K., et al. 1977. Virology 82:431-448.
5. Burmester, B. R., et al. 1946. Cancer Res. 6:189-196.
6. Crittenden, L. B., et al. 1974. Virology 57:128-138.
7. Dougherty, R. M., and R. Rasmussen. 1964. Natl. Cancer Inst. Monogr. 17:337-350.
8. Duff, R. G., and P. K. Vogt. 1969. Virology 39:18-30.
9. Engelbreth-Holm, J., and A. Rothe-Meyer. 1935. Acta Pathol. Microbiol. Scand. 12:352-365.
10. Fujita, D. J., et al. 1974. Virology 60:558-571.
11. Graf, T. 1973. Ibid. 54:398-413.
12. Graf, T., and H. Beug. 1978. Biochim. Biophys. Acta 516:269-299.
13. Graf, T., et al. 1976. Virology 71:423-433.
14. Graf, T., et al. 1977. Ibid. 83:96-109.
15. Hanafusa, H. 1965. Ibid. 25:248-255.
16. Hanafusa, H., and T. Hanafusa. 1966. Proc. Natl. Acad. Sci. USA 55:532-538.
17. Hanafusa, T. Unpublished. Rockefeller Univ., New York, 1977.
18. Hanafusa, T., and H. Hanafusa. 1973. Virology 51:247-251.
19. Hanafusa, T., et al. 1970. Proc. Natl. Acad. Sci. USA 67:1797-1803.
20. Hayman, M. J., et al. 1979. Virology 92:31-45.
21. Hayward, W. S., and H. Hanafusa. 1975. J. Virol. 15:1367-1377.
22. Hu, S. S. F., and P. K. Vogt. 1979. Virology 92:278-284.
23. Hu, S. S. F., et al. 1978. Ibid. 89:162-178.
24. Ishizaki, R., and T. Shimizu. 1970. Cancer Res. 30:2827-2831.
25. Ishizaki, R., and P. K. Vogt. 1966. Virology 30:375-387.
26. Ishizaki, R., et al. 1971. J. Virol. 8:821-827.
27. Ivanov, X., et al. 1964. Bull. Inst. Pathol. Comp. Anim. 10:5-38.
28. Keshet, E., and H. M. Temin. 1977. J. Virol. 24:505-513.
29. Lolinger, H. C. 1964. Dtsch. Tieraerztl. Wochenschr. 71:207-212.
30. Moscovici, C., and P. K. Vogt. 1968. Virology 35:487-497.
31. Moscovici, C., et al. 1975. Ibid. 68:173-181.
32. Murray, J. A., and A. M. Begg. 1930. Sci. Rep. Cancer Res. Found. London 9:1-13.
33. Oker-Blom, N., et al. 1975. Intervirology 5:342-353.
34. Oker-Blom, N., et al. 1978. J. Gen. Virol. 40:623-633.
35. Reamer, R. H., et al. 1967. Virology 33:363-364.
36. Rubin, H. 1960. Proc. Natl. Acad. Sci. USA 46:1105-1119.
37. Rubin, H., and P. K. Vogt. 1962. Virology 17:184-194.
38. Shoyab, M., and M. A. Baluda. 1975. J. Virol. 16:1492-1502.
39. Vogt, P. K. 1965. Virology 25:237-247.
40. Vogt, P. K., and R. R. Friis. 1971. Ibid. 43:223-234.
41. Vogt, P. K., and R. Ishizaki. 1965. Ibid. 26:664-672.
42. Vogt, P. K., and R. Ishizaki. 1966. Ibid. 30:368-374.

Name: RSV = Rous sarcoma virus. **Subgroup:** Mix = not cloned; NA = not applicable. **Oncogenicity:** Predominant neoplasm, or neoplasm for which strain is known, is placed first; ON = other neoplasms, which may include endothelioma, erythroblastosis, fibrosarcoma, nephroblastoma, or osteopetrosis; Low = little or no evidence of oncogenicity; NT = not tested in vivo. **Origin:** "Wild type" implies not cloned. **Holder:** For full name, *see* list of HOLDERS at front of book.

Name	Symbol	Subgroup	Oncogenicity	Origin	Holder	Reference
Leukosis-Sarcoma Virus Group						
Avian erythroblastosis virus	AEV	B	Erythroblastosis; lymphoid leukosis	Wild type	DUKE, DKFZ	16
Avian myeloblastosis virus	AMV	A + B	Myeloblastosis; lymphoid leukosis; ON	Wild type	VA, LSI, HPRS	21
Avian myeloblastosis virus-A	AMV-A	A	Myeloblastosis	Cloned	DUKE	18
Avian myeloblastosis virus-B	AMV-B	B	Myeloblastosis; lymphoid leukosis; ON	Cloned	VA	21
Avian sarcoma virus Bratislava 77	B-77	C	Fibrosarcoma	Cloned	USC, HPRS	8
		Mix	Fibrosarcoma	Wild type	USC	
Avian sarcoma virus Bratislava 77—high titer	B-77-19	C	Fibrosarcoma	Cloned	JLV	1
Bryan high titer strain RSV	BH-RSV	Mix	Fibrosarcoma	Wild type	RPRL	18
Bryan high titer strain RSV (−)[1]	BH-RSV(−)	NA	Fibrosarcoma	Replication-defective[2]	R, RPRL, USC, ICRL	12,13, 36
Bryan high titer strain RSVa (−)	BH-RSVa(−)	NA	Fibrosarcoma	Replication-defective[2]	R	36
Bryan standard strain RSV	BS-RSV	Mix	Fibrosarcoma	Wild type	RPRL, HPRS	18
Bryan standard strain RSV (−)	BS-RSV(−)	NA	Fibrosarcoma	Replication-defective[2]	....	13
Carr-Zilber associated virus	CZAV	D	NT	Cloned	USC	8
Carr-Zilber strain RSV	CZ-RSV	Mix	Fibrosarcoma	Wild type	USC	8
Carr-Zilber strain RSV-D	CZ-RSV-D	D	Fibrosarcoma	Cloned	USC	8
Engelbreth-Holm strain RSV	EH-RSV	Mix	Fibrosarcoma	Wild type	HPRS	20
Erythroblastosis-sarcoma virus-4	ES-4	Mix	Fibrosarcoma; ON	Wild type	HPRS	9
Fujinami associated virus-1	FAV-1	A	NT	Cloned	USC	38
Fujinami strain sarcoma virus	FUSV	Mix	Fibrosarcoma	Cloned	USC, HPRS	18
Fujinami strain sarcoma virus (−)	FUSV(−)	NA	Fibrosarcoma	Replication-defective[2]	....	13
Harris strain RSV	HA-RSV	Mix	Fibrosarcoma	Wild type	USC	38
Harris strain RSV (−)	HA-RSV(−)	NA	Fibrosarcoma	Replication-defective[2]	....	13
Houghton Poultry Research Station-B-15	HPRS-B-15	Mix	Lymphoid leukosis; ON	Wild type	HPRS	3
Houghton Poultry Research Station-F42	HPRS-F42	A	Lymphoid leukosis; ON	Wild type	HPRS	3,7
Houghton Poultry Research Station-F45	HPRS-F45	Mix	Lymphoid leukosis; ON	Wild type	HPRS	3
Los Angeles-23[3]	LA-23	A	Fibrosarcoma	Temperature-sensitive defect in transformation	USC	30,36, 39

[1] Two continuous lines of Japanese quail cells containing BH-RSV (−) [R(−)Q] are available: line 23-16 [ref. 23] and clone 3 [ref. 12]. [2] Replication-defective virus stocks are non-infectious. [3] Only representative mutants of each type are given; consult reference 36 for complete review and partial listing.

continued

Name	Symbol	Sub-group	Oncogenicity	Origin	Holder	Reference
Los Angeles-338m[3]	LA-338m	C	Fibrosarcoma	Temperature-sensitive co-ordinate defects in trans-formation & replication	USC	30,36, 39
Los Angeles-3342[3]	LA-3342	C	Fibrosarcoma	Temperature-sensitive defect in replication	USC	30,36, 39
Los Angeles 5509-1[3]	LA5509-1	NA	Lymphoid leukosis	Transformation-defective	USC	30,36, 39
Mill Hill strain RSV-2	MH-2	Mix	ON	Wild type	USC, HPRS	26
Myeloblastosis associated virus-1	MAV-1	A	Lymphoid leukosis; ON	Cloned	DUKE	21,33
Myeloblastosis associated virus-2	MAV-2	B	Lymphoid leukosis; nephro-blastoma; osteopetrosis; ON	Cloned	DUKE	21,33
Myeloblastosis associated virus-2(O)	MAV-2(O)	B	Osteopetrosis; nephroblastoma; lymphoid leukosis	Cloned	DUKE	34
Myeloblastosis associated virus-2(N)	MAV-2(N)	B	Nephroblastoma; osteopetrosis	Cloned	JLV	11,24, 35
Myelocytomatosis associated virus (i)	MC29-AV(i)	A	NT	Cloned	DUKE	19
Myelocytomatosis associated virus (L)	MC29-AV(L)	Mix	NT	Wild type	DUKE	19
Myelocytomatosis associated virus-B	MCAV-B	B	NT	Cloned	DKFZ	11
Myelocytomatosis virus-B	MCV-B	B	Myelocytomatosis	Cloned	DKFZ	11
Myelocytomatosis virus-29	MC29	A + B	Myelocytomatosis	Wild type	DUKE	19
Myelocytomatosis virus-29-A	MC29-A	A	Myelocytomatosis	Cloned	DUKE	19
Myelocytomatosis virus-29-B	MC29-B	B	Myelocytomatosis	Cloned	DUKE	19
New York-8	NY-8	NA	Fibrosarcoma	Replication-defective[2]	R	36
New York-8a	NY-8a	NA	Fibrosarcoma	Replication-defective[2]	R	36
Osteopetrosis virus	....	Mix	ON	Wild type	HPRS	4
Poultry Research Centre-2	PRC-2	Mix	Fibrosarcoma	Wild type	HPRS	5,38
Poultry Research Centre-4	PRC-4	Mix	Fibrosarcoma	Wild type	HPRS	5
Prague strain RSV	PR-RSV	Mix	Fibrosarcoma	Wild type	USC	8
Prague strain RSV-A	PR-RSV-A	A	Fibrosarcoma	Cloned	USC	8
Prague strain RSV-B	PR-RSV-B	B	Fibrosarcoma	Cloned	USC	8
Prague strain RSV-C	PR-RSV-C	C	Fibrosarcoma	Cloned	USC	8
Regional Poultry Laboratory strain-12	RPL-12	A	Lymphoid leukosis; ON	Wild type	RPRL; HPRS	28
Regional Poultry Laboratory strain-25	RPL-25	A + B	Lymphoid leukosis; ON	Wild type	RPRL; HPRS	27
Regional Poultry Laboratory strain-28	RPL-28	A	Lymphoid leukosis; ON	Wild type	RPRL; HPRS	27
Regional Poultry Laboratory strain-29	RPL-29	A	Lymphoid leukosis; ON	Wild type	RPRL; HPRS	27
Regional Poultry Laboratory strain-30	RPL-30	A	Lymphoid leukosis; ON	Wild type	RPRL; HPRS	27
Resistance-inducing factor	RIF	A + B	Lymphoid leukosis; ON	Wild type	USC	32
Resistance-inducing factor-1	RIF-1	A	NT	Cloned	USC	38
Resistance-inducing factor-2	RIF-2	B	NT	Cloned	USC	38

[2] Replication-defective virus stocks are non-infectious. [3] Only representative mutants of each type are given; consult reference 36 for complete review and partial listing.

continued

Name	Symbol	Sub-group	Oncogenicity	Origin	Holder	Reference
Rous associated virus-0	RAV-0	E	Low	Spontaneously released	RPRL	22,30, 37
Rous associated virus-1	RAV-1	A	Lymphoid leukosis; ON	Cloned	ATCC[4]	18,30, 31,38
Rous associated virus-2	RAV-2	B	Lymphoid leukosis; ON	Cloned	ATCC[4]	18,30, 38
Rous associated virus-3	RAV-3	A	NT	Cloned	USC[4]	18,38
Rous associated virus-5	RAV-5	A	NT	Cloned	USC	18,38
Rous associated virus-7	RAV-7	C	Lymphoid leukosis; ON	Cloned	USC[4]	4,30
Rous associated virus-49	RAV-49	C	Lymphoid leukosis; ON	Cloned	ATCC[4]	8,30
Rous associated virus-50	RAV-50	D	Lymphoid leukosis; ON	Cloned	ATCC[4]	8,30
Rous associated virus-60	RAV-60	E	Low	Recombinant	R[4]	14,30
Rous associated virus-61	RAV-61	F	Lymphoid leukosis; ON	Recombinant	R	15
Rous sarcoma virus-29	RSV-29	Mix	Fibrosarcoma	Wild type	HPRS	25
Schmidt-Ruppin strain RSV	SR-RSV	Mix	Fibrosarcoma	Wild type	USC	38
Schmidt-Ruppin strain RSV-1	SR-RSV-A	A	Fibrosarcoma	Cloned	USC	18,38
Schmidt-Ruppin strain RSV-2	SR-RSV-B	B	Fibrosarcoma	Cloned	USC	18,38
Schmidt-Ruppin strain RSV-D	SR-RSV-D	D	Fibrosarcoma	Cloned	USC	8
Schmidt-Ruppin strain RSV-H	SR-RSV-H	D	Fibrosarcoma	Cloned	JLV	2
Reticuloendotheliosis Virus Group						
Chick syncytial virus	REV-CS	NA	Reticuloendotheliosis	Wild type	RPRL	29
Duck infectious anemia virus	REV-DIA	NA	Reticuloendotheliosis	Wild type	RPRL	29
Duck spleen necrosis virus	REV-SN	NA	Reticuloendotheliosis	Wild type	RPRL	29
Turkey strain T REV[5]	REV-T	NA	Reticuloendotheliosis	Wild type	RPRL	29
Pheasant Virus Group						
Amherst pheasant virus	APV	G	NT	Rescued by RSV(−)	R	15
Golden pheasant virus	GPV	G	Low	Rescued by RSV(−)	USC	10,15
Golden pheasant virus-ny	GPV-ny	G	NT	Rescued by RSV(−)	R	15
Ring neck pheasant virus	RPV	F	Low	Rescued by RSV(−)	USC	10
Group Unknown						
Chinese quail virus	CHQV	?	NT	Spontaneously released	USC	6
Ghighi pheasant virus	GIPV	G	NT	Spontaneously released	USC	6
Swinhoe pheasant virus	SWPV	?	NT	Rescued by RSV(−)	USC	6

[4] Also available at a number of other laboratories. [5] Synonym: REV-Tweihaus.

Contributor: L. B. Crittenden

References

1. Bauer, H. Unpublished. Max-Planck-Institut für Virusforschung, Tübingen, West Germany, 1979.
2. Bauer, H., and T. Graf. 1969. Virology 37:157-161.
3. Biggs, P. N., and L. N. Payne. 1964. Natl. Cancer Inst. Monogr. 17:83-98.
4. Campbell, J. G., et al. 1964. J. Comp. Pathol. Ther. 74:263-279.
5. Carr, J. G., and J. G. Campbell. 1958. Br. J. Cancer 12:631-635.
6. Chen, Y. C., and P. K. Vogt. 1977. Virology 76:740-750.
7. Dougherty, R. M., and H. S. DiStefano. 1967. Cancer Res. 27:322-332.
8. Duff, R. C., and P. K. Vogt. 1969. Virology 39:18-30.

continued

9. Engelbreth-Holm, J., and A. R. Meyer. 1935. Acta Pathol. Microbiol. Scand. 12:352-365.
10. Fujita, D. J., et al. 1974. Virology 60:558-571.
11. Graf, T. 1973. Ibid. 54:398-413.
12. Halpern, M. S., et al. 1976. J. Virol. 18:504-510.
13. Hanafusa, H. 1975. Cancer 2:49-90.
14. Hanafusa, H., et al. 1971. In L. G. Silvestri, ed. The Biology of Oncogenic Viruses. North Holland, Amsterdam. pp. 170-175.
15. Hanafusa, T., et al. 1976. Proc. Natl. Acad. Sci. USA 73:1333-1337.
16. Ishizaki, R., and T. Shimizu. 1970. Cancer Res. 30:2827-2831.
17. Ishizaki, R., and P. K. Vogt. 1966. Virology 30:375-387.
18. Ishizaki, R., et al. 1975. J. Virol. 15:906-912.
19. Langlois, A. J., et al. 1971. Ibid. 8:821-827.
20. Morgan, J. R., and W. Traub. 1964. Natl. Cancer Inst. Monogr. 17:392-393.
21. Moscovici, C., et al. 1975. Virology 68:173-181.
22. Motta, J. V., et al. 1975. J. Natl. Cancer Inst. 55:685-689.
23. Murphy, H. M. 1976. Anim. Virol. ICN-UCLA Symp. Mol. Cell. Biol. 4:243-256.
24. Ogura, H., et al. 1974. Intervirology 4:69-74.
25. Payne, L. N. Unpublished. Houghton Poultry Research Station, Huntingdon, Cambridgeshire, England, 1979.
26. Payne, L. N., and P. M. Biggs. 1970. J. Gen. Virol. 7:177-185.
27. Payne, L. N., et al. 1968. J. Natl. Cancer Inst. 40:907-916.
28. Purchase, H. G., and B. R. Burmester. 1972. In M. S. Hofstad, et al., ed. Diseases of Poultry. Ed. 6. Iowa State Univ., Ames. pp. 502-568.
29. Purchase, H. G., and R. L. Witter. 1975. Curr. Top. Microbiol. Immunol. 71:103-124.
30. Purchase, H. G., et al. 1977. Infect. Immun. 15:423-428.
31. Rubin, H., and P. K. Vogt. 1962. Virology 17:184-194.
32. Rubin, H., et al. 1962. Ibid. 17:143-156.
33. Smith, R. E., and C. Moscovici. 1969. Cancer Res. 29:1356-1366.
34. Smith, R. E., et al. 1976. J. Virol. 17:160-167.
35. Smith, R. E., et al. 1976. Abstr. Annu. Meet. Am. Soc. Microbiol., p. 215(S67).
36. Vogt, P. K. 1977. In H. Fraenkel-Conrat and R. R. Wagner, ed. Comprehensive Virology. Plenum, New York. v. 9, pp. 341-455.
37. Vogt, P. K., and R. R. Friis. 1971. Virology 43:223-234.
38. Vogt, P. K., and R. Ishizaki. 1966. Ibid. 30:368-374.
39. Vogt, P. K., et al. 1974. J. Virol. 13:551-554.

170. GENES DETERMINING AVIAN SARCOMA VIRUS AND AVIAN LEUKOSIS VIRUS SUSCEPTIBILITY AND PRODUCTION OF ENDOGENOUS VIRUSES: CHICKEN

Two independent genes—*gs* and *h-E*—have been identified as being responsible for the level of expression of endogenous virus. Recent studies have established that these expressions are determined by several independent endogenous provirus genes, designated as *ev1* to *ev10* [32-34]. The endogenous proviruses synthesize viral components—internal viral proteins and glycoproteins [ref. 2, 9, 10, 11, 20, 27, 30]—but not complete virions. RAV-60 [ref. 13, 14] is considered to be a group of viruses produced as a result of recombination between these endogenous genes and exogenous virus [ref. 15], and is therefore to be distinguished from RAV-0 [ref. 28]. RAV-0 production is also genetically controlled by the *V* gene.

Susceptibility of chicken cells to subgroup A, B, C, and E tumor viruses are known to be determined by independent *Tv* ("tumor virus") genes. The term C/O is used for those susceptible to viruses of all subgroups; C/A for those susceptible to all except A; C/ABE for those susceptible to all except for A, B, and E, etc. [ref. 29]. Thus far, the types C/O, C/C, C/AC, C/AE, C/BE, and C/ABE have been identified. Figures in heavy brackets are additional reference numbers.

Gene Symbol	Allele	Phenotypic Expression	Reference
Gr-E	*Gr-E*	Permissive for the growth of endogenous subgroup E virus	22
	gr-E	Restrictive for the growth of endogenous subgroup E virus	
gs	*Gs*	Expression of gs antigen & chicken helper factor (chf) (gs⁺chf⁺ type)	10,12,20,
	gs	No expression of gs antigen & chf (gs⁻chf⁻ type)	30,31
h-E	*H-E*	Expression of chf without gs antigen (gs⁻chf⁺ type)	1,12,23
	h-E	No expression of chf	

continued

170. GENES DETERMINING AVIAN SARCOMA VIRUS AND AVIAN LEUKOSIS VIRUS SUSCEPTIBILITY AND PRODUCTION OF ENDOGENOUS VIRUSES: CHICKEN

Gene Symbol	Allele	Phenotypic Expression	Reference
I-E	I-E	Epistatic inhibitor of Tv-E gene	6,16,17, 21
	i-E	No epistatic inhibition	
Tv-A	Tv-A^s	Susceptible to subgroup A virus	4
	tv-A^r	Resistant to subgroup A virus	
Tv-B	Tv-B^{s1}	Susceptible to subgroup B & E virus; linked to R₁ erythrocyte antigen [5]	3,4,6,18, 25
	Tv-B^{s2}	Susceptible to subgroup B & E virus; not linked to R₁ antigen [3]	
	Tv-B^{s3}	Susceptible to subgroup B, but resistant to subgroup E virus [3]	
	tv-B^r	Resistant to subgroup B & E virus	
Tv-C	Tv-C^s	Susceptible to subgroup C virus	7,19
	tv-C^r	Resistant to subgroup C virus	
Tv-E	Tv-E^s	Susceptible to subgroup E virus	21
	tv-E^r	Resistant to subgroup E virus	
V	V-EC	Spontaneous production of RAV-0 in Reaseheath line C ⟨RH-C⟩	7,8,24, 26,28
	v-EC	Absence of production of RAV-0 specific to RH-C	
	V-E7	Spontaneous production of RAV-0 in RPRL-7	
	v-E7	Absence of production of RAV-0 specific to RPRL-7	
	V-15	Inducible for 15-ILV ⟨induced leukosis virus⟩ in RPRL-15 by bromodeoxyuridine ⟨BrdUrd⟩[1/]	
	v-15	Not inducible for 15-ILV by bromodeoxyuridine	

[1/] A virus produced from RPRL-15 after BrdUrd treatment is not identical to RAV-0 [24].

Contributor: Hidesaburo Hanafusa

References

1. Ando, T., and K. Toyoshima. 1976. Virology 73: 521-527.
2. Chen, J. H., et al. 1974. J. Virol. 14:1419-1429.
3. Crittenden, L. B., and J. V. Motta. 1975. Virology 67:327-334.
4. Crittenden, L. B., et al. 1967. J. Virol. 1:898-904.
5. Crittenden, L. B., et al. 1970. Science 169:1324-1325.
6. Crittenden, L. B., et al. 1973. Virology 52:373-384.
7. Crittenden, L. B., et al. 1974. Ibid. 57:128-138.
8. Crittenden, L. B., et al. 1977. Ibid. 76:90-97.
9. Dougherty, R. M., and H. S. DiStefano. 1966. Ibid. 29:586-595.
10. Hanafusa, H., et al. 1970. Proc. Natl. Acad. Sci. USA 66:314-321.
11. Hanafusa, H., et al. 1973. Virology 56:22-32.
12. Hanafusa, H., et al. 1974. Ibid. 58:439-448.
13. Hanafusa, T., et al. 1970. Proc. Natl. Acad. Sci. USA 67:1797-1803.
14. Hanafusa, T., et al. 1972. Virology 47:475-482.
15. Hayward, W. S., and H. Hanafusa. 1975. J. Virol. 15: 1367-1377.
16. Pani, P. K. 1974. J. Gen. Virol. 23:33-40.
17. Pani, P. K., and L. N. Payne. 1973. Ibid. 19:235-244.
18. Payne, L. N., and P. M. Biggs. 1964. Virology 24:610-616.
19. Payne, L. N., and P. M. Biggs. 1970. J. Gen. Virol. 7: 177-185.
20. Payne, L. N., and R. C. Chubb. 1968. Ibid. 3:379-391.
21. Payne, L. N., et al. 1971. Ibid. 13:455-462.
22. Robinson, H. L. 1976. J. Virol. 18:856-866.
23. Robinson, H. L., and W. F. Lamoreux. 1976. Virology 69:50-62.
24. Robinson, H. L., et al. 1976. Ibid. 63:63-74.
25. Rubin, H. 1965. Ibid. 26:270-276.
26. Smith, E. J., et al. 1974. Ibid. 61:594-596.
27. Smith, E. J., et al. 1976. Ibid. 70:493-501.
28. Vogt, P. K., and R. R. Friis. 1971. Ibid. 43:223-234.
29. Vogt, P. K., and R. Ishizaki. 1965. Ibid. 26:664-672.
30. Weiss, R. A. 1969. J. Gen. Virol. 5:511-528.
31. Weiss, R. A., and L. N. Payne. 1971. Virology 45:508-515.
32. Astrin, S. M. 1978. Proc. Natl. Acad. Sci. USA 75: 5941-5945.
33. Astrin, S. M., et al. 1979. Cold Spring Harbor Symp. Quant. Biol. 44:(in press).
34. Hayward, W. S., et al. 1979. Ibid. 44:(in press).

171. SUSCEPTIBILITY TO AVIAN RNA TUMOR VIRUSES: CHICKEN

The data below characterize chicken strains for susceptibility to infection by five subgroups of avian RNA type C tumor viruses. Other lines of chickens are not included because they either are not kept under specific-pathogen-free

continued

171. SUSCEPTIBILITY TO AVIAN RNA TUMOR VIRUSES: CHICKEN

conditions or are not well-characterized for susceptibility. **Holder:** For full name, *see* list of HOLDERS at front of book. **Susceptibility to Subgroup:** S = susceptible; R = resistant; SR = low level of susceptibility; Seg = segregating for resistance and susceptibility; NT = not thoroughly tested.

Strain		Holder	Susceptibility to Subgroup					Reference
Symbol	Name		A	B	C	D	E	
Br L	Houghton Brown Leghorn	HPRS	S	S	S	S	R	5
K-16	Kimber Line 16	WFEB	S	Seg	S	NT	R	6
K-18	Kimber Line 18	WFEB	S	Seg	S	NT	R	6
K-28	Kimber Line 28	WFEB	S	Seg	S	NT	Seg	6
RH-C	Reaseheath Line C	HPRS, RPRL	R	S	S	S	R	2,4,5
RPRL-6	Regional Poultry Research Laboratory 6	RPRL	S	S	S	S	R	2
RPRL-7_1	Regional Poultry Research Laboratory 7_1	RPRL	R	S	S	SR	NT	1
RPRL-7_2	Regional Poultry Research Laboratory 7_2	RPRL, HPRS	R	R	S	SR	R	2
RPRL-15_B	Regional Poultry Research Laboratory 15_B	RPRL	S	S	R	S	S	2
RPRL-100_B	Regional Poultry Research Laboratory 100_B	RPRL	Seg	Seg	S	SR	Seg	2
SPAFAS	Specific Pathogen Free Supply	SPAFAS	S	S	S	S	R	3

Contributor: L. B. Crittenden

References

1. Crittenden, L. B. Unpublished. Regional Poultry Research Laboratory, East Lansing, MI, 1979.
2. Crittenden, L. B., et al. 1974. Virology 57:128-138.
3. Okazaki, W., et al. 1975. Avian Dis. 19:311-317.
4. Pani, P. K. 1976. J. Gen. Virol. 32:441-453.
5. Pani, P. K., and L. J. N. Ross. 1976. Ibid. 32:97-107.
6. Robinson, H. L., and W. F. Lamoreux. 1976. Virology 69:50-62.

172. ENDOGENOUS VIRUSES: CHICKEN

The following data characterize chicken strains for expression of endogenous virus. **Holder:** For full name, *see* list of HOLDERS at front of book. **Phenotype:** Single-dominant gene controls the coordinate expression of viral group-specific antigen (**gs**) and subgroup E envelope glycoprotein (**chf**); single-dominant gene controls the expression of subgroup E envelope glycoprotein (**chf**) alone. **V:** Two single-gene loci control the expression of complete subgroup E virus (*V-E7, V-EC*); another locus controls the expression of a defective virus (*V-15*); dominant alleles control virus expression in each case; V$^-$ = no virus production. *Abbreviations:* NT = not thoroughly tested; Seg = segregating.

Strain		Holder	Phenotype			Reference
Symbol	Name		gs	chf	V	
K-16	Kimber Line 16	WFEB	Seg	chf$^-$	V$^-$	5-8
K-18	Kimber Line 18	WFEB	Seg	Seg	V$^-$	5-8
K-28	Kimber Line 28	WFEB	Seg	Seg	V$^-$	5-8
RH-C	Reaseheath Line C	HPRS, RPRL	gs$^-$	chf$^-$	V-EC$^+$	2,5
RPRL-6	Regional Poultry Research Laboratory 6	RPRL, HPRS	gs$^+$	chf$^+$	V$^-$	1,5
RPRL-7_1	Regional Poultry Research Laboratory 7_1	RPRL	NT	chf$^-$	V-E7$^+$	3,5
RPRL-7_2	Regional Poultry Research Laboratory 7_2	RPRL, HPRS	gs$^-$	chf$^-$	V-E7$^+$	1,2,5
RPRL-15_B	Regional Poultry Research Laboratory 15_B	RPRL	gs$^-$	chf$^-$	V-15$^+$	1,2,5-8
RPRL-15_1	Regional Poultry Research Laboratory 15_1	RPRL	gs$^+$	chf$^+$	V$^-$	3,5
RPRL-$15I_4$	Regional Poultry Research Laboratory $15I_4$	RPRL	gs$^-$	chf$^+$	V-E15I$_4$	3,5
RPRL-$15I_5$	Regional Poultry Research Laboratory $15I_5$	RPRL	gs$^-$	chf$^+$	Seg	3,5
RPRL-100_B	Regional Poultry Research Laboratory 100_B	RPRL	gs$^-$	chf$^-$	V-E7$^+$	1,5-8
SPAFAS	Specific Pathogen Free Supply	SPAFAS	gs$^-$	Seg	V$^-$	4,5

Contributor: L. B. Crittenden

continued

172. ENDOGENOUS VIRUSES: CHICKEN

References

1. Crittenden, L. B., et al. 1974. Virology 57:128-138.
2. Crittenden, L. B., et al. 1977. Ibid. 76:90-97.
3. Crittenden, L. B., et al. Unpublished. Regional Poultry Research Laboratory, East Lansing, MI, 1979.
4. Hanafusa, H., et al. 1974. Virology 58:439-448.
5. Robinson, H. L. 1978. Curr. Top. Microbiol. Immunol. 83:1-36.
6. Robinson, H. L., and W. F. Lamoreux. 1976. Virology 69:50-62.
7. Robinson, H. L., et al. 1976. Ibid. 69:63-74.
8. Robinson, H. L., et al. 1976. J. Virol. 18:856-866.

173. NOMENCLATURE AND PROPERTIES OF STRUCTURAL PROTEINS OF AVIAN SARCOMA VIRUSES AND AVIAN LEUKOSIS VIRUSES: CHICKEN

Protein Name: The nomenclature was adopted [ref. 1] to designate each protein with p (protein) or gp (glycoprotein) and its molecular weight (in thousands). Figures in heavy brackets are reference numbers.

Protein Name	Molecular Weight daltons	No. of Molecules per Virion	Antigenicity	Location in Virions
gp85	85,000	1000	Type (subgroup) and group specific	Envelope
gp37	37,000	400	....	Envelope
p27	27,000	3000	Group specific	Core shell
p19	19,000	1800	Group specific	Virion interior
p15	15,000[1/]	3000	Group specific	Core shell
p12	12,000[1/]	2000	Group specific	Core interior (associated with RNA)
p10	10,000	1500	....	Envelope (?)
[1]	[1, 3, 6, 7, 9]	[7]	[2, 7, 8, 12]	[4, 5, 10, 11]

[1/] This estimate of molecular weight was based on data obtained from gel-filtration in agarose-guanidine hydrochloride rather than those from sodium dodecyl sulfate-acrylamide gel electrophoresis, in which this protein behaves anomalously.

Contributor: Hidesaburo Hanafusa

References

1. August, J. T., et al. 1974. Virology 60:595-601.
2. Bauer, H., and D. P. Bolognesi. 1970. Ibid. 42:1113-1126.
3. Bolognesi, D. P., and Bauer, H. 1970. Ibid. 42:1097-1112.
4. Bolognesi, D. P., et al. 1972. Ibid. 47:551-566.
5. Bolognesi, D. P., et al. 1975. Ibid. 64:349-357.
6. Duesberg, P. H., et al. 1968. Ibid. 36:73-86.
7. Fleissner, E. 1971. J. Virol. 8:778-785.
8. Huebner, R. J., et al. 1964. Proc. Natl. Acad. Sci. USA 51:742-749.
9. Hung, P. P., et al. 1971. Virology 43:251-266.
10. Rifkin, D. B., and Compans, R. W. 1971. Ibid. 46:485-489.
11. Stromberg, K., et al. 1974. J. Virol. 13:513-528.
12. Tozawa, H., et al. 1970. Virology 40:530-539.

174. STRAINS OF MAREK'S DISEASE VIRUS ISOLATES: CHICKEN

Virulence: H = high; M = medium; L = low; A = apathogenic; the criteria for determining virulence—particularly the criterion for A—are variable and depend on the test host used. **Remarks:** CEF = chicken embryo fibroblast cell

continued

culture; CK = chicken kidney cell culture; DEF = duck embryo fibroblast cell culture; QEF = quail embryo fibroblast cell culture; MD = Marek's disease. **Holder**: For full name, see list of HOLDERS at front of book. Data in brackets refer to the column heading in brackets.

Virus		Viru-lence	Remarks	Holder	Refer-ence
Strain Symbol [Strain Name] ⟨Synonym⟩					
AL-1 [Alabama-1]		H	....	UGA	19
AM-1		H	....	UQA	31
AM-1 att.		A	....	UQA	32
BC-1(A-MDV) [British Columbia-1 Attenuated MDV]		A	Passaged 50-64 times in CK	ACC	50
BC-1(V-MDV) [British Columbia-1 Virulent MDV]		H	....	ACC, OUJ[1]	1,51
[Beckenham]		A	Originally apathogenic. No spread.	WRE	7
[Biken C2D]		A	Adapted to DEF. Large plaques in DEF, small in QEF. Protects against MD.	OUJ	23,34
[Biken C2DQ]		A	Biken C2D passaged 120 times in QEF	OUJ	23,24
[Biken C2DQts]		A	Temperature-sensitive mutant of Biken C2DQ. Little growth at 41°C. Lacks infectivity for chicks.	OUJ	23,36
[Biken VI]		H	Very small plaques	OUJ	35
Cal-1(Type 1PPA) [California-1(Type 1 plaque-producing agent)]		H	Small plaques, slow growth, few inclusions, little cell-free virus.	UCDM	3,28
Cal-1(Type 2PPA) [California-1(Type 2 plaque-producing agent)]		L	Large plaques, rapid growth, more inclusions, some cell-free virus	UCDM	3,28
CM		H	....	MUM	26
Conn-A [Connecticut A]		H	....	UCS	15
Conn-B [Connecticut B]		H	....	UCS	20
CPRL II HP [Copenhagen Poultry Research Laboratory II High Passage]		A	Passaged 45-60 times in CK. Large plaques. No spread. A-antigen lost.	CUD	45
CPRL II LP [Copenhagen Poultry Research Laboratory II Low Passage]		H	Passaged 10 times in CK. Small plaques. Spreads. Produces A-antigen.	CUD	43
CPRL VII		H	....	CUD	44
CR 64		H	Viscerotropic	CBC, RPM	37
CU1 [Cornell University 1]		L	Cloned. <11 passages in CK. Neurotropic.	NYS	12
CU2 [Cornell University 2]		L	Cloned. <8 passages in CK. Neurotropic.	NYS	12,48, 49
CVI 988 [Central Veterinary Institute 988]		A	Mild strain passaged in DEF. Produces A-antigen. Spreads.	CDN	40
D-2		H	....	SVC	25
DM 7/11		H	....	TBH	2
FC 50 [Field Case 50]		H	....	RPM	37
FC 127 [Field Case 127]		H	From chickens housed adjacent to turkeys	RPM	54
FM 46		A	Mild strain passaged in CK, CEF, & DEF	WRE	7
GA [Georgia]		H	Small plaques. Produces A-antigen. Viscerotropic.	ATCC[2], UGA[1]	13,18, 39
GA-5 [Georgia-5]		H	Small plaques. Produces A-antigen. Viscerotropic.	NYS	48
GA-22 [Georgia clone 22]		H	Cloned 3 times in CEF & DEF; total <16 passages	RPM	39
GA (A⁻) [GA lacking A antigen]		A	Passaged in culture. Lacks A-antigen. No spread.	HPRS	11
GM-1 to GM-5		L	Isolates from Red Jungle Fowl. Small cell plaques in CEF.	WSU	13

[1] Also generally available at several other laboratories. [2] Line VR-624.

continued

Virus		Remarks	Holder	Reference
Strain Symbol [Strain Name] ⟨Synonym⟩	Virulence			
GS-1	L	Isolate from Ceylon Jungle Fowl. Small cell plaques in CEF.	WSU	13
HN [Heisdorf & Nelson]	L	Large cell plaques in CEF	WSU, HNW	13,14
HPRS B14 [Houghton Poultry Research Station B14]	H-L	Classical MD. Neurotropic. Produces A-antigen. Spreads.	HPRS	5
HPRS 16 [Houghton Poultry Research Station 16]	H	Viscerotropic. Produces A-antigen. Spreads.	HPRS	16,38
HPRS 16/att [HPRS 16 attenuated]	A	Attenuated by ∿30 passages in CK. Lacks A-antigen. No spread. Large plaques.	HPRS	4,6,11, 17
HPRS 17	L	....	HPRS	38
HPRS 18, HPRS 19, & HPRS 20	H		HPRS	38
HPRS 24	A	Small, slow-developing plaques. Some cell-free virus. Produces A-antigen different from other MD strains.	HPRS	9,10
HPRS 27 ⟨BBB5⟩	A	....	HPRS	4
Id-1 [Idaho-1]	H	Small cell plaques in CEF. Dermotropic.	WSU	13,47
JMHP [JM High Passage] ⟨JM/att. [JM attenuated]⟩	A	Passaged 40-100 times in DEF. Lacks A-antigen. Large plaques.	RPM, HPRS	11,33, 39
JMLP [JM Low Passage]	H	Neurotropic & viscerotropic. Spreads. Produces A-antigen.	ATCC[3/], UMAS[1/]	33,46
JM 10	H	Cloned	NYS	12,48
JM 19	H	Cloned 3 times in CEF & DEF; total <13 passages	RPM	39
JM-102W	H	Cloned 3 times in chicks & DEF	RPM	52
JS-1 to JS-5	L	Isolates from Japanese Silkies. Small cell plaques in CEF.	WSU	13
K	H	....	RIT	59
[Kekava]	M	....	AMU	56
LATV-1	H	Isolate from poultry dust	CASM	30
LCBS-212 [Laboratorio richerche Cip-Zoo, Breschia-212]	H	....	UMI	57
LCBS 216/68	A	Passaged 47 times in CK. Lacks A-antigen.	UMI	58
MD-X	H		CASM	29
MD 7/1970	H		VRH	53
MSD₁ [Merck, Sharpe & Dohme 1]	H		MSD	37
NB ["Normal Bird"] ⟨Cook No. 10436⟩	H		MUM	27
[Oldenberg]	H		HPRS	10
PA-3	A		INM	41
PA4 & PA5	H		INM	42
PQ-1 [Quebec-1]	H	....	ACC	51
RPL 39 [Regional Poultry Laboratory 39]	H	Viscerotropic. Spreads. Produces A-antigen. Cloned 3 times in CEF & DEF; total <16 passages.	RPM	37
S11	L	Cloned in CK; total <8 passages	NYS	12,49
TK 809	H	Isolated from turkeys	RPM	55
VC I & VC II	H	Classical strains. Neurotropic.	BVG	8
VC II/8	A	VC II passaged 8 times in chicken embryos. Spreads.	BVG	8
VUB-70 [Veterinári ústav, Brno-70]	M	....	VUC	21,22
WSU-GF [Washington State University-Game Fowl]	H	Classical strain. Neurotropic. Small cell plaques.	WSU	13

[1/] Also generally available at several other laboratories. [3/] Line VR-585.

Contributor: H. Graham Purchase

continued

174. STRAINS OF MAREK'S DISEASE VIRUS ISOLATES: CHICKEN

References

1. Akiyama, Y., et al. 1973. Biken J. 16:177-179.
2. Antal, S., and V. Andras. 1973. Magy. Allatorv. Lapja 28:533-538.
3. Bankowski, R. A., et al. 1969. Am. J. Vet. Res. 30: 1667-1676.
4. Biggs, P. M., and B. S. Milne. 1972. IARC Sci. Publ. 2:88-94.
5. Biggs, P. M., and L. N. Payne. 1963. Vet. Rec. 75: 177-179.
6. Biggs, P. M., et al. 1970. Ibid. 87:704-709.
7. Blaxland, J. F., et al. 1972. Ibid. 90:431-437.
8. Bulow, V. V. 1971. Am. J. Vet. Res. 32:1275-1288.
9. Bulow, V. V. 1975. IARC Sci. Publ. 11:329-336.
10. Bulow, V. V., and P. M. Biggs. 1975. Avian Pathol. 4: 133-146.
11. Bulow, V. V., and P. M. Biggs. 1975. Ibid. 4:147-162.
12. Calnek, B. W., et al. 1977. Avian Dis. 21:346-358.
13. Cho, B. R. 1976. Ibid. 20:324-331.
14. Cho, B. R., and S. G. Kenzy. 1972. Appl. Microbiol. 24:299-306.
15. Chomiak, T. W., et al. 1967. Avian Dis. 11:646-653.
16. Churchill, A. E. 1968. J. Natl. Cancer Inst. 41:939-950.
17. Churchill, A. E., et al. 1969. J. Gen. Virol. 4:557-564.
18. Eidson, C. S., and S. C. Schmittle. 1968. Avian Dis. 12:467-476.
19. Eidson, C. S., et al. 1971. Poult. Sci. 50:693-699.
20. Jakowski, R. M., et al. 1970. Avian Dis. 14:374.
21. Jurajda, V. 1976. Vet. Med. (Prague) 21:107-118.
22. Jurajda, V., and J. Jurajdeva. 1971. Acta Vet. Brno 40:433-437.
23. Kato, S. 1973. Anal. Exp. Epidemiol. Cancer Proc. 3rd Int. Symp. Princess Takamatsu, pp. 259-267.
24. Konobe, T., et al. 1972. Jpn. J. Vet. Sci. 34 (suppl): 98.
25. Lesnik, F., et al. 1974. Vet. Med. (Prague) 19:661-666.
26. Marquardt, W. W. 1972. Appl. Microbiol. 23:942-945.
27. Marquardt, W. W., and J. A. Newman. 1972. Avian Dis. 16:986-996.
28. Mikami, T., and R. Bankowski. 1971. Am. J. Vet. Res. 32:303-317.
29. Mlozanek, I., and V. Sovova. 1974. Folia Biol. (Prague) 20:51-58.
30. Mlozanek, I., et al. 1973. Ibid. 19:118.
31. Mustaffa-Babjee, A. 1970. Aust. Vet. J. 46:587.
32. Mustaffa-Babjee, A., and P. B. Spradbrow. 1973. Ibid. 49:347-353.
33. Nazerian, K. 1970. J. Natl. Cancer Inst. 44:1257-1267.
34. Ono, K., et al. 1974. Jpn. J. Vet. Sci. 36:407-420.
35. Onoda, T., et al. 1971. Biken J. 14:167-176.
36. Onoda, T., et al. 1971. Ibid. 14:357-360.
37. Purchase, H. G. 1969. J. Virol. 3:557-565.
38. Purchase, H. G., and P. M. Biggs. 1967. Res. Vet. Sci. 8:440-449.
39. Purchase, H. G., et al. 1971. Infect. Immun. 3:295-303.
40. Rispens, B. H., et al. 1972. Avian Dis. 16:108-125.
41. Schat, K. A., et al. 1974. Proc. Abstr. 15th World's Poult. Congr. Expo., pp. 49-50.
42. Schat, K. A., et al. 1974. Avian Dis. 18:531-535.
43. Settnes, O. P. 1970. Acta Pathol. Microbiol. Scand. B78:495-503.
44. Settnes, O. P. 1972. Ibid. B80:817-822.
45. Settnes, O. P. 1975. Nord. Veterinaermed. 27:26-30.
46. Sevoian, M., et al. 1962. Vet. Med. 57:500-501.
47. Sharma, J. M., et al. 1970. J. Natl. Cancer Inst. 44: 901-912.
48. Smith, M. W., and B. W. Calnek. 1974. Ibid. 52:1595-1603.
49. Smith, M. W., and B. W. Calnek. 1974. Avian Pathol. 3:229-246.
50. Spencer, J. L., and A. Robertson. 1972. Am. J. Vet. Res. 33:393-400.
51. Spencer, J. L., et al. 1972. Avian Dis. 16:94-107.
52. Stephens, E. A., et al. 1976. J. Natl. Cancer Inst. 57: 815-874.
53. Thakur, H. N. 1973. Curr. Sci. 42:687-688.
54. Witter, R. L., et al. 1970. Am. J. Vet. Res. 31:525-538.
55. Witter, R. L., et al. 1974. Ibid. 35:1325-1332.
56. Yakovleva, L. S., et al. 1975. Acta Virol. 19:293-298.
57. Zanella, A. 1969. Arch. Vet. Ital. 20:431-444.
58. Zanella, A. 1972. Prog. Immunobiol. Stand. 5:149-155.
59. Zygraich, N., et al. 1972. Ibid. 5:136-140.

175. STRAINS OF TURKEY HERPESVIRUS USED AS VACCINES AGAINST MAREK'S DISEASE: CHICKEN

Although turkeys are the natural hosts of these viruses, their primary importance is their use as vaccines against Marek's disease in chickens. Some virus strains protect more effectively than others. **Virulence:** A = apathogenic;

continued

175. STRAINS OF TURKEY HERPESVIRUS USED AS VACCINES AGAINST MAREK'S DISEASE: CHICKEN

UK = unknown. **Remarks:** CEF = chicken embryo fibroblast cell culture; DEF = duck embryo fibroblast cell culture; QEF = quail embryo fibroblast cell culture; TK = turkey kidney cell culture. **Holder:** For full name, *see* list of HOLDERS at front of book. Data in brackets refer to the column heading in brackets.

Virus		Remarks	Holder	Reference
Strain Symbol [Strain Name]	Virulence			
AC 16	A	....	RPM	18
AC 18	A	....	RPM	18
[Biken T-3]	A	....	OUJ	14
C3-1	A	....	IIB	9
FC-126 [Field Case 126]	A	Large plaques	ATCC[1], RPM[2]	18
HPRS 26 [Houghton Poultry Research Station 26]	A	Large plaques	HPRS	1
HVT 01	A	Medium plaques on DEF & QEF; large giant cells in DEF	OUJ	10,14
HVT-4	A	Clone from FC-126	NYS	17
HVT(A⁻)	A	FC-126 passaged 5 times in CEF. Lacks A-antigen.	HPRS	3,4
LCBS 42/70	A	....	UMI	19
NSW-1/70 [New South Wales-1/70]	A	....	USA	8,16
PB 1 [Poultry Biologicals 1]	A	Passaged 12 times in CEF	PBE	5
PT-4	A	Passaged 5 times in CEF	LVR	15
TAM-1 & TAM-2	A	....	UQA	12,13
TK/A	A	....	WRE	2
WHG [Wisconsin-Harvard-Georgia]	A	WTHV-1 passaged 60 times in CEF	UGA	6,11
WTHV-1	A	Passaged 21 times in TK	UGA	11
WTV [Wild Turkey Virus]	UK	....	IAF	7

[1] Line VR-584. [2] Also generally available at several other laboratories.

Contributor: H. Graham Purchase

References

1. Biggs, P. M., and B. S. Milne. 1972. IARC Sci. Publ. 2:88-94.
2. Blaxland, J. D., et al. 1975. Vet. Rec. 97:50-52.
3. Bulow, V. V., and P. M. Biggs. 1975. Avian Pathol. 4: 133-146.
4. Bulow, V. V., and P. M. Biggs. 1975. Ibid. 4:147-162.
5. Churchill, A. E., et al. 1973. Vet. Rec. 92:327-334.
6. Eidson, C. S., and D. P. Anderson. 1971. Avian Dis. 15:68-81.
7. Grant, H. G., et al. 1975. J. Wildl. Dis. 11:562-565.
8. Harman, D., et al. 1973. Aust. Vet. J. 49:520-524.
9. Kasabov, R., et al. 1976. Vet. Med. Nauki 13:53-58.
10. Kato, S. 1973. Anal. Exp. Epidemiol. Cancer Proc. 3rd Int. Symp. Princess Takamatsu, pp. 259-267.
11. Kawamura, H., et al. 1969. Avian Dis. 13:853-863.
12. Mustaffa-Babjee, A., and P. B. Spradbrow. 1973. Aust. Vet. J. 49:347-353.
13. Mustaffa-Babjee, A., et al. 1971. Ibid. 47:125.
14. Ono, K., et al. 1974. Jpn. J. Vet. Sci. 36:407-420.
15. Patrascu, I. V., et al. 1974. Acta Vet. (Brno) 43:171-182.
16. Sinkovic, B., and N. F. Jones. 1972. Proc. Aust. Poult. Sci. Conv. (Auckland, N.Z.), p. 2.
17. Smith, M. W., and B. W. Calnek. 1974. J. Natl. Cancer Inst. 52:1595-1603.
18. Witter, R. L., et al. 1970. Am. J. Vet. Res. 31:525-538.
19. Zanella, A. 1972. Prog. Immunobiol. Stand. 5:149-155.

176. TRANSPLANTABLE TUMORS AND CELL LINES OF MAREK'S DISEASE VIRUS ORIGIN: CHICKEN

Cell Line or Tumor: New Symbol designation is according to reference 24; MDCC = Marek's disease chicken cell line; MDCT = Marek's disease chicken transplant. **Cell Type:** T = thymus-dependent lymphoid cell. **Holder:** For full name, *see* list of HOLDERS at front of book. Data in brackets refer to the column heading in brackets.

continued

| Cell Line or Tumor Symbol [New Symbol] | Source | | Cell Type | Sex | Chromosome | | Antigens Positive, % | | | C-Type Virus | Holder | Reference |
	Virus	Organ			No.	Aberration	Viral Capsid	Viral Membrane	Tumor			
Cell Lines												
CUCL-1 [MDCC-CU2]	....	Lympho-ma	..	......	.....	....	...	...	.....	..	NYS	4
GACL-1 [MDCC-CU1]	CU7	....	..	......	.....	....	...	...	.....	..	NYS	4
GACL-4 [MDCC-CU4]	GA	....	..	......	.....	....	...	...	.....	..	NYS	4
GACL-6 [MDCC-CU6]	GA	Blood	..	......	.....	....	...	...	.....	..	NYS	4
GBCL-1 [MDCC-CU5]	GB1	....	..	......	.....	....	...	...	.....	..	NYS	4
GBT [MDCC-SK3]	....	Tumor & spleen	..	♀ ⟨ZW⟩	145	3Z, 2W, short no. 3	0	...	.....	..	MSC	8
HPRS line 1 [MDCC-HP1]	HPRS 16	Ovary	T	♀ ⟨ZW⟩	52-62	Longer no. 3 & no. 5	0	0	94-97	..	HPRS, OUJ, RPM	13,16, 17,21
HPRS line 2 [MDCC-HP2]	HPRS 16	Ovary	T	♀ ⟨ZW⟩	53-60	Longer no. 5	0	0	92-95	..	HPRS, OUJ, RPM	13,16, 17,21
JM-1	....	Lympho-ma	..	......	.....	....	...	...	.....	..	UMAS	14
JMCL-1 [MDCC-CU3]	JM	....	..	......	.....	....	...	...	.....	..	NYS	4
JMV-1	JMV	....	..	......	.....	....	...	...	.....	..	UMAS	14
JM-VLC$_8$ [MDCC-SK1]	JMV	Blood	..	♀ ⟨ZW⟩	145	....	0	...	.....	..	MSC	7
MKT-1 [MDCC-LS1]	....	Kidney	..	......	.....	....	...	...	.....	..	FLA	22
MOB-1 [MDCC-MOB1]	BC-1	Ovary	T	♀ ⟨ZW⟩	73-80	Longer no. 1	0.4	0.5	54-92	−	OUJ	1,2,12, 21
MOB-2 [MDCC-MOB2]	MSB-1	Ovary	T	♀ ⟨ZW⟩	66-79	Trisomy no. 1	0.2	0.1	71-89	+	OUJ	10,12, 21
MOB-3 [MDCC-MOB3]	MSB-1	Ovary	T	♀ ⟨ZW⟩	68-75	None	1.2	0.6	81-95	−	OUJ	13,21
MSB-1 [MDCC-MSB1]	MOB-1	Spleen	T	♀ ⟨ZW⟩	69-78	Longer no. 1	2.0	1.0	73-92	−	OUJ, RPM, HPRS[1]	1,2,12, 13,21
RPL-1 [MDCC-RP1]	JMV	Spleen	T	......	.....	....	0	0	Fn[2]	−	RPM	15,20
Transplants												
GA/Tr-1 [MDCT-CU7]	GA-5	Lympho-ma	..	......	.....	....	...	...	.....	..	NYS	6
GA/Tr-2 [MDCT-CU9]	....	Lympho-ma	..	......	.....	....	...	...	.....	..	NYS	6
JMCT [MDCT-CU8]	....	Lympho-ma	..	......	.....	....	...	...	.....	..	NYS	3

[1] Also generally available at several other laboratories. [2] Positive antigens were detected, but percentages are not available.

continued

| Cell Line or Tumor Symbol [New Symbol] | Source | | Cell Type | Sex | Chromosome | | Antigens Positive, % | | | C-Type Virus | Holder | Reference |
	Virus	Organ			No.	Aberration	Viral Capsid	Viral Membrane	Tumor			
JMV	JM	Lympho-ma	..	......	.....	Breaks	0	0	20-85	−	RPM, HPRS	18,20, 25
JMV-A	JMV	Yolk	..	......	.....	....	...	...	.....	..	UMAS, HPRS	9,19
MDT-198 [MDCT-NYM1]	Conn-B	Muscle & wing web	..	......	.....	....	...	...	.....	..	MCN, UCS	3,5,11, 23

Contributor: H. Graham Purchase

References

 1. Akiyama, Y., and S. Kato. 1974. Biken J. 17:105-116.
 2. Akiyama, Y., et al. 1973. Ibid. 16:177-179.
 3. Calnek, B. W., et al. 1969. Am. J. Vet. Res. 30:1403-1412.
 4. Calnek, B. W., et al. 1978. Int. J. Cancer 21:100-107.
 5. Calnek, B. W., et al. 1978. J. Natl. Cancer Inst. 60:623-631.
 6. Fabricant, J., et al. 1978. Avian Dis. 22:646-658.
 7. Hahn, E. C., et al. 1977. J. Natl. Cancer Inst. 59:267-271.
 8. Hahn, E. C., et al. 1978. Avian Dis. 22:409-421.
 9. Hamdy, F., and M. Sevoian. 1973. Ibid. 17:476-485.
10. Ikuta, K., et al. 1976. Biken J. 19:33-37.
11. Jakowski, R. M., et al. 1974. J. Natl. Cancer Inst. 53:783-789.
12. Kato, S., and Y. Akiyama. 1975. IARC Sci. Publ. 11:101-108.
13. Matsuda, H., et al. 1976. Biken J. 19:119-123.
14. Munch, D., et al. 1978. Infect. Immun. 20:315-318.
15. Nazerian, K., et al. 1977. Avian Dis. 21:69-76.
16. Powell, P. C., et al. 1974. Nature (London) 251:79-80.
17. Powell, P. C., et al. 1975. IARC Sci. Publ. 11:89-99.
18. Sevoian, M., et al. 1964. Proc. 101st Annu. Meet. Am. Vet. Med. Assoc., p. 342.
19. Shieh, H. K., and M. Sevoian. 1975. Poult. Sci. 54:69-77.
20. Stephens, E. A., et al. 1976. J. Natl. Cancer Inst. 57:865-874.
21. Tagaki, N., et al. 1977. Biken J. 20:21-28.
22. Tanaka, A., et al. 1978. Virology 88:19-24.
23. Theis, G. A., et al. 1974. J. Immunol. 113:1710-1715.
24. Witter, R. L., et al. 1979. Avian Pathol. 8:(in press).
25. Yoon, J. W., et al. 1976. J. Natl. Cancer Inst. 56:757-762.

177. GENETIC FACTORS IN SUSCEPTIBILITY TO MAREK'S DISEASE VIRUS: CHICKEN

Holder: For full name, *see* list of HOLDERS in front of book. Susceptibility to Marek's Disease: R = resistant; RS = intermediate; S = susceptible. Figures in heavy brackets are reference numbers.

Chicken Strain or Line ⟨Synonym⟩	Holder	Susceptibility to Marek's Disease	B Complex Locus Allele Frequency	Remarks
Inbred				
Cornell C-resistant	NYS	RS [6, 12, 14]	....	....
Cornell K-resistant	NYS, ARC	R [6, 16]	B^{15}: High [19]	Partly dominant to Cornell S-susceptible

continued

Chicken Strain or Line ⟨Synonym⟩	Holder	Susceptibility to Marek's Disease	B Complex Locus Allele Frequency	Remarks
Cornell S-susceptible	NYS, ARC	S [12, 16, 17, 19]	B^1; B^{13} [19]	....
Ottawa Leghorn line GF ⟨Ott GF⟩	ARC	R [22]	....	Derived from Ott 3
Ottawa Leghorn line GH ⟨Ott GH⟩	ARC	S [10]	....	Derived from Ott 3
Ottawa Leghorn line LD ⟨Ott LD⟩	ARC	R [22]	....	Derived from Ott 4
Regional Poultry Research Laboratory 6 ⟨RPRL-6⟩	RPM, HPRS	R [2, 8, 16, 20, 23]	B^2: 1.00 [2, 19]	Partly dominant to RPRL-7
Regional Poultry Research Laboratory 7 ⟨RPRL-7⟩	RPM, HPRS	S [2, 8, 16, 20, 23]	B^2: 1.00 [2, 19]	....
Outbred				
Athens Canadian Control	UGA	S [9, 15]	....	Similar to Ott K
Cornell JM-N	RPM	R [2-7, 14, 18]	B^{21}: 1.00 [3, 19]	Partly dominant to Cornell JM-P. B^{21} associated with resistance.
Cornell JM-P	RPM	S [2-7, 14, 18]	B^{19}: 0.97; B^{13}: 0.03 [3, 19]	....
Houghton Rhode Island Red ⟨HPRS-RIR⟩	HPRS	S [1]	....	....
Ottawa Leghorn selected strain 3 ⟨Ott 3⟩	ARC	S [12, 13, 21]	....	Selected for egg production
Ottawa Leghorn selected strain 4 ⟨Ott 4; ARI 4⟩	ARC	R [12, 13, 21]	....	Selected for egg production
Ottawa Leghorn Control strain 5 ⟨Ott 5; ARI 5⟩	ARC	S [12, 13, 21]	....	Random-bred control
Ottawa NH	ARC	S [12, 13, 21]	....	Meat strain
Ottawa Strain K Meat Control ⟨Ott K; OMC⟩	ARC	S [11, 12]	....	Meat strain
Poultry Disease Research Center ⟨PDRC⟩	NYS	R [4, 5]	....	Resistance comparable to Cornell JM-N

Contributor: H. Graham Purchase

References

1. Biggs, P. M., and L. N. Payne. 1967. J. Natl. Cancer Inst. 39:237-280.
2. Briles, W. E., and H. A. Stone. Unpublished. Northern Illinois Univ., DeKalb, 1973.
3. Briles, W. E., et al. 1977. Science 195:193-195.
4. Calnek, B. W. 1972. IARC Sci. Publ. 2:129-136.
5. Calnek, B. W. 1973. J. Natl. Cancer Inst. 51:927-939.
6. Cole, R. K. 1968. Avian Dis. 12:9-28.
7. Cole, R. K. 1972. IARC Sci. Publ. 2:123-128.
8. Crittenden, L. B., et al. 1972. Poult. Sci. 51:261-267.
9. Eidson, C. S., and S. C. Schmittle. 1968. Avian Dis. 12:467-476.
10. Gavora, J. S. Unpublished. Animal Research Institute, Ottawa, ON, Canada, 1977.
11. Gavora, J. S., et al. 1975. Br. Poult. Sci. 16:375-388.
12. Grunder, A. A., et al. 1972. Can. J. Anim. Sci. 52:1-10.
13. Grunder, A. A., et al. 1974. Br. Poult. Sci. 15:167-175.
14. Hansen, M. P., et al. 1967. Poult. Sci. 46:1268.
15. Hess, C. W. 1962. World's Poult. Sci. J. 18:147-152.
16. Hutt, F. B., and R. K. Cole. 1947. Science 106:379-384.
17. Longenecker, B. M., et al. 1975. Infect. Immun. 11:922-931.
18. Longenecker, B. M., et al. 1976. Immunogenetics 3:401-407.
19. Pazderka, F., et al. 1975. Ibid. 2:93-100.
20. Schmittle, S. C., and C. S. Eidson. 1968. Avian Dis. 12:571.
21. Spencer, J. L., et al. 1974. Ibid. 33:44.
22. Spencer, J. L., et al. 1976. Ibid. 20:265-285.
23. Stone, H. A. 1975. U.S. Dep. Agric. Tech. Bull. 1514.

SPECIALIZED JOURNALS AND REFERENCE SOURCES: CHICKEN

Articles describing investigations in which chicken and other avian species were used can be found in the general biochemical literature. Specialized journals and other reference sources on avian research are listed below.

Publication	Compiler & Publisher	Year
Avian Chromosome Newsletter	Poultry Science Dept., Cornell Univ., Ithaca, NY	1972-
Avian Diseases	American Society of Avian Pathologists, Inc., College Station, TX	1957-
Avian Tumors and Tumor Viruses	USDA Regional Poultry Research Laboratory, E. Lansing, MI	1972-
British Poultry Science	Longman Group Ltd., Edinburgh, Scotland	1960-
Catalogue of Poultry Stocks Held at Research and Teaching Institutions in Canada, 10th ed.	R. D. Crawford, Dept. of Poultry Science, Univ. of Saskatchewan, Saskatoon, Saskatchewan, Canada	1977
Current Cancer Research on Avian Tumor Viruses (NCI/ICRDB/SL-206)	USDHEW National Cancer Institute, Silver Spring, MD	1979
Japanese Poultry Science	Japan Poultry Science Association, Chiba, Japan	1964-
Poultry Science	Poultry Science Association, Inc., Champaign, IL	1921-
Registry of Poultry Genetic Stocks, 3rd ed. (Bulletin 446)	R. G. Somes, Jr., Storrs Agricultural Experiment Station, Univ. of Connecticut, Storrs, CT	1978
World's Poultry Science Journal	World's Poultry Science Association, Stope Mandeville, Aylesbury, Bucks, England	1945-

Contributor: Raymond A. McBride

INDEX

Animal Strains
To facilitate location of related strains and substrains, animal strain designations are presented in the following order:

> Major strain
> Substrains
> Hybrids

Major animal strain designations are listed alphabetically within the index. Their substrains and hybrids are presented alphabetically within each category.

Virus Strains
Designations for virus strains are listed alphabetically within the index. They are not grouped with related strains and substrains.

Genes
Gene symbols are given in italics, and are accompanied, where available, by the pertinent gene name in brackets. Dominant and recessive gene symbols of the same locus appear together. Gene names and symbols are listed alphabetically within the index.

Designations Containing Numbers
Designations *commencing* with a number can be found at the end of the index, after the listing for the letter "Z":

> Zymotypes
> 1 (strain)
> 1 (tumor line)
> 1-T1,m (strain)

With the exception of gene symbols and chemical names, designations commencing with a letter or letters but *con-*

taining numbers are listed numerically after the last entry bearing the same initial letter or letters:

> Bwamba virus   Estrous cycle
> *By* [brachydactyly]   ES-4 (virus)
> B-77 (virus)   *Et* [ear-tuft]

Numbers in gene symbols are disregarded in the alphabetization unless they appear in sequence:

> AMV-BAI (virus)
> *Amy-1* [amylase-1]
> *Amy-2* [amylase-2]
> Amygdala lesions

Numbers and italicized symbols in chemical names do not alter the letter-by-letter alphabetization of entries:

> 3-Methylcholanthrene
> Methyl methanesulfonate
> N-Methyl-N'-nitro-N-nitrosoguanidine
> 4-Methylumbelliferyl esters

Designations Containing Greek Letters
With the exception of chemical names, designations containing Greek letters are alphabetized as though the written form had been used:

> Lakenvelder (breed)   CMII (virus)
> λc (gene) $C_\mu Ms$ (gene)
> λ light chains $C_\mu n$ (gene)
> Langshan (breed)   *cn* [crooked-neck dwarf]

In chemical names, Greek letters are ignored in the alphabetization.

*	indicates diagram or graph
fn	indicates footnote material
hn	indicates headnote material

AK [adenylate kinase] (gene): rabbit, 585

Ak or *ak* (gene): rabbit
    Ak (wild type), 577
    ak [acrobat], 577

Akp or *akp* [alkaline phosphatase] (gene): chicken, 628-632, 639

Akp-2 or *akp-2* [alkaline phosphatase-2] (gene): chicken, 639

ALA [alkaline lipolytic activity] (gene): rabbit, 588

Alabama-1 (virus): chicken, 677

ALAC (strain): hamster, 433 hn
    ALAC/Lac, 448 hn, 449-450

Alanine, immunoglobulin
    chicken, 659
    rabbit, 596, 601

Alanine aminotransferase: rabbit, 578 hn

Alanine-containing polymers: guinea pig, 511 hn, 544 hn, 545-546

Alb [serum albumin] (gene): chicken
        independent segregation, 628, 630-631, 633-635, 637
        research studies, 640

Albinism: chicken (see *a; s^al*: chicken)

Albino
    guinea pig
        controlling locus, 531, 533
        strain association, 511-512
    hamster, 433
    rabbit, 567-568 (see also *c*: rabbit)

Albino, synthetic: guinea pig, 515, 531

Albumin (gene): chicken (see *Alb*)

Albumin, anti-bovine serum: chicken response, 658 hn, 660

Albumin, bovine serum
    chicken response, 658
    guinea pig response, 545-546

Albumin, egg
    guinea pig response, 548
    hamster response, 470, 472

Albumin, human serum
    chicken response, 654 hn, 655-656
    guinea pig response, 545

Albumin, poly(L-lysyl) rabbit serum: guinea pig response, 545

Alcohol consumption: hamster, 460

Aliesterase: rabbit, 584

Alkaline lipolytic activity: rabbit, 588

Alkaline phosphatase: chicken (see *Akp* or *akp; Akp-2* or *akp-2*)

Alkaline phosphatase, capillary: chicken, 620

Allantois: hamster, 442

Alleles (*see also* specific gene)
    chicken
        autoimmune thyroiditis, 657 hn
        erythrocyte alloantigens, 651
        immunoglobulin allotypic specificities, 662 hn, 662-664
        lymphocyte alloantigens, 664-665
        major histocompatibility locus, 611 hn
        Marek's disease, 682-683
        mutant gene tester strains, 615
        nomenclature, 654 hn
        segregation, 611 hn

guinea pig
    coat/eye color, 531-532
    complement factors, 543
    histocompatibility antigens, 543
rabbit
    blood group systems, 590-591
    immunoglobulin allotypes, 593 hn, 593-603
    major histocompatibility, 592
    protein control, 579-588

Allergic encephalomyelitis
    chicken, 658
    guinea pig, 508, 547, 560

Allergic orchitis: guinea pig, 560

Allergic parathyroiditis: chicken, 658

Allergic thyroiditis: chicken, 658

Alloantibodies
    hamster, 469 hn, 469
    rabbit, 594

Alloantigens, erythrocyte: chicken, 650-651

Alloantigens, immunoglobulin: rabbit, 599

Alloantigens, lymphocyte: chicken, 664-665

Alloantisera: rabbit, 593-603, 606 fn

Allograft rejection: chicken, 653

Allografts, skin: hamster, 469 hn

Allogroups, Ig heavy-chain chromosomal region: rabbit, 605-606

Allotypes, immunoglobulin
    guinea pig, 508
    rabbit, 592-603, 605-606, 606 fn

Allotypes, serum globulin: chicken, 612 hn

Allotypic marker: guinea pig, 533

Alloxan diabetes: hamster, 426

α-chain constant region, IgA: rabbit, 598

Alphaviruses
    guinea pig, 549
    hamster, 473-474, 496-497

Alternaria solani: guinea pig, 551

ALV-RPL12 (virus): chicken, 668

AL-1 (virus): chicken, 677

Am [α_2-macroglobulin] (gene): rabbit, 583

am [muscular dystrophy] (gene): chicken
        breed holder, 641
        independent segregation, 628-629, 632-635, 637

Amapari virus: guinea pig, 549

Amber: hamster, 433, 452 fn

Ambulation, open-field: hamster, 468

Amelanosis: hamster, 455

American Game (breed): chicken, 644

American rabbits, 597, 601 (see also *Oryctolagus*)

Ametapodia: chicken (see *Mp*: chicken)

Amherst pheasant virus: chicken, 672

Amine oxidase inhibitors: hamster, 467

Amino acids: rabbit (*see also* specific amino acid)
        hemoglobin, 586
        immunoglobulins, 593 hn, 593-594, 596, 601-602

Amino acids, free: chicken, 620

Amino acids, N-terminal: chicken, 659

p-Aminobenzoic acid N-acetyltransferase: rabbit, 587

p-Aminobenzoic acid conjugate of chicken gamma globulin: chicken response, 654 hn, 655-656

Aminopeptidase (cytosol): chicken (see *Lap* or *lap*)

Amoeba infections: guinea pig, 508, 551

Amphetamine: hamster, 462

Binding site, immunoglobulin G: chicken, 660
BIOAC (strain): guinea pig, 511, 542-544
BIOAD (strain): guinea pig, 512, 542-544
BIOB (strain): guinea pig, 512, 542-544
BIOC (strain): guinea pig, 512, 542-544
Biochemical defects: guinea pig, 513 hn, 513-514
Biochemical genetics: guinea pig, 506
Biochemical polymorphisms: guinea pig, 533-534
Biochemical traits: chicken, 639-641
Biological clock: hamster, 461 (see also Circadian rhythm)
BIO IPI (strain): hamster, 433
BIO PD4 (strain): hamster, 432, 434, 489
BIO X.3 (strain): hamster, 433, 451, 500
BIO X.68 (strain): hamster, 433, 451
BIO XX.B (strain): hamster, 433, 490
BIO 1.14 (strain): hamster, 435
BIO 1.26 (strain): hamster, 433, 450
BIO 1.5 (strain): hamster, 433, 448, 450, 489
BIO 1.50 (strain): hamster, 454
BIO 1.83 (strain): hamster, 435
BIO 2.4 (strain): hamster, 433, 451, 489, 500 (see also LSH)
BIO 4.22 (strain): hamster, 433, 451, 489-490, 500
BIO 4.24 (strain): hamster, 433, 451, 500
BIO 7.88 (strain): hamster, 433, 448, 489
BIO 10.37 (strain): hamster, 433
BIO 11.10 (strain): hamster, 433
BIO 11.34 (strain): hamster, 435
BIO 12.14 (strain): hamster, 433, 451, 489, 500
BIO 14.6 (strain): hamster, 433, 447-448, 454
BIO 15.16 (strain): hamster, 433, 447-448, 489-490, 500
BIO 29.66 (strain): hamster, 435
BIO 35.97 (strain): hamster, 435
BIO 37.39 (strain): hamster, 435
BIO 40.54 (strain): hamster, 433, 448, 454
BIO 41.56 (strain): hamster, 433
BIO 45.5 (strain): hamster, 433, 451, 489, 500
BIO 53.58 (strain): hamster, 433, 454
BIO 54.7 (strain): hamster, 433, 451, 489-490
BIO 65.67 (strain): hamster, 435 fn
BIO 65.67B (strain): hamster, 435
BIO 72.29 (strain): hamster, 433, 447-448, 489
BIO 82.62 (strain): hamster, 433, 448, 454, 500
BIO 82.73 (strain): hamster, 433, 451, 489
BIO 84.9 (strain): hamster, 433, 489
BIO 86.93 (strain): hamster, 433, 451, 489
BIO 87.20 (strain): hamster, 433, 447-448, 451, 489-490, 500
Birchen (variety): chicken, 646
Birchen (gene): chicken (see E^R)
Birth canal: guinea pig, 521
Bj (strain): rabbit, 569*
BK (virus): hamster, 490, 495
B-L [major histocompatibility complex leukocyte-specific antigen B-L] (gene): chicken, 625, 651 fn, 664
Bl [blue; blue plumage] (gene): chicken
      breed association, 646
      independent segregation, 629, 632-637
Black (variety): chicken, 646
Black
    guinea pig, 531-532 (see also a: guinea pig)
    rabbit, 567-568, 574
Black and tan: rabbit (see a^t)
Black-breasted Red (variety): chicken, 646

Black-eyed white: guinea pig, 533
Black Minorca (breed): chicken, 611 hn, 612, 646
Black Polish, White-crested (breed): chicken, 645 fn, 646
Black Spanish (breed): chicken, 611 hn, 612
Black Spanish, White-faced (breed): chicken, 644
Bladder, urinary: hamster, 483
Bladder weight: guinea pig, 528-529
Blastocyst(s)
    hamster, 441-442
    rabbit, 573
Blastomyces dermatitidis
    guinea pig, 550
    hamster, 476 fn
Blastomycosis: guinea pig, 508
bli [blindness] (gene): chicken, 641
Blindness
    chicken (see bli)
    hamster, 457-458, 461-462, 467
Blood
    chicken
        cell line source, 681
        composition, 616-617
    guinea pig
        characteristics, 534-536
        mutant genes, 513 hn, 513-514
        protozoan infection, 558
    hamster
        characteristics, 432
        estrous cycle, 438
    rabbit, 587
Blood glucose regulation: hamster, 504
Blood group A (gene): chicken (see Ea-A)
Blood group B (gene): chicken (see Ea-B)
Blood group C (gene): chicken (see Ea-C)
Blood group D (gene): chicken (see Ea-D)
Blood group E (gene): chicken (see Ea-E)
Blood group genotype(s)
    chicken, 652 hn, 652-653
    rabbit, 567 fn, 591-592
Blood group H (gene): chicken (see Ea-H)
Blood group I (gene): chicken (see Ea-I)
Blood group J (gene): chicken (see Ea-J)
Blood group K (gene): chicken (see Ea-K)
Blood group L (gene): chicken (see Ea-L)
Blood group P (gene): chicken (see Ea-P)
Blood group systems
    chicken, 611 hn-612 hn, 650-653
    rabbit, 590-592
Blood group types
    chicken, 610 hn-612 hn, 652-653
    rabbit, 591-592
Blue (variety): chicken, 646
Blue (gene): chicken (see Bl)
Blue egg shell: chicken (see O)
Blue-eyed white: rabbit, 567
Blue nevus, cellular: hamster, 481
Blue Polish, White-crested (breed): chicken, 645 fn
Blue plumage: chicken (see Bl)
Blue-splashed White (variety): chicken, 646
Blue tongue virus, sheep: hamster response, 496
B lymphocytes
    chicken, 651 fn, 664-665
    guinea pig, 537, 544 hn
Body composition: chicken, 617

Chinchilla race V: rabbit, 567, 569 fn
Chinese hamster
 chromosomes & karyology, 435-436
 diabetes mellitus, 504
 meiosis & mitosis, 502
 phenotypic characteristics, 501 hn, 502
 research studies, 501 hn
 taxonomic location, 425
Chinese quail virus: chicken response, 672
Chin IIb (strain): rabbit, 568 hn, 569*
Chirodiscoides caviae: guinea pig, 558
Chlamydia infections
 guinea pig, 508, 550
 hamster, 475
Chloride, plasma: guinea pig, 536
1-Chloro-2,4-dinitrobenzene: guinea pig, 546
Chlorpromazine: hamster, 460
Chlortetracycline: hamster, 475
Chocolate (coat color): guinea pig, 530, 533
Cholangiocarcinoma: hamster, 482
Cholangioma: hamster, 481, 493-494
Cholinesterase: chicken, 620 hn
Chondrodystrophy
 chicken (see *ch*)
 rabbit, 576 (see also *cd:* rabbit)
Chondrodystrophy, sex-linked: chicken (see *chz*)
Chondroplastic dwarf: rabbit, 578
Chondrosarcoma: hamster, 483, 494 fn
Chorio-allantoic plate: hamster, 442
Choriomeningitis virus, lymphocytic
 guinea pig, 508, 549
 hamster, 474, 484 hn, 497, 499
Chorion: hamster, 442
Chorionic gonadotropin, human: rabbit response, 573
CHQV (virus): chicken, 672
Chromatids
 chicken, 638
 hamster, 502
Chromosomal regions, Ig heavy-chain: rabbit, 593, 596, 598-599, 601, 605-606
Chromosome(s) (*see also* Sex chromosomes)
 chicken
  abnormalities, 638-639
  congenic line development, 607
  gene & linkage group assignment, 621-622, 623 fn, 625 fn, 639 fn, 641 fn-647 fn
  morphology, 621-622
  number, 628 hn
  translocation, 638-639
 guinea pig, 515 hn-516 hn, 516*-519*, 520
 hamster
  karyology, 435-436, 502
  meiosis & mitosis, 502
  number, 435-436
 rabbit
  aberrations, 573
  karyotype, 571 hn-572 hn, 572*
  number, 571 hn
Chromosome rearrangement strains: chicken, 614
chz [sex-linked chondrodystrophy] (gene): chicken, 624, 642
CI [blood group I] (gene): chicken, 629-632, 634-637
Cigarette smoke: hamster, 489, 500

Cilia, vestibular: guinea pig, 561
Ciliate infections: guinea pig, 551
Cinnamon: hamster, 452 fn
Cinnamon agouti: guinea pig, 533
Circadian rhythm: hamster, 458, 461, 467
Circling: guinea pig, 508, 513 hn, 514, 562
Cirrhosis, hepatic: hamster, 433
CJ [blood group J] (gene): chicken, 629-632, 634-637
CK [blood group K] (gene): chicken, 629-632, 634-637
CL [blood group L] (gene): chicken, 629-632, 634-637
Cl [Cornish lethal] (gene): chicken, 642
cla [congenital leg anomaly] (gene): chicken, 641
CLAC (strain): hamster, 433 hn
  CLAC/Lac, 448 hn, 449-450
Cleft palate: chicken, 643
Clostridium perfringens: guinea pig, 550
C. tetani: hamster, 475
CM (virus): chicken, 677
cm [coloboma; sex-linked coloboma] (gene): chicken, 624, 642
Cm-1 [immunoglobulin M] (gene): chicken, 625 fn
CMII (virus): chicken, 668
$C_\mu Ms$ (immunoglobulin gene): rabbit, 599
$C_\mu n$ (immunoglobulin gene): rabbit, 599, 605 fn-606 fn
cn [crooked-neck dwarf] (gene): chicken, 642
Co [Columbian restriction] (gene): chicken, 615, 646
co [cornea abnormality] (gene): guinea pig, 513
Co-2 [C2 polymorphism] (gene): guinea pig, 533
co-3 [C3 deficiency] (gene): guinea pig, 513, 533
Co-4 [C4 deficiency] (gene): guinea pig, 513, 533
Coagulative necrosis, liver: guinea pig, 560
Coat color
 guinea pig, 508, 511-515, 530-533
 hamster, 425, 433-434, 451-455
 rabbit, 567-568, 574-575
Coat length: guinea pig, 514
Coat texture: guinea pig, 508, 513 hn, 514
coc [congenital crippling] (gene): chicken, 641
Cocaine: rabbit, 579 hn, 581
Cocaine esterase: rabbit, 580 (see also *Est-1; As:* rabbit)
Cocal virus: guinea pig, 549
Coccidioides immitis
 guinea pig, 551
 hamster, 476 fn
Coccidioidomycosis: guinea pig, 508
Cochin (breed): chicken, 644-646
Cochin, Laced (breed): chicken, 646
Cochlear nerve: guinea pig, 561
Cochlear neurons: guinea pig, 530
Cochlear nuclei: guinea pig, 561
Coefficients (*see* specific coefficient)
Colchicine: hamster, 426
Cold (ambient temperature): hamster, 431, 459-461
Cold symptoms: hamster, 496
Coliform infections: hamster, 475
Collagen biosynthesis: guinea pig, 509
Coloboma, sex-linked: chicken (see *cm*)
Coloboma of the iris: chicken, 642
Colon, distended: guinea pig, 507
Color (*see* Coat color; Eye)
Colorado tick fever virus: hamster, 426, 473, 496
Colored: rabbit, 574
Colostrum: hamster, 471

taxonomic location, 425
Golden Leghorn (breed): chicken, 646
Golden pheasant virus: chicken response, 672
Golden pheasant virus-ny: chicken response, 672
Golden Polish (breed): chicken, 646
Golden Spangled Hamburg (breed): chicken, 646
Gonadal primordia: hamster, 437
Gonadectomy: hamster (*see also* Castration; Ovariectomy)
    eating behavior, 460
    lordosis, 467
    nest building, 459
    sex-typical activity patterns, 461
Gonadotropic hormone antisera: hamster, 465
Gonadotropins: hamster, 439, 441 hn
Gongylonema pulchrum: guinea pig, 552
Gout: chicken, 608, 642
Gout, diet-induced: chicken (see *go*)
GPγ_2-1 (gene): guinea pig, 533
GPHLV (virus): guinea pig, 548
GPIC (virus): guinea pig, 550
GPIr-1 [immune response] (gene): guinea pig, 513
GPLA [major histocompatibility locus] (gene): guinea pig
    antigens, 543-544
    complement factors, 542-543
    strain distribution, 511 hn, 511-513
GPPLV (virus): guinea pig, 548
GPV (virus): chicken, 672
GPV-ny (virus): chicken, 672
Gr [ginger] (gene): chicken, 646
Gr or *gr* (gene): guinea pig
    Gr (wild type), 532
    gr [grizzled]: guinea pig, 532
Graft rejection: guinea pig, 543 hn
Graft survival: hamster, 469 hn, 469
Graft-versus-host reactions
    chicken
        histocompatibility antigens, 653
        WL sublines, 611 hn
    guinea pig, 512
    hamster
        immunogenetics research, 426-427
        strain combinations, 469 hn, 469
Granulocytes: guinea pig, 538
Granulosa cells: hamster, 482
Gray hamster, 501 hn (*see also* Armenian hamster)
Gray long-tailed hamster, 425
Gr-E (gene): chicken, 673
Green shank: chicken (see *id^c*)
Green spotting: chicken (see *id^a*)
Grizzled: guinea pig (see *gr*)
Grooming activity: hamster, 462
Group-specific antigen: chicken (see *gs*)
Growth (*see also* Age)
    guinea pig, 523-526
    hamster, 449, 501 hn
Growth defects: guinea pig, 513 hn, 514
Growth hormone: hamster, 504
gs [group-specific antigen] (gene): chicken
    linkage relationships, 625
    virus susceptibility, 673 hn, 673
gs (antigen): chicken, 673
GS-1 (virus): chicken, 678
GT (antigen): guinea pig, 544 hn, 546
Gt [non-limited growth; long tail] (gene): chicken, 645

Guanidine: chicken
    immunoglobulin dissociation, 660
    immunoglobulin extinction coefficient, 659
Guinea pig (*see* specific condition, gene, strain; *Cavia*)
Guinea pig albumin, dinitrophenyl derivative of: guinea
    pig response, 544 hn, 544-545
Guinea pig herpes-like virus: guinea pig response, 548
Guinea pig inclusion conjunctivitis virus: guinea pig response, 550
Guinea pig leukocyte antigens: guinea pig response,
    542 hn, 542-543 (*see also* Major histocompatibility
    complex: guinea pig)
Guinea pig pox-like virus: guinea pig response, 548
Guinea pig skin protein conjugates, dinitrophenylated:
    guinea pig response, 545
Guinea pig type C virus: guinea pig response, 549
Gut mucosa: rabbit, 579, 587
Gyropus ovalis: guinea pig, 558
G-1 (immunoglobulin specificities): chicken, 661-662
g74 (immunoglobulin specificity): rabbit, 598
g75 (immunoglobulin specificity): rabbit, 598
g77 (immunoglobulin specificity): rabbit, 605 fn-606 fn

h [silkiness; hookless] (gene): chicken
    breed, 645
    chromosome assignment, 621, 627*
    independent segregation, 629, 633-637
    linkage group, 623, 627*
    related genes, 623
Ha or *ha* (gene): rabbit
    Ha (wild type), 576
    ha [hemolytic anemia], 567-568, 576
Haemobartonella: hamster, 475
Hair
    guinea pig
        abnormalities, 513 hn, 514
        gene affecting color, 531-532
        rosette patterns, 514
    hamster, 452, 455
    rabbit, 574-575
Hair cell, organ of Corti: guinea pig, 560-561
Hairless (gene): hamster (see *hr*)
Half-life, immunoglobulin
    chicken, 660
    hamster, 470
Hamburg (breed): chicken, 644, 646-647
Hamburg, Golden Spangled (breed): chicken, 646
Hamburg, Penciled (breed): chicken, 646
Hamburg, Silver Spangled (breed): chicken, 646
Hamster (*see* specific condition, gene, strain; Chinese
    hamster; Syrian hamster)
Haploid abnormalities: chicken, 638 hn, 638
Haploidy: rabbit, 573
Haplotypes
    chicken, 611 hn-612 hn
    rabbit
        immunoglobulins, 596-597, 603, 605-606
        major histocompatibility complex, 592
        serum proteins, 580 fn, 583-584
Haptoglobin
    chicken (see *Hp*)
    hamster, 432
    rabbit, 579, 582
Harderian gland: hamster, 480, 493

Harelip: guinea pig, 530
Harris strain RSV (virus): chicken
    characteristics, 666 hn, 666
    oncogenicity, 670 hn, 670
    origin, 670 hn, 670
Harris strain RSV(−) (virus): chicken, 670 hn, 670
HA-RSV (virus): chicken
    characteristics, 666 hn, 666
    oncogenicity, 670 hn, 670
    origin, 670 hn, 670
HA-RSV(−) (virus): chicken, 670 hn, 670
Hartley (strain): guinea pig, 515, 547-548
    Hartley F, 563
    Hartley outbred, 516 hn, 519*
    (Hartley x 2)F$_1$, 547
Hatchability: chicken
    associated gene, 651
    strain association, 616-618
Hatching: chicken, 658 fn
HB (virus): hamster, 495
H-B [major histocompatibility complex]: chicken, 654 hn
Hb [hemoglobin] (gene): chicken, 641
Hb [Hb blood group] (gene): rabbit
    linkage group, 570*, 571
    phenotypes, 591
*Hb*α [hemoglobin α-chain] (gene): rabbit, 581, 586
*Hb*β [hemoglobin β-chain] (gene): rabbit, 586
Hb blood group: rabbit (see *Hb:* rabbit)
H blood group: chicken (see *Ea-H*)
Hbp [heme-binding protein] (gene): rabbit, 582
Hc [Hc blood group] (gene): rabbit, 591
Hd or *hd* (gene): rabbit
    Hd [hydrops fetalis], 576
    hd (wild type), 576
He [He blood group] (gene): rabbit, 570*, 571, 591
He or *he* (gene): chicken
    He⁺ [rugged rose-combed], 644
    he^l [smooth rose-combed], 644
h-E (gene): chicken, 673 hn, 673
HEA (protein): hamster, 472
Head
    guinea pig
        abnormalities, 530, 561
        rosette hair patterns, 514
    hamster, 493
    rabbit, 565
Head-spot: chicken (see *Hs*)
Head streak: chicken (see *ko*)
Hearing
    guinea pig, 560-561
    hamster, 453, 455
Heart; heart tissue
    guinea pig, 528-529
    hamster (*see also* Cardiac arrhythmia; Cardiomyopathy)
        research suitability, 427
        sarcoma, 485
        weight, 450-451
Heart cells, embryonic: rabbit, 573 fn
"Heat" (*see also* Estrous cycle)
    guinea pig, 562
    hamster
        activity rhythm, 461
        aggressive behavior, 458

    determination, 438 hn, 439
    pseudopregnancy, 444 hn
Heavy chains, immunoglobulin
    chicken
        amino acids, 659
        constant regions, 661, 662 hn, 662, 663 hn
        molecular weight, 659
    guinea pig, 537
    rabbit
        allotypes, 593 hn, 593-601
        constant regions, 596-600
        variable region, 593-596
He blood group: rabbit (see *He:* rabbit)
Hectopsylla eskeyi: guinea pig, 558
Heisdorf and Nelson (virus): chicken, 678
Helminth infections
    guinea pig, 508-509, 551-552, 558
    hamster, 477-478
Helper viruses: chicken, 668
Hemangioendothelioma: hamster, 483
Hemangioma: hamster, 481, 485, 494, 494 fn
Hemangiopericytoma: hamster, 483, 494 fn
Hematocrit
    guinea pig, 534-535
    hamster, 432
Hematologic mutations: rabbit, 576
Hematologic values: hamster, 432
Hematopoiesis: guinea pig, 507
Hematopoietic system infection: hamster, 474
Heme-binding protein: rabbit, 582
Hemocyanin, keyhole limpet: hamster, 472
Hemoglobin
    guinea pig
        blood concentration, 535
        congenital abnormality, 530
    hamster, 432
Hemoglobin (gene): chicken (see *Hb:* chicken)
Hemoglobin α-chain: rabbit, 586
Hemoglobin β-chain: rabbit, 586
Hemoglobin synthesis: chicken, 608
Hemolysis: hamster, 475
Hemolytic anemia
    hamster, 477
    rabbit (see *ha*)
β-Hemolytic *Staphylococcus:* guinea pig, 550
Hemopexin: rabbit, 582 (see also *Hx*)
Hemorrhagic fevers: hamster, 497 fn
Hemorrhagic fever virus, Omsk: guinea pig, 549
Hen egg albumin: hamster response, 471 fn, 472
Hen feathering: chicken (see *Hf*)
Hepatic (*see also* Liver)
Hepatic adenocarcinomas: hamster, 487
Hepatic amyloidosis: hamster, 433
Hepatic cirrhosis: hamster, 433
Hepatic sarcomas: hamster, 487
Hepatitis: hamster, 473-475, 477
Hepatocarcinoma
    guinea pig, 562-563
    hamster, 482, 501 hn, 502
Hepatocellular tumors: hamster, 487, 494
Hepatoenteritis: guinea pig, 549, 558
Hereditary autoimmune thyroiditis: chicken, 642
Hereditary gonad hypoplasia: chicken (see *Hgh*)
Hereditary uricemia and articular gout: chicken, 642

Mammillary bodies: hamster, 438 hn
Mandible: guinea pig
    abnormality, 530
    length, 528
Mandibular molars: hamster, 454
Mandibular prognathism: rabbit (see *mp*)
Mannose, immunoglobulin: chicken, 659
Mannosephosphate isomerase: rabbit, 588
Manzanilla virus: guinea pig, 549
Marans (breed): chicken, 644
Marbled down: chicken (see *ma*)
Marburg virus
    guinea pig, 549
    hamster, 474
Marek's disease: chicken
    associated gene, 651
    strain resistance, 612 hn
    strain susceptibility, 611 hn, 619
Marek's disease virus: chicken
    cell lines, 681
    susceptibility, 682-683
    tumors, 681-682
Marek's disease virus, strain JM: chicken, 639
Marek's disease virus isolates: chicken, 676-678
Marker, allotypic: guinea pig, 533
Marrow, bone: hamster, 502
Mastadenovirus: hamster, 496
Mast cells
    guinea pig, 537-538
    hamster
        estrous cycle, 438-439
        immunoglobulins, 470
        pregnancy, 441-442
Mastitis: hamster, 476
Maternal behavior: hamster, 459
Mating behavior
    guinea pig, 562 hn
    hamster, 440 hn, 455-458, 465-466
MAV-1 (virus): chicken, 668, 671
MAV-2 (virus): chicken, 668, 671
MAV-2(N) (virus): chicken, 671
MAV-2(O) (virus): chicken, 671
Maxilla abnormalities: guinea pig, 530
Maxillary molars: hamster, 454
Maze learning: hamster, 426, 462
Mb [muffs and beard] (gene): chicken
    associated breeds, 645
    linkage group tester strain, 614
    linkage relationships, 623, 628-637
M blood group: chicken (see *Ea-M*)
Mc or *mc* (gene): rabbit
    Mc (wild type), 577
    mc [lethal muscle contracture], 577
MC-A (tumor): guinea pig, 563
MCA-A (tumor): guinea pig, 563
MCAV-B (virus): chicken, 671
MCA-25 (tumor): guinea pig, 563
MC-D (tumor): guinea pig, 563
MC-E (tumor): guinea pig, 563
MCV-B (virus): chicken, 671
MC29 (virus): chicken, 668, 671
MC29-A (virus): chicken, 671
MC29 associated virus-A: chicken, 668

MC29 associated virus-B: chicken, 668
MC29-AV-A (virus): chicken, 668
MC29-AV-B (virus): chicken, 668
MC29-AV(i) (virus): chicken, 671
MC29-AV(L) (virus): chicken, 671
MC29-B (virus): chicken, 671
md [missing mandible] (gene): chicken, 642
MDCC-CU1 (cell line): chicken, 681
MDCC-CU2 (cell line): chicken, 681
MDCC-CU3 (cell line): chicken, 681
MDCC-CU4 (cell line): chicken, 681
MDCC-CU5 (cell line): chicken, 681
MDCC-CU6 (cell line): chicken, 681
MDCC-HP1 (cell line): chicken, 681
MDCC-HP2 (cell line): chicken, 681
MDCC-LS1 (cell line): chicken, 681
MDCC-MOB1 (cell line): chicken, 681
MDCC-MOB2 (cell line): chicken, 681
MDCC-MOB3 (cell line): chicken, 681
MDCC-MSB1 (cell line): chicken, 681
MDCC-RP1 (cell line): chicken, 681
MDCC-SK1 (cell line): chicken, 681
MDCC-SK3 (cell line): chicken, 681
MDCT-CU7 (tumor transplant): chicken, 681
MDCT-CU8 (tumor transplant): chicken, 681
MDCT-CU9 (tumor transplant): chicken, 681
MDCT-NYM1 (tumor transplant): chicken, 682
MDT-198 (tumor transplant): chicken, 682
MD-X (virus): chicken, 678
MD 7/1970 (virus): chicken, 678
Measles virus: hamster, 474, 497, 499
Meat production stocks: chicken, 617-618
MeBPA (antigen): guinea pig, 546
Median forebrain bundle: hamster, 468
Mediterranean kala-azar: hamster, 501 hn
Medium chinchilla: rabbit (see *c^{chm}*)
Meiosis: hamster, 502
Melanin-forming tissue: hamster, 481
Melanoma: hamster, 488, 493
Melanotic: chicken (see *Ml*)
Melatonin: hamster, 426
Membrane damage: guinea pig, 541
Membranes, cell: chicken, 657 hn
Merck, Sharpe & Dohme 1 (virus): chicken, 678
Mercuric chloride: guinea pig, 546
Mesenchymal tumors: hamster, 494
Mesentery: hamster, 481
Mesocricetus auratus (*see also* Syrian hamster)
    chromosomes & karyology, 436
    research suitability, 431
    taxonomic location, 425
M. auratus auratus, 501 hn (*see also* Syrian hamster)
M. brandti
    chromosomes & karyology, 436
    hibernation research, 431
    taxonomic location, 425
M. newtoni, 425
Mesometrial arteries: hamster, 442
Mesotheliomas: hamster, 494 fn
Metabolic half-life, immunoglobulin G: chicken, 660
Metabolic investigations: chicken, 608
Metabolic traits: chicken, 641-642
Metabolism, fatty acid: hamster, 504

Metastases: guinea pig, 562-563
Metastrongylus apri: guinea pig, 552
Methionine: rabbit, 596
3-Methylcholanthrene
    guinea pig, 562 hn, 563
    hamster, 489-490
Methyl methanesulfonate: chicken, 638
N-Methyl-*N'*-nitro-*N*-nitrosoguanidine: guinea pig, 562 hn, 563
4-Methylumbelliferyl esters: rabbit, 584
mf [frizzle modifier] (gene): chicken, 645
Mh [mahogany] (gene): chicken
        breed association, 646
        mutant gene tester strain, 615
MHA (strain): hamster
        immunogenetics, 469-470
        viral infection, 474
        MHA/SsLak, 434
MHC (*see also* Major histocompatibility complex)
        chicken, 607, 657 hn
        hamster, 427, 469 hn
MH-RSV (virus): chicken, 666
MH2 (virus): chicken
        characteristics, 668
        oncogenicity, 671
        origin, 671
mi [bilateral microphthalmia] (gene): chicken, 642
Mi-2 [dominant microphthalmia] (gene): chicken, 641
mi-3 [microphthalmia-3] (gene): chicken, 641
Microchromosomes: chicken
        congenic line development, 607
        linkage groups, 622, 625 fn, 627 fn
        translocation, 639
Microcirculation: hamster, 426, 501 hn
Micrococci: hamster, 476
Micrococcus luteus: rabbit, 588
M. lysodeikticus: rabbit, 588 fn
Micromelia
    chicken, 608
    guinea pig, 530
Micromelia - Asmundson: chicken, 643
Micromelia - California: chicken (see *mm-A*)
Micromelia - Hays: chicken (see *mm-H*)
Micromelia - Kawahara: chicken (see *mm-K*)
Micromelia VII: chicken (see *mm-VII*)
Microphthalmia
    guinea pig, 515, 529-530
    hamster, 434, 453
Microphthalmia, dominant: chicken (see *Mi-2*)
Microphthalmia-3: chicken (see *mi-3*)
Microsporidians: guinea pig, 551
Microsporum audouinii: guinea pig, 550
M. canis: guinea pig, 550-551
M. cookei: guinea pig, 550
M. distortum: guinea pig, 550
M. gypseum: guinea pig, 550
M. nanum: guinea pig, 550
Middleburg virus: guinea pig, 549
Milk immunoglobulins: guinea pig, 537
Milk lines: hamster, 437
Mille Fleur (variety): chicken, 646
Mille fleur (gene): chicken (see *mo*)

Mill Hill Dunkin-Hartley (strain): guinea pig, 523, 525
Mill Hill strain RSV (virus): chicken, 666 hn, 666
Mill-Hill strain RSV-2 (virus): chicken, 670 hn, 671
Mink encephalopathy, transmissible: hamster response, 499
Minnesota marker males: chicken, 639
Minnesota rearrangement strains: chicken, 614, 639
Minorca (breed): chicken, 644-647
Minorca, Black (breed): chicken
        genetic traits, 646
        inbred-line progenitor, 611 hn, 612
Minorca, Buff (breed): chicken, 646
Minor histocompatibility system: chicken, 651, 653, 665
Minute virus of mice: hamster response, 495
Missing mandible: chicken (see *md*)
Missing maxillae: chicken (see *mx*)
Mitogen response-1: chicken (see *Mr-1*)
Mitogens: hamster, 471 hn, 471-472
Mitosis: hamster, 502
Mitotic index aberration: rabbit, 573
Mixed leukocyte reaction: chicken, 653
Mixed lymphocyte reaction: hamster, 469 hn, 469, 472
Mixoploidy: rabbit, 573
MKT-1 (cell line): chicken, 681
Ml [melanotic] (gene): chicken
        breed association, 646
        linkage relationships, 625
        mutant gene tester strain, 615
mm-A [micromelia - California] (gene): chicken, 642
mm-H [micromelia - Hays] (gene): chicken, 643
mm-K [micromelia - Kawahara] (gene): chicken, 643
mm-VII [micromelia VII] (gene): chicken, 643
Mo [mottled white] (gene): hamster, 435, 452
mo [mottling; mille fleur; speckling] (gene): chicken
        breed association, 646
        independent segregation, 629, 632-635
MOB-1 (cell line): chicken, 681
MOB-2 (cell line): chicken, 681
MOB-3 (cell line): chicken, 681
Mod-1 [malate dehydrogenase, cytoplasmic] (gene): rabbit, 587
Mod-2 [malate dehydrogenase, mitochondrial] (gene): rabbit, 587
Modern Game (breed): chicken, 646
Modified slow feathering: chicken, 645
Molars: hamster, 454, 560
Molecular formula, immunoglobulin: guinea pig, 537
Molecular weight
    chicken
        avian virus structural proteins, 676
        immunoglobulins, 659
        polypeptide chains, immunoglobulin, 664-665
    guinea pig
        complement proteins, 541
        immunoglobulins, 536-537
Moloney leukemia: hamster, 497
Mongolism: hamster, 495
"Mongoloid" osteolytic cerebellar hypoplasia: hamster, 473
Monilia: hamster, 501 hn
Moniliformis dubius: hamster, 478
Monoacetylmorphine esterase: rabbit, 579 hn

Monoamine oxidase: hamster, 467 fn
Monocercomonas caviae: guinea pig, 551
M. minuta: guinea pig, 551
M. pistillum: guinea pig, 551
Monocercomonoides caviae: guinea pig, 551
M. exilis: guinea pig, 551
M. quadrifunilis: guinea pig, 551
M. wenrichi: guinea pig, 551
Monocyte-mediated phagocytosis: guinea pig, 538
Monocytes
    chicken, 651 fn, 664
    hamster, 432
Mononuclear peritoneal cells: guinea pig, 541
Mononucleosis cell transplantation, human infectious: hamster, 427
Monosomic abnormalities: chicken, 638 hn, 638
Monsters: guinea pig, 530
Morbillivirus: hamster, 497
Morphological traits: chicken, 617-618 (*see also* specific trait)
Mortality
    chicken, 651
    guinea pig
        anemia, 530
        at birth, 524
        pre-weaning, 522
    hamster, 484 hn (*see also* Death; Life-span; Longevity)
Mosaics, chromosome
    chicken, 638 hn, 638
    rabbit, 573
Motor end plates: chicken, 620 hn
Mottled (variety): chicken, 646
Mottled white: hamster (see *Mo*)
Mottling: chicken (see *mo*)
Mount Elgon bat virus: guinea pig, 549
Mounting
    guinea pig, 562
    hamster, 456-457
Mouse-like hamster, 435
Mouse viruses
    guinea pig response, 549 (*see also* Murine viruses)
    hamster response, 485, 495, 497
Mp [ametapodia] (gene): chicken
        breed holder, 643
        linkage relationships, 622, 629, 633-635
Mp or *mp* (gene): rabbit
    Mp (wild type), 576
    mp [mandibular prognathism], 568, 576
Mpi-1 [mannosephosphate isomerase] (gene): rabbit, 588
Mr-1 [mitogen response-1] (gene): chicken, 628, 630-631, 633-634
Ms (immunoglobulin gene): rabbit, 599
MSB-1 (cell line): chicken, 681
MSD$_1$ (virus): chicken, 678
Ms1 to Ms6 (immunoglobulin specificities): rabbit, 599-601
Ms16 to Ms17 (immunoglobulin specificities): rabbit, 599
Ms21 to Ms26 (immunoglobulin specificities): rabbit, 599, 605-606
mt [non-molt] (gene): chicken, 645
Mtz [α_2-macroglobulin] (gene): rabbit
        controlled protein, 583-584
        linked genes, 579, 582-583, 601
μ chains, immunoglobulin: rabbit, 599-601

Mucosa, gut: rabbit, 579, 587
Muffs and beard: chicken (see *Mb*)
Multifocal leukoencephalopathy, progressive: hamster, 485 fn, 499
Multiple spurs: chicken (see *M*)
Mumps virus: hamster, 474, 497
Murine viruses (*see also* Mouse viruses)
    guinea pig response, 562 hn, 563
    hamster response, 497
Murray Valley encephalitis virus: guinea pig, 549
Muscle, uterine: hamster, 439
Muscle contracture: rabbit, 577
Muscle degeneration: hamster, 426
Muscle fibers: chicken, 619 hn-620 hn
Muscle hypoplasia: chicken, 608
Muscle tumor source: chicken, 682
Muscular conditions: chicken, 608
Muscular diseases: guinea pig, 560
Muscular dystrophy: chicken, 608, 619-620 (see also *am*)
Musculoskeletal traits: chicken, 643
Mutagens: chicken, 614
Mutant gene (*see also* specific gene)
    chicken, 615
    guinea pig, 513-514, 529-532, 560-561
    hamster, 435, 451-453, 455
Mutational load: rabbit, 565
Mutation studies: hamster, 427
MVM (virus): hamster, 495
mx [missing maxillae] (gene): chicken, 643
my [myopathy] (gene): hamster, 433
Myasthenia, autoimmune: guinea pig, 547
Mycobacterium bovis, strain BCG: hamster, 476
M. kansasii: hamster, 476
M. leprae: hamster, 475 fn
M. paratuberculosis
    guinea pig, 550
    hamster, 476
M. tuberculosis var. *bovis:* hamster, 476
M. tuberculosis var. *humanum:* hamster, 476
Mycoplasma: hamster, 475
M. caviae: guinea pig, 550
M. pneumoniae: hamster, 475
M. pulmonis: guinea pig, 550
Mycoplasmas: guinea pig, 550, 558 fn
Mycoses: guinea pig, 508, 550-551
Myeloblastosis: chicken, 670
Myeloblastosis associated virus-1: chicken, 671
Myeloblastosis associated virus-2: chicken, 671
Myeloblastosis associated virus-2(N): chicken, 671
Myeloblastosis associated virus-2(O): chicken, 671
Myeloblastosis virus, avian: chicken, 668, 670
Myelocytomatosis: chicken, 671
Myelocytomatosis associated virus-B: chicken, 671
Myelocytomatosis associated virus (i): chicken, 671
Myelocytomatosis associated virus (L): chicken, 671
Myelocytomatosis associated viruses, avian: chicken, 668
Myelocytomatosis virus, avian: chicken, 668
Myelocytomatosis virus-B: chicken, 671
Myelocytomatosis virus-29: chicken, 671
Myelocytomatosis virus-29-A: chicken, 671
Myelocytomatosis virus-29-B: chicken, 671
Myeloid leukemia virus: chicken, 668
Myocarditis: hamster, 477
Myoclonic tremors, hamster, 497

Purine-nucleoside phosphorylase: rabbit, 579 hn
PVM (virus)
    guinea pig, 549
    hamster, 474 fn, 497
PWM (chemical): hamster, 472
Px [polydactyly] (gene): guinea pig, 513 hn, 514, 530
px [paroxysm] (gene): chicken
        breed holder, 642
        linkage relationships, 622, 624, 627*
Pyruvate: rabbit, 587

Q blood group (gene): chicken (see *Ea-Q*)
Quail (variety): chicken, 645 fn
Quail pattern: chicken, 645 fn
Quaranfil virus: guinea pig, 550
Quebec-1 (virus): chicken, 678

R (strain): rabbit
        genealogy, 569*
        litter size, 565*
        skeletal malformations, 565
    R/J, 569*
R [rose comb] (gene): chicken
        breed association, 644
        linkage group tester strain, 614
        linkage relationships, 622, 627*, 628-637
R [rough] (gene): guinea pig, 513 hn, 514
r [rust] (gene): hamster, 433 fn, 451 fn
R-1 or *r-1* (gene): rabbit
    R-1 (wild type), 574
    r-1 [rex-1; French rex], 570*, 571, 574
R¹ (gene): chicken (see *Ea-R*)
R¹ or *r¹* (gene): rabbit (see *R-1* or *r-1*)
R-2 or *r-2* (gene): rabbit
    R-2 (wild type), 574
    r-2 [rex-2; German rex]
        linkage group, 570*, 571, 574
        strain association, 568
R² or *r²* (gene): rabbit (see *R-2* or *r-2*)
R-3 or *r-3* (gene): rabbit
    R-3 (wild type), 574
    r-3 [rex-3; Normandy rex], 574
R³ or *r³* (gene): rabbit (see *R-3* or *r-3*)
R67 [high-density lipoprotein] (gene): rabbit, 582-583
RA (strain): guinea pig, 544
Rabbit (*see* specific condition, gene, strain; *Oryctolagus*)
Rabbit serum albumin, poly(L-lysyl): guinea pig response, 545
Rabbit tubular basement membrane: guinea pig response, 548
Rabies virus
    guinea pig, 549
    hamster, 426, 470, 473 fn, 497, 501 hn
Radiation
    hamster, 488-489
    rabbit, 574
Ragged wing: chicken (see *rw*)
Random-bred
    chicken, 616-618
    guinea pig
        body weight, 505
        immune reactions, 547-548
    hamster
        chemical carcinogens, 489-490
        copulatory behavior, 466

        saccharin, 468
        toxic substances, 500
    laboratory animals, 419-421
    rabbit
        immunoglobulin allotypes, 596
        protein characteristics, 586-587
Rapid feathering: chicken (see *k⁺*)
Rat virus: hamster response, 495
Rauscher erythroleukemia virus: hamster, 497
RAV-0 (virus): chicken
        characteristics, 668
        controlling gene, 673 hn, 674, 674 fn
        oncongenicity, 672
        origin, 672
RAV-1 (virus): chicken, 668, 672
RAV-2 (virus): chicken, 668, 672
RAV-3 (virus): chicken, 668, 672
RAV-4 (virus): chicken, 668
RAV-5 (virus): chicken, 669, 672
RAV-6 (virus): chicken, 669
RAV-7 (virus): chicken, 669, 672
RAV-49 (virus): chicken, 669, 672
RAV-50 (virus): chicken, 669, 672
RAV-60 (virus): chicken, 669, 672, 673 hn
RAV-61 (virus): chicken, 669, 672
RAV-62 (virus): chicken, 669
RBC (*see* Erythrocytes)
Rc or *rc* (gene): rabbit
    Rc (wild type), 576
    rc [renal cysts]
        description, 576
        strain association, 567
rc [induced retinal mutation] (gene): chicken, 641
rd [riboflavinuria] (gene): chicken, 638, 641
Re or *re* (gene): rabbit
    Re (wild type), 574
    re [red eye], 574
Reagents, typing: rabbit, 590-591
Reaseheath line C: chicken (*see also* RH-C)
        avian viruses, 674
        endogenous virus, 675
        erythrocyte alloantigens, 652
        tumor virus susceptibility, 675
REAV (virus): chicken, 668
Recessive dwarfism: chicken (see *td*)
Recessive genes: rabbit, 565-566 (*see also* specific gene)
Recessive rumplessness: chicken (see *rp-2*)
Recessive sex-linked dwarfism: chicken (see *rg*)
Recessive waltzer (strain): guinea pig, 561
Recessive waltzing: guinea pig (see *wtz*)
Recessive wheaten (strain): chicken, 615
Recessive wheaten (gene): chicken (see *eʸ*)
Recessive white: chicken (see *c:* chicken)
Recessive white lethal: chicken (see *l:* chicken)
Recessive white spotting: rabbit (see *du; duᵈ; duʷ*)
Recombinants, genetic: chicken, 653
Red (variety): chicken, 646
Red blood cell antigens: chicken, 610 hn
Red-brown complex: chicken, 647
Red coat color: guinea pig, 530-533
Red earlobes: chicken, 644
Red eye
    chicken, 644
    guinea pig, 531-532
    rabbit (see *re*)

S blood group (gene): chicken (see *Ea-S*)
sc [scaleless] (gene): chicken
      breed holders, 645
      independent segregation, 629-630, 632-636
Scaleless: chicken (see *sc*)
Scarpa's ganglion: guinea pig, 561
Scent marking: hamster, 458, 462, 467
Schaumann bodies: hamster, 476-477
Schistosoma haematobium
    guinea pig, 551
    hamster, 477 fn
S. japonicum: hamster, 477 fn
S. mansoni
    guinea pig, 551
    hamster, 478
Schistosomiasis: hamster, 426
Schizotrypanum cruzi: guinea pig, 551
Schmidt-Ruppin strain RSV (virus): chicken, 667, 670,
    672
Schmidt-Ruppin strain RSV-D (virus): chicken, 672
Schmidt-Ruppin strain RSV-H (virus): chicken, 672
Schmidt-Ruppin strain RSV-1 (virus): chicken, 672
Schmidt-Ruppin strain RSV-2 (virus): chicken, 672
Schwannoma: hamster, 481
Sclerosing panencephalitis, subacute: hamster, 499
Sco or *sco* (gene): rabbit
    Sco (wild type), 578
    sco [scoliosis], 578
Scoliosis
    chicken, 608
    rabbit, 567 fn (see also *sco*)
Scrapie: hamster, 499
Scrapie virus: hamster, 426, 475
Scrotum: hamster, 475
se [sleepy-eye] (gene): chicken
    breed holder, 644
    linkage relationships, 623, 627*, 629-630, 632-
      636
Sebaceous flank glands: hamster, 458
Sebright (breed): chicken, 643-646
Secretions (*see* specific secretion)
Secretory IgA: rabbit, 599
Secretory immunoglobulin: chicken, 658 hn (*see also* Im-
    munoglobulin A: chicken)
Sedimentation coefficients, immunoglobulin
    chicken, 659
    guinea pig, 536
Sedimentation coefficients, complement factors: guinea
    pig, 541 hn, 541
Segregating genes
    guinea pig, 505
    rabbit, 567-568
Segregation, gene: chicken
    avian RNA tumor virus subgroup, 675
    dermal melanin strain, 615 fn
    disease patterns, 619 hn, 619
    Ea-B locus, 656
    endogenous viruses, 675
    erythrocyte alloantigens, 652 hn, 652-653
    gene independence, 628-637
    inbred lines, 611 hn-612 hn, 612 fn
    leukosis/sarcoma virus subgroups, 619
    linkage group tester strains, 614

Segregational genetic load: rabbit, 565
Seizure: hamster, 455, 501 hn, 502 (see also *sz*)
Selenomonas ruminantium: guinea pig, 551
Self-Blue (variety): chicken, 646
Self dubbing: chicken, 644
Self golden: guinea pig, 533
Semen: chicken, 639
Seminal emission: hamster, 456 (*see also* Ejaculation)
Seminal vesiculitis: guinea pig, 560
Seminoma: hamster, 494 fn
Semliki Forest virus: guinea pig, 549
Sendai virus
    guinea pig, 549
    hamster, 474, 497
Sepik virus: guinea pig, 549
Septal lesions: hamster
      aggressive behavior, 457
      avoidance response, 462
      circadian rhythm, 461
      food hoarding, 459
Serine
    chicken, 659
    rabbit, 586, 601
Serine ethanolamine phosphate: chicken, 620
Serum, anti-hamster thymocyte: hamster response, 490
Serum, anti-lymphocyte: hamster, 474
Serum albumin: chicken (see *Alb*)
Serum albumin, anti-bovine: chicken response, 658 hn,
    660
Serum albumin, bovine
    chicken response, 658
    guinea pig response, 545
Serum albumin, human
    chicken response, 654 hn, 655-656
    guinea pig response, 545
Serum albumin, poly(L-lysyl) rabbit: guinea pig response,
    545
Serum albumin, trinitrophenyl-bovine: hamster response,
    472
Serum blocking activity: hamster, 490
Serum esterases: rabbit, 579-581
Serum factor(s)
    guinea pig, 509
    hamster, 472
Serum factor-hypersensitivity: guinea pig (see S^{hy})
Serum globulin allotypes: chicken, 612 hn
Serum hormones: hamster
      estrous cycle, 438-439
      lactation, 446
      pregnancy, 441
Serum immunoglobulins
    chicken, 660
    guinea pig, 537
    hamster, 432, 471
Serum lipoproteins: rabbit, 582-583
Serum protein(s) (*see also* specific protein)
    hamster, 432, 504
    rabbit, 579-584 (see also *Prt*)
Serum sickness glomerulonephritis: chicken, 658
sex [sex-linked lethal-Bernier] (gene): chicken, 625, 643
Sex chromosome(s)
    chicken, 621-622, 623 fn (*see also* W chromosome;
    Z chromosome)

Small Silver (strain): rabbit, 568, 568 hn-569 hn, 569*
Smooth rose-combed: chicken (see *he^l*)
sn [sunsuit] (gene): chicken
      feathers, 645
      independent segregation, 629-630, 633, 636
sno [snub nose] (gene): chicken, 643
Snow-white down: chicken (see *sw*)
Snub nose: chicken (see *sno*)
Sodium, plasma: guinea pig, 536
Soft tissue tumors: hamster, 494
Sooty yellow: rabbit, 568
Sp [spangling] (gene): chicken, 646
SPAFAS (strain): chicken, 675
Spangled Old English Game (breed): chicken, 646
Spangling: chicken (see *Sp*)
Spanish, Barred (breed): chicken, 612
Spanish, Black (breed): chicken, 611 hn, 612
Spanish, White-faced Black (breed): chicken, 644
Spastic paralysis, asymmetrical: rabbit, 577
Specificities, immunoglobulin
    chicken, 661-664
    rabbit, 593-603
Specific Pathogen Free, Supply (strain): chicken, 675
Specific pathogen-free stock: guinea pig, 507, 522 fn, 534 hn
Speckled head: chicken (see *e^s*)
Speckled Sussex (breed): chicken, 646
Speckling: chicken (see *mo*)
Sperm
    guinea pig, 520-521
    hamster, 437, 441, 501 hn
    rabbit, 573
Sperm acrosome: guinea pig, 548
Spermatogenic hypoplasia: guinea pig, 530
Sperm-egg contact: hamster, *Part 1*, 52 hn
Sphaeromonas communis: guinea pig, 551
Spicule, lung bony: guinea pig, 560
Spike blade comb: chicken (see *sb:* chicken)
Spina bifida: rabbit (see *sb:* rabbit)
Spinal column: guinea pig, 530
Spinal cord, bovine (antigen): chicken response, 658
Spindle cell carcinoma: hamster, 482
Spiral ganglia cell degeneration: guinea pig, 561
Spiromonas augusta: guinea pig, 551
Spitzhauben (breed): chicken, 645-646
Spleen; spleen tissue
    chicken, 681
    guinea pig
        transplantable tumor, 562
        weight, 528-529
    hamster
        cytotoxicity, 490
        immune response assay, 471-472
        infections, 474, 476-477, 496
        tumors, 481, 483, 488, 494
        weight, 437 hn, 450
Spleen cells, embryonic: rabbit, 573 fn
Splenectomy: hamster, 477
Splitfoot: chicken (see *sf*)
Spondweni virus: guinea pig, 549
Spongiform encephalopathy: hamster, 499
Spontaneous seizure: hamster (see *sz*)
Spontaneous tumors
    guinea pig, 507
    hamster, 480-483, 493-494

Sporothrix schenckii: hamster, 476 fn
Sporotrichum schenckii: hamster, 476 fn
Sporozoa infections: guinea pig, 551
Spotting, white: rabbit, 574
Spring-summer encephalitis virus, Russian: guinea pig, 549
Spurlessness: chicken (see *sl*)
Squamous cell carcinoma: hamster, 482, 488, 493 fn
SR-RSV (virus): chicken, 667, 672
SR-RSV-A (virus): chicken, 672
SR-RSV-B (virus): chicken, 672
SR-RSV-D (virus): chicken, 672
SR-RSV-H (virus): chicken, 672
SSPE (disease): hamster, 499
St [star] (gene): guinea pig, 514
st [stringy] (gene): chicken, 645
st-2 [stringy-2] (gene): chicken, 645
Staphylococcus
    guinea pig, 550
    hamster, 426, 476
S. aureus: guinea pig, 550
Star: guinea pig (see *St*)
Starvation: hamster, 438 hn, 460
Steel: rabbit (see *E^S*)
Stenosis, aqueductal: hamster, 473-474
Sterility
    guinea pig
        mutant gene, 513 hn, 513-514, 530
        spermatogenic hypoplasia, 530
    hamster, 434
Steroids
    guinea pig, 507
    hamster, 440 hn
Stickiness: chicken (see *sy:* chicken)
Sticky coat: guinea pig (see *sk*)
Stillborn: guinea pig, 521, 524
Stillborn monsters: guinea pig, 530
Stippling: chicken (see *Sg^+*)
St. Louis encephalitis virus
    guinea pig, 549
    hamster, 426, 497
St. Louis virus
    guinea pig, 549
    hamster, 474, 497
Stomach; stomach tissue
    guinea pig, 528
    hamster
        induced tumors, 485, 489
        spontaneous tumors, 480-482, 493 fn
Strawberry comb: chicken, 644
Streptobacillus moniliformis: guinea pig, 550
Streptococcal polysaccharides: rabbit, 603
Streptococcus
    guinea pig, 508, 550, 558
    hamster, 476
S. agalactiae: hamster, 476
S. pneumoniae
    guinea pig, 550
    hamster, 476
S. zooepidemicus: guinea pig, 550
Stress
    guinea pig, 509
    hamster, 460, 504
Stria vascularis lesions: guinea pig, 561
Stringy: chicken (see *st; st-2*)
Striped-back hamster, 500 hn (*see also* Chinese hamster)

Tetanus vaccine: hamster, 476
Tetraploid abnormalities: chicken, 638 hn, 638-639
Tf [transferrin-conalbumin] (gene): chicken
       breed holder, 641
       independent segregation, 628, 633, 635, 637
(T,G)-A—L (chemical): guinea pig, 545
Th-1 [thymocyte antigen-1] (gene): chicken
       linkage relationship, 625
       tissue distribution, 665
Thalidomide: hamster, 500
Thecoma: hamster, 481, 494
Theileria: guinea pig, 551
Thermoregulation, behavioral: hamster, 460
Thorax: guinea pig, 532
Threonine
    chicken, 659
    rabbit, 586, 596
Thrombophlebitis, pulmonary: hamster, 476
Thymectomy: chicken, 657 hn-658 hn
Thymic adenoma: hamster, 494 fn
Thymidine: hamster, 439
Thymidine, radioactive: hamster, 439, 471-472
Thymidine kinase activity: chicken, 620 hn (see also
    Tk-F)
Thymocyte antigen-1: chicken (see *Th-1*)
Thymocytes: chicken, 665
Thymocyte serum, anti-hamster: hamster response, 490
Thymus; thymus tissue
    guinea pig
        human similarity, 507
        weight, 528-529
    hamster, 471-472
    rabbit, 588
Thymus-dependent lymphoid cell: chicken, 680 hn, 681
Thyroglobulin: chicken, 654 hn, 654, 657 hn
Thyroglobulin antibody: chicken, 657 hn, 657
Thyroid extract: chicken, 658
Thyroid gland; thyroid tissue
    chicken, 657 hn
    hamster
        mitotic cycle, 502
        tumors, 480, 482, 494
Thyroiditis
    chicken, 657 hn, 658
    guinea pig, 508, 547, 560
Thyrotropin sensitivity: chicken (see *Tsh*)
Tibia abnormality: guinea pig, 530
Tibial dyschondroplasia: chicken, 643
Ticked-bellied agouti: guinea pig (see *A*ʳ)
Tick fever virus, Colorado: hamster, 426, 496
tip [tipsy] (gene): chicken, 642
Tipsy: chicken (see *tip*)
TK/A (virus): chicken, 680
Tk-F [cytosol thymidine kinase F] (gene): chicken, 622,
    625, 627*, 641
TK 809 (virus): chicken, 678
T lymphocytes
    chicken, 665
    guinea pig, 544 hn
TME (disease): hamster, 499
TN (disease): guinea pig, 548
TNP-Brucella: hamster, 472
TNP-BSA (chemical): hamster, 472
TNP-Ficoll (chemical): hamster, 472

To [tortoiseshell] (gene): hamster, 435, 453
Togaviruses: guinea pig, 549
Tooth (*see also* Dental entries)
    hamster
        eruption, 454
        transplantation, 427
    rabbit, 578
Tortoiseshell
    guinea pig, 531, 533
    hamster (see *To*)
Tortoiseshell and white: guinea pig, 533
Toxic inhalants: guinea pig, 509
Toxocara canis: guinea pig, 552
Toxoplasma gondii
    guinea pig, 508, 551, 558
    hamster, 477
Toxoplasmosis: guinea pig, 508
Tr or *tr* (gene): rabbit
    Tr (wild type), 577
    tr [shaking palsy], 577
Tracheal cancer: hamster, 426
Tracheobronchitis: hamster, 474
Trachoma: guinea pig, 508, 550
Träger: hamster, 442
Transferrin: rabbit, 579 hn, 584
Transferrin-conalbumin: chicken (see *Tf*)
Transformation-defective virus: chicken, 666 hn
Translocation, chromosome
    chicken, 638-639
    hamster, 502
Transmissible mink encephalopathy: hamster, 499
Transplantable tumors
    chicken, 682
    guinea pig, 562-563
Transplantation antigens
    guinea pig, 508
    hamster, 490, 492 hn, 492
Transplantation studies: hamster, 427, 484 hn, 490
Trembling: rabbit, 577
Tremors
    guinea pig, 561
    hamster, 497
Treponema pallidum: hamster, 476
Trichinella: hamster, 426, 501 hn
T. spiralis
    guinea pig, 508-509, 538, 552, 558
    hamster, 477 fn
Trichlorofluoromethane: hamster, 500
Trichomonas: hamster, 477
T. caviae: guinea pig, 551
T. flagelliphora: guinea pig, 551
T. foetus: hamster, 477
T. vaginalis: guinea pig, 551
Trichomoniasis: guinea pig, 508
Trichophyton equinum: guinea pig, 550
T. megninii: guinea pig, 550
T. mentagrophytes: guinea pig, 508, 550-551
T. rubrum: guinea pig, 550
T. verrucosum: guinea pig, 551
T. violaceum: guinea pig, 550
Trichostrongylus colubriformis: guinea pig, 509, 552, 558
Triethylenemelamine: chicken, 614 hn, 614, 639
Triglycerides: chicken, 620
Trimenopon hispidum: guinea pig, 558